China and Japan

China and Japan:
Search For Balance Since World War I

Alvin D. Coox and Hilary Conroy, Editors

ABC-Clio, Inc.

SANTA BARBARA, CALIF.
OXFORD, ENGLAND

Library of Congress Cataloging in Publication Data
Main entry under title:

China and Japan.

   Includes bibliographical references and index.
   1. China—Foreign relations—Japan—Addresses, essays, lectures. 2. Japan—Foreign relations—China—Addresses, essays, lectures. I. Coox, Alvin D. II. Conroy, Francis Hilary, 1919–
DS740.5.J3C3975   327.51′052   77-10006
ISBN 0-87436-275-X

Clio Books
American Bibliographical Center—Clio Press
2040 Alameda Padre Serra
Santa Barbara, California 93103
European Bibliographical Center—Clio Press
Woodside House, Hinksey Hill
Oxford OX1 5BE, England
Manufactured in the United States of America

Contents

List of Photographs

Foreword

This collection was conceived in July 1972, when we met at the University of California, Irvine, and discovered our mutual interest in the interactions between China and Japan. During our initial discussions we shared our knowledge of several original research projects completed by young scholars on various aspects of Sino-Japanese relations in the twentieth century and concluded that that research, much of which was based on primary Chinese and Japanese sources, merited wide circulation. We proceeded to prepare a list of potential contributors. We subsequently concluded that the "normalization" of relations between Peking and Tokyo, which stemmed from former Prime Minister Tanaka's "breakthrough" visit to China in September 1972, suggested that the vital findings contained in these studies should be published as soon as possible.

In developing the format of the proposed volume, we strove for balance. We elected to include original work developed from multiarchival and multilingual sources by young scholars along with older scholars' opinion pieces and commentary based on their long acquaintance with the general field. We also elected to accentuate the positive aspects of the continuing, and dynamic, relations between China and Japan and we asked our contributors to keep those themes in mind while preparing their essays. Some of the contributors paid more attention to the guidelines than others; yet we believe that because of that emphasis, the positive elements embedded in the generally bleak record of Sino-Japanese relations from the late nineteenth century until the "breakthrough" in 1972 will not now be lost from view.

China and Japan achieved a momentary and illusory paper "balance" in their relations following the first modern treaty (1871), but Japan's participation in the dismemberment of the Chinese Empire soon brought the two nations into an imbalance that has persisted. In the interest of keeping this volume to a manageable size, we were obliged to focus attention on the period following the breakup of China's Confucian international system in the late nineteenth century. Japan's seizure of the Ryukyu Islands, Taiwan, and Korea played a major role in that breakup. The transition from Confucian to Western-style diplomacy brings to mind the interpretation contributed by K. H. Kim of the University of California, Davis. Kim demonstrates that Japanese diplomacy was a game of maneuver, even in 1871.[1] From that time until 1945, Sino-Japanese relationships were characterized by the increasing power and predatory policies of Japan and the weakness and frequent internal chaos of China.

The collection of essays in this volume lends itself to substantive and chronological categorization. The initial overview by Chalmers Johnson provides an overview of the long course of Sino-Japanese relations and the way these two nations perceived each other. Part II relates the specific issues of the pre–1931 era. Japan operated within the larger international framework of treaty-power relationships with China until the Manchurian Incident (1931). Japan sought a favored position and utilized an ambivalent institutional approach—through administration, government, and diplomacy—to gain her ends.

Part III explores stereotypes of China and Japan, Japanese attitudes toward China, and China's failure to resist Japanese aggression in Manchuria, which undermined institutional approaches to diplomacy. Part IV covers the post-Manchurian period to 1945, during which mutual hostility broadens into war, intergovernmental communication breaks down, and Chinese and Japanese "experts and meddlers" evolve schemes for restoring peace. Some of those schemes seemed close to achieving their purpose but in Part V the "faces of force" underlying Japan's aggressive foreign policies are shown to be the dominant aspect of Sino-Japanese relations.

The postwar period covered in Part VI was characterized by "chill and thaw," the increasingly complicated interactions between Japan, Nationalist China, and the People's Republic. The concluding essay sketches Sino-Japanese relationships in the 1970s and formulates a new approach toward ways of thinking about them.

ALVIN D. COOX
HILARY CONROY

Notes

1.   Key Hiuk Kim, "The Last Phase of the East Asian World Order: Sino-Japanese Rivalry in Korea, 1870–1882" (Ph.D. diss., University of California, Davis, 1975), especially Chap. 4, part 3. An earlier study covering a longer time span is Hilary Conroy, *The Japanese Seizure of Korea, 1868–1910: A Study of Realism and Idealism in International Relations* (Philadelphia, 1960; paperback edition, 1974). The classsis study, now somewhat dated, is M. Frederick Nelson, *Korea and the Old Orders in Eastern Asia* (Baton Rouge, 1946).

Acknowledgments

The editors are grateful for the special and extensive efforts extended by a number of individuals to this book. They wish to make public note of their thanks to:

Robert A. Scalapino for his Introduction; Barbara Phillips for copy editing; Charlotte Conroy, Stephen Feldman, Richard Henriques, Wayne Patterson, and Sharlie C. Ushioda for proof reading; Mrs. Billie K. Walsh for compiling the Index.

Introduction

Robert A. Scalapino

The course of Sino-Japanese relations has swept through the history of Asia like a mighty river. At times, its currents have borne the ships and men of peace. The products of such intercourse have been commerce and wide-ranging cultural borrowing, from language and religion to political values and institutions. At other times, the turbulent waters have signaled estrangement and open strife. Whether in peace or war, however, the relations between these two societies have had a deep impact, first upon the immediate northeast Asian region, then upon East Asia as a whole, and in modern times, upon the larger world as well.

In the long history of contact between these two related but dissimilar peoples, the opening stages were dominated by China. The reasons for the early advance of Chinese civilization need not detain us here. Suffice it to note that along with a very few other societies, such as Egypt and Mesopotamia, the Chinese developed a truly remarkable ancient culture, justifying that element of self-satisfaction, even arrogance, that is epito-mized in the very designation of their nation—Chūgoku (Middle King-dom). China was the sun around which all lesser bodies should gravitate. To the Chinese elite, the Japanese were but one of the barbarian peoples who inhabited the peripheries of the empire, and owed allegiance to it.

When barbarians were discerning and well behaved, rewards were available: trips to the celestial center, an exchange of gifts, and above all the opportunity to borrow from China's cultural font. When they misbehaved, the application of punishments was equally in order, with the all-important variant being China's capacity to apply them effectively.

If we were to leave the description at this point, however, we would have merely an idealized version of the Chinese interaction with neighboring peoples. In point of fact, as is well known, this version fully applied only when China was reasonably well governed and unified, having the requisites of political health and strength. When the Chinese polity was ailing—and this was not infrequent—the barbarians progressively impinged upon the celestial kingdom and occasionally conquered the capitol, taking the reins of power from a fading dynasty.

In traditional times, however, conquests were traded. The barbarian conquered China—but then China conquered the barbarian, not militarily but by forcing him to adapt to the Chinese way. Similarly, with peoples like the Japanese, who were not involved in mainland conquest prior to the modern era beyond the ill-fated effort to subjugate Korea, the cultural conquest was that of China. To the Japanese, China transmitted language, religion, a political ideology, and a host of other aspects of Chinese civilization. To be sure, the process of cultural borrowing was scarcely less complex in earlier centuries than in our times. Most of the Chinese adaptations bore a distinct Japanese cast by the time they had been assimilated. Some were found to be unsuited to Japanese conditions, moreover, and were discarded. Nevertheless, the Japanese acquired a profound cultural debt to China, one that has played a significant psychological role in shaping contemporary Japanese attitudes and policies toward the Chinese, at least until recently.

Is that debt about to be repaid? Again, some historical background is in order. The Sino-Japanese War of 1894–1895 marked the great watershed not merely in the relations between these two states, but in China's relations with the world. Poverty, corruption, lax organization, an effete military—these could be accepted by the Chinese elite of the late nineteenth century with considerable equanimity as the prices to be paid for a system which—all things considered—was superior to any within their (highly limited) range of knowledge. But military defeat at the hands of the Japanese, a people whom they had always viewed with a high degree of condescension, could not be accepted by the elite, especially by that younger element that stood on the threshold of governance. This defeat, moreover, symbolized but the most prominent among many external threats, threats that raised in graphic form the issue of survival itself.

Almost immediately, the cultural stream was reversed. Thousands of young Chinese poured into Japan in an effort to discern the mysteries of modernization. Military studies were particularly in vogue, but science and technology in all of their facets were not ignored; nor were political ideas and the institutions accompanying them. The monarchy itself sought to borrow extensively from the Japanese model, attempting to move toward constitutionalism down the path pursued by the Meiji leaders. That effort failed, primarily because of its timing, but also because China was under Manchu rule, and the issue of nationalism now swept forward, dominating the political scene.

In every sense, however, the preparations for the revolution of 1911 were incomplete. Consequently, all of the deficiencies implicit in a vast, backward empire made themselves manifest in the ensuing years, and once again, a familiar interaction followed: internal weaknesses and divisions precipitated external intervention, which in turn further aggravated internal weaknesses.

Japan, of course, was one of the principal interveners. Throughout Japanese history, one of the central issues for Japan has always been: involvement with or aloofness from the Asian continent? In this sense, the Japanese dilemma has been similar to that of the British with respect to the European continent, and both societies have answered the question differently at various points in their evolution. In modern times, however, the Japanese became progressively involved in the continent, both for economic and strategic reasons. As in other cases, the Japanese Empire came into being as an incremental process, with each acquisition raising new costs and problems as well as new "prestige" and power.

The initial key was Korea. Once Korea had been absorbed into the Japanese Empire, Japan was physically present on the continent of Asia, and from this point on, the issue of continental stability became a preoccupation of successive Japanese leaders. By stability, of course, Tokyo's leaders meant the development of political regimes that were, on the one hand, sufficiently friendly with Japan to interact positively on both economic and political fronts and, on the other hand, capable of maintaining that degree of political order and economic development necessary to sustain the government against internal and external threat.

The Japanese leaders prior to World War II were not so shortsighted as to have a single model in mind in seeking to achieve these objectives. It was not necessary, for example, that Manchuria or North China be incorporated directly into the empire, in the fashion of Korea. On the contrary, almost all Japanese political and military leaders recognized the impracticality of such an act. Rather, the effort was to cultivate a series of client states, preferably discreet in size and closely interrelated to Japan economically, politically, and strategically. If this plan was frequently marred by the overzealousness of various elements within the Japanese hierarchy, both military and civilian, it was not totally unsophisticated, especially when it was coupled with a strong appeal to Asian nationalism, an appeal that made an attack upon Western imperialism its keynote.

Any attempt to portray the Japanese political-military elite as singular in their views regarding China, or monolithic in their actions is a serious distortion, as many of the articles in the volume illustrate. Moreover, the division was not merely one between the advocates of "soft" and "tough" policies, or a reflection of different personalities operating in or upon a foreign culture. There were also major differences in the perceptions of how Japan and China could and should interact. Many of those Japanese who could be labeled not inaccurately "expansionists" genuinely thought of themselves as "friends of China," individuals who knew and greatly appreciated Chinese culture and numerous individual Chinese. Their task, as they saw it, was to preserve that culture against communism, that foreign ingredient with a Russian imprint, while simultaneously freeing China from Western imperialism and helping it to embark upon the path of modernization.

This idealism was expressed in a variety of ways. It found voices in men like Ōkuma Shigenobu and Inukai Tsuyoshi. It was manifested in the *Kokuryukai* (Amur River Society). Still other expressions came from Shidehara Kijūrō and men of his type. Nor was it absent by any means from the concept of the Greater East Asia Co-Prosperity Sphere. And it was reciprocated at various times, in various degrees, by Sun Yat-sen himself and by many who came after, among them Chiang Kai-shek and Wang Ch'ing-wei.

Yet in the final analysis, this idealism was blighted by the "Rape of Nanking" and the flames that engulfed Shanghai. The Japanese, torn and divided among themselves, and with the military in the general ascendancy, could not find a method of translating their goals into actions compatible with the mainstream of Chinese nationalism, or with peaceful coexistence between these two major societies. Consequently, in what must be the supreme irony of the mid-century, they—the most staunch opponents of Asian communism—made possible the massive victory of the Communists in China.

In that process, however, and in its aftermath, the fundamental changes in Sino-Japanese relations that were unleashed by the events of 1894–1895 have not been reversed. Today, the leaders of the People's Republic of China are once again looking to Japan for support in their goal of making China "a strong and prosperous nation by the end of the twentieth century." Indeed, *in certain respects,* Japan has become a model, since the goal itself is one that recalls the driving principle behind the Meiji Restoration.

One must stress the phrase "in certain respects," since the current Chinese leadership has no intention of borrowing Japanese political values or institutions at this point, nor indeed, of adapting its basic economic system. However, from the time that the decision was made in Peking to diverge from the Soviet modernization model, a decision that was implicit in the commune program, Japan did offer an alternative model. It was the Japanese who had pioneered the encouraging of small and medium industry based upon low capitalization and with access to a rural labor supply. It was the Japanese who had managed to keep a significant element of their political culture intact while turning outward to borrow Western science and technology on a massive scale. And it was Japan as a nation that had placed a premium upon a stern, competitive higher education system designed to cultivate the type of elites—scientific, technological, managerial—so essential if economic development on a rapid scale was to take place.

Many technical questions remain with respect to the problem of scientific and technological borrowing. It is not sufficient as the Japanese discovered long ago, merely to copy a foreign machine or transplant a foreign method of production. The entire level of scientific-technological capacity is the critical determinant in the final analysis, and thus borrowing is not only likely to be long-term, but it must also be the agent for an indigenous transformation that ultimately brings "backward" societies abreast of "advanced" ones.

For the moment, however, the technical questions in this field are secondary to the political ones insofar as the People's Republic of China is concerned. Contemporary China rides two horses. If the basic goals are akin to those of the Meiji Restoration, the rhetoric is MLM (Marxist-Leninist-Maoist). In some important respects, moreover, rhetoric is fortified by political culture. Hence, the emphasis upon "self-reliance," and the resistance to any large-scale foreign presence, even in the form of technicians or foreign loans, is both a reflection of China's experiences with Western imperialism and its historic xenophobia. The Maoist quest for egalitarianism and the insistence upon "politics in command" have a more contemporary, Communist ring, but even these are not without their indigenous roots.

Yet at this point, China's overwhelming need is for a rational economic development program. Thus, it is understandable that Peking's leaders would look to Japan, given what most observers have termed "the new pragmatic leadership" that is presently ascendant in this initial post-Mao period. Japan has both a geographic and a cultural proximity, notwithstanding the major differences that characterize these two societies. Given its proclivity toward separating economics and politics, moreover, and its eagerness to direct its export-oriented energies toward the late-developing countries, Japan is already playing an important role in the Chinese economy and, more broadly speaking, in China's technological revolution. Currently, the prospects are for an increase in that role in the years immediately ahead. In these terms, the process of cultural transfer continues to operate in a direction opposite to that of the premodern era. The "debt" is in the process of being repaid.

Meanwhile, the contemporary leaders of China have shifted their view of Japanese foreign policy in dramatic fashion. Up to a few years ago, the central theme emanating from Peking was the menace of "Japanese militarism," abetted and encouraged by "American imperialism." It was continuously charged that the American role in Asia was being passed to the Japanese, with the result that once again Japan was likely to become an aggressive force throughout East Asia. Today, the Chinese government is openly encouraging Japan to strengthen its defenses, assuming that it will direct those defenses against "Soviet social-imperialism." Criticism of the U.S.-Japan Mutual Security Treaty, moreover, has ceased, with the PRC acknowledging that the United States should retain its commitments to Japan for the time being.

China's leaders are forthright in proclaiming that their present goal is the broadest possible united front against the Soviet Union. And here, interestingly enough, they draw a direct analogy with China's needs at the time of the Sino-Japanese conflict which recommenced in 1937. The tripartite division of the world today was then paralleled by the divisions within China. To oppose *the primary enemy* (then Japan, now the USSR), it was necessary to form a tactical alliance with the strongest countervailing force (then the Kuomintang, now the United States), and also to enlist the support of the national bourgeoisie (then China's intelligentsia and business community, now the so-called Second World of advanced capitalist states, namely, Japan and Western Europe). Finally, it was critical that the Chinese Communist Party itself assume the leadership of the peasants and proletariat, appealing primarily to their nationalist sentiments but also catering to their economic interests when possible, with this class currently depicted internationally as the Third World, that cluster of late-developing states with which China identifies and whom it seeks to guide.

The united front strategy and the image of the world which underwrites it are the very heart of the balance of power- and national interest-oriented foreign policy presently pursued by the People's Republic of China. Setting aside its other dimensions, what does such a policy portend in terms of Sino-Japanese relations? I belong to the school of thought that regards those relations as likely to be characterized by a mixture of competition and cooperation for the foreseeable future, not the relations of alliance, but not those of unalleviated confrontation either.

As many of the papers in this book indicate, the vision of a Sino-Japanese alliance has long been held by certain individuals of both nationalities, either as a part of or somewhat apart from a larger Pan-Asianism. That vision is not entirely dead, as witness men like Utsunomiya and elements within the Kōmeitō. Yet such a vision seems to ignore the limited mutuality currently existing between China and Japan. Even in the economic field, the linkage will be a complex one, hampered in some degree by China's economic and political constraints, natural and self-imposed. But the strongest potential linkage lies there. Political ties can be forged mainly around a negative concern, the Soviet threat, that same concern which links China and the United States. Even a modest convergence of ideology or political institutions is not yet in sight. Nor does China have the capacity to provide Japan with the type of security guarantees that are important to the American-Japanese alliance.

On the other hand, a full-fledged confrontation—even one short of war—is not in the interests of either nation. Troublesome issues are not absent, to be sure; some of them relate to basic economic and security concerns. One is Korea; another is Taiwan. For understandable reasons, Japan leans strongly to the status-quo in both situations, and any use of force designed to change the present equilibrium would be regarded in Tokyo as dangerous—although Japan would not take any drastic actions to prevent such an occurrence. That, it leaves up to the United States. Assuming, however, that China's preoccupations for the decade ahead will be primarily with internal development, that the Sino-Soviet cleavage cannot be fundamentally healed, and that the United States maintains a predictable, credible presence in Asia, it should be possible to contain the Korean and Taiwan issues so that a forced solution is not attempted by any party.

To contain issues, however, is not necessarily to resolve them, and it would be most extraordinary if from their quite different vantage points China and Japan were able to reach a wholly compatible position with respect to these perennial problems. Other potential issues are on the horizon: maritime jurisdiction; approaches to the question of "a new international economic order"; and attitudes toward the Soviet Union.

Concerning the latter question, Japan is likely to avoid, if at all possible, a sustained partisan position with respect to the Sino-Soviet struggle. Its interests lie in some degree of balance in its relations with the two major Communist states. Recent events have indicated how difficult it is to achieve and maintain such a position. Currently, anti-Soviet sentiment runs high in Japan as a result of the northern territory and fisheries issues. Nevertheless, an alliance with China, de jure or de facto, would greatly complicate Japan's relations with the USSR, and with few discernible advantages. On balance, therefore—both for intrinsic strategic reasons and because of the complex overlay of issues that can unite and divide them, China and Japan are likely to continue a relationship that harbors both cooperation and contention.

One of the admirable qualities of the essays that follow is the freshness and diversity which they bring to bear upon both contemporary issues, such as those just discussed, and issues embedded in the history of Sino-Japanese relations that serve as a vital background to current developments. In part, this is due to the fact that the editors have enlisted individuals of different ethnic backgrounds as well as from different disciplines. Different generations are also represented, bringing to bear yet another variable. Thus, the reader can detect not merely differences of opinion but differences of nuance, emphasis, even cultural perspective. At a time when few views concerning modern Asia are unanimously held, it is good to be confronted with well-argued diversity.

**

Robert A. Scalapino is Robson Research Professor of Government and Director of the Institute of East Asian Studies at the University of California, Berkeley. He is also the editor of *Asian Survey* and the author of numerous books and articles on Japan, China, Korea, and U.S. policy in Asia.

China and Japan

I. Overview

1.

The first essay, by Chalmers Johnson, characterizes the establishment of diplomatic relations between Japan and the People's Republic of China as "the single greatest result of the so-called Nixon–Kissinger policy of détente toward the PRC" and places the event itself in the broad setting of the history of East Asian–global international relations.

The first part of the essay, with minor changes, is reprinted with permission from *Foreign Affairs,* July 1972; copyright 1972 by Council on Foreign Relations, Inc. The second part was entirely rewritten for this collection.

Professor Johnson's works on China and Japan include *Peasant Nationalism and Communist Power* (1962), *An Instance of Treason* (1964), *Conspiracy at Matsukawa* (1972), and *Autopsy on People's War* (1973). He is chairman of the Department of Political Science and was from 1967 to 1972 chairman of the Center for Chinese Studies at the University of California, Berkeley.

How China and Japan See Each Other

Chalmers Johnson

I.

Over the past century the politics of East Asia have been influenced more profoundly by the Sino-Japanese relationship than by any other single factor. Because both present-day societies have roots in classical Chinese civilization—only a "heritage" for each today—Chinese and Japanese politicians before World War II often argued that there was a special binding relationship between them. Japan's written language and much of its religious, artistic, and moral civilization derive from Chinese culture, while Japan was the primary influence both positively and negatively on whole generations of Chinese revolutionaries, some of whom are still active today. Perhaps because of this common heritage of civilization and mutual influence, the enormous misunderstandings, wars, threats, and depredations that have characterized Sino-Japanese relations for a century have tended to take on the ferocity of a family or civil feud. Even though well-educated Chinese and Japanese can learn each other's language rather easily, it is doubtful whether any two peoples in the twentieth century have approached each other with more profoundly misleading stereotypes.

Three specific historical occurrences continue to mold Chinese and Japanese attitudes toward each other, in addition to the broader pressures of different ideologies and national interests. First, China and Japan reacted to the influence of Western imperialism in the nineteenth century in almost diametrically opposite ways. Within a few decades after the Western intrusion, Japan had accommodated herself to and incorporated modern technology, whereas China disintegrated as a social system and required a century before she could begin her own modernization under conditions of

5

national unity. Second, prior to World War I, Japan served as an exemplar and model for many Chinese modernizers, a role that the Soviet Union took over after the Bolshevik Revolution; and just as in the case of the Sino-Soviet conflict, this earlier relationship has tended to color later antagonisms with feelings of ingratitude on the one hand and betrayal on the other. Third, Japan's ultimate betrayal, in the eyes of Chinese revolutionaries, was her military intervention in China between 1937 and 1945 in order to suppress by force the Chinese anti-imperialist nationalist movement—a savage crucible in which the Chinese Communist Party obtained a mass following by championing resistance to Japan.

Of these three elements, perhaps the first is of the greatest long-term significance. Premodern China and premodern Japan were sociologically quite different societies, and Western imperialist pressure impinged upon them in different ways. Nonetheless, they were similar enough—common Sinitic civilization, closed to foreign intercourse since the seventeenth century, and forced open by the West in the 1840s and 1850s—to cause members of each society to make invidious comparisons about the performance of the other in the face of common challenges. The Chinese, supremely confident of the superiority of their own culture, reacted with various antiforeign movements until the end of the century, while the Japanese, after a brief experiment with antiforeignism, gave it up as a lost cause and quickly modernized along Western lines.

Among the humiliations suffered by the Chinese, none was more galling than the defeat in 1895 of the "Celestial Empire" (China) by the "Wa dwarfs" (Japanese, as seen by the Chinese), a defeat that resulted in the ceding of Taiwan to Japan. The initial Chinese reaction to this defeat, which brought the first true Chinese revolutionary movements into being, was to blame their own inept government; and after 1895, thousands of Chinese students flocked to Japan to learn about the modern world. Over time and in light of Japan's subsequent development as an imperialist power in her own right, Chinese admiration of the Japanese modernization effort changed to hatred of Japan, the quintessential imperialist villain who kept China weak in order to usurp her resources.

China and Japan offer two of the clearest archetypes in the so-called Third World of alternative responses to Western imperialism. Japan adopted the reformist strategy, grafting Western institutions onto an essentially feudal social structure, changing in subtle ways but at the same time maintaining a distinctive national identity and continuity with the past. China rejected reform, since it seemed to imply an unacceptable accommodation of Confucian culture to barbarian (uncivilized) mores, and implacable imperialist pressure ultimately forced China to revolution—a revolution in which the traditional culture was to be totally dismantled and replaced with a new culture that could prevent the incessant foreign "humiliations" and restore a sense of national dignity.

Reform and revolution remain the two broad alternatives open to the so-called modernizing nations; and Japan and China, the one perhaps the most reformist nation in modern history and the other the most revolutionary, exemplify for them and for other nations the strengths and weaknesses of each strategy.

The attitudes that grew up along with these divergent histories persist to the present time and will have an important influence on any future process of Sino-Japanese reconciliation. To the Chinese, the Japanese "economic miracle" is not only a threat; it is also an insult. Today the Chinese trade more with Japan than with any other nation, but they do not praise Japan for her economic success, nor do they appear willing to put Sino-Japanese economic cooperation on a stable long-term footing. For that matter, the Chinese do not display much understanding of why Japan's economy continues to grow as fast as it does. Many Chinese leaders think that Japan's economic power is an inevitable precursor of remilitarization and imperialism, and the Chinese have not thus far shown the slightest willingness to adjust to the fact that Japan's GNP is larger than China's and will continue indefinitely to be so.

The Japanese, on the other hand, seem to be befogged by an equally long-standing inability to take the Chinese seriously. It is perhaps not too farfetched to describe Japanese attitudes toward their continental neighbors as somewhat comparable to the English or German industrialist's attitude toward an Italian or Spanish aristocrat recently gone into commerce. He admires, and is slightly intimidated by, the ancient cultural achievements to which his modern counterpart is heir, but he finds it almost impossible in the company boardroom to suggest seriously that the new boy might become a competitor or a threat. Japan today is interested in doing business with China but her interest in the China business is only a slight fraction of her interest in business generally, and Japanese commercial representatives seem quite willing to sign humiliating Chinese communiqués or other anti-Japanese pronouncements drafted by Peking in order to get what trade there is—presumably because the Japanese do not take these Chinese pronouncements very seriously. The Japanese are more concerned about the possibility that another nation might get ahead of them in the China trade than that the Chinese might compete with them successfully in the rest of Asia.

Even Chinese nuclear weapons do not appear to have caused the Japanese to view China as a potential threat, although the Japanese dislike atomic testing by anybody. One sign of this Japanese self-confidence vis-à-vis China is the underdeveloped state of postwar Japanese research on the Chinese Revolution. Japan's academic and governmental specialists on Chinese Communist developments are among the most knowledgeable in the world, but all of them complain of students' and the Japanese public's relatively slight interest in scholarship on China. Even when Chinese events reach the headlines, they are likely to be regarded as mere "news," and not as developments that might vitally affect Japan as a nation.

None of this is to suggest that the major sources of tension between China and Japan are attitudinal and that there are no real problems. It is rather to point out that the Chinese tend to regard Japan, for good historical reasons, with the utmost suspicion, remembering how quickly the old samurai of the nineteenth century armed themselves with Western weapons and turned these against China. China's stereotypes of Japan seem to preclude a realistic Chinese assessment of how Japan has changed and of the ways in which she may change in the future, always coming back to the underlying suspicion that Japan's achievements are likely to be at China's expense. Conversely, the Japanese regard the Chinese as still struggling with their interminable revolutions and are inclined to take the Chinese deadly seriously only when it looks as if the Chinese are about to form an alliance with a non-Asian power, say, the Soviet Union or the United States, for that might greatly restrict Japan's freedom of access and maneuver in international commerce.

The other two main historical influences affecting Sino-Japanese relations—Japan's erstwhile role as model and leader of an "Asian renaissance," and the second Sino-Japanese war—reinforce and provide sustenance for the deeper suspicions arising out of the two nations' differing responses to the West. From approximately 1895 to the Treaty of Versailles (1919), and persisting in an attenuated form until Japan's seizure of Manchuria in 1931, Chinese and Asian nationalists of many different political hues traveled to Tokyo to learn modern scientific culture and political ideas. During this period, Japan herself was wrestling with the problem of what kind of foreign policy she might appropriately pursue in the world. Should she use her newly acquired power to lead the rest of Asia toward independence and modernity? Or should she, having achieved the industrial underpinnings of Great Power status, join the imperialists? Despite what one may think with the benefit of hindsight, the answer was not a foregone conclusion.

Prior to World War I (and Japan's discovery of how easy it was to step into the enclaves vacated by the then-distracted European imperialists), some Japanese gave considerable aid and assistance to Chinese revolutionaries such as Sun Yat-sen. Equally important, Japan herself provided the climate for political discussion and ideological exploration that was so essential to the education of revolutionary leaders. In fact, much of the contemporary Chinese vocabulary of politics—such terms as anarchism, socialism, communism, nationalism—derives from Japanese renderings of these European words. Even when the Japanese began to lean toward an imperialist rather than an Asian role, many Chinese tried to continue to work with them.

Japan's progression from the Twenty-one Demands on China in 1915 to the seizure of Manchuria in 1931 ultimately filled all Chinese nationalists with enmity against Japan, a sentiment bolstered by fury against Japan's parvenu imperialism and betrayal of her fellow Asians. When, in the 1930s, Japanese militarists tried to revive an anti-Western Asian nationalism, they were too late. In Chinese eyes, Japan was no longer Asian; she was imperialist, pure and simple.

The Sino-Japanese War (1937–1945) itself bred further animosities that continue to influence perceptions, but it would be wrong to interpret the war's effects solely in terms of its brutalities. The war's more lasting contribution was its cognitive or ideological structure. Virtually all adult Japanese acknowledge and wish to atone for Japan's military actions on the continent, but many fewer will agree that Japan was fighting for a totally worthless national cause. They recall that in the depression era of "economic nationalism," every area of East Asia from India to the Philippines, with the exception of China and Thailand, was a European or American colony and that Japan was threatened with being frozen out in each of these territories. When China, the last country open to Japanese economic activity, began to develop a powerful, quasi-Marxist, anti-imperialist, anti-Japanese social movement—one enjoying the sympathy and sometimes the encouragement of the United States—Japan reacted with panic. Fears of international isolation and of alliances working against Japan's needs as a resource-poor, overpopulated, insular, industrial economy lay very close to the surface, as they do today. Thus the mentality of "Japan, Inc." and protectionism remain powerful despite Japan's present global economic outreach.

On the Chinese side, World War II tended irresistibly to recommend Marxist and especially Leninist modes of thought to Chinese nationalists, since the progress of Japan from feudalism to capitalism to imperialism seemed to be a compelling confirmation of Marxist-Leninist ideology. Even with the decline of ideological rigidity in the Communist world and the Sino-Soviet schism, China continues to believe that there is an economic inevitability about Japan's being a menace to China, regardless of what the Japanese (or representatives of other economically advanced nations) profess. Needless to say, Japan's postwar alliance with the United States and America's own deep postwar antagonism to the Chinese Communists did nothing to lessen the hold of this ideological cast of mind.

Chinese Communist ideology is a complex subject, and no suggestion is intended that it is unchanged or that it is the primary influence on Chinese behavior in the world. Rather, what should be stressed is that the heritage of World War II in Sino-Japanese relations has an ideological dimension and that such set patterns of thinking may be more important in future contacts between China and Japan than wartime memories. For example, Japan today has a vested interest in international stability, a prerequisite for the global commerce on which Japan depends and thrives.

So Japan is increasingly making available foreign aid to the established governments of such countries as Indonesia, Malaysia, and Thailand, and is opposed to revolutionary movements. How does China interpret these Japanese activities—say, economic aid to South Korea or to Thailand? Inevitably, the Chinese explain Japan's posture in ideological terms, as a reflection of the "capitalist-imperialist-reactionary syndrome." China does not and probably will not soon accept the legitimacy of Japan's close commercial and aid ties with the other nations of Asia.

On the other hand, China's efforts to promote revolution throughout the Third World strike Japan as evidence of China's continuing Communist-based hostility to nations such as Japan. China is not—yet—a stability-promoting force in the world, and this stance of China's directly conflicts with a basic Japanese national interest. The Japanese recall what happened to their important prewar China market under revolutionary conditions, and they are not the least bit reasssured by the continued virulence of Communist ideology on the mainland. In short, both China and Japan have good reasons to fear a recurrence of such international conditions as existed in the 1930s; both nations' perceptions of that possibility are, however, colored by their respective ideological explanations of why those conditions ever came about in the first place.

II.

One needs to bear this heritage in mind when looking at recent East Asian developments. October 1, 1974, the twenty-fifth anniversary of the founding of the People's Republic of China, was also the second anniversary (plus two days) of the establishment of diplomatic relations between Japan and China. It does not seem an exaggeration to say that the agreement signed in Peking on September 29, 1972, at the time of former Prime Minister Tanaka's visit, whereby Japan broke relations with the Republic of China on Taiwan and recognized the People's Republic of China, was one of the most significant events in modern Asian history. Although both the Chinese and Japanese refer to this exchange of ambassadors as a "normalization" of relations, it is hard to imagine a period in which relations between Japan and China were ever "normal." Normalization, of course, means creation of ties comparable to those that exist between other nation-states at peace, and not the restoration of some preexisting normal state of Sino-Japanese relations, since such a state never existed at any time in the past.

Indeed, in light of the bitter relations between China and Japan during the first three-quarters of this century that have dominated the

politics of the rest of eastern Asia, the single greatest result of the so-called
Nixon–Kissinger policy of détente toward the PRC has been precisely the
establishment of diplomatic ties between Peking and Tokyo. It is of course
true that the American government was strongly criticized for failing to
coordinate its change in China policy with its Japanese allies and that the
Americans' primary motivation was not to effect an improvement in Sino-
Japanese relations. Nonetheless, the most important, even if unintended,
consequence of the Nixon trip to China in February 1972 was to deliver a
seismic shock to the Japanese government, causing it to take steps that
ended a longer and much more dangerous impasse in China's foreign
relations than ever existed between China and the United States. Before
1972, some Japanese and some Americans—notably former U.S. Ambassador to Japan Edwin O. Reischauer—used to talk of Japan serving as a
bridge between China and the United States. A moment of serious
reflection would have revealed that this was a bridge no Chinese was ever
likely to set foot on. A much more likely scenario was that the United States
would serve as a bridge between China and Japan. This is precisely what
happened.

It should be recalled that only seven months before Prime Minister
Tanaka's trip to Peking, in the Sino-American communiqué of Shanghai
(February 28, 1972), the Chinese wrote that "The Chinese People's
Republic firmly opposes the revival and outward expansion of Japanese
militarism and firmly supports the Japanese people's desire to build an
independent, democratic, peaceful and neutral Japan." A few months later,
Peking not only dropped all mention of the "revival of Japanese militarism," it also no longer wished Japan to become neutral. Much to the
embarrassment of leftist parties within Japan, Peking became an open
champion of the Japanese-American security treaty. What brought about
this sudden and unforeseen improvement in Sino-Japanese relations? And
what are the prospects for the future?

The easy answer to the first question is that the change in American
policy caused the change in Japanese policy, but this is inadequate for at
least two reasons: it overly personalizes the change in American policy,
centering on former President Nixon (as, for example, in Japanese references to the so-called Nixon shocks), and it offers no explanation at all for
China's changed attitudes toward Japan. There were, of course, many
factors leading up to the unfreezing of Sino-Japanese relations, but the
most fundamental seems to have been the Sino-Soviet dispute. As in so
many other areas of East Asian politics, it is impossible to overstate the
significance of the rupture between the two Communist superpowers; that
dispute remains the most important determinant of East Asian international relations and, in fact, of much of the politics of the world as a whole.

Prior to 1960, Japan was dominated by feelings of remorse toward
China and by a desire to establish a basis of friendship. The American-

imposed policy of embargo against China was heartily disliked within Japan, and many elements in Japanese society wanted to reestablish trade relations with China. The embargo was pursued solely because the United States demanded it and because the Japanese felt that Japan required the friendship and protection of the United States. The 1950s were also the heyday of Japan's ban-the-bomb movement and the period when Japan's antirearmament movement was the strongest. As one authority wrote, "Contrition, humility, nostalgia, and sympathy had combined in early postwar Japan to induce among the Japanese people a sympathetic attitude toward their Chinese neighbors. Neither China's domestic policies nor her entry into the Korean War seemed to shake Japan's unreciprocated feelings of friendship."[1]

The Sino-Soviet split of 1960 ended this mood, first and most directly by dividing the Japanese peace movement into many warring factions over such issues as whether Soviet nuclear tests were to be opposed as seriously as American tests. More important than this propaganda fallout, China became committed to the development of a domestic arms industry of superpower proportions. In addition to developing a nuclear weapons capacity, China by the late 1960s was able to supply a very significant proportion of the small arms and ammunition used by the Communist side in the Vietnam War, a capacity China did not have at the time of Korea, when the Chinese were themselves armed by the Russians.

China's development of an advanced weapons capacity caused the Japanese during the 1960s to see China, for the first time, as a potential threat. There was never any likelihood of an invasion of Japan, but China increasingly had the capacity to destroy Japan through the use of nuclear weapons or to exercise a nuclear blackmail. Some Japanese speculated openly about the possibility of Japan's acquiring a nuclear capacity, particularly now that Japan had the industrial base from which to do so. This reaction within Japan, slow developing though it was throughout the 1960s, in turn produced the late–1960s reaction in China to the alleged dangers of "revived Japanese militarism." Chou En-lai made this explicit in his famous proclamations in Pyongyang in April 1970 about how the Satō government was "planning to follow the old road of Japanese militarism, trying again to reconstruct the old illusion of a Greater East Asia Co-Prosperity Sphere."

Chou's statement ushered in a Chinese propaganda campaign of vituperation against Japan that lasted until 1972. It was characterized by attacks on Japanese films and culture, worries about the various communiqués issued by Satō and Nixon, hysterical reactions to the suicide of novelist Yukio Mishima on November 25, 1970, and various other attempts to sound an alarm against Japan's alleged preparations for aggressive war. By far the clearest and most dispassionate statement of this Chinese policy came in the interview between Premier Chou En-lai and columnist James Reston of the *New York Times* on August 5, 1971. Chou pointed out, first, that the United States had strengthened the Japanese reactionaries in the postwar world and that Japan's great economic expansion would inevitably induce the growth of militarism. Second, Chou argued that the United States had promoted such growth by prolonging indefinitely its security treaty with Japan. Reston countered by suggesting that without the pact, Japan's incentive to "go nuclear" would increase. Chou called this a "forced argument," but he was unconvincing in his attempt to refute it.

The original Chinese decision to go nuclear, the Japanese reaction to this development, and the Chinese reaction to the Japanese reaction can all be traced to unintended consequences of the Sino-Soviet split in 1960. But that dispute also had a more direct effect: the real possibility from about 1969 on that China and the Soviet Union might become engaged in a nuclear war. It was this development above all others that changed Chinese attitudes toward Japan and made China receptive to overtures of peace from President Nixon of the United States and Prime Minister Tanaka of Japan. The Sino-Soviet dispute also explains why in October 1973 Premier Chou En-lai told a visiting delegation of Japanese Diet members representing all parties except the Japanese Communist Party that Japan should maintain indefinitely the Japanese-American security treaty and should also build up its own defense forces. Chou said that these measures were necessary to counter the threat of Soviet social imperialism, which he defined as the greatest threat to world peace. It further explains why the Chinese have gone out of their way to strengthen the pro-Peking forces within the Japanese Liberal Democratic Party (LDP), why they have been so lenient on Japan's trade relations with Taiwan, and why they have been so alarmed by the Japanese Communist Party's growing strength.

Relations between the Japanese and Chinese Communist parties form an important component of this very complex picture. Before the Sino-Soviet dispute, China defined U.S. imperialism as the primary enemy of Communist forces. After 1960, Soviet "social imperialism" progressively displaced U.S. imperialism for top billing as the enemy. From about 1961 until 1966, the Japanese Communist Party (JCP) tended to agree with the Chinese position in the then primarily ideological Sino-Soviet dispute, and during this period it purged from its own ranks about 600 pro-Soviet members. However, this period of interparty cordiality ended abruptly in April 1966. At that time, JCP Secretary-General Miyamoto Kenji led a JCP delegation to Pyongyang, Hanoi, and ultimately Peking, where it had a historic confrontation with the Chinese leadership. The Japanese were critical of the Cultural Revolution, were extremely disturbed by the so-called September 30 Incident (1965), which initiated the destruction of the Indonesian Communist Party in the course of following Mao Tse-tung's policies, and wanted an international Communist front in support of North Vietnam in the Vietnam War. Mao countered by urging the Japanese Communists to open guerrilla warfare in Japan, something the Japanese could only view as a suicidal gesture. The JCP delegation went home and denounced Mao and his leadership; the Chinese Communists in turn raised the JCP to the level of one of China's primary enemies. The split became irreversible on October 10, 1967, with the JCP's publication of its Central Committee Thesis, *Konnichi no Mō Taku-tō rōsen to kokusai kyōsanshugi undō* [Mao Tse-tung's line today and the international Communist movement]. In this document, the JCP accuses Mao of representing a faction opposed to Marxism-Leninism and characterizes the Chinese Cultural Revolution as a revisionist heresy.

All of this might be of only marginal interest to students of Communist factionalism, except for the facts that the dispute between the two parties has continued and deepened and that the Japanese Communist Party is one of Japan's leading opposition parties. The JCP increased its strength in the Diet in the December 1972 general election, and again in the 1974 upper house election. And the JCP is a severe critic of both the LDP's China policy and China's current line. At its Twelfth Congress in November 1973, the JCP Central Committee denounced the Chinese for their alleged "beautification" *(bika)* of U.S. imperialism in supporting the security treaty and urging Japan to maintain the *kaku no kasa* ("nuclear umbrella") of the United States. The JCP accused the Chinese of lacking principles, of revisionism, of the betrayal of Asian socialist states and national liberation movements, and of being "Nixon lovers." These attacks are important because the JCP commands a respect in Japan that goes well beyond its electoral strength. It has formally renounced violent revolution, is actively competing in parliamentary contests, and has emerged as a champion of consumer and citizen needs. The JCP's *Akahata* is one of the most widely read newspapers in the country—partly because it has an outstanding sports page—and its attacks against China have weakened the LDP's basis of support for its pro-Peking policies.

Although the Sino-Soviet dispute was and remains the single most important force pulling the Americans, the Japanese, and the Chinese together, other, more immediate forces made possible Tanaka's initiative of 1972. First and foremost was pure political opportunism. The announcement by President Nixon in July 1971 that Kissinger had secretly visited Peking and that the president himself had accepted an invitation to visit China, all without consulting the leading American ally in East Asia, doomed the Satō government then and there. Tanaka ran for the Liberal Democratic Party presidency the following July on a platform of "not missing the boat to China"—in fact, of surpassing the Americans in the race to win friends in Peking. Tanaka was aware, as was Nixon, that the China initiatives created an enormous, although as it turned out fleeting, public interest in China, which had been for so long obscured from public view; and it satisfied the citizens' demands for novelty, all of which could be translated into votes. Backing up Tanaka in Japan, as in the case of Nixon in the United States, was a major China boom in the mass media centering on pandas, acupuncture, the Great Wall, Chinese food, and Chou En-lai's renowned good manners and civility. Tanaka defeated Satō's designated successor, Fukuda Takeo, simply by promising to recognize the Peking government.

More substantive, and indispensable for the success of the LDP's new policy, was a major wave of enthusiasm that swept the Japanese trading and industrial world for the expansion of the China market. Japan had already been China's leading trade partner since the Sino-Soviet dispute, but throughout 1971 and 1972, Japanese economic circles came to believe that China trade was about to expand enormously and that Japan must be in the forefront of all nations hoping to establish commercial ties with China. Actually, this was an old refrain in Japan, and the *zaikai* ("financial world") was not at all unified on it. For many years a segment of Japanese business and of the Japanese government, notably the Ministry of International Trade and Industry, wanted to promote closer economic relations with China. They were horrified to find the United States in advance of Japan on the march to China, since they had themselves held off only in order not to offend the Americans. This pro-China group was centered mostly in the so-called *Kansai zaikai,* that is, the industrial and commercial interests of the Osaka and Kobe areas. These pro-Chinese views were not nearly so strongly held in Tokyo industrial circles, however, where there were major doubts about the size of the China market and also close ties to Taiwan. In 1972, the Nixon shocks and the Tanaka candidacy caused the Kansai interests to overwhelm the Tokyo interests and to bring virtually the entire business community into line in support of the Liberal Democratic Party and of Prime Minister Tanaka.

What about the future of Sino-Japanese relations? This is first of all an economic question because the relations between China and Japan are above all economic in character. Japan's total exports during 1973 were valued at US$36.9 billion. Of this amount, Taiwan bought 4.4 percent and the People's Republic of China, 2.8 percent. Japan's total imports for 1973 were valued at US$38.3 billion, of which 2.5 percent came from the PRC and 2.3 percent from Taiwan.

Japan's economic relations with the two Chinas could go in any of several directions, depending on whether Taiwan maintains its separate status, whether the Sino-Soviet dispute continues, whether the successors to Mao and Chou En-lai maintain China's foreign policies of the mid-1970s, and whether the Chinese will be willing to export to Japan some of their newly discovered petroleum resources at stable prices and amounts. A basis for future cooperative relations between China and Japan was laid by the initiatives of Nixon, Tanaka, and Chou En-lai during 1972. Whether these contacts will actually develop into mutually advantageous relations is one of the truly significant questions for the last quarter of the twentieth century. Meanwhile, it is well to remember that China and Japan have been interacting with each other and misunderstanding each other for a century, during which both have undergone dramatic changes. There is little evidence that either country "understands" the other any better than it did in the past. If China will coexist with Japan only on Chinese terms, then the recent Japanese position of adaptability is likely to wither and tensions between the two countries will grow. If China is prepared to compromise with Japan, then the Japanese will surely make concessions in order to see that conditions improve. Whatever the outcome of particular negotiations, however, the long-standing rivalries between the two nations are likely to persist.

Notes

1. John Emmerson and Leonard Humphreys, *Will Japan Rearm?* (Washington, D.C., 1973), p. 17.

II. Administration, Government, Diplomacy to 1931

2.

Tsing Yuan, born in Peking, is the son of the late distinguished bibliographer of Chinese studies, T. L. Yuan. After undergraduate study at Harvard and George Washington University, and an M.A. from the latter, Tsing Yuan entered the Ph.D. program in East Asian history at the University of Pennsylvania, receiving his doctorate in 1969. From 1966 to 1972 he taught at Swarthmore College and has been promoted to associate professor of history at Wright State University, Ohio. He had an American Council of Learned Societies fellowship in 1970.

In the following essay he discusses the Shantung question of the World War I era, which so greatly embittered Chinese-Japanese relations, from the standpoint of what Japan actually did in replacing the Germans as occupiers of Shantung.

The Japanese Intervention in Shantung during World War I

Tsing Yuan

I.

World War I represented a turning point in the power balance in East Asia. By removing the Europeans from the Chinese scene, the outbreak of the Great War left Japan as the paramount power in the area. Indeed, Japan lost little time in pressing her claims on the young Chinese Republic from Manchuria and Mongolia in the north to Fukien in the south. The Kiaochow area of Shantung, under German control since 1898, appeared a tempting prize once Germany and Japan's ally, Great Britain, were at war. On the basis of the Anglo-Japanese Alliance, begun in 1902 and renewed in 1905 and again in 1911, Japan felt justified in intervening in Kiaochow.[1]

There have been several studies on the Japanese presentation of the Twenty-one Demands on China in 1915 as well as on the so-called Shantung question at the Paris Peace Conference and the Washington Conference.[2] But thus far, academic inquiry has focused on the diplomatic ramifications of the Japanese occupation of Kiaochow, November 1914 to June 1922, when the Japanese government promised withdrawal. The principal concerns here are, however, the administrative and economic aspects of the Japanese occupation. Moreover, the present study seeks to make use of the vast archives of the Japanese Ministry of Foreign Affairs, now readily available on microfilm, as well as a number of Japanese contemporary research surveys of the Kiaochow area.

Finally, this essay raises the general question of "intervention" in light of the Shantung case. The notion itself implies organized and systematic activities to enhance one's own power and to undercut that of the other side. In retrospect, the great disparity between Chinese and Japanese power in

1914 created the opportunity for the Japanese to intervene. The manner in which economic domination followed military conquest has yet to be illumined. We shall first examine the Japanese military and civil administration of the Kiaochow area and the evolution of a long-term policy for the territory.

Three days after the surrender of the German garrison at Tsingtao on November 7, 1914, the Japanese military command converted its original Independent 16th Division, which had conquered the territory, into the Tsingtao Military Garrison Forces. Henceforth, the new military headquarters would have direct jurisdiction over local police, the Tsingtao Customs, the Tsingtao-Tsinan Railway linking the port with the provincial capital, as well as sanitation and postal services.[3] The new command would encompass an infantry of 4000 men, a cavalry of 150 men, a light artillery of 300, a heavy artillery of 300, an engineering unit of 200, and a railway corps of 200.[4]

The issuance, on November 19, 1914, of "Regulations of the Japanese Administration of Kiaochow" gave the first indication that the intervention was no temporary affair. These regulations divided the Kiaochow territory into two districts, Tsingtao and Litsun, each of which was to be supervised by a military administrator directly responsible to the commander in chief of the Tsingtao garrison. The regulations empowered the two administrators to levy taxes, public rates, and special assessments.[5] The preservation of law and order was obviously a major concern of the Japanese authorities, and the administrators were instructed to carry out existing Chinese laws as long as they did not interfere with Japanese requirements.

Before long, the right of Japanese citizens to lease land within Kiaochow gained official recognition. In view of the unsettled conditions created by the steady influx of Japanese migrants into the territory, the military authorities issued on January 26, 1915, a set of regulations governing leasing. The applicant must be a respectable citizen of Japan and he and the Chinese landowner must sign his application, with a statement on the dimensions of the land and the period of the contract.[6] The purpose of the new ruling was to curtail illegal seizures by the Japanese migrants and thereby alleviate Chinese discontent.

The inauguration of a civil administration in late September 1917 was convincing proof that the government headed by Prime Minister Terauchi Masatake had no intention of withdrawing from Shantung. In preparation for the administrative change, the Terauchi cabinet appointed General Hongō Fusatarō (1860–1931), the vice-minister of war, as the new commander in chief of the Tsingtao garrison.[7] A professional soldier, General Hongō had fought in the Russo-Japanese War, becoming a major general in 1905 and a lieutenant general in 1912. Arriving in Tsingtao on September 9, 1917, Hongō's major task was to create a civil administration that would give longer-range stability to the Japanese intervention.

The new civil administration was, however, intended not to replace the Tsingtao garrison but to be subordinate to it, in accordance with the imperial ordinance issued by the Taishō emperor on September 29.[8] The civilian authority was to take over the management of the railway and communications, as well as the post office and the wharves. The new civil administrator was Akiyama Masanosuke (1866–1937), a distinguished jurist and Japanese representative at the Red Cross Congress in Washington in 1912. Of his staff of 600, as many as 400 were in positions connected with the operation of the Tsingtao-Tsinan Railway. Akiyama himself left no doubt that he was subordinate to the commander in chief. In a speech he gave before the Military Club of Tsingtao on October 11, he said:

> . . . as long as the present war lasts, this place will be dealt with as in military occupation and the occupied territory should be administered by the Military Commander, that is, the will of the Military Commander is the law to be enforced in the occupied territory according to the principle of international law in war time.[9]

Because there was no Sino-Japanese agreement on the status of Kiaochow, the creation of a civil administration naturally gave rise to speculation about its significance. The Chinese suspected that the administrative shuffle meant a change from temporary military occupation to a more permanent peacetime status. To allay that suspicion, General Hongō gave the reassurance that only a desire for the improvement of Sino-Japanese relations had prompted the change. During an official inspection trip, from November 9 to November 11, which took him to the provincial capital Tsinan as well as to the Tomb of Confucius in Chufou, General Hongō asserted that military officers were not experts in the execution of administrative tasks and were liable to make mistakes that could hinder international cooperation.[10] Civilians, being more adaptable, could correct misunderstandings that might exist between the Chinese and the Japanese. Moreover, the Japanese commander in chief acknowledged the increasing influx of Japanese into Shantung and explained that the civil administration would look after their affairs.

II.

As the Japanese government placed the Kiaochow territory under a more permanent administrative structure, the intervention and the eventual disposition of this territory became subjects of discussion within Japan. A number of Japanese publicists, including Matsumoto Tadao, dwelt on the sacrifices Japan had made in the war with Germany and argued that these losses justified Japan's retention of Kiaochow.[11] Yet to a disinterested observer of the immense loss of men in Europe at the time, Japanese casualties in the entire campaign involving Shantung and the Carolines, the Marshalls, and the Marianas were infinitesimal: 12 officers killed, 40 officers wounded, and some 1472 men either killed or wounded among the rank and file.[12] It was obvious that in the hour of patriotism, any loss would be considered a "sacrifice."

More forceful in his arguments was Ninagawa Arata, a renowned scholar of international law. In his article in *Gaikō Jihō*, he systematically demolished the various arguments that had been advanced for the return of Kiaochow to China. Countering the notion of preserving Chinese sovereignty, Ninagawa posed the rhetorical question, Why doesn't Japan give up all her concessions and leased territories in China?[13] In answer to the argument that Japan would win praise from the rest of the world, he cited the example of Britain's retention of Gibraltar. Refuting the argument that the war against Germany had been waged on behalf of justice, Ninagawa expounded the philosophy of *Realpolitik,* asserting that wars among nations were always fought for the sake of power.[14] The article is of interest because of its nationalistic tenor and because Ninagawa felt the need to counter the more moderate and pacifistic views being aired in Japan.

Although Ninagawa gave little weight to world opinion, more thoughtful Japanese leaders must have pondered the reaction of the United States to Japan's intervention in Shantung. In his article on Kiaochow Bay, Suehiro Shigeo cited the Root–Takahira Agreement of 1908. He argued that the new developments in Kiaochow had not contravened the clause of the agreement advocating preservation of the status quo in the Pacific: "If the United States should protest the Japanese occupation of a stretch of the China coast bordering on the Pacific, we should also be able to reproach the United States for any action she might take in Central or South America, which also border on the Pacific."[15] In this context of self-righteous justification of the intervention, the Japanese presented the notorious Twenty-one Demands to China in January 1915.

III.

Before 1914, the number of Japanese in German-held Kiaochow was insignificant. In 1901, only 50 to 60 Japanese could be found in Tsingtao; by 1913 the German census placed the number of Japanese in Tsingtao at

316, a very small proportion in a population of 55,672 Chinese and 4470 Europeans.[16] The lot of these Japanese was not easy, for the Germans, according to a Japanese authority, placed various restrictions on the Japanese and forbade them to work without special licenses.[17]

As soon as Japan took possession of the Kiaochow territory, the number of Japanese migrants grew. By February 1915, the number in Tsingtao itself had grown to 5275, while a corresponding increase took place in the rest of the territory and in Shantung province as a whole.[18] The statistics on the number of Japanese in the territory during the years 1915 to 1918 are revealing:[19]

December 1915:	15,738
December 1916:	21,812
December 1917:	25,329
December 1918:	25,899

These emigrants came from all walks of life. In mid-October 1914, the Chinese government noted that Japanese merchants were buying land and property in areas through which Japanese troops had just passed.[20] But later, the migration was more proletarian in color. Early in 1915, one Japanese newspaper reported that Tsingtao was being overrun by "penniless adventurers hungry for employment."[21] Another eyewitness noted that "all grades of Japanese are to be seen, including coolies and artisans, and ricksha-pullers."[22] In fact, many of the Japanese emigrants were barely able to pay for their passage to Tsingtao. In one sense, this influx was predictable, for the Japanese migration to the Liaotung Peninsula or Kwantung Leased Territory after the Russo-Japanese War followed a similar pattern. Before 1904, the number of Japanese in the vicinity of Port Arthur and Dairen was insignificant, but after the Japanese occupation, it grew by 1916 to 53,658.[23]

By 1918, the Japanese newcomers in Shantung could be found in almost every occupation. Within the Kiaochow territory itself, those engaged in commerce numbered 6575 and thus constituted the largest single occupational group; those in entertainment came next with 1385, followed closely by those connected with the Japanese administration, numbering 1341.[24] Among other occupations, 406 Japanese were in industry, 299 in transportation, 233 in agriculture, and 213 in fisheries. With Kiaochow safely in their hands, the Japanese could turn the territory into a base of operations for the economic penetration of the Shantung interior.

It is important to consider the economic ramifications of the Shantung intervention. Between November 1914 and the end of 1918 some fifty-two Japanese joint-stock companies were established in the Kiaochow territory. Twenty-eight of these each had investment capital of over 1,000,000 yen; eight had capital exceeding 10,000,000 yen; and three had capital exceeding 100,000,000 yen.[25] The last three were branches of giant concerns. The subsidiary of the Nippon Yūsen Kaisha at Tsingtao had 100,000,000 yen, that of the Mitsui had a similar share; while the harbor affairs branch of the South Manchurian Railway had as much as 200,000,000 yen.[26] Less well financed but still impressive were the branches of the Yokohama Specie Bank (48,000,000 yen) and the Bank of Chōsen (40,000,000 yen). But more representative of the new Japanese companies in Kiaochow were those capitalized at between 500,000 yen and 4,000,000 yen. Most of the salt-manufacturing companies belonged to this group, such as the Dai Nihon, the Tōa, and the Chintō companies.[27] Though smaller in comparison with the giants, they dwarfed by far their Chinese competitors.

Besides the salt-manufacturing companies, Japanese enterprises covered a wide range—flour mills, spinning mills, chemical factories, soap and match factories, rice mills, tanneries, ice factories, and canneries. Sometimes, the Japanese would take over old German companies and rework them. Thus, for example the Dai Nippon Brewery Company of Tokyo bought the Germania Beer Brewery in September 1916. More often Japanese merchants bought up Chinese concerns and operated them as Sino-Japanese companies.

Trade statistics reflected Japan's increasing share of the Tsingtao market. While cotton clothes imported from Great Britain declined from $392,992 in 1913 to a mere $87,826 in 1916, the same products imported from Japan during the same period increased from $25,813 to $181,620.[28] Similarly, imports from American cotton mills dwindled from $22,814 in 1913 to almost nothing in 1916, but imports from Japanese mills increased during the same years from $4,710 to $13,282. In this trade competition with other powers, Japan's control of the Tsingtao Customs no doubt proved to be a tremendous advantage. When the Japanese forces took Tsingtao, all the records and documents of the customs office were impounded and Chinese employees dismissed.[29] In a subsequent agreement in July 1915, the Chinese government agreed to the appointment of a Japanese commissioner of customs at Tsingtao and the retention of the Japanese personnel already appointed during the interim period.[30]

In addition, most of Tsingtao's exports went to Japan. Notable among these exports were foodstuffs, particularly beef, eggs, and salt. The shortage of salt in Japan and Korea created a great demand for that commodity, as shown by the proliferation of Japanese companies in Kiaochow. By 1921, at least 55 percent of the salt production in Shantung was in Japanese hands.[31] Of the salt exported from Tsingtao, 123,595 tons went to Japan, 43,093 tons to Korea, and only 27,243 tons were sent elsewhere.

Most of Tsingtao's imports and exports were carried by Japanese shipping lines. In 1913, Japanese ships accounted for 29 percent of all the vessels and 18 percent of the tonnage in Tsingtao's shipping; German ships enjoyed 33 percent and 42 percent, respectively. But by 1921, the Japanese share was 74 percent of all the vessels and 64 percent of all the tonnage.[32]

Far behind was the British share, 12 percent and 17 percent, respectively. Among the Japanese steamship lines operating between Tsingtao and various Japanese ports were Nippon Yūsen Kaisha, Chōsen Yūsen Kaisha, Harada Steamship Company, Dairen Steamship Company, Awa Steamship Company, and Osaka Shōsen Kaisha. They accounted for almost all the traffic between Tsingtao and such cities as Kobe, Osaka, Chemulpo, and Dairen, as well as Tientsin, Shanghai, and Hong Kong.

Making maximum use of their privileged position at Tsingtao, the Japanese authorities thought of various devices to curb foreign competition. One was the requirement that every foreign ship carry a special permit each time it gained entry to Tsingtao harbor. As late as September 1915, almost a year after the Japanese conquered Tsingtao, British ships were still required to produce this permit.[33] As a consequence, only two British lines— Jardine Matheson and Company and Butterfield and Swire—operated occasional steamers between Tsingtao and Shanghai.

Just as Japanese ships linked Tsingtao with the Japanese economy, so the Tsingtao-Tsinan Railway, under new Japanese management, served as the outlet for Japanese products in the Shantung interior. The Japanese also took over the mines located within the railway zone. The Japanese, contending that the Chinese were loyal to the Germans and hence could not be trusted, transferred their own employees from the South Manchurian Railway to replace the dismissed Chinese ticket inspectors, locomotive firemen, and railway policemen.[34]

China protested the seizure of a private company, in which the Chinese were also shareholders, arguing that as such, the railway could not be considered a prize of war.[35] But the Japanese legation dismissed the protest with the statement that the railway company was "entirely and purely a German company, possessing the nature of public property under direct control of the German Government."[36] Indeed, the Japanese also took over the private company that had operated the mines.

The Tsingtao-Tsinan Railway services experienced some improvement under Japanese management. Cushion seats replaced wooden benches in the second-class coaches and wooden benches were provided in the third-class cars, where under German management there had been none.[37] The Japanese increased the number of passenger cars from 102 in 1913 to 143 in 1921; during the same period the number of locomotives was increased from 46 to 94.[38] In 1914, under German management, the Tsingtao-Tsinan schedule listed 1 passenger train and 5 freight trains for an average working day; under the Japanese, there were 3 daily passenger trains and 10 daily freight trains. There was a definite increase in passenger traffic, estimated at 2,065,654 for 1917.[39] The gross receipts that year from both passenger and freight traffic amounted to 8,196,146 yen.[40] Moreover, possession of the railroad enabled the Japanese to control the economic pulse of Shantung.

IV.

Although Chinese opposition to the Japanese presence in Shantung did not crystallize until the May 4 Movement in 1919, there were stirrings of protest by the fall of 1917. The Japanese institution of a civil administration was the immediate occasion for an outpouring of Chinese indignation. Heretofore, Chinese protests in Shantung had been feeble and poorly directed; they were to become both more vocal and better organized. Earlier, Chinese protests were made mainly by the central government, but from October 1917 onward, popular participation in the anti-Japanese movement increased. Interestingly, it was not the students, who assumed an active role in the May 4 Movement, but the merchants and the local gentry who first took up the Japanese challenge. Among the prominent organizations participating in meetings and petitioning the Peking government were the Shantung Chamber of Commerce, the Farmers' League, and the Provincial Educational Association.[41] But the galvanizing influence was the Shantung Provincial Assembly, whose members were both responsive to popular pressure and able to mobilize public opinion.

Chinese opposition arose mainly because the Japanese had extended their jurisdiction beyond the Kiaochow territory into the interior of Shantung. To promote their control of the railway zone, the Japanese set up offices for civil administration in such interior towns as Fangtze, Changtien, and even in the provincial capital Tsinan.[42] In addition, the Japanese authorities in Kiaochow requested Chinese compliance for a census in the interior of the province. They also demanded that the chamber of commerce make daily reports of market fluctuations and exchange rates.[43] The Japanese had grandiose plans for afforestation and for the construction of roads, schools, and hospitals. The Chinese voiced their objections not because these efforts were not useful but because they obviously impinged on Chinese sovereignty.

As early as October 6, 1917, Consul Hayashi Kyujirō in Tsinan reported to Foreign Minister Motono that the Chinese had misconstrued Japanese intentions and could think only of the worst aspects of the civil administration.[44] For example, the Chinese daily in Tsinan, the *Ta-tung Jih-pao* (of October 5), had excoriated Japanese designs on Shantung. On November 10, Hayashi reported a mass rally held in Tsinan, which passed a number of resolutions condemning the Japanese establishment of a civil administration.[45] The rally ended only after the crowd decided to petition President Feng Kuo-chang, urging him to negotiate for the withdrawal of the Japanese administration.

If the appeal to a powerless president was futile, a more effective weapon, the boycott, was at hand. On November 18, a giant rally took place at Tsinan, attended by representatives of some sixty different organizations. Among them were the publisher of the *Ta-tung Jih-pao,* the head of the local chapter of the Chinese YMCA, and the board chairman of the Shantung Bank, as well as representatives from the chamber of commerce, the Provincial Educational Association, and the Shantung Provincial Assembly. The leaders announced the adoption of a boycott against Japanese goods, a measure that caused Hayashi deep concern.[46]

These rallies served to heighten Chinese national consciousness and to focus the prevailing anti-Japanese sentiments, and brought support from other areas of China. On November 15, 1917, the Chihli Provincial Assembly telegraphed its Shantung counterpart, pledging complete support.[47] Before the month was out, support had also come from Shansi, Shensi, Hupei, and Kirin provinces.[48] By the time World War I ended, anti-Japanese rallies and demonstrations were common occurrences. When the Allies awarded the Kiaochow territory to Japan at the Paris Peace Conference, the seeds of Chinese mass protest burst into full flower.[49]

Although the Japanese government promised to return the Kiaochow territory to China at the Washington Conference (1921–1922), the Japanese had already laid the economic infrastructure for control of Shantung province. This essay suggests that in light of their economic stranglehold, they could afford political and military concessions without jeopardizing their economic interests. To be sure, other considerations at the time of the Washington Conference probably influenced the Japanese decision for withdrawal: the emergence of party government in Japan, the return of the Western powers to the Pacific area after the Great War, and the stalemate of the Siberian intervention, as well as the increasing vehemence of Chinese nationalism. Yet in the final analysis, it was not simply idealism or internationalism alone, but pragmatic considerations that prompted Japan to relinquish her claims to Shantung and to withdraw her troops from the area. There was, after all, no strong central authority in China to challenge the growth of Japan's economic influence in Shantung in spite of her military withdrawal.

Apologists of intervention often tended to make a virtue of necessity. Japanese defenders of the Kiaochow intervention harped on the themes of opportunity, *Realpolitik,* and a Japanese version of the Monroe Doctrine. They left largely unsaid what was perhaps from an objective viewpoint an even more crucial factor in any intervention—the disparity in power between the parties intervening and those intervened against. Most, if not all, apologiae sounded alike and constituted minor variations from the same refrain: the importance of "security" and "proximity," or of conferring "enlightenment and order" upon those intervened against. Indeed, there can be little meeting ground between morality and intervention.[50]

To be sure, the historian can afford to indulge in hindsight. But looking at the initial American acquisition of the Philippines, for example, one notes how tenuous was the American connection to these islands in 1898 and how weighty the arguments to acquire them for the sake of civilizing and benefiting the natives.[51] The historical problem often is that such idealistic considerations tend to take precedence over more strategic and pragmatic motivations, at least in the public imagination. Thus Japanese publicists justified their government's actions in Shantung at the expense of a weak neighbor. Whatever their arguments, the Kiaochow intervention brought out Japan's best and worst qualities: a gift for enterprise and efficiency, but also high-handedness, greed, and self-infatuation.

Notes

1. On the history of the Anglo-Japanese Alliance, see the two definitive studies by Ian H. Nish, *The Anglo-Japanese Alliance: The Diplomacy of Two Island Empires, 1894–1907* (London, 1966), and *Alliance in Decline: A Study in Anglo-Japanese Relations, 1908–1923* (London, 1972).

2. Among the outstanding studies are Madeleine Chi, *China Diplomacy, 1914–1918* (Cambridge, Mass., 1970); Li Yü-shu, *Chung-Jih erh-shih-i t'iao chiao-she* [The Sino-Japanese negotiations on the Twenty-one Demands] (1966); T'ien-i Li, *Woodrow Wilson's China Policy, 1913–1917* (Kansas City, Mo., 1952); Russell H. Fifield, *Woodrow Wilson and the Far East* (Hamden, Conn., 1952).

3. *Chintō senryō go no shisei narabi ni zengo shobun zakken* [Miscellaneous documents relating to administration and reform measures after the occupation of Tsingtao], Gaimushō Archives (Library of Congress microfilm), MT 5.2.6.25:40.

4. Ibid., MT 5.2.6.25:42.

5. An English translation of the regulations can be found in Carnegie Endowment for International Peace, comp., *Shantung: Treaties and Agreements* (Washington, D.C., 1921), p. 72.

6. Ibid., p. 73.

7. Consul Willys Peck to Secretary of State Robert Lansing, 14 November 1917, Enclosure no. 13, U.S. Department of State Files (National Archives, Washington, D.C.), Decimal File 862a.01/3.

8. The original Japanese ordinance 175 can be found in *Nichi-Doku Sen'eki senryō-chi shisei ikken* [Documents relating to the administration of occupied areas resulting from the Japanese-German War], Gaimushō Archives, MT 5.2.6.221:106–13; an English translation of the ordinance can be found in *Papers Relating to the Foreign Relations of the United States, 1918* (Washington, D.C., 1930), pp. 216–18.

9. Peck to Lansing, 14 November 1917, Enclosure no. 14; the speech also appeared in *North China Herald,* 20 October 1917, p. 176.

31

10. Peck to Lansing, 14 November 1917, Enclosure no. 5.

11. Matsumoto Tadao, *Nisshi shinokōshō ni yoru teikoku no riken* [The rights and interests of the empire in reference to the recent Sino-Japanese negotiations] (Tokyo, 1921), pp. 11–12.

12. *The Japan Year Book, 1918* (Tokyo, 1919), p. 759.

13. Ninagawa Arata, "Ko-shū wan no zōyo" [The gift of Kiaochow Bay], *Gaikō Jihō* 21 (1915): 1307.

14. Ibid., p. 1308.

15. Suehiro Shigeo, "Ko-shū wan no shobun to Nibei kyōyaku" [The disposal of Kiaochow Bay and the Japanese-American Agreement], *Gaikō Jihō* 21 (1915): 260.

16. Tahara Teijirō, *Ko-shū wan* [Kiaochow Bay] (Tokyo, 1914), pp. 535, 540.

17. Ibid., p. 545.

18. *Japan Weekly Mail*, 20 February 1915, p. 15.

19. Chintō Shubigun [Tsingtao Military Headquarters], *Nempō, 1918* [Annual Report, 1918] (1920), p. 17.

20. Sun Pao-ch'i to Minister in Peking Hioki Eki, 11 October 1914, enclosed in Hioki to Foreign Minister Katō Taka'akira, 13 October 1914, Gaimushō Archives, MT 5.2.6.25:4.

21. *Japan Weekly Mail*, 23 January 1915, p. 60.

22. Peck to Secretary of State William Jennings Bryan, 11 February 1915, Decimal File 862a.00/8.

23. *The Japan Year Book, 1919–1920* (Tokyo, 1921), p. 739.

24. *Nempō, 1918,* pp. 169–72.

25. Ibid.

26. Ibid.

27. Ibid.

28. Julian Arnold, *Commercial Handbook of China* (1919), 1:626.

29. Liu Yen, *Ou-chan ch'i-chien Chung-Jih chiao-she shih* [A history of Sino-Japanese negotiations during the European war] (1921), p. 9.

30. *Japan Weekly Mail*, 3 July 1915, p. 67.

31. T'an T'ien-k'ai, *Shan-tung wen-t'i shih-mo* [The beginning and end of the Shantung problem] (1935), p. 45.

32. "The Maritime Customs of China," *Decennial Reports, 1912–1921* (1924), p. 209.

33. Norman to Prime Minister Ōkuma Shigenobu, 10 September 1915, Japanese Army and Navy Archives (Library of Congress microfilm), T319, F12330.

34. T'an T'ien-k'ai, op. cit., p. 41.

35. "Japan and the Shantung Railway," *Journal of the American Asiatic Association,* 15 February 1915, p. 22.

36. Ibid.

37. *Decennial Reports, 1912–1921,* p. 224.

38. Ibid.

39. Chintō Shubigun, *Nempō, 1917* [Annual Report, 1917] (1918), p. 11.

40. Ibid.

41. Peck to Lansing, 14 November 1917, Memorandum, p. 6, Decimal File 862a.01/3.

42. Ibid.

43. Peck to Lansing, 18 December 1917, Memorandum, p. 2. Decimal File 862a.01/4.

44. Consul Hayashi Kyujirō to Foreign Minister Motono Ichirō, 6 October 1917, Gaimushō Archives, MT 5.2.6.221:254.

45. Hayashi to Motono, 10 November 1917, ibid., MT 5.2.6.221:254.

46. Hayashi to Motono, 22 November 1917, ibid., MT 5.2.6.221:313.

47. Attaché Matsudaira Tsuneo to Motono, 16 November 1917, ibid., MT 5.2.6.221:250.

48. Hayashi to Motono, 12 December 1917, ibid., MT 5.2.6.221:367.

49. A thorough treatment of this movement can be found in Tse-tsung Chow, *The May Fourth Movement: Intellectual Revolution in Modern China* (Cambridge, Mass., 1960).

50. Manfred Halpern, *The Morality and Politics of Intervention* (New York, 1963), p. 10.

51. See John A. S. Grenville and George Berkeley Young, "The Influence of Strategy upon History: The Acquisition of the Philippines," in *American Expansionism: The Critical Issues,* ed. Marilyn B. Young (Boston, 1973), pp. 53–71. Also see Yamamoto Shirō, "Sansen nijūichikajō yōkyū to rikugun" [Participation in World War I, the Twenty-one Demands, and the army], *Shirin* 57:3 (1974):351–83.

3.

In her essay Hsi-ping Shao explores the attempts at Sino-Japanese cooperation during World War I, with special reference to the career of Tuan Ch'i-
jui.

Shao was born in Shanghai, but received her B.A. from National
Taiwan Normal University in 1959. After coming to the United States, she
enrolled in graduate studies at the University of Pennsylvania and completed her M.A. in East Asian history in 1964. The following study is based
on her doctoral dissertation, completed in 1976, entitled "Tuan Ch'i-jui,
1912–1918: A Case Study of the Military Influence on the Chinese Political
Development."

Her research for this study was made possible by a Shirley Farr
Fellowship from the American Association of University Women.

From the Twenty-one Demands to the Sino-Japanese Military Agreements, 1915–1918: Ambivalent Relations

Hsi-ping Shao

Since the late nineteenth century, the relationship between China and Japan has been characterized by repeated attempts to achieve mutual understanding and accommodation in the face of Western powers in the Far East. On the other hand, the China policy pursued by Japan collided sharply with China's desire to preserve her national interests and administrative integrity. For decades, Japan constituted an important factor in China's diplomatic relations as well as in her domestic politics. A succession of Chinese political leaders from Li Hung-chang and Yüan Shih-k'ai to Tuan Ch'i-jui rose and fell on their handling of the Japanese question. All of them, during the course of their political careers, veered from policies of direct confrontation to reconciliation with Japan. All of them tried, at one time or other, to utilize the time-honored tactics of *i-i chih-i* (playing one foreign power against the other) and *yüan-chiao chin-kung* (befriending the far and attacking the near). But in the end, they all foundered on the same knotty issue—how to maintain a precarious balance between cooperation with and capitulation to Japan.

The period from 1915 to 1918 provides good examples of the element of ambivalence in Sino-Japanese relations. The outbreak of World War I turned the attention of the Western powers to the armed struggles in Europe. This shift in the balance of power in Far Eastern international relations left Japan relatively free to pursue a unilateral policy in China, which created tensions and friction between the two nations. This diplomatic scene was further complicated by the deep Japanese involvement in China's internal politics. Personal ambitions and human frailties of Chi-

37

nese political figures also influenced their dealings with Japan, adding a peculiar poignancy to Sino-Japanese diplomatic relations of this period.

Yüan Shih-k'ai began his career as a military attaché to General Wu Ch'ang-ch'ing, commander of the Chinese expeditionary forces in Korea. Wu's task was to put down Korean internal disturbances instigated by the Taewongun in 1881. This experience gave Yüan his first insight into the intensity and nature of Sino-Japanese rivalry, and it made a lasting impression upon him. Viewed in retrospect, Yüan's meteoric rise was closely linked to the growing menace posed by Japan to the security of China. Perhaps more than any other political leader of his time, Yüan possessed a personal, firsthand knowledge of Japan's objectives in the Far East. He was also more aware of China's inadequacy to meet this serious challenge.[1]

After Yüan Shih-k'ai became president of the Chinese Republic, Japan regarded his administration with great misgiving, scarcely alleviated by the rapport he established with Sir John N. Jordan, British minister in Peking. For his part, Yüan was constantly on the alert for any chance to stave off the increasing Japanese pressure on China. In August 1914, Peking became apprehensive after learning of Japan's decision to attack the Germans in Shantung on the basis of the Anglo-Japanese Alliance. It was feared that Japan might also become active in Fukien province, where she had earlier attempted to acquire a foothold. Yüan offered to join the Allied military operations against Germany, hoping thereby to establish China's position among the Entente Powers. However, Sir John Jordan advised Yüan to do nothing;[2] without the necessary British support, Yüan laid the matter to rest. Officially, China established a policy of neutrality.[3]

On September 3 [in China], 1914, Japanese expeditionary troops landed at Lungkow on the northern coast of the Shantung Peninsula, in violation of China's neutrality. The Peking government reacted by delimiting a "war zone" for the belligerents,[4] which Japan contemptuously ignored. By early November, the Japanese troops had captured all the German leased territory in Shantung and were pushing westward along the Tsingtao-Tsinan Railway.[5] The Japanese took the position that the railway and all adjacent areas were part of the German leased territory in Shantung. Therefore, the Japanese government, having declared war against Germany, was justified in taking possession of and controlling the railway.[6] The Japanese military command even arrested and court-martialed Chinese citizens outside those areas on charges of spying. Chinese guards were also forced to withdraw from the railway zone.[7]

The outrageous Japanese activities in Shantung aroused great apprehension and resentment throughout the country. The members of the Council of State (Ts'an-cheng-yüan), under the leadership of Liang Ch'i-ch'ao, formally demanded an immediate answer from the government about steps being taken to safeguard China's territorial integrity against Japanese aggression.[8] Feng Kuo-chang, the powerful governor-general of Kiangsu, and several other senior military leaders also addressed a joint telegram to Yüan Shih-k'ai, pressing for the withdrawal of Japanese troops from Weihsien and Tsinan, both of which were situated outside the declared war zone.[9]

Under increasing domestic pressure for positive action, the Peking government repeatedly indicated to Japan that the war zone should return to normal conditions,[10] but to no avail. Therefore, the Waichiaopu (Ministry of Foreign Affairs) made a unilateral move on January 7, 1915, by informing the belligerents of the abolition of the war zone and asking for the withdrawal of Japanese troops from it.[11] Japanese Foreign Minister Katō Taka'akira refused to accept its validity. He instructed Hioki Eki, Japanese minister in Peking, to inform China that the Japanese troops would remain as long as necessary, and were in no way restricted by the declaration.[12]

On January 18, Hioki handed Yüan Shih-k'ai a series of demands, now well-known as the Twenty-one Demands. He wanted speedy action and total secrecy concerning the whole matter.[13] The first four groups consisted of a total of fourteen demands representing a wide range of rights and privileges sought by Japan in Shantung, southern Manchuria and Inner Mongolia, the Yangtze Valley, and the coastal province of Fukien. The most drastic, contained in the fifth group, directly infringed upon China's sovereignty and administrative integrity.[14]

In order to place Yüan Shih-k'ai's handling of the Japanese demands in its proper perspective, it is essential to view the episode against the background of Chinese domestic political developments. The Twenty-one Demands could not have come at a more awkward time for Yüan. Since his crushing defeat of the so-called Second Revolution led by the Kuomintang in 1913, Yüan had worked systematically to centralize political power in his own hands through a series of ingenious administrative reforms. By 1915, Yüan had succeeded in curtailing the authority of the territorial military commanders by stripping them of control over financial and civil matters in the provinces. At the national level, he had done away with the troublesome Parliament and replaced it with a quasi legislature, the Council of State, made up primarily of politicians of the old regime. The cabinet system was abolished, and the Administrative Court (Cheng-shih-t'ang) was set up with a secretary of state as its head, responsible directly and only to the president.[15] All such reforms were to pave the way for his monarchical scheme, already under way when the Twenty-one Demands were presented to him. These two seemingly isolated issues were subtly entangled. The arbitrary and high-handed manner in which Japan made these demands left Yüan with no illusions as to the ultimate Japanese objectives in China.

Yüan was unceremoniously reminded that he was not exactly the master of his own house. Whatever Yüan's political plans, it was clear that Japan's blessing would be vital to him.

The formal discussions concerning the Japanese demands began in February and continued through mid-April. In pressing for China's total acquiescence, Hioki employed all possible tactics of coercion—on April 17, for example, the negotiations were broken off at his insistence. Throughout, however, Yüan's hands were tied. No positive support from any of the Entente Powers was forthcoming, and China by herself was in no position to ward off Japan. Furthermore, there were warnings of an impending Japanese ultimatum.[16] At this point, Yüan was prepared to make almost any concessions. On May 5, Ts'ao Ju-lin, vice-minister of foreign affairs, was instructed to inform Hioki that China would be willing to reopen negotiations and even to consider the demands in Group V. Ironically, the Japanese government could no longer take advantage of Ts'ao's offer: earlier, Japan had made the content of the drafted ultimatum to China known to London, Paris, Petrograd, and Washington with the understanding that Group V was to be reserved for future consideration only.[17]

When Yüan was finally presented with the Japanese ultimatum on May 7, he was greatly relieved. Japan's temporary withdrawal of Group V was received with considerable personal satisfaction. In fact, he even interpreted this as a diplomatic victory of sorts.[18] On the following day, Yüan called a high-level meeting and indicated his readiness to accept the ultimatum. The majority of the participants went along with him.[19] The only dissident was Tuan Ch'i-jui, minister of war, who insisted on the rejection of the ultimatum and who proposed military resistance to Japan. Yüan pointedly reminded him that the head of the Chinese Army should have a more realistic assessment of China's military capability. In the end, Yüan's decision prevailed.[20] China accepted the Japanese ultimatum on May 9, and subsequently signed a series of treaties and notes with Japan.

On that same day, Tuan Ch'i-jui sent a personal circular telegram to the provincial military authorities deploring the government's decision and reiterating his reasons for advocating military resistance to Japan.[21] This, of course, had no effect, but Tuan soon resigned and withdrew from public affairs.[22] Yüan Shih-k'ai saw in the settlement of the Twenty-one Demands an indication that Japan, satisfied with the arrangements, would develop a cordial relationship with Yüan's government. Lu Tsung-yü, Chinese minister in Tokyo, was even told by Okuma Shigenobu, then Japanese prime minister, that he would be happy to see Yüan's monarchical plans carried out successfully and that he was willing to provide assistance to Yüan if the latter desired it.[23] As if by coincidence, Hioki in a speech given at a banquet in Peking made a suggestive comment: "The bulk of the Chinese nation do not appreciate the difference between a republican and a monarchical regime. It is all one to them whether they have over them a president or an emperor."[24] Such encouragement from responsible Japanese officials led Yüan to believe that the Japanese government tacitly backed the constitutional changes he had envisioned.

Yüan's illusion of Japanese goodwill soon dissipated. When his stage-managed monarchical melodrama was far advanced, Japan chose to strike again. On October 28, 1915, at the insistence of Japan, the diplomatic representatives of Japan, Great Britain, and Russia jointly advised the Waichiaopu against a monarchical government.[25] A day later, the Gaimushō (Ministry of Foreign Affairs) issued an official communiqué in Tokyo openly questioning the wisdom of attempting "at present" to establish a monarchy in China, in light of information possessed by the Japanese government.[26] Yüan interpreted this obvious inconsistency as a desire on the part of Japan to strike a bargain at the critical moment. Peking therefore decided to dispatch Chou Tzu-ch'i, minister of agriculture and commerce, as a high-ranking special envoy to Japan. Ostensibly Chou's mission was to present the highest Chinese decoration to the Japanese emperor. Still, the timing of Chou's trip gave rise to speculation that his real assignment was to offer the Japanese certain concessions.[27]

At first, Chou's proposed trip was given a green light by both the Gaimushō and the Japanese Army.[28] However, on January 16, 1916, just before the scheduled departure of the Chinese mission, Peking was advised by Hioki to cancel the trip.[29] Yüan's government was greatly embarrassed by Japan's rejection of his diplomatic overture; worse still, all his political opponents saw this act as a clear indication of Japan's readiness to eliminate Yüan from the scene. Thus, it gave a tremendous psychological boost to the anti-Yüan groups. Yüan's monarchical undertaking ended in fiasco, and he died a discredited and humiliated man (June 6, 1916).

Whatever political stability Yüan had achieved prior to his imperial venture was soon lost. Amid the general chaos and confusion, Tuan Ch'i-jui emerged from his self-imposed seclusion to become the premier. His seniority in the Peiyang Army and distinguished record of military service, combined with his well-known personal integrity and long-standing opposition to Yüan's monarchical designs, made him the only person acceptable to both the north and the south. He was looked upon as the strong man who could bring China together again, while Li Yüan-hung, the new president, was treated as the figurehead of the Republic.

Tuan's primary concern in foreign affairs was the question of Japan. The threat of a renewed Japanese request for Group V of the Twenty-one Demands was forever present.[30] On numerous occasions, Japan skillfully pressed her unfulfilled demands in disguised forms, as though to test China's will to resist. One case in point was the persistent Japanese attempt to obtain police rights in China. In 1916, the Japanese consul, without the knowledge or the consent of the Chinese government, arbitrarily set up police stations and houses of detention in Amoy, Fukien. When confronted with vigorous Chinese protests, the Japanese legation in Peking justified this action by contending that their police rights were the logical extension of the existing extraterritorial and consular rights.[31]

Another blatant revelation of Japanese objectives in China came after the Chengchiatun (or Liaoyuan) Incident (August 13, 1916). In this small town near the border of Inner Mongolia, a quarrel between a Japanese resident and a local street vendor became a full-fledged conflict involving the soldiers of the Chinese 28th Army Division stationed there and local Japanese police and military forces. From various field reports, the Japanese soldiers appeared to be in the wrong throughout the dispute. First of all, Japan had no treaty or other legal right to have troops present. Second, Japanese soldiers forced their way into the Chinese barracks and attacked the sentries. Third, the Japanese held hostage the local Chinese civil administrator who went to their headquarters to mediate. Fourth, Japan used the incident as a pretext to dispatch large military reinforcements to Chengchiatun and forced the Chinese army units to evacuate the area within a radius of thirty miles along the railway line from Szepingkai to Chengchiatun.[32]

In the wake of the incident, the Japanese claimed that Chinese troops had surrounded and fired on the Japanese barracks in Chengchiatun.[33] On September 2, Hioki Eki, Japanese minister in Peking, handed an aide-mémoire to the Waichiaopu. The conditions for settlement of the incident bore a striking resemblance to the most critical points embodied in Group V of the original Twenty-one Demands. Japan asked that the commander of the Chinese 28th Army Division be punished, all officers involved in the incident be dismissed, and orders be issued throughout South Manchuria and eastern Inner Mongolia forbidding all Chinese soldiers and civilians to provoke the Japanese. In addition, the note demanded that China agree to the "stationing of Japanese police officers in South Manchuria and eastern Inner Mongolia . . . [and] the engagement of Japanese political advisers by the officials of South Manchuria." Attached to the note were four Japanese desiderata, among them, "(1) Chinese troops stationed in South Manchuria and eastern Inner Mongolia to employ a certain number of Japanese military officers as advisers; (2) Chinese military cadet schools to employ a certain number of Japanese military officers as instructors."[34]

From the beginning, Tuan Ch'i-jui was suspicious of Japan's real motives. He anticipated that Japan would use the incident as an excuse to demand additional rights and privileges in China. He therefore instructed the Waichiaopu to expose the false Japanese accusations and to be firm in its negotiations.[35] Tuan was inclined to be conciliatory on the less important points such as punishment of the responsible Chinese officers and compensation for the Japanese victims and their families. However, he stood firm on the vital issues.[36]

The settlement of the Chengchiatun Incident became bogged down in the lengthy negotiations. On January 5, 1917, the Japanese minister restated emphatically his earlier demands. On the question of establishing police stations and the appointment of police officers, Japan again argued that these rights lay "within the scope of extraterritoriality." The note also stated, "If the Chinese government hesitates or disapproves, the Imperial Government will be obliged to establish police stations and appoint police officers according to necessity."[37] There was "no ground for argument."[38]

In its reply of January 12, Peking declared that China reserved the right not to employ any foreign advisers at all in South Manchuria, and that China had no intention of hiring any foreigners in the military cadet schools. The Chinese government argued that there was "no necessity to station Japanese police officers" in South Manchuria and eastern Inner Mongolia, and that such functions were not a necessary corollary of the right of extraterritoriality.[39] With the formal exchange of notes on January 22, 1917, the Chengchiatun Incident was officially closed.[40] Nevertheless, the basic issues were left unresolved.

Early in February 1917, after the United States severed diplomatic relations with Germany, neutral countries were invited by the American government to associate themselves with the American action of protest. When this instruction reached Paul S. Reinsch, American minister in Peking, on February 4, he took it seriously and interpreted it as "more than pious wish" on the part of Washington.[41] Reinsch devoted himself wholeheartedly to the task of saving China from the "thraldom of Japan."[42]

Reinsch's proposal that China ally herself with the United States struck a responsive chord in Tuan Ch'i-jui.[43] Like his political mentor and predecessor Yüan Shih-k'ai, Tuan sought to thwart Japanese aggression by allying China with a country strong enough to challenge Japan. During the ensuing negotiations with Reinsch, Tuan and his cabinet members managed to exact from the American minister pledges guaranteeing China her "national independence" and American financial assistance.[44] On February 9, a Chinese protest against German submarine warfare was delivered to Admiral von Hintze by the Waichiaopu. This marked the first step toward a total break with Germany.

During the discussions between Reinsch and the Peking government, the influence of the "Young China" elements prevailed. These Western-educated politicians tended to follow the American lead, to the exclusion of Japan. Significantly, Tuan Ch'i-jui accepted and acted on the advice given by the pro-American faction. Peking had asked Great Britain and Japan for their opinions on the American proposal, yet at no time did the Peking government reveal its intent.[45] Only one hour before the delivery of China's protest to Germany, Japan was perfunctorily informed by Chang Tsung-hsiang, Chinese minister in Tokyo.[46] Japan was not unaware of the ongoing Sino-American parleys, and regarded Peking's move as an indication of Tuan's desire to break the Japanese hold over China. Japanese Foreign

Minister Motono Ichirō conveyed his "deep regrets" to Chang that China had failed to take Japan into her confidence on such an important diplomatic move.[47]

Unfortunately, Reinsch's enthusiasm was neither fully shared nor supported by Washington. Both President Wilson and Secretary of State Robert Lansing were of the opinion that hasty action on the part of China would only antagonize Japan and that the American government was not in a position to defend Chinese interests. They decided that no assurance of any kind should be given to China. Instead, China was cautioned against imprudence.[48]

The episode gave added impetus to Japan's secret diplomatic dealings. In late January and early February 1917, Motono sought assurances from the British government for Japan's succession to German rights in Shantung and possession of islands north of the equator at a future peace conference.[49] Since Tokyo indicated that British assurances were linked to Japanese naval assistance, it was not difficult for London to make its choice. On February 14, the Japanese ambassador in London was informed by the British Foreign Office that His Majesty's government "accede with pleasure" to the Japanese request for support.[50] Subsequently, Japan received the desired assurances from France, Russia, and Italy.[51]

Reinsch's inability to deliver on his earlier promises placed Tuan in an awkward position. To abandon China's original course of neutrality, Tuan had to overcome strong domestic opposition from many quarters. Thus, Tuan banked heavily on obtaining some tangible concessions from the Allies in order to silence the outcries of his opponents as well as to win over the skeptical. Liang Ch'i-ch'ao, principal architect of Tuan's policy of war participation, convinced Tuan of the advisability of employing diplomacy to advance China's national interests. As the Entente Powers were apparently eager to have China on their side, Tuan was advised to propose a quid pro quo to the Entente: Chinese participation in return for postponement of the Boxer indemnity, increase of Chinese customs tariffs, and modification of all restrictive clauses in the Boxer Protocol of 1901. The first two points were communicated to Tokyo on February 14, with the understanding that China was contemplating a break with Germany and was prepared for the possibility of war.[52] Meanwhile Lu Cheng-hsiang, acting as Tuan Ch'i-jui's personal representative, presented the Chinese desiderata to the Entente embassies in Peking.[53]

The Entente ministers responded vaguely in a memorandum which promised "to consider favorably" the Chinese requests in the event that China effectively severed relations with Germany and Austria-Hungary.[54] Motono, however, told Chang Tsung-hsiang on various occasions that the government of Japan agreed in principle to the proposed Chinese terms. He also offered the good offices of Japan to smooth away any possible difficulties with the Entente Powers on the condition that China first break with Germany. Nevertheless, Motono was careful to make no definite concessions to China's desiderata.[55]

The combined pressure of domestic opposition to his German policy and the diplomatic impasse forced Tuan's hand. The promised assistance from Tokyo seemed the only way out. Thereupon Tuan devised a two-step countermeasure. As a gesture of good faith, China promised to sever diplomatic relations with Germany immediately but stopped short of war. Once the Entente Powers agreed to all the Chinese conditions, China would declare war on Germany.[56] A telegram to this effect was drafted for transmission to Tokyo.[57] This decision precipitated a serious rift between President Li and the cabinet. Tuan was forced by events to submit the whole question to Parliament before he could secure any assurances from the Entente Powers.

On March 14, immediately following the severing of diplomatic ties with Germany, Wu T'ing-fang, Chinese minister of foreign affairs, handed a formal note embracing the Chinese desiderata to the Entente ministers in Peking.[58] Simultaneously, Chinese ministers accredited to the Entente Powers were instructed to enter into direct negotiations with their host countries. Again the responses were vague and noncommittal,[59] and Tuan began to pin his hope for a successful diplomatic bargain solely on the goodwill of Japan. More and more, he came under the influence of a pro-Japanese group, including Ts'ao Ju-lin, Chang Tsung-hsiang, and Lu Tsung-yü, who had personal connections and contacts with both Japanese official and financial circles. Subsequent negotiations between China and Japan were conducted increasingly through these people on a semiofficial basis instead of through the normal channel of the Waichiaopu.

But Japan remained as evasive as ever, and began to assume a tough and businesslike attitude toward the Chinese requests.[60] At times, Motono even accused Peking of trickery and insincerity for having deliberately presented Japan with unacceptable demands. The Boxer indemnity, he maintained, constituted a part of the Japanese government budget, and it could not be suspended for ten years, as suggested by Peking.[61] Finally, Motono outlined a proposal in which China's original three demands were drastically scaled down. He advised Chang Tsung-hsiang that if Tuan Ch'i-jui found it acceptable, this new proposal should be officially communicated to the Entente Powers as a basis for further negotiation.[62] The pliable Chang was more than ready to accept the new offer. He felt optimistic that with the help pledged by his Japanese friends, the Entente would accept the Chinese demands. Thus Chang strongly urged Ts'ao Ju-lin to obtain Tuan's consent to the Motono plan.[63]

The Motono proposal fell far short of Tuan's original expectations, but since the credibility of his administration hinged on his ability to deliver the promised diplomatic gains, he was disposed to meet Japan halfway. He agreed to use the proposal as a basis for negotiation. Tuan insisted, however, that the Motono plan be officially communicated to Peking as a Japanese reply to the previous Chinese inquiries on the subject. In addition, Tuan wanted the payments of the Boxer indemnity to be suspended for a period of at least five to six years, and tariff rates set at 7.5 percent *ad valorem*. In return, Tuan agreed to abolish the *likin* (local Chinese tax).[64]

After Tuan's response was communicated to Tokyo, Motono reacted cautiously. On the question of tariff revision, he indicated that he might accept Tuan's demand with one qualification—duty-free exportation from China of certain raw materials. He adhered to his earlier position on the Boxer indemnity. Once again, Motono volunteered to smooth the way for China in her negotiations with the other Entente Powers. But first of all, Motono desired a personal assurance that Tuan indeed had the determination to declare war on the Central Powers despite domestic opposition.[65]

By this time, Tuan was willing to declare war, but he had miscalculated the mood of the country. His awkward tactics of forcing Parliament to adopt his war policy not only goaded the members to revolt against him, it also set off a chain of extraordinary events. Tuan himself was forced out of office. In an attempt to reconstruct a cabinet acceptable to all factions, President Li appealed to Chang Hsün, intractable, royalist tuchün (military governor) of Anhwei. This blatant mistake on Li's part resulted in the dissolution of Parliament and the brief imperial restoration in the summer of 1917. Ironically, the restoration afforded Tuan an opportunity to stage his political comeback. It was Tuan who provided the much-needed leadership and determination at the critical time to bring the royalist venture to a quick end. On July 13, Tuan returned to Peking as the savior of the Republic. With his newly won political prestige, it was clear that Tuan could pursue his war-entry policy to its logical end. Once again, however, the question of war participation was linked to internal political developments.

Tuan's past difficulties with Parliament had been so great that he was determined to strip this legislative body of its constitutional authority by revising the fundamental laws governing its organization. On the other hand, his political opponents insisted on the revival of the dissolved Parliament. In the south, Sun Yat-sen formed an uneasy alliance with the dissident tuchüns and proclaimed the establishment of a provisional military government in Canton on September 1, 1917. Tuan was in no mood to compromise. It became clear that Tuan was prepared to use his war policy as an instrument to achieve his ultimate domestic goal of unification.

Chinese political developments coincided with a reorientation of Japanese policy toward China. When the Terauchi cabinet came to power in October 1916, it adopted a more conciliatory and moderate attitude toward China but did not abandon the objectives of political and economic supremacy. At a cabinet meeting on January 1, 1917, the basic guidelines of the Japanese policy were adopted formally. The leaders reaffirmed Japan's "paramount position" in China, the maintenance of "Japan's special privileges in South Manchuria, Eastern Inner Mongolia and Fukien."[66] In view of Tuan's dramatic political comeback in July 1917, the Terauchi cabinet deemed it opportune to throw its full support behind him and to be more accommodating than ever. A new Japanese diplomatic course, charted at a cabinet meeting held on July 27, 1917, called for immediate cessation of official Japanese cooperation with the southern anti-Peking political factions and an offer of economic and military aid to Peking to regain China's goodwill. It should be noted that the new policy once again stressed Japan's economic expansion in China.[67]

As the Peking government was perennially in financial straits to meet normal administrative expenditures, its only recourse for any military undertaking was to borrow from foreign monetary markets. Tuan's first option was to secure loans from Western countries, especially from the United States. His repeated efforts proved to be unfruitful.[68] Thus, Japan's readiness to offer Tuan financial assistance in the form of loans was the only alternative. The result of this phase of Sino-Japanese cooperation was the much-maligned Nishihara Loans.

The term "Nishihara Loans" is a misnomer. Between 1917 and 1918, the Terauchi cabinet invested in China over 200,000,000 yen through various Japanese banking groups. The Nishihara Loans represented but a portion of this investment. Second, Nishihara Kamezō was employed by Terauchi to act as his unofficial go-between in order to establish contacts with Peking and facilitate his economic diplomacy in China. As Nishihara's name never appeared in any of the signed contracts, it is impossible to identify all the loans which were concluded through his personal manipulation. However, over the years, the term "Nishihara Loans" came to indicate reckless borrowing at tremendous sacrifice of China's natural resources and administrative integrity, the borrowed money being squandered in internal political strife.

According to Ts'ao Ju-lin, who played a crucial part in the negotiations of the Nishihara Loans, the initial financial transaction concluded through the intercession of Nishihara was the second Bank of Communications Reorganization Loan signed with a Japanese syndicate[69] in the amount of 20,000,000 yen on September 28, 1917. The readiness of Japanese banking firms to furnish the Peking government with money, the low interest rate, and the liberal borrowing terms convinced Ts'ao as well as Tuan Ch'i-jui that Nishihara was indeed acting as Terauchi's special emissary.[70] The Yokohama Specie Bank advanced 10,000,000 yen in August 1917 as part of the second Reorganization Loan yet to be negotiated with the Four-Nation Consortium, which had held an option for this loan since

1913. During the following twelve months, two additional advances totalling another 20,000,000 yen were made by Japan under the same conditions.[71]

Revival of the Reorganization Loan was proposed initially by Liang Ch'i-ch'ao, minister of finance. According to Liang's original plan, the loan was to fund currency reform.[72] Unfortunately, at this time Tuan Ch'i-jui was not interested in financial reforms. He was occupied with suppressing the southern dissidents. Troops had already been dispatched to Hunan and Szechwan to reestablish Peking as the only source of political authority. In Kwangtung, Tuan also tried to aid Lung Chi-kuang, who challenged the rebelling tuchün. Financially, Peking was incapable of sustaining such large-scale military activities. According to the draft budget submitted by Liang Ch'i-ch'ao for September 1917–June 1918, national revenues were estimated at $70,000,000 silver, while regular military expenditures totalled $49,000,000 silver, nearly 70 percent of the total income of the Peking government. Yet the estimated military outlay did not include expenditures incurred as the result of any military contingencies. Not surprisingly, as a consequence of Tuan's military campaigns in the southwestern provinces, all funds advanced by the Yokohama Specie Bank were spent by the Ministry of War.[73]

The financial needs of Tuan Ch'i-jui grew in proportion to his military

Major Sino-Japanese Loans, 1917–1918

Date	Loan	Amount (Yen)
8/28/1917	1st advance, Second Reorganization Loan	10,000,000
9/28/1917	2d Bank of Communications Reorganization Loan	20,000,000
10/12/1917	Kirin-Changchun Railway Loan	4,511,250
12/30/1917	1st Taihei Firearms Loan	14,866,798
1/6/1918	2d advance, Second Reorganization Loan	10,000,000
4/30/1918	Cable Telegraph Loan	20,000,000
6/18/1918	Kirin-Huining Railway Loan	10,000,000
7/5/1918	3d advance, Second Reorganization Loan	10,000,000
7/30/1918	2d Taihei Firearms Loan	22,420,702
8/2/1918	Kirin-Heilungkiang Gold Mine and Forestry Loan	30,000,000
9/22/1918	War Participation Loan	20,000,000
9/28/1918	Shantung Railways Loan	20,000,000
9/28/1918	Manchuria-Mongolia Railways Loan	20,000,000
	Total	211,798,750

Figures are based on Wang Yü-tung, *Chung-kuo tui-Jih chih chai-wu wen-t'i* [The question of Chinese debts to Japan] (Shanghai, 1936), pp. 67–69, 91–93. All figures are substantiated by existing loan contracts in the Waichiaopu Archives.

activities. The campaigns in Hunan and Szechwan did not go as well as he had hoped, largely because Tuan was unable to gain total cooperation from the field commanders who belonged to the Chihli military faction. Thus Tuan embarked on a plan to create a military force to be trained, armed, and controlled directly by him and his close associates. To acquire the needed funds, Tuan resorted to reckless borrowing (see table, Sino-Japanese Loans).

The Japanese were shrewd enough to turn Tuan's financial need to their own advantage. If viewed purely from the standpoint of conventional business practices, the loans advanced by the Japanese banking groups seemed to defy common sense and prudence. The real significance of the Nishihara Loans must be assessed in terms of the potential economic and political implications. For instance, the railway loans gave Japan undisputed control over strategic lines in Manchuria, Mongolia, and Shantung. Under the Japanese reorganization plan of April 1917, the administration of the Korean railway system was merged with that of the South Manchurian Railway.[74]

Through the Kirin-Changchun Railway and Kirin-Huining Railway loans with China, Japan acquired the rights to establish the vital physical link between Korea and Manchuria. Furthermore, through the Manchurian-Mongolian Railways Loan, the Japanese were permitted to construct five additional lines: (1) from Szepingkai, via Chengchiatun, to Taonan; (2) from Jehol to Taonan; (3) from Kaiyuan to Heilungkiang and Heilung to Kirin; (4) from Changchun to Taonan; and (5) from a point on the Taonan-Jehol line to a seaport.[75] These lines were to become branch lines of the South Manchurian Railway crisscrossing the vast heartland of Manchuria and Inner Mongolia. If all the plans were carried out, the comprehensive railway system linking Korea with North China would be completely financed, controlled, operated, and policed by Japan. That was not all. The Shantung Railways Loan included two proposed lines. One was from Kaomi to Hsuchow, which would connect the Japanese-controlled Tsingtao-Tsinan Railway with the Tientsin-Nanking line. The other was from Tsinan to Shunteh, connecting the Tsingtao-Tsinan Railway to the Peking-Hankow line.[76] The political, military, and economic implications of these proposed railways were so obvious, there was no doubt that the Japanese government had carefully planned and executed every move with overall objectives in mind.

The success of Terauchi's diplomacy reached its high point with the exchange of notes between China and Japan in March 1918 declaring their mutual desire to cooperate militarily in defense against a common enemy. Early in February, General Tanaka Giichi, Japanese vice-chief of the general staff, first proposed to Chang Tsung-hsiang a Sino-Japanese military alliance in view of the situation in Siberia.[77] In Peking, General

Aoki Nobuzumi approached acting President Feng Kuo-chang with the same suggestion.[78] Peking desired only a temporary military arrangement with Japan to deal with the emergent situation in Siberia. Peking also wanted the scope of the proposed joint undertaking clearly "limited to events occurring outside of the Chinese territory."[79] The agreement would terminate as soon as the world war came to an end.[80] Military delegates from the two countries would work out the details of the informal agreement of cooperation, though both governments would give it official sanction.[81]

Despite Peking's initial caution, Japan maneuvered Peking into accepting a military alliance on Japanese terms. The exchange of notes took place on March 25, 1918; the Sino-Japanese army and navy joint defensive agreements were signed on May 16 and 19, respectively. Japanese military and naval forces were permitted to operate in Chinese territories. Furthermore, Chinese local officials in the military areas were required "to do their best to aid the Japanese troops . . . so that no obstacles shall arise to impede their movements. . . ."[82]

This was a remarkable diplomatic achievement for the Terauchi cabinet. The military agreements provided a legal basis for Japanese troop deployment in China. And Japan did not wait long to use this newly acquired privilege to its fullest advantage. On the excuse of military needs in Siberia, some 16,000 Japanese troops began massing along the borders of Kirin and Heilungkiang and the Eastern Manchurian Railway. Wherever they went, Japanese forces took over the barracks occupied by Chinese troops and set up patrol outposts at strategic points.[83] In some cases, police stations were established.[84]

Although all the military actions were supposed to be joint undertakings, Japanese troop movements in northern Manchuria were arbitrary and unilateral.[85] Japan maintained that the decision to send troops to Siberia had nothing whatsoever to do with the Sino-Japanese military agreements, and thus consultation with China was not required.[86] In addition, Japan tried to discourage Peking from dispatching even a token expeditionary force to Siberia.[87] When Peking asked the South Manchurian Railway to provide transportation for some 1700 troops to be sent to Vladivostok, Japan was reluctant to comply.[88]

Tuan Ch'i-jui and his clique, instrumental in bringing about the Sino-Japanese military agreements, were again amply rewarded by Japan. On September 28, 1918, the Peking authorities concluded the War Participation Loan of 20,000,000 yen with the Japanese banking syndicate. The preamble of the loan contract stated:

> In accordance with the Sino-Japanese Joint Army Military Agreement, the Chinese government . . . for the purpose of securing funds for organizing a fully coordinated

national defense army and for meeting the expenses in the participation of the war, has entered into a loan contract with . . . the Bank of Chosen, the Industrial Bank of Japan, and the Bank of Taiwan.[89]

The most significant part of the transaction was a provision appended to the contract: "The proceeds of the entire loan are to be handed over to the chief of the Chinese government agency which directly supervises the national defense army."[90] In other words, Tuan Ch'i-jui, chief of the War Participation Bureau, was given absolute control over the loan.

Against the background of such dubious dealings with Japan, Tuan's vigorous military campaigns against the insurgent south and the attempt of the An-fu Club (the political arm of the Tuan clique) to capture Parliament in the 1918 election became sinister. Although Tuan had been accused of Peiyang partisanship, his personal integrity was seldom challenged. Yet the extremely unpopular Nishihara Loans and the Sino-Japanese military agreements turned Chinese public opinion irrevocably against Tuan.

Coinciding with the growing domestic opposition to Tuan Ch'i-jui and his pro-Japanese cabinet members was the downfall of the Terauchi cabinet in September 1918. The new China policy formulated by the Hara cabinet called for Japanese cooperation with the other powers to seek reconciliation between the north and the south.[91] Under both domestic and diplomatic pressure, Tuan once again resigned (October 10, 1918).

Tuan's retirement ended another unsuccessful attempt at Sino-Japanese cooperation. From the beginning, it was doomed by conflicts of national interest, further aggravated by the deep-rooted Chinese mistrust of and antipathy toward Japan. The Japanese, for their part, were not farsighted enough to uphold by deeds as well as by words the true principles of mutual interest. Instead, Japan chose to secure its objectives by establishing political and military supremacy over China through whatever means were available. Its reckless display of military might and devious diplomatic tactics had indeed achieved some immediate tangible results. Viewed in retrospect, however, the gains were short-lived, while the imprint of suspicion and hostility toward Japan was indelible.

Notes

1. For a detailed account of Yüan Shih-k'ai's early life and political career, see Shen Tsu-hsien and Wu K'ai-sheng, eds., *Yung-an ti-tzu-chi* [A biographical account of Yüan Shih-k'ai by his disciples] (Taipei, 1962). Jerome Chen's *Yüan Shih-k'ai, 1859–1916: Brutus Assumes the Purple* (Stanford, 1961) provides a reasonably good summary of Yüan's career. For a collection of Yüan's official papers and documents prior to the Republican period, see *Yang-shou-yüan tsou-yi chi-yao* [Collection of important memorials and proposals of Yüan Shih-k'ai] (Taipei, 1966). Also see *Li Wen-chung-kung ch'üan-shu* [The complete collection of the official papers of Li Hung-chang] (Taipei, 1965). The Li collection includes some telegrams sent by Yüan while he served as commercial commissioner in Korea.

2. Ian H. Nish, "Dr. Morrison and China's Entry into the World War, 1915–1917," in *Studies in Diplomatic History,* ed. Ragnhild Hatton and M. S. Anderson (Hamden, Conn., 1970), p. 325. Also see *North China Herald,* 15 August 1914, pp. 539–40.

3. For an English translation of Yüan's presidential mandate (August 6, 1914), see *North China Herald,* 8 and 22 August 1914, pp. 463, 575.

4. Circular note from Waichiaopu (Ministry of Foreign Affairs) to the belligerents, 3 September 1914. See Sir John N. Jordan to Secretary of State for Foreign Affairs Sir Edward Grey, 4 September 1914, British Government Documents, Foreign Office File, 1914–1919 (Public Record Office, London), 371, 46142/23. Hereafter cited as FO.

5. *North China Herald,* 3, 10, and 17 October 1914, pp. 7, 83, 99, 128, 137, 201.

6. Ibid., 3 and 10 October 1914, pp. 56, 83.

7. Ibid., 24 and 31 October 1914, pp. 227, 360.

8. Ting Wen-chiang, *Liang Jen-kung hsien-sheng nien-pu ch'ang'pien ch'u-kao* [Draft of the chronological biography of Liang Ch'i-ch'ao] (Taipei, 1962), 2: 436–38.

9. *North China Herald,* 24 October 1914, p. 284.

10. Vice-Foreign Minister Ts'ao Ju-lin to Minister in Tokyo Lu Tsung-yü, 12 December 1914; Lu to Ts'ao, 14 December 1914; and Ts'ao to Lu, 29 December 1914, in Wang Yün-sheng, *Liu-shih nien lai Chung-kuo yü Jih-pen* [China and Japan in the last sixty years] (Tientsin, 1934), 6: 74–76. Also First Secretary Obata Torikichi to Foreign Minister Katō Taka'akira, 26 November 1914, Gaimushō Archives, Papers of Matsumoto Tadao (Library of Congress microfilm), 12–7, pp. 2702–3; and Minister in Peking Hioki Eki to Katō, 8 January 1915, ibid., 12–7, pp. 2713–15.

11. *North China Herald,* 30 January 1915, p. 341.

12. Katō to Hioki, 8 January 1915, Gaimushō Archives, Matsumoto Papers, 12–7, p. 2722.

13. Hioki to Katō, 19 January 1915, 12–11, pp. 4320–30. Also see Ting Wen-chiang, op. cit., 2: 221.

14. *Papers Relating to the Foreign Relations of the United States, 1915* (Washington, D.C., 1928), pp. 160–61. Hereafter cited as *FRUS.*

15. Li Chien-nung, *Chung-kuo chin pai-nien cheng-chih-shih* [A political history of China in the last century] (Taipei, 1965), 2: 406–17. Also see Li Shou-k'ung, *Min-ch'u chih kuo-hui* [The national assemblies of the early Republican period] (Taipei, 1964), pp. 134–41; *Huang Yüan-sheng yi-chu* [Collection of writings of Huang Yüan-sheng] (Taipei, 1962), 1: 207–8, 275–81, and 2: 8–13, 189–90, 212–15, 222–29.

16. Lu Tsung-yü to Waichiaopu, 4 and 5 May 1915, in Wang Yün-sheng, op. cit., 6: 297–99.

17. See "The Activities of the Chinese Government before the Delivery of the Ultimatum," Memorandum, Gaimushō Archives, Matsumoto Papers, 12–8, pp. 2932–37.

18. Jordan to Langley, 10 June 1915, FO 350, vol. 13.

19. Ts'ao Ju-lin to Lu Tsung-yü, 10 May 1915, in Wang Yün-sheng, op. cit., 6: 311–12.

20. Ts'ao Ju-lin, *I-sheng chih hui-i* [Reminiscences of my life] (Hong Kong, 1966), pp. 128–29.

21. Huang Chi-lu, ed., *Ko-ming wen-hsien* [Documents on Chinese revolution], series no. 46, pt. 1, "T'ao-Yüan shih-liao" [Historical documents on anti-Yüan campaigns] (Taipei, 1969), pp. 541–42.

22. Wu T'ing-hsieh, ed., *Ho-fei chih-cheng nien-pu* [A chronological biography of Tuan Ch'i-jui] (Taipei, 1962), pp. 29–30.

23. Lu Tsung-yü, *Wu-shih tzu-hsü-chi* [Reminiscences at fifty] (Peking, 1925), pp. 16–17. Also see Ch'in Hsüeh-lü, ed., *San-shui Liang Yen-sun hsien-sheng nien-pu* [A chronological biography of Liang Shih-yi] (Taipei, 1962), 1: 296.

24. *North China Herald,* 6 November 1915, p. 382.

25. Jordan complained that the Entente representatives were "so many puppets pulled by the Japanese strings." See Jordan to Alston, 21 December 1915, Private Correspondence, FO 350, vol. 13. See also *North China Herald,* 6 November 1915, pp. 382, 436, 438; Ch'in Hsüeh-lü, op. cit., 1: 280–81.

26. *North China Herald,* 6 November 1915, pp. 436–37.

27. *Hu-kuo-chün chi-shih* [Chronicles of the National Preservation Army] (Shanghai, 1916), 1 (pt. 2): 20–22, and 1 (pt. 5): 3–25. Also see Ch'in Hsüeh-lü, op. cit., 1: 294–95; Li Chien-nung, op. cit., 2: 439–41; and Paul S. Reinsch, *An American Diplomat in China* (New York, 1922), pp. 184–85.

28. Vice-Chief of the General Staff Tanaka Giichi to Banzai Rihachirō, 18 December 1915, Gaimushō Archives, Matsumoto Papers, 12–16, p. 6409; also Waichiaopu to Lu Tsung-yü, 4 January 1916, in Wang Yün-sheng, op. cit., 7:29.

29. Foreign Minister Ishii Kikujirō to Hioki, 15 January 1916, Gaimushō Archives, Matsumoto Papers, 12–16, pp. 6484, 6505–7; Lu Tsung-yü to Waichiaopu, 16 January 1916, in Wang Yün-sheng, op. cit., 7: 34–35; *North China Herald*, 22 January 1916, p. 198.

30. Group V consisted of a total of seven articles. Among other things, China was asked to employ Japanese advisers in political, financial, and military affairs, to administer jointly with Japan the Chinese police forces, to purchase Japanese firearms or to establish a joint arsenal, and so forth. Even though these demands were not embodied in the series of Sino-Japanese treaties and notes signed on May 25, 1915, Japan nevertheless reserved the right to bring them up in future negotiations.

31. Aide-mémoire from Waichiaopu to the Japanese legation, 1 February 1917; minutes of interview between Secretary Shih Lü-pen and Chargé d'Affaires Yoshizawa Kenkichi, 3 February 1917; and cabinet directive to Waichiaopu, 9 February 1917, "Jih-pen tsai Hsia-men she-ching-an" [File on the establishment of Japanese police stations in Amoy], Waichiaopu Archives (Institute of Modern History, Academia Sinica, Taipei), C-3-3. Also see Westel W. Willoughby, *Foreign Rights and Interests in China* (Baltimore, 1927), 2: 588–90.

32. Report of Chief of Commission for Foreign Affairs in Fengtien Hsieh Tzu-yüan to Waichiaopu, covering the events of August 13 to August 19, 1916; telegrams from Chief of Staff Tung Chi-ch'ing (Chengchiatun Military Garrison), 13 and 14 August 1916; from the special representative of Waichiaopu in Fengtien, 14, 16, 17, and 21 August 1916; and from Chang Tso-lin (*tuchün* of Fengtien) to Waichiaopu, 21 and 25 August 1916, "Liaoyüan Chung-Jih-ping ch'ung-t'u-an" [File on the Sino-Japanese military conflicts in Liaoyuan], Waichiaopu Archives, C-4-5.

33. V. K. Wellington Koo to Waichiaopu, 18 August 1916, and Minister in Tokyo Chang Tsung-hsiang to Waichiaopu, 25 August 1916, ibid., C-4-5.

34. Aide-mémoire, ibid., C-4-5.

35. Cabinet directive, 30 August 1916, Official Correspondence no. 701, ibid., C-4-5.

36. Cabinet directive, 6 September 1916, Official Correspondence no. 751, ibid., C-4-5.

37. Willoughby, op. cit., 2: 592–93.

38. *NCH,* 27 January and 3 February 1917, pp. 172, 215–16.

39. Willoughby, op. cit., 1: 207–8, and 2: 593–94; *North China Herald*, 3 February 1917, p. 216.

40. *North China Herald,* 27 January and 3 February 1917, pp. 172, 215.

41. Reinsch, op. cit., p. 241.

42. Alston to Balfour, 20 April 1917, FO 371, 82069/10.

43. Reinsch, op. cit., pp. 244–46.

44. Ibid., pp. 247–50; also Reinsch to Lansing, 7 February 1917, *FRUS, 1917*, Supp. 1 (Washington, D.C., 1931), pp. 403–4.

45. See Foreign Office Minutes, 6 February 1917, FO 371, 28850/10; also Chang Tsung-hsiang to cabinet, 9 February 1917, in Wang Yün-sheng, op. cit., 7: 92.

46. Cabinet and Waichiaopu to Chang Tsung-hsiang, 9 February 1917, ibid., 7: 93–94.

47. Chang Tsung-hsiang to cabinet, and to Waichiaopu, 9 February 1917, ibid., 7: 94–95.

48. Wilson to Lansing, 9 February 1917, in U.S. Department of State Files, 1914–1919 (National Archives Microfilm Publications), 763.72/3245.

49. Greene to Balfour, 27 January 1917, FO 371, 22099/23, 22137/23; Greene to Balfour, 2 February 1917, FO 371, 27203/23, 27683/23.

50. Memorandum, 14 February 1917, FO 371, 36133/23.

51. Willoughby, op. cit., 1: 269–71.

52. Cabinet and Waichiaopu to Chang Tsung-hsiang, 14 February 1917; Ts'ao Ju-lin to Chang, and Chang to cabinet, 14 February 1917, in Wang Yün-sheng, op. cit., 7: 97–99.

53. Ts'ao to Chang, 16 February 1917, and Chang to cabinet, 17 February 1917, ibid., 1: 100–101. Also see Nish, op. cit., p. 336.

54. *North China Herald,* 3 March 1917, p. 447.

55. Chang to cabinet, 17, 20, and 27 February and 3 March 1917, in Wang Yün-sheng, op. cit., 7: 100–103.

56. Liang Ch'i-ch'ao to Tuan Ch'i-jui, March 1917, cited in Ting Wen-chiang, op. cit., 2: 512.

57. Ibid.; also see Li Chien-nung, op. cit., 2: 490; *North China Herald,* 10 and 17 March 1917, pp. 503, 568.

58. Minutes of an interview given by Dr. Wu T'ing-fang to the Entente ministers in Peking, 14 March 1917, "Huan-fu keng-tzu p'ei-k'uan yü tseng-kai kuan-shui-an" [File on the postpone-ment of the Boxer indemnity and the revision of the Chinese customs tariffs], Waichiaopu Archives, no. Pei-1454.

59. Chinese ministers in Paris, London, and Rome to Waichiaopu, 16 March 1917, and from the Chinese minister in Washington to Waichiaopu, 20 March 1917, ibid., no. Pei-1454.

60. The specific Chinese desiderata were outlined in an aide-mémoire to Tokyo dated March 8, 1917, in three categories. (1) The Boxer indemnity payments to Germany and Austria-Hungary were to be cancelled permanently, while payments to the Entente Powers were to be postponed for ten years. Thereafter, the payments were to be resumed without any additional interest. (2) Port duties were to be increased immediately to an effective 5 percent. After the revision of the customs tariffs, the duties would be raised to 7.5 percent *ad valorem.* After the *likin* (local Chinese tax) was abolished, the duties would be raised to an effective 12.5 percent. (3) The provisions of the Boxer Protocol (1901) regarding the prohibition of Chinese troops stationed within a 20-*li* radius of Tientsin and the presence of foreign troops in the legations and along the railways should be abolished. See enclosure, cabinet and Waichiaopu to Chang Tsung-hsiang, 8 March 1917, in Wang Yün-sheng, op. cit., 7: 104–5.

61. Chang Tsung-hsiang to cabinet and Waichiaopu, 20 and 22 March 1917, Waichiaopu Archives, no. Pei-1454. Also Chang to cabinet, 16, 20, and 22 March 1917, and Chang to Ts'ao Ju-lin, 27 March 1917, in Wang Yün-sheng, op. cit., 7: 105–8.

62. The points contained in Motono's proposal were (1) request the Entente Powers to appoint delegates to a conference on tariff revision which was to take place after China's participation in the war; (2) postpone for a period of three years the Boxer indemnity payments to the Entente Powers; (3) the question of the Chinese right to station troops in and around Tientsin was to be dealt with by the Entente diplomatic corps in Peking. See telegram from Chang to Ts'ao, 27 March 1917, ibid., 7: 108–9.

63. Chang to Ts'ao, 30 March 1917, ibid., 7: 109–10.

64. Ts'ao to Chang, 8 April 1917, ibid., 7: 110.

65. Chang to Ts'ao, 9 April 1917, ibid., 7: 110–12.

66. Record of the Japanese cabinet decision of 1 January 1917, Gaimushō Archives, Matsumoto Papers, 12–4, pp. 1877–79.

67. Hara Kei (Takashi), *Hara Kei nikki* [The diary of Hara Kei (Takashi)] (Tokyo, 1965), 4: 308–9.

68. Tuan Ch'i-jui first hoped that China would qualify for U.S. financial aid to the Entente countries by an early entrance into the war, but domestic opposition to war participation was too strong. See "Chüeh-chiao-an" [File on severance of diplomatic relations with the Central Powers], Waichiaopu Archives, E-1-3. Then private American banking concerns made several attempts to float loans. Negotiations were bogged down by excessive American demands regarding securities and control over Chinese financial reorganization. See "Pi-chih chieh-k'uan" [File on currency reform loan], ibid., E-7-4, and "Yen-chiu chieh-k'uan" [File on tobacco and wine loan], E-6-4. Also see Burton F. Beers, *Vain Endeavor: Robert Lansing's Attempt to End the American-Japanese Rivalry* (Durham, N.C., 1962).

69. It consisted of the Industrial Bank of Japan, the Bank of Chosen, and the Bank of Taiwan.

70. Ts'ao Ju-lin, op. cit., pp. 169–71. Also see "Chiao-tung yin-hang yü Jih Yin-hang . . . chieh-k'uan-an" [File on the Bank of Communications Loan with the Japanese syndicate], Waichiaopu Archives, E-6-5.

71. See "Shan-hou hsü-chieh-k'uan yi erh san tz'u tien-k'uan ho-tung" [File on the extension of contracts of the first, second and third advances made toward the second Reorganization Loan], ibid., E-6-5, no. Pei-1354.

72. Ting Wen-chiang, op. cit., 2: 532–34.

73. Ibid., 2: 535–37.

74. See "Nan-man t'ieh-lu-an, pt. 1" [File on South Manchurian Railway, pt. 1], Waichiaopu Archives, G-2-4, no. Pei-2127.

75. Willoughby, op. cit., 1: 216.

76. Ibid., 1: 266.

77. Chang Tsung-hsiang to Waichiaopu, 6 February 1918, in *Chung-Jih chün-shih hsieh-ting-an* [The Sino-Japanese military agreements] (Peking, 1921), p. 1.

78. Waichiaopu to Chang, 22 February 1918, ibid.

79. Ibid.

80. Waichiaopu to Chang, 11 March 1918, ibid., pp. 4–5.

81. Waichiaopu to Chang, 2, 11, 13, and 17 March 1918, ibid., pp. 3–7.

82. Article III of the Sino-Japanese army agreement (signed May 16, 1918), ibid., p. 56. See pp. 55–60, 60–67 for an English translation of the texts of the agreements.

83. Pao Kuei-ch'ing (*tuchün* of Heilungkiang) to Waichiaopu, 6 September 1918, and Meng En-yüan (*tuchün* of Kirin) and Ko Tsung-hsi (civil administrator of Kirin) to Waichiaopu, 8 September 1918, "Hsieh-yüeh-kuo kung-tung ch'u-ping-an" [File on joint military expedition of the allies], Waichiaopu Archives, C-8-3. Also see Chief of Staff to Chang Tsung-hsiang, 15 August 1918, and Waichiaopu to Wellington Koo, 19 August 1918, "Hsieh-shang-kuo ch'u-ping Hsi-po-li-ya an" [File on the Siberian expedition of the allies], Waichiaopu Archives, pt. 2.

84. Chief of Staff to Meng, 23 August 1918, ibid., pt. 2.

85. Minutes of interviews between the French minister in Peking and Chinese Foreign Minister Lu Cheng-hsiang, 2 and 3 September 1918, ibid., pt. 4.

86. Chang Tsung-hsiang to Waichiaopu, 24 July 1918, ibid., pt. 1.

87. Minutes of interview between Hayashi and Secretary Liu of Waichiaopu, 20 July 1918, ibid.

88. Waichiaopu to Wellington Koo, 19 August 1918, ibid.

89. Contract of the War Participation Loan (September 22, 1918), "Tai-p'ing chün-chieh chi ts'an-chan chieh-k'uan" [File on the Taihei Firearms Loans and the War Participation Loan], Waichiaopu Archives, E-6-5, no. Pei-267.

90. Ibid.

91. Hara Kei, op. cit., 5: 28–29.

4.

In the following essay Pao-chin Chu indicates the process by which the pro-Japanese diplomats, who were guiding Chinese foreign policy at the end of World War I, were replaced by an Anglo-American-educated and -oriented group. And the question emerges, Did their style of diplomacy hurt or eliminate the possibility of finding a viable Sino-Japanese balance in the 1920s?

Another interesting point in Chu's paper, which comes up again in Wray's, is the idea that China was not an "organized state" and therefore could not be counted on to keep agreements, which Japan's delegate Matsuoka tried to sell to the League of Nations. The continuity of China's foreign policy, as shown by Chu, seems to invalidate this hypothesis, so fondly articulated by certain Japanese intellectual and political leaders, including, as Shumpei Okamoto has shown, Japan's leading Sinologist, Professor Naitō Torajirō.*

Chu, a native of China, is a graduate of National Taiwan University. He received his Ph.D. in international relations at the University of Pennsylvania in 1970 and is currently associate professor of Chinese history at San Diego State University.

---

*Professor Okamoto, who teaches at Temple University, gave a fascinating paper on this theme at the winter (1974–1975) meeting of the Oriental Club of Philadelphia. He is preparing it for publication.

From the Paris Peace Conference to the Manchurian Incident: The Beginnings of China's Diplomacy of Resistance against Japan

Pao-chin Chu

I.

When the Armistice was signed on November 11, 1918, World War I finally came to an end with the understanding that President Wilson's Fourteen Points would serve as the guideline for rebuilding the postwar world for both the victors and the defeated.[1] China, as a victorious power, immediately faced the problem of representation at the Paris Peace Conference. Against the wishes of the rebellious Canton government, the Peking government appointed all five delegates—Lu Cheng-hsiang, foreign minister; Sao-ke Alfred Sze, minister in London; V. K. Wellington Koo, minister in Washington; and Suntchou Wei, minister in Brussels—but included C. T. Wang, who had been sent to Washington by Canton to lobby for representation. A preparatory conference was held by President Hsü Shih-ch'ang, who had succeeded Feng Kuo-chang as president of the Peking government on October 10, 1918. It was attended by members of the pro-Japan faction including Tuan Ch'i-jui, head of the An-fu Party and chief of the War Participation Bureau, and Ts'ao Ju-lin, minister of communications. Except for general proposals on China's territorial integrity and preservation of sovereign rights, and on economic and fiscal independence, no definite decision on Shantung was made.[2]

Despite Japan's objections, the Chinese delegation was invited to present its view on the problem of Shantung to two consecutive sessions of the Council of Ten (January 27 and 28) and to the session of the Council of Four (April 22, 1919). In view of the Japanese wartime effort and "achievements in destroying German bases in the Extreme Orient and the South Seas," Baron Makino Nobuaki claimed "the unconditional cession of the leased territory of Kiaochow together with the railways, and other rights possessed by Germany in respect to Shantung."[3] Japan's strength at the end of the war was based in part on the renewed Anglo-Japanese Alliance; on secret agreements (1917) with Great Britain and France which approved her claims to German rights in Shantung; and on secret treaties with China (1915, 1918).

As the weight of President Wilson's influence at the conference became obvious to the Chinese delegation and Lu's health deteriorated, Koo and Wang were selected to speak on behalf of China.[4] At the Council of Ten, Koo asked for the restoration to China of the leased territory of Kiaochow, the railway in Shantung, and all rights Germany had in that area. Koo argued that the territories in question, integral to China's heritage, the national economy, and national defense, had been taken by force,[5] and that the Chinese government had accepted the treaties and notes resulting from negotiations on the Twenty-one Demands (1915) only after an ultimatum from Japan. They were at best only provisional arrangements subject to final review by the conference; China's declaration of war on Germany meant that they could not be enforced on the principle of *rebus sic statibus*.[6]

Koo secured the sympathy of President Wilson and of Secretary of State Robert Lansing through many interviews before and during the crucial period. However, Sze, disheartened by the overlooking of his seniority, failed to convince Prime Minister Lloyd George to break the British engagement with Japan. Lu, a student of the traditional diplomatic school and good mainly for diplomatic ceremonies, also failed to persuade "Tiger" Georges Clemenceau not to follow the example of his British colleague.[7]

Wilson, faced with a Japanese "ultimatum"[8] and Italy's absence and Belgium's defection, finally withdrew his support of China's position. Shantung was to be ceded to Japan by the treaty, although Japan promised to return Kiaochow to China and to control the Shantung Railway in actual "partnership" with China. The concern for a speedy peace after a disastrous war, the maintenance of an allied front against anarchy, and the establishment of the League of Nations were paid for at the expense of the fundamental principles of Wilson's Fourteen Points.[9] A series of proposals by the Chinese delegation to sign the treaty with certain conditions were not accepted.[10]

In the meantime, news of the decision of the Big Three on Shantung reached China. During a routine business meeting of the Kuo-min tsa-chih she (National Monthly Society), Chang Kuo-t'ao, then a student at National Peking University, moved for a general demonstration, which eventually brought 3000 college students into the streets.[11] On May 6, a special session was held in Shanghai by peace delegates, to try to effect a peaceful unification of the two rival regimes. Instead, the two chief delegates, Chu Ch'i-ch'ien, who represented the Peking government, and T'ang Shao-i, who represented the Canton government, signed a cablegram to the Chinese delegates at Paris opposing the signing of the treaty.[12] For the first time in twentieth-century China, people from all walks of life joined in a patriotic movement which eventually caused the downfall of pro-Japan diplomacy and diplomats, including Ts'ao Ju-lin and Chang Tsung-hsiang.[13] Clearly against the instructions of Peking, the Chinese delegates were absent from the Hall of Mirrors in the Palace of Versailles at the signing of the treaty.

The most profound effect of the Paris Peace Conference on Chinese diplomatic history was that Chinese foreign policy shifted from pro-Japan policies to a pro-Anglo-American course led by English-speaking and American-trained diplomats such as Koo, Sze, and Wang. No pro-Japan faction has been influential for any lengthy period in any Chinese government save the "puppet governments" during the World War II era. The precedent of an independent line of nationalistic diplomacy was established by the Anglo-American-trained diplomats. They held themselves above parties and politics and generally did not resist the pressure of public opinion. The resulting popular mandate further strengthened their control of China's foreign policy and, to some degree, resulted in a loss of flexibility in their international diplomacy.

II.

The Paris Peace Conference left many problems unsolved. As a result of the war, the balance of power among England, Germany, and Russia shifted to a competition among England, the United States, and Japan in international trade, overseas investment, and armament. President Warren G. Harding sent invitations on August 11, 1921, to the governments of Great Britain, France, Italy, and Japan to participate in a conference on the limitation of armament. He also invited China, Belgium, the Netherlands, Portugal, and the four above-mentioned powers to discuss Pacific and Far Eastern questions.[14] In the meantime, in Peking, Foreign Minister W. W. Yen was appointed director of the newly established Division for the Preparation of the Conference on the Limitation of Armament.[15] Sze was appointed head of the Chinese delegation, which included Koo and Wang Ch'ung-hui, Chief Justice of the Chinese Supreme Court. Contributions to finance the Chinese delegation of 132 came from the warlords of sixteen provinces, from Manchuria to the Yangtze River Valley, except from those areas under the rival Canton government.[16]

Sze submitted China's Ten Points to the Committee on Pacific and Far Eastern Questions, including principles such as observance of territorial integrity, political and administrative independence, and China's acceptance and application of the Open Door policy. These served as the basis of the Root Resolution, which included four points: (1) respect for China's sovereignty and integrity; (2) the fullest opportunity for China to develop and maintain a stable government; (3) restraint from using present conditions to seek special rights or privileges; (4) maintenance of the principle of equal opportunity for commerce and industry of all nations.[17]

Perhaps China's only solid gain from the open conference was the increase of Chinese import tariff duty from 3.5 percent to 5 percent. Koo stated on November 23, 1921, at the meeting of the Committee on Pacific and Far Eastern Questions that the existing situation in China constituted an infringement of China's sovereign right to set tariffs and deprived China of the power to make reciprocal arrangements. Further, Koo argued, a uniform rate that did not distinguish luxuries and necessities failed to take into consideration the needs of the Chinese people. Moreover, revision of tariffs was most difficult.[18] Koo proposed an immediate increase to 12.5 percent and eventual restoration of tariff autonomy.

Sir Robert Borden, a Canadian delegate, agreed that the tariff should be made effective at 5 percent at once, with future revision possible every seven years. Upon abolition of the *likin,* a special conference would be called to raise the duty to 12.5 percent. Masunosuke Odagiri, director of the Yokohama Specie Bank, retorted that Japanese trade with China accounted for more than 30 percent of China's foreign trade and that such a sudden increase in tariff would mean high prices for Chinese purchasers and would exert serious pressures on Japanese industry. Therefore he proposed to levy a surtax of 30 percent on all trade.[19] He also insisted that additional customs revenues should first be used for the service of foreign loans, and that Japan should have a fair share in the custodian banks and a proportion of the foreign nationals employed on the customs staff. Consequently, a committee of revision was called to meet at Shanghai to revise the present tariff to a basis of 5 percent, effective two months after publication of the agreement. Long-range revision would involve a special conference charged with abolition of the *likin* and effecting a 2.5 percent surtax and a special surtax on luxuries not exceeding 5 percent.[20]

China also sought the withdrawal of Japan from Shantung province. China had refused to sign the Treaty of Versailles and had refused to engage in direct negotiations with Japan afterward, fearing that she might become the isolated victim of Japanese imperialism. Japan did not want to be "on trial" at the Washington Conference and tried to settle this matter. After initial contacts, Baron Shidehara Kijūrō, Japanese ambassador in Washington, on August 18 offered Secretary of State Charles Evans Hughes an outline of a proposed settlement of the Shantung question.[21] It included the restoration of Kiaochow Bay to China with the promise that it be opened for international trade and that the Tsingtao-Tsinan Railway and all appurtenant mines be worked as joint Sino-Japanese enterprises, to be guarded by a special Sino-Japanese police force. Other reservations were the opening of more ports in Shantung, the construction of several railways under the International Consortium, special status for the customshouse at Tsingtao, and special arrangements on maintenance and operation of public works. Nevertheless, Yen found the Japanese plans fundamentally unacceptable and again China refused to negotiate directly with Japan.[22]

Finally, a formula worked out by Secretary Hughes and Arthur Balfour, head of the British delegation, was accepted by Katō Tomosaburō of Japan and by Sze. The first Sino-Japanese negotiations were opened on December 1, 1921, under the sponsorship of Hughes and Balfour and under the observation of Anglo-American delegates, J. V. A. MacMurray and Edward Bell for the United States and Sir John Jordan and Miles Lampson for the British Empire.[23]

Fear and suspicion of the Japanese still pervaded China, however, and the Chinese people at home and abroad, opposing direct negotiations with Japan, insisted upon taking the case of Shantung to the conference. When news of the Washington Conference reached China, public opinion was initially hopeful of a settlement. Numerous societies were formed from trade unions, educational circles, and commercial establishments, and finally consolidated into the National Association for Chinese People's Diplomacy on November 11, 1921, in Shanghai.[24]

On October 12, the National Association of Teachers and Merchants elected Yü Jih-chang and Chiang Meng-lin as representatives and sent them to Washington to disseminate the opinion of the Chinese people.[25] They were convinced that Japan would employ a strategy of delay at the negotiation table until the conference was over, that the Peking government, deceived by Japanese diplomacy, would lose China's sovereignty over Shantung, and that any direct negotiation would mean China's recognition of the Twenty-one Demands and the Treaty of Versailles and thus the abandonment of the basis of the international law for which China had been struggling. However, their demonstration on December 1 only briefly delayed the first Sino-Japanese meeting.

The question of the Tsingtao-Tsinan Railway occupied most of the thirty-six meetings of the negotiators and brought the meetings to a halt at least three times in two months. Before the long adjournment on December 20, Baron Shidehara summarized the negotiations:

The Japanese Government originally proposed a plan of joint enterprise. They have not yet withdrawn that proposal. But the Japanese Delegation . . . expressed joint enterprise plan, a plan of railway loan agreement to be concluded between the Chinese Government and Japanese capitalists, on the basis of the terms contained in railway loan agreements of comparatively recent dates which China has entered into with various foreign capitalists.[26]

Shidehara failed to mention the significant conditions attached to his plan: (1) the term to be fifteen years with option of redemption after five years; (2) a Japanese traffic manager and a Japanese chief accountant to be appointed; (3) details to be worked out in Peking.

The Chinese delegates did not expect the long adjournment caused by the Japanese delegates, and they did not have an opportunity to present their own statement until the meeting was resumed after the new year:

Plan I—Cash Payment—Japan to transfer to China the railway and its branches together with all properties appurtenant thereto . . . China to pay Japan a cash payment for the railway properties, consisting of the sum of 53,406,141 gold marks plus expenditures for permanent improvements and additions to the railway properties under Japanese administration. No undertaking is to be given by China to employ upon the railway any officials of Japanese nationality.

Plan II—Deferred Payment—The same as Plan I, except that payment is to be made by China in installments in Chinese Government treasury notes extending over twelve years, with an option on the part of China at any time after three years, upon giving six months' notice, to pay all remaining unpaid installments. China herself to select and to employ in the service of the railway, a district engineer of Japanese nationality.[27]

In Peking at the end of December, Obata Torikichi, Japanese minister in Peking, was pressing Foreign Minister Yen and newly appointed Premier Liang Shih-yi to accept a Japanese plan-loan agreement between the Chinese government and the Japanese capitalists, with Japanese personnel serving as traffic manager, chief accountant, and chief engineer.[28] When on January 4 Baron Shidehara told Hughes that Premier Liang had accepted the Japanese proposal, the representatives of the Chinese students and people in Washington took to "berating the delegates for their weak-kneed policy toward Japan." In China, the warlords of the Chihli Party, under the powerful Inspector-General Wu P'ei-fu, started to move troops and demanded Premier Liang's immediate removal from office. Liang's telegrams denying the rumor were not heeded and he was forced out of office on January 12. Yen served as acting prime minister. The removal of the Fengtien-supported premier was one cause of the Fengtien-Chihli war three months later between Marshal Chang Tso-lin's Manchurian Army and General Wu P'ei-fu's Chihli Army, which resulted in the complete domination of the Peking government by the Chihli Party.[29]

When the negotiations again came to a standstill at the nineteenth meeting, Balfour and Hughes instructed Jordan and MacMurray to visit both delegations and proposed several compromise formulas. Under pressure from Secretary Hughes and President Harding's personal intervention in Washington and Peking, the Chinese government accepted Japan's final formula. The matters of Chinese treasury notes and of appointing accountants for the railway embodied the conditions attached to Shidehara's plan. In addition, provisions were made for the appointment of Japanese and Chinese traffic managers.[30]

Other settlements regarding Shantung included restitution to China of the Kiaochow leased territory and the fifty-kilometer zone around Kiaochow Bay within six months under a special commission, as Baron Shidehara had offered; the transfer to China by Japan of all public properties in the leased territories except those reserved for the Japanese consulate and community including public schools, shrines, and cemeteries; the complete withdrawal, also within six months, of Japanese troops stationed along the Tsingtao-Tsinan Railway. The customshouse at Tsingtao was to be an integral part of Chinese maritime customs, while providing Japanese traders with Japanese-speaking staff. Tsinan-Shunteh and Kaomi-Hsuchow railway concessions were to be open to an international financial group on terms to be arranged by the Chinese government and the group; the mines of Szechwan, Fangtze, and Chinlingchen were to be handed over to a company under a special charter in which Japanese capital might not exceed the amount of Chinese capital. The interests of Japanese salt-manufacturing companies at Kiaochow Bay were to be purchased by the Chinese government at fair compensation and the exportation to Japan of a quantity of salt was to be permitted on reasonable terms. Agreements were also reached concerning opening an international trading port, and the Chinese purchase of undersea cables between Tsingtao and Chefoo and between Tsingtao and Shanghai.[31]

In regard to negotiation with the Japanese on the restoration of Shantung and the acceptance of the railway settlement, the policy of Koo, Sze, and Wang was basically sound. By refusing any direct negotiation, China might have offered Japan an excuse to boycott the conference entirely. When the case of the Manchurian Incident is considered, a Chinese appeal to the League of Nations would probably not have produced concrete results. But for the Washington agreements, the Shantung question would have remained unsettled until after World War II, and the area would have been completely under Japanese exploitation. Consequently China would have had to face the difficult problems presented by a Japanized generation.[32] China would also have lost the annual revenue of the Shantung administration, the Tsingtao-Tsinan Railway, and the Tsingtao salt tax, as well as 2000 positions with the railway that Japanese nationals held.

Baron Shidehara's diplomacy of disarmament, international cooperation with the Western powers, and noninterference in China provided China the best possible opportunity to settle the problem of Shantung on reasonable terms. An influential ruling elite with popular support, however, was leading Japan toward arrogance. The Japanese delegates at Washington probably experienced as much difficulty as did the Chinese diplomats. Foreign Minister Uchida Yasuya told American Ambassador Warren in Tokyo that "the Japanese Delegates to the Washington Conference had exceeded their powers in proposing terms of payments."[33] As for the proposal of Shidehara to employ Japanese experts as associate engineer and associate accountant of the railway, Obata informed Yen that while "it was the intention of the Japanese representatives, the Japanese Government would never give its consent."[34] The Japanese government insisted that Japanese citizens should be appointed traffic manager, chief accountant, and chief engineer.

III.

Three matters occupied the diplomats in Peking during the remaining years of the warlord government, namely, the restoration of Sino-Russian relations, the gold franc controversy, and the tariff conference. Although Japan was against China on all of these issues, only in the case of the tariff was she particularly opposed to change.

As China's fortunes declined amid wars of defeat and imposition of unequal treaties, the relatively cordial relationship along the 4150-mile Sino-Russian border ended. The problems of Mongolia and the Chinese Eastern Railway assumed serious proportions. The independence of Outer Mongolia had been declared in 1911 by the Living Buddha, and by the terms of the agreement signed in June 1915 by China, Outer Mongolia, and Russia, Outer Mongolia accepted China's suzerainty and China recognized Outer Mongolia's autonomy.[35] Mongolian collaboration with White Russian forces under General Roman Nikolaus von Ungern-Sternberg, to restore the independence abolished during the Russian Revolution in 1917, only offered a pretext for the Soviet Army's seizure of Outer Mongolia.[36] The Chinese Eastern Railway had been Li Hung-chang's payment for the secret Sino-Russian defensive alliance (1896) after China's defeat in the Sino-Japanese War.[37] Taking advantage of the Russian Revolution, China recovered both the administration and the police power of the line in 1920.

Seeking allies against the foreign troops in Siberia, Lev Mikhailovich Karakhan, acting commissar of foreign affairs, proposed to the governments at Peking and Canton that all unequal treaties between China and Imperial Russia be abolished. Thus the Soviet government would return the Chinese Eastern Railway, and would abandon the Boxer indemnity and the principle of extraterritoriality.[38] As the White resistance in Siberia began to collapse, Karakhan sent the Chinese governments a second, less cordial proposal (September 27, 1920).[39] In neither declaration were the problems of Outer Mongolia mentioned. Because of Russian troops in Outer Mongolia and the opposition of the diplomatic corps in Peking, the Peking government did not designate a director-general for Sino-Soviet negotiations (C. T. Wang) until March 27, 1923, when the Sun-Joffe Declaration concerning cooperation between the Kuomintang and the Communists was made known.[40]

Karakhan, who succeeded Adolf Abrahamovich Joffe as the Soviet representative to China, arrived on September 2, 1923. Objections of the diplomatic corps in Peking to Karakhan's dealings with Japan, however, delayed the exchange of opinions between Wang and Karakhan until the Russians threatened to establish relations with the Kuomintang regime.[41] After several revisions, Wang and Karakhan signed draft agreements to settle their differences. Due to the long-standing rivalry of Koo and Wang, the final instruments were not signed until May 31, by which time Koo had ousted Wang and taken the negotiations in his own hands.[42]

Besides the articles on normalization of relations, abolition of concessions, the Boxer indemnity, extraterritoriality, and the fixed tariff rate, the USSR recognized that Outer Mongolia was an integral part of China and that a complete withdrawal of Russian troops would be effected as soon as conditions for the withdrawal were agreed upon. The Chinese Eastern Railway became a jointly operated commercial enterprise, with the possibility of redemption by China.[43]

After five years' postponement because of the European war, China's Boxer indemnity payment was due again in 1923. A dispute between China and France arose as a result of the devaluation of the franc to one-third of its prewar level. In coordination with Japan and the other ten signatories of the protocol, France demanded the debt be paid in gold. The British inspector-general of customs withheld the surplus of the customs duties and the gabelle on behalf of the French in order to press the Peking government, which depended largely upon this surplus for survival.[44]

According to Article VI of the Final Protocol for the Settlement of the Disturbances of 1900 (Boxer Uprising),

> China agreed to pay the Powers an indemnity of four hundred and fifty millions of Haikwan Taels. . . . These four hundred and fifty millions constitute a gold debt calculated at the rate of the Haikwan tael to the gold currency of each country, indicated below. Haikwan tael = 3.055 marks, 3.75 francs, etc. This sum in gold shall bear interest at four percent per annum, and the capital shall be payable in gold or at the rates of exchange corresponding to the dates on the first of January, 1903. . . .[45]

The exchange between France and China in July 1905 concerning the method of payment read:

> Recognizing that the sum of 450,000,000 taels constitutes a debt to gold . . . (1) That is to say, for each Haikwan tael due to each of the Powers, China must pay in gold . . . (4)

China will make these payments, calculated on the basis set for the above which fixed
the value of the Haikwan Protocol tael in relation to the money of each country, either
in silver according to the price of silver on the London market, or in gold bills, or in
telegraphic transfers, at the choice of each Power. . . .[46]

France had chosen telegraphic transfers, and China had complied for
eighteen years without any problems.

On June 22, 1922, however, the French requested conversion of the
remaining indemnity payment into American dollars, on condition that
part of the payment be used for restoring the Sino-French Enterprises Bank
and Sino-French cultural activities. Foreign Minister W. W. Yen, not fully
aware of the French intrigue, simply forwarded part of the payment to the
ministry of finance, which made no commitment.[47] In the subsequent Sino-
French agreement, the franc was not defined. On July 13, the first French
request for gold francs was sent to the Chinese government and was rejected
by then Foreign Minister Wang, in his note of December 28, 1922, to the
French minister and envoys of the other powers including Yoshida
Shigeru.[48] In subsequent notes from the envoys signed by Yoshida on
February 24 and November 5, 1923, the envoys insisted that the indemnity
was a gold debt. Then, anxious that the customs surplus be released to the
Peking government and that the French agree to the conference on tariffs
arranged at the Washington Conference, the cabinet of Premier Chang
Shao-tseng decided to accept the French request. This action caused
turmoil in Parliament.[49] Pending solution, the case passed from one to
another when Koo became foreign minister in January 1924 in Sun Pao-
ch'i's cabinet and, in July, acting premier under warlord President Ts'ao
K'un. Public opinion was intense but Koo resisted pressure on the
beleaguered president and his Chihli Party to accept the French demand.

In the Capital Revolution (October 24, 1924), Marshal Feng Yü-
hsiang ousted President Ts'ao; General Wu P'ei-fu ordered his Chihli Army
to recover Peking. Feng, fearing the threat posed by Wu, invited Tuan Ch'i-
jui, former head of the An-fu Party, to be chief executive. Thus General
Cheng Shih-ch'i, military governor of Shantung and a lieutenant of Tuan's
An-fu Party, could be brought into the coalition against General Wu.[50] On
April 11, 1925, the chief executive directed both his finance minister, Li
Szu-hao, and his foreign minister, Shen Jui-lin, to notify the French
minister of China's acceptance of the gold franc demand. Consequently,
the $10,000,000 held up by the inspector-general of customs on behalf of
France and the $5,000,000 held up for the other powers were immediately
released to Tuan's government.[51] Due to the stability of the yuan, Japan
was not a major recipient of the monetary profit, nor did she change her
method of payment with respect to her part of the indemnity. Nevertheless,
as a signatory of the Boxer Protocol, Japan collaborated with the French
envoy throughout the so-called gold franc controversy.

According to Article X of the Treaty of Nanking (1842), China agreed to "a fair and regular tariff of import and export customs and other dues."[52] The fixed tariff rate was at the expense of China, without reciprocity. While import duty in Shanghai on one pound of British tobacco was only one-third yuan, the same quantity of Chinese tobacco found its way blocked by a high wall of protection, three yuan. Further, the uniform import tariff rate made no distinction between raw materials and manufactured goods or between necessities and luxury goods. Consequently, China was not in a position to raise the tariff rate for luxury goods and imported goods, such as liquor and opium, which severely harmed China's infant industry and social order. Native Chinese products for export usually paid multiple transit duties according to their market value as they journeyed from their origin through numerous ports and at the ultimate port of exit; yet foreign goods paid only the fixed low import duty plus 2.5 percent transit dues. Even the export trade was mainly in the hands of foreign merchants. The situation became critical when foreign export trading was subsidized by home government policies through lower or free export tariffs or reduced transportation charges.[53]

At the Paris Peace Conference, China failed to obtain a hearing from her European allies for her case for tariff autonomy.[54] The Washington Conference granted China an effective duty rate of 5 percent and a surtax of 2.5 percent plus an addition for luxury goods if authorized by a "special conference." After the gold franc controversy was settled and the French government had ratified the terms of the Washington Conference, the Peking government sent invitations to Italy, France, the United States, Japan, Belgium, Holland, the United Kingdom, and Portugal on August 18, 1925, to attend such a special conference. The special conference finally opened in Peking on October 26, 1925, after three years' delay.[55] The Chinese delegation included W. W. Yen and C. T. Wang, as well as General Huang Fu, who served as the link between the Chinese delegation and the Kuominchün under Marshal Feng Yü-hsiang, who was in actual control of Peking.[56]

Wang presented the Chinese proposal: (1) the powers' recognition of China's tariff autonomy; (2) China's promise to abolish the *likin* as of January 1, 1929; (3) a surtax of 5 percent to be added to general commodities, 20 percent to luxury goods, and 30 percent to liquors and tobacco products within three months after the signing of the present agreement.[57] In the meantime, the Peking government issued its Tariff Rate Regulations and Tobacco and Liquor Import Regulations on October 24, 1925.[58] Wang's proposal caused broad opposition by all the powers in general and by Japan in particular. Wang, however, pressed the foreign delegates at the subsequent meetings of the various subcommittees and utilized Chinese public opinion to voice the determination of the Chinese government to set its own tariff rate, in case the powers failed to pass the proposal. As a result, the powers were forced to honor the principle of China's tariff autonomy:

> Each and all the Powers recognize China's right to enjoy tariff autonomy, permit liquidating all tariff restraints in the various existing treaties and agreements between China and the Powers, and further permit tariff rates of the Chinese Government to be effective on January 1, 1929.
>
> The Chinese Government declares that the abolishment of *likin* will be carried out simultaneously with the tariff autonomy of the Chinese Government. The abolishment of *likin* should be completed before January 1, 1929.[59]

Nevertheless, the powers were stalemated on the question of surtax rate, how to make up local resources after abolition of the *likin*, and how to dispose of the surtax and ensure its safekeeping. Since China was the importer of more than 40 percent of the goods exported by Japan, and the cheaper and lower-grade Japanese goods could find markets only in China and could be easily manufactured by Chinese under a protective tariff, it is understandable that Japan was the archopponent of China's tariff autonomy.[60] The Japanese delegation, under Hioki and Yoshizawa, presented a counterproposal in which Japan reiterated that during the transitional period (prior to full tariff autonomy) China could collect only the 2.5 percent surtax as designated by the Washington Conference; that China should enter into a new bilateral agreement with Japan establishing a lower tax for Japan's imports from China, such as cotton, rice, soy beans, and iron ore, and for Japanese industrial exports to China; that the surtax should service China's unsecured loans for Japan; that the Yokohama Specie Bank should be one of the depositors of the surtax; and that a Japanese should be hired as inspector-general of Chinese maritime customs, since Japan had replaced Great Britain as the largest trading partner of China.[61]

The American proposal would have allowed China to raise customs duties from the current 5 percent to 12.5 percent for imports and from 5 percent to 7.5 percent for exports effective three months after the agreement, prior to full implementation of tariff autonomy in China. It also included articles specifying the use of part of the surtax to compensate the provinces for their lost *likin* income and to repay the unsecured loans.[62] But civil war caused the end of the conference in April 1926, as a new alliance of old foes, Marshal Chang Tso-lin of Manchuria and General Wu P'ei-fu of the revived Chihli Party, drove the Kuominchün of their former ally, Marshal Feng Yü-hsiang, out of Peking.[63] Under Generalissimo Chang, the new dictator of Peking, a committee for a special tariff conference was established (July 14, 1926) by Finance Minister Wellington Koo, who established (February 24, 1927) a surtax committee, in order to forestall Japanese ambitions. But no powers sent delegates to Peking throughout the remaining months of the warlord government in Peking.[64]

IV.

As Chinese nationalism gained momentum throughout China, the struggle of Chinese diplomats in Peking to restore Chinese sovereign power and abolish unequal treaties was matched in the south. In the Declaration of the First National Assembly (January 21, 1924), the Nationalist Party asserted that the abolition of unequal treaties, such as concessions, consular jurisdiction, and fixed tariff was a fundamental policy. The same principle was reiterated in Dr. Sun's declaration of the Northern Expedition (September 18, 1924), and of the journey to Peking (November 10, 1924). In accordance with Dr. Sun's will, the Kuomintang's Central Executive Committee on June 25, 1925, invited the powers to revise the unequal treaties and declared abolition of such treaties as the primary goal of its national revolution on July 1, when the Nationalist government was founded.[65] This upheaval was attended by a series of demonstrations and massacres from Shanghai and the Yangtze River Valley to Canton between May 30 and July 31, 1925, as well as by the resulting restoration of British concessions in Hankow, Kiukiang, and Chenchiang in early 1927.[66]

The growth of Chinese nationalism was matched by an expansion of Japanese militarism, which eventually annulled Shidehara's peace policy. On January 18, 1927, Shidehara, foreign minister of Premier Wakatsuki's Kenseikai cabinet, made public his China policy: (1) to respect China's sovereign independence and territorial integrity; (2) to refrain from intervening in China's civil strife; (3) to improve Sino-Japanese relations and economic cooperation; (4) to develop Japanese sympathy toward the Chinese and help the Chinese to achieve their proper aspirations; (5) to treat the current Chinese situation with patience and tolerance while protecting the proper rights of the Japanese in China through rational means.[67] Shidehara's China policy was affirmed by nonparticipation of Japanese warships in the American-British bombardment of Nanking on March 24, 1927, when the consulates were destroyed by the victorious Northern Expeditionary Forces' 6th Army.[68]

Nevertheless, the unification of China was furthered when the Northern Expeditionary Forces crossed the Yangtze and entered Shantung. Tanaka Giichi, leader of the Seiyukai, came to power after the fall of the Wakatsuki ministry and resolved on April 20, 1927, to dispatch 2000 Kwantung Army men to Shantung in the name of protecting 2196 Japanese subjects and their property in Tsinan.[69] Both Foreign Minister C. C. Wu (Wu Ch'ao-ch'u) of the Nationalist government and Foreign

Minister Koo of the Peking government under Generalissimo Chang sent protests to Japan. Taking advantage of the rivalry between Chiang Kai-shek's government in Nanking and Wang Ching-wei's government in Wuhan, the fleeing warlord Sun Ch'uan-fang began a counterattack to recover his lost territory. The Japanese Army, reassured by the favorable trend, withdrew from Shantung on August 30, 1927.[70]

When the Northern Expedition was resumed under Chiang and his forces entered Shantung in April 1928, the Japanese government once again sent troops to Tsinan. The clash resulted in 4704 recorded deaths and property damage amounting to $26,000,000. The Chinese field political affairs commissioner and head of the foreign affairs division, Ts'ai Kung-shih, and his staff were killed and Chiang's foreign minister Huang Fu and his staff were disarmed, detained, and, at bayonet point, forced to sign statements absolving the Japanese of responsibility.[71] A full-fledged war was avoided only when Chiang ordered his men out of Tsinan and they crossed the Yellow River to continue the Northern Expedition.

Having failed to settle the Tsinan Incident, Huang Fu, the first veteran diplomat of the warlord government in Peking to work for Chiang, resigned. Marshal Feng Yü-hsiang of the Second National Revolutionary Army Group recommended C. T. Wang to succeed Huang on June 6. After long negotiation, a Sino-Japanese agreement on the Tsinan Incident was signed by C. T. Wang and Yoshizawa Kenkichi, Japanese minister to China, on March 28, 1929. Articles containing a Japanese apology for the death of Ts'ai and an indemnity were eliminated from the document. Only a joint investigation commission was formed to do an on-the-spot study.[72]

The positive Manchurian and Mongolian policies of Tanaka's cabinet were developed at the Eastern Conference (June 27–July 7, 1927), attended by the military governor of the Kwantung Leased Territory, the Japanese consuls-general at Shanghai and Mukden, and Yoshizawa, and at an executive conference at Dairen, which also included the two Japanese advisers of Chang Tso-lin. The conference agreed to Japanese rights to construct six railways in Manchuria; to manage forests in Kirin and Heilungkiang; to materialize the existing rights over leased land; to cancel plans for Chinese railways parallel to the South Manchurian Railway; and to exchange the right of inland residence of Japanese subjects for the abolition of extraterritoriality.[73] Yoshizawa negotiated with Yang Yü-t'ing, Generalissimo Chang's chief of staff, but without result because of the pressure of public opinion. Even on the last day of Chang's fatal journey from Peking, Yoshizawa was still pressing the Old Marshal for his consent to these terms.

Shigemitsu Mamoru explained Premier Tanaka's policy toward Manchuria in his *Shōwa no dōran:*

> The policy of Premier Tanaka toward Manchurian problems is to consider Man-
> churia a special area, separated from China proper, and to settle all issues with Marshal

Chang Tso-lin, the actual ruler of Manchuria. Therefore, Tanaka disagreed with Chang's extending his ambition toward Peking. He only wished that through Japanese assistance, Chang might become independent in Manchuria, separating from the Chinese Central Government, and establish special relations with Japan to settle Manchurian problems according to Japanese wishes. . . . Consequently, Premier Tanaka . . . had dispatched General Yamanishi, former Army Minister, to Peking, advising Marshal Chang to hurry back to Manchuria, minding his home order. Yet Chang already was sworn in as the Generalissimo and considered himself chief of the Chinese state. . . . Resentful of Chang's arrogance, General Yamanishi, back empty-handed, reported everything to Tokyo. . . .

On the other hand, Minister Yoshizawa, shouldering a mission similar to General Yamanishi's, was ordered to execute Premier Tanaka's instructions on May 18, 1928. The instructions state that in case Chang refused to take the Premier's advice and consequently was forced back to Manchuria after his defeat, the Japanese Army might prevent his withdrawal at Shanhaikuan on the Great Wall. . . . The Kwantung Army was convinced that the Manchurian problems would not be settled unless Marshal Chang was eliminated.[74]

On June 4, Marshal Chang and many of his staff were victims of an explosion arranged by Colonel Kōmoto Daisaku, senior staff officer of the Kwantung Army, when the marshal's special train was passing under the bridge of the South Manchurian Railway near Mukden.[75]

The quick succession of the Young Marshal, Chang Hsueh-liang, spoiled the scheme of the Kwantung Army to take over Manchuria during the chaos following the Old Marshal's death. But because he refused to negotiate with the Japanese to settle the so-called Manchurian problem and because he stayed in Peking after intervening in the civil war in 1930 between Chiang and his rivals, Marshals Feng Yü-hsiang and Yen Hsi-shan, his rule over Manchuria lasted only three years.[76] Convinced that the Kwantung Army had murdered his father, the Young Marshal rejected the warnings of Hayashi Kyūjirō, Japanese consul-general in Mukden, and ordered the flying of the Nationalist flag over all Manchuria on December 29, 1928. The failure of Tanaka's positive China policy resulted in the fall of his cabinet, and he was replaced by Hamaguchi Osachi (Yūkō) of the Minseito in July 1929. Once again, Shidehara was appointed foreign minister and again he was able to try his peace policy toward China. His thesis, "Sino-Japanese Non-Aggression Pact," was made public in October 1929 with Shigemitsu Mamoru as the executive officer in China.[77] Shidehara's peace policy, however, ended in the Manchurian Incident (September 18, 1931).

The Manchurian Incident finally brought Yen and Koo, the last two anti-Japanese veteran diplomats of the warlord government, to the Nationalist government. On November 30, 1931, Koo was appointed acting foreign minister and Yen was sent to Washington to strengthen the diplomatic front. Strangely, most of the important diplomatic posts in the major capitals, including Washington, Paris, Berlin, and Moscow, were vacant at the time.[78]

In Geneva, Sao-ke Alfred Sze, the Chinese representative to the League of Nations, first brought the issue before the council. Following Japanese occupation of Chinchou, Secretary of State Henry L. Stimson, in notes to China and Japan on January 7, 1932, set forth his nonrecognition doctrine. The Japanese responded by landing troops in Shanghai on January 28. Yen was rushed to Geneva to replace Sze, an indication of China's faith in U.S.-League support. Yen asked that Articles 10 and 15 of the Covenant be applied, so that a special arrangement could be made in order to settle the long-standing controversy in the council. But Japan created "Manchukuo" and signed a military alliance with the puppet state while Koo was accompanying the Lytton Commission to the Far East.[79]

Finally the council met on November 21 to discuss the Lytton Report. Matsuoka Yōsuke, now Japan's representative, condemned the report. Because China was not an organized state, usual solutions were inapplicable. In addition, Matsuoka insisted, Manchuria was not by definition part of China and the actions of the Kwantung Army were based on self-defense, not on an attempt to manufacture a movement for independence. Koo, appointed to argue for the commission's findings, cited the report:

> Although, at present, China is split, the central authority is not, at least openly, repudiated. . . . As for the relations of Manchuria to the rest of China, it is shown that the influence of Chinese culture and civilization has been strong in Manchuria long before it became formally a part of China in 1644. . . . When the Republic was established, the Manchurian authorities accepted the fait accompli and voluntarily followed the leadership of Yüan Shih-k'ai. . . .
>
> On the night of September 18, the Japanese military operations could not be regarded as measures of legitimate defense and a carefully prepared plan was put into operation with swiftness and precision. . . . A group of Japanese civil and military officials, both active and retired, who were in close touch with the new political movement in Japan to which reference was made, conceived, organized and carried through this movement [Manchukuo], as a solution to the situation in Manchuria as it existed after the event of September 18. . . . While there were a number of factors which contributed to the creation of Manchukuo, the two which, in combination, were most effective, and without which, in our judgment, the new State could not have been formed, were the presence of Japanese troops and the activities of Japanese officials, both civil and military.[80]

When the assembly adopted the report on February 24, 1933, Matsuoka and the entire Japanese delegation withdrew.[81] But the Kwantung Army occupied Jehol, and the Chinese province, linking Manchuria with China Proper, was declared part of Manchukuo.[82]

Anti-Japanese and national-salvation movements and organizations had existed since the intervention of the Japanese Army in Shantung during the Northern Expedition. The September 18 affair finally caused the anti-Japanese movement to explode. College students, Kuomintang officials, the various trade unions, and the armed forces including police in Peking, Shanghai, and Nanking held mass meetings, strikes, and demonstrations. The movement soon spread to inland cities and to large ports such as Hankow, Hsuchow, and Taiyuan.[83] They demanded national mobilization against Japan, volunteer corps for military training, a boycott of Japanese goods, punishment of sovereignty-selling diplomats, and no direct negotiation with Japan. By the end of September, 3000 delegates representing nineteen colleges and universities in Shanghai and Peking traveled to Nanking to petition and critically injured Foreign Minister C. T. Wang, who soon resigned.[84] The national mood and public opinion under the influence of the students and the newspapers were so inflamed that any direct negotiation between China and Japan was considered an act of treason and a national disgrace.

Meanwhile, Japan's chief delegate in Geneva, Yoshizawa Kenkichi, reiterated to the League's council that the government favored "direct negotiation with the Nanking Government regarding the Sino-Japanese crisis in Manchuria," and that "Japan will not tolerate the mediation or interference of any other party or Government in the negotiations."[85] But the Nanking government under the Kuomintang stubbornly resisted. T. V. Soong, finance minister and deputy premier, who was in actual control of foreign affairs, was misled into believing that the League would be all-powerful against aggression. The Kuomintang authorities were convinced that "party strategy toward this incident must follow public opinion. Without the support of public opinion, the party would lose its political power, and the National Government would also be diminished."[86] The peace approach devised by farsighted Japanese as well as Chinese was now either neglected or destroyed by greedy Japanese militarists and a self-perpetuation-minded Kuomintang.[87] Throughout the period from the Paris Peace Conference to the Manchurian Incident, Far Eastern peace was endangered by growing Japanese militarism and Chinese nationalism. The focus was on Manchuria, the meeting ground of the two rivals. The diplomats of the Anglo-American school who formerly served the warlord governments in Peking, such as C. T. Wang, W. W. Yen, and Wellington Koo, first replaced the pro-Japanese diplomats in control of Chinese foreign policy. They then transferred themselves one after another from Peking to Nanking, the site of the new revolutionary Nationalist government. Neither knowing nor trusting Japan, the central government and the diplomats of the Anglo-American school put their faith in the League of Nations and refused to conduct direct negotiations with the enemy.[88] As a result, flexibility, an essential element of international politics, was lost. Lost also was the Shidehara peace faction of the Japanese government, China's Manchurian provinces with their 30,000,000 population, and peace in the Far East.

Notes

1. The Fourteen Points emerged from the presidential address to Congress, "Five Demands and Four Principles" (February 11, 1918); the presidential address at Mount Vernon, "Four Ends" (July 4, 1918); the presidential address in New York, "Five Particulars" (September 27, 1918); and the presidential addresses in Manchester, England (December 30, 1918) and in Rome (January 3, 1919) on abolition of the balance of power. Herbert Hoover, *The Ordeal of Woodrow Wilson* (New York, 1958), pp. 23–27.

2. Ts'ao Ju-lin, *I-sheng chih hui-i* [Reminiscences of my life] (Hong Kong, 1966), p. 188.

3. Secretary's note (British) of a convention held in M. Pichon's room at Quai d'Orsay, Paris, 27 January 1919, in Wunsz King Collection of V. K. Wellington Koo Papers (copy in author's possession), no. 7, pp. 16–18.

4. Besides the understandable suspicion between the delegates from the north and Wang from the south, the northern delegates were also involved in the question of seniority. V. K. Wellington Koo to the author, 19 May and 16 June 1969.

5. See Wunsz King Collection, no. 9, pp. 21–22.

6. Ray Stannard Baker, *Woodrow Wilson and World Settlement* (New York, 1923), 2:231.

7. *Papers Relating to the Foreign Relations of the United States: The Paris Peace Conference*, 1919 (Washington, D.C., 1946), 5:142–43. Hereafter cited as *FRUS*.

8. Baker, op. cit., 2:241, 260–61, indicates that the Japanese would not sign the treaty if settlement of the Shantung question favored China.

9. Robert Lansing, *The Peace Negotiations: A Personal Narrative* (Boston, 1921), pp. 256, 262.

10. Koo's interview with Dutasta, 24 June 1919, Wunsz King Collection, no. 23, pp. 68–69.

11. Chang Kuo-t'ao, "O-te hui-i" [Memoir of Chang Kuo-t'ao], *Ming-pao yüeh-k'an* [Ming-pao Monthly] 1:4 (1966):88–91. Chang was a founder of the Chinese Communist Party.

12. Consul-General Thomas Sammons to Secretary of State Robert Lansing, 14 June 1919, *National Archives Microfilm Publications Microcopy No. 329, Records of the Department of State Relating to Internal Affairs of China, 1910–1929*, reel 21, 893.00/3119.

13. Lo Kuang, *Lu Cheng-hsiang chuan* [Biography of Lu Cheng-hsiang] (Taipei, 1967), pp. 113–14.

14. U.S. Department of State, *Conference on the Limitation of Armament, Washington, November 12, 1921–February 6, 1922* (Washington, D.C., 1922), pp. 4–8.

15. *Cheng-fu kung-pao* [Government Gazette], nos. 1966 and 1971, 14 and 19 August 1921.

16. *Wai-chiao kung-pao* [Foreign Affairs Gazette], no. 11, May 1922.

17. *Conference on the Limitation of Armament*, pp. 866–68.

18. Ibid.

19. Ibid., pp. 544–46, 558–64.

20. Ibid., pp. 1162–64.

21. Shidehara to Hughes, *FRUS, 1921* (Washington, D.C., 1936), 1:617–18.

22. Foreign Minister W. W. Yen to Minister in Peking Obata Torikichi, 3 September 1921, ibid., 1:632–35.

23. Hughes to Ambassador to Japan Charles B. Warren, 20 November 1921, *FRUS, 1922* (Washington, D.C., 1938), 1:937.

24. Ch'in Hsüeh-lü, *San-shui Liang Yen-sun hsien-sheng nien-p'u* [A chronological biography of Liang Shih-yi] (Taipei, 1962), 2:171.

25. Ho Szu-yüan, "Hua-sheng-tun hui-i chung Shantung wen-t'i chih ching-kuo" [The problem of Shantung during the Washington Disarmament Conference], *Tung-fang tsa-chih* 19:2 (1922):54–65.

26. *Conversations between the Chinese and Japanese Representatives in Regard to the Shantung Question, Treaty for Settlement of Outstanding Questions Relative to Shantung, Agreed Terms of Understanding Recorded in the Minutes of the Japanese and Chinese Delegations Concerning the Conclusion of the Treaty for the Settlement of Outstanding Questions Relative to Shantung; Minutes Prepared by the Japanese Delegation* (Washington, D.C., 1922), pp. 166–67.

27. Ibid., pp. 182–83.

28. Waichiaopu (Ministry of Foreign Affairs) to Sze, Koo, and Wang, 31 December 1921, Waichiaopu Archives (Institute of Modern History, Academia Sinica, Taipei).

29. *Wu P'ei-fu chuan* [Biography of Wu P'ei-fu] (Taipei, 1963), pp. 61–65.

30. Chia Shih-i, *Hua-hui chien-wen lu* [Reminiscence pertaining to the Washington Disarmament Conference] (Shanghai, 1928), pp. 149–50.

31. *Conversations,* pp. 263, 266, 276, 366, 377, 23–24, 34–35, 28, 37, 210–13, 228–39, 125–26, 215, 218, 227, 218–19, 226, 378, 16–17, 20–22, 230–36, 277, 379, 281–82, 294, 59–61, 73–75, 305–13, 54–56, 238, 251, 380–81.

32. Pao-chin Chu, "V. K. Wellington Koo: A Study of the Diplomat and Diplomacy of Warlord China, During His Early Career, 1919–1924" (Ph.D. diss., University of Pennsylvania, 1970), pp. 183–84.

33. Warren to Hughes, 26 December 1921, *FRUS, 1922,* 1:938.

34. Record of interview between Yen and Obata, 27 December 1921, Waichiaopu Archives.

35. John V. A. MacMurray, *Treaties and Agreements with and concerning China, 1894–1919* (New York, 1921), 2:1066–67.

36. Ch'en Lu, *Chih-shih pi-chi* [Notes of Ch'en Lu] (Taipei, n.d.), pp. 182–87.

37. Sergei Witte, *The Memoir of Count Witte,* tr. and ed. Abraham Yarmolinsky (New York, 1967), p. 89.

38. Chung-O hui-i ts'an-k'ao wen-chien [Documents prepared for the Sino-Russian conference], vol. 2, Chung-O wen-t'i lai-wang wen-chien [Documents on the Sino-Russian problems], pp. 1a–3a.

39. Ibid., vol. 2, pp. 4a–4b.

40. Wang Yü-chün, *Chung-Su wai-chiao ti hsü-mu: Ts'ung Yu-lin tao Yüeh-fei* [The beginning of Sino-Soviet diplomacy: From Yurin to Joffe] (Taipei, 1963). A comprehensive and scholarly study of Sino-Soviet negotiations.

41. *Hua-kuo yüeh-k'an* [Hua-kuo Monthly], no. 3, 16 September 1923, p. 9.

42. *Wai-chiao kung-pao,* no. 36, June 1924, Special Documents, pp. 1–9, 13–23, 36–39.

43. Ibid., pp. 13–22.

44. (Meng) Hsin-shih, "Chin-fo-lang an" [On the case of the gold francs], *Tung-fang tsa-chih* 20:24 (1923):111–14.

45. MacMurray, op. cit., 1:278–84.

46. Wu Tien-fang, "Chin-fo-lang wen-t'i" [On the question of the gold francs], *Tung-fang tsa-chih* 21:8 (1924):23–24.

47. W. W. Yen, "Yen Hui-ch'ing tzu-chuan" [Autobiography of W. W. Yen], trans. Yao Sung-lin, *Chuan-chi wen-hsüeh* [Biographical Literature] 19:6 (December 1971):55–56.

48. *Wai-chiao kung-pao,* no. 32, February 1924, Commercial, pp. 5–6.

49. Shen I-yün, *I-yün hui-i* [Memoirs] (Taipei, 1968), pp. 184–220.

50. Ibid.

51. *Cheng-fu kung-pao,* no. 3258, 27 April 1925, Official Dispatches.

52. Inspector-General of Customs, *Treaties, Conventions, etc., between China and Foreign States* (Shanghai, 1917), 1:355.

53. Li P'ei-en, "Kuan-shui tzu-chu" [Tariff autonomy], *Tung-fang tsa-chih* 22:12 (1925):35–40.

54. Wunsz King (Chin Wen-szu), *Ts'ung Pa-li ho-hui tao Kuo-lien* [From the Paris Peace Conference to the League of Nations] (Taipei, 1967), p. 5.

55. Shen Yün-lung, ed., *Chin-tai Chung-kuo shih-liao ts'ung-k'an: Kuan-shui t'e-pieh hui-i i-shih-lu* [Modern China historical materials series: Special tariff conference minutes] (Taipei, 1968), 1:11–37.

56. Shen I-yün, op. cit., 1:183–231.

57. Shen Yün-lung, op. cit., 1:57–58.

58. *Cheng-fu kung-pao,* no. 3434, 25 October 1925, Official Dispatches.

59. *Tung-fang tsa-chih* 22:23 (1925):3–5, News Reviews.

60. Lu Hua-chin, "Chung-Jih kuan-shui chiao-she chih kuo-ch'ü yu wei-lai" [Sino-Japanese tariff negotiations, past and future], *Tung-fang tsa-chih* 25:23 (1928):32–33.

61. Chou Keng-sheng, "Kuan-shui tzu-chu yu kuan-shui hui-i" [Tariff autonomy and tariff conference], *Hsien-tai p'ing-lun* [Contemporary Review], special issue for special tariff conference (October 1925):3–12; Wei Shen-fu, "Hai-kuan yung-jen hsing-cheng-ch'üan shou-hui chih pu-tsou" [Stages for restoration of the hiring power of customs], same issue, pp. 17–20.

62. *Wai-chiao kung-pao,* nos. 8–10, 3 November 1925, Special Documents Issued by the Tariff Conference.

63. Wang T'ieh-han, "Tung-pei chün-shih shih-liao" [A general history of the Northeastern Army], *Chuan-chi wen-hsüeh* 18:6 (June 1971):34–35.

64. *Cheng-fu kung-pao,* no. 3693, 24 July 1926, Documents, and no. 3896, 25 February 1927, Dispatches.

65. Fu Ch'i-hsüeh, *Chung-kuo wai-chiao shih* [Diplomatic History of China] (Taipei, 1966), pp. 360–64.

66. The May 30 Movement was touched off by the killing of a striking worker, Ku Cheng-hung, at the Japanese textile mill in Shanghai. The British also used weapons to disperse demonstrators, with fatal results, at the Shanghai International Settlement, in Hankow (June 11), in Kiukiang (June 13), in Canton Shamien (June 23), in Chungking (July 2), and in Nanking (July 31). A massacre in Hankow (January 3, 1927) resulted in the restoration of British concessions in Hankow on January 4, in Kiukiang on June 2, and Chenchiang on February 24, 1927.

67. Fu Ch'i-hsüeh, op. cit., p. 370.

68. John B. Powell, *My Twenty-Five Years in China* (New York, 1945), p. 149.

69. Liang Ching-tun, "Chi-an chih chien-cheng" [An eyewitness on the case of Tsinan], *Tung-fang tsa-chih* 25:11 (1928):14–15.

70. Fu Ch'i-hsüeh, op. cit., p. 394.

71. *Ko-ming wen-hsien* [Revolutionary documents] (Taipei, 1958), no. 19, p. 1411.

72. Ibid., pp. 1371–72.

73. Fu Ch'i-hsüeh, op. cit., pp. 396–97.

74. Shigemitsu Mamoru, *Shōwa no dōran* [The Shōwa upheavals] (Tokyo, 1952), 1:34–35.

75. Sadako N. Ogata, *Defiance in Manchuria: The Making of Japanese Foreign Policy, 1931–1932* (Berkeley, 1964), p. 13.

76. Liu Shih, *O-te hui-i* [My reminiscence] (Taipei, 1966), pp. 82–116.

77. Fu Ch'i-hsüeh, op. cit., pp. 402–3.

78. Yen, op. cit., 20:4 (April 1972):101–2.

79. Ibid., 20:5 (April 1972):95–96.

80. Westel W. Willoughby, *The Sino-Japanese Controversy and the League of Nations* (Baltimore, 1935), pp. 385–88, 408–13.

81. Yen, op. cit., 20:5 (May 1972):96–97.

82. Assembly Report, 24 February 1933, on the Sino-Japanese Dispute, *Ko-ming wen-hsien,* no. 40, p. 2903.

83. *Shen Pao* [Shanghai Daily], 20–24 September 1931.

84. Ibid., 28 September 1931, pp. 4, 12.

85. *North China Herald,* 22–29 September 1931, pp. 366–444.

86. Yen, op. cit., 20:4 (April 1972):101–2.

87. Shen I-yün, op. cit., 2:425–26.

88. Yen, op. cit., 20:4 (April 1972):101. Yen criticized Soong's confidence in the League's power as a significant factor in his failure to open other avenues of settlement.

III. Japanese Attitudes and Chinese Resistance

5.

In her essay Frances Moulder offers a number of challenging ideas and interpretations concerning the negative image late Manchu and early Republican China had to bear in comparison with Japan. She questions whether this was fair or accurate. When first presented in preliminary form at a meeting of the Columbia University Seminar on Modern Japan in the spring of 1974, her paper was regarded as a challenge to the Princeton series on Japanese modernization, which tend to credit Japan's traditional society and institutions with significant contribution to its modernization process. The paper evoked both positive and negative comment from scholars who heard it, and the discussion that ensued was something of an intellectual feast.

Moulder received her Ph.D. from Columbia University and has been assistant professor of sociology at the Livingston College of Rutgers University. Her revised dissertation, titled "Development and Underdevelopment in Japan and China," is scheduled for publication by the Cambridge University Press.

Comparing Japan and China: Some Theoretical and Methodological Issues

Frances V. Moulder

I.

The case of Japan is of critical importance to theories of economic development and underdevelopment, for several reasons. Japan was the *first* non-Western nation to achieve the position of a major industrial power. Japan's industrialization was almost contemporaneous with the industrialization of Western nations such as the United States, Germany, and France. "Takeoff" occurred in the late nineteenth century, and industrialization was well under way by World War I. Today, Japan is still the only non-Western society to have become a major industrial state. Although considerable economic progress has been made in several other non-Western nations since World War II (for instance, China, India, Brazil), none is highly industrialized, and only China can be regarded as a major world power.

Moreover, Japan was the first so-called Third World nation to become an industrial power. The term "Third World" refers to those countries of Asia, Africa, and Latin America that have been economically and politically dominated by the industrial capitalist nations. Today it is often forgotten (at least outside Japan) that Japan was partially controlled by the Western capitalist nations during the nineteenth century. Although Japan never became a formal colony, a set of treaties reduced national autonomy and blocked industrial development. Western observers during the nineteenth century were as confident of their sway over Japan as any of the other areas of Asia, Latin America, and Africa. "The Japanese are a happy race and being content with little, are not likely to achieve much," wrote the *Japan Herald* in 1881.[1]

How is it possible that Japan became an important industrial state? Why do other nations of the Third World remain underdeveloped? Any theory of development must provide a framework for answering these interlocked questions.

Since World War II, the sociology of economic development in America and Western Europe has been dominated by a concern with the way "traditional" social, cultural, and personality factors affect economic development and underdevelopment. The case of Japan has generally been studied from this point of view. "Traditional society" theorists regard the poverty and underdevelopment prevailing among Third World countries as a result of "traditional" sociocultural forces. According to these theorists, the industrial nations have supplied a stimulus to economic growth in the non-Western world. Underdevelopment persists because Third World societies are basically "traditional" rather than "modern"; that is, they fail to encourage change and innovation. Traditional society theorists have seen the case of Japan as the exception that proves the rule, as the only non-Western society with a tradition that promoted rather than hindered change.

The "traditional society" view of Japan's unique development has often been buttressed through comparative study—primarily of Japan and Imperial China. Japan's nineteenth-century development and China's spectacular decline and misery have been interpreted as a result of the divergent traditional societies of the two nations on the eve of the Western impact. For example, it has been popular to contrast dynamic economic transformation of "feudal" Japan with economic stagnation in "bureaucratic" China.[2]

Such theories have been challenged in recent years by another perspective which emphasizes the relationship of Third World societies to the world political economy. "World economy" theorists argue that Western nations have provided not a stimulus to development but a knockout blow. Underdevelopment has been caused by the forcible incorporation of Third World nations into a world economy that disproportionately benefits the industrial capitalist nations. The non-Western nations have become agrarian satellites exploited as sources of raw materials, while their own economic development has been thwarted and neglected. Any industrial development has been backward and dependent, and a gap remains which is never closed.

"World economy" theorists have paid little attention to the case of Japan. But to the few who have discussed Japan, Japan is again the exception that proves the rule; in this case, the only Third World nation to have escaped pressures to become a satellite of the industrial capitalist nations.[3]

The "world economy" perspective raises important issues, and it requires us to rethink many of the assumptions we have shared about Japanese and Chinese development. The purpose of this paper is to consider some of those issues. The comparative studies of Japan and China have, above all, failed to consider systematically whether there might have been differences in the relationships of China and Japan to the world economy, and the probable effects of these differences on Chinese and Japanese economic development. After the presentation of evidence that such differences did exist—that Japan enjoyed relatively greater autonomy within the world economy than did China—and their probable effects, attention will be given to the implications for the interpretations made by "traditional society" scholars of Japanese versus Chinese development.

II.

For some authors, excluding the question of China and Japan in the world economy is a matter of emphasis. For others, however, the exclusion is explicit. Levy, for instance, says, "In both China and Japan *the external sources were virtually identical*. They were the factors involved in modern industrialization."[4] In the words of Fairbank and Reischauer:

> One cannot but be struck by the great differences among the various countries of East Asia in the speed and nature of their responses to the West in the past century. . . . These variations in response *must be* attributed mainly to the differences in the traditional societies of the countries of East Asia. Only such differences can explain why *a basically similar impact* could have brought such varied initial results . . . why relatively small Japan, for example, soon became a world power, while China sank to the status of an international problem. [5]

Occasionally, authors point out that the Western impact on Japan was much smaller than on China, but they deny that this has any analytic significance:

> As compared with the Chinese experience, the initial impact of the West on Japan in the middle of the nineteenth century was gentle. No wars were fought, no smuggling trade developed, no territory was forfeited. . . . And yet, Japan's response was far quicker and greater than that of China. . . . This startling paradox—that Japan's greater response followed a less violent impact than in China—has posed difficult questions of historical interpretation. What forces at work in Japan produced so great a ferment? Obviously, Japan in the mid-nineteenth century, even though it had derived a large part of its higher culture from China, was a very different country, capable of very different responses to the Western challenge.[6]

Are these assumptions valid? *Did* Japan and China stand in the same relationship to the world economy and the Western powers during the nineteenth century? Or was Japan more autonomous than China? And if so, did Japan's greater autonomy contribute to development, in contrast to China's underdevelopment?

Let us first consider how we might define and measure a society's "incorporation" as a satellite into the world political economy, then discuss whether Japan and China were incorporated to the same degree.

"Incorporation" has two basic dimensions, an economic and a political dimension. The world political economy that has emerged since the sixteenth century constitutes, first of all, a world division of labor: advanced industrial nations (the "metropoles") and their primary producing and industrially dependent satellites. Second, there is an accompanying political division: dominant industrial metropoles and their satellites, in which sovereign powers have been reduced or eliminated.

The degree to which a Third World country is incorporated as a satellite depends on its importance to the metropolitan countries in terms of the extent and nature of their trade and investments there. The larger and more staple the trade, the larger and more interrelated the investments, the more pronounced is the country's satellite status.

Trade. The size of the trade is important, as is its nature—above all, whether the objects traded are important *staple* items or not. Staple goods can be defined as commodities that are either consumed or produced on a large scale in the Western nations, or are otherwise vital in some way to the functioning of their economies. Staples are distinct from "precicosities," luxury items of less significance in those economies.

The exchange of staples rather than precicosities has formed the foundation of the world division of labor and the basis for imperialist efforts to subordinate satellite nations politically. The mere existence of trade relations with the West has never meant that a non-Western area was significant in the world political economy. For example, in the sixteenth century the nations of the West traded with many countries around the world, but only a small part of the globe (the Mediterranean islands and parts of the Caribbean) became satellite areas, producing a large trade in staple products. Trade with the rest of the world was still an exchange of precious and luxury items, not yet of vital importance to the Western economies, and did not lead to efforts at political incorporation.[7]

Investments. Again, the size is important, and so is the character, especially whether the investments form an interrelated complex, or large "stake," as opposed to random, isolated ventures. For example, investments in oil fields, in refineries in nearby seaports, in shipping from the seaports to the metropole, and in docking and repair facilities in the port constitute an interrelated investment complex of considerable significance, as compared, let us say, to investment in an oil well here and a factory there. The existence of significant and interconnected investments is the hallmark of a strongly incorporated satellite.

"World economy" theorists have noted that political incorporation usually accompanies, and promotes, economic incorporation. Two aspects of political incorporation seem to have been important in the nineteenth century.

Political encroachment. This means the degree to which the industrial capitalist nations assumed rulership of or otherwise encroached on the fiscal, administrative, legal, and military powers of native governments, and includes the territory proper of the country as well as colonies and hinterlands that the government of the country has historically claimed to rule. This aspect is sometimes considered irrelevant to a discussion of economic development in the country proper; but since the concept of an obligation to defend or expand national territory has internal political and economic consequences, it cannot be neglected.

Missionary encroachment. This refers to the degree to which the area was penetrated by Catholic or Protestant missionaries, those "pickets or advance guards for the . . . phalanx of national power."[8] Missionaries are a significant indicator of the economic and political importance of a satellite. Nineteenth-century European governments provided military protection only when they thought missionary influence would further their political economic aims.

Having defined somewhat more precisely the concept of incorporation, let us now consider some of the evidence that Japan was less "incorporated" than China as a satellite in the nineteenth-century world political economy.

The initial Western interest in China was in trade. The China trade, of course, was very large and lucrative; for the nations concerned, it was also a staple trade, and was soon followed by the emergence of a large investment complex. In contrast, the initial Western interest in Japan was not in trade. Westerners saw Japan as a way station for naval, whaling, and merchant ships going elsewhere, especially to China. When trade of any significance did develop with Japan, it was small by comparison to the China trade, and was not of a staple nature for the nations involved. Western investments in Japan similarly lagged behind investments in China throughout the nineteenth century.

The story of China's incorporation has often been told, and the details need only be summarized here. Chinese-Western trade during the seventeenth and eighteenth centuries was primarily an exchange of precicosities. Western gold, silver, and "sing-songs" (e.g., fancy clocks) were exchanged for Chinese goods regarded as luxuries in the West, such as silk, porcelains, tea, and cotton fabrics. The trade was small and grew slowly prior to the late eighteenth century. Western merchants were restricted by the Chinese government to the frontiers of the country—to the seaports of Canton and Macao, and to the "landports" of Kiakhta and Nerchinsk on the Russian frontier—and their activities were supervised closely in order to ensure a steady flow of revenue and to prevent the Westerners from doing anything that might endanger the government's economic policies or infringe upon its sovereignty.

In the late eighteenth and early nineteenth centuries, China's trade relations with the West were transformed totally: the trade became a staple trade, it expanded quickly, and government restrictions were overcome. This transformation, primarily on the initiative of Great Britain, had two aspects. First, tea consumption in Britain was such that tea became a staple commodity. In the seventeenth century, beer was the staple drink of the poor. By the mid-eighteenth century, however, tea "was not uncommon in the countryside, even among labourers," and about a pound was consumed each year per capita.[9] In the nineteenth century, tea became the national drink: the East India Company was required by an act of Parliament always to keep a year's supply in stock.[10] Consumption reached almost 5 pounds per capita in the 1860s, 6 pounds in the 1880s, and nearly 11 pounds in the 1920s.[11]

As is well known, the establishment of a mass market for Chinese tea in Great Britain posed a large problem for the mercantilist-oriented British government—how to avoid a continual drain of specie to China to pay for the tea, a problem solved by linking the China trade to the interests of the emerging British colony in India. It was discovered that there was a market in China for Indian raw cotton and, above all, opium. Once the British gained control of the opium-producing territories of India in the 1750s, they applied themselves vigorously to increasing the output of opium in India, simultaneously preventing its consumption by the Indian producers and increasing the market for it in China.

The second aspect concerned China's imports of British textiles and was related directly to British industrialization in the late eighteenth and early nineteenth centuries. As Britain industrialized, there was a strong drive to find foreign markets for her products, particularly for cotton textiles. Eyes fell upon China with its population of "400 million" as a vast potential market. Moreover, after the 1870s, France, the United States, and Germany also began to industrialize rapidly and joined Britain in the effort to open the China market.

The cotton textiles industry was the key industry in Britain's industrial revolution, and its development was intimately related to the development of the British world empire. Raw cotton was almost entirely derived from colonial sources, mainly the slave plantations of the West Indies and the United States. From the 1790s, the British cotton industry exported most of its output—by the late nineteenth century, almost 90 percent of it. "From time to time, it broke into the rewarding markets of Europe and the U.S.A., but wars and the rise of native competition put a brake on such expansion, and the industry returned time and time again to some old or new region of the undeveloped world."[12] And the East, especially India and China, came to consume a large part of the industry's exports.

The vision of many Western manufacturers—of the entire Chinese population dressed in Western textiles—never materialized. The Chinese handicraft industry continued to supply the bulk of China's needs. Even so, China's consumption of Western goods was hardly small; it expanded greatly during the century, and Western merchants never gave up their dreams of China's potential.

Following the expansion of trade, a considerable complex of Western (and, later, Japanese) investments developed in China, primarily surrounding the needs of China's commerce with the West. Westerners invested in shipping, not only in the export-import area but also in China's domestic commerce, which was "one of the chief foreign stakes in China,"[13] and in shipbuilding and repairs in the treaty ports. There were also investments in the processing of exports and in the manufacturing of goods, at first for the Western residents of the treaty ports, and later also for the domestic market. In addition, Western-owned banks funded the export-import trade, handled foreign-exchange deals, and also issued banknotes, which enjoyed widespread use in the latter part of the century. Finally, investments occurred in railways and mines, and in loans to the Chinese government, a good part of which were used to fund railway construction.[14]

Thus China came to be strongly incorporated as an agrarian satellite of the Western nations, especially Great Britain. The story of Japan is very different. Unimportant to the West in the seventeenth and eighteenth centuries as compared to China, Japan remained so after the Western expansion into East Asia in the nineteenth century.

On the eve of the Western drive into Asia, Japan's trade with the Western nations was much more limited than China's. Early in the Tokugawa period, Japan's rulers closed the country to all traders but Chinese and Dutch, and severely restricted their operations. However, trading with Japan had long been regarded by the Western nations as of little consequence. The British East India Company, for example, established a factory in Japan in 1613, but closed it in 1623 because it did not prove profitable.

Dutch activities in Japan were also in marked contrast to Dutch activities in other areas of the world, such as Indonesia. During the eighteenth century, while the Dutch turned Indonesia into a vast plantation producing coffee and other staples and ruled it through dependent native rulers, and during the nineteenth century while they established direct rule over the country, Dutch traders in Japan were still living meekly in accordance with the restrictions of the Tokugawa shoguns. Moreover, the Dutch traders were primarily involved in exchanging Japanese objects for Chinese, rather than developing a trade between Holland and Japan.[15]

In the 1850s, when China's incorporation had already been under way for more than a generation, the governments of the various Western nations finally determined that trading with Japan was important enough to overturn the Tokugawa seclusion policy. However, although Western trade with Japan grew rapidly after Japan was "opened," it was far smaller than the China trade during most of the century, and much of it did not constitute a staple trade for the nations involved. For example, the size of Japan's trade with America and Britain, her major trading partners, was much smaller than their trade with China. The value of British exports to China was at least two to three times greater than the value of exports to Japan until the 1880s, and the value of British imports from China at least thirteen to twenty-five times greater. The value of U.S. exports to China was at least two to sixteen times greater than the value of those to Japan through the 1870s, and the value of U.S. imports from China three to twenty times greater.[16]

One of the most interesting aspects of the "opening" of Japan is that the British did not attempt to import Japanese tea. That major Japanese export item went mainly to the United States, where it was not an important staple commodity. In 1821, for instance, per capita tea consumption in the United States was only about .5 pound, approximately what it had been in Britain in 1750. By 1882, consumption had risen to only 1.5 pounds per year per capita. At the same time, coffee consumption in the United States rose from 1.29 pounds per capita in 1821 to 8.25 pounds in 1882.[17] The United States has been a nation of coffee-drinkers since the nineteenth century, and coffee has been closely connected with U.S. imperialism, while tea has not. (British coffee consumption in 1926 was about what American consumption had been in 1821, something over a pound per capita.)[18]

Why were the British not interested in importing Japanese tea? The reasons seem to lie in a trend toward importing tea from British colonial territories. In 1866 only 4 percent of the tea imported into the United Kingdom was from India; the rest was from China. But by 1903, the figures were 60 percent from India, 30 percent from Ceylon, and only 10 percent from China. Thus it is not surprising that there was not much effort to import Japanese tea.[19]

The British also made no effort to develop an opium market in Japan. No opium-smuggling trade ever developed, nor did treaties legitimize the import of opium into Japan as they did into China. The British lack of interest in Japanese tea probably accounts for this, since the desire to find a "return" for the tea had given rise to the import of opium into China.

Western investments in Japan were neither large nor interrelated. For example, there was no railway construction by Westerners in Japan, or opening of mines. The only exception was one coal mine initially opened in 1868 in Saga prefecture, with funds from Glover and Company, a subsidiary of Jardine Matheson and Company. The firm was unable to maintain itself, sustained heavy losses, and sold out to the Mitsubishi Steamship Company in 1881.[20]

Manufacturing in Japan by Western firms was also limited during the nineteenth century, as compared with China: "direct participation by Western firms in Japan's industrial expansion, though always limited to a small number of industries, was considerably more important in the twentieth century, especially after the First World War, than at any time during the nineteenth century."[21] Although Japan's foreign trade was largely carried in Western ships until the twentieth century, Japanese *domestic* shipping remained primarily in Japanese hands. Several Western steamship companies established lines between China and Japan, and between Japan and Europe. But there do not appear to have been any Western companies of any importance engaged exclusively in the Japanese coastal trade.[22]

Shipbuilding and repairing generally remained in Japanese hands throughout the nineteenth century. Western investment in the processing of tea, silk, and other export goods was more limited in Japan than in China. There were also foreign banks in Japan: they financed foreign trade and handled exchange dealings, as they did in China, but they did not issue banknotes.[23]

It is often assumed that China and Japan equally lost political autonomy due to the establishment of a treaty port system in both countries. This system included the loss of tariff autonomy; extraterritoriality, or the loss of jurisdiction over Western residents; the opening of a number of ports to Western trade and residence (treaty ports); and the establishment of Western diplomatic units in the capitals and ports. But Western political encroachment on Japan began and ended with this system, while China suffered many additional forms of encroachment.

China's foreign customs came under Western administration in the 1850s. This alone might not have constituted a severe loss of autonomy for the Chinese government. The indemnities levied by Westerners on China as punishment for resisting encroachment were collected by securing them on the customs revenues. The late nineteenth-century practice of loaning money to the Chinese government secured on the customs revenues had the same effect.

Indemnities were levied on China not only after defeat in war but also in punishment for antimissionary rebellions. In the 1860s alone, the total was 877,000 taels, for thirty-four incidents that had involved the deaths of 24 foreign and 130 Chinese Christians.[24] The treaties between the Western nations and Japan did not permit missionaries or traders to settle in the interior of the country, taking their extraterritoriality with them and causing problems.

The Western powers (and, later, Japan) compelled the Chinese government virtually to give up its ability to control China's own processes of economic development. From the 1890s, railroad and mining concessions gave the receiving power spheres of influence, the first chance to undertake economic activities in certain areas. The Treaty of Shimonoseki (1895) permitted foreign nationals to undertake manufacturing in the treaty ports. None of these impositions occurred in Japan.

The Western powers (and, later, Japan) continually snipped away at the outlying territories of Ch'ing China. Tibet, Manchuria, Indochina, Mongolia, Burma, and Ili were gradually disengaged from Chinese control, in whole or in part, despite the Chinese government's military and diplomatic resistance. Moreover, Hong Kong was taken from China and made a British colony. No such phenomena occurred in Japan. Japan's peripheries, such as the Kuril Islands, Sakhalin, Hokkaidō, the Bonin Islands, and the Ryukyu Islands, were not so vigorously attacked by the Western powers, and no part of Japan proper was ever seized as a colony. Disputes in the Meiji period were generally settled through negotiations and on an equal basis, and some of the Western nations, especially the United States, encouraged Japan in efforts to maintain or regain territories. The Americans also encouraged Japan's expansion to Taiwan.[25]

Finally, it should be noted that Western encroachment on China generally took a violent form. It took two wars to establish the initial set of commercial treaties with China, and to secure the colony of Hong Kong. Warfare led to the Treaty of Shimonoseki that permitted manufacturing in the ports; warfare accompanied the disengagement of Indochina from Chinese control. In contrast, the "opening of Japan" was carried out primarily through negotiations, and only a few incidents of large-scale violence occurred. Thus there is a certain amount of evidence that Japan was relatively more autonomous than China within the nineteenth-century world political economy.

III.

Among the many social changes associated with the rise of an industrial economy, two seem to be of great significance: first, the emergence of a centralized national state having the capacity to exercise strong control over the society and its economic processes; second, government efforts to encourage national industrial development. It seems that government economic policies promoting national industrialization have everywhere been critical in the development process; their success has depended, in turn, on the strength of the state. State economic policies were important in encouraging national industrial development in Europe and the United States in three respects.

First, the development of national industries and an industrial infrastructure of railways, shipping, public utilities, etc., was encouraged by policies in the following areas.

Capital accumulation. Prior to the modern era, merchants in Europe and elsewhere were usually reluctant to invest in industry, as opposed to commerce and land. Industrial investment required large sums and involved unknown risks. Government efforts to stimulate private investment included various subsidies to industry, ranging from outright monetary grants, to tax exemptions, grants of land (as along railway routes), low-cost loans; government-sponsored pilot projects; and the establishment of banking systems that funded industrial investments.

Protectionism. The major weapon was perhaps tariff policy, but other mechanisms were also important, such as government purchase policies favoring national over foreign industries, and policies such as the British Navigation Laws that prevented foreign ships from moving in and out of British ports.

Expansion. The pursuit of colonial policies enabled national industries to expand their capacity and output significantly, farther and faster than the initial narrowness of the home market permitted, and to control sources of industrial raw materials not available, or available in insufficient quantities, at home. It also provided the colonizing powers with windfall gains from plunder, taxation, indemnities, etc., that could then be plowed into industrial development at home.

Diffusion of technology. Efforts here included the import of technicians, creation of native technical schools, sending students abroad, purchase or pirating of inventions, and the reverse—restricting the emigration of skilled technicians ("brain drain"), and preventing important technological innovations from leaving the country.

Second, governmental efforts were important in the development of national markets. On the negative side, this involved the abolition of internal tariffs and tolls, and the unification of currency, weights, and measures. On the positive side, the government sought to improve internal transport and communications—canal, highway, and railway construction, shipping, telephone and telegraph service.

Third, the government encouraged the formation of an industrial work force, by creating welfare systems that made relief more horrible than factory work and by establishing compulsory educational systems and military conscription, both of which contributed to effective factory discipline.

All these processes depend on the existence of a strong national state for their success. For example, without a strong state capable of taxing the nation and directing the proceeds of taxation into subsidies, capital accumulation cannot be furthered. Without control over tariffs or central institutions capable of providing large markets, industry cannot be protected from foreign competition. Without a strong central military apparatus, expansion cannot be furthered, nor can the nation be defended from the depredations of other powers.

Of these areas of activity, the first seems of paramount importance in creating a developed industrial economy. That is, without national industries, the creation of a national market would simply result in a country becoming a unified market for the consumption of foreign manufactures; without national industries, the "industrial proletariat" would amount merely to an underemployed or unemployed urban *lumpenproletariat.*

On the eve of the Western expansion, China's Ch'ing rulers lacked the ability to exercise strong control over the nation. Like previous dynasties, they ruled through an officialdom drawn from China's "gentry," a landed and educated upper class with strong local and provincial ties. The seesaw of power inherent in this system was never resolved in favor of the central government, and there was a great deal of provincial and local autonomy. This autonomy tended, moreover, to increase as time passed. Japan's Tokugawa rulers were also unable to control the nation strongly. The *han,* or feudal domains, retained autonomy in financial and other affairs; as time passed, some became increasingly wealthy and powerful.

The Western expansion into China and Japan in the nineteenth century led to profound internal changes in both countries. In both cases, periods of conflict and upheaval ensued. In China, the Taiping Rebellion (1850–1864) nearly overturned the dynasty before being defeated by the efforts of provincial and local gentry-led armies. In Japan, a revolt successfully overturned the rule of the Tokugawa—the Meiji Restoration (1868). The aftermath of these periods of disorder was very different in the two societies, however. The new Meiji rulers in Japan embarked on a path of successful centralization; the essential fiscal, legal, and military powers of state were removed from the *han* and grasped by the new central government, thus laying the groundwork for a successful national industrial policy. In China, however, the central government never recovered the powers it had held before the rebellion, and the seesaw of power increasingly ended in favor of the local levels.

By the late nineteenth century, the contrast between Chinese decentralization and Japanese centralization was striking, particularly in the area of fiscal affairs. After the restoration, the Japanese central government gained control of the land taxes paid by the nation's peasants and turned these taxes, originally payable in kind, into a money payment. Thus revenues were increased and were highly predictable. (The procedure hurt the peasants, since taxes were no longer flexible in times of crop failure.) The land tax came to provide the new government with 70 to 80 percent of its total revenues during the nineteenth century. The central government also terminated payment of stipends to the upper class of daimyo and samurai, thus freeing funds for new, centrally determined investments.

Chinese revenues, in contrast, were dispersed domestically among a variety of regional and local gentry, politicians, and military commanders, and were also, as noted above, partially under foreign control. For example, after the Taiping Rebellion, the land tax, once about 75 percent of central revenues, shrank to about 40 percent, and the commercial taxes that made up the difference came under increasing control of the foreign powers. [26]

These divergent processes—centralization in Japan and collapse in China—are often treated as though "dynastic decline" in Ch'ing China, or the "decline of feudalism and rise of capitalism" in Japan, would have occurred in much the same fashion independent of the ways in which Japan and China were being incorporated into the world political economy. This view is somewhat one-sided. The centralization process would probably not have occurred in Japan had Japan been so strongly incorporated as was China. The major reason is that centralization requires great effort, since resistance by those who are losing power is inevitable. Yet the incorporation of China effectively sent the energies of China's rulers into many other directions.

China's rulers were engaged in almost continuous battles from the 1830s, both against the Western powers and against the Chinese peasantry. Losses of money and life were vast, as was ecological destruction, and enormous efforts were required to restore the peasant economy in devastated places to its former state.

The size and ferocity of the Taiping Rebellion were related intimately to the intensive character of China's incorporation into the world economy from 1820 to 1850. The opium and tea trade caused a large outflow of specie, a deflation, and a depression, which led to a tax increase that hit the peasantry severely. The shift in trade routes after new ports were opened under the treaties caused widespread loss of employment. Warfare with the West led to internal banditry and disorder.[27]

Japan's incorporation involved the peasantry to a lesser extent. There was no deflation in Japan, and no depression. There was no large, long-term outflow of specie, and no loss of employment over large areas of the countryside.[28] No great nationwide peasant rebellion thus threatened Japan's rulers. The major economic result of Japan's opening to Western trade was an inflation, the burden of which was felt primarily by the daimyo and samurai, who lived on fixed stipends. Thus, in contrast to the Chinese upheaval, the Meiji Restoration was a tempest in a teapot—a struggle within the upper class soon won by one faction and involving relatively little loss of life and funds or economic destruction.

After the 1870s, China's leadership still had to deal with continual "incidents" caused by missionaries and adventurers; with French, British, Russian, and Japanese encroachment on outlying territories; with Western efforts to revise treaties so as to take more powers away from China; and with Western efforts to construct railways and open mines (efforts the Chinese government successfully thwarted up to the late 1890s). Such Western pressures on Japan were virtually nonexistent, and Japan's rulers enjoyed a period of relative isolation or, in E.H. Norman's words, a "breathing space" in which the process of centralization might be pursued.

After establishment of the Meiji regime, government activities became important in developing Japan's modern industries. The focus will be on the government's contribution to capital accumulation and protectionism, possible because of the strong position of the Meiji government in the nation, and the relative autonomy the government enjoyed in its relationship to the Western nations. The Chinese central government and various provincial and regional rulers made similar efforts to contribute to China's industrialization; it cannot be said that the Chinese leadership was less ideologically motivated to do this than the Japanese. However, the prevailing decentralization of power in China after the rebellion, together with the progressive encroachment of the Western powers (and, later, Japan), prevented them from succeeding.

The Meiji government provided subsidies to modern industries and the industrial infrastructure, ran industrial pilot projects, and founded a system of banks, including industrial banks that would provide long-term loans to private industrial investors. These efforts were ultimately successful in sparking national industrialization, and in stimulating the investment of private capital in industry.

The business undertakings sponsored by the Chinese government frequently suffered protracted delays, their production stagnated, and profits were small. Hsü expresses a view predominant among China scholars as to why this was so:

> These government-supervised merchant enterprises were a hybrid operation which smacked of strong official overtones and the usual bureaucratic inefficiency, corruption and nepotism. Being profit-oriented, they discouraged private competition and tended to monopolize business through government favor or intervention. . . .[29]

Accounts of the operation of these enterprises reveal that many of their troubles were rooted in a continuous state of financial crisis. In contrast to the Japanese government, which subsidized industries with outright grants of money, Chinese authorities tended to rely upon loans and demanded repayment, often with interest, after very short periods. Subsidies were limited in China because of the greater unpredictability and inaccessibility of revenues due to their dispersal among a variety of authorities, and to their partial control by the Western powers.

The absence of a centralized fiscal structure in China meant that the financing of government-sponsored industries was always precarious. For example, initial funds for the Hanyang Ironworks (established by Chang Chih-tung, governor-general of Hupei) came from a variety of sources: provincial funds under Chang's control, allocations from the central government, and from the capital of an arsenal and a textile mill also controlled by Chang. Substantial amounts were also procured from salt merchants of the Lianghuai area and from the "defense funds" of Kiangsu and Chekiang. The firm always lacked sufficient capital; it turned to Chinese native banks for credit, and eventually began to borrow from the Japanese. After the turn of the century, the firm became a purely merchant-operated undertaking, and it came to be effectively controlled by Japanese creditors; almost the entire output of the ironworks and an iron mine associated with it went to Japan, where it was worked up by the Yawata Iron and Steel Mill.[30]

Another example is the China Merchants Steamship Navigation Company. The initial capital for this *kuan-tu shang-pan* (state-supervised, commercially operated) enterprise came in part from shares purchased by private persons, but the most important portion came from government loans procured from the treasuries of at least four provincial governments, as well as from the customs revenues.[31]

Both China and Japan were deprived of the major weapon of protection during the nineteenth century tariff policy. Nevertheless, the Japanese government managed to protect Japanese industry. First, government purchase policies favored national industries whenever possible. Second, the government enacted laws and regulations designed to encourage Japanese citizens to purchase the products and services of native industries, and to discourage Western citizens from developing industries in Japan. Neither of these actions would have been successful had Western encroachment on Japan been as great as on China.

In effect, "the government subsidized private industry by becoming its chief customer."[32] In the early years of Japan's industrialization, a large home market for the output of modern industry existed perhaps only for textiles. Electrical industry, paper, glass, leather, cement, bricks, modern shipping, and so forth met with such a small market that large-scale production was not conceivable. Had there been no government purchase policy, most of these businesses would not have come into existence.

The Chinese government also tried to protect national industries by purchase policies but was unsuccessful. China's growing fiscal and military weakness, first, meant that the effect of government purchases on the economy was small. Second, when important sectors of the modern Chinese economy came under Western control and when the government began to borrow from the West, the government's ability to exercise its purchasing power to stimulate domestic industrialization was severely restricted. For example, since much of China's railways, shipping, and manufacturing came under foreign control, purchase of supplies and equipment for them tended to be made in the West, not China. The Japanese government was not burdened with this problem and could make purchases in the home market. Moreover, loans to China came with many "strings attached," with requirements that purchases be made from the creditor country with the funds granted. Thus, when the Hanyang Ironworks was established, the imperial government guaranteed that all government railway projects would purchase iron and steel only from Hanyang. However, when railroads began to be built with foreign loans, the contracts qualified this privilege out of existence. Only the Peking-Hankow line was built with Hanyang iron and steel.[33]

Another method of protection used by the Japanese was to enact laws encouraging Japanese citizens to purchase Japanese products. The shipping industry provides a good example of how a Japanese-owned industry was protected in this way. Japan's domestic shippers had some competition during the early Meiji years from American and British steamship lines. The government established a set of regulations in 1876 that hampered the ability of Japanese people to use foreign ships. With the help of this and heavy subsidies, Mitsubishi was able to buy out a British shipping company operating in Japan.[34]

The shipping industry also provides a good example of why government efforts at protection failed in China. In the early days of the expansion of Western shipping in China, Chinese authorities made an effort to forbid Chinese shipping on Western vessels, but the Western consuls objected and, under pressure, the Chinese were forced to give in.[35] In his discussion of the rise of the China Merchants Company in the 1870s and 1880s, Liu points out that its government sponsors could not put pressure on Chinese merchants to ship with the company, because the Western powers would have objected to this as a violation of the treaties.[36]

The Chinese government tried to support the China Merchants Company by certain tax exemptions: tea shipped north into Tientsin on the way to Russia was exempted from inland duties, for example. Its services were also purchased; grain tribute going to the capital from the south was shipped on the line at a rate twice that charged by Western lines. Still, the major business of the domestic shipping companies was domestic commerce, and here the government was forced to compete against Western firms without any special advantage.

In addition, the Japanese recovered tariff autonomy almost a generation before the Chinese did. The Japanese government's attempts were blocked by the British government, which refused to permit recovery throughout the nineteenth century. In the 1890s, Britain's situation in Asia began to change. Russia was becoming an increasing threat to British hegemony in Asia, and the British began searching for allies. Thus when renewed negotiations with Japan over treaty revision began in 1892, the British reversed their policy. Extraterritoriality was ended in 1899 and tariff autonomy was regained in 1911. The new tariff was of greater importance in the expansion of certain industries—above all, textiles, the iron and steel industries, copper, sugar, and dyestuffs.[37]

It is sometimes noted that the Chinese government does not seem to have made an equally vigorous effort to achieve the goal of tariff autonomy. Whereas the Japanese engaged in almost continual negotiations from the 1870s on this question, the Chinese hardly raised it. It is, however, misleading to trace this to Chinese bureaucratic backwardness versus Japanese enlightenment. First, various Western governments encouraged Japan to pursue the question. Second, treaty revision in China was always an occasion for ruthless pressure on the Chinese negotiators to give up more national rights. Since Chinese officials were struggling to avoid giving away more, it is not surprising that an effort to recover something lost was far from their minds.[38]

In sum, Japan's relative autonomy within the nineteenth-century world political economy facilitated centralization of power and the carrying out of government policies to encourage national industrialization. China's strong incorporation hampered centralization and blocked the successful execution of government policies.

From the "world economy" perspective, the use of traditional sociocultural variables as a general explanation of Japan's unique development appears questionable. The key factor in Japan's development was the country's relative autonomy within the world system as compared with other Third World nations. Moreover, the reasons for Japan's autonomy lie outside Japanese society, in the dynamics of the development of the world political economy, together perhaps with Japan's size and other material and geographic qualities. The social characteristics of the Japanese people had little to do with it.

The development of the world political economy from ca. 1800 to ca. 1918 could be divided into two phases.[39] In each phase the dynamics of world economy development were such as to exclude Japan from incorporation. The first phase, termed the "Imperialism of Free Trade," lasted until the 1880s. The major integrating factor was trade, especially in the manufactures of Western countries for tropical staples such as sugar, and traditional products such as silk and tea. At this time, there were fewer efforts than later to establish formal colonial control over satellite areas, because Britain was so powerful that it was able to maintain hegemony in many areas of the world even though formal colonial powers were lacking.

During this first phase, Japan was shielded from incorporation by other areas that had been reached first and appeared to Western merchants to be more lucrative than Japan, especially China, India, and Indonesia. Even after Japan was "opened" in the late 1850s, China, India, and other areas of the East continued to bear the brunt of Western exploitation in Asia.

Fortunately for Japan, the country escaped the "New Imperialism" of the 1880s and 1890s, which was of a different nature. In this second phase, other Western nations—the United States, Germany, France, Russia—began to industrialize and to give England increasing competition. Simultaneously, Western industry was shifting from a base of coal and iron to one of steel, oil, chemicals, and electricity. The new base depended on a continuing supply of materials and sources of energy from the non-Western world, such as oil, nickel, nitrates, rubber, and tin. Ideologists stressed the need for integrated, self-sufficient empires that would eliminate dependence on enemies for supplies and provide secure colonial markets for surplus capital. The result was a competitive struggle among the Western nations formally to carve up and control the world, in which many areas—the lucrative as well as territories barren of worthy resources—were annexed by one or another Western power.

During this second phase, many areas of the world as resource-poor and small as Japan were incorporated into the world economy as colonial satellites and deprived of their autonomy. Had the Western nations reached Japan at this time, rather than in the 1850s, Japan might today be burdened with an English, French, or German colonial heritage. By the 1880s, however, Japan's new army and navy, while probably not formidable enough to withstand a serious European effort at conquest, were sufficiently strong to deter such an effort.[40] At the same time, Japan's military forces had proved themselves formidable enough to defeat China in the 1890s. Thus Japan was a likely candidate for an ally or "junior partner" of some European power in the competitive race to carve up China and the rest of the world. Fortuitously for Japan, Great Britain was looking for such a partner in Asia by the mid-1890s; Japan, rather than being conquered as it might have been, was bolstered.

From the "world economy" perspective, many differences in Chinese and Japanese social or cultural patterns may have contributed to Chinese underdevelopment and Japanese development (e.g., China's governmental decentralization after the Taiping Rebellion as compared with Japan's centralization). However, such patterns are analyzed in terms of the operation of the world economy—how they are created, transformed, reconstructed, or constructed by its operation, and vice versa. In this context, many of the "traditional" differences between China and Japan emphasized by the "traditional society" theorists do not seem of great significance. It is shortsighted to blame China's underdevelopment on government "bureaucracy" or "monopoly," in the light of the total world situation in which the government existed. Two other examples of "traditional" factors appear to be of diminished significance once China's and

Japan's positions in the world economy are taken into account: (1) Levy's emphasis on the existence of a merchant class "able and willing" to invest in industry in Japan, and its absence in China, and his argument that a system of feudal loyalties in Japan maintained an order conducive to economic growth, while the gap between family and bureaucratic state in China led to disorder and social breakdown; (2) Fairbank's and Reischauer's comments on the more "pragmatic" and "goal-oriented" quality of Japan's "nationalistic" leaders and population.[41]

If Levy is correct in his assumptions that the Japanese merchant class was inherently more "willing and able" than the Chinese to invest, or that the population of Japan was inherently more loyal, disciplined, and orderly than the population of China, under what conditions would they be relevant to Japan's nineteenth-century economic development? For example, would Japan have been orderly, the population loyal and willing, if confronted with the import of opium on a mass scale, a veritable invasion of missionaries, and several wars with the Western powers? Under these conditions, would the Japanese regime have been able to provide the subsidies to merchants that stimulated their "willingness and ability" to invest? Conversely, had China not been so subjected, would the alleged gap between family and state in China have led to disorder and breakdown? It seems unlikely. In any case, Levy's argument needs to be restated in the light of the world economy perspective.

Nothing may appear more obvious than the pragmatic and single-minded obsession of Japan's nineteenth-century leaders with the development of Japan's national industrial and political power as compared with the apparently bumbling, self-interested activities of the Chinese bureaucrats. However, what would have happened had the Western nations been obsessed with blocking it as they were elsewhere in the world? Moreover, the ineffective and bumbling quality of Chinese leadership stems from a failure to appreciate the world situation. Again, the argument needs to be restated in the light of the world economy perspective.

IV.

A good design for comparative research involves "comparing the comparables." If a theorist is investigating the influence of phenomenon A on phenomenon B through comparative research, he or she must proceed in the following way. First, some logic must be involved in the selection of the countries to be used in the comparison. Second, evidence of phenomena A and B in both countries must be collected. Third, the two countries must be compared to one another in regard to A and B, and at comparable time periods.

The "world economy" perspective compels a certain discipline with regard to these matters, especially the last, since the world economy is conceived of as a phenomenon developing through time. However, the "traditional society" studies have taken a great deal of leeway in their interpretation of comparative research. Some "traditional society" scholars have neglected to compare China and Japan at comparable time periods. Sheldon, for instance, compares the social organization of shipping in Japan before the Western impact and the Meiji Restoration to that in China after the Western impact.[42]

Others have failed to compare China and Japan to one another. For example, a careful examination of Fairbank, Reischauer, and Craig's argument in *East Asia: The Modern Transformation* reveals that it is in part built up by comparing traditional China with early modern Europe and then Japan with China! By this method China looks much more backward than would be the case had Japan and China been carefully compared with one another, and then each compared to Europe.[43]

Many scholars have violated the principle of collecting evidence on both A and B. For example, there is the familiar argument that "bureaucracy" or "centralization," in contrast to "feudalism," impedes the rise of commerce and a commercial bourgeoisie. Much attention has been lavished upon the evidence for commercialization in Japan. But little effort has been devoted to collecting evidence on the lack of commercial development in China; instead, its lack has largely been assumed. The high degree of "centralization" in imperial China has also largely been assumed.

Finally, why have China and Japan been compared to one another anyway? Few authors bother to give a reason; the comparison has become ritualistic. Why not compare China systematically with India? Or Japan with Brazil, Egypt, Indonesia, or Turkey? The fact that China and Japan are close geographically is no compelling reason per se to compare them. And other reasons—their entrance into the world political economy and their social structures—should lead us to include still other countries, such as India, Egypt, Indochina, Indonesia, and Korea.

Much could be learned from systematic comparisons of nineteenth-century Japan with other Third World countries. Thus, if Japan were compared with Egypt, more light might be shed on the significance of Japan's autonomy within the world system.[44] During the early nineteenth century, Mohammed Ali (Viceroy, 1805–1848) led the country through a series of efforts designed to modernize the country that do not appear to be greatly different from Japan's achievements prior to the 1890s. For instance, he established a number of industries with the help of European technicians and imported European equipment (including textiles, paper, arsenals, foundries, chemicals, machinery and parts, and glass). By the 1830s, these industries employed as many as 30,000 to 40,000 workers. Funds were supplied from the proceeds of government monopolies in external and internal commerce, and by centralizing control over tax revenues, formerly in the hands of tax farmers. Markets for the new industries were supplied by government purchases (especially, supplies for the army) and by excluding foreign imports. Students were also sent to Europe to study; and military and naval academies, language and technical schools were established in Egypt. Agricultural production was increased by the construction of new irrigation works.

What happened? In 1841, Egypt lost its autonomy. It was defeated in war and compelled to reduce its armed forces. This removed much of the market for the foundries and textile mills, and thus much of the stimulus to industrialization. Foreigners were permitted to move into the interior of the country to trade, and were allowed to purchase land. Barriers to the import of foreign manufactures were removed. The result of all this was the decline of the industries established by Mohammed Ali; Egypt was integrated into the world economy as an agrarian satellite dependent upon the production of cotton.

The comparison with Egypt indicates, perhaps more strongly than the comparison with China, the significance for Japan's development of the country's autonomy within the world system. Comparisons of both China and Japan with other countries would undoubtedly lead to many fruitful insights. All of these methodological problems must be corrected if comparative study of Japan and China is to contribute to the understanding of Japan's unique development.

"Traditional society" theories have frequently compared Japan with China in order to explain that Japan's unique development is due to the country's unique traditional institutions. It has been argued here that those theorists are making several assumptions that appear invalid: (1) that China and Japan stood in the same relationship to the Western powers during the nineteenth century; and (2) that Japan's greater autonomy within the world political economic system had no effect on the country's development. Instead, Japan's relative autonomy within the world political economy facilitated her development to an important extent, while China's strong incorporation led to her underdevelopment. The arguments here cast doubt on the validity of using "traditional" sociocultural factors as general explanations of Japanese versus Chinese development.

Notes

1. Cited by George C. Allen and Audrey G. Donnithorne in *Western Enterprise in Far Eastern Economic Development* (London, 1954), p. 225. The term "Third World" implies a "Second World"—the socialist industrial nations such as the Soviet Union and the nations of Eastern Europe—as well as the "First World" of the capitalist industrial nations. At the time Japan was opened to Western influence, of course, a "Second World" did not exist, and thus the use of the term "Third World" for nineteenth-century Japan is not entirely appropriate.

2. Comparisons of Japan and China from the "traditional society" perspective include: Marion Levy, "Contrasting Factors in the Modernization of China and Japan," in *Economic Growth: Brazil, India, Japan*, ed. S. Kuznets, B. Moore, and J. J. Spengler (Durham, N.C., 1955), pp. 496–536; Marion Levy, "Some Aspects of 'Individualism' and the Problem of Modernization in China and Japan," *Economic Development and Cultural Change* 10:3 (April 1962); Robert Holt and John E. Turner, *The Political Basis of Economic Development* (Princeton, 1966), a comparison of Japan, China, England, and France; Norman Jacobs, *The Origin of Modern Capitalism and Eastern Asia* (Hong Kong, 1958); John K. Fairbank and Edwin O. Reischauer, *East Asia: The Great Tradition* (Boston, 1958); John K. Fairbank, Edwin O. Reischauer, and Albert M. Craig, *East Asia: The Modern Transformation* (Boston, 1965); James Nakamura and Masao Miyamoto, "Social Institutions, Population Change and Economic Growth: A Comparative Study of Tokugawa Japan and Ch'ing China" (unpublished ms.); Charles D. Sheldon, "Some Economic Reasons for the Marked Contrast in Japanese and Chinese Modernization," *Kyoto University Economic Review* 23 (1953): 30–60; Barrington Moore, *The Social Origins of Dictatorship and Democracy* (Boston, 1967), Chapters 4–5; William W. Lockwood, "Japan's Response to the West: The Contrast with China," *World Politics* 9 (1956): 37–54; Joseph Levenson, ed., *European Expansion and the Counter-Example of Asia, 1300–1600* (Englewood Cliffs, 1967); Allen and Donnithorne, op. cit. Comparative references abound in the monographic literature, especially works on China written in the "traditional society" vein, among them: Rhoads Murphey, *The Treaty Ports and China's Modernization—What Went Wrong?* (Ann Arbor, 1970); John K. Fairbank, Alexander Eckstein, and L. S. Yang, "Economic Change in Early Modern China: An Analytic Framework," *Economic Development and Cultural*

Change 9 (1960); Albert Feuerwerker, *China's Early industrialization* (Cambridge, Mass., 1958); S. N. Eisenstadt, "Tradition, Change and Modernity: Reflections on the Chinese Experience," in *China in Crisis*, ed. Ho Ping-ti and Tang Tsou (Chicago, 1968), 1:753–74; E. H. Norman, *Japan's Emergence as a Modern State* (New York, 1940).

3. Comparisons of Japan and China from the "world economy" perspective include: Paul Baran, *The Political Economy of Growth* (New York, 1957), pp. 134–62; Shigeki Toyama, "Politics, Economics and the International Environment in the Meiji and Taisho Periods," *Developing Economies* 4: 4 (December 1966); Huang I-feng and Chiang To, "Chung-kuo yang-wu yün-tung yü Jih-pen Mei-chih wei-hsin tsai ching-chi fa-chan sang ti pi-chiao" [A comparison of economic development in China's industrialization movement and in the Japanese Meiji Restoration], *Ching-chi Yen-chiu* 1 (1963): 27–47, summarized at length in Feuerwerker, *History in Communist China* (Cambridge, Mass., 1968), pp. 235–36.

4. Levy, "Contrasting Factors," p. 498 (emphasis added).

5. Fairbank and Reischauer, op. cit., p. 670 (emphasis added).

6. Fairbank, Reischauer, and Craig, op. cit., p. 180.

7. Immanuel Wallerstein, *The Modern World System* (New York, 1974), p. 41.

8. Paul Reinsch, *Colonial Government* (New York, 1902), p. 43.

9. Eric Hobsbawm, *Industry and Empire* (London, 1969), p. 28.

10. Michael Greenberg, *British Trade and the Opening of China* (Cambridge, 1951), p. 3.

11. Great Britain, Central Statistical Office, *Annual Abstract of Statistics,* no. 16, pp. 24–25; no. 31, pp. 44–45; no. 44, p. 67; no. 71, p. 315.

12. Hobsbawm, op. cit., p. 58.

13. John K. Fairbank, *Trade and Diplomacy on the China Coast* (Stanford, 1969), p. 311.

14. A good recent summary of Western investments in China can be found in Hou Chi-ming, *Foreign Investment and Economic Development in China, 1840–1937* (Cambridge, Mass., 1965). See also C. F. Remer, *Foreign Investment in China* (New York, 1933).

15. W. G. Beasley, *Great Britain and the Opening of Japan* (London, 1951), pp. xiv–xix, 28–29, 4–5; M. Paske-Smith, *Western Barbarians in Japan and Formosa in Tokugawa Days* (Kobe, 1930), pp. 196–98; Y. Takekoshi, *The Economic Aspects of the History of the Civilization of Japan*, 2: 409–15.

16. Compiled from Great Britain, Board of Trade, *British and Foreign Trade and Industry, 1854–1908* (London, 1909), pp. 40–43, 30–33; Grace Fox, *Great Britain and Japan* (Oxford, 1969), p. 368; U.S. Bureau of the Census, *Historical Statistics of the United States, Colonial Times to 1957* (Washington, D.C., 1960), pp. 550–53. Nineteenth-century statistics of British and American trade with China exclude exports and imports that went through Hong Kong and Macao. But these ports handled an important part of China's total foreign trade. The statistics cited also exclude the value of imports from India—i.e., the opium trade—also an enormous omission. Thus the value of the China trade, as compared to the Japan trade, is undoubtedly far larger than the estimates given.

17. U.S. Bureau of Statistics, *Statements of Imports of Tea and Coffee into the U.S. Each Year from 1789 to 1882* (Washington, D.C., 1883).

18. Calculated from figures in Great Britain, Central Statistical Office, *Annual Abstract of Statistics,* no. 71.

19. D. R. Gadgil, *Industrial Evolution of India* (London, 1934), p. 52.

20. See John McMaster, "The Takashima Mine: British Capital and Japanese Industrialization," *Business History Review* 37 (1963): 217–39.

21. Allen and Donnithorne, op. cit., p. 223.

22. Ibid., p. 218.

23. Ibid., pp. 215, 226.

24. Paul A. Cohen, *China and Christianity* (Cambridge, Mass., 1963), pp. 275–76.

25. This account is based on Mary E. Harbert, "The Open Door Policy—The Means for Attaining Nineteenth Century American Objectives in Japan" (Ph.D. diss., University of Oregon, 1967), p. 282.

26. Wang Yeh-chien, "China's Land Taxation in the Late Ch'ing Era" (Ph.D. diss., Harvard University, 1969), p. 129.

27. Ichisada Miyazaki, "The Nature of the Taiping Rebellion,"*Acta Asiatica* 8 (1965); Frederic Wakeman, Jr., *Strangers at the Gate* (Berkeley, 1966); Grace Fox, *British Admirals and Chinese Pirates* (London, 1940), p. 85; Lo Wan, "Communal Strife in Mid-Nineteenth Century Kwangtung," *Papers on China* 19 (1965): 85–119.

28. John McMaster, "The Japanese Gold Rush of 1859," *Journal of Asian Studies* 19 (1960): 273–87; Fox, *Britain and Japan,* pp. 331–34.

29. Imanuel C. Y. Hsü, *The Rise of Modern China* (New York, 1970), p. 345.

30. Albert Feuerwerker, "China's Nineteenth Century Industrialization: The Case of the Hanyehping Coal and Iron Company Limited," in *The Economic Development of China and Japan,* ed. C. D. Cowan (New York, 1964).

31. Liu Kwang-ching, "Steamship Enterprise in Nineteenth Century China," *Journal of Asian Studies* 18 (1959): 438–40, 448–50.

32. Johannes Hirschmeier, *The Origins of Entrepreneurship in Meiji Japan* (Cambridge, Mass., 1964), p. 153.

33. Feuerwerker, "China's Nineteenth Century Industrialization," p. 101.

34. Kozo Yamamura, "The Founding of Mitsubishi: A Case Study in Japanese Business History," *Business History Review* 41 (1967): 150.

35. Fairbank, op. cit., pp. 313–18.

36. Liu Kwang-ching, op. cit., p. 442.

37. George C. Allen, *A Short Economic History of Japan* (London, 1966), pp. 121–23.

38. Imanuel C. Y. Hsü, *China's Entrance into the Family of Nations* (Cambridge, Mass., 1960), p. 143.

39. This discussion is based on Geoffrey Barraclough, *An Introduction to Contemporary History* (Baltimore, 1967), p. 43.

40. Hyman Kublin, "The 'Modern' Army of Early Meiji Japan," *Far Eastern Quarterly* 9 (1949): 20–41.

41. See Levy, "Contrasting Factors" and "Some Aspects of 'Individualism' "; and Fairbank and Reischauer, op. cit.

42. See Sheldon, op. cit.

43. Fairbank, Reischauer, and Craig, op. cit., pp. 89–96, 189–91.

44. Charles Issawi, "Egypt Since 1800," *Journal of Economic History* 21 (1961): 1–25.

6.

The following essays, though discrete, are presented as parts of a single chapter because they both portray early twentieth-century Japanese attitudes toward China and the Chinese.

Harry Wray utilizes Japanese school textbooks to reveal that these outlooks are generally critical, condescending, or both. It is noteworthy that they elaborate in various ways the idea, alluded to in Chapter 4, that China was a disorganized state and needed guidance by Japan. The essay makes clear that although these are elementary texts, they carried with them the authority of the Japanese government, whose Ministry of Education not only controlled but, through its Editorial Division, actually wrote and rewrote them from 1903 to 1945.

Dr. Wray's essay is based on his doctoral dissertation, completed at the University of Hawaii in 1971. He is associate professor of East Asian history at Illinois State University.

In his "Notes on the Cultural Relationship," which constitutes the second essay in this chapter, Ryōzō Kurai gives a brief, though not uncomplicated, historical account of the organized activity of Japanese "friends" of China, many of whom were high-ranking and influential people. Their general approach may be discerned from the term *dōbun* ("the same written language" or "common culture"), which was frequently used in the organizational names under which they operated and in their publications. The idea they wished to promote was that Japan and China, being closely related by language and culture, should be good friends, but a corollary was that Japan, being stronger, should help China. While this was somewhat condescending, it should be noted that the "Dōbun" Japanese greatly honored Chinese culture and even used the term "Chūgoku" (Middle Kingdom) for China on occasion, as in Chūnichi Gakuin (China-Japan School), described in the essay.

The author, Ryōzō Kurai, is a member of the Tokyo staff of the newspaper *Asahi Shimbun;* he is also vice-president of the Tōa Gakuin, East Asian Academy (or Institute), which is a latter-day descendant of the organizations he describes in his essay. It is interesting that, like Kurai, many Chinese expatriates in Japan remember the old "Dōbun" days fondly, and together they have such organizations as "Friends of Shanghai" which help them reminisce. Kurai wrote this essay in Japanese; a Chinese friend of his and former Shanghai journalist, Wan-chiu Tsui, took charge of having it translated into English, the draft translation being done by Umeko Suzuki of Tokyo.

China in Japanese Textbooks

Harry Wray

I.

> When China received insults from foreign countries and the country was threatened, Japan always shielded her and used her power especially to support peace in East Asia and for the independence of China. From earliest times it has been inclined to disorder. Further, many Chinese have continued to live a pitiful life. Japan is trying now to save the Chinese. Yet, without understanding the true spirit of Japan a part of the Chinese people do not come to their senses today and are using the power of such countries as Great Britain and the United States to resist the Japanese. We must make these people wake up as quickly as possible and together advance in the building of a Greater East Asia.[1]

These statements, expressed in a sixth-grade history textbook written in 1943, clearly indicate two facts about Japanese textbook attitudes toward and Japanese government views of China. First, the quotation illustrates what wartime Japanese leadership sought to teach schoolchildren as a sympathetic, objective, and balanced understanding of China. Second, it reveals the care which the Japanese Ministry of Education and its instrument, the Editorial Division, exercised at even the lowest educational level to create "proper" attitudes toward China.

The purpose of this study is to illustrate the attitudes that the Editorial Division expressed toward China in successive editions of textbooks during the period 1903–1945. There is much merit in such an approach. After 1903 only the Japanese government could prepare elementary textbooks and it was responsible for producing five editions of morals and national-language readers and six editions of history and geography textbooks during this forty-two-year period. These textbooks therefore provide the student of Japan with an accurate measure of the official government attitude toward

China (or at least what it wanted taught) at the time the textbooks were issued, and how the messages about China it wished to convey to Japanese children were altered or kept constant in each edition.[2] The information about and images of China contained therein may have been simplistic, stereotyped, patronizing, myopic, and distorted, but the student of Japan cannot ignore or deny their impact. For most of the Japanese people, the elementary-level textbooks provided the highest level of instruction they would ever receive about China.

This point is graphically illustrated by some statistics. After 1907 the textbooks were read by over 97 percent of all Japanese youth and occupied 50 percent of the students' daily classroom study time in the fifth and sixth grades and 46 percent in the first four grades.[3] The elitist nature of prewar education meant that as late as 1935, only 17.9 percent of all the Japanese people had received an education which went beyond the first six years of compulsory education.[4]

The first edition of textbooks prepared by the government appeared in 1903. The attitude toward China is explicitly and implicitly the least favorable, hopeful, or balanced of any subsequent textbook edition. The 1903 textbooks clearly reflect an attitude of still seeking to emulate the West while dissociating the Japanese people from all other Asians, including the Chinese. The Editorial Division's way of acknowledging the low esteem in which Chinese were held was illustrated by the inclusion of only one Chinese hero for both the morals and national-language textbooks, compared to thirteen and three Western heroes, respectively, in the same 1903 textbooks. In striking contrast, a reader published in 1881, before people like Fukuzawa Yukichi began to preach dissociation from Asians, included forty-four Chinese figures.[5] The Japanese people did not wish to have Westerners associate them with the values, institutions, and retarded social and economic development of the Chinese people; nor did they feel compelled at this time to propound a historical destiny in any part of Asia.

The attempt to dissociate Japan from China's backward and un-enlightened condition is further illustrated by the very limited treatment of China in any of the subject-matter areas of the textbooks, as well as by the invidious comparisons. Japan alone in East Asia had a constitution and Diet, the textbook authors boasted; China's devastating defeats at the hands of well-trained, brave Japanese troops in the Sino-Japanese War and Boxer Rebellion were ample proof of her military weakness. She refused to abandon an outmoded "Middle Kingdom" (Chūgoku) concept as well as duplicity in her diplomacy. China had "violated her agreement with our country" *(waga kuni to no yakusoku ni somuite)* and, by being "very rude [*anmari Shinkoku ga burei da*], finally caused Japan to send a great many troops into Korea to confront China to go to war." She claimed both Taiwan and Korea

as vassals when it was to her advantage and as independent states when
that policy was disadvantageous. The Editorial Division refused to be a
party to the idea of China as the Middle Kingdom, studiously avoiding the
use of the Chinese characters for Chūgoku, using instead the characters for
"country of the Manchus," (Shinkoku), and later the even more derogatory
ones for the phonetic sound, "Shina."[6]

The textbooks did admit a debt to China in Japan's early history, but
found the Chinese of the contemporary world a people who tried to hold
back progress not only in their own country but in nearby areas and
countries as well.

> At this time Taiwan was a possession of China, but China said they [the Taiwanese]
> were a barbaric people outside their civilization and therefore would not consider their
> actions in the slightest. However, when the Japanese government sent troops to . . .
> punish the barbarians of Taiwan, then China suddenly presented a contrary opinion.
> Finally, there were peace talks, they paid an indemnity, and we withdrew our troops.[7]

In Korea the Chinese government had encouraged the reactionary and
"subservient" (jidai) faction to oppose the "independent" (dokuritsu)
faction, which was progressive and wanted to learn from the Japanese
people. Indeed, the Chinese were supposedly responsible for encouraging
the Sino-Japanese War (1894–1895), for landing troops in Korea in 1894
without notifying Japan as required by treaty, and for precipitating the war
by attacking Japanese ships.[8]

Obviously, the images of China in the 1903 textbook were not
flattering; more insulting, the Japanese authors did not find merit in
arousing in the children any interest about China. Later editions continued
the patronizing, negative attitude, but they tried to balance that attitude
by emphasizing China's importance to Japan. The precise nature of
China's importance varied from edition to edition and reflected a changing
world and Japan's vital interests.

In 1909 Ōkuma Shigenobu, founder of the Progressive Party and of
Waseda University, wrote:

> We desire, by the cooperation of our Anglo-Saxon friends, to engage in a glorious
> humanitarian work of civilization and developing two Oriental nations [Korea and
> China] now deeply sunk in misery, so that they, too, may someday be able to write semi-
> centennial stories of progress as we are now doing.[9]

Analysis of the 1910 textbooks shows that the Editorial Division decided to
complement the negative message of 1903 with Ōkuma's more positive
view that Japan and the Japanese people should show a keener interest in
their neighbor, help the Chinese people, and recognize China's relevance to
the peace of East Asia.

The greater interest in "Shina" was illustrated by more coverage of

China as well as an increase in the number of lessons on Orientals in the national-language readers from zero in 1903 to seven in the 1910 edition. In view of Japan's increased role on the continent, the authors expanded the coverage of Kwantung and Manchuria; the emphasis was justified by their "geographic propinquity" and importance to the peace of East Asia.[10] Japan's growing economic ambitions led the authors to exhort merchants to look to China as a market where they could fulfill their duty "to develop foreign trade and to greatly increase the nation's wealth."[11] The myth of the China trade was thus to be held up to generations of Japanese youth to delude them into expectations far beyond the realities. When that trade did not meet the Japanese textbooks' unrealistic expectations, the blame (as was charged in the West too) had to be placed on an uncooperative Chinese government.

The control of new areas of East Asia, including Taiwan and Manchuria, was also justified by their inferiority. Taiwanese were aborigines who soon would be uplifted by Japanese education and contacts. A letter from a settler in Sakhalin (Karafuto) encouraged future Japanese settlement in Taiwan and Sakhalin for the enlightenment and civilization Japan could bring to those areas.[12] The poem "Fifty Million Countrymen" reflected Japan's rising aspirations and expanded destiny:

> The God-given mission of peace in East Asia rests on the shoulders of such a people as us. Japan has a heavy responsibility in advancing the civilization of the East. . . .[13]

According to the textbooks, Japan's increasing involvement in China and East Asia stemmed from another new mission, namely, preserving the peace of East Asia. Japan's brilliant accomplishments between 1895 and 1910 had finally brought Japan to the role of a Great Power, but such strength entailed a heavy responsibility for East Asia. That responsibility had driven Japan to negotiate frequently with Russia between 1900 and 1902, but when Russia proved uncooperative, Japan had made her alliance with Great Britain.[14]

The textbooks of 1910 carried the negative messages about China of the 1903 edition. The Chinese were smug, guileful in diplomacy, and insincere toward Japan. These characteristics caused the Chinese people's failure to recognize Japan's true desires to promote peace and enlightenment in East Asia.[15] The pupils reading the textbooks learned of Chinese military incompetence, devious Chinese diplomatic efforts in Korea at Japan's expense, and Chinese responsibility for precipitating the war with Japan by their arrogance, antiquarianism, and willful desire to misunderstand Japan's pure motives. The Editorial Division strongly implied that China did not know what was good for her and for the peace of East Asia. That message did not yet say that such attitudes would justify a more active Japanese effort to teach them what was best for China. Each subsequent pre–1945 edition would advance that message. It remained to be seen how the post–World War I Japanese textbook edition would handle the topic.

Following the Great War the world and Japan had changed sufficiently that the Ministry of Education deemed it advisable to develop new textbook editions. Those textbooks written and published between 1918 and 1923 presented the least patronizing and negative images of China and the most balanced treatment of the Middle Kingdom of any of the 1903–1945 editions. Thus the textbooks reflected a general attempt by all the 1918–1923 authors to achieve a balance between nationalism and internationalism that was not characteristic of other editions.[16] The textbooks did, however, support a more activist role in one part of China, Manchuria.

It may come as a surprise for some observers of Japanese history to discover how clearly at this early date the textbook authors spelled out the importance of Manchuria to Japan, but an examination of the texts themselves leaves no doubt about that emphasis.

The Japanese and Manchurian economies, it was repeated again and again, were mutually beneficial. Developments in railroad building, port construction, and shipping had created close ties between them. Sparse settlement of Manchuria had invited Japanese settlement; already the Japanese and the nation's technical and economic assistance had contributed to a high level of Manchurian development.[17] Japanese were still fewer in number than the Chinese, but the authors predicted that that would change. Furthermore, although Dairen was not a part of Manchuria, the authors tried to draw the children's attention to its importance for Japan and Manchuria. A lesson called "News from Dairen" stressed that city's key role as the link between Manchuria and Japan, its developing transportation system, and its Western appearance.[18]

Manchuria in turn was important because of its relevance to China Proper and to Japan. The authors stressed Japan's long historical relationship with China and the latter's cooperation with Japan which had allowed Japanese bases and leases on the Liaotung Peninsula, permitted the South Manchurian Railway, and aided in the growing mutual trade between the two countries.[19] Manchuria was seen as a tie between the two countries.

The post–World War I textbooks emphasized more than before China's commercial importance to Japan. One story provided a detailed account of the Yangtze River, the adjacent regions, and the commercial role of Hankow and Shanghai. Chinese acquiescence in programs promoting greater Sino-Japanese trade and Chinese development were building a better China and a cooperative policy which involved keeping out the West.[20]

This treatment of Manchuria stressed the positive aspects of China, and Japanese and Chinese cooperation in China Proper and Manchuria, but in the history textbook Japan's ambivalent attitude toward China continued to be expressed in negative descriptions and stereotypes. Balance there was, but it was on Japanese terms and goodwill toward the Chinese existed as long as China saw the world and her interests in the same manner as Japan. That negativism toward China was also an expression of Japan's own enhanced self-esteem and historical experiences.

The textbook authors praised Motoori Norinaga (the great Tokugawa scholar) for leading the reaction against a slavish acceptance of China. They criticized China's policy in Korea prior to the Sino-Japanese War; her insincerity and culpability for ignoring Japanese proposals and thus providing major reasons for the war; and her poor military showing during that conflict.[21] The textbooks also strengthened a previous argument found in more sketchy form in the 1910 textbooks. As a weak and practically defenseless nation, China had suffered and had drawn Japan willy-nilly into activities on the continent. By the Anglo-Japanese Alliance, Japan had sought to preserve the lands of China and Korea but eventually had found it necessary to fight Russia to protect both areas. In justifying Japan's entry into World War I, the authors pointed out that Japan had gone to war with Germany because her ships "threatened the peace in the Far East."[22]

The Editorial Division had gone beyond the 1910 edition and the messages of Japan's mission on the continent and its responsibility for peace in East Asia. The textbooks became an instrument for preparing future citizens for a more active role in China and inculcated in the minds of the young the view that Manchuria was a vital area for Japan. Indeed, they came very close to asserting a Japanese Monroe Doctrine for East Asia. The next set of textbooks, issued after the Manchurian Incident of September 18, 1931, would not hesitate to make that assertion clearly and vigorously.

By 1933, domestic and international developments made the textbooks published between 1918 and 1923 anachronistic. A new wave of nationalism at home and commitment in Manchuria resulted in a decision by the Ministry of Education to write new textbooks which abandoned the cooperative, conciliatory, and cosmopolitan tone of the post–World War I edition and substituted a more assertive, exclusive, and totalitarian type of nationalism. Backed into a corner by her Manchurian policy, Japan now believed it was unrealistic to rely on the goodwill of other nations; wisdom dictated an independent foreign policy. Isolated by a mostly hostile world opinion, Japan became self-righteous and defensively aggressive, features reflected in the new textbook edition.

This more assertive nature and more clearly defined roles and images of the future can be found especially in the fifth- and sixth-grade morals and national-language textbooks and a fifth edition of the geography textbook, all of which were published between 1937 and 1939. These slightly more advanced grades allowed more elaborate and sophisticated expression in the textbooks. More important, however, the texts produced between 1933 and 1936 did not reflect with sufficient clarity the strong post–Manchurian Incident views and aggressive nationalism to which the Japanese government and a critical and hostile world committed Japan after 1933–1935.[23] The later texts voiced emphatically and didactically new attitudes and policies growing out of Japan's increasing involvement on the continent.

According to the post–Manchurian Incident textbook edition, Japan was to pursue an independent foreign policy, to create a self-sufficient empire, and to ensure peace and development in East Asia, the implementation of which would require China to play a great role. The empire would allow Japan to overcome scarcities, achieve a balanced development, and attain greater national power. Japan, however, was not selfish. The peoples of China, Manchuria, and Korea would benefit through greater development of their economies, a higher standard of living, security from hostile outside powers, and a higher form of culture. The best part of the bargain for the Chinese, indeed for the whole world, was that Japan's peacekeeping role in East Asia would guarantee peace not only in East Asia, as the previous textbook edition had claimed, but also in the world.

Japan was a great world power, a member of the Big Three with Britain and the United States, and the Japanese people were a "great people." There was little to criticize about Japan, but much wrong with other powers.[24] Japan, formerly taught by the West, had become independently great and a leader. Strong in herself, strong among nations, Japan had a special claim to greatness, the new textbook edition believed. She was the "oldest country in the world," and her national honor had not been stained "even once" by foreign occupation. She was great also because of the purity of spirit of the Japanese people, the brilliance of the Meiji emperor, her uniqueness, and the new claim that it was "god country."[25] The Editorial Division stressed Japanese culture, exploits, and heroes because it believed Japan had far less to learn from the outside world and much more to teach. From such an attitude, Japan approached China in this period.

II.

One of the most striking differences in the textbook attitudes toward China was the assertion that Japan was *solely* responsible for the peace of the Far East, a fact which would preserve world peace. The authors argued that Japan would be untrue to her responsibilities if she sacrificed world peace and her own assessment of the actual situation in East Asia before, during, and after the Manchurian Incident by accepting the mistaken analysis of the League of Nations and world opinion. For that reason, the morals textbook stated, "We have decided to carry out and undertake the peace of the world in the Far East from an independent standpoint. . . . In order to establish international peace it is necessary for us to maintain the stability of East Asia."[26] When the Chinese (as the textbooks falsely asserted) blew up the South Manchurian Railway and Manchurians created a new nation, the situation in the Far East "suddenly changed." Japan decided to recognize Manchukuo in order to implement her goal of making peace firmer in the Far East. The last chapter of the history textbook, entitled "The People's Resolution," after summing up a number of great deeds and battles, emphasized Japan's responsibility for peace in East Asia:

> Now our national prosperity is increasing all the more and our country, alone, is responsible for the peace of East Asia. Along with England, and the United States, we occupy the most important position in the world.[27]

The Japanese argument that they alone had responsibility for the peace of East Asia obviously entailed a need—nay, a mission—to interfere in China and to ignore any Chinese point of view which conflicted with their own. This was myopic and arrogant on the part of the textbook authors. There was no sensitivity to the Chinese position.

The Editorial Division took pains to show that preserving peace in the Far East and the world required Japan to develop and promote the prosperity of China and Manchukuo (the latter was not treated as a separate nation in the geography textbook). Hence Japan had signed a mutual defense treaty with Manchukuo and was tightening the ties of friendship with China.[28] Japan had paid dearly in the past—three wars—for not recognizing that the strength of China, Manchuria, and Korea was vital to the security of Japan and East Asia. China's weakness had created an undesirable power vacuum in Manchuria. In turn, Manchuria's geographical propinquity, lack of development, and "extremely intimate relationship" with Japan in industry and defense had motivated Japan's deep concern.[29]

If Japan, Manchukuo, and China would cooperate, their security would be enhanced and coordination of their complementary economies would redound to their mutual prosperity. Japan had wealth and industries; Manchukuo and China had rich natural resources. All three needed one another badly:

> Thus our industries have developed and our national wealth has increased tremendously, but our land area is small and we are not rich in natural resources. However, our neighboring countries, Manchukuo and China, have vast natural resources. In spite of this fact, their development has been retarded and industry underdeveloped. Therefore, these countries are desirous of developing their natural resources and bringing prosperity to their countries with the aid of our country. In the future, it will be

necessary to have the cooperation of Japan, Manchukuo and China to have prosperity in Asia.[30]

No doubt was left in the minds of the students that Manchukuo was reaping benefits from Japanese development. A lesson, "Riding on the [train] 'Asia,'" provided an opportunity to show how much more beneficially Japan had altered the landscape than had the Russians during their occupation. There was the ultramodern Japanese train, as well as a Japanese agricultural development station, a well-planned and beautiful capital, and everywhere one received the impression of a happy, vibrant, purposeful society.[31] The authors emphasized developments in irrigation, agriculture, maritime industry, trade, coal mining, iron works, and the timber industry; all of these were the result of Japanese capital, engineers, and laborers.[32] Today's students could help Japan fulfill her destiny by emigrating to Manchukuo and duplicating the achievements of their fathers and older brothers. Moreover, what had been accomplished in Manchukuo could also be achieved in China.

China was weak and underdeveloped, but that unhappy condition, argued the authors, could be overcome by coordinating China, Japan, and Manchukuo, by common efforts to preserve the peace, and by utilizing Japanese wealth, engineering, and leadership.[33] The children were taught that the Japanese people had an obligation to help China in order to preserve peace in East Asia, and because Japan had borrowed so much from China in earlier times. Times had changed and lately the nation had been "paying dearly in order to develop China." Fifty thousand loyal Japanese were living in China now to promote Chinese industry, mutual trade, and cultural intercourse. Japan was deficient in food supplies, land area, and natural resources for her increasing population; those students who went to the continent would strengthen those nations' economies, overcome shortages for Japan, and help to build a brilliant future for Japan.[34] The fact that the latter point was so strongly stressed illustrated Japan's priorities; China was secondary to Japan's needs.

China also played a role in the theme of a greater East Asia because she, along with Manchukuo and Japan, would help to "develop a great culture in East Asia."[35] Proclaiming its necessity *(hitsuyō)*, the authors failed to clarify "the great East Asian culture." This ambiguity was not restricted to the textbooks; any reader of the propagandistic *Kokutai no hongi* [Cardinal principles of the national entity] encounters the same frustration in trying to define Japan's cultural mission.

The apparent meaning for China, however, was that promoting a great world culture meant such things as sublimating Occidental culture, synthesizing a "purified" Western culture and the old and new cultures of East Asia, clarifying the national entity, helping China achieve the original purity of Japan, and giving full play to the Japanese mission *(shimei)*. The fusion, the textbooks taught, would not offer East Asians shoddy Western materialism and disruptive individualism. The ambiguity of the language feeds the suspicion that Chinese culture was also to be "purified." In view of developments in Manchukuo and Korea, giving "full play to our way" meant exporting Japanese culture. The Pan-Asianism in the 1933–1939 textbooks, rejected in the 1903 edition,[36] was intensified in the subsequent wartime textbook editions of 1941–1945.

Wartime conditions placed a heavy burden on the Ministry of Education. Its Editorial Division found it necessary to keep up with the expansion of the Japanese Empire, to select appropriate materials to bolster national morale, and to rationalize Japan's war mission and Greater East Asia Co-Prosperity Sphere (GEACPS) to the schoolchildren. Consequently, the ministry began to prepare in 1941 a fifth edition of the morals, national-language, and history textbooks and then, in unprecedented fashion, produced a sixth edition for history in 1943 and for geography in 1944. Such activity emphasized the importance which the government attached to the messages and attitudes the textbooks could carry.

The new textbooks were infused with the authors' desire to revive the peoples of Asia and the Pacific. They vented anger at the Western colonial powers for breaking the "organic relationship" that had existed among Asian peoples, for destroying their economic, political, and social fabric, and for putting them into a deep slumber and decay. The textbook authors exhibited a deep frustration at the anesthetizing of Asian peoples such as the Chinese, because the conditions limited the fulfillment of Japanese ambitions to revive other Asian peoples. All these emotions are vividly illustrated by a passage in the 1943 history textbook:

> Only four hundred years ago first Portugal and Spain, followed by the Netherlands, England, Russia and finally America gnawed away furiously at East Asia. Our country promptly saw through their ambitions and strengthened the defense of the country, stimulated East Asian countries and worked to expel the influence of the West. Thus, even now for the purpose of completing this great work we are bearing various difficulties and are carrying on the Greater East Asian War. The way to the stability of East Asia and prosperity of the Japanese Empire will be opened by this war.[37]

Wartime textbooks had rediscovered all the Asian peoples. They taught that the GEACPS could not fail. Japan would help restore the dynamic intraregional commerce that flourished prior to the arrival of the Europeans; furthermore, Japan would protect the native rulers and revive the old spirit of Asian brotherhood. The Japanese students discovered that their interests were in a larger Asia and that all the people of Asia were their blood brothers. Japan's activities in Asia were logical; her location with relation to China, Manchukuo, and Korea bestowed upon her a natural role of protector. Manchukuo had been strengthened against attacks from the north and its natural resources combined with Japanese capital and skill brought mutual prosperity.

The textbooks' extensive treatment of Manchukuo and China illustrated clearly that these two areas were the most important in Asia; indeed, they had a "completely inseparable relationship with Japan" (. . . *Shina wa Nihon to mattaku fukabun no kankei ni aru*).[38] The Japanese textbooks were proud of Japan's economic and social development of Manchukuo. Their activity in Manchukuo was particularly important and advantageous because it provided a model of the benefits accruing from membership in the GEACPS. The authors worked to stress the common origins and culture of the Chinese and Japanese people *(jinshu to shite mo chikaku, moji mo kyōtsū no mono o tsukatte ire);* moreover, their economies were mutually beneficial. China exported commodities and natural resources which Japan lacked such as raw wool, wood oil, tungsten, coal, and iron; Japan exported factory products to her. But the authors unconsciously revealed China's junior relationship by the telling statement:

> Moreover, nothing could be more useful for building a Greater East Asia than if the great resources and manpower of China can be developed hereafter through powerful Japanese capital and exceptional Japanese engineers.[39]

The Chinese were to be hewers of wood.

Both Manchukuo and China were assigned an elder brother's role within the GEACPS. They would be brought into the world brotherhood of *hakkō ichiu* (eight corners of the world under one roof). This slogan meant that in practice all people subject to Japanese liberation would become members of one large Confucian family. Japan and the emperor were the parents; they would dominate in order to bring protection, harmony, stability, prosperity, and a higher moral code to the greater family. Japan would transfer its concept of the *kokutai* (national polity), in which all the Japanese were one big, happy family and all self-interest was submerged in the larger GEACPS. China and Manchukuo deserved higher status within that family because of their geographical propinquity, common racial origins, and historical interrelationships.[40] While the previous edition discussed developing "one great East Asian culture" *(Tōa ni ichi dai bunka),* the wartime textbooks propounded instead the concept of a harmonious, Confucian family held together by the individual units denying their own self-interest and taking their place in a hierarchical ranking system with Japan at the apex.

Despite the high position of China in that hierarchy, the textbook authors could not refrain from expressing their anger at the Chinese people. Unlike the peoples of Southeast Asia and the Pacific, many were not sympathetic to the concept of GEACPS. The textbooks could not admit too much Chinese defiance, though; hence the disappointment expressed above was quickly countered by the statement that the "majority of Chinese are relying on us."[41]

The authors tried to keep up the pretense of Manchukuo's independence but they frequently gave themselves away. One story, "The Night Singapore Fell," must have strained some of the young Japanese students' credulity: the Manchukuo emperor, (Henry) P'u-yi, hearing of the fall of Singapore, cried profusely from joy and awakened the Japanese officers (their presence belied his freedom to act) to tell them of the congratulatory letter he had just written to the Japanese emperor. After encouraging the officers to bow in the direction of the Japanese palace, he went off to worship at the Japanese-built shrine honoring the Sun Goddess.[42] Another story related how the emperor of Manchukuo went to Japan on the 2600th anniversary of Jimmu Tennō's founding of Japan and how on his return he told his people that he desired to govern the country in the same spirit as the Japanese emperor.[43]

If Chinese students had read the Japanese textbooks, they would have been greatly angered by the justification for Japan's presence in Manchuria. They would also have been disappointed to learn that Manchukuo was to be detached permanently from China. Japan's presence there was legitimized by "100,000 brave and loyal" Japanese soldiers losing their lives and expending "an enormous amount of the country's wealth" during the Russo-Japanese War, and by the "mistaken Anti Japanese thought . . . scorn and insult" expressed by the Chinese prior to the Manchurian Incident.[44] In addition, Japanese soldiers and citizens had been welcomed heartily by the emperor and people of Manchukuo, who were eagerly studying the Japanese language and acquiring Japanese skills. Land and natural resources were plentiful, but the need was great; accordingly, Japanese would have to work in Manchuria at least another twenty years.[45]

The textbooks, enthusiastic about the cooperation of other nations in the GEACPS, expressed discouragement and frequent frustration with China and the Chinese people. China presented the biggest obstacle to the fulfillment of the GEACPS. The authors were ambivalent about China. On the one hand, there was indebtedness to China, the great size, scale, and wealth of the land, and the admirable perseverance of the Chinese despite adversity. The Chinese people were relaxed, natural, expansive, enterprising, and good-natured: Chinese youth, it was claimed, were grateful for the Japanese efforts to awaken China.[46] Three essays on China in the appendix of the fifth-grade reader were sympathetic to the Chinese people and praised the youth corps and women and children, who were organized by Japanese soldiers, for keeping open China's roads—as important to the country "as blood vessels to the body."[47]

On the other hand, China was always inclined to disorder and her people's lives were pitiful. Worse yet, they refused to recognize their own best interests and senselessly relied upon Great Britain and the United States to help them resist the Japanese. Too many older Chinese could not rid themselves of the Middle Kingdom conceit that China was the greatest country in the world and had nothing to learn from others.[48] The Chinese were obstinate, uncooperative, and disposed to face-saving and fatalism. These invidious comparisons reflected value judgments and Japan's own contrary image of herself. This point was also illustrated by the argument that the main problem of the Chinese was their limited sense of loyalty. The allegation was followed by the condescending remark that perhaps the Chinese should not be criticized too severely, since over the centuries Chinese were only concerned with themselves and their immediate environment.

Despite these debilitating and intransigent Chinese attitudes, which made it difficult to ". . . make these people wake up as quickly as possible and together advance in the building of a Greater East Asia," the textbook authors professed optimism. The reason for high expectations was that the Chinese people had other redeeming qualities. China was a literate country and her people were skillful in propaganda, diplomacy, and social intercourse. Most encouraging, despite the repeated efforts of the Chinese administration to sabotage the efforts of sincere Japanese living in China and to encourage anti-Japanese feelings, were the Chinese youth, who were "developing splendid characters and . . . trying to clasp the hands of the Japanese people."[49] Further, the Chinese were "deeply moved by our sincerity" (seii) and at long last were opening their eyes to the "new order" (shin chitsujo) in East Asia; the proof lay in the fact that the Chinese had formed a new government under Wang Ching-wei in March 1940.[50]

New historical interpretations made the Chinese seem capable of redemption. The Editorial Division decided that the textbooks produced after 1943 would no longer portray China as the chief villain of the Sino-Japanese War and the Boxer Rebellion. For the history of East Asia from approximately 1885 to 1918, Russia enjoyed that dubious distinction.[51] After that date the United States and, to a lesser extent, Great Britain occupied the villain's role.

The textbook authors also saw some hope for China's future in her slow but growing recognition that it was not in her best interests to rely upon the United States and England. China was misled by the hypocritical concern of the United States for China's territorial integrity; the United States was only prospering at China's expense, as she had during World War I.[52] Even Japan had not recognized the will of the United States and England to dominate and to deceive in such examples as the self-seeking proposals at both the Washington and London naval conferences. Innocence and frequent military victories in the past made the Japanese people careless and able to see only the "surface of world movements"; Japan, even now, needed to perform more research on the importance of East Asia, "especially on China."[53] The implication of these statements was that an alert, realistic Japan could and would lead a confused, misguided China, prevent the United States from skillfully manipulating China, and keep the Chinese government from inciting anti-Japanese sentiment among its populace.

The Editorial Division labored assiduously to convince the students that Japanese perseverance and Chinese introspection would create an intimate relationship, preserve peace in the Far East, and fulfill the goals of the GEACPS. The Japanese, who were trying to understand the "customs, manners and national characteristics of the Chinese," could achieve their objectives with and in China, despite Chinese rudeness, by keeping their minds fixed on the long-range goals. Chinese youth were cooperating, the Wang Ching-wei government had come into existence, and Japan was making headway in forcing the Chinese to analyze their own character, actions, and long-range interests. "Our country," the textbooks claimed, "is encouraging introspection by China and is working with all her might to uplift the country under our mission of establishing eternal peace in the Far East. We are gradually achieving that objective."[54]

Today, we can see that it was not China that was misguided, but rather an aggressive Japan, which came to be so myopic that she saw her narrow interests as the only legitimate ones for China and the Chinese people. The textbook authors in each edition from 1903 to 1945 seemed to be genuinely sincere in their desire to have the Japanese schoolchildren understand China, its history, people, and national characteristics. They wanted the students to feel a brotherhood with the Chinese people and to understand that what happened in China affected Japan's vital interests and the peace of East Asia.

Despite the seeming goodwill and intentions, the textbook authors did not accomplish those objectives. Instead, they were responsible for developing and perpetuating unflattering stereotypes of and condescending attitudes toward a misguided, confused, and disorderly Chinese society and government. They did not succeed in really informing the students about the aspirations of the Chinese people or their intense effort to realize nationalist hopes that encompassed the unity of all of China including Manchuria. They pictured a China in decay rather than the real China, which was exploding with life and moving toward unification. Furthermore, the textbooks did not try to explain from a Chinese perspective why China believed her best interests lay in resisting Japanese leadership and allying herself with the United States and Great Britain. On the contrary, the textbooks constantly portrayed the Chinese as an obtuse people because they failed to recognize that their own interests coincided exactly with those of Japan. The Japanese textbooks were a faithful instrument of Japanese policy. In the short run they proved to be a dependable vehicle for promoting Japanese expansion in China; in the long run they served neither Japan nor China well.

Notes

1. *Kaigō tokiomi, Nihon kyōkasho taikei-kindai hen* [Outline of Japanese textbooks: The modern period], (Tokyo, 1962), 20:374. Hereafter cited as *NKT*. This twenty-four-volume collection, the principal source for this study, includes textbooks published from 1872 and all moral-education, national-language, geography, and history textbooks for grades one through six for the period 1903–1945, when the Ministry of Education possessed a monopoly on authorship of elementary textbooks. The subject matter of the volumes is as follows: morals (vol. 3); national language (vols. 6–8); geography (vols. 16, 17); history (vols. 19, 20).

2. For a fuller discussion of the background leading to government-written textbooks and a discussion of many other items found in the textbooks, see Harold J. Wray, "Changes and Continuity in Japanese Images of the *Kokutai* Textbooks, 1903–1945" (Ph.D. diss., University of Hawaii, 1971).

3. General Headquarters, Supreme Commander for the Allied Powers, Civil Information and Education Section, Education Division, *Education in the New Japan* (Tokyo, 1948), 2: Appendix, p. 423.

4. Tsurumi Kazuko, *Social Change and the Individual: Japan, Before and After Defeat in World War II* (Princeton, 1970), pp. 112–13.

5. Karasawa Tomitarō, *Kyōkasho no rekishi* [A history of textbooks] (Tokyo, 1960), pp. 725, 728, 733. Fukuzawa Yukichi, *Autobiography of Fukuzawa Yukichi,* tr. Kiyooka Eiichi (Tokyo, 1947), p. 231; Miwa Kimitada, "Fukuzawa Yukichi's 'Departure from Asia': A Prelude to the Sino-Japanese War," in *Japan's Modern Century,* ed. Edmund Skrzypczak (Tokyo, 1968), pp. 1–26.

6. *NKT,* 3: 477–78, 548, 609; 19: 471, 489–90.

7. Ibid., 19: 489.

8. Ibid., 19: 488, 491.

9. Ōkuma Shigenobu, *Fifty Years of New Japan* (London, 1909), 1: 53.

10. *NKT,* 16: 414–26.

11. Ibid., 7: 242. "Our country as an island country has a very great use of foreign trade. Above all we are near the large country of China which possesses a population of 400 million. The future of foreign trade is a very promising prospect." *NKT,* 16: 241–42.

12. Ibid., 8: 206, 222. In the history text, there was a strong implication that the Taiwanese did not fight hard against the Japanese troops because they preferred Japanese to Chinese rule. The authors also boasted—as they would in subsequent editions—that the Taiwanese were no match for the Japanese troops, and neither were the Chinese.

13. Ibid., 7: 226–27.

14. Ibid., 19: 557–58.

15. Ibid., 19: 491, 550, 554.

16. On the ambivalence of the 1918–1923 textbooks and the effort to maintain a balance between nationalism and internationalism, see Harry Wray, "Nationalism and Internationalism in Japanese Elementary Textbooks, 1918–1931." *Asian Forum* 5:4 (October–December): 46–62.

17. *NKT,* 16: 467–71.

18. Ibid., 7: 380–81.

19. Ibid., 16: 471.

20. Ibid., 8: 401–2; 473–74; 16: 468–71.

21. Ibid., 7: 478; 19: 719–20.

22. Ibid., 19: 731.

23. The publication of two geography textbook editions, the first between 1934 and 1936, was unprecedented, but reflected a desire to bring the textbook up to date for Japan's greater involvement in Asia. The morals texts were published each year from 1934 to correspond to each grade level; the same practice applied for the national readers, which were published in two volumes each year from 1933.

24. *NKT,* 3: 299, 351–54.

25. Ibid., 3: 259, 295–96.

26. Ibid., 3: 345–46.

27. Ibid., 20: 121. The intensity of feeling for the divine mission of Japan in East Asia by 1940 is dramatically illustrated by inclusion of the following statement as fact in the English examination questions for entrance to college: "What Japan seeks is the establishment of a new order which will ensure the permanent stability of East Asia. . . . The new order has for its foundations a tripartite relationship of mutual aid and coordination between Japan, Manchukuo and China in political, economic and other fields. Its object is to secure international justice to perfect the joint defense against communism, and to create a new culture and realize a close economic cohesion throughout East Asia. This indeed is the way to contribute toward the stabilization of East Asia and the progress of the world." Robert K. Hall, *Education for a New Japan* (New Haven, 1949), p. 117.

28. *NKT,* 3: 346.

29. Ibid., 16: 549–52; 20: 112–22.

30. Ibid., 3: 353–54.

31. Ibid., 8: 150–53.

32. Ibid., 3: 353; 16: 548; 20: 120.

33. Ibid., 16: 551–52; 3: 492.

34. Ibid., 16: 552; 3: 252.

35. Ibid., 3: 354.

36. Ibid., 3: 493. Simultaneously an educational study group *(kyōiku kenkyū kai)* proposed as a part of its fundamental reform plan for education in December 1936 that "our recent rise in intellectual status reminds us of the increasing importance of our world mission. Another aim of the educational reform is to break out of our insularity, cultivate the magnanimity and insight of the broad-minded citizenry, and at the same time to demonstrate further our traditional talent for amalgamating foreign and domestic culture and contributing to a new growth of world civilization." Herbert Passin, *Society and Education in Japan* (New York, 1965), p. 255.

37. *NKT,* 3: 374.

38. Ibid., 17: 56.

39. Ibid., 17: 79.

40. Ibid., 3: 432.

41. Ibid., 17: 80.

42. Ibid., 8: 695–96.

43. Ibid., 8: 234.

44. Ibid., 17: 70.

45. Ibid., 8: 523, 585; 17: 67, 69.

46. Ibid., 17: 73; 3: 430.

47. Ibid., 17: 80.

48. Ibid., 20: 354.

49. Ibid., 17: 80. Such indoctrination did not stop with the textbooks, but also found its way into the entrance examination for a South Manchurian Higher Technical School. Hall, op. cit., p. 122.

50. *NKT,* 20: 370.

51. Ibid., 20: 353–55, 356, 358, 360.

52. Ibid., 20: 365–66. The people of the United States were selfish, arrogant, prejudiced, discriminatory; their government was viewed in the textbooks as the chief threat to peace in Asia and the Pacific.

53. Ibid., 20: 366–67.

54. Ibid., 17: 80.

Notes on the Cultural Relationship Between Japan and China

Ryōzō Kurai

I.

Japanese culture derives totally from that of China, whence it continued to flow for over a thousand years. Chinese cultural influence was pervasive, whether in religion, art, philosophy, manners, customs, or ways of life, until approximately the time of the Meiji Restoration in 1868. Thereafter, the cultural flow began to be reversed: Japan absorbed advanced Western civilization and successfully established a modern nation, whereas China was only starting to learn Western culture through Japan. The Sino-Japanese War (1894–1895) marked a turning point. Early in the seventh century, the Japanese central government dispatched its first official envoy, Ono Imoko, to the Sui court. In 1896, almost 1300 years later, the first official student from Ch'ing China arrived in Tokyo. By the early 1900s, several thousand Chinese students had come to Japan.

Earlier, some farseeing Japanese formulated a new approach to China. Although Japan, in theory, had established a unified modern nation by the time of the Meiji Restoration, the basis was not solid enough to withstand the relentless European powers invading Asia at that time. In particular, the Japanese were apprehensive lest the European penetration of China directly affect the safety of Japan. This fear led to the concept known as "Protection of East Asia." Already in 1878 the Shin-a-sha was established by agreement between Ōkubo Toshimichi, the most forceful leader of Japan, and Ho Ju-chang, the first minister to represent the Ch'ing in Japan, with a view to the promotion of cultural exchange between the two

133

countries. Two years later, the Shin-a-sha became the Kō-a-kai, which in turn developed into the Asia Association.

Inukai Tsuyoshi (later prime minister) and a number of journalists established the Tōa-kai in 1897. In the same year, the Dō-bun-kai was founded by Prince Konoe Atsumaro, chairman of the House of Peers, Arao Sei, and others. In 1898 these two institutions combined to become the Tōa-dō-bun-kai. The Asia Association also joined the Tōa-dō-bun-kai, which became the only civilian body for organized cultural exchange between the two countries.

Two famous members of the Tōa-kai were K'ang Yu-wei and Liang Ch'i-ch'ao, refugees from the Ch'ing government impeached for their part in the "self-strengthening" and "modernization" movements. When the Tōa-kai was incorporated with the Tōa-dō-bun-kai, it adopted a rule of not engaging in any direct political activities; therefore the Chinese members became associate members, as did over forty Chinese and thirty Persian members of the Asia Association.

The presidents of the Tōa-dō-bun-kai were among the highest political leaders in Japan: the first president, Konoe Atsumaro, was followed by Viscount Aoki Shūzō, Marquis Nabeshima Naodai, Count Makino Nobuaki, and Prince Konoe Fumimaro. The vice presidents, chairmen, and directors were also men of power: Viscount Kiyoura Keigo (later prime minister), Prince Hosokawa Morinari, General Abe Nobuyuki (later prime minister) and leading financiers such as Ogura Masatsune, Kodama Kenji, and Fujiyama Aiichirō (a postwar foreign minister). The Dō-bun-kai was a membership organization established as an institutional juridical person. By October 1943, there were more than 4000 members.

Although the Dō-bun-kai consisted of top-level politicians and financiers, its activities were restricted to the cultural field, with a special emphasis on education. The Tōa-dō-bun-shoin was established in Shanghai as an educational center.

The Sino-Japanese Trade Research Institute was already in existence in Shanghai, founded in 1890 by Arao Sei, who was close to Konoe Atsumaro and Nezu Hajime. After the death of Arao in 1896, Konoe and Nezu established the Tōa-dō-bun-kai and Tōa-dō-bun-shoin, respectively, in accordance with his will.

When Arao, then a lieutenant attached to the Army General Staff, was sent to China in 1886, he stayed at the Gakuzendō Company's Shanghai branch operated by Kishida Ginka, later a renowned journalist. Gakuzendō, originally a small trading firm on the Ginza in Tokyo in 1877, expanded and Kishida's office was the forerunner of the Sino-Japanese Trading Company. Kishida was a man of profound knowledge, of noble and generous character; his lofty ideals propelled him beyond the small commercial world into cultural and political activities. Dozens of ambitious youth from Japan were always gathered at the Shanghai Gakuzendō, so a new office was opened in Hankow as a base for inland activities. Branch offices were set up in Peking, Tientsin, Chungking, Changsha, and Foochow. Their goal was to develop trade as well as to introduce to the world China and her people. They were eager to help the development and improve the life of the Chinese people. Nezu edited the results and published *Summary of the Commercial Trade of the Ch'ing Dynasty*, which totaled five volumes and 2000 pages.

Arao devoted himself to studies of China around the Gakuzendō for three full years. In April 1889, when he was ordered to return to Japan, Arao decided to leave the army in order to devote himself to the protection of Asia and the conduct of studies on China. His motivation can be seen clearly in his Report of Mission submitted to the general staff:

> Although the American and European powers are pouring in, inside China nothing is organized, things are vacant, policy is rotten and the people are on the verge of poverty; but outwardly China is making a bluff and despising Japan on the self-centered assumption that China is the only land of true civilization, which makes it difficult to unify the Orient. Even though the situation is such, it does not mean that we can use violence to oppress China. Violence should never be put into practice. The only way is to promote commercial trade and to recommend the establishment of a "Sino-Japanese Trade Firm."

Arao himself was eager to participate in the establishment of this firm and, despite his elite status as a lieutenant, a graduate of the Military Academy, he resigned from the army.

The Sino-Japanese Research Institute was thought to be an educational subdivision of the Sino-Japanese Trade Firm projected by Arao. Arao talked Prime Minister Kuroda Kiyotaka into offering the help of the government, and during the course of a year, he recruited over 300 youth volunteers. About 150 were selected and dispatched to Shanghai under the leadership of Arao in September 1890; after three years of training, 89 graduated in June 1893. Because of financial difficulties, the institute was obliged to close temporarily; the outbreak of the Sino-Japanese War in 1894 brought the whole project to an end. Subsequently, however, Tōa-dō-bun-kai and Tōa-dō-bun-shoin were established.

During the active initiation period, the Tōa-dō-bun-kai decided to establish local chapters in the major cities of China and to send students to Shanghai, but insufficient funds prevented these activities. Instead, the magazine *Tōa Current Views* was published and study meetings were held once or twice a month. In 1899 the following projects were started: the Hankow chapter published a Chinese-character paper, "Han Report"; the Shanghai chapter published "A-tō [Asia East] Current Report," decided to support the Tōbun Gakudō and "Fukien Report" of Foochow, and to send students to Hankow and Canton; in Korea, it was decided to publish *Kanjo*

Monthly, to establish Japanese-language schools in Pyongyang and Peishan, and to support the Kyungsung-gaku-dō.

In July 1899, four students were sent to Shanghai for a period of three years. During the fall of the same year, Konoe Atsumaro stopped in Shanghai on his way back from a tour of Europe and the United States with an observation group. He paid a visit in Nanking to Governor-General Liu K'un-i, and in Wuchang to Governor-General Chang Chih-tung, to explain the activities of the Tōa-dō-bun-kai and to ask for their cooperation, especially in establishing a school in Nanking. Liu's answer was that he would give all possible assistance.

In May 1900, the Nanking School opened with students representing each prefecture, trainees from the Ministry of Agriculture and Commerce, Dō-bun-kai students, and self-supported students—fifteen in all; Nezu Hajime was appointed president. A temple among the central belltowers of Nanking was used for classrooms. A branch school for Chinese students was opened separately, and over thirty were enrolled. The outbreak of the Boxer Rebellion in August, however, forced them to withdraw from Nanking and they had to move to Shanghai. Even after the termination of the rebellion, the school remained in Shanghai, its name being changed to the Tōa-dō-bun-shoin. The school was expanded and only Japanese students were accepted. For Chinese students, the Tokyo Dōbun-shoin was established. Government-scholarship students were recruited from all over the nation and seventy to eighty were sent to Shanghai in April 1901. The school was located in a suburb of Shanghai, near the Kiang-Nan Bureau of Machine Tools, housed in a building of the French Girls School.

Nezu Hajime served as president, except for Sugiura Jyūgo's one-year term, until 1923, when he resigned because of illness. In 1921 Tōa-dō-bun-shoin became a recognized school designated by the Specialized School Code of the Ministry of Education; in 1939, by the University Act, the school became a university. Up to 1945, when the school was abolished upon Japan's surrender, 4638 students graduated in the 46 classes, all imbued with the spirit of Nezu, the founder.

In *Prospectus on the Founding of the School* and *Principles of Education* (both in Chinese), Nezu's intentions can be seen clearly; both pieces were published on the occasion of the opening of the school. According to the opening sentence of the *Prospectus:* "By giving lectures on the facts of the nation and the situation abroad, the education of the intellectuals in both Japan and China is intended to establish a foundation for the development of China as well as to create a strong bond of cooperation between Japan and China." Nezu reveals his concept of the Protection of China as follows: "China will become desperate when her territory is ceded, whereupon disputes in Asia cannot be avoided, which in turn may lead to a disturbance of the peace of the world. The protection of China means securing the

safety of Asia, which is equivalent to maintaining the peace of the world."
Further,

> In terms of Asia, the biggest nation is China and the strongest is Japan. Through the
> collaboration of the two countries, self-enforcement can be maintained with outer
> nations, which is the main contribution the two nations can make for East Asia.
> However, the national power of China has waned dreadfully and her future is without
> hope. Even if the two countries tried to collaborate, it would be difficult to bring about
> total success, though there might be several small advances. Collaboration may bring
> temporary security but no hope of permanent safety for East Asia. Now is the only time
> to recover China and bring back prosperity; otherwise the collaboration of Japan and
> China would be in vain. The role of anxious people who are concerned about Asia is to
> establish the foundation of China for further development and to lay a solid basis for
> cooperation between Japan and China. This is the first and urgent thing to be done.
> There are various ways to bring about national prosperity but the most direct and
> effective way is to open a school and to educate competent people.

In his *Principles of Education* Nezu says, "Moral culture is of utmost importance, and mental training is subordinate." Thus he foresaw a defect of
modern education—overemphasis on mental training.

The Tōa-dō-bun-kai established other educational institutions besides
the Shanghai Tōa-dō-bun-shoin. As mentioned earlier, a Tokyo Dō-bun-
shoin was established in 1901 for Chinese students. Its president was Nezu
Hajime, who was also chief secretary of the Dō-bun-kai.

The forerunner of the China-Japan School was established in 1921 in
Tientsin to educate Chinese students and to develop understanding toward
Japan. The Tientsin Dō-bun-shoin offered high school liberal education
and Japanese language. In 1926, when the school became a joint operation
of Japanese and Chinese, the name was changed to Chūnichi Gakuin (the
China-Japan School). In 1927 the school was given official approval by the
Department of Education of China, enabling both Chinese and Japanese
youth to enter. The graduates were qualified to go on to Japanese high
schools, specialized schools, or a Chinese university. Despite these privileges
afforded by the Chūnichi Gakuin, many students still were entering the
Tōa-dō-bun-shoin. As of 1943, fifty-five Chinese students were graduated
from the Tokyo Dō-bun-shoin.

The Hankow Dō-bun-shoin was established in 1923, with the same
prospectus as the Tientsin Dō-bun-shoin. Three years later, the organization was changed and a board of directors was established with both
Japanese and Chinese members. The school was renamed the Kiang-Han
Senior Middle School. In 1929 it became a government-designated middle
school. Adding a junior middle school, it became the Kiang-Han Middle
School. The school was closed between 1937 and 1941, when it was
reviewed.

The Cultural Department of the Ministry of Foreign Affairs established a system of sending Japanese elementary school graduates to China.

Japanese children residing in Shanghai, Chingtao, and Manchuria were to enter the Chūnichi Gakuin and Kiang-Han School. In 1931, as a first attempt, seven students entered the former and two the latter. Later, entering students became the first graders of the middle school. As of 1943, sixteen students were said to be attending the Chūnichi Gakuin, and the graduates went on to Peking University or to the Tōa-dō-bun-shoin.

The North China High School of Industry was established in 1943 by the Specialized School Code of the Japanese Ministry of Education. When the Pacific War broke out, the Japanese authorities took over the British-founded Lester Industrial School, whose operation was entrusted to the Tōa-dō-bun-kai. It became the Tōa Industrial School in 1942 under the presidency of Yada Hichitarō, also president of the Tōa-dō-bun-shoin University. The Bun-ka-kai, set up in Tokyo in 1937, was attended by Chinese students studying in Japan who were graduates of the Chūnichi Gakuin and Kiang-Han Middle School, both operated by the Tōa-dō-bun-kai. Its purpose was to promote friendly relations between the two countries and to study Japan. As of 1943, its membership exceeded the forty students who were studying at the Tokyo University of Commerce, the present Hitotsubashi University, at the Tokyo University of Technology, and at other public and private universities and specialized schools.

As we have seen, the purpose of the Tōa-dō-bun-kai was to educate intellectuals in the schools of the Tōa-dō-bun-shoin, as well as to make China better known abroad. A biweekly magazine *China* was published; it was considered the most authoritative magazine on Chinese problems in Japan at the time. Other publications included the 12-volume *Complete Survey on the Economics of China* (1907), the 18-volume *Complete Geographical Survey of China by Provinces* (1920); the 2000-page *Year Book of China* was published nine times, the *Who's Who in China* was published several times. Four series of *Reminiscences of China* gave details of the Japanese people who were active in promoting goodwill with China, and their activities since the early years of the Meiji Era. In all, more than 100 publications were issued.[1]

Notes

1. Matsumoto Shigeharu recently published his memoirs of days as a Domei correspondent in China: *Shanhai jidai shi* [My time in Shanghai], 3 vols. (Tokyo, 1974–1975).

7.

Chong-Sik Lee utilizes hitherto untapped Chinese and Japanese source material to engage in an in-depth analysis of Chinese resistance to Japanese aggression in Manchuria in 1931 and of the Chinese Communist policy toward it. He suggests that the Chinese Communist Party was totally unprepared for the situation and that the CCP's strategy directed primarily against the Kuomintang was not conducive to winning over the masses to the Communist side.

After completing his Ph.D. at the University of California, Berkeley, Lee in 1963 joined the faculty of the University of Pennsylvania, where he is now a professor of political science. He is the author of *The Politics of Korean Nationalism* (1963) and coauthor with Robert A. Scalapino of *Communism in Korea* (1973). The latter won for its authors the Woodrow Wilson Foundation award of the American Political Association for the best work in political science for 1973.

The present essay is part of Lee's book-in-progress on the revolutionary struggle in Manchuria, 1917–1941. He wishes to acknowledge the generous financial assistance provided by the Committee on Contemporary China of the Social Science Research Council and the American Council of Learned Societies, which made it possible for him to prepare this essay. Of course, he alone is responsible for its content.

The Chinese Communist Party and the Anti-Japanese Movement in Manchuria: The Initial Stage

Chong-Sik Lee

I.

The Chinese Communist Party had argued for a long time that Manchuria was in effect a Japanese colony, and that the Kuomintang (KMT) and the Manchurian warlord Chang Hsueh-liang were tools of Japanese and other imperialists. Acting on these assumptions, the CCP leadership had ordered the party's Manchurian Provincial Committee to organize the workers and poor peasants as party recruits or members of party-controlled groups and to prepare them for leading positions in a bourgeois revolution. In this revolution the party in Manchuria would be fighting against the KMT, the Chang Hsueh-liang regime, the imperialists, the capitalists, the rural landlords, and the rich peasants.

The Japanese ultranationalists saw the situation in a different light. There was no doubt that the Japanese position in Manchuria was overwhelming, particularly in the economic sphere. But the political situation there and in China had been turning against Japanese interests since Japanese Kwantung Army officers masterminded the assassination of Chang Tso-lin in 1928. Chang Hsueh-liang was becoming increasingly nationalistic,[1] and the KMT government in Nanking was making demands concerning tariffs, unequal treaties, and other matters that were sure to cost Japan her special position in Manchuria which had been won in wars against China (1894–1895) and against Russia (1904–1905). Under the influence, if not the aegis, of the KMT, strong anti-Japanese sentiments had developed in China during the 1920s, and the boycott of Japanese goods was inflicting severe economic damage upon Japan. The KMT and the Chang Hsueh-liang regime were encouraging public demands for Chinese

143

ownership of the South Manchurian Railway, the return of the Kwantung Leased Territory to China, and an end to the privileges enjoyed by the Japanese. Hence, the ultranationalists, whose ranks included many young army officers, were demanding strong measures to turn the tide in favor of Japan. But the cabinet in Tokyo, unwilling to accommodate them, relied on conciliatory diplomacy toward China and other powers and was actively trying to reduce the size of the army and the navy. Meanwhile, beginning in 1930, the worldwide economic depression was severely affecting the shop-keepers, small businessmen, farmers, and workers in Japan—the classes from which most of the officers had emerged. To the ultranationalists, the conquest of Manchuria presented itself as a panacea: it would radically improve the political and economic position of Japan in Manchuria and consequently boost the ailing economy at home. A conquest undertaken without the prior consent of the cabinet would also alter the character of Japanese politics. The effeminate rule of the political parties must be brought to an end.[2]

On September 18, 1931, the Japanese Kwantung Army reported a mysterious explosion on the South Manchurian Railroad at Liutiaokou, near Mukden. Alleging that the explosion was the work of Chang Hsueh-liang forces in Mukden, the Kwantung Army Command began what it called a punitive or retaliatory action. In spite of the desperate plea of the KMT government for a settlement and attempts by the Tokyo government to localize the incident, Japanese troops occupied Mukden, Changchun, Yingkou, and Kirin within three days. On the third day, the Japanese "Korea Army" (Chōsengun) dispatched a brigade to assist the Kwantung Army. The cabinet in Tokyo acquiesced to the development in Manchuria, and the era of militarist expansion began. The incident had been staged by Kwantung Army officers.

Immediately after fomenting the Manchurian Incident and occupy-ing major cities, the Kwantung Army established a puppet government. At first, some important Chinese figures were induced or intimidated to declare their independence from the KMT government, which by virtue of Chang Hsueh-liang's declaration of allegiance in 1928, held claim to authority over Manchuria. On September 24, Yüan Chin-k'ai, the former adviser to Chang's Mukden government and an influential "elder states-man" of Manchuria, was made to organize the Mukden District Peace Preservation Committee, which in December became the Fengtien Provin-cial Government. On September 28, Hsi Hsia, acting governor of Kirin province and chief of staff of the Kirin Army, was induced to declare the independence of that province. On September 29, Chang Ching-hui, governor of the Northern Manchuria Special District, proclaimed the formation of the Self-Rule Committee. On October 1, Chang Hai-p'eng, commander of the Taoliao Garrison at Taonan in western Manchuria, was induced to declare independence. These actions paved the way for the organization of the Northeastern Administrative Committee in February 1932, and the establishment of Manchukuo in March. Henry P'u-yi was brought to Changchun from Tientsin to be installed as "chief executive." He immediately handed a letter to the commander of the Kwantung Army requesting him to oversee the defense, maintain public security, and manage the railroads for the new state.[3] Two years later, on March 1, 1934, P'u-yi was enthroned as emperor and the title of the state was changed to Manchou Tikuo (Manchu Empire).

Although the Kwantung Army succeeded in bringing a number of important Chinese leaders into its fold, it encountered the determined resistance of many others. Even before the Manchurian Incident, the Chinese populace had been inflamed against the Japanese by the Wan-paoshan affair (July 1931). A dispute between the local Chinese and Korean farmers at Wanpaoshan had led to large-scale anti-Chinese riots in Korea, encouraged, it was suspected, by the Japanese government. The Chinese also regarded the increasingly numerous Korean immigrants in Manchuria as agents of Japanese imperialism.[4] Now the open aggression in Manchuria by the Japanese Army brought the anti-Japanese feelings among the Chinese to a higher intensity, presenting the CCP with new challenges and opportunities. In this essay we shall examine first the reaction of the Chinese populace to the Japanese takeover, and then the actions taken by the CCP. In view of the fact that the Japanese takeover of Manchuria in 1931 was only a harbinger of the full-scale attack against China in 1937, the lessons from Manchuria, even though they were mostly the lessons of failures, were of special value to the CCP in later years.

II.

Such Chinese leaders as Chiang Kai-shek and Chang Hsueh-liang are likely to have shared the anger of the masses against Japan, but they chose not to resist the Japanese with arms. Chiang Kai-shek evidently concluded that Japan possessed too mighty an army for divided and weakened China, and that priority must be given to unifying the country by bringing down the warlords in the north and annihilating the Communists in the hinterlands of Kiangsi. Chiang Kai-shek, in any event, adopted a policy of nonresistance and appealed to the League of Nations for sanctions against

Japan. The League in turn sent the Lytton Commission to investigate, and conducted deliberations on the problem, but was not able to offer any solutions. In the meantime, Chiang ordered Chang Hsueh-liang to follow his policy of nonresistance. Chiang Kai-shek, it should be noted, was the effective leader of the KMT forces. He was the chairman of the State Council and ex-officio president of the National government, chairman of the Standing Committee of the KMT Central Executive Committee, and commander in chief of the Nationalist armies.

Like his father before him, Chang Hsueh-liang was deeply involved in Chinese domestic politics. Since September 1930 he had been in Peking, and 120,000 of his best-equipped troops were in North China poised against the warlords of the northwest. He still had 50,000 troops in southern Manchuria, and commanded the allegiance of an additional 80,000 in Kirin (under his uncle, Chang Tso-hsiang) and 30,000 in Heilungkiang (under Chang's subordinate Wan Fu-lin).[5] Still, he ordered the troops under his direct command in Manchuria and northern China to follow Chiang's directive. He then established his advance headquarters and 30,000 men in Chinchou at the western end of Manchuria just outside the Great Wall. But when the Japanese Kwantung Army launched an attack against Chinchou (December 1931), Chang withdrew these troops and attempted no effective resistance, permitting the Japanese to take over the city.

While his troops were confined inside the Great Wall, Chang appears to have encouraged the spontaneous resistance movement that spread rapidly throughout Manchuria. Former military officers, police chiefs, bandits, and members of secret groups such as the Big Sword Society began to mobilize destitute farmers in their vicinity to offer resistance to the Japanese and their Chinese collaborators. In addition to general anger against the Japanese, economic conditions favored the leaders of the resistance movement. The worldwide depression was creating financial distress in Manchuria, and serious floods in northern Manchuria in 1932 added to the confusion created by the battles and movements of Japanese troops and Chinese fighters and made farming impossible in many areas.[6]

As of December 1931, Wang Yung-ch'ing, former commander of the 7th Cavalry Brigade of the Kirin Army, reportedly had mobilized 2000 volunteers in Lishu, north of Szepingkai; Ya Tung-yang, former chief of police in Chengchiatun, had 1600 men in Huaite; about 1000 defectors from Chang Hai-p'eng's Taonan forces were in Chengchiatun. Approximately 4000 volunteers were reported in Tungliao and 3000 others in Hsinmin. The bandit chieftains Lao Pei Feng ("Old Northern Wind," alias of Chiang Hai-fu) and Ta Ch'ing Shan ("Great Blue Mountain," alias of Hsiang Chung-i) wielded great strength in Haicheng and Taian prefectures in the lower reaches of the Liao River (near Yingkou), obstructing railroad transportation and harassing the Japanese. The latter alleged that both

Table 1

Strength of the Anti-Japanese Forces in Manchuria, June 1932

Region	Number of Men	Composition
Liaoning Province		
Liaohsi (west of the Liao River)	53,500	Former bandits such as Lao Pei Feng and volunteers such as Cheng Kuei-lin
Liaonan (south of the Liao)	27,700	Former bandits, police forces, and volunteers
Liaopeh (north of the Liao)	26,100	Mostly former bandits
Liaotung (east of the Liao)	15,100	Mostly former police forces, with 4000 former bandits, 3000 volunteers, and 1500 Korean independence fighters
Total	122,400	
Heilungkiang Province	69,500	50,000 under Ma Chan-shan, 10,000 under Su Ping-wen, 8500 volunteers, and 1000 former bandits
Kirin Province	107,000	All under former military leaders
Grand Total	298,900	

Source: "Kwangtung Fu-yuan Tung-pei I-yung-t'uan" [The Kwangtung Volunteers Corps to Aid the Northeast], *Tung-pei chin-ch'ing pao-kao* [Report on the recent conditions in the Northeast], (n.p., 1932), pp. 20–26.

Jehol, not included in the Three Northeastern Provinces, had an additional 29,700 dissidents. The total including Jehol would be 328,600.

Table 2

Social Composition of Anti-Japanese Fighters in Manchuria, 1932 (in percentages)

	She I-tse	Lei Ting
Bankrupt and unemployed farmers	50	50–60
Former military personnel	25	50
Former bandits	20	30–40
Intelligentsia	5	4–5
Workers		6
	100	140–161

Sources: She I-tse, ed., *Tung-pei shih-k'uang yü ti-k'ang* [The loss of the Northeast and resistance] (Shanghai [?], 1932), p. 245; Lei Ting, *Tung-pei i-yung-chün shih-hua* [Historical account of the Northeastern Volunteers' Army] (Shanghai, 1932), p. 22. The date of publication of the latter work is obviously wrong because the book covers events up to 1936. There apparently is an overlap in Lei Ting's categories.

these bandits were "bought off" by Chang Hsueh-liang, but they undoubtedly were patriotic heroes in Chinese eyes.[7] In June 1932, Teng T'ieh-mei, former chief of police in Fengcheng prefecture, declared his resolve to counter the Japanese and raised 15,000 men. Chang Hsueh-liang appointed him commander of the 25th Route Army of the Northeastern People's National Salvation Self-Defense Army (Tung-pei Min-chung Chiu-kuo Tzu-wei-chün). His forces and those under Liu Ching-wen, former governor of Hsiuyen prefecture, commanding the 56th Route Army, and Li Tzu-jung, commanding the 35th Route Army, posed a considerable threat to the Japanese operations. They reportedly received weapons and ammunition from Chang Hsueh-liang by waterway and maintained active contacts with the Big Sword Society and the Red Spear Society (Hung-ch'iang-hui).[8] Such major cities as Mukden and Fushun were not immune from Chinese attacks. In August 1932 some 1000 "bandits" attacked the Mukden airfield and destroyed all the airplanes on the ground. In September, 1000 Big Sword Society members attacked the Fushun mines and created havoc.[9] Security of southern Manchuria was to require considerable effort on the part of the Japanese.

Nor was the situation in northern Manchuria placid. When Hsi Hsia, a Manchurian bannerman (ch'i-jen) and graduate of the Japanese Military Academy, willingly allowed the Kwantung Army to occupy Kirin and placed the province under Japanese control, his actions were opposed by Chang Tso-hsiang, then in Yingkou, and by many of Chang's subordinates. The Kirin provincial army was almost evenly split, the anti-Japanese forces being led by such prominent figures as Li Tu, commander of the 24th Infantry Brigade and defense commissioner (chen-shou-shih) of Ilan; Feng Chan-hai, head of the governor's guard unit; Su Ping-wen, commander of the 2d Infantry Brigade in Hulan; and Ting Ch'ao, commander of the 28th Brigade and of the Chinese Eastern Railway Guard Unit. The 1st, 25th, and 26th Infantry brigades as well as the 7th Cavalry Brigade also rose against Hsi Hsia. In Heilungkiang province, Wu Sung-lin, the commander of the 1st Cavalry Brigade, fought the Japanese. After some vacillation, Ma Chan-shan, commander of the 3d Infantry Brigade in Heiho, rose against the Japanese too, boosting the morale of the anti-Japanese forces. A contemporary Chinese estimate of the strength of the anti-Japanese forces in different regions as of June 1932 is given in table 1.

The social composition of these forces as estimated by two contemporary Chinese sources is summarized in table 2. While the estimates vary, both sources agree that destitute farmers comprised the largest element in the anti-Japanese forces, followed by soldiers and officers (mostly from Kirin and Heilungkiang provinces in the north), and then by former bandits. The intelligentsia and workers obviously were few in number, and only Lei Ting, a Marxist author, included workers in his estimate.

The social composition of the forces determined their ability and resilience, the nature of the warfare, and the results. Naturally, those of military background were better equipped and trained, and were capable of engaging in large-scale battles against the enemy. The bandits, on the other hand, were skilled partisan fighters, seasoned by experience in harsh circumstances. The farmers had neither training nor experience in warfare, were poorly equipped, and in most cases were badly disciplined and commanded. Unless led by able and experienced men, they were bound to be less effective in inflicting damage on the enemy and more prone to attrition, particularly when confronted by a modern army. These various anti-Japanese fighters offered formidable resistance in the first year and a half of Japanese occupation. Chart 1 lists the principal encounters between the Japanese and the anti-Japanese forces.

The second item on the chart, the rebellion in Tungpientao, needs elaboration. The term "Tungpientao" (Eastern Border District) refers to the region of the Changpai Mountains along the Korean border, including Kuantien, Huanjen, Chian, Tunghua, Linchiang, and Changpai prefectures. The dense forests, the ravines and ridges, and the ever-present midges and gadflies of the region provide natural barriers against attacks.[10] Not surprisingly, soon after the Japanese began to take over Manchuria, anti-Japanese forces began to congregate in this region. Tungpientao thus became one of the most troublesome spots for the Japanese.

It should be added that T'ang Chü-wu, general commander of the Northeastern People's National Salvation Army, had been commander of the Kirin Army's 1st Regiment at Huanjen. Wang Feng-ke, the grand master (tsung-fa-shih) of the Big Sword Society, had been chief of police in Tunghua prefecture.[11] This was the group with which the Manchurian Provinces Committee of the CCP sought to establish working relations between 1927 and 1928, until it was prevented by the party leaders in Shanghai.

The case of Ma Chan-shan also merits attention. In October 1931 Ma was appointed by Governor Wan Fu-lin, then in North China, to command the entire provincial forces of Heilungkiang province. Ma was also appointed acting governor by the Chinese government. Because of his popularity in the area, the Japanese made every effort to enlist his support, appointing him defense minister in the Manchukuo cabinet. In February 1932 their hopes were raised when he participated in the meeting of the Japanese-sponsored Northeastern Political Affairs Committee (Tung-pei Cheng-wu Wei-yuan-hui) in Mukden. According to Yen Ying's detailed biography, Ma feigned collaboration to obtain badly needed food, weapons, and ammunition for his troops.[12]

In April, Ma raised the banner of resistance against Japan and began to fight the Kirin Army and the Kwantung Army, which had dispatched

Table 3

Appearances of the Anti-Japanese Forces in Manchuria, 1932–1934

Year	No. of times reported	Cumulative no. of resistants reported	Average no. of resistants per appearance
1932	3,816	3,774,184	989
1933	13,072	2,668,633	204
1934	13,395	900,204	67

Source: Manshūkoku-shi Hensan Kankōkai [The Society to Edit and Publish the History of Manchukuo], *Manshūkoku-shi* [History of Manchukuo] (Tokyo, 1971), 2 (Kaku-ron): 312.

Chart 1

Japanese Listing of Important Military Operations in Manchuria, March 1932–November 1933

Operation	Opposing Forces and Leaders	Strength of Opposing Force
Subjugation of anti-Kirin Army	Anti-Kirin Army: Li Tu Ting Ch'ao Ma Hsien-chang Li Cheng-sheng	20,000
First Tungpientao clearance	Northeastern People's National Salvation Army T'ang Chü-wu Big Sword Society Wang Feng-ke	20,000
Ma Chan-shan subjugation	1st Route Army Ma Chan-shan 2d Route Army Li Hai-ch'ing 3d Route Army Wu Sung-lin	Main Strength 6000 The Li forces 10,000
Li Hai-ch'ing subjugation	2d Route Army Ma Chan-shan Li Hai-ch'ing	10,000
Feng Chan-hai subjugation near Yushu	Feng Chan-hai Kung Chang-hsi	15,000
Subjugation of remnants of Li Hai-ch'ing	Remnants of Li force	2000
First Feng Chan-hai subjugation	Feng Chan-hai Kung Chang-hsi	15,000
Mongolian bandits subjugation	Hu Pao-shan Hai Pao-tou Li Pao-ting	2000

Attack of Tien Ch'en bandits	Tien Ch'en	3500
Second Feng Chan-hai subjugation	Feng Chan-hai Kung Chang-hsi	10,000

Su Ping-wen sub-jugation (Manchouli Incident)	Su Ping-wen army
	    Su Ping-wen
	    Chang Tien-chiu
		20,000

Second Tungpientao subjugation	Northeastern People's National Salvation Army: T'ang Chü-wu	20,000
Li Hai-ch'ing subjugation	Li Hai-ch'ing	3000
Kirin-Changchun-Hailung region subjugation	Shan Chiang-hao Tien Ch'en Sung Kuo-jung Hung troops	5000
Third Tungpientao subjugation	Bandits operating in Tungpientao	20,000
Jehol subjugation	T'ang Yu-lin Army Former Northeastern Army Regular Army of Republic of China National Salvation Army	130,000
Kirin province subjugation	Bandits in the entire province of Kirin	20,000

Operation Period	Note on Operation
March–June 1932	Manchukuo troops operating jointly with Japanese troops drove the anti-Kirin troops to the northern parts of Kirin province and secured control of the Sungari River and occupied Ilan.
May–June 1932	Former Tunghua regiment commander T'ang Chü-wu rebelled and surrounded the Japanese consulate at Tunghua. Japanese police forces advanced from two different routes and commenced the clearing of the Tungpientao region. The insurgent bandits being strong, the Fengtien Army met defeats at various points.
Late April–early July 1932	Ma ran away from Tsitsihar [Chichihaerh] on April 3, gathered his former troops, and opposed the Japanese and Manchukuo troops. Two detachments of the Heilungkiang Army attacked the Hailun district,

	the base of Ma's operation, and, cooperating with Japanese troops, routed his forces. Confusion was caused in many parts because the Heilungkiang Army constantly changed sides.
May 1932	Bandits under Li occupied Chaotung, in southern Heilungkiang, and Fuyu, in Kirin, and became very powerful. The Heilungkiang and Kirin armies attacked from three sides, with the participation of Japanese troops, and managed to disperse the enemy and regain the district.
June 20–25, 1932	To subjugate the 30,000 anti-Kirin troops gathered in the district south of Harbin, the Kirin Army under the command of Lieutenant Ogawa met bandits on its way to Ssuhocheng, after passing Yushu. In the whole day's battle both sides suffered much damage; the Manchukuo troops' casualties reached 150, including Lieutenant Ogawa. Enemy deaths reached about 1000.
Mid-July, 1932	Insurgents under Li ran away to the Lanshih district of Heilungkiang province, where they were attacked. 50 of Li's troops were killed and two leaders were arrested.
Late June– early July 1932	Manchukuo troops cooperating with Japanese troops cleared the districts of Shuangcheng, Acheng, Yushu, Wuchang, and Shulan of insurgents.
Late August 1932	Insurgents had occupied Tanyuhsiencheng and caused destruction in the districts along the Ssutao railway line. The Taoliao Army, with the cooperation of Japanese troops, attacked those insurgents and recovered Tanyuhsiencheng on November 1.
Late August 1932	The Tien Ch'en bandits surrounded Shuangyang-hsien-cheng for several days, and the troops and police of the district held their ground against them. One regiment of cavalry attacked the bandits, without developing a serious battle. The Tien Ch'en forces retreated.
September 2, 1932	Realizing that the Feng Chan-hai bandits were attempting to move to Jehol province, the Kirin Army in cooperation with Japanese troops surrounded the Kirin district, but the bandits ran away to Jehol via the Nungan district, along the North Manchurian Railway. Nungancheng was surrounded by the bandits, but the Liu cavalry brigade succeeded in protecting it.
September 30– December 6, 1932	Su Ping-wen rebelled and caused the Manchouli Incident. Cooperating with the operations of Japanese troops along the western line of the North Manchurian Railway, Manchukuo forces participated in battle in the Fulaerhchi district. The

	Hsingan Army joined with the Solun Detachment and, cooperating with the operations of Japanese detachments, advanced from Solun to Hailar. Su Ping-wen was defeated on December 5; he ran away to Soviet territory.
October 1932	Cooperating with Japanese troops, Manchukuo troops carried out a major subjugation activity in the Tungpientao district, and made T'ang Wu-chen and his 1000 subordinates surrender, while more than 270 were shot.
October 1932	Subjugation activity was carried on in Anta, Chaotung, and Chaochou against the Li bandits, who attempted to threaten the Japanese and Manchukuo troops from behind, in the southern part of Heilungkiang province, scheming together with Su Ping-wen. The Li bandits ran away to distant parts of Jehol province.
November 6– 20, 1932	To cooperate with the Japanese Independent Guard Corps in subjugating the bandits active in the triangular area formed by Kirin-Changchun-Hailung, Manchukuo troops were dispatched from the Fengtien and Kirin armies.
November 22– December 5, 1932	Small groups of bandits became active, taking advantage of the fact that military strength in southern Manchuria was weakened on account of the Su Ping-wen affair. They were attacked and 1799 bandits were deprived of their arms.
February 20– March 28, 1933	For subjugating Jehol Province, Manchukuo troops were divided into the Southern and Northern forces. Cooperating with Japanese troops, they advanced into Jehol and, fighting at various places for one month, drove out all rebels and pacified Jehol.
Mid-October –mid-November, 1933	Manchukuo troops cooperating with Japanese troops attacked bandits of Kirin province at various places. Particularly, the subjugations of the Suining, Pinkiang, and Kicha districts were successful. Tien Ch'en was killed, Sun Chao-yang was captured, and Pi Ching-shan was brought to surrender. Small groups of bandits were either scattered or annihilated.

Note: In this chart are given only the principal military operations participated in by the Manchukuo Army to the end of 1933. Operations for the subjugation of bandits by various troops besides those mentioned here were numerous. The figures given are very rough estimates.

Source: The chart and the note are reproduced with slight changes from Tō-a Keizai Chōsakyoku [East Asia Economic Investigation Bureau], *Manchukuo Year Book, 1934* (Tokyo, 1934), pp. 142–147. Such terms as "bandits" and "insurgents" were used in the original source.

two divisions to northern Manchuria. However, by the end of 1932 the Japanese had succeeded in defeating most of the principal forces opposing them.[13] The arrival of sixty-six anti-Japanese leaders and subordinates in Berlin on April 20, 1933, including Ma Chan-shan,[14] Li Tu, Su Ping-wen, Wang Te-lin,[15] and Chang Tien-chiu,[16] signaled the end of organized resistance in northern Manchuria. These men, who fled the battlefields for the Soviet Union between late 1932 and early 1933, were allowed to return to China Proper via Europe. The anti-Japanese struggle in Manchuria continued after the departure of the leaders, but the scale of the resistance forces became much smaller.

The intensity of the struggle can be seen from tables 3 and 4, which present statistics concerning the appearances of the anti-Japanese forces and the casualties suffered by them. While these statistics undoubtedly are neither complete nor accurate, they do indicate something of the intensity of the struggle.

Table 3 shows that the anti-Japanese operations in 1932 were mostly on a large scale, involving an average of nearly 1000 troops on each occasion of reported appearance. During the next two years the size of the groups became smaller, while the number of reported cases increased greatly. Moreover, as table 4 shows, casualties mounted steadily, indicating the determination of each side to destroy the other. According to a Japanese account, many of the captured anti-Japanese fighters were murdered at the

Table 4

Damages Suffered by the Anti-Japanese Forces in Manchuria, 1932–1934

Year	Killed	Wounded	Captured	Rifles captured	Ammunition captured (rounds)	Horses captured
1932	7591	5160	831	3642	8238	1558
1933	8728	2381	1461	5970	174,288	2731
1934	8909	4264	1435	3153	36,107	2889

Source: *Manshūkoku-shi*, 2:312.

discretion of the unit commanders.[17] If the losses on the Japanese side were heavy, proportional reprisals were inflicted on the captured. Captured troops and civilians as well were often murdered on suspicion of having contacts with the enemy. In some instances, according to the same account, the captured Chinese were murdered in the most gruesome manner, sometimes to "test the raw nerves of the new recruits" or simply to satisfy the whims of the soldiers.[18]

This was the background against which the CCP had to orient itself. Obviously the party leadership in Shanghai could not anticipate all the events, and sometimes events moved too swiftly for the party to react properly.[19] Even so, the Manchurian Incident and subsequent developments were of such momentous proportions that clearly delineated policies were required.

III.

The CCP leadership at this time was in disarray. The Fourth Plenum of the Central Committee, held in January 1931, finally repudiated the Li Li-shan line and removed Li from the position of leadership, but internecine struggles involving the twenty-eight "returned students" from the Soviet Union, who constituted the mainstream of leaders, and such veteran figures as Ho Meng-hsiung and Lo Chang-lung, among others, continued to plague the party.[20] To aggravate the problems, Ku Shun-chang, the head of the Secret Service of the Central Committee, who had overall control of the party's communications and traffic, was arrested in April by the KMT, to which he subsequently defected. Hsiang Chung-fa, secretary-general of the CCP, was arrested and executed by the KMT government in June, and the others were exposed to the constant danger of arrest. For the first time since its founding in 1921, the CCP found it necessary to abandon Shanghai as the party's headquarters. During August and September of 1931 many central leaders, including Chou En-lai, fled to Juichin, the seat of the Kiangsi soviet base under Chu Teh and Mao Tse-tung.[21] Other important figures had left earlier. Pavel Mif, the Comintern representative in China, and Ch'en Shao-yü (Wang Ming), Mif's protégé and the ringleader of the "returned students," went to Moscow soon after the Fourth Plenum.[22] Chang Kuo-t'ao, who returned to Shanghai from Moscow in late January and participated in important decisions of the party, left for the Oyuwan soviet in the Honan-Hupei border region in April. Only Chang Wen-t'ien and Ch'in Pang-hsien appear to have stayed in Shanghai, where they maintained the Provisional Central Political Bureau until 1933.[23] The twenty-four-year-old Ch'in (known in the party as Po Ku) headed the bureau.

In a consideration of the policies adopted by CCP leaders with respect to the Japanese conquest of Manchuria, it is essential to bear in mind the intensity of the bitterness between the KMT and the CCP at this time. After the split of the united front in 1927, the KMT government suppressed with extreme severity any manifestation of Communism in China. KMT authorities nearly succeeded in eradicating the Communist movement in the urban centers, and the CCP, in turn, all but gave up hope of organizing workers in the "white areas." Only the rural soviets in Kiangsi and a few other enclaves offered the CCP a ray of hope, and these areas were also under constant threat of a KMT attack. The idea of compromise, of course, did not exist. Since the KMT clearly had the upper hand, negotiations under such conditions would have meant a total surrender for the CCP.

It is indeed doubtful that the CCP leaders had had a chance at this time to reflect deeply on the momentous events in Manchuria. The new developments probably seemed to them simply to confirm their predictions, and if so, no change in the party policy would have been thought necessary. The more urgent problem for the central leadership was to consolidate the soviet regime in Kiangsi, on which the fate of the CCP depended, and to defend it against the onslaught of the KMT forces.

It is not surprising that the resolution of the party headquarters on September 22, 1931, simply parroted the line of policies that the CCP had been issuing for the previous few years. The resolution characterized the Manchurian Incident as a "product of the Japanese imperialists' positive colonial policy, an unabashed expression of the Japanese plan to seize all Manchuria and eastern Mongolia and by colonizing Manchuria to turn it into a military base for attack on the Soviet Union."[24] Also, "by relying on various strategically important points in Manchuria," they intended to "prepare for aggression against the Soviet Union, for imperialist plundering of markets, and for a robbers' war for colonies, as well as for direct military interference in the revolutionary war in China." Therefore, the CCP argued, the Manchurian Incident was the "beginning of the carving up of China by various imperialists for colonies, the prelude to the anti-Soviet war, and the first step in a new imperialist robbers' war."

In spite of this position, the CCP did not see fit to call for a united struggle of all anti-Japanese forces. The KMT was charged with failure to prevent the Japanese aggression in Manchuria and with actual participation in it. The resolution said:

> Unhindered execution of policy by Japan cannot but be attributed to the shameless surrender of the Kuomintang to imperialism and its sale of the national interest. The Kuomintang government has participated in the Japanese plan for the seizure of Manchuria beforehand and ordered its troops to surrender unconditionally to the enemy, permitting millions of working masses to suffer trampling, massacre, rape, and

fleecing by Japanese imperialists. Afterward, they lodged empty protests, carried out "calm" diplomacy, begged of the robbers' agency [the League of Nations], hoped that the United States would uphold equity, or wailed at memorial meetings. But in practice they tightened their cruel suppression of the masses' national awareness and anti-imperial struggles. The Kuomintang government's surrender to imperialism and the shameless sale of national interest has opened the way for the Japanese imperialists' colonial policy and armed seizure.

The Central Committee also harped on the theme that the imperialist attack was a prelude to war against the Soviet Union:

. . . Utilizing [the existing consensus among] various imperialist powers for the war against the Soviet Union and seizing the opportunity when [other] imperialist nations [were absorbed in other areas and hence] had no time to look after the situation in the East, Japan has seized Manchuria. This seizure and military action is a most unabashed prelude to the anti-Soviet war. Through seizure of various strategically important locations, dispatch of Japanese troops to northern Manchuria, seizure of the southern part of the Chinese Eastern Railway, and massacre of the railroad workers and employees, Japanese imperialism has everywhere indulged in provocative military adventures against the Soviet Union. The mad utterances of important Japanese military commanders against the Soviet Union, the British imperialists' decision to stop the exchange of cash for gold, and the activities of the German chief of staff tell us that preparation for the war against the Soviet Union has already been made.

What was to be done? The formula offered by the committee was more of the same policies the leadership had been exhorting the party branches to implement, namely, "to arm and protect the Soviet Union, to oppose the imperialist robbers' war; to oppose Japanese colonial butchery policy; to annihilate . . . the reactionary Kuomintang government; and to carry out anti-imperialist land reform, which will bring about complete emancipation of the nation, the proletariat, and the working masses."

Throughout the long and repetitious document, no precise formula for opposing the Japanese was offered. In fact, the resolution prescribed more anti-Kuomintang than anti-Japanese actions. The paragraph that dealt with anti-Japanese operations, for instance, allocated only two sentences to anti-Japanese operations and three to those against the KMT. The directive on the anti-Japanese movement simply stated:

Carry out a broad movement against Japanese imperialist brutality. Do not in the least be afraid of the nationalist passion of the masses; on the contrary, the national consciousness of the masses must be further awakened and led to anti-imperial struggles.

This was followed by a directive on the anti-KMT movement:

At the same time, steadfastly oppose all the militarist propaganda of the Kuomintang. Indicate to the broad masses that only by their own power can victory against imperialist aggression be attained and national emancipation obtained, only through the soviet regime can the imperialist regime be thoroughly opposed. Calculating the masses' enmity and passion, present slogans to arm the masses. Turn the armed mass organizations into guerrilla units and workers' self-defense units.

The Central Committee also ordered the party to intensify its activities among the KMT soldiers. It declared that the troops had long been subjected to the deceitful propaganda of their officers, and predicted that once they recognized the servility and shamelessness of the KMT, they were bound to be rebellious and angry. Provincial committees were directed to infiltrate large numbers of comrades into what was disparagingly called the "White Army," to ignite struggle among the soldiers and organize them for guerrilla warfare. This, according to the Central Committee, was "one of the ways to engage true support for the Soviet Union with arms and to turn the imperialist war into a domestic war." The resolution declared further that "only by overthrowing the Kuomintang government, which is that of the landlord-bourgeois class, can true revolutionary-national war be carried out." The anti-imperialist movement was to be expanded and intensified, but the more immediate objective was to fight the KMT. Thus the Central Committee declared that "without overthrowing the proprietorship of the landlords, imperialism cannot be fundamentally eliminated from the villages; without overthrowing imperialist rule, victory in land reform cannot be permanent."

The position of the central leaders influenced by the "returned students," in short, was that (1) the struggle against Japanese imperialism was only an aspect of the struggle against all imperialists; (2) the KMT was the puppet of imperialism and the overthrow of the KMT was a precondition for anti-Japanese and anti-imperialist struggle; and (3) the (Chinese) Soviet government and the Red Army were the basic leading forces of the national revolutionary war and only the workers and farmers constituted the revolutionary core. The national bourgeoisie was regarded in general as the enemy of the revolution.[25]

But what was the condition of the Manchurian Provincial Committee? How did it react to the momentous events and these instructions?

The Manchurian committee suffered a mass arrest in April 1930. In June 1931 the Chinese police again arrested some of the officers of the committee in Mukden and, according to a Japanese source, the committee's activities declined. The central leaders reportedly dispatched Chang Meng-kuan, who along with two survivors from the previous committee, Li Ch'eng-hsiang and Liu I-ch'eng, reconstructed the group.[26] According to the same source, Chang became the chairman, Li the head of the organization department, and Liu the head of the propaganda department.[27] At the headquarters in Mukden, committees were established to deal with specific targets: workers, "oppressed minority nationalities," the commercial district, and Japanese soldiers. By September the Manchurian committee had reestablished connections with the special committee for southern, northern, and eastern Manchuria, and for the Liaohsi (west of the Liao River) and Jehol regions.[28]

Details are not available, but the East Manchurian Special Committee

Table 5
Communist Strength in Chientao, June 1931

	Party Members	Youth Corps	Red Militia*	Anti-Imperial League or Farmers' Association	Total
East Manchurian Special Comm.	7 (5)	3			10 (5)
Yen-ho Prefectural Comm.	2	2			
Laotaokou Dist.	70 (1)	75	200	2,500	2,845 (1)
Weng-sheng-la-tzu Dist.	30	25	70	300	425
Shantaokou Dist.	40	130	150	2,400	2,720
Pingkiang Dist.	80	215	40	2,000 (6)	2,335 (6)
Lungching Dist.	13	15	35	117	180
Yenchi Dist.	45 (5)	80 (10)	300	800	1,225 (15)
Kaishantun Dist.	50	80	250	1,300	1,680
Ta-la-tzu Dist.	30	60	55	—	145
Wangtsing Prefectural Comm.	200	1,100	600	2,600	4,500
Hunchun Prefectural Comm.	20	50	30	50	150
Total	587 (11)	1,835 (10)	1,730	12,067 (6)	16,215 (27)

Note: Figures in parentheses indicate Chinese members; the remainder are Korean.
Source: Report, Consul-General Okada Kenichi to Foreign Minister Shidehara Kijurō, 2 June 1931, Gaimushō Archives, reel S374, file S9452-6, pp. 428–29.
*Red Militia refers to members of the party or its auxiliary organizations who were either armed or given military training.

still appeared to have the largest number of party members and followers because of the presence of Korean Communists in that area.[29] A report filed by the Japanese consul-general in Chientao on June 2, 1931, cited a total of nine CCP prefectural committees in Mengchiang, Omu, Changpai, Fusung, Yen-ho (Yenchi and Holung), Tunghua, Antu, Wangching, and Hunchun, and provided figures on membership in the party and auxiliary organizations (see table 5).

Because, as noted earlier, Chientao was a stronghold of the Korean nationalist and Communist movements, the CCP strength in these prefectures was atypical. It is evident that the Anti-Imperialist League and the Farmers' Associations enlisted substantial numbers of the Korean farmers in the region. Recruits from these organizations were highly important when the Communist movement entered the guerrilla phase later.[30]

As was to be expected, the Manchurian Provincial Committee and the subordinate organizations that had eluded the authorities promptly reacted against the Japanese invasion by distributing leaflets in which the Communist declarations and slogans were printed. Chart 2 summarizes these activities.

These leaflets, issued in the name of the CCP's Manchurian Committee, Northern Manchurian Special Committee, Eastern Manchurian Spe-

Chart 2

Declarations and Leaflets Issued by the
Communists in Manchuria after the Japanese Invasion, 1931

Date	Place	Organization	Groups Addressed or Theme of Material
Sept. 20	Mukden	MC/CCP-CYC	To the Korean workers, the farmers, students, and all working masses.
Sept. 21	Harbin	NMC/CCP	All citizens—arm and demonstrate
Sept. 23	Mukden	MC/CCP	To the Japanese soldiers
Sept. 23	Harbin	NMC/CCP	To the workers in Harbin
Sept. 23	Harbin	no org. indicated	Slogans for revolution
Sept. 25	Harbin	NMC/CCP	To the working masses in Harbin
Sept. 25	Mukden	Mukden Anti-Japanese Society	Destroy Kuomintang
Sept. 26	Harbin	Harbin Anti-Japanese Society	Citizens: Rise, Advance
Sept. 26	Harbin	NMC/CCP	Oppose Massacre of the Chinese masses
Sept. 30	Dairen	Dairen Branch, CCP	To the workers of Dairen
early Oct.	Mukden	MC/CYC	To the Chinese and Korean workers, farmers, soldiers
Oct. 10	Kirin	MC/CCP	To the Japanese soldiers
Oct. 27	Harbin	NMC/CCP	October Revolution Pictorial "Imperialism and the Soviet Red Army"
Oct. 27	Harbin	NMC/CYC	To the Young Students in Northern Manchuria
Oct. 28	Hailung	Hailung Prefectural Committee	To the soldiers in the Northeastern Army
Oct. 25	Harbin	NMC/CCP	To the soldiers on the 14th anniversary of the Soviet revolution
Nov. 7	Harbin	NMC/CCP	"Workers' Conditions" (October Revolution Pictorial)

Nov. 7	Mukden	Mukden Commercial District Committee	Commemorating the Russian Revolution and the establishment of the Chinese Soviet Republic
early Nov.	Dairen	Dairen Branch, CCP	To the Japanese Seamen
late Nov.	?	CCP	"To the People"—by the Chinese Soviet Government
December	?	MC/CCP-CYC	To the Kuomintang Soldiers

MC = Manchurian Committee; CCP = Chinese Communist Party; CYC = Communist Youth Corps; NMC = Northern Manchurian Special Committee.

The original source refers to Fuchiatien rather than Harbin in some entries. Fuchiatien is the Chinese section of Harbin.

Source: Compiled from Ōsaka Taishi Keizai Remmei, *Sa-Rempō to Shina Manshū no kyōsan undō* (Tokyo, 1934), pp. 578–84. Not all the materials noted in the source are listed above.

cial Committee, and other auxiliary organizations such as the anti-Japanese societies, seem to have been printed in considerable quantity at Mukden and transported to the areas where the party had branches. The Japanese consul-generals for Chientao (in Yenchi) and Chilin, and their branch consulates, collected some of these and sent copies to the Foreign Ministry in Tokyo.[31] The position taken by the Communists in Manchuria, therefore, can be easily determined.

In general, the Manchurian organizations simply reiterated the themes stressed by the central headquarters: Japanese imperialism must be opposed; the KMT must be destroyed; soviets must be established; the Soviet Union must be defended. The September 20 declaration of the Manchurian committee, addressed to the Korean workers, the farmers, students, and all working masses, urged them to rise:

Under the leadership of the Chinese Communist Party, in unison with the broad [masses of] worker-farmer brothers of China, directly participate in the great Chinese Soviet revolution. Destroy Kuomintang imperialism and win true liberation. The CCP's political platform on national self-determination will guarantee your equal political power after the success of the Chinese revolution. If you hesitate, only terror and massacre will come to you. Fight for the great historical task! Unite with the Chinese revolutionary worker-farmer brethren! Directly participate in the Chinese revolution! Oppose unemployment! Oppose the rise in price of rice! Do not pay tenant fees and taxes! Eat the grain of the landlords without payment! Demand refunds of students' dormitory fees! Oppose the Japanese imperialists' occupation of Manchuria through strikes! Oppose the [threatened] attack on the Soviet Union! Protect the Soviet Union with arms! Oppose the robbers' war of imperialists! Rise in guerrilla war! Execute land reform! Destroy the Kuomintang! Destroy Japanese imperialism and all imperialisms! Join the Boys' Vanguard Units and Children's Corps! Join the Anti-Imperialist League, Red Labor Unions, and Farmers' Associations![32]

The Communist Youth Corps' declaration of October particularly denounced the KMT warlords' alleged "massacre of the Korean masses" and decried the KMT's alleged policy of driving a wedge between the Korean and Chinese peoples. The leaflet issued by the Mukden Anti-Japanese Society held the KMT responsible for the suffering of the masses in Manchuria under imperialists and called on the people to destroy the KMT. The leaflet addressed to the KMT soldiers in December called for the soldiers to disobey their superiors' "order to disarm" (probably referring to the order not to fight the Japanese aggressors), to mutiny and kill the warlord generals, and to participate in the establishment of a soviet government. Policemen were urged to strike and stop being tools of the imperialist KMT. Slogans of the call for revolt were "Chinese Soldiers Rise in Unity!" "Oppose the Second World War!" "Oppose Japanese Imperialism!" "Oppose the Attack on the Soviet Union!"[33]

These materials are consistent with the Central Committee's resolution of September 22, though some were issued before that date. Faithfully reflecting the attitude of the central leaders, the Manchurian leadership focused primarily on fighting the KMT and protecting the Soviet Union. Although in its September 20 declaration the Manchurian committee analyzed the motives of the Japanese aggression in detail, it was not ready to call for concerted attack against Japan.

The Japanese action in Manchuria obviously required further strengthening of the leadership in Manchuria, and the Central Committee dispatched a party man of some prominence, Lo Teng-hsien. Lo, a hero of the Hong Kong strike of 1925 and the Canton uprising of 1927, was elected, according to some CCP accounts, a member of the Politburo of the Central Committee of the CCP at the Sixth Congress.[34] In January 1931, he was also appointed chairman of the All-China Federation of Labor. Evidently Lo was dispatched soon after the Manchurian Incident erupted because Feng Chung-yün, a party worker in Harbin during this period, says that Lo was in Harbin a few days after September 18. Another party worker of this period, Hsueh Wen, recollected that Lo arrived in Harbin in early fall of that year.[35] It is curious that Lo Teng-hsien decided to work in Harbin even though the Manchurian Provincial Committee was still located in Mukden. It is possible that the leaders in Manchuria were making preparations to relocate the committee in Harbin. Lo, however, does not appear to have taken command of the Manchurian committee until later when some leaders were arrested.[36]

Be that as it may, someone at the central headquarters saw that a mistake was being committed in Manchuria although the leaders in Manchuria were in fact closely following the line established by the Central Committee. The November 20, 1931, issue of the party organ *Hung-ch'i chou-pao* carried an article by a Su Kwang entitled "The Central Tasks of the Manchurian Party in the Struggle against the Japanese Imperialists' Occupation of Manchuria."[37] Although the identity of Su Kwang has not been established, presumably he was in an authoritative position and obviously he had read all the pronouncements issued by the Manchurian committee and its subordinate organizations. Liu Shao-ch'i requested earlier, when he was in charge of the Manchurian committee, that the Central Committee publish its directives in *Hung-ch'i* because the Manchurian committee was too shorthanded to rewrite and transmit the directives to local organizations.

The principal criticism offered by Su Kwang was that the Manchurian committee failed to stress the "central task of fighting Japanese imperialism" in spite of the fact that previous instructions had defined the central task to be that of fighting the KMT. In his article (which bears the date of October 22), Su accused the committee of having improperly evaluated the heightening of anti-Japanese sentiment among the oppressed masses of the entire nation. While the committee properly attacked the KMT for having suppressed the anti-imperialist movement, it failed to observe the great discontent and resistance of the masses. Because the anti-Japanese movement among the masses was underevaluated, the committee failed to devise a single slogan on the central task of the moment, according to Su. Instead of presenting abstract slogans such as "Oppose the Imperialists' Occupation of Manchuria through Strikes," "Drive out the Army and Navy of the Japanese and All Other Imperialists," or "Establish an All-Nation Soviet Regime," the committee "must properly grasp the central point and call on the masses in Manchuria to arm themselves, drive out Japanese imperialism, and establish their own government." Although the committee was correct in presenting numerous "partial demands" of the masses, such as opposing unemployment, it was failing to lead them from the struggle for partial demands to the struggle for taking over weapons and establishing a soviet regime. Also, the vague call for opposition to Japanese imperialism, or connecting Japanese imperialism with other imperialisms in the same slogan, slighted the foremost task in Manchuria—to oppose Japan. Su Kwang then presented a number of specific slogans centered on the task of fighting against Japan.

While approving the Manchurian committee's propaganda work regarding the Chinese soviet, Su Kwang also called on the committee to intensify the uprisings and guerrilla wars of the masses so as to encircle and disturb the cities and key transportation points. The party should also lead the soldiers, who were engaged in movements against surrender or disarmament, into mutinies; the rebellious soldiers should be led to the villages with their rifles in order that they might join the farmers' war, implement land reform, and establish new soviet districts.

The Manchurian committee was also urged to mobilize workers, indigents, revolutionary students, and all the oppressed masses in the cities and towns of Manchuria, as well as the farmers in the suburbs, to form revolutionary anti-Japanese societies and organizations of their own, whether these were labor unions, farmers' associations, associations of the poor, or revolutionary students' associations. These revolutionary organizations then should form a representatives' congress to counter all the governmental organizations in Manchuria put up by Japanese imperialists. The oppressed masses should also organize their own armed self-defense corps. The Manchurian committee was warned, however, that the landlords, bourgeoisie, and any persons who had surrendered to imperialism should never be allowed to join any of the revolutionary organizations or the representatives' congresses. These organizations should become a genuine agency of the masses, managing their own affairs, taking over the arms of the enemy, and establishing a soviet regime. Su Kwang expected the Japanese to prohibit these organizations, but he saw clear possibilities for them in areas where the Japanese had not yet entrenched themselves and where the old regime had lost all effective control. In areas under strong Japanese control, organizational movements should be conducted in secret. In northern Manchuria, which the Japanese had not yet occupied, a broad movement should be carried out to link the anti-Japanese movement with the struggle against the Chang Hsueh-liang regime.

Finally, Su Kwang directed the Manchurian committee to emphasize the unity of the oppressed masses of China and Korea—rather than simply call for the unity of the oppressed Chinese and Korean peoples—and make every effort to arouse the Japanese workers and the soldiers in Manchuria to overthrow Japanese imperialist rule.

It is likely that the cadres in Manchuria reacted to Su's article with enthusiasm. This was the first time the Manchurian committee had been told in unequivocal terms to fight the Japanese. Although Su still insisted on opposing the KMT, the Chang Hsueh-liang regime, the landlords, and the bourgeoisie, the emphasis was shifted from fighting the KMT or Chang Hsueh-liang forces in Manchuria to the struggle against the Japanese. Devoid of the heavy ideological overtones that characterized earlier directives, Su's article set forth strategies, tactics, and slogans that appealed predominantly to the anti-Japanese feelings among the masses in Manchuria. It should be recalled that the Central Committee's resolution of September 22 defined the historical task of the proletariat and the working masses in China as that of arming and protecting the Soviet Union, of opposing the "imperialist robbers' war," of opposing Japanese "colonial butchery policy," of annihilating the "reactionary KMT government," and of carrying out "anti-imperialist land reform," which would "bring about complete emancipation of the nation, the proletariat, and the working masses." In contrast to this were the slogans presented by Su Kwang:

> Workers, farmers, soldiers, and all oppressed people in Manchuria! Strike [in all lines of work and study] and resist the Japanese imperialists' occupation of Manchuria and the massacre of the masses!
>
> The masses! Arm yourselves and chase off Japanese imperialism! Drive out the Japanese army, navy and air force!

Confiscate all banks, factories, and enterprises of Japanese imperialism!

Cancel all privileges of Japanese imperialism in China! Recover the concessions and leased territories in China granted to Japanese imperialism!

Oppose the League of Nations that carves up the weaker peoples!

Oppose the American and all other imperialisms that engage in stealing at a fire!

Never recognize secret treaties concluded between the KMT and Japan!

The masses in Manchuria! Rise on your own and restore the friendship with the Soviet Union!

The oppressed masses of China, Japan and Korea! Rise in unison and overthrow the direct rule of Manchuria by Japan!

Do not recognize the new tool of Japanese imperialism in Manchuria—the "independent government in Manchuria"!

The KMT government that sold out Manchuria is no longer wanted. Establish a [soviet] government that represents the workers, farmers, soldiers, and all oppressed people in Manchuria!

Except for three slogans dealing specifically with the Soviet Union and the KMT, all the others were straight anti-Japanese slogans that could be readily accepted by any of the anti-Japanese groups that were mushrooming all over Manchuria.[38]

The committee, however, was not in a position to put into action the new line of policy contained in Su Kwang's article. The Japanese takeover of Manchuria, while thrusting new responsibilities and challenges upon the committee, also heightened the risk of police suppression. The takeover of Mukden in September particularly made the Communist operation there more dangerous. While the Chang Hsueh-liang regime was neither less severe nor less efficient in its pursuit of Communists (local authorities in other areas, of course, were another matter), the presence of different authorities with different jurisdictions (the Japanese police in the South Manchurian Railway zone and the Chinese police in the Chinese section of the city) had offered distinct advantages to the Communists. There had been the usual jurisdictional rivalries and lack of cooperation and coordination.[39] These propensities naturally became intensified when anti-Japanese sentiment among the Chinese became more pronounced. Now the Japanese gendarmes appear to have arrested some of the Communist leaders in Mukden, Dairen, and Fushun.[40] Another roundup, on November 21, netted Chang Meng-kuan, Liu I-ch'eng, and Huang Yun-teng, the principal leaders of the Manchurian committee.[41] The committee, therefore, decided to move to safer ground in Harbin, which was still in turmoil. The Japanese were able to dispatch a division of their forces to Harbin only in February 1932, and even after that, until the summer of that year, various forces vied for control of the city and vicinity.[42]

Before moving to Harbin, the Manchurian committee in December 1931 directed the Northern Manchurian Special Committee to establish a soviet district in Tu-mu-ho, Hulin prefecture, near the Russo-Manchurian border, and relocated the special committee officers there. The preparations being completed, the Manchurian committees of the CCP and the CYC were moved to Harbin. The Harbin City Committee, fourteen prefectural committees, and twelve branches that had been under the special committee were now placed directly under the Manchurian committee headed by Lo Teng-hsien,[43] thus in effect abolishing the special committee. In addition to the two other special committees—those for southern Manchuria (in Huang-ku-tun near Mukden) and eastern Manchuria (near Yenchi)—a new committee was created in Liaohsi (west of the Liao River) in Taian in January 1932. The city committee in Dairen was still operating.[44]

The relocating of the committee headquarters and minor reorganization in the party structure do not appear to have cured the problems that the Manchurian Provincial Committee faced. Further reorganizations between March and July 1932 suggest that the committee was struggling with some internal problems. According to one source, an inspector from the center arrived in Manchuria in March and reestablished the Northern Manchurian Special Committee. Then, according to the same source, the party suffered a "major blow" from the Japanese Army. Presumably another round of arrests took place. Meanwhile, the inspector discovered many "anti-party and impure elements" among the party ranks and judged that party activities in Manchuria were in error in many aspects. Party work, therefore, was held in abeyance.[45] The party in Manchuria was obviously due for a purge and reorganization.

Thus response by the Manchurian committee to such a momentous event as the open aggression by Japan and the mounting resistance movement in wide segments of society was almost nonexistent. Until early 1932, the CCP played virtually no role in the spontaneous rise of anti-Japanese struggles. While various agencies of the CCP distributed declarations and slogans against the Japanese, the efforts of the CCP were of little consequence. Instead of arousing, organizing, and leading the masses, the CCP cadres in Manchuria dealt mainly with managing their own survival, moving the regional headquarters from Mukden to Harbin, and shuffling the organizational tables of the various agencies under their jurisdiction. Indeed, one wonders how the Communist cadres managed to exist under such conditions.

Of course, the CCP leaders advanced their own explanations for this deplorable situation and presented their versions of corrective measures. As is true in most such cases, the central leaders blamed the front-line cadres rather than defects in the strategies that they had themselves advocated. The Manchurian Provincial Committee thus failed to move beyond the stage of conspiratorial coteries not simply because of the shortcomings of the front-line cadres but primarily because of weaknesses in the party strategies. The CCP's urban-centered, anti-KMT and putschist strategies alienated virtually every class of Chinese society except perhaps those who were totally uninterested in political rhetoric of any type. The hope of the

CCP lay precisely here, but more powerful inducements, arguments, and organizational skills were needed to break through the apathy among the "oppressed" classes. The central leaders had failed to provide these.

The reasons why the CCP leaders failed to come up with more realistic and effective strategies have been forcefully stated in Mao Tse-tung's postmortem analysis presented in 1945:

> Meanwhile, with the invasion of Japanese imperialists, begun on September 18, 1931, the movement for democracy and national independence throughout the country reached a new climax. *The new Central Committee from the very beginning made a completely mistaken appraisal of the new situation arising out of these events. It exaggerated the crisis of the Kuomintang's rule and the growth of the revolutionary forces,* and, neglecting the sharpening of national contradictions between China and Japan and the demand of the intermediate classes since September 18, 1931, for resistance and democracy, *stressed that Japan and other imperialist powers would unanimously attack the Soviet Union and that the imperialist powers and reactionary cliques and even the intermediate groups in China would unanimously attack the Chinese revolutionary forces, and asserted that the intermediate groups were the most dangerous enemy of Chinese revolution.* Hence it insisted on "down with everything," in the belief that at that time a "life-and-death struggle between the revolution and counter-revolution forms the innermost centre of the political situation in China," and once again put forth a number of adventurist proposals, including the seizure of major cities by the Red Army to win victory first in one or several provinces and, in the White areas, the arming of workers and peasants everywhere and the declaration of a general strike in all enterprises.[46]

Considering the developments in Manchuria and China Proper between 1931 and 1945, it would be difficult to refute these criticisms. However, it should be added that the CCP Central Committee began to modify its Manchurian strategy in 1934, a year after the Comintern had done so. Thereafter the situation improved gradually for the Communists in Manchuria and by 1935 the CCP had become the predominant element in the anti-Japanese struggle there.

Notes

1. A compilation of anti-Japanese instructions by the Chang regime is in Kantō-chō, Keimukyoku [Bureau of Police Affairs, Kwantung Leased Territory], *Tōhoku kanken no hai-Nichi kunrei-shū* [Compendium of anti-Japanese instructions by northeastern authorities (January-September 1931)] (n.p., n.d., mimeographed, 123 leaves). The original is at the Library of Congress.

2. For detailed discussion of the complicated events, see Nihon Kokusai Seiji Gakkai [Japanese Association for the Study of International Relations], *Taiheiyō sensō e no michi* [The road to the Pacific War] (Tokyo, 1963), 1:327–440, hereafter cited as *TSM,* and Sadako N. Ogata, *Defiance in Manchuria: The Making of Japanese Foreign Policy, 1931–1932* (Berkeley, 1964). About the role of the ultranationalist Japanese in Manchuria, see Hirano Kenichirō, "The Movements and Attitudes of Japanese Residents in Manchuria, 1929–1931," in Nihon Kokusai Seiji Gakkai, *Kokusai Seiji* [International politics], no. 1, 1970, pp. 51–76.

3. See "Chronological Table on the Manchurian Incident," in *TSM,* 2:414. For details, see Sanbō Honbu [Army General Staff], *Manshū jihen-shi* [History of the Manchurian Incident], vol. 5, reprinted in Inaba Masao, Kobayashi Tatsuo, and Shimada Toshihiko, comps., *Gendaishi shiryō* [Documents on contemporary history] (Tokyo, 1965), 11:299–489. See pp. 410–18, 487–89 for negotiations with Chinese political figures in Manchuria.

4. In addition to various accounts of anti-Japanese actions described previously, see "Documents Relating to Anti-Japanese Feeling and Boycotts in Manchuria: Reports from [Japanese] Diplomatic Establishments, May 1928–July 1931," in Gaimushō Archives (Library of Congress microfilm), reel S470, and "Documents Relating to the Protection, Evacuation, and Escape of Japanese Residents, and to Injuries Suffered by Them," reels S473–476 (section on Manchuria). On the Wanpaoshan affair, see Whitewall Wang, *Wanpaoshan Incident and the Anti-Chinese Riots in Korea* (Nanking, n.d.).

5. See Ranseikai [Orchid Star Society], *Manshūkokugun* [The Manchukuo Army] (Tokyo, 1970), p. 3. Ranseikai is an association of former Manchukuo Army officers in Japan. This 952-page publication is a compendium of recollections and documents gathered by these men two decades after their return to Japan. It provides much information not available elsewhere.

6. Destitution among the farmers in the region west of the Liao River is described vividly in Kwangtung Fu-yuan Tung-pei I-yung-t'uan [The Kwangtung Volunteers Corps to Aid the Northeast], *Tung-pei chin-ch'ing pao-kao* [Report on recent conditions in the Northeast] (n.p., 1932), pp. 32–34. This volunteer group consisted of students from Kwangtung who went to join the anti-Japanese fighters in Manchuria.

7. Manshūkoku-shi Hensan Kankōkai [The Society to Edit and Publish the History of Manchukuo], *Manshūkoku-shi* [History of Manchukuo] (Tokyo, 1971), 2 (Kaku-ron): 316. This comprehensive two-volume work (880, 1291 pp.) is based on recollections and documents gathered by former officials of Manchukuo since their return to Japan. Some information dealing with security overlaps *Manshūkokugun*. A very valuable source of information.

8. *Manshūkoku-shi*, 2:316. The designation of "armies" in this period does not appear to have been based on any orderly system. Each leader was free to choose the name of his own group, and many different kinds of "armies" emerged in this period. In spite of the report cited above, Chang Hsueh-liang's role in the anti-Japanese struggle in Manchuria is not clear.

According to *Manshūkokugun* (p. 261), the Red Spear Society was not operating in Manchuria until early 1932, when the society dispatched 200 to 300 "priests" *(fa-shih)* from northern China. By the summer of the same year, however, the society was reported to have recruited 20,000 to 30,000 followers.

9. *Manshūkoku-shi*, 2:315. The Japanese had their "My Lai affair" at this time. A detachment from the Fushun garrison was sent in pursuit of the Big Sword Society troops and at Pingtingshan, which was suspected of harboring them, the lieutenant in charge ordered a massacre of the villagers. The Chinese war crimes court in Mukden determined on December 14, 1947, that Japanese troops had burned the village and slaughtered 2800 villagers. This incident received wide publicity in China at the time. The organ of the Northern Bureau of the CCP, *Pei-fang hung-ch'i* [Northern Red Flag], nos. 17–18, 11 December 1932, pp. 88, 109–10, cites *Shen pao*, 7 November, and presents almost identical information. The number of killed is reported to be 2500. In nearby Chienchinchai, another 1000 reportedly were massacred.

10. Henry Evan M. James, *The Long White Mountain* (London, 1888), pp. 230–76, gives a vivid account of the rigors of traveling in Tungpientao, having been attacked by millions of midges and gadflies that "bite like fiends." The Long White Mountain is a translation of Changpaishan. Also see Francis E. Younghusband, *The Heart of a Continent* (New York, 1896), pp. 12–13.

11. *Manshūkoku-shi*, 2:314; *Manshūkokugun*, p. 118. See also "Daitōkai-hi ni tsuite" [Concerning the Tataohui bandits], by the Staff Department (Sanbō-bu) of the Kwantung Army, October 1932, in the Archives of the Japanese Army and Navy (Library of Congress microfilm), reel 107, frames 16841–875.

12. Yen Ying, *Tung-pei I-yung-chün chan-shi* [Battle history of the Northeastern Volunteer Army] (Hong Kong, 1963), pp. 120–21. This is a well researched work, intended for the general reader; the author spent two years among the anti-Japanese fighters. While the numerous conversations quoted in the book are likely to be fictitious, many of the facts cited are accurate. According to Yen, who is very sympathetic to Ma Chan-shan, Ma joined a band of Robin Hood–type bandits early in life and eventually became a renowned bandit leader. He was appointed commander of a cavalry regiment by Wu Chün-sheng, the Kirin warlord who had the same background as Ma, and advanced rapidly in rank.

13. For very detailed accounts of the battles in northern Manchuria, see *Manshūkokugun*, pp. 85–116. A Chinese magazine called *Hei-pai pan-yüeh-kan* [Black and White Semi-Monthly], Shanghai (?), which appears to have been published by expatriates from Manchuria, devoted

much space to the developments in Manchuria after September 1931. Most of the issues (1932–1933) contain news about the anti-Japanese forces. For a good description and analysis of the anti-Japanese resistance, see Lei Ting, *Tung-pei i-yung-chün shih-hua* [Historical account of the Northeastern Volunteers' Army] (Shanghai, 1932), pp. 21–67.

14. In 1937, Ma was appointed deputy commander of the Second War Zone in the Kuomintang Army under Yen Hsi-shan. After 1945, he was in Manchuria as deputy commanding general of the Northeastern Security Command. Ma died in Peking in 1950. See Yen Ying, op. cit., p. 121. Another biography is available in Li Chih, *Tung-pei k'ang-pao lieh-chuan* [Biographies of the anti-tyranny figures of the Northeast] (Taichung, 1966), pp. 1–7.

15. Wang was a battalion commander in the 27th Brigade of the Kirin Army. According to a report from the Japanese consul-general in Chientao to Foreign Minister Shidehara, 21 May 1931, Wang had been in Yenchi for eighteen years and maintained amicable relations with the Japanese authorities there, particularly in controlling the Communists. He rebelled in February 1932 and engulfed the Chientao region in turmoil. By April his original force of 1200 rose to 5000. A Japanese report also related that he was negotiating on collaboration with the Manchurian Provincial Committee of the CCP. Gaimushō Archives, reel SP103, file SP205-5, frame 7795. Other on-the-spot reports about Wang Te-lin are in frames 7067, 7645, 7724–27, 7731–32, 7738–45 (particularly detailed), 7773, 7793–95. For a brief biography in Chinese, see Li Chih, op. cit., pp. 17–19.

16. Chang was the commander of the 1st Brigade of the Kirin Army, stationed at Cha-lan-tun.

17. *Manshūkokugun,* p. 292.

18. Ibid.

19. For example, *Pei-fang hung-ch'i,* no. 31, 11 March 1932, bitterly denounced Ma Chan-shan for having joined Chang Ching-hui, Hsi Hsia, and others in declaring the "independence of Manchuria and Mongolia." See Fan K'ang's article, "From Ma Chan-shan to Ts'ai T'ing-k'ai," pp. 38–39.

20. For a lively discussion of the factional struggles of this era, see Chang Kuo-t'ao, *The Rise of the Chinese Communist Party, 1928–1938,* vol. 2 of *Autobiography of Chang Kuo-t'ao* (Lawrence, Kansas, 1972), Chapter 3.

21. Ibid., p. 262. Kai-yu Hsu, *Chou En-lai: China's Gray Eminence* (New York, 1968), pp. 97–105, says Chou En-lai left for Kiangsi with his wife in September. Hsu cites Kung Ch'u, *Wo yü Hung-chün* [I and the Red Army] (Hong Kong, 1955), p. 256. Kung was active in the Kiangsi soviet at this time.

22. Chang Kuo-t'ao, op. cit., p. 145. James Pinckney Harrison, in his excellent work, *The Long March to Power: A History of the Chinese Communist Party, 1921–1972* (New York, 1972), says Ch'en Shao-yü left for Moscow in September (p. 218), but Chang Kuo-t'ao appears to have a vivid memory of the situation in Shanghai at this time.

23. Donald W. Klein and Anne B. Clark, *Biographic Dictionary of Chinese Communism 1921–1965* (Cambridge, Mass., 1971), 1:63–197. Chang Kuo-t'ao heard in the Oyuwan soviet that Ch'in Pang-hsien and Chang Wen-t'ien also fled to Juichin in August 1931, but Chang Wen-t'ien (Lo Fu) told Nym Wales in 1937 that he remained in Shanghai until 1933. See Wales, *Inside Red China* (New York, 1939), p. 228.

24. Text of the resolution is in *Hung-ch'i chou-pao,* no. 19, 18 October 1931, and Wang Chien-min, *Chung-kuo Kung-ch'an-tang shih-kao* [A draft history of the Chinese Communist Party] (Taipei, 1966), 3:12–16.

25. An excellent exposition of the anti-Japanese and anti-imperialist line of the CCP between 1931 and 1935 is in Ishikawa Tadao, *Chūgoku Kyōsantō-shi kenkyū* [A study of the history of the Chinese Communist Party] (Tokyo, 1959), Chapter 4.

26. Sasaki Hideo, "Manshūkoku o shisatsu shite" [Having inspected Manchukuo], in Chōsen Sōtokufu, Kōtō Hōin, Kenjikyoku [Prosecutor's Bureau, High Court, Government-General of Korea], *Shisō ihō* [Thought Report], no. 3, June 1935, pp. 112–72.

27. Ibid.

28. Ibid. The Liaohsi and Jehol special committees apparently were new creations; an account of the party organization, as of June 1930, mentions only the special committees for northern, southern, and eastern Manchuria. Chūō Keimu Tōsei Iinkai [Central Police Affairs Control Committee, Manchukuo], *Manshū ni okeru kyōsan undō no suii gaikyō* [Summary survey of the changes in the Communist movement in Manchuria] (n.p., 1937), p. 16.

29. As of 1931, there were 395,847 Koreans and 120,394 Chinese in the Chientao area. Because the area was separated from the other regions by mountains and forests, which made travel very arduous, and land was abundant elsewhere in Manchuria, relatively few Chinese had been attracted to it until the Kirin-Tunghua Railway was opened in 1929. Thus, in 1926, there were 356,016 Koreans and 86,347 Chinese. *Manshū kyōsanhi no kenkyū*, p. 544.

30. The consulate police raided the Yen-ho Prefectural Committee on May 28, 1931, and arrested 78 members, including Yu Chi-won (Liu Chih-yuan, if Chinese), the new head of the committee. As a result, some of the district committees disbanded, but the Communists soon began regrouping. The district committees in Pingkiang, Laotaokou, Ta-la-tzu, and Kaishan-tun were reported to have held meetings of branch chiefs and decided to mobilize new members of revolutionary character, "guiding the masses with earnestness instead of resorting to deceitful means as in the past," and collecting revolutionary funds on a large scale for the guerrilla units. Members of guerrilla units under the military departments in each district were reported to be staying in the forests during the day and with the local people at night. They were also said to be collecting funds from the rich through intimidation and threats. Gaimushō Archives, reel S374, file S9452-6, pp. 452–55.

31. Many leaflets listed in chart 2 are in Gaimushō Archives, reel S374, file S9452-6. The Manchurian committee's declaration of September 20 (see chart 6) is on pp. 506–13; To the Chinese and Korean Workers, Farmers, and Revolutionary Soldiers, pp. 513–15; Slogans of the Central Executive Committee of the CCP, dated October 1931, pp. 526–30; Appeal of the East Manchurian Committee on the anniversary of the October Revolution, pp. 542–48; Northern Manchurian Committee's September 25 declaration, pp. 492–95; Slogans for the same anniversary by the Panshih Special Committee, reel S382, file S9452-12, pp. 843–45; and Joint Declaration of the Chinese and Japanese Communist Parties to the Chinese and Japanese masses, n.d., reel S374, file S9452-7, pp. 9–33.

32. Ibid., reel S386, file S9452-6, pp. 506–12.

33. Ibid., pp. 578–84.

34. Feng Chung-yün, "Remembering Comrade Lo Teng-hsien," in Hua Ying-shen, ed., *Chung-kuo Kung-ch'an-tang lieh-shih-chuan* [Biographies of Chinese Communist Party martyrs] (Hong Kong, 1949), pp. 197–99; Klein and Clark, op. cit., 2:655, citing Wang Ming in *Lieh-shih chuan* [Biographies of martyrs] (Moscow [?], 1936), pp. 154–61. Chang Kuo-t'ao, op. cit., 2:82, says, on the other hand, that Lo was elected an alternate member of the Central Executive Committee at the Sixth Congress, but not to the Politburo.

35. See Feng Chung-yün, op. cit., and Hsueh Wen, op. cit.

36. Sasaki Hideo, op. cit. This Japanese source says that Chang Meng-kuan was in command of the Manchurian committee until his arrest in November.

37. *Hung-ch'i chou-pao,* no. 23, pp. 9–16. The Chinese term for the "Manchurian Party" was *Manchou tang-pu.*

38. There is, incidentally, a strong possibility that the article is the same as that Feng Chung-yün mentions in his recollections of Lo Teng-hsien. According to Feng (p. 198), Lo came back to Harbin from Mukden in the spring of 1932 with an issue of *Hung-ch'i chou-pao* which carried an article by Chou En-lai instructing the Manchurian committee to direct a national revolutionary war in Manchuria against the Japanese and drive them out. On the basis of this directive, according to Feng, Lo ordered the CCP members in Manchuria to go down to the villages and promote anti-Japanese guerrilla war. It is quite possible that the November 20, 1931, issue of *Hung-ch'i chou-pao* reached Manchuria only in the beginning of 1932 and that Lo had received this issue before he returned to Harbin. A check of later issues of *Hung-ch'i chou-pao* does not reveal any article of similar nature or that appears to have been written by Chou. There is a distinct possibility, therefore, that "Su Kwang" was an alias of Chou En-lai.

39. Some cooperation existed between the Japanese and the Chang Hsueh-liang regime, but some Japanese writers complained of the lack of it. See, for example, South Manchurian Railway Company, Research Section, General Affairs Department, *Manshū ni okeru sekka senden jijō gaiyō* [Summary of the condition of Communist propaganda in Manchuria] (Dairen, 1927), p. 8. When the Chinese police arrested the Communist leaders in April 1930, the Japanese were forced to wait for the release of details. See *Gaiji keisatsuhō* [External Police Report], no. 95, May–June 1930, p. 105.

40. Sasaki Hideo, op. cit., and *Suii gaikyō,* p. 39.

41. Ibid.

42. *Manshūkokugun,* pp. 86–103.

43. Sasaki Hideo, op. cit. The Japanese sources, incidentally, never cite Lo Teng-hsien by name or by his pseudonym, Ta P'ing. Evidently the true identity of the man who headed the operation in Manchuria at this time was not known to the Japanese. The locations of prefectural committees and branches (in actuality, cell-type organizations in Harbin) are recorded in *Suii gaikyō,* p. 39.

44. Ibid., p. 40.

45. Manshūkoku Kyōwakai [Concordia Association, Manchukuo], *Senmetsu kyōhi* [Annihilate Communist Bandits] (Changchun [?], 1933), p. 8.

46. "Resolution on Some Questions in the History of Our Party," adopted by the Enlarged Plenary Session of the Central Committee of the CCP, seventh since the sixth Congress, April 20, 1945, in *Selected Works of Mao Tse-tung* (London, 1956), 4:184 (emphasis added).

IV. "Experts and Meddlers"

8.

The so-called North China Autonomy Movement is the subject of the essay by B. Winston Kahn. In it we meet a Japanese military officer, Doihara Kenji, who was thought of in Japanese military and governmental circles as a "China expert" and whose *modus operandi* was in the style of military intelligence. Doihara promoted a scheme whereby Japan would cooperate with conservative (i.e., pro-Japanese) Chinese to counterbalance "radical" nationalist and Communist movements in the China of the mid-1930s.

Kahn, an assistant professor of history at Arizona State University, was born in Hsin-shih, Formosa, graduated from National Taiwan University, and did postgraduate work at the University of Minnesota and the University of Pennsylvania, where he completed his Ph.D. in international relations. His essay is based on his dissertation. He is also the author of "Formosan Nationalism: a Reappraisal," which appeared in Yung-hwan Jo, ed., *Taiwan's Future?* (1974).

The author wishes to thank the Arizona State University's Grants Committee for financial assistance during the summer of 1971.

Doihara Kenji and the North China Autonomy Movement, 1935–1936

B. Winston Kahn

I.

In tracing the turbulent course of Sino-Japanese relations in the 1930s, one is bound to discern the steady growth, almost in direct proportion to each other, of two diametrically opposed forces, i.e., Japanese militarism, which attempted to impose Japan's hegemony on China, and Chinese nationalism, which resolved to eradicate Japan's influence from Chinese soil. The ultimate clash of these two forces at the Marco Polo Bridge on July 7, 1937, was by no means coincidental; it should be understood in the context of Japan's historical relations with China, her recent growth as an empire, and China's painful but determined efforts to recover her sovereignty in modern times. Perhaps no event had aroused stronger Chinese nationalistic reaction in the mid-1930s than the so-called North China Autonomy Movement, a machination of the Japanese Army to detach the five North China provinces of Hopei, Chahar, Suiyuan, Shantung, and Shansi from the jurisdiction of the Nanking government by setting up an "autonomous government" under the nominal control of the North China leaders. At a time when China was torn by civil strife, with Chiang Kai-shek still preoccupied by his "extermination campaign" against the Communists in the wake of their successful Long March to the northwest, the foreign intrigue in North China did much to awaken the Chinese populace to the peril of national disintegration. This in turn brought the dissident Chinese together in a united front against the Japanese Army. The central figure in the Japanese maneuver was General Doihara Kenji,[1] then chief of the Kwantung Army's Mukden Special Service Organ, whose previous secret activities in Manchuria had won him the nickname of "Lawrence of Manchuria."[2]

As one of the Japanese Army's "old China hands," Doihara was seemingly well qualified to take charge of the scheme. His contact with China began in 1913, when, after graduation from the army staff college, he was sent to Peking by the general staff for a five-year period of study and residence.[3] Thereafter, until the Mukden incident, he served on a number of occasions as an adviser to various leaders of North China who were involved in the old-style warlord politics for control of China. Through these years of firsthand experience, he gained sufficient knowledge of China's political situation and established such a wide circle of acquaintance with many opportunistic leaders of North China that his services were essential when the Japanese Army decided in 1935 to renew its thrust into North China. This study makes a heretofore unattempted assessment of Doihara's role and motivations in the North China Autonomy Movement.

II.

The conclusion of the Tangku Truce between the Kwantung Army and the Chinese Army on May 31, 1933, marked the end of the first phase of Japanese expansion since the Mukden incident. It halted temporarily the Japanese southward advance into North China by creating a demilitarized zone south of the Great Wall. A period of relative calm ensued for about two years. Obviously, the Kwantung Army was still absorbed in the construction of its puppet regime, Manchukuo, and was not prepared to make the next move. In the meantime, Japan's new foreign minister, Hirota Kōki, intent on restoring friendly relations with China, undertook a new peace initiative. After he became foreign minister, succeeding Uchida Yasuya on September 14, 1933, Hirota had announced a principle of "peace and cooperation" as the cornerstone of his new foreign policy.[4] He was particularly concerned with Japan's interests in China and wanted to settle the disputes peacefully and also to normalize relations between the two countries. On October 20, Hirota managed to have the Five Ministers' Conference approve his new foreign policy; on the following day, it was endorsed officially by the Saitō cabinet.[5]

Hirota's foreign policy, however, was not devoid of contradictions. During the cabinet meeting of October 21, while arguing for the promotion of friendly relations with China, the Soviet Union, and the United States, he stressed the necessity for taking "a resolute attitude, thereby giving the Nanking government no alternative but to suspend its anti-Japanese policy and to suppress the anti-Japanese activities of its people." To contradict himself further, Hirota defined the goal of his foreign policy as the promotion of peace in East Asia through the creation of a triangular relationship of "mutual assistance and cooperation among Japan, Man-chukuo, and China,"[6] but with a clear implication that this must come under the leadership of Japan. The logical extension of this approach suggests that the realization of peace in East Asia would be possible only on Japan's terms. In other words, what Hirota sought in the end was *Pax Japonica*, the imposition of Japan's hegemony on East Asia.

Despite its inner contradictions, Hirota's foreign policy received generally favorable response from Chinese official circles.[7] In the face of mounting domestic economic crisis and potential Communist menace, the Nanking government under Chiang Kai-shek evidently decided to seek rapprochement with Japan so that urgent domestic problems could be settled. Nanking's conciliatory attitude also reflected the sentiment of the "pro-Japanese faction" which, headed by Foreign Minister Wang Ching-wei, still exercised considerable influence in foreign policy matters. In late 1933, Nanking began to make some friendly gestures toward Japan;[8] and by early 1935, the Sino-Japanese rapprochement had resulted in a series of negotiations held in both Nanking and Tokyo. On January 21 and 22, 1935, Suma Yakichirō, Japanese consul-general in Nanking, had a preliminary talk with Wang Ching-wei on problems of mutual concern; on January 30, a higher-level meeting took place between Ariyoshi Akira, Japanese minister to China, and Chiang Kai-shek.[9] Subsequently in Tokyo, Wang Ch'ung-hui, Chinese representative to the Permanent Court of Interna-tional Justice, called on Hirota on February 26, while en route to The Hague.[10] As the personal emissary of Chiang Kai-shek, Wang proposed to Hirota that the two countries restore friendly relations on the basis of the following three principles: (1) mutual respect for the other's territorial integrity and absolute independence; (2) genuine friendship to be demon-strated by reciprocal measures, such as China's suppression of anti-Japanese activities and Japan's cessation of assistance to "regional govern-ments" in China; (3) peaceful settlement of disputes through the normal channels of diplomacy.[11] Wang also expressed China's desire to exchange ambassadors with Japan as a first step toward the restoration of friendly relations.[12] In spite of the reasonableness of Wang's proposal, Hirota's response was rather ambivalent, agreeing in general but remaining non-committal on the specific issues.[13]

The ensuing months saw Nanking's growing interest in restoring friendly relations with Japan. Previously, on February 20, the Chinese authorities had already issued a nationwide order, prohibiting newspaper publication of anti-Japanese speeches; and on February 28, Shao Yüan-

ch'ung, propaganda minister of the Kuomintang who had been responsible
for directing anti-Japanese activities, was removed from his post and
replaced by Yeh Ch'u-ts'ang, former secretary-general of the party.[14] This
spirit of goodwill finally culminated in the announcement in Tokyo and
Nanking on May 18, 1935, of the exchange of ambassadors between the two
countries.

It was the intention of the Okada cabinet to encourage the development of Sino-Japanese friendship and, at the same time, to demonstrate to
the Chinese that Japan alone, as compared with the Western powers,
remained their real friend in East Asia. Ironically for Japan, this marked
the turning point in Sino-Japanese negotiations. Thereafter, the diplomatic
initiative shifted to China, and Japan's defensive stance resulted from the
contradictions inherent in Hirota's China policy. Having established
formal diplomatic relations, Nanking now insisted on settlement on its
terms of the basic issues confronting the two countries, namely, the Sino-
Japanese disputes over Manchuria. This became clear on September 7,
when Chiang Tso-pin, China's newly appointed minister to Japan, paid a
visit to Hirota. Chiang reiterated China's desire to settle pending issues
with Japan on the basis of the three principles proposed by Wang Ch'ung-
hui on February 26.[15]

In the face of China's diplomatic counteroffensive, Hirota remained
unwilling to accept Wang's three principles, for fear that this might
jeopardize Japan's position in China; at the same time he was unable to do
so, as he came under increasing pressure from the army. To take the
initiative away from China, on October 4 Hirota drafted his famous three
principles as the basis for Sino-Japanese negotiations: (1) China's cessation
of anti-Japanese activities, (2) China's de facto recognition of Manchukuo,
and (3) Sino-Japanese cooperation in suppressing Communist activities.[16]
Unfortunately, Hirota's three principles reflected the ideas of the army and
the navy as much as his own. In fact, he was forced to accept the demand for
stiff terms, especially by the army: it was obvious to him that the support of
the military was essential to the success of his policy.[17] Ironically, Hirota's
three principles satisfied neither the Nanking government nor the Japanese
Army; the field officers of the Kwantung Army and the Tientsin garrison
felt that the terms were too conciliatory to the Chinese and decided to
frustrate his peace efforts.[18] In the final analysis, Hirota's peace initiative
lacked both courage and imagination; it failed to restore friendly relations
with China and contributed only to increasing discontent in the Japanese
Army.

The army central authorities reckoned that peace with China at this
stage, when the tide of anti-Japanese sentiment was still running high, was
premature and could only endanger Japan's interests in China.[19] To offset
Hirota's peace efforts, War Minister Araki Sadao succeeded in having the

Saitō cabinet accept, on November 30, 1933, as an amendment to its decision of October 21, the army's view that Japan promote political decentralization in China, i.e., assist "regional governments" to counter anti-Japanese activities.[20] Araki's amendment, when carried out, would no doubt antagonize Nanking and thereby aggravate the already fragile Sino-Japanese relationship. On December 7, 1934, the succeeding Okada cabinet reaffirmed the army's position when it approved the memorandum "Taishi seisaku ni kansuru ken" [Matters concerning Japan's China policy][21] drafted by the section chiefs of the Ministries of War, Navy, and Foreign Affairs, but under the predominant influence of the army.

At the same time, the Kwantung Army began to promote "regional autonomy" in North China. It was necessary to strike a blow at Hirota's policy before any agreement could be reached between Tokyo and Nanking that might compromise the Kwantung Army's position in Manchuria. Second, creation of "autonomous governments" in North China would serve the purpose of "divide and rule," thereby ruining China's ability to put up unified resistance to Japanese expansion. Third, almost two years had elapsed since the conclusion of the Tangku Truce, and the Kwantung Army officers were anxious for a new venture, especially when there appeared to be no imminent danger of foreign intervention in support of China.

In February 1935, Doihara made a special trip to North China at the order of the general staff, to assess the situation there in the light of recent Sino-Japanese negotiations. His subsequent report to the Kwantung Army resulted in the formulation on March 30 of "Kantōgun taishi seisaku" [China policy of the Kwantung Army], which contained three recommendations: (1) to take a wait-and-see attitude toward the friendship policy of the Nanking government; (2) to further political and economic expansion into North China by establishing a regional government absolutely subordinate to Japan and by promoting the development of cotton and steel industries there; and (3) to support the "Southwest" clique against the Nanking government by providing military and economic assistance.[22]

The China policy of the Kwantung Army revealed doubt as to the sincerity of the Nanking government concerning Sino-Japanese friendship and showed that concealed behind the facade of regional autonomy was the economic motive to exploit the natural resources and manpower of North China, under the administration of a single regional government. This policy also marked the emergence of Doihara as indispensable to the execution of the Kwantung Army's scheme in North China, and laid down a plan for the Kwantung Army's eventual move into South China, to reduce the Nanking government to a mere regional government in the Yangtze Valley.

III.

After the formulation of its China policy, the Kwantung Army began seriously looking for a pretext to enter North China. Meanwhile, Doihara continued in his familiar post as chief of the Mukden Special Service Organ. The announcement of the exchange of ambassadors between Tokyo and Nanking on May 18 incensed the Kwantung Army officers, who saw in this a deliberate plan by Nanking to undermine by diplomatic means Japan's interests in China.[23] Encouraged next month by the success of the Tientsin garrison in getting General Ho Ying-ch'in, chairman of the Peking Military Council, to submit to a list of demands which had the effect of banishing the Nationalist Army and the Kuomintang organizations from the province of Hopei (the Ho–Umezu agreement), Doihara obtained similar concessions for the Kwantung Army in the neighboring province of Chahar.

Chahar was regarded by the Kwantung Army as strategic not only for the defense of Manchuria but also for its access to Inner Mongolia and North China. In late 1934, the situation in Chahar was aggravated by a series of incidents caused by the illegal entry of Japanese Army officers into the province. The occurrence of an episode on June 5, 1935, the so-called Second Changpei Incident, finally provided a pretext for the Kwantung Army to remove, once and for all, the Chinese forces from the province. On May 31, 1935, four Kwantung Army officers, stationed at the Abakar Special Service Organ, set out on a trip of unknown nature through Chahar province to its capital, Kalgan (Changchiakou). This party did not carry entry permits required by the Chinese authorities in Chahar. When they reached Changpei on June 5, they were detained by soldiers of General Sung Che-yüan, commander of the 29th Army and governor of the province. After overnight detention, they were released at the order of Sung with a warning that appropriate permits must be obtained in the future.

The incident itself was trivial indeed, especially in view of the illegality of the Japanese entry in the first place. However, the Kwantung Army was eager to seize any pretext to carry out its China policy of March 30. Since a group of Kwantung Army staff officers headed by Major General Itagaki Seishirō was also conspiring to support Prince Te's Inner Mongolia Autonomous Movement, control of Chahar province became imperative.[24] On June 17, General Minami Jirō, commander of the Kwantung Army, invited Colonel Sakai Takashi, chief of staff of the Tientsin garrison, Lieutenant Colonel Matsui Tadao, chief of the Kwantung Army's Special

Service Organ at Kalgan, and his own staff officers to a meeting in Hsinking (Changchun) to decide on measures to be taken against Sung.[25] The meeting resulted in the drafting (June 18) of "Sō Tetsugen ni taisuru kōshō yōryō" [Guideline for conducting negotiations with Sung Che-yüan]. Its provisions were as follows.

A. Objective:
   To expect absolute nondisturbance hereafter by Sung Che-yüan's army to our movements within Chahar province.

B. Demands:
   (a) Withdrawal of Sung Che-yüan's army from the regions east of the extension of the Tangku Truce line and north of the northern Great Wall line to the southwestern region.
   (b) Complete dissolution of such anti-Japanese organs as the Northeast Military Police, the Blue Shirts, the Kuomintang, etc.
   (c) Apology by Sung Che-yüan and punishment of the responsible persons without delay.
   (d) Fulfillment of items (a) and (b) within two weeks from the day of the presentation of the demands.

C. Negotiations:
   (a) To assign Major General Doihara, in close contact with the Tientsin garrison, etc., to open direct negotiations with Sung Che-yüan.
   (b) In order to expect speedy completion of the negotiation and to assure China's compliance [with our demands], part of the Kwantung Army forces shall proceed toward Jehol province.
   (c) Furthermore, to make efforts to prevent the influx of migrants from Shantung province [to Chahar province], even though this is not directly related to the anti-Japanese activities.[26]

This guideline was significant in three respects: the Kwantung Army was determined to extend its control to the province of Chahar; although Doihara was not present at the meeting, he was to be in charge of negotiations; the Kwantung Army was prepared to use the threat of force to support Doihara's assignment. Subsequent developments, however, proved that there was no need for coercion.

In order to alleviate the tension and also to assert its authority over the province of Chahar, the Nanking government quickly took control of the situation. On June 18, the same day that the Kwantung Army's guideline was drafted, the Chinese removed Sung Che-yüan from his posts and appointed General Ch'in Te-ch'un as acting governor of Chahar province and deputy commander of the 29th Army.[27] This gesture of conciliation, however, did not alter the attitude of the Kwantung Army. On June 23, Doihara called on Ch'in at his residence in Peking and presented to him a set of demands as specified in the Kwantung Army's guideline.[28] Ch'in in turn expressed regret for the recent incident and promised that a formal reply would be made upon receiving instructions from Nanking.[29] Dissatisfied with Ch'in's response, Doihara continued to press the local Chinese authorities. On June 25, he called on Wang K'o-min, acting chairman of

the Peking Political Readjustment Council (later known as the Peking
Political Council), to protest Nanking's procrastination.[30] Doihara's efforts
yielded speedy results; Wang promised to cable Nanking immediately. On
June 27, having received Nanking's approval, Ch'in visited the office of
Major Takahashi Tan in Peking and delivered a formal acceptance of
Doihara's demands.[31]

This so-called Ch'in–Doihara agreement, by expelling Sung Che-
yüan's forces and the Kuomintang affiliates fom the province of Chahar,
gave the Kwantung Army a foothold in North China. It was the work of
Doihara, who took command of the negotiations and exacted concessions
from the local Chinese authorities. After this initial success, Doihara turned
to other provinces of North China in the ensuing months to seek the
realization of the China policy of the Kwantung Army.

The conclusion of the Ho–Umezu and Ch'in–Doihara agreements
enabled the Japanese Army to proceed to the final stage of its scheme to
create an "autonomous government" in North China. This program was
hampered from the beginning, however, by mutual antagonism and rivalry
between the Tientsin garrison and the Kwantung Army. The scheme was
revealed to the public for the first time on September 24 by Lieutenant
General Tada Hayao, newly appointed commander of the Tientsin garrison. During a press conference with some twenty Japanese reporters
touring the Peking-Tientsin area, Tada made an unusually strong statement, asserting that Japan should disregard Nanking's pretentious gesture
of friendship and start to create "a paradise for coexistence and mutual
prosperity between the two countries" in North China. Tada added: "Such
a step will help the healthy growth of Manchukuo in the north and
demonstrate to that part of China lying to the south that a happy state of
mutual dependence for existence and the cooperation among Japan,
China, and Manchukuo with the Empire [Japan] as the center of gravity
can warrant peace in Eastern Asia."[32]

Tada's statement provoked such sharp criticism from abroad, especially from the Nanking government, that Foreign Minister Hirota was
prompted to dissociate himself from it and, in turn, to criticize the press for
misquoting Tada.[33] Meanwhile, unsolicited support for Tada came from
General Minami, who recognized the necessity for creating an "autonomous," pro-Japanese regime in North China as the best guarantee for the
security of Manchukuo. In line with the China policy of the Kwantung
Army, he ordered Doihara in late September to undertake this important
mission.[34] Minami's order, however, did not please Tada, who had been
privately contacting various North China leaders since he succeeded
General Umezu in August as commander of the Tientsin garrison. Tada
saw Doihara's coming to North China as an intrusion by the Kwantung
Army upon the "jurisdiction" of the Tientsin garrison.[35] He therefore urged
Minami not to send Doihara, insisting that an "autonomous government"

would soon be established in North China. Minami, nevertheless, decided to send Doihara to Tientsin, ostensibly to assist Tada and at the same time to act as liaison between the Kwantung Army and the Tientsin garrison.[36] Minami's decision reflected the growing uneasiness of the Kwantung Army toward Tada and its determination to dictate the outcome of the North China situation. Tada's displeasure with the Kwantung Army was to be manifested more and more in his personal bickering with Doihara in the months to come.

At this time, there were four dominant political figures in North China whose collaboration would be vital to the success of Doihara's mission: Sung Che-yüan, former governor of Chahar province and currently commander of the Chinese garrison forces in the Peking-Tientsin area; Yen Hsi-shan of Shansi, Han Fu-chü of Shantung, and Shang Chen of Hopei, governors of their respective provinces. Doihara left Mukden for Peking on September 25, where he conferred with Lieutenant Colonel Takahashi Tan, the Japanese military attaché. He flew to Taiyuan, where he tried to induce his old acquaintance, Yen Hsi-shan, to join the scheme.[37] Yen remained noncommittal, presumably fearing that any rash response to Doihara's overture might arouse strong nationalistic reaction and thereby jeopardize his position.

Doihara returned to Mukden on September 29, still hoping that Yen would eventually collaborate. After having reported to Minami, he told a group of reporters abut the Kwantung Army's plan to create an "autonomous government" in North China, involving the five provinces of Hopei, Chahar, Suiyuan, Shantung, and Shansi. "With regard to the North China situation," Doihara declared, "I express my satisfaction with the steps taken for the establishment of a fixed policy in that region. It is also necessary for the stabilization of North China that a joint self-administrative body be created in the five provinces of North China."[38] Doihara's remarks clarified Tada's previous statement by specifying the five provinces as the base on which "a paradise for coexistence and mutual prosperity between the two countries" would be created in North China. Just why these five provinces were chosen, Doihara did not explain; but in view of the situation of North China, it is not difficult to understand. Aside from their strategic importance to the security of Manchuria and their potential for Japan's economic exploitation, they constituted the core of North China previously administered by the Peking Political Readjustment Council, the branch office of the Nanking government founded after the Tangku Truce.

Following a brief period in Mukden, presumably for further instructions from Minami and the Kwantung Army general staff regarding the details of his mission, Doihara left for Tientsin around October 10, accompanied by his personal aide, Major Morota Moritoshi.[39] He quickly discovered the lack of progress of the "autonomous movement" undertaken by the Tientsin garrison. The conversation he had with Tada disappointed him. Tada told him that he had received separate assurances from Sung Che-yüan, Yen Hsi-shan, Han Fu-chü, and Shang Chen that they would participate in the formation of an "autonomous government," providing the other three would agree. Obviously Tada thought this was a definite sign of success. Doihara thought otherwise; he felt that these North China leaders were prone to give their consent whenever they were approached individually, but would afterwards often break their promise as a group. Consequently he decided to take a new approach.[40]

The essential problem that confronted Doihara was how to bring the North China leaders together for a common accord on the "autonomy" scheme. The regional differences among them and the mounting pressure by the Nanking government for noncollaboration with the Japanese made it a difficult task. Nevertheless, Doihara believed that if one leader could be persuaded, regional government on a limited scale could be established and serve as the basis for eventual control of the five provinces of North China.[41] Hence Doihara began to search for that leader. His early hope for Yen Hsi-shan's collaboration was soon shattered by Yen's rebuff. Having learned of Doihara's secret meeting with Yen, Chiang Kai-shek himself flew to Taiyuan in mid-October and tried to dissuade Yen from making any commitment to Doihara.[42] It was reported in the press that in return for Yen's pledged loyalty to the Nanking government, Chiang promised him extensive authority over those five provinces of North China plus a considerable amount of money for his military expenditures.[43] Evidently Chiang's efforts were successful; Yen subsequently left for Nanking, allegedly to attend the Sixth Plenary Session of the Kuomintang Central Executive Committee scheduled to open on November 1.[44]

With Yen's temporary absence from North China, followed by the departure of Shang Chen for Nanking presumably under the same pretext, the collaboration of Sung Che-yüan became imperative. His forces were in control of the vitally important Peking-Tientsin area.[45] Moreover, as a former subordinate of Feng Yü-hsiang, who fought against Chiang Kai-shek's forces in the late 1920s, Sung seemed to be the ideal man for Doihara to approach. It is significant to note, however, that after the Mukden incident Sung became increasingly anti-Japanese, as manifested by his support of Chang Hsueh-liang's forces against the Kwantung Army along the Great Wall.[46] Conceivably Doihara did not take Sung's defiance seriously, or he may have thought that Sung could be swayed.

Doihara could also approach Han Fu-chü, governor of Shantung province; but inasmuch as he was to carry out his mission from Tientsin, Han's participation did not appear urgent. Doihara also had his eye on Yin Ju-keng, a lesser but reliable figure. Yin was a graduate of Waseda University and currently administrative commissioner of the Luantung district of the demilitarized zone. Educated in Japan and married to a

Japanese woman, he was known for his pro-Japanese attitude. In fact, he had been secretly receiving assistance and guidance from the Kwantung Army for some time and had made a fortune by smuggling illegal Japanese goods through his district into North China, so his reliability was never doubted by the Kwantung Army.[47] In the meantime, Doihara decided to work on Sung, a dominant figure whose support was essential to the success of his mission.[48]

Around October 20, Doihara received a message from the Kwantung Army headquarters inquiring about the progress of his mission. He therefore sent Morota to explain the difficulty of forming a regional government with the participation of all the North China leaders. An alternate plan was to be suggested: Sung and Yin establish a government as the first step toward eventual inclusion of the other leaders.[49] Kwantung Army headquarters approved his plan and ordered him to accomplish the task by the middle of November,[50] as Morota reported near the end of October. Since the autonomy scheme was a joint project, Doihara sent Morota to brief Tada on the decision of the Kwantung Army.[51] This failed to satisfy Tada, for the obvious reason that he resented Doihara's meddling in his business. But Tada also disagreed with Doihara's plan for handling the North China leaders. The lack of coordination between them was to become apparent when Doihara decided to move to Peking, where he spent most of his time dealing with the North China leaders and reporting developments to the Kwantung Army headquarters through the office of the Japanese military attaché.[52]

With a promise of economic and military assistance, Doihara approached Sung, trying to cajole him into forming a regional government; but Sung was reluctant to commit himself in view of the volatile nature of the North China situation.[53] By the beginning of November, it became obvious to Doihara that unless certain coercive measures were taken, there was no possibility of Sung's collaboration.

Meanwhile, initiation of monetary reform by the Nanking government gave Doihara timely impetus to take strong measures.[54] In the fall of 1935, China's financial situation was in total disarray; the country had yet to recover from the impact of the world depression. To cope with this situation, T. V. Soong, board chairman of the Bank of China, and several other financial experts in the Nanking government concluded that a sweeping reform designed to introduce a managed paper currency, the yuan, was urgently needed. Such a reform would require considerable foreign assistance in terms of loans and technical advice. Since Great Britain still held very large interests in China and, moreover, was sympathetic to China's predicament, Nanking naturally turned to London for help. The British dispatched an economic advisory mission headed by Sir Frederick Leith-Ross. This mission arrived in China in late September and conferred with Chinese officials and businessmen. As a result, Nanking announced on November 3 the initiation of monetary reform designed to nationalize silver and regulate paper currency.

In the eyes of the Japanese Army, this reform, which must also have had political unification in mind, aimed more at eradicating Japanese influence from North China than solving the domestic economic crisis. Inasmuch as the reform was to be directed to T. V. Soong, a dominant member of the "pro-Western faction" within the Nanking government, and since it had the support of the British government, it could be taken as a sign of Nanking's increasingly pro-Western and anti-Japanese posture. Within a few days of Nanking's announcement, the Japanese military attachés in North China urged the North China leaders to boycott Nanking's monetary reform. By November 10, most of the North China leaders had issued restraining orders prohibiting the shipment of silver from their respective provinces to Nanking.[55]

The apparent vulnerability of the North China leaders was an encouragement to Doihara, who on November 12 visited Hsiao Chen-ying and Chen Chüeh-sheng, confidants of Sung, and pressed them to collaborate.[56] To support Doihara, Minami on the same day ordered the 1st Independent Mixed Brigade of the Kwantung Army, consisting of about 15,000 troops from infantry, tank, artillery, and engineer units, to concentrate at Shanhaikuan by November 15 in preparation for an advance into the Peking-Tientsin area.[57] Exactly what Doihara said to Hsiao and Chen is not clear, but his thoughts at this juncture were revealed on the following day during his meeting in Peking with Secretary Wakasugi Kaname of the Japanese embassy. According to Wakasugi's report to Foreign Minister Hirota,[58] Doihara appeared optimistic about the outcome of his dealings with the North China leaders. There was not the slightest possibility, he told Wakasugi, that Nanking would dispatch troops to suppress the autonomy movement, since it was still preoccupied with other urgent domestic problems. Doihara went on to explain the process by which the autonomous government would be created. He maintained that this should begin with the formation of the Anti-Communist Autonomous Committee in Hopei province by Sung Che-yüan and Shang Chen, gradually expanding its membership to include such notable figures from other provinces as Han Fu-chü, Wu P'ei-fu, Ts'ao K'un, Ts'ao Ju-lin, and even Yen Hsi-shan, though recently he had shown signs of leaning toward Nanking. Doihara added that unless certain formalities were followed to express the "will of the people," the movement could be suspected as the mere machination of the North China leaders.

Doihara's remarks threw some light on his dealings with Sung. Obviously Doihara wanted Sung to issue some sort of "autonomy manifesto" as soon as possible so that he would have the psychological edge vis-à-vis Nanking—to show that the people of North China were willing to support the scheme of the Japanese Army. Second, he still hoped to lure other North China leaders into participation. Yet, as Wakasugi had pointed out, even some of the Japanese military attachés in China were skeptical about the sincerity of collaboration on the part of Sung and other North China leaders.[59] Doihara's confidence seems misplaced, but perhaps he misjudged the thinking of the North China leaders, or perhaps he did not wish to admit the existence of a problem to a diplomatic official for fear that his efforts might be compromised by unfavorable publicity.

Doihara's apparent optimism soon proved to be ill-founded, in spite of support by Minami, who on November 16 decided to increase the pressure by ordering two squadrons each of air reconnaissance and heavy bombers to concentrate near the North China border.[60] Sung remained unwilling to issue the "autonomy manifesto" immediately, suggesting instead that it would be more appropriate to wait until after the Fifth Party Congress of the Kuomintang, scheduled to end on November 25.[61] Doihara decided to renew the threat of force made earlier by Minami, but in even stronger and more definitive terms. On November 18, he delivered a verbal "ultimatum" to Hsiao Chen-ying, announcing that if Sung and other North China leaders did not issue the "autonomy manifesto" by noon on November 20, the Kwantung Army would "come pouring through the Great Wall into North China" and take matters into their own hands.[62] Doihara must have known that, since many of the Kuomintang members attending the congress were beginning to intensify their appeals to the nation for unity and solidarity in the face of a national crisis,[63] it was likely that the North China leaders—most of whom were nominally members of the Kuomintang—might be wooed to pledge support of Nanking in consonance with the rising nationalism.

The events of the following days were less than encouraging to Doihara. Upon receiving Doihara's "ultimatum" through his confidant Hsiao, Sung cabled Nanking to explain that "under the Japanese pressure he could not help but declare autonomy between November 20 and 22."[64] By reporting directly to Nanking about the critical situation, Sung expected aid, however slight, in case he refused to yield to Doihara's demand. It is also possible that Sung was hoping for concessions from Nanking, which, lacking firm control over North China, would probably choose to give him more authority in exchange for his noncollaboration with Doihara. In either case, Sung would be able to enhance his position vis-à-vis Doihara and Nanking.

On November 19, Doihara kept in close touch with Hsiao, waiting for a formal reply from Sung. It was now obvious that Sung was trying to avoid direct contact with Doihara by having either Hsiao or Chen handle the actual negotiations. Conceivably, Sung did not want to commit himself while still awaiting Nanking's response. But, for Doihara, time was running out—he already had orders from the Kwantung Army headquarters to complete his mission by the middle of November. In an interview given to reporters in Peking that afternoon, Doihara, without any promise from Sung, stated that "the Chinese plans for the autonomy of North China" had been completed and that he expected a formal announcement very soon.[65] Doihara's presumptuous remark only hastened Nanking's promise of support to Sung and in the end killed whatever chance he might have had of making a deal with Sung. On the evening of November 19, Nanking's position became clear. In a telegram addressed to all the North China leaders, Chiang Kai-shek urged them to suspend negotiations with Doihara, since the problem of North China was being taken up in Nanking between the Chinese Foreign Ministry and the Japanese ambassador, Ariyoshi Akira.[66] Chiang's telegram echoed the growing anti-Japanese sentiment that prevailed among the members of the Fifth Party Congress. In his speech to the congress earlier that day, Chiang emphasized that China would not give up her hope for peace with Japan, but was determined to make whatever sacrifice necessary to preserve her territorial integrity if peace with Japan became impossible.[67]

Nanking's statement indicated to Doihara that since the five provinces of North China were an integral part of China, only Nanking had the authority to enter into agreements affecting their future, but with the Japanese government in Tokyo, not the army. In maintaining this posture, Nanking was also encouraged by the attempts of the Japanese War, Navy, and Foreign Ministries to control the situation from Tokyo. On November 18, all the major newspapers in Japan carried the story of Doihara's ultimatum and the expected issuance of an "autonomy manifesto" by the North China leaders on November 20.[68] Fearing international repercussions and the possible intervention by Nanking if the current North China situation remained uncontrolled, the three ministries held a joint consultation on the same day and decided on the following measures: (1) to postpone the date for issuing the autonomy manifesto until after Ariyoshi conferred with Chiang Kai-shek; (2) to take a gradual approach to the autonomy movement.[69] This decision indicated that Tokyo was still capable of exerting some pressure on the field officers. Although in the process the Foreign Ministry had to go along with the army's plan to issue the autonomy manifesto, it succeeded in winning the support of the War and Navy Ministries to try to postpone the date and to control the autonomy movement from the Japanese capital. On the other hand, the War Ministry, while it approved the policy of political decentralization of China, was concerned about the potentially dangerous situation in North China and opted to side with the Foreign Ministry. Subsequently, in a telegram transmitting the decision to the Kwantung Army and the Tientsin garrison, the vice-minister of war counseled them to exercise prudence and cautioned against independent action.[70]

These welcome developments were by no means ignored by the

Nanking authorities, who must have concluded, after Ariyoshi met with Chiang on November 19 for preliminary conversations, that Doihara's ultimatum lacked the official sanction of the Japanese government. Without that endorsement the Kwantung Army would be reluctant to back up Doihara's ultimatum.

Nanking's instructions brought the North China leaders together. Most of them were experienced in warlord politics, a common phenomenon during the early Republican era. They had fought not only against each other but also against Chiang Kai-shek for control of North China. Even after national unification by Chiang, they had remained centrifugal groups whose allegiance to Nanking was questionable. Now, however, in view of Nanking's firm opposition and the tide of anti-Japanese sentiment, it was obvious to the North China leaders that collaboration with Doihara would either result in Nanking's retaliation or incur the wrath of the Chinese people. It is also probable that they felt, by following Nanking's instructions, they could stay behind its protective shield while maneuvering themselves into a position of power. Consequently, they decided to ignore Doihara's ultimatum; when the deadline arrived at noon on November 20, they had not yet gathered in Peking to issue the autonomy manifesto. Shang Chen was allegedly ill, and Han Fu-chü simply decided to remain in Shantung, while Sung Che-yüan had secretly left for Tientsin.[71]

On the morning of November 20, Doihara left for Tientsin and there was no advance by the Kwantung Army into the Peking-Tientsin area. Tokyo's effort to control the situation had forestalled a showdown between the Kwantung Army and Nanking. Interviewed by reporters before his departure, Doihara admitted that it would be necessary to postpone the date for issuing the "autonomy manifesto" because of the failure of Han Fu-chü and Shang Chen to show up.[72] One wonders if he was misled by Sung, who had repeatedly avoided him and skillfully procrastinated. Perhaps Sung's reluctance to refuse him outright led him to misjudge the situation. Despite his reputation as one of the Japanese Army's "old China hands," Doihara failed to understand the mentality of the North China leaders, whose opportunistic yet realistic thinking had convinced them of the advantage of siding with Nanking.

Doihara's North China mission was temporarily halted despite his cajoling, pressure, and intimidation. The problem of mutual antagonism and jurisdictional rivalry between the Tientsin garrison and the Kwantung Army was aggravated by Doihara's predominant role. Officially, he was the liaison officer whose duty was to assist Tada in the autonomy scheme. But, in actuality, Doihara went his own way and after the middle of October he virtually took over the negotiations in Peking, leaving Tada as a bystander. His unscrupulous use of intimidation and, above all, his proclivity for self-assertion aroused such jealousy and resentment among the Tientsin garrison officers that they refused to give him the strong support that he needed so badly. Even Takahashi became openly critical of him. On the night of November 20, Takahashi made a remark to a United Press correspondent that "Doihara was in North China in a private capacity only, and not on any official mission."[73] On the following day, he bluntly said: "Major-General Doihara has no authority to negotiate with Chinese officials."[74] Clearly, Doihara would have to take alternative measures now in order to accomplish his mission.

IV.

Having been disappointed by Sung, Shang, and Han, Doihara turned to Yin Ju-keng. It was necessary for Doihara to show some progress in order to retain the confidence of the Kwantung Army; he also felt that Yin's participation, which he had never doubted, would encourage Sung to come forward in defiance of Nanking.[75]

Upon his arrival in Tientsin on November 20, Doihara immediately approached Yin. As expected, Yin's response was positive. On the night of November 23, Yin called commanders of the various units of the Peace Preservation Corps in the DMZ to a meeting in Tientsin, and prevailed upon them to issue an "autonomy manifesto" on November 25.[76] On the night of November 24, Yin met with Doihara in his hotel in Tientsin for final arrangements; after a jovial toast for success, he hastily returned to Tungchou, where he was scheduled to make his announcement the following day.[77] Doihara then went to the Tientsin garrison headquarters to inform Tada of the latest development. According to Doihara's aide, Tada obviously did not like Doihara's plan to use Yin alone and voiced his discontent with Doihara's arbitrary methods of handling such a sensitive matter; Doihara did not return to his hotel until late.[78]

On the evening of November 25, Yin declared autonomy for the demilitarized zone plus the three nearby prefectures of Yenching, Lungmen, and Chihcheng, to be administered by the East Hopei Anti-Communist Autonomous Council, consisting of nine members with Yin as chairman.[79] Doihara thus scored his first success with no difficulty. The term Anti-Communist served the purpose of the Japanese Army well, for it would distract the Chinese nationalists and could be used as a pretext to suppress the anti-Japanese movement of the Chinese people. After his announcement, Yin told reporters that he had sent a circular telegram to the North China leaders, urging them to join him. If they refused, he and his associates would carry on the autonomy movement and cooperate with the Japanese.[80]

The council was not so much an autonomous government as a puppet of the Japanese Army. Moreover, the formation of such a regime in the DMZ was a clear violation of the Tangku Truce (1933). The Nanking government, irritated by Yin's announcement, on the following day decided to abolish the Peking Military Council and transfer its functions to the Nanking Military Council; to appoint Ho Ying-ch'in resident representative of the Executive Yuan in Peking; to appoint Sung Che-yüan pacification commissioner of Hopei and Chahar provinces; and to order Yin's arrest.[81]

Nanking's measures were designed to ostracize Yin as a traitor while appeasing Sung and other North China leaders, and to centralize its own control over North China. Immediately after Yin's announcement, Shang Chen urged Sung to suppress the autonomy movement by force if necessary; simultaneously, he sent a circular dispatch to all the prefectural magistrates and commanders of the Peace Preservation Corps, directing them to boycott Yin's council.[82] Shang's reaction is understandable: these territories in the DMZ were still a part of Hopei province, of which he was governor. In response to Shang's urging, a number of prefectural magistrates withdrew from the council.[83] To Doihara's disappointment, Sung also refused to join the council and seemed content with his new post which gave him greater authority in the Nanking administration. Yin's announcement had touched off a wave of nationalistic protest which made it clear that any support given to Yin would be tantamount to political suicide. Earlier, on November 24, some twenty Chinese educational and cultural leaders in the Peking area met to pass a resolution opposing any movement designed to detach Chinese territory from the jurisdiction of Nanking. The day after Yin made his announcement, student organizations in the Peking-Tientsin area also issued a manifesto denouncing him.[84] Thus, Nanking's effort to ostracize Yin was a success. It remained to be seen, however, whether or not Nanking would be able to centralize its control over North China under favorable circumstances.

Meanwhile, the East Hopei Anti-Communist Autonomous Council lasted until December 25, when it was renamed the East Hopei Anti-Communist Autonomous Government.[85] Doihara once more turned to Sung, hoping to expand the autonomy movement to the provinces of Hopei and Chahar.

Doihara's obsession with an autonomous government centered on Sung continued to hinder his success. It is not clear what sort of measures Doihara had in mind to attain his goal. However, in his report to Foreign Minister Hirota on November 28, Secretary Mutō of the Japanese consulate in Peking observed that a group of army officers were planning to take punitive action against Sung in case he refused to declare autonomy. Mutō concluded that the situation in the Peking-Tientsin area was so tense that unexpected incidents might occur at any moment.[86] Mutō's report suggests that Doihara's measures perhaps fell short of a true verbal ultimatum.

Toward the end of November, Doihara's pressure on Sung began to yield some results. On the twenty-seventh, Sung told Doihara that he would cable Nanking in a few days to demand autonomy for North China and that he would resign as pacification commissioner of Hopei and Chahar provinces and would also cable Han and Shang, inviting their participation.[87] It is possible that Sung was only temporarily succumbing to the pressure while trying to alert the Chinese central authorities. On November 30, Sung sent the following telegram to Nanking:

> The situation here is becoming increasingly tense as various arguments in favor of autonomy or self-determination are being raised. It is difficult to maintain the situation by verbal promises as it is no longer possible to suppress these arguments. The situation is so hopeless that unless appropriate measures are taken to meet the demands of the people, it is feared there will be troubles both at home and abroad.[88]

Sung's telegram reflected some reluctance on his part to declare autonomy, but whether this was a subtle attempt to invite Nanking's intervention is a moot point. Nanking's response was prompt: a four-man delegation consisting of Ho Ying-ch'in as its head, Ch'en Yi, Hsiung Shih-hui, and Yin T'ung was to go to Peking to settle the problems of North China on the basis of the following principles: (1) Sino-Japanese cooperation in common defense against Communism; (2) appropriate modification of the monetary reform for application in North China; (3) harmonization of the economic relationship between North China and Manchuria; (4) considerable financial autonomy for North China; (5) local settlement of pending issues between China and foreign powers; and (6) opening of all public offices to men of ability for the realization of an ideal government.[89] Nanking's policy was conciliatory enough to alleviate the tension; from Doihara's point of view, it fell short of granting complete separation to North China.

The ensuing months witnessed maneuvers and countermaneuvers between the two parties in an effort to maximize their respective influence on the fate of North China. The delegation arrived in Peking on December 3 after Ho held preliminary talks with some of the North China leaders in Paoting.[90] Once in Peking, he conducted a series of discussions with Sung Che-yüan, Hsiao Chen-ying, and Ch'in Te-ch'un. It became clear to Ho that Sung was under tremendous pressure from Doihara to declare autonomy. To force his hand, Sung on December 5 resigned his post as pacification commissioner and temporarily dropped out of sight. Soon, Hsiao demanded autonomy, with a warning that the North China leaders would resign unless Nanking complied.[91]

During his meeting with Secretary Mutō on December 4, Doihara gave the following account:

> Since the beginning, Sung Che-yüan has been in favor of autonomy, but he wants to avoid entanglement with Nanking; and in order to make Nanking believe that

autonomy is inevitable, he is trying to impress Nanking that it is utterly impossible for him to suppress the demand for autonomy of North China. Concerning the problem arising from Ho Ying-ch'in's arrival in Peking, our policy is to have Sung appeal to him for understanding the difficulty of saving the situation, thereby making him give up all his hope in despair and recognize the absolute necessity for granting autonomy to Sung.

And when Mutō asked him about the rumor that the Tientsin garrison, convinced of Sung's lack of sincerity with respect to declaring "autonomy," was planning to take punitive action against Sung, Doihara replied:

We should not think that Sung will not declare autonomy. It is necessary to be patient in dealing with the Chinese and I think Sung will definitely carry it out. But in case he fails to do so, it will be necessary to give him considerable encouragement. I therefore intend to press for an immediate joint resignation by Sung's clique as a first step toward carrying out the autonomy plan announced by Sung. Should he refuse to declare autonomy no matter how we encourage him, then if he has deceived others, it would be necessary to take punitive action against him. But even so, there is no reason for military action. Instead, when that happens, it would be necessary to find some pretext for taking action against him personally.[92]

On December 5, the day Sung disappeared, Doihara again met with Mutō and told him privately: "Sung's departure from Peking marks the beginning of the so-called second stage of the autonomy movement which will be followed by a joint resignation by Sung's clique."[93] Doihara's candor is amazing in revealing the army's secrets to a diplomatic official, yet two generalizations may be derived from his account. First, it was Doihara who remained behind the scenes and directed Sung's resignation and subsequent threat of a joint resignation; and second, Doihara had yet to change his mind about Sung's sincerity. Even the Japanese diplomatic officials in China became concerned about Sung's reliability. Consul-General in Tientsin Kawagoe Shigeru reported to Hirota on December 5 that, according to the Chinese newspapers, Sung had said the day before that he would "absolutely obey the orders of Nanking" and would strive to serve in the post of pacification commissioner under the leadership of Ho. Kawagoe warned that if this was true, Ho's mission to Peking must have been a success, and it would be a great mistake to think that the situation in North China had been settled.[94] If that newspaper account was correct, why did Sung resign the following day? Obviously, Sung was under such pressure from Doihara and Ho that he had to do some double-dealing with them in order to survive. His dropping out of sight meant that he avoided making a commitment to either side.

On the basis of the "pro- and anti-autonomy" demonstrations,[95] Ho perceived a new crisis in North China. He realized that some form of autonomous status must be granted Sung's administration, if Nanking was to continue to exercise its jurisdiction over the area under his control. On the night of December 5, he met with Hsiao, who had temporarily assumed Sung's official duties, and they agreed early in the morning of December 6 to create the Hopei-Chahar Political Council with Sung as chairman.[96] This was duly reported to Sung, Doihara, and Tada by Hsiao; Ho also recommended that Nanking approve.[97]

Ho's recommendation exceeded his authority according to Nanking's six principles. But recognizing Ho's lack of maneuverability under the circumstances, Nanking promptly notified him on December 6 of its approval.[98] Problems remained, however, concerning the council's autonomy, its relationship with the Nanking government and with the Japanese Army. While Ho was willing to concede limited autonomy to the council, Doihara was insistent on broadening the scope of the council's activities to include such functions as personnel, military affairs, finance, and diplomacy.[99] Moreover, taking advantage of Nanking's conciliatory attitude, Doihara on December 7 urged Sung (who was still in "secret hiding") not to give up the principle of "North China autonomy for the people of North China,"[100] an indication that Doihara still intended to carry the autonomy movement for the rest of North China. Regarding the council's relationship with Nanking, the two sides remained firm in their respective positions. Since Ho was trying to keep the council under Nanking's jurisdiction, Doihara contended that the council should only recognize the "suzerainty" of China, leaving itself fully autonomous.[101] Ho's stand on the council's relationship with the Japanese Army was more flexible; he appeared to be yielding to Doihara's demand that Sung conclude an accord with him as a guarantee of the Japanese Army's role in the council's activities.[102] It was reported that Ho had decided to remain in Peking for a few days until the pact was signed.[103] Such an agreement would no doubt have legitimized Japanese control over the council and eventually led to its complete separation from Nanking, as Doihara would have liked, At this juncture the Nanking government suddenly decided to step in. On December 11, it appointed seventeen members to the council, with Sung as chairman and including such other familiar figures as Wan Fu-lin, Wang K'o-min, Hsiao Chen-ying, and Ch'in Te-ch'un.[104] Although the power of the council was not defined until the announcement of its provisional organization on January 17 of the following year, Nanking strongly indicated that it intended to maintain direct control. On December 18, the Hopei-Chahar Political Council was officially inaugurated in Peking in a simple ceremony attended by the council members and a small group of business leaders.[105]

Thus, Nanking was able to forestall conclusion of an agreement between Sung and Doihara and to make some progress in its own effort to control North China. Meanwhile, the development of the disagreement between Doihara and Tada received much publicity. On December 19, Reuters reported that Tada arrived in Peking to meet with Doihara in order to remove a misunderstanding that had arisen between them following the collapse of the "pro-autonomy" demonstrations in Tientsin. Doihara was said to have been displeased by Tada's failure to render assistance to the demonstrators; this had caused the general staff in Tokyo to dispatch Colonel Kita Seiichi, chief of the China Section, to North China to mediate their differences.[106] Though neither the Kwantung Army nor the Tientsin garrison confirmed this, subsequent developments only emphasized the significance of the Reuters report. In the months that followed, the North China autonomy movement was an anticlimax, characterized by increasing frustrations and antagonism between Doihara and Tada that resulted in the former's departure from North China.

V.

The creation of the East Hopei Anti-Communist Autonomous Council and the Hopei-Chahar Political Council was directly or indirectly the result of Doihara's efforts. Nevertheless, the two councils differed in their political orientation. While the former was a Japanese puppet over which Nanking had no effective control, the latter was a subsidiary organ of the Executive Yuan under Nanking. Doihara's task hereafter was to convert the Hopei-Chahar Political Council to the cause of autonomy and to seek its merger with the East Hopei Anti-Communist Autonomous Council. As he had reported to Minami, he hoped the Hopei-Chahar Political Council, though far from satisfactory, would eventually become the basis for an autonomous government of North China.[107] Nanking also wanted a merger of the two councils, to bring the East Hopei Anti-Communist Autonomous Council back to Nanking. The two irreconcilable motives nullified any possibility of the merger.

The question of abolishing the East Hopei Anti-Communist Autonomous Council was brought to Doihara by Ch'in Te-ch'un and Hsiao Chen-ying, members of the Hopei-Chahar Political Council, immediately after its formation on December 18. Doihara was reported to have expressed his willingness to discuss the matter with Yin provided that the Hopei-Chahar Political Council change its name to the Hopei-Chahar Anti-Communist Self-Governing Council, thus making it appear more autonomous of Nanking's jurisdiction.[108] But on the same day he bluntly told a foreign correspondent that Japan had no intention of dissolving the East Hopei Anti-Communist Autonomous Council, and that, on the contrary, he expected it to absorb the Hopei-Chahar Political Council eventually.[109] To strengthen his bargaining position, the East Hopei Anti-Communist Autonomous Council was renamed the East Hopei Anti-Communist Autonomous Government on December 25.

Meanwhile, the merger negotiations continued in Tientsin between Sung and Doihara, occasionally replaced by Tada in the latter's absence. It appeared that the two sides agreed in principle, but remained apart on the question of how the merger was to be carried out. As Doihara told reporters in Mukden on December 26, during his return trip to the Kwantung Army headquarters for consultation, he expected to see Yin's government merge with the Hopei-Chahar Political Council "as soon as both groups agree on the underlying spirit of autonomy for North China."[110] Later, Ch'in Te-ch'un, a council member and concurrently mayor of Peking, also announced agreement in principle but admitted that various problems needed to be ironed out.[111] As he told Mutō earlier, Doihara was demanding that the council appoint a number of Japanese advisers as a hedge against Nanking's control.[112] Doihara's wishful thinking even led him to urge Han Fu-chü and Yen Hsi-shan to join the council.[113] Faced with their pro-Nanking stance, Doihara began publicly questioning the feasibility of merger. He was quoted by Reuters as stating that the two regimes were "fundamentally opposed to each other," and that he did not think it possible for them to reach accord in the near future.[114]

The arbitrary manner in which Doihara conducted his negotiations naturally caused resentment among the Tientsin garrison officers, especially when the negotiations were not proceeding well. On February 18, the *Shanghai Evening Post* reported alleged dissensions between Doihara and Tada over the merger. The Chinese reports indicated that Tada was inclined to accept the "proposal with conditions more acceptable to Chinese authorities than those advanced by Major-General Doihara."[115] And on February 23 Tada told Chinese reporters in Peking that Doihara had no authority to represent the Kwantung Army in discussions concerning the Hopei-Chahar issues.[116] It is doubtful that Tada, a strong advocate of a hard-line policy toward Sung and other North China leaders, would suddenly be willing to compromise Japan's interests in North China, as reported in the Chinese press. The logical explanation seems to be that Tada's opposition to Doihara was motivated not so much by any real difference on policy matters as by his personal dissatisfaction with Doihara's involvement in North China affairs. Certainly in the eyes of the Tientsin garrison officers, Doihara was tampering with their business, and he should bear the blame for Japan's failure in North China.

In the spring of 1936, when the routine reshuffling of army personnel was to take place, the army central authorities in Tokyo made two major changes. Doihara was recalled to Tokyo to be attached to the headquarters of the 12th Division, and Minami was made a reserve general and likewise ordered to return to Tokyo.[117] It is interesting to note that Tada continued in his post as commander of the Tientsin garrison until May of that year. Although these transfers may seem to be merely routine, the army central authorities were obviously annoyed by the Kwantung Army's activities in

North China. On March 3, Doihara left Peking for Mukden, thus ending almost six months of personal adventure in North China. As he bade farewell to the Japanese reporters in Peking, Doihara said:

> Japan does not aim at making North China a second "Manchukuo," completely separated from Nanking, but is seeking to make the region an experimental ground for actual Sino-Japanese rapprochement by means of economic and military cooperation. . . . I am confident that the situation in North China, where all necessary fundamental measures have been taken, will soon see a decided improvement. . . . The Hopei-Chahar Political Council, however, will face serious difficulties, I am afraid, in reconciling the questions of the East-Chahar [sic] administration and the demands of the Nanking Government. However, I am sure that, with good faith and honesty, the authorities in power will be able to overcome all these obstacles in the realization of real Sino-Japanese cooperation in North China.[118]

Behind the façade of cautious optimism, one could sense Doihara's anxiety. It goes without saying that he was gravely concerned about Nanking's growing influence on the council members who were attempting to incorporate Yin's regime against the interest of the Japanese Army. He was also bitter about the newspapers' widespread criticism of his activities. Before his departure from Peking, he told a Reuters reporter that he was not a firebrand and not antiforeign, but was for peace and progress, and he hoped that people would understand this.[119] What could be more frustrating than to have realized that his self-righteous mission in North China was being "misunderstood" by the Chinese people? When he arrived at Dairen on March 8, en route to Tokyo, Doihara was less than optimistic. He told reporters that the two North China regimes would probably be united soon, "but it will take time before they are able to become a region contributing to peace in the Orient. It is a question of time, and it is no use rushing matters now."[120] Meanwhile, Doihara's departure gave new hope to the North China leaders. The *Shanghai Evening Post* reported on March 8 that the Chinese leaders were optimistic about the early abolition of the East Hopei Anti-Communist Autonomous Government, following preliminary negotiations with Tada.[121] It was obvious that the North China leaders felt they could deal better with the Tientsin garrison than with the powerful Kwantung Army.

VI.

The North China Autonomy Movement offers an interesting example of how the Kwantung Army undertook actions without formal approval from the army central authorities in Tokyo, even though they might have common goals, as in this particular case. Throughout the movement, the army central authorities remained bystanders, vacillating from mild encouragement to caution, but always submitting to the actions of the Kwantung Army.

Doihara played a major role in the overall movement, from the formulation of the China policy of the Kwantung Army on March 30, 1935, to his ultimate departure from North China on March 3, 1936. Although under the command of General Minami, he was the Kwantung Army's chief agent in North China, having a free hand in dealing with the North China leaders.

Writing in the March 1937 issue of *Bungei Shunjū*, Doihara explained his personal views of the autonomy scheme. He maintained that the army's actions in North China were motivated by the desire to create a model for regional Sino-Japanese cooperation which would eventually spread to the rest of China. Such cooperation, according to him, was indispensable in order to check Communist expansion and would ultimately become the cornerstone of peace in the Orient. "Without Japan, there could be no peace in the Orient," Doihara continued, but "without China, there could be no peace for Japan. Close cooperation with China would be the only basis for peace in the Orient."[122] These words explain Doihara's state of mind, his motivations, and his assessment of the situation, but they could not justify his actions. Beneath the surface of Sino-Japanese cooperation was his concept of Pan-Asianism—the idea of Japan's "mission" in Asia—which became a convenient justification for Japanese expansion in the decade before World War II. One wonders whether there was any difference between his concept of Pan-Asianism and Japan's desire to impose her hegemony on China.

Doihara's idea of Japan's "mission" in Asia, as expressed in terms of Pan-Asianism or its subtheme, anti-Communism, offered little attraction to the North China leaders when compared to the strong appeal of Chinese nationalism in the 1930s. A man like Sung Che-yüan, despite his warlord background from which he once challenged Nanking's authority, became acutely aware of rising anti-Japanese sentiment and growing hostility toward collaborators, and so in turn was drawn into the vortex of the national movement. This development was also facilitated by Nanking's successful attempt to counter Doihara's promise of assistance with an offer of a better position and more power in the regional government. Thus the conversion of the North China leaders to the cause of nationalism was the result of realistic as well as idealistic considerations of China's political situation. It is fair to say that Doihara was as much misled as double-crossed by Sung. Finally, his view that in a country as big as China, whose people were still living in a "semi-feudal" society, regional interests would prevail over national interest[123] proved to be anachronistic in an age of Chinese nationalism. Perhaps he would have had a better chance of success in the earlier "era of warlordism."

Both the East Hopei Anti-Communist Autonomous Government and the Hopei-Chahar Political Council were dissolved by the Japanese Army after the Marco Polo Bridge Incident of 1937 and were subsequently incorporated into the newly created Provisional Government of the Chinese Republic at Peking. If there was any lesson to be learned from the experience of the North China Autonomy Movement, it was the futility of "divide and rule" tactics in an ethnocentric society like China, where foreign interference in domestic affairs would only stimulate national unity. The events that followed, however, were to demonstrate that the Japanese Army was determined not to take heed of such lessons, as it continued to create puppet regimes in China.

Notes

1. His family name, "Doihara," could also be pronounced "Dohihara." When questioned about this during the Tokyo trial, Doihara replied: "My original name as written in the Chinese character was pronounced 'Doihara.' However, when I established my own home, in order to eliminate the confusion in the pronunciation, I decided to adopt the pronunciation of 'Dohihara' as characters written." Consequently, his name appeared as "Dohihara" in all the Tokyo trial records. See his interrogation in International Military Tribunal for the Far East, *Exhibit* No. 2190, 12 February 1946. Hereafter cited as IMTFE. This study, however, adopts the conventional pronunciation and consequently the spelling of "Doihara" as it has appeared in English newspapers and journals.

2. Doihara earned the nickname because his skill in instigating incidents and devising plots was comparable to that of T. E. Lawrence, the British intelligence officer during World War I who staged the famous "revolt in the desert" in Arabia against the Ottoman Empire.

3. For the chronological background of Doihara's early career in China, see Cabinet Secretariat Personnel File for Doihara Kenji, IMTFE, *Exhibit* No. 104; and Interrogation of Doihara Kenji, IMTFE, *Exhibit* No. 2190, 11, 13, 18 January and 2, 5, 12 February 1946.

4. Nihon Kokusai Seiji Gakkai [Japan Association for the Study of International Politics], *Taiheiyō sensō e no michi* [The road to the Pacific War], (Tokyo, 1963), 3:70. Hereafter cited as *TSM.*

5. Ibid., p. 70.

6. Ibid., p. 71.

7. Ibid., p. 72.

8. Ibid.

9. Ibid., pp. 85–86.

10. Ibid.

11. *Teikoku no taiShi seisaku kankei no ken* [Concerning the China policy of Japan], 4, "Hirota daijin O Chō-kei kaidan yōroku" [Digest of Foreign Minister Hirota's talk with Wang Ch'ung-hui], 26 February 1935, Gaimushō Archives, cited by James B. Crowley, *Japan's Quest for Autonomy* (Princeton, 1966), pp. 211–12.

12. Ibid.

13. Ibid.

14. *TSM*, 3:87.

15. Hata Ikuhiko, *Nit-chū sensōshi* [A history of the Sino-Japanese War] (Tokyo, 1961), p. 50.

16. Ibid., pp. 49–50.

17. Ibid., pp. 51–52.

18. Ibid.

19. Ibid., p. 11.

20. Crowley, op. cit., p. 194.

21. Inaba Masao, Kobayashi Tatsuo, and Shimada Toshihiko, comps., *Gendaishi shiryō* [Documents on contemporary history] (Tokyo, 1964), 8:22–24. Hereafter cited as *Gendaishi*.

22. *TSM*, 3:92–93. It was reported that in early January 1935, the staff officers of the Kwantung Army held a secret meeting in Dairen to map strategy for the Kwantung Army's advance into North China. To date, no detailed information is available regarding the meeting. See Shigemitsu Mamoru, *Gaikō kaisōroku* [Diplomatic memoirs] (Tokyo, 1953), p. 188; and *Ta Kung Pao*, 17 January 1935.

23. *TSM*, 3:91.

24. Ibid., pp. 114–15.

25. Ibid., pp. 116–17.

26. Telegram from Chief of Staff of Kwantung Army Nishio Juzō to Vice-Chief of Army General Staff Sugiyama Gen (Hajime), 19 June 1935, *Gendaishi*, 8:96–97 (author's translation).

27. Telegram from Consul-General Suma Yakichirō to Foreign Minister Hirota Kōki, no. 599, 19 June 1935, cited in *TSM*, 3:117.

28. Telegram from Military Attaché in Peking Takahashi to Sugiyama, 25 June 1935, *Gendaishi*, 8:98–99.

29. Ibid.

30. Ibid.

31. Telegram from Takahashi to Sugiyama, 27 June 1935, ibid., p. 100.

32. For complete text of Tada's statement, see *China Weekly Review*, 2 November 1935, pp. 306–12.

33. Ibid., 12 October 1935, p. 184.

34. Testimony of Tanaka Ryūkichi, Kyokutō Kokusai Gunji Saiban Kōhan Kiroku Kankōkai [Association for the Publication of the Record of the Proceedings of the International Military Tribunal for the Far East], *Kyokutō Kokusai gunji saiban kōhan kiroku* [Record of the proceedings of

the International Military Tribunal for the Far East] (Tokyo, 1948-1949), 2:65 (hereafter cited as *Kyokutō kokusai gunji saiban*); Mitarai Tatsuo, *Minami Jirō denki* [A biography of Minami Jirō] (Tokyo, 1957), p. 397; and Morota Moritoshi, "Shin-Nichi Kahoku seiken juritsu no yume kuzureru" [Awaken from the dream of establishing a pro-Japanese North China regime], *Bessatsu Chisei,* December 1956, pp. 139-40.

35. Morota, op. cit., pp. 139-40. The Tientsin garrison claimed "jurisdiction" over the Peking-Tientsin area, since it had the right, based on the Boxer Protocol, to protect the Japanese legation and nationals in the area. This view was not accepted by the Kwantung Army in Manchuria, which was anxious to extend its control to North China.

36. Ibid.

37. *China Weekly Review,* 28 September 1935, p. 119.

38. Ibid., 5 October 1935, p. 154.

39. Hata Ikuhiko, op. cit., p. 60; and Morota, op. cit., p. 142.

40. Morota, ibid., pp. 140-41.

41. Ibid., p. 142.

42. *Gendaishi,* 8:130. For the best account of Yen Hsi-shan's relations with the Japanese army, see Donald G. Gillin, *Warlord Yen Hsi-shan in Shansi Province, 1911-1949* (Princeton, 1967), pp. 208-18.

43. For details of the alleged agreement between Chiang Kai-shek and Yen Hsi-shan, see *China Weekly Review,* 16 November 1935, pp. 375-76.

44. *Gendaishi,* 8:130.

45. Morota, op. cit., p. 142.

46. For Sung Che-yüan's background, see *Gendaishi,* 8:129-30.

47. For Yin's connection with the Kwantung Army and his involvement in smuggling, see Morota, op. cit., pp. 141-43.

48. Ibid., p. 142.

49. Ibid.

50. Ibid.

51. Ibid., p. 143.

52. Ibid.

53. Testimony of Tanaka Ryūkichi, *Kyokutō kokusai gunji saiban,* 2:65; and Affidavit of Ch'in Te-ch'un, ibid., pp. 122-23.

54. For details about Nanking's monetary reform, see Harley F. MacNair and Donald F. Lach, *Modern Far Eastern International Relations,* 2d ed. (New York, 1955), pp. 373-79.

55. *TSM,* 3:142-44, 147-48.

56. Affidavit of Ch'in Te-ch'un, *Kyokutō kokusai gunji saiban,* 2:122-23.

57. *TSM,* 3:149-50; Hata Ikuhiko, op. cit., pp. 61-62.

58. Telegram from Secretary Wakasugi to Hirota, no. 387 (1 and 2), 16 November 1935, Gaimushō Archives, PVM 40, *Kahoku mondai* [North China Problems], pp. 1346-51.

59. Telegram from Wakasugi to Hirota, ibid.

60. Hata Ikuhiko, op. cit., p. 61.

61. Telegram from Wakasugi to Hirota, no. 387 (1 and 2), 16 November 1935, *Kahoku mondai*, pp. 1346–51.

62. *North China Star*, 19 November 1935; and T. A. Bisson, *Japan in China* (New York, 1938), p. 91.

63. For the rising nationalistic sentiment in the congress, see "Special Kuomintang Sessions Supplement," *China Press Weekly*, 1 December 1935, p. 46.

64. *Gendaishi*, 8:131.

65. *China Weekly Review*, 23 November 1935, p. 414.

66. *North China Star*, 20 November 1935.

67. "Tui-wai kwan-hsi chi pao-kao" [Report on foreign relations], Chiang Tsung-t'ung-chi Pien-chi Wei-yüan-hui [Committee for the Compilation of the Collected Speeches and Writings of President Chiang], comp., *Chiang Tsung-t'ung-chi* [Collected speeches and writings of President Chiang] (Taipei, 1960), 1:920–21.

68. For example, see *Asahi Shimbun*, 18 November 1935.

69. *TSM*, 3:152–53.

70. Telegram from Vice-Minister of War Furushō Motoo to Chiefs of Staff of Kwantung Army and Tientsin Garrison, and to Military Attachés in Peking and Shanghai (no date or number of telegram given), *Kahoku mondai*, pp. 1337–40.

71. *China Weekly Review*, 23 November 1935, p. 414.

72. *North China Star*, 21 November 1935.

73. Ibid.

74. Ibid., 22 November 1935.

75. Morota, op. cit., pp. 143–44.

76. Testimony of Tanaka Ryūkichi, *Kyokutō kokusai gunji saiban*, 2:65; Mitarai Tatsuo, op. cit., p. 398.

77. Morota, op. cit., p. 144.

78. Ibid.

79. *China Weekly Review*, 30 November 1935, p. 477; and *Gendaishi*, 8:132.

80. *China Weekly Review*, 30 November 1935, p. 477.

81. *Gendaishi*, 8:132.

82. *China Weekly Review*, 30 November 1935, p. 478.

83. Ibid.

84. Bisson, op. cit., p. 99.

85. *TSM*, 3:165–66; and Hata Ikuhiko, op. cit., p. 67.

86. Telegram from Secretary Mutō to Hirota, no. 409, 28 November 1935, *Kahoku mondai,* pp. 1470–72.

87. *TSM,* 3:161–62.

88. Telegram from Mutō to Hirota, no. 414, 30 November 1935, *Kahoku mondai,* p. 1478.

89. *Gendaishi,* 8:132–33.

90. *China Weekly Review,* 7 December 1935, p. 7.

91. *Gendaishi,* 8:133.

92. Telegram from Mutō to Hirota, no. 427, 4 December 1935, *Kahoku mondai,* pp. 1543–47.

93. Telegram from Mutō to Hirota, no. 430, 5 December 1935, ibid., pp. 1548–49.

94. Telegram from Consul-General Kawagoe to Hirota, no. 374, 5 December 1935, ibid., pp. 1550–52.

95. *TSM,* 3:163.

96. Hata Ikuhiko, op. cit., p. 71.

97. *Gendaishi,* 8:133.

98. Telegram from Mutō to Hirota, no. 431, 7 December 1935, *Kahoku mondai,* pp. 1587–89.

99. Telegram from Mutō to Hirota, no. 432, 8 December 1935, ibid., pp. 1600–1608.

100. Telegram from Mutō to Hirota, no. 431, 7 December 1935, ibid., pp. 1587–89.

101. Telegram from Mutō to Hirota, no. 432, 8 December 1935, ibid., pp. 1600–1608.

102. Ibid.

103. Ibid.

104. *TSM,* 3:163.

105. *China Weekly Review,* 21 December 1935, p. 79.

106. Telegram from Ambassador in Shanghai Ariyoshi Akira to Hirota, no. 1131, 20 December 1935, Gaimushō Archives, SI. I. I. 0–73, *Kahoku mondai: yoron narabi ni shimbun ronchō* [North China problems: Public opinion and press comments], pp. 701–2.

107. Testimony of Tanaka Ryūkichi, *Kyokutō kokusai gunji saiban,* 2:66, 79–80.

108. *China Weekly Review,* 28 December 1935, p. 119.

109. Ibid., 4 January 1936, p. 153.

110. Ibid., pp. 156–57.

111. Ibid., 1 February 1936, p. 299.

112. Telegram from Mutō to Hirota, no. 432, 8 December 1935, *Kahoku mondai,* pp. 1600–1608.

113. *China Weekly Review,* 1 February 1936, p. 299.

114. Ibid., 15 February 1936, p. 371.

115. Ibid., 22 February 1936, p. 410.

116. Ibid., 29 February 1936, p. 442.

117. Ibid., 7 March 1936, p. 10.

118. Ibid.

119. Ibid., p. 36.

120. Ibid., 14 March 1936, p. 48.

121. Ibid.

122. Doihara Kenji, "Taishi kōsaku no saiken" [Reconstruction of our work in China], *Bungei Shunjū*, March 1937, pp. 62–69.

123. Ibid.

9.

In his essay, Han-sheng Lin suggests that the Kuomintang sought consistently to solicit Japanese support for the revolution, despite the Twenty-one Demands and the Shantung issue. Matters changed after the Tsinan Incident (May 3, 1928), partly because Chiang Kai-shek possessed virtually no policy toward Japan and partly because the anti-Japanese movement was so severe that Chiang conveniently used the Anglo-American experts to ease domestic pressures—a way of applying the West, one might say, against Japan. Lin points out that the Chinese left-wingers had inherited Sun Yat-sen's policies of socialism at home and of peace and collaboration with Japan. Efforts were made to put these policies into effect in the early 1930s during Wang Ching-wei's premiership, but an attempt on Wang's life led to his retirement from public life and terminated a progressive and pacific era.

The skill of Chinese diplomats in preserving national interests by peaceful means, Dr. Lin feels, has not been sufficiently appreciated either in China or abroad. Chinese leaders resorted to excessive rhetoric because of a great literary tradition and, more important, because domestic struggles for power required the appearance of diplomatic victory. The Sian Incident (December 1936) marked a turning point in Chinese policy toward Japan. Chiang Kai-shek's most trusted subordinates urged Wang Ching-wei to return to lead the Nationalist government, while the Communists and Wang's old enemies were obliged to join Chiang to preserve their power, thereby deciding the Japan policy. Wang Ching-wei's subsequent peace efforts and collaboration with the Japanese represented a continuation of the early policies of Sun Yat-sen and the leftists. Thus Wang's program carried its historical background to its logical conclusion. Most enlightened Chinese leaders did not consider temporary concessions to be a betrayal of the country. Lin is strongly of the opinion that if the KMT leftists had succeeded in their social reforms and peaceful cooperation with the powers, particularly Japan, China could have achieved modernization and industrialization much sooner and without bloodshed. He is convinced that if Wang and his followers had continued in power in 1935, the history of Sino-Japanese relations would have been vastly different.

Lin is a professor of history at California State College, Sonoma. He has served as managing editor of *Peace and Change: A Journal of Peace Research* and is executive vice-president of the Interchange for Pacific Scholarship. He is the author of "Chou Fo-hai: The Diplomacy of Survival" in Richard D. Burns and Edward M. Bennett, eds., *Diplomats in Crisis* (1974) and of a forthcoming book on ways of peacemaking in China.

A New Look at Chinese Nationalist "Appeasers"

Han-sheng Lin

I.

Analysis of the Nationalist period (1925–1949) has generally focused on the dictatorship of Chiang Kai-shek, the second Sino-Japanese war (1937–1945), and the Communist victory (1945–1949). Other aspects of early Nationalist activities, which might have led China into an era of democracy, progress, and prosperity at home and peace and international cooperation abroad, have been to a large extent neglected by scholars. Still obscure is the significant role of Wang Ching-wei, veteran revolutionary leader, champion of republicanism, democracy, and national independence, and first chairman of the Nationalist government. Scant attention has been paid to Wang's close associates in the Kai-tsu p'ai (Reorganization Group) who assisted him in restraining Chiang and other military leaders from assuming dictatorship in the 1920s and in pursuing a progressive and conciliatory policy at home and abroad in the early 1930s. The Japanese peace efforts of Huang Fu and his colleagues in the Cheng-hsüeh hsi (Political Science Clique) have been virtually ignored; worse yet, scholars have taken for granted that the Ou-mei p'ai (European-American Group) was instrumental in helping the generalissimo engage in war and dictatorship. This ignorance has led to many erroneous interpretations of the fall of the Kuomintang and has resulted in failure to learn valuable lessons from the Chinese "appeasement policy" which might be useful in national reconstruction and in the achievement of change through peace and cooperation in developing countries today.[1]

Sun Yat-sen, the founder of the Republic of China and leader of the Nationalist Party (T'ung-meng Hui, 1905; Chung-hua ko-ming-tang,

1913; Kuomintang, 1923), inaugurated the Nationalist appeasement policy. In 1917, in his celebrated book, *Chung-kuo ts'un-wang wen-t'i* [The problems of China's survival], Sun urged China and Japan to cooperate as brothers, despite the controversy over the Shantung issue and the notorious Twenty-one Demands. In January 1923, he signed the famous Sun–Joffe Declaration in Shanghai to promote Sino-Soviet collaboration, and in November of the same year he delivered a cordial speech at Kobe in Japan, advocating Pan Asianism.[2] Wang Ching-wei helped develop the principal ideology for the reorganization of the Nationalist Party: first in the Manifesto of the First National Congress of the Kuomintang in 1924 and then in the will of Sun Yat-sen in 1925. Both documents advocated abolition of "unequal treaties," awakening of the masses to national liberation, and cooperation with those nations which had treated China on equal terms.[3]

Meanwhile, the workers and students also rose in protest against imperialist exploitation and organized a strike against foreign owners for higher wages and more humane treatment. On May 30, 1925, a large group of demonstrators confronted British police at the Shanghai International Settlement, where a British lieutenant, perhaps out of panic, ordered his men to open fire. Seven demonstrators were killed on the spot; eight others died in the hospital and many more received wounds.[4] This tragic incident, soon known as the May 30 Movement, triggered the "Great Revolution" of 1925–1927. Instead of offering compromises to cool the situation, the Western powers chose to suppress the revolutionaries by force. On June 19, workers in Hong Kong and Canton initiated the longest strike in history, lasting sixteen months. On June 23, British and French garrison forces in Canton Shamien fired on the demonstrators, taking the lives of 52 Chinese and leaving more than 150 wounded.[5] Chinese radical forces grew rapidly, and the infant Chinese Communist Party suddenly became a major force. In contrast, Japan, under the guidance of Shidehara Kijūrō, then foreign minister, adopted a cautious and conciliatory policy toward the May 30 incident by paying condolence money to the families of the deceased, by reimbursing striking workers, and by granting the right to organize unions.[6]

Under these tense circumstances, Wang Ching-wei became chairman of the Nationalist government in July 1925, and concurrently presided over the Central Political Council, the highest decision-making body, the Central Executive Committee of the Kuomintang, and its Military Council. Wang chose a moderate course in dealing with the Western powers. His first act was to support the Hong Kong-Canton strike in order to rally the discontented workers and students, as well as to control them and avoid violence. He continued Sun Yat-sen's new policy of collaboration with the Soviet Union, of cooperation with the Chinese Communist Party, and of assistance to workers and peasants.[7] Wang published his celebrated book

China and the Nations, in which he articulated his foreign policy. He opposed the Open Door policy, which meant equal foreign exploitation, and the Washington Conference (1921–1922), which entailed joint domination of China. Further, he condemned the collusion of the warlords and the imperialists.[8] In his early revolutionary activities, as a student and polemical writer in Japan, Wang was popular with the Japanese people; according to Henry P'u-yi, the last Ch'ing emperor, Wang's life had been spared in the Peking imperial prison partly because of Japanese intervention.[9] Wang was abroad and inactive in politics during the Twenty-one Demands controversy. After his return to China in 1917, he was Sun Yat-sen's adviser, and evidently shared Sun's ideas on Pan-Asianism. Therefore it could be assumed that Wang would cooperate with Shidehara to resolve the differences between China and Japan.

Wang, however, did not survive the political pressures in China to deal directly with Shidehara. On August 20, 1925, right-wingers closely connected with Hu Han-min, another of Sun's principal lieutenants, assassinated Wang's friend and associate, Liao Chung-k'ai, a firm believer in socialism, a powerful figure in Kuomintang politics, and the architect of collaboration with the Soviet Union.[10] In November, the Western Hills group, a right-wing organization, expelled Wang from their "Kuomintang" on the grounds that he had allied himself with the Chinese Communist Party. Wang initially met the rightist challenges with considerable success. His lieutenants Ch'en Kung-po and Ku Meng-yü and his Communist allies, notably Li Ta-chao and Mao Tse-tung, won significant elective positions in the Second National Congress of the Kuomintang, held in January 1926 at Canton, and his followers constituted a large majority in the Central Executive Committee.[11] The rightists, however, continued to conspire with Wang's military lieutenant, Chiang Kai-shek, to trigger the March 20, 1926, coup d'état in an attempt to alter the new policy of the Kuomintang. Chiang detained the Soviet advisers, arrested the Chinese Communists, and declared martial law in Canton without Wang's authorization. Chiang claimed that Wang was ill at the time and that he had had to take emergency measures. Wang, however, immediately summoned a meeting of the Central Political Council at his residence and denounced Chiang's abuse of power, which, he contended, would lead eventually to a military dictatorship. Then he submitted his resignation. Although Chiang apologized for his rash act and the council declined Wang's resignation, Wang took a leave of absence to recuperate from his illness and traveled to France in order to avoid a direct confrontation inside the party.[12]

Wang's left-wing followers, however, remained strong within the Kuomintang, and Chiang needed their support, to avoid becoming a puppet of the rightists. In May 1926, Chiang negotiated a compromise with Wang's followers. Chinese Communists would not occupy ministerial positions in both the Kuomintang and the Nationalist government and he authorized an expedition to subdue the warlords in the north. In return, Chiang would support the policy of reorganization and join the leftists in asking Wang's return to China to lead the revolution.[13] During the Northern Expedition, the leftist generals of the 4th Army, notably Chang Fa-k'uei, commander of the "Ironsides," and their Communist allies scored many victories and thereby further strengthened Wang's political basis.

Chiang Kai-shek first consolidated his political base among his cadets at the Whampoa Military Academy by organizing special agents known later as the Blue Shirts to oversee the activities of his political opponents. He then recruited the European-American group, which had not looked down on the military as most traditional scholars did, to serve him in various civilian functions. The group, however, was divided into at least five categories. First were the career diplomats, including C. T. Wang (Wang Cheng-t'ing), Wellington Koo (Ku Wei-chün), Lo Wen-kan, and Wang Ch'ung-hui, who had served both the Peking and Nationalist governments without ideological considerations. Second were the Chekiang-Kiangsu financiers, the core of the rightists. Third was the C.C. (Central Club) clique, under the leadership of Tuan Hsi-p'eng, Ch'en Li-fu, and Ch'eng T'ien-fang, partly reorganized from the notorious Anti-Bolshevik League to extinguish the Communists through subversion and counterspying and to destroy domestic opponents through extraordinary means. Fourth was the American group, led by T. V. Soong (Soong Tsu-wen) and K'ung Hsiang-hsi, relatives of Sun Yat-sen. Fifth were the missionaries and their Chinese converts, who exerted considerable influence on Chinese higher education. Chiang initially could rely only on the support of the C.C. clique because of their ideological affiliation. The other European-American elements assisted him either because of mutual interests or simply because he happened to be in power.

Chiang's long association, however, with Ch'en Ch'i-mei, a prominent revolutionary leader in the Shanghai area, gained him considerable power; his background as a student in both the Kanbu Gakkō and the Shikan Gakkō (Military Academy) in Japan attracted many Japanese-educated military leaders; and his close contacts with members of the secret societies, particularly Tu Yüeh-sheng, were also valuable. After Ch'en's death, his military and civilian associates began to follow Chiang's leadership. For example, Huang Fu and Chang Ch'ün, who attended military schools in Japan and served in the Peking government and with the "Christian general" Feng Yü-hsiang, later returned to help Chiang in his power struggle against the leftists. Chang Ching-chiang and Tai Chi-t'ao, two principal civilian leaders under Ch'en Ch'i-mei, also came to assist Chiang because of ideological and regional power struggles. Ch'en's nephews,

Ch'en Kuo-fu and Ch'en Li-fu, later became Chiang's most effective organizers. Ho Ying-ch'in, a Japanese-trained commander, rallied under Chiang's banner and helped him build the strength of his Whampoa cadets, while his friends among the secret societies supplied him with unlimited manpower for subversive activities and occasionally with financial assistance. Chiang's strong belief in nationalism and his political skill united this highly divergent group while he gradually developed a simple ideology and a relatively flexible policy to satisfy the varying aspirations of his supporters.

Chiang's nationalism, no longer Sun Yat-sen's anti-imperialism, became an effort to restore China's traditional virtues and Confucianism. It would serve his anti-Communism and would reduce sharp conflict against the imperialists. Chiang's military strategies encompassed Tseng Kuo-fan's *tzu-ti p'ing* (soldiers of brothers and sons) and the elitist-troop approach of Germany and Japan; he therefore became notorious for supporting his Whampoa cadets at the expense of other Nationalist troops. His economic policy combined China's traditional state monopolies with modern profit-oriented capitalism, to produce the famous bureaucratic capitalism. Chiang's foreign policy, nonetheless, was pragmatic. He would favor a cooperative policy with Japan, provided the latter would not violate China's sovereignty, but he would not hesitate to seek assistance and cooperation from the West. It is significant, however, that most of Chiang's followers opposed the Chinese Communists in part because they believed that the Comintern dominated Communist activities in China.

II.

Although Chiang Kai-shek possessed considerable strength, the leftists continued to control the Nationalist government at Canton and then in Wuhan because they commanded parts of the Nationalist Army, controlled most of the political commissars, and received the support of a significant number of Whampoa cadets. They also attracted enthusiastic responses from students, petty merchants, shopkeepers, most of the press, and university professors; and they maintained cordial relationships with the Soviet advisers and the Chinese Communist Party. In addition, the leftists dominated the Central Executive Committee of the Kuomintang; Wang Ching-wei's leave of absence did not diminish his popularity throughout the country. The leftists moved ahead with the new policy of supporting the workers and peasants, insisted on the return of Wang Ching-wei, and advocated a strong policy of anti-imperialism together with a flexible attitude toward foreigners. For example, in Hankow, when the revolutionaries moved to recover the British concession, Ch'en Kung-po, Wang's ardent follower, personally restrained the mob from committing violence against foreigners. This action paved the way for Eugene Chen (Ch'en Yu-jen), then foreign minister of the Nationalist government and a renowned anti-imperialist propagandist, to negotiate with the British authorities for the successful recovery of the concession.[14] The Nationalists also recovered the British concessions in Kiukiang and later in Chenchiang, Weihaiwei, and Amoy, confiscated the customs surplus, and imposed surtaxes—all without forcefully confronting the foreign powers. Japanese diplomats under the guidance of Shidehara appreciated the Nationalists' aspirations and their flexible foreign policy, and adopted a conciliatory policy toward China in the hope that the Nationalists would resume their intimate relationship with Japan.

Shidehara's first significant move was to offer to abolish extraterritoriality and concede tariff autonomy to the Peking government. He instructed his representative to grant tariff autonomy in principle on the grounds that "the Chinese people are gradually awakening to political affairs."[15] In 1926, at the time of the Wanhsien Incident, a British gunboat leveled the city in retaliation for Chinese detention of two British ships and the British government wanted other powers to take strong measures against China; Shidehara refused to sanction the brutal action or to support the British proposal.[16] When the Nationalists arrived in the Yangtze region in October 1926, the Japanese government decided not to intervene, not to use force to protect Japanese nationals in the area, and not to join the British defense of the Shanghai International Settlement. After the famous and somewhat conciliatory Chamberlain "Christmas Memorandum" (1926), Shidehara enunciated his government's China policy under the principle of "coexistence and coprosperity." He was prepared to negotiate with the Nationalists on equal terms, provided the latter would protect Japanese economic interests in China. Shidehara was further convinced that no foreign power could dictate policy to China for any length of time.[17]

In the Nanking Incident (March 24, 1927), a group of Chinese soldiers killed several foreigners during the battle to occupy the city. British and American gunboats retaliated immediately and shelled Nanking, but the Tokyo government again refrained from military action. At Shidehara's request, unarmed Japanese marines were landed in Nanking to withdraw their nationals and, at his suggestion, the Japanese consul-general in Shanghai, Yada Shichitarō, privately advised Chiang Kai-shek to initiate a settlement. When the Western countries decided to adopt such strong measures as setting a deadline for Nationalist compliance with their demands for apologies, indemnities, and possible sanctions, however, Japan declined to concur.[18] Thus the incident did not become a major conflict, and a reasonable settlement was reached.

Chiang Kai-shek was ready to heed Shidehara's advice, but he had to deal with the growing threat posed by the leftist-controlled Wuhan government. Perhaps out of necessity and desperation, Chiang joined the leftists in urging Wang Ching-wei to return and to lead the revolution. Wang arrived in Shanghai on April 1, whereupon Chiang and his friends immediately visited him and told him that the Chinese Communist Party constituted a threat to the existence of the Kuomintang. On April 5, however, Wang and Ch'en Tu-hsiu, secretary-general of the Chinese Communist Party, issued a joint declaration in Shanghai reaffirming the principles of the reorganization and restating the cooperation of the Kuomintang with the party.[19] Four days later, Wang arrived in Wuhan, and Eugene Chen sought Japanese mediation the following day to settle the Nanking Incident. Both Chiang Kai-shek and Wang Ching-wei seemed to appreciate Shidehara's conciliatory policy, but domestic problems prevented their active cooperation with the Japanese moderates.

On April 12, Chiang Kai-shek and his conservative allies initiated a bloody coup d'état, indiscriminately purging and shooting Communists and leftists in Shanghai and metropolitan areas throughout South China. On April 18, they established their rival Nationalist government in Nanking with Hu Han-min as titular head. Meanwhile, Huang Fu played a major role in the effort to split the warlords of North China. Using his influence in the Peking government, Huang advised Feng Yü-hsiang to trigger a coup against the Chihli leaders in 1926. Feng subsequently declared his allegiance to the Kuomintang. Yen Hsi-shan, governor of Shansi province and a member of the original T'ung-meng Hui, also accepted an appointment from the Nationalist government. In Wuhan, Wang Ching-wei directed his generals to continue the Northern Expedition rather than to attack Chiang Kai-shek in Nanking, while Chiang dispatched his troops into Shantung province.

The Wakatsuki cabinet in Japan, meanwhile, fell in April 1927, because of the financial crisis and the controversy over Shidehara's "weak-kneed" diplomacy. General Tanaka Giichi, who succeeded Wakatsuki as prime minister, advocated a "positive" policy toward China. Tanaka valued traditional virtues, feared the spread of Communism, and would not hesitate to use force to protect Japanese interests and "to intimidate the disdainful Chinese by demonstrating Japan's military power."[20] In May 1927, he ordered 2000 Japanese marines to Tsingtao to obstruct Chiang's advance through Tsinan, where many Japanese nationals resided. The goodwill created by Shidehara's diplomacy evaporated in China, and a wave of anti-Japanese movements followed. In June, Tanaka convened the Eastern Conference to find ways to deal with the "rampant Communists . . . responsible for the revolutionary atmosphere in China and at the same time to establish a defense for Japan's 'position' in Manchuria."[21] This conference provided Chinese propagandists an opportunity to coin the famous "Tanaka Memorial" to discredit the Japanese government. It was unfortunate that Tanaka did not bother to review the facts that Chiang Kai-shek had already purged the Communists, while Wang Ching-wei in Wuhan soon undertook similar action to curtail Communist influence.

In June, Joseph Stalin delivered an ultimatum to Wang through a representative of the Comintern, M. N. Roy, demanding that the Wuhan government be reorganized to include a majority of Chinese Communists, to sanction strikes against Chinese factories, and to confiscate the land of Chinese landlords.[22] Wang, although sympathetic to those Communist goals, which were similar to Sun's three principles, would not accept the domination of the Comintern. Further, he viewed class struggle as extreme, a cause of bloodshed, and the dictatorship of the proletariat as undemocratic because workers constituted less than 1 percent of the Chinese population. Wang advocated radicalism in political revolution, but he believed in gradual economic development because it would not cause too severe an upheaval within society. In addition, Wang was under pressure from Generals Feng Yü-hsiang and T'ang Sheng-chih, commander of the 8th Army, to eject the Communists. Feng's troops marched into Honan province and he shared the spoils of victory over Marshal Chang Tso-lin; through Huang Fu's skillful arrangement, Feng met Chiang Kai-shek in Hsuchow to secure an understanding. Subsequently Feng demanded that the Communists be purged from the Wuhan government and that the Wuhan and Nanking governments be reunited.[23] T'ang's lieutenants, landlords in Hunan and Hupei provinces, objected to Communist demands for land reform. Wang had no alternative. In July, after careful preparations, he decided to send all Soviet advisers, including Michael Borodin, back to the Soviet Union and to purge the Chinese Communists from the Kuomintang.[24]

Despite the expulsion of the Communists from both the Nanking and Wuhan governments, Tanaka did not alter his "positive" policy by accommodating the Nationalists. In August 1927, when Chiang's troops marched toward Shantung, Tanaka promptly dispatched his second Shantung expedition, which caused another anti-Japanese wave to spread throughout China. The Shantung warlord, Chang Tsung-ch'ang, however, defeated Chiang's forces and temporarily prevented a direct confrontation between the Japanese and Nationalist armies. Chiang then retired from the Nanking government to pave the way for the unification of the Nationalist Party, to seek a personal interview with Tanaka in Japan, and to arrange his own marriage to T. V. Soong's sister.

The Wuhan and Nanking governments were finally unified under a special committee but Wang Ching-wei's left-wing lieutenants disliked the inclusion of the Western Hills group and refused to cooperate. Accordingly, Wang sent General Chang Fa-k'uei to establish a base in Canton and then demanded the dissolution of the committee. In retaliation General Li Tsung-jen, a member of the Kwangsi group and a strong ally of the Western Hills group, attacked General T'ang in Hupei. Civil war within the Kuomintang was imminent.

Meanwhile, Chiang Kai-shek, as a result of his meeting with Tanaka, believed that Tanaka, impressed by his anti-Communist stand, would not interfere with the Nationalist efforts to unify China.[25] Chiang also denounced the Special Committee, in return for which Wang urged him to resume the post of commander in chief of the Nationalist Army. In December, Chiang's marriage made him a relative of the most powerful revolutionary family. He could now count on T. V. Soong to rally the support of the European-American group and to effect a rapprochement with Wang.

Unexpectedly, however, the Canton Commune uprising erupted in December 1927, under the direction of such veteran Communist leaders as Yeh Chien-ying, Chou En-lai, Chang T'ai-lei, and Yen T'ing. Many lives and much property were lost in the upheaval. The rightists immediately blamed General Chang Fa-k'uei for the catastrophe despite the latter's efforts to restore order within five days, and the Kwangsi generals even tried to arrest Wang in Shanghai. Although Wang escaped unharmed and exiled himself to France again, the possibility of a Wang–Chiang coalition had disappeared.

III.

In January 1928, at the Fourth Plenary Session of the Central Committee of the Kuomintang in Nanking, Chiang emerged supreme. He was elected chairman of the Central Executive Committee, chairman of the Nationalist government, and commander in chief of the Nationalist Army. Consequently Chiang became a dictator. Most liberals, including Chiang's new brother-in-law T. V. Soong, were unhappy with these developments. Hu Shih, a non-Kuomintang liberal leader, wrote:

> I met Professor Manley O. Hudson of the Harvard Law School, who had just come from Shanghai, in the Tokyo Imperial Hotel. He told me, "The political change in China recently is very reactionary!" I asked: "How do you know?" He replied: "I personally listened to Mr. Sung Tzu-wen [T. V. Soong] who lamented and said: 'The aim of the Nationalist revolution is to rule the military through the party; i.e., to restrain the generals by civilian leaders. Everything is now changed. The situation of restraining the generals by civilian leaders is completely destroyed.' "[26]

After a tour of the Yangtze region, John V. A. MacMurray, then U.S.

minister to China, commented in April in a telegram to Washington that

among the leaders in the South as in the North there is today no guiding purpose or
principle outside of the self-interest of certain militarists who have grouped themselves
together for their own common profit though with no faith in each other's loyalty. . . .
One who is sympathetic with the temper of the Chinese and has a certain acquaintance
with them cannot escape the feeling that here is China at its worst. . . .[27]

Nevertheless, foreign observers failed to appreciate other aspects of the Nationalist development. Despite Soong's bitter complaints, for example, he joined the Chiang regime to reorganize its finances. Further, Chiang brought Huang Fu and his friends of the political science clique into the Nationalist government. Huang served as mayor of Shanghai and then as Chiang's foreign minister. He and Soong wielded considerable power and influence in Chiang's domestic and foreign policies. Wang Ching-wei's followers, particularly Ch'en Kung-po, published *Ko-ming p'ing-lun* [Revolutionary critics] and organized the Kai-tsu p'ai to challenge Chiang's dictatorial power.

Chiang Kai-shek, Li Tsung-jen, Feng Yü-hsiang, Yen Hsi-shan, and the leftist generals finally cooperated to complete the Northern Expedition. Before moving into Shantung province, Chiang dispatched his confidant Chang Ch'ün to Tokyo to notify the Japanese leaders and thus avoid any misunderstanding. Before Chang's arrival, however, General Fukuda Hirosuke's division marched from Tsingtao to Tsinan, in spite of Chiang's repeated promise to protect Japanese lives and property, and regardless of Tanaka's explicit order not to advance to Tsinan without further instructions. Fukuda's insubordination proved to be the first signal of Japan's military unrest. No sooner had the Japanese troops arrived in the provincial capital than they clashed with the Chinese armed forces, and the conflict spread. On May 3, Japanese soldiers murdered China's negotiator, Ts'ai Kung-shih, and his associates in Tsinan. The Tsinan Incident aroused an intense anti-Japanese movement in China. Huang Fu personally directed peace negotiations in Tsinan, halted the shooting, and recommended the withdrawal of the Chinese troops from Tsinan to minimize the conflict. Chiang accordingly moved his armies by another route toward Peking.[28]

Chang Ch'ün arrived in Tokyo on May 5 and immediately went to the Japanese Foreign Ministry and Tanaka in an attempt to resolve the conflict. Tanaka sent General Matsui Iwane as his representative to negotiate in Tsinan. Chang finally persuaded Matsui to restrain the Japanese Army and to settle the issue through regular diplomatic channels.[29] Huang Fu was so disappointed by this tragic incident that he submitted his resignation and retired to the mountains.

Tanaka's main interests, however, remained in Manchuria; evidently he would exchange the potential advantage in North China for Japanese domination of Manchuria if the Nationalists agreed. For example, Tanaka's private representative, Yamamoto Jōtarō, pressed Marshal Chang Tso-lin to sign an agreement allowing the Japanese to construct five railway lines in Manchuria, thereby rendering the region a Japanese protectorate. At the May 18 cabinet meeting, Tanaka adopted a resolution of support for Chang in Manchuria and of noninterference in the Chinese civil war. Colonel Kōmoto Daisaku of the Kwantung Army, however, failed to comprehend Tanaka's scheme and undertook "direct action" to protect the Japanese "lifeline" in Manchuria. On June 4, Kōmoto conspired to blow up Chang Tso-lin's railroad car as it arrived in the South Manchurian Railway zone near Mukden; Chang died shortly afterward. The assassination of the marshal was the second indication of the insubordination of Japanese military officers. The expected confusion in Manchuria after the death of Chang Tso-lin, however, did not develop. Chang's son, the Young Marshal Chang Hsueh-liang, proved to be resourceful and assumed command of the Manchurian Army with an active interest in negotiating with the Nationalist government for China's unification.[30]

On June 6, the Nationalists occupied Peking. On June 7, Chiang Kai-shek appointed C. T. Wang, a Yale-educated career diplomat, as foreign minister. Wang had participated in revolutionary activities and understood the value of propaganda. No sooner had he been named foreign minister than he issued a manifesto abolishing "unequal treaties." Tanaka immediately denounced this unilateral action and refused to negotiate any new treaties with the Nationalist government until China withdrew this announcement. Wang's "revolutionary diplomacy," however, was intended mainly for domestic consumption. The Nationalist government did not want to provoke a confrontation with Japan.[31]

In August, in accordance with the teachings of Sun Yat-sen, the Central Executive Committee of the Kuomintang declared the termination of the military campaign and initiated the tutelage period. The Nationalist government was to be reorganized with a sixteen-member political council as the highest decision-making body and a five-power executive branch to include Executive, Legislative, Judicial, Control, and Examination Yuan. The local governments at the district level would hold a general election. In October 1929, the Central Political Council elected Chiang Kai-shek president of the Nationalist government.

Within the Nanking administration, T. V. Soong had been hard at work. Worried about the country's financial state, he pointed out that in 1929 China had over two million soldiers and required 643,000,000 Chinese dollars to support them; but the central government had an income of only 450,000,000 Chinese dollars of which 300,000,000 had to be allocated toward the payment of foreign debts.[32] Soong therefore proposed a severe cut in military expenditures based upon vigorous demobilization. Chiang would consent only if the budget of other military leaders was cut and the troops of other generals were demobilized. This shortsighted policy on Chiang's part helped to bring on a bloody civil war among the Nationalists.

Earlier, in February 1929, the Kwangsi generals started a revolt and, in March, Ch'en Kuo-fu and Hu Han-min attempted to pack the forthcoming Third National Congress of the Kuomintang to assure the domination of the rightists and Chiang's dictatorship. Upon learning of this arbitrary and illegal measure, Wang circulated a telegram from France denouncing Chiang's action. Fifteen of eighteen provincial Kuomintang headquarters quickly responded and publicly denounced Chiang's manipulation of the delegates.[33] During his campaign against the Kwangsi generals, Chang Fa-k'uei, commander in the south, demanded that Chiang change his "immoral and outrageous" policy and that the duly elected leftist delegates be included in the Third National Congress. When his demands were not satisfactorily answered, Chang shifted his troops to attack Chiang's military allies at Canton. T'ang Sheng-chih, who had recently accepted Chiang's appointment as commander in North China, followed suit and declared independence in Honan. Feng Yü-hsiang, deserted by many of his able generals, belatedly joined the anti-Chiang campaign. Since Huang Fu was no longer available to mediate the conflict, the tragic battle of the Northern Plain began.

Marshal Chang Hsueh-liang, in the meantime, defied Tanaka's various inducements and threats to become an "autonomous" ruler in Manchuria under Japan's auspices. In December 1928 he declared his allegiance to the Nationalist government and raised the Nationalist flag. The Young Marshal also transferred his negotiations with Japan to Nanking. Tanaka temporarily laid aside the thorny Manchurian issue and proceeded to settle other outstanding matters with the Nationalists. In the cases of the Tsinan and Nanking incidents, Tanaka proved conciliatory. The Nationalist government agreed to pay a small indemnity to the families of the injured, the Japanese government would withdraw its troops from Tsinan immediately, and both the Nanking and Tokyo governments would issue apologies for the incidents.[34] The tariff autonomy issue, however, proved difficult because of Japan's traditional policy of connecting it with Chinese willingness to abolish the *likin* (transit taxes of the local government), to guarantee payment of previous debts, and to maintain the most-favored-nation clause. In any case, Tanaka was out of power by July because he could not explain satisfactorily the assassination of Chang Tso-lin and, ironically, discipline the Japanese military. Hamaguchi Osachi (Yūkō) succeeded him and Shidehara returned as foreign minister. The resumption of the Shidehara diplomacy appeared to strengthen the prospects for improving Sino-Japanese relations.

Meanwhile, Chiang Kai-shek attempted to demonstrate his hostility toward the Soviet Union as a means of appeasing both Japan and the West. He instructed Marshal Chang Hsueh-liang to search the Soviet consulate in Harbin, to march his troops into the Chinese Eastern Railway zone, to arbitrarily replace Soviet personnel, and to confiscate Soviet commercial interests. The Soviet Union retaliated by promptly crushing Chang's troops, and, to Chiang's dismay and surprise, Japan and the Western powers expressed sympathy for the Soviet Union rather than for Nanking, because of their primary interest in maintaining the treaty rights.[35]

Chiang compounded his error in judgment by committing another unnecessary act in regard to Japan. In October, Shidehara appointed Saburi Sadao, a China expert and friend of the Nationalists, as minister to Nanking. Chiang received him cordially and expressed his anxieties about Sino-Japanese relations. T. V. Soong indicated readiness to set aside some funds for the repayment of China's debts once the income from the tariffs increased. Saburi, however, was found dead while vacationing in Japan, and Shidehara nominated Obata Yūkichi, another China specialist, to succeed him. The Chinese press opposed Obata's nomination because of his participation in the Twenty-one Demands negotiations in 1915, and the Nanking government refused to receive him, without investigating the fact that Obata had personally opposed the demands. This action so outraged the Japanese public that Shidehara appointed Shigemitsu Mamoru, consul-general in Shanghai, as temporary chargé d'affaires for the Nanking embassy. Shigemitsu proved conciliatory and effective, and proceeded to resolve the tariff issue.[36]

The Nationalist government, ever conscious of the propaganda value of strong diplomacy and hard-pressed by civil strife, in December 1929 unilaterally announced the abolition of extraterritoriality effective January 1, 1930. Japan and other foreign powers, alarmed by this arbitrary measure, quickly united in denouncing Nanking's action. C. T. Wang then declared that China had merely indicated that in principle extraterritoriality should be abolished by January 1 but that in practice China was ready to negotiate with foreign powers for its gradual implementation.[37] Wang's explanation temporarily silenced the protests of the powers, but the issue remained unresolved.

Amid these diplomatic difficulties, Wang Ching-wei returned to China in February 1930 and thus intensified the domestic power struggles. Wang united all of Chiang's opponents including the Western Hills group, the Kwangsi generals, Yen Hsi-shan and Feng Yü-hsiang, and convened an enlarged conference of the Kuomintang at Peking. The leftists virtually dominated the conference and managed to pass a series of progressive programs. The most significant were to convene a people's conference, to put the provisional constitution into practice immediately at the provincial level, to protect the people's rights and liberties, and to initiate social and economic reforms.[38] The Communists also recovered from their 1927 debacle. Mao Tse-tung built up a red army and a regional base at Chingkangshan; Li Li-shan and other Communist leaders organized red armies, revolutionary bases, and cells. Li ordered the red armies to assault various southern cities during the battle of the Northern Plain, but the

Western powers intervened and dispatched gunboats to shell the Communists in Changsha and environs under the pretext of protecting lives and property of their nationals.[39] The Communists rose with considerable strength, but the intervention impressed both Chiang Kai-shek and his opponents in the Kuomintang. Marshal Chang Hsueh-liang, after a period of hesitation and hard bargaining, helped Chiang terminate the battle of the Northern Plain by marching his Manchurian troops to Peking on September 18.[40] Wang Ching-wei fled to Yen Hsi-shan's stronghold in Shansi.

Meanwhile, Yang Yung-t'ai, a veteran politician of the political science clique, joined Chiang's entourage through the influence of Huang Fu. Chou Fo-hai, a founding member of the Chinese Communist Party and a leading pro-Japanese figure, emerged as Chiang's political confidant. Immediately after his victory, Chiang had second thoughts about the split of the party. His personal army was on the verge of exhaustion, and Marshal Chang was at best an unreliable ally. Furthermore, Wang and his programs, enunciated in the conference at Peking, were exceptionally popular, and the Communist threat was serious. Chiang's new adviser, Yang Yung-t'ai, known for his statecraft and moderation, perhaps exerted some influence on his thinking. In any event, on October 3, without consulting his conservative allies in Nanking, particularly Hu Han-min, Chiang circulated a telegram from his military headquarters accepting all of Wang's proposals as the basis of the Nationalist government policy.[41] Hu Han-min, a recent critic of Wang's programs, particularly the provisional constitution, was angered by Chiang's appointing the Young Marshal as deputy generalissimo and chairman of the Peking Political Council in exchange for his service in the battle of the Northern Plain. Chiang's retaliation, detaining Hu at Tangshan, provoked a political storm in the south. Hu's followers established a rival government in Canton and elected Wang Ching-wei chairman. Wang, however, was not interested in the politics of the right-wing Kuomintang and, through his principal lieutenant Ku Meng-yü, he had resumed negotiations with Chiang's representatives. Because of Chiang's negligence, the relationship with Japan suddenly became critical and the young officers of the Kwantung Army took direct action.

IV.

On September 18, 1931, under the guidance of Colonels Ishiwara Kanji and Itagaki Seishirō, the Kwantung Army occupied Mukden under the pretext that the Chinese had set off an explosion on the railroad tracks near Mukden. The Japanese moved rapidly, in part because of Chiang's policy of "nonresistance," but mainly because Ishiwara had planned so well for the conquest of Manchuria. In Japan, in the midst of public opposition to the London naval treaty, Premier Hamaguchi was shot (November 1930) and Wakatsuki again assumed the premiership. Although Shidehara remained in office and continued to maintain that Japan had no right to violate the sovereignty of China in Manchuria, he was unable to restrain the young officers from taking military action.

In China, the Nanking government was beset by internecine strife and natural disasters. In 1931, drought in North China and floods in Central China occurred with unprecedented severity, and the world depression affected the Chinese market and currency. The Wanpaoshan and Nakamura affairs alarmed the Nanking authorities, and Soong and Shigemitsu attempted personally to travel to Manchuria to inspect the situation. It was too late. After the Manchurian Incident, Chiang created a special committee on foreign affairs with Tai Chi-t'ao as chairman to assume full responsibility for negotiating peace. Tai recommended continuing reliance on the League of Nations, on the goodwill of Shidehara to restrain the Japanese military, and on "non-resistance and non-negotiation."[42] The Fourth National Congress of the Kuomintang approved Tai's recommendations, but the policy of "non-resistance and non-negotiation" evidently was not popular with the Chinese people. In retrospect, the strategy of "non-negotiation" with Japan was also a major mistake. First, this policy weakened Shidehara's position in Japan because he was unable to resolve the Manchurian issue through negotiations. Second, it gave the Japanese military the time necessary to consolidate the occupation of Manchuria. Third, once the Japanese Army completely occupied the three eastern provinces of Manchuria, Japanese diplomats, whether Shidehara or his successors, could only defend the accomplished fact.

Chinese public reaction to the Japanese invasion of Manchuria was violent in its denunciation of the Nationalist government. Students marched into Nanking, destroyed the headquarters of the Kuomintang, assaulted C. T. Wang, and demanded a meeting with Chiang Kai-shek. Chiang replaced Wang with Ku Wei-chün as foreign minister, and declared that he needed time to prepare for war. The press then demanded the end of civil war within the Kuomintang and the convening of a national conference including Wang Ching-wei, Hu Han-min, and Chiang Kai-shek to cope with the Manchurian crisis. Under these pressures, Chiang released Hu Han-min from Tangshan, traveled to Shanghai to meet Wang Ching-wei, and arranged a national conference in Shanghai at the end of the year.

At the Shanghai Conference, Wang, Hu and Chiang reached a compromise agreement. Chiang was to accept the supremacy of civilian rule and to relinquish his power in the party. The Central Political Council was to be reorganized to include three permanent members, Wang, Hu, and Chiang, with equal authority or veto power in important matters. The Nationalist government was to be reconstructed to reduce its chairman to a figurehead and to entrust its real power to the Executive Yuan or the cabinet. A constitution was to be drafted but before constitutional government was established, a provisional constitution should be instituted at the provincial level.[43] After the conference Hu left for Canton, where he joined his Cantonese followers in issuing a demand that Chiang immediately resign as commander in chief, in the interest of national unity. Chiang complied and retired from politics. The Canton government dissolved itself.

After Hu and Chiang's retirement from government (although not from the party) while Wang was ill in Shanghai, the Kuomintang selected Sun Fo, son of Sun Yat-sen, as the first premier of the Executive Yuan, and Lin Shen, a leader of the Western Hills group, as figurehead chairman of the Nationalist government. The Sun cabinet with Eugene Chen as foreign minister failed to inspire public confidence, particularly among the financiers of the Nanking-Shanghai area. Meanwhile, the Wakatsuki ministry resigned in December 1931 because it could not settle the Manchurian episode, and Japanese naval authorities in Shanghai pressed the Nanking government to resolve local differences arising from the killing of a Japanese monk. Unable to secure financial support to defray governmental expenditures and incapable of resolving a potentially explosive incident with Japan, the Sun cabinet resigned after a month's trial.[44] China faced a national crisis without a central government.

On January 16, 1932, Wang Ching-wei initiated a personal meeting with Chiang Kai-shek in Hangchow, where they decided that Wang would take charge of civilian matters in the Executive Yuan while Chiang led the army. They journeyed to Nanking to take over the responsibilities of the Nationalist government. Wang was inaugurated premier on February 1, three days after fighting began between Chinese and Japanese troops in Shanghai. On March 6, Chiang became chairman of the Military Affairs Commission or generalissimo directly under the Nationalist government, and Yang Yung-t'ai served as his chief secretary. It is clear that the Nanking government was a coalition of Wang and Chiang, that it consisted of progressive and conciliatory members of the Kai-tsu p'ai, the Ou-mei p'ai, and of the Cheng-hsüeh hsi, and that its domestic and foreign policies were substantially different from those under Chiang's dictatorship. Ch'en Kung-po and Ku Meng-yü, Wang's two principal lieutenants, were in charge of the ministries of railways and industry, and other members of the Reorganization group such as Kan Nai-kuang and Ch'en Shu-jen also occupied ministerial posts. T. V. Soong and Kung Hsiang-hsi continued in their finance and economic-development positions; other returned students such as Wang Shih-chieh and Chu Chia-hua controlled education and communications. Yang Yung-t'ai, Chang Ch'ün, and Huang Fu exerted considerable influence on the policy making of the Generalissimo through their service in Chiang's inner circle. Lo Wen-kan, a principal figure in the Peking government and a leader of the European-American group, became foreign minister; he worked under Marshal Chang Hsueh-liang in Manchuria for several years.

Wang articulated his Japanese policy as *i-mien ti-k'ang i-mien chiao-she* (resistance on the one hand and negotiation on the other), while his domestic program focused on *yu-chien-she erh t'ung-i* (unification through reconstruction). Wang brought honesty and moral virtues into the Nanking government and he tried by almost every imaginable means to fulfill his promises. Confronted with the severe fighting in Shanghai, Wang recommended that the capital of the Nationalist government be removed to Loyang at once in order to avoid a direct Japanese threat. He ordered the 19th Route Army, previously a division of the 4th Army, to resist the Japanese aggression in Shanghai. For months, despite considerable reinforcement, Japan was unable to subdue the 19th Route Army. Chiang Kai-shek's 5th Army joined the Shanghai defense, and the fighting spirit of the Chinese soldiers startled foreign observers throughout the world. Sleeping China appeared to have awakened, as Napoleon Bonaparte had feared a century ago.

Wang's main hope, however, remained in negotiations to settle the conflict peacefully. Wang and his foreign minister traveled to Shanghai and solicited the assistance of the League of Nations. Japanese negotiators under the leadership of Admiral Nomura Kichisaburō and Shigemitsu proved moderate and reasonable, and Japan's new prime minister, Inukai Tsuyoshi, a friend of Sun Yat-sen and Wang Ching-wei, was eager to end the fighting. Thus the Shanghai Incident ended quickly with a compromise in May 1932; Japanese troops were to be withdrawn from Shanghai while China would remove the 19th Route Army to the interior and demilitarize the greater Shanghai area.[45]

Wang was determined to observe the agreement. When General Ch'en Ming-shu, deputy premier, minister of communications, and commander in chief of the Nanking-Shanghai theater, who had directly commanded the 19th Route Army, attempted to sabotage the peace settlement, Wang promptly removed him from all his official responsibilities in the central government.[46] Japanese pressures had barely subsided in the south, however, when they appeared again in North China. The Kwantung Army in January 1932 had already occupied Chinchou near the Great Wall, and on March 9 the Japanese authorities in Manchuria, under the guidance of Itagaki and Doihara Kenji, created Manchukuo and appointed Henry P'u-yi as chief of state. Thus they attempted in part to cover up Japanese aggression in Manchuria because the League of Nations established a team to investigate the Manchurian Incident. But the strategy of Itagaki and Doihara also attempted to coerce both Nanking and Tokyo into confronting the realities in Manchuria. Wang denounced the creation of Manchukuo and refused to recognize the puppet government, but he realized that the Nationalist government was too weak militarily to go beyond nonrecognition.[47]

Still, Wang would not allow the expenditure of the central government's meager resources by the military commander in North China to build up a huge army unless he offered a gesture of resistance against the enemy. In August 1932, Wang publicly disclosed the excessive spending by the Young Marshal and demanded his resignation. According to Chiang's biographer, Tung Hsien-kuang, Nanking erupted into chaos, and Chiang Kai-shek reluctantly accepted Marshal Chang Hsueh-liang's resignation.[48] Wang also took a leave of absence to go abroad to recuperate from his chronic illness.

Japanese pressure on North China continued. After the assassination of Inukai Tsuyoshi and other prominent leaders in May 1932, Japan's party government collapsed. The Kwantung Army became virtually free to pursue its objectives in North China. In January 1933, the Japanese initiated a massive attack at the first gate of the Great Wall. T. V. Soong, acting premier, and his colleagues believed that if the Chinese Army showed its determination to resist Japanese aggression, both the League of Nations and the United States might be more sympathetic to the Nationalist cause and thus might grant assistance to China. But after three months of intensive fighting, no aid from the Western powers was forthcoming. Soong then urged Wang to return to China immediately and summoned Huang Fu from retirement to formulate a new policy to end the war.

On March 20, Wang arrived in Nanking and resumed the premiership. On March 31, the Tokyo government sent a special envoy, Hosokawa Kenkitsu, to China to discuss secretly with Huang Fu the possibilities of a cease-fire. The Japanese Army, meanwhile, continued to press forward on the battlefield. Wang personally assessed the battles in North China and became disturbed because many Chinese soldiers were slaughtered before they even saw the enemy. Although China was virtually united against Japanese aggression, the discrepancy in weaponry was insurmountable. Wang was determined to bring the war to a speedy conclusion by almost any means. On May 26, he announced that the Nanking government would be willing to negotiate a truce, subject to the principle of nonviolation of China's territorial integrity and sovereignty. This announcement constituted a shift from his policy of "resistance and negotiation" to one of appeasement. On May 28, Wang, Chiang, Sun Fo, and other prominent leaders of the Kuomintang convened a summit meeting at Lushan in Kiangsi province, and on May 31 they authorized the local commander to sign the infamous Tangku Truce, negotiated by Huang Fu and Hosokawa. The agreement designated the area from the Great Wall to Peking as a demilitarized zone to be patrolled by Chinese police and security forces.[49] Lo Wen-kan resigned as foreign minister, and Wang Ching-wei himself assumed this difficult post concurrently; Huang Fu was appointed chairman of the Peking Political Council to handle the delicate regional problems, particularly those concerning Japan in North China.

The Tangku Truce caused the military, the rightists, and some liberal leaders who had been his strong supporters to criticize Wang for his "weak-kneed" diplomacy. The military challenge to the policy of Wang and Chiang ranged from verbal abuse to active revolts. Shortly after Wang's announcement on May 28, Feng Yü-hsiang and his generals organized an army, the People's Anti-Japanese Alliance, and bitterly denounced the Tangku Truce as soon as it was signed. The Kwangsi generals and their allies on the Southwest Political Council immediately responded to Feng's call for war. Both Wang and Chiang, however, tired of civil war with the Kuomintang, circulated their famous *chin-tien* (telegram of July 20) urging Feng to support the government's policy. Public opinion also condemned Feng's tactics. Through Huang Fu's personal mediation, Feng finally accepted the "persuasion" of the Nanking government to retire to Taishan and thus avoid more civil strife at a time of national crisis.[50]

Then Ch'en Ming-shu of the 19th Route Army and other notable leaders of the Kuomintang such as Eugene Chen, Li Chi-shen, and Hsü Ch'ien organized a "People's Government" in Fukien province and solicited the support of the Southwest Political Council and the Chinese Communist Party in forming a united front against both the Nanking government and the Japanese. Hu Han-min refused his endorsement because of the close relationship of the "People's Government" with the Chinese Communist Party. Without Hu's support, the generals of the Southwest Political Council would take no action. Moreover, the Chinese Communist leadership, with Mao Tse-tung out of favor, was slow in reaching a decision. The public was extremely critical of this rebellion, and many of Wang's loyal followers who had served in the 19th Route Army also voiced their opposition to the overt revolt. When one of the division commanders refused to join in the action against Wang, the rebellion collapsed.[51]

The appeasement policy of Wang, Chiang, and Huang had its limits, however. They adopted this policy because they thought that war would only bring further disaster and humiliation to China, while peace probably would provide an opportunity for the nation to reconstruct itself and thereby to survive. The Nanking government therefore attempted to strengthen itself in various other ways. Soong was in Europe and the United States seeking financial and technical support for China's reconstruction and alerting the Western powers to Japan's ambitions in China. Soong succeeded in negotiating cotton and wheat loans totalling $50,000,000 from the United States, and in securing the continued technical assistance of the League of Nations. Furthermore, the Nanking government resumed diplomatic relations with the Soviet Union and widened its diplomatic activities. The Japanese government became alarmed and issued the Amau declaration on April 18, 1934, warning the Wang cabinet:

> Thus, we oppose China's use of other countries' power in an attempt to resist Japan in any way. We also oppose China's attempting to use one country against another. . . . As for supplying military airplanes to China, building airfields in China, sending military training officers or advisers to China, and loaning money for Chinese political expenses, these obviously can split the friendship of China and Japan and other countries, with the effect of disturbing peace and order in East Asia. Japan will oppose all these activities.[52]

Wang sharply refuted the Japanese accusations when he asserted that "Japan adds insult to injury by accusing China of still pursuing the old policy of 'playing one barbarian against another.' . . . For it is Japan who is brow-beating China, and it is China, like one in danger, who is crying out for help. Should she be prohibited even from crying out for help?"[53]

Wang continued to maintain the appeasement policy toward Japan, to solicit support from other countries to reconstruct China, and to avoid civil strife within the Nationalist Party. Chiang Kai-shek likewise expressed his strong support of the appeasement policy in his celebrated article, "Ti-hu yu-hu?" [Enemy or friend?]; he reiterated that "Japan cannot be our enemy, and that cooperation with Japan is a necessity."[54] Hu Shih wrote a series of articles in the *Tu-li p'ing-lun* [Independent Critics] about his approval of the conciliatory policy and his condemnation of the war advocates.[55] Wang concentrated on "unification through reconstruction"; Chiang on suppressing the growing power of the Communists. Wang believed that China's peaceful reconstruction alone would allow her to avoid foreign invasion and humiliation.

Chiang's war machine gradually pushed into Kiangsi and forced the Chinese Communists into the famous Long March (begun October 16, 1934). The Nationalist Army followed the retreating army and occupied the territory of the warlords in the interior; thus the power and influence of the Nanking government extended slowly beyond the east coast. Assisted by Yang Yung-t'ai, Chiang initiated the New Life Movement in an attempt to restore China's ancient virtues to counter the new ideology of Communism. More important, however, Wang's domestic reconstruction programs appeared promising; they stressed modern ideas rather than ancient virtues, and the importance of the masses rather than the elite. In rural areas, he started the Central Agricultural Experimental Bureau, Agricultural Cooperative Enterprises, and the Chinese Agricultural Bank, all of which experienced some success by 1936. The exorbitant levies and miscellaneous taxes on the farmers were first abolished in Kiangsi province in 1934 and then in other provinces. The conservation projects also produced results.[56] In short, the grain and industrial production indexes during Wang's tenure were impressive.[57]

In fiscal matters, the Wang cabinet stabilized the currency and implemented the *fa-pei* (legal tender) by the end of 1935. Despite heavy military spending and numerous economic activities, Wang managed to balance the budget in the last two years of his premiership, an extraordinary feat in Republican China. Railroad and highway construction in the coastal areas, increased expenditure for public education, and heightened morale in government were among his other main achievements. The Nationalist government moved to complete the legal code protecting women's rights, sanctioning collective bargaining for workers, prohibiting such social ills as footbinding, infanticide, parental abuses of power, and superstition, safeguarding civil rights and liberty, and enforcing varying political rights and responsibilities.[58] It must be pointed out, however, that Japanese aggression and the campaigns against the Communists prevented many provinces from carrying out the provisions of the new legal code. Nonetheless, Wang hoped that all provisions would be enforced and that the long-sought goal of ending extraterritoriality would be realized. At the Fifth National Congress, to be held in November 1935, Wang was prepared to propose the adoption of constitutional government.

The major problem of the Wang cabinet remained the effective containment of Japanese aggression. This issue divided the nation and many worthy programs were not developed because of it. Wang's personal relationship with Japanese leaders in Tokyo was good, but neither the Kwantung Army leaders nor other Japanese officials in North China and Manchuria would necessarily follow Tokyo's instructions. So he worked at improving Sino-Japanese relations through national and local channels. In Tokyo, he attempted to negotiate with the highest Japanese authorities in laying down certain principles for cooperation and mutual prosperity. At the local level in North China, he relied on Huang Fu and then on Ho Ying-ch'in to accommodate Japanese aspirations. In December 1934, Huang Fu signed an agreement with Manchukuo to resume postal and train services, an act which aroused considerable condemnation. Wang, however, insisted that this local settlement did not constitute recognition of Manchukuo by the Nanking government. In January 1935, Wang sent a goodwill mission headed by Wang Ch'ung-hui to confer with the Japanese foreign minister, Hirota Kōki. The latter proposed the famous three principles of Sino-Japanese relations: anti-Comintern pact, economic cooperation, and neighborliness. On February 20, at a meeting of the Central Political Council, Wang responded enthusiastically: "We wish to dedicate our sincerity fully to employing a peaceful means and a normal procedure to solve all the outstanding disputes between China and Japan."[59] On March

2, Chiang Kai-shek sent a telegram to Wang expressing his complete support of the policy articulated in the council.[60] The Japanese, however, continued to press China at the local level.

The Kwantung Army attempted to eject all Kuomintang influence from North China; Doihara Kenji promoted separationist movements in various Chinese provinces, particularly in the north; and Japanese *ronin*, a sort of masterless samurai, fomented disorder, especially smuggling in North China. Huang Fu, mentally and physically exhausted by his efforts to contain Japanese aggression in North China, returned to the mountains. Ho Ying-ch'in, chairman of the Peking Military Council, subsequently assumed responsibility for negotiating with the Japanese at the local level. In June 1935, Wang instructed Ho to sign the Ho–Umezu agreement, by which both the Kuomintang and the Nationalist Army were banned from Hopei province.[61] Wang also approved the Ch'in–Doihara agreement (June 23) to exclude all Nationalist troops and the Kuomintang headquarters from Chahar province.[62] The smuggling problem and the issue of separationist movements remained to be resolved. Anti-Wang sentiment grew rapidly and, on November 1, a would-be assassin, Sun Feng-ming, shot Wang three times. This tragic incident caused the termination of a colorful and progressive era: Wang resigned the premiership to recuperate in Europe, although he remained chairman of the Central Political Council.[63]

Chiang Kai-shek succeeded Wang and wished to maintain the coalition government. But Wang's lieutenants Ch'en Kung-po and Ku Meng-yü declined to serve him, in part because they suspected that Chiang might have been involved in the assassination attempt against Wang.[64] This internal split in the Kuomintang proved a serious blow to the Sino-Japanese relationship and to the future of the Nationalist government. Chiang also wanted to pursue the appeasement policy, and on November 20 he declared: "Until we reach the point of absolute hopelessness, we shall resolutely not give up the idea of peace; until we reach the final moment for sacrifice, we shall not speak lightly of sacrifice."[65] Chiang appointed Chang Ch'ün as foreign minister; Yang Yung-t'ai became governor of Hupei province. Chiang packed the cabinet with his military subordinates and the Chekiang-Kiangsu financiers, and ended the social and economic reforms of the Wang era. Moreover, the generals lacked the ability to articulate their policy in public and tended to adopt military measures to cope with civilian problems. For example, when student unrest became widespread, as during the December 9 Movement, Chiang chose to employ force to suppress it. But he failed to discipline other military leaders. When the Kiangsi generals joined the Southwest Political Council in denouncing the appeasement policy and in mounting armed revolt, Chiang accommodated them by promotion, financial rewards, and promise of strong action against Japan.[66] Chiang's ignorance of civilian strength in the struggle for national survival proved to be his greatest weakness.

The inability of the Chiang cabinet to guide patriotism toward constructive purposes was bad enough for the country; its suppressive measures stimulated anti-Japanese violence. On August 24, an unexpected incident flared up in Chengtu in Szechwan province, where some Chinese "patriots" wounded four Japanese travelers, two of whom died. On September 3, a mob in Peihai in Kwangtung province murdered a Japanese national. Other incidents occurred in Hankow, Shanghai, and other major Chinese cities. The Chinese and Japanese authorities soon realized that military confrontation would be inevitable. Chang Ch'ün and Japanese Ambassador Kawagoe Shigeru on September 15 initiated negotiations aimed at improving relations,[67] but the violence continued. On September 23, the eve of the third meeting of the delegations, a Chinese mob assaulted a group of Japanese nationals in Shanghai and wounded two of them, one of whom died shortly afterwards. On October 25, an assassin killed Yang Yung-t'ai in Hankow. This senseless murder destroyed the last hope of moderation. Kung Te-po, a prominent journalist and Japan specialist, observed that only Yang Yung-t'ai and Wang Ching-wei had the power and prestige to restrain Chiang Kai-shek and the Chinese military from engaging in war with Japan, but Yang's death and Wang's early retirement determined the fatal war between China and Japan.[68]

The Chinese military took action against the Japanese. In November 1936, General Fu Tso-yi's army defeated Wang Ying and Li Shou-hsin in Suiyuan. This action elated the Chinese people but enraged the Kwantung Army, which had equipped and supported the armies of Wang and Li. Numerous patriotic demonstrations throughout the country celebrated the "victory" and demanded that the government adopt a positive policy. Chiang Kai-shek blamed the intellectuals for the demonstrations, and on November 23 he ordered the arrest of seven intellectual leaders, including Tsou T'ao-fan and Li Kung-po, two prominent editors of anti-Japanese magazines in Shanghai. The public praised the scholars as "seven superior men" and made them martyrs to a great patriotic cause.[69] Chinese workers joined the students and intellectuals to boycott Japanese goods and to strike at Japanese factories. On December 2, before the eighth meeting of the Sino-Japanese negotiators, 23,000 Chinese workers went on strike in Tsingtao, causing the Tokyo government to dispatch marines to protect Japanese nationals and property there. This action in turn aroused Chinese fear, suspicion, and tension. The marines, nonetheless, remained in Tsingtao until December 23.

In this charged atmosphere, the negotiators continued their work with considerable restraint. On December 3, Kawagoe submitted a memorandum focusing on the vital areas of aviation, tariffs, employment of Japanese advisers, prohibition of Korean activities in China, and restriction of anti-Japanese movements; Chang would not agree to an anti-Comintern pact because he feared Japanese intervention in Chinese domestic affairs.[70] Wang Ching-wei, Yang Yung-t'ai, or Huang Fu might have persuaded Chiang and other military leaders to compromise, but Chang Ch'ün had neither the power nor the influence to do so, and Huang Fu died on December 6 after a long illness. The deadlock ended negotiations—both Kawagoe and Chang awaited further instructions. On December 12, Marshal Chang Hsueh-liang and his allies kidnapped Chiang Kai-shek in Sian and demanded that the civil war against the Chinese Communists be terminated, that a united front against Japan be formed, and that all political prisoners be released.[71]

The Chinese public, stunned by this military coup in time of national crisis, demanded that Chiang be released unconditionally at once. The Comintern and the Chinese Communist Party wanted to rescue Chiang because they regarded Japan as the fatal enemy of the Communist movement and believed that ending the civil war would relieve the pressure on the infant Yenan government. Mao Tse-tung therefore sent Chou En-lai to Sian to negotiate with both sides for Chiang's freedom.[72] The Tokyo government unexpectedly refrained from any rash action during the crisis. The immediate concern, of course, was the leadership of the Kuomintang. In a series of meetings at Nanking, two widely different approaches became apparent. Soong Mei-ling (Madame Chiang) and T. V. Soong, fearing for Chiang's life, sought negotiations and concessions for his safety. Ho Ying-ch'in and Tai Chi-t'ao, evidently troubled about the future of the National-ist government, proposed air and ground attacks on Sian, as well as the immediate recall of Wang Ching-wei to China to assume responsibility for the administration. The Nanking authorities finally adopted a modified form of both approaches.

Soong requested that William Henry Donald, Chiang's Australian adviser who had served Marshal Chang Hsueh-liang in Manchuria, go to Sian to negotiate for Chiang's release. As a result of Donald's efforts and the Communist pressures, Chang allowed Chiang's wife and T. V. Soong to come to Sian for further negotiations. Ho's movement of troops and Wang's impending return appeared to be the main reasons for Marshal Chang's unconditional release of Chiang Kai-shek on December 25.[73] The advance of Nationalist armies into the northwest would destroy the warlords' domination, as indicated by the movement of the Nationalist troops into Kweichow, Szechwan, and other southeastern provinces during the Long March. The expected arrival of Wang Ching-wei and his resumption of power in Nanking signaled a continuation of his appeasement policy regardless of the fate of Chiang Kai-shek; and Chang, Wang's bitter enemy for many years, would have virtually no bargaining power once Wang took over the central government. Moreover, Soong handled Chang's personal finances abroad; if Chang persisted in his present course, he might well lose his foreign investments.[74] In sum, it was unwise for him to continue to detain Chiang either for the cause of war against Japan or for personal reasons. Besides, it now became apparent that only Chiang's prompt release could forestall the powerful coalition of Wang, Ho, and Tai in the

Nationalist government. Thus, after his conversation with Soong, Chang decided to escort Chiang back to Nanking personally, even before Wang arrived on Chinese soil.

As a consequence of this episode, Chiang's attitude toward both Japan and the Communists changed. Chiang obviously believed his release was the result of popular demand for his leadership against Japanese invasion and the mediation of Chou En-lai. He became more conscious of popular clamor for war and he received Chou En-lai in Nanking to organize the second united front between the Chinese Communist Party and the Kuomintang.[75] Chiang probably also suspected the personal loyalty of his "pro-Japanese" advisers, but he could not disregard their considerable hold over the army and the party. Ho and Tai could easily transfer their power and influence to Wang in any power struggle. Chiang therefore proceeded cautiously to rebuild his power bases. At first, he relied heavily upon the European-American experts to carry on the daily functions of the government, replaced Chang Ch'ün with Wang Ch'ung-hui as foreign minister, and brought Soong back into government service. Gradually, however, Chiang shifted his dependence to those people who had proved their personal loyalty to him. He put Ch'en Kuo-fu in charge of personnel of the administration; utilized the special agents of Ch'en Li-fu in the party and Tai Li in the army to discipline his opponents; and appointed General Ch'en Ch'eng, whose sole virtue was unquestioned personal loyalty, to take charge of political affairs and later to organize the notorious San-min chu-i ch'ing-nien t'uan (Youth Guards of the Three Principles for the People), to sustain Chiang's personal power.

On January 3, 1937, Wang Ching-wei arrived in China, and immediately launched a campaign urging his countrymen to continue his previous efforts to defeat the Communists, to reconstruct the economy, to work for a constitutional and democratic government, and to cooperate with Japan. Wang's Japanese policy was not popular with the masses, but his vigorous efforts produced two notable results. Some liberals under the leadership of Hu Shih rallied to his support, and the younger members of Chiang's entourage, particularly Chou Fo-hai, Mei Ssu-p'ing, and Kao Tsung-wu, joined him in his advocacy of peace.

Meanwhile, Chiang implemented Marshal Chang's demands by releasing political prisoners, formulating the second united front against Japan, and intensifying political and military training for war. The local commanders in North China moved to enlarge the sphere of conflict when the Marco Polo Bridge Incident (July 7, 1937) occurred, and war began between China and Japan. Chiang's loyal followers promptly seized the opportunity presented by hostilities and made him dictator in April 1938. Wang Ching-wei and Chou Fo-hai then looked elsewhere to launch their peace offensive, which eventually led them to collaborate with Japan in occupied Nanking.[76]

In conclusion, Wang Ching-wei's domestic and foreign policies represented a development of Sun Yat-sen's early theory and practice; his strength evolved during the power struggle both in and out of the government in the 1920s, and his bases of power were relatively broad. In contrast, Chiang Kai-shek, although he grasped Sun's nationalism, virtually abandoned the other teachings. Later, Chiang's attempted modification of modern nationalism with ancient Confucian virtues proved to be a miserable failure. He did not regenerate the morale in his administration or raise the level of consciousness of the people. Chiang's considerable power and influence in the Nationalist government rested on his army and his special agents and the persistent support of the financiers, but his political base was extremely narrow. Before the Manchurian Incident, Chiang had not developed a comprehensive Japanese policy, in part because of the insecurity of his political position at home; after the traumatic episode of 1931, the Nationalist government was controlled by the coalition of Wang and Chiang.

The meager achievements of the Nationalist government in the early 1930s, such as they were, derived from the combination of Wang's pragmatism and political skill in peace negotiations and Chiang's military power. Above all, it was the appeasement policy rather than military strength that effectively contained the Japanese in Shanghai and in North China, and this containment provided the Nationalists breathing space in which to perform the miracle of "unification through reconstruction." It is erroneous, therefore, to assume that Chiang was a dictator in the Nationalist government and that the fruits of the progressive era were the result of his military power, which maintained law and order and thereby produced political stability and economic prosperity. It appears reasonable to conclude that without the early retirement of Wang after the assassination attempt and without the deaths of Yang Yung-t'ai and Huang Fu, the coalition government of Wang and Chiang might have been maintained, the appeasement policy continued, and China spared the turbulence of war and revolution. Finally, Chiang's loss of power should have been abundantly evident shortly after the Sian Incident, when he chose to narrow his political base, to value personal loyalty rather than talent, and to abandon the peace policy. The Sino-Japanese War merely accelerated his political demise. During the next decade, at terrible human sacrifice, the Chinese Communist Party became the natural successor to the most progressive era in Republican China through its own efforts at military discipline and innovation, social and economic reform, moral regeneration and humanistic concern, political accommodation and foreign collaboration, and, above all, through its brilliant leadership.[77]

Notes

1. Professor C. Martin Wilbur summarizes current interpretations of Chiang's fall from power when he says that Sun Yat-sen's "main successor, Chiang Kai-shek, devoted twenty-five harassed years struggling to unify the country and might have succeeded except for Japanese, American, and Russian interference." *China in Crisis,* ed. Ho Ping-ti and Tang Tsou (Chicago, 1968), 1:220. Two popular textbooks appear to have generally ignored the power and influence of Wang Ching-wei in the Nationalist government. Professor Edmund Clubb even implies that Wang's service was terminated by his leave of absence in October 1932. O. Edmund Clubb, *Twentieth Century China* (New York and London, 1972), p. 183. John K. Fairbank, Edwin O. Reischauer, and Albert M. Craig, *East Asia: The Modern Transformation* (Boston, 1965), pp. 691–95.

2. Sun Yat-sen, *Kuo-fu ch'üan-chi* [Collected works of the Founding Father of the Republic] (Taipei, 1965), 2 (section 7):87; section 8, pp. 306–15.

3. Ibid., (section 4):44–51, 74; Jerome Chen, "The Left-Wing Kuomintang—A Definition," *Bulletin of School of Oriental and African Studies* (London University) (October 1962), pp. 557–76.

4. Liang Hsiao-ming, *Wu-san-shih yün-tung* [The May Thirtieth Movement] (Peking, 1955), pp. 20–21; Ch'en K'o-hua, *Chung-kuo hsien-tai ko-ming yün-tung shih-shih* [Revolutionary records of modern Chinese history] (Hong Kong, 1964), 1:92–94.

5. Liang, op. cit., pp. 28–29; Chung-kuo hsien-tai shih yen-chiu wei-yüan hui [Committee on Modern Chinese Historical Studies], ed., *Chung-kuo hsien-tai ko-ming yün-tung shih* [A history of modern Chinese Revolutionary movements] (Hong Kong, 1949), p. 194; Ch'en K'o-hua, op. cit., 1:92–94.

6. Bamba Nobuya, *Japanese Diplomacy in a Dilemma: New Light on Japan's China Policy, 1924–1929* (Vancouver, 1972), p. 244.

7. T'ang Liang-li, *The Inner History of the Chinese Revolution* (London, 1930), pp. 207–9.

8. Wang Ching-wei, *China and the Nations,* trans. and ed. I-sen Teng and John N. Smith (New York, 1927). This book was originally a draft to be submitted to the People's Conference in

1925 for approval as a guideline for China's foreign policy. The conference was never held; the work was subsequently published as Wang's personal views.

9. Ai-hsin chüeh-lo P'u-i, *Wo te ch'ien-pan-sheng* [The first half of my life] (Hong Kong, 1964), 1:37–38.

10. T'ang, op. cit., pp. 214–21; Ch'en, op. cit., 1:83.

11. Ch'en, op. cit., 1:86–89; T'ang, op. cit., pp. 215–41; *Chung-kuo hsien-tai ko-ming yün-tung shih,* pp. 205–6.

12. T'ang, op. cit., pp. 241–47; Tung Hsien-kuang, *Chiang Tsung-t'ung Chuan* [A biography of President Chiang Kai-shek], rev. ed. (Taipei, 1952), p. 71.

13. Ch'en, op. cit., 1:113–18.

14. Ch'en Kung-po, *Han-feng chi* [Collected essays] (Shanghai, 1944), p. 268; Liu Yen et al., *Chung-kuo wai-chiao shih* [Diplomatic history of China], rev. ed. (Taipei, 1962), 2:833–37; Wang Yün-sheng, "Chung-kuo Kuo-min-tang wai-chiao chih hui-ku" [A study of the Kuomintang diplomacy], *Kuo-wen chou-pao* [National News Weekly] 9:1, pp. 3–4.

15. Dai-Nihon Teikoku Gikai-shi Kankō-kai, ed., *Dai-Nihon Teikoku Gikai-shi* [The Diet record of the Great Japanese Empire] (Tokyo, 1930), 21 January 1926; see Bamba, op. cit., p. 247.

16. *Chung-kuo hsien-tai ko-ming yün-tung shih,* pp. 214–15; Akira Iriye, *After Imperialism* (New York, 1969), pp. 118–19.

17. Iriye, op. cit., pp. 110–11, 130–31; *Nihon Gaikō-shi* [Japanese diplomatic history] (Tokyo, 1971), 17:176–77.

18. *Nihon Gaikō-shi,* 17:177–84; Iriye, op. cit., pp. 132–34.

19. Chiang Kai-shek (Chiang Chung-cheng), *A Summing-up at Seventy: Soviet Russia in China* (London, 1957), pp. 48–49; T'ang, op. cit., pp. 265–67.

20. Bamba, op. cit., p. 301.

21. Ibid., p. 295.

22. M. N. Roy, *Revolution and Counterrevolution in China* (Calcutta, 1946), pp. 519–20; T'ang, op. cit., pp. 280–81; Robert C. North, *Moscow and Chinese Communists* (Stanford, 1953), p. 106; Conrad Brandt, *Stalin's Failure in China, 1924–1927* (Cambridge, Mass., 1958), p. 138.

23. James Sheridan, *Chinese Warlord: The Career of Feng Yü-hsiang* (Stanford, 1966), p. 228.

24. Roy, op. cit., pp. 519–20; T'ang, op. cit., pp. 280–81; Chiang, op. cit., pp. 50–51.

25. Iriye, op. cit., pp. 157–58; Gaimushō, ed., *Nihon gaikō nenpyō narabi ni shuyō bunshō* [Chronology and main documents of Japanese foreign policy] (Tokyo, 1955), 2:102–6.

26. Hu Shih et al., *Wu Chih-hui hsien-sheng chi-nien chi* [A collection of memorial essays of Mr. Wu Chih-hui] (Taipei, 1954), p. 15.

27. MacMurray to Secretary of State Frank B. Kellogg, 7 April 1928, U.S. Department of State Files (National Archives, Washington, D.C.), 893.00/9859; cf. Iriye, op. cit., p. 217.

28. Wang Yün-sheng, op. cit., pp. 4–5; Ch'en K'o-hua, op. cit., 2:71–72; Iriye, op. cit., pp. 198–205; Nihon Kokusai Seiji Gakkai, ed., *Taiheiyō sensō e no michi* [The road to the Pacific War] (Tokyo, 1963), 1:300–302, hereafter cited as *TSM;* Shen I-ÿün, *I-yün hui-i* [Memoirs] (Taipei, 1968), p. 372.

29. Shen I-ÿün, op. cit., pp. 388–96; *Pe-nien-lai Chung-Jih kuan-hsi lun-wen chi* [Collected essays on Sino-Japanese relations in the past hundred years] (n.p., n.d.), pp. 11–12.

30. Bamba, op. cit., pp. 337–45.

31. Wang Yün-sheng, op. cit., pp. 5–6; Shigemitsu Mamoru, *Japan and Her Destiny* (New York, 1958), pp. 58–59.

32. Ch'en Kung-lu, *Chung-kuo chin-tai shih* [History of modern China] (Shanghai, 1935), p. 789.

33. Tung, op. cit., pp. 141–42.

34. Wang Yün-sheng, op. cit., pp. 6–7; Iriye, op. cit., pp. 114–17; Shen, op. cit., pp. 349–97.

35. Iriye, op. cit., pp. 264–68; Ch'en Kung-lu, op. cit., p. 797; Chiang, op. cit., p. 58; Wang Yün-sheng, op. cit., pp. 8–10.

36. Shigemitsu, op. cit., p. 56; Bamba, op. cit., p. 358.

37. Wang Yün-sheng, op. cit., pp. 7–8; Ch'en Kung-lu, op. cit., p. 796.

38. Li Tse-feng, *Chung-Jih kuan-hsi shih* [History of Sino-Japanese relations] (Taipei, 1970), pp. 162–78. For details, see Wang Ching-wei et al., *The Chinese National Revolution: Essays and Documents,* ed. T'ang Liang-li (Peking, 1931).

39. "Chung-yang t'ung-kuo te pa-shih-ssu hao" [Central Circular Note, No. 84], *Kung-fei huo-kuo shih-liao hui-pien* [Collected historical materials on the Communist bandits who damage the country] (Taipei, 1961), 2:34–41; Chiang, op. cit., pp. 58–59; Jerome Chen, *Mao and the Chinese Revolution* (Oxford, 1965), pp. 160–71.

40. Lei, op. cit., pp. 161–78. Chou Fo-hai accompanied Chiang Kai-shek on various campaigns and considered the defeat of Chiang's opponents the result of poor coordination, Chang Hsueh-liang's participation on Chiang's side at the decisive moment, and bad luck. Many times, chance kept Chiang from being defeated. Chou Fo-hai, *Sheng-shuai yüeh-chin hua ts'ang-sang* [Talks on the violent changes of the thriving and declining through experience] (Hong Kong, 1956), pp. 51–56.

41. Chou, ibid., p. 62. According to Chou, if Yen Hsi-shan's representative was willing to spend as much money as Chiang's, Chang's allegiance to Nanking was far from certain. Chiang's telegram can be found in Lei, pp. 179–80. Chiang's biographer, Tung Hsien-kuang, also acknowledges this telegram and Chiang's intention of accepting Wang's programs (pp. 158–60). Professor Hsu Dau-lin, a close associate of Chiang for a long time, estimates that Chiang's army suffered 80,000 casualties; his opponents, 150,000 (*China in Crisis,* 1:274). Wang Ching-wei in the meantime was tired of the civil war and expressed his deep grief and sorrow for the great loss of human lives, in his famous poem, "Kuo Yen-meng Kuan" [Through the Yen-Meng Pass], *Shuang-chao-lou shih-tzu kao* [Drafted poems of the Shuang-chao Studio] (Hong Kong, n.d.), p. 47.

42. Liang Ching-tun, *Chiu-i-pa shih-pien shih-shu* [The Manchurian affairs] (New York, 1964), pp. 116–17; *Kuo-wen chou-pao* 10:37; *TSM,* 2:268.

43. Lei, op. cit., pp. 208–10. A more detailed description of the Shanghai Conference appears in *Kuo-wen chou-pao* 8:42, 43, 44.

44. Lei, op. cit., p. 211.

45. Wang Ching-wei, *Wang Ching-wei hsien-sheng chiang-yen chi* [Collected speeches of Wang Ching-wei] (Shanghai, 1936), pp. 9–16. The objectives of Wang's foreign policy also appeared in his book, *China's Problems and Their Solution,* ed. T'ang Liang-li (Shanghai, 1934).

46. Chin Hsiung-pai, *Wang Cheng-ch'üan te k'ai-ch'ang yü shou-ch'ang* [The beginning and end of the Wang regime] (Hong Kong, 1959–1964), 2:176; Lei, op. cit., pp. 212–13; Ch'en K'o-hua, op. cit., 2:135.

47. Wang Ching-wei, *Wang Ching-wei hsien-sheng chiang-yen chi,* pp. 71–76.

48. Tung, op. cit., p. 172.

49. Liu Yen, op. cit., pp. 893–94; *Shen-pao yüeh-k'an* 2:6, pp. 129–31; *Kuo-wen chou-pao* 10:22. For Huang Fu's role in this negotiation, see James T. C. Liu, "Sino-Japanese Diplomacy during the Appeasement Period, 1933–1937" (Ph.D. diss., University of Pittsburgh, 1950); Shen, op. cit., pp. 467–500.

50. *Kuo-wen chou-pao* 10:31; Ch'en K'o-hua, op. cit., 3:24–25; Tung, op. cit., pp. 227–28.

51. *Kuo-wen chou-pao* 11:1,2; Tung, op. cit., p. 173; Ts'ai T'ing-k'ai, *Ts'ai T'ing-k'ai tzu-chuan* [Autobiography of Ts'ai T'ing-k'ai], pp. 383–84.

52. Li Chih-chung, *Jih-pen wai-chiao* [Japanese diplomacy] (Changsha, 1938), pp. 383–84; Li, op. cit., p. 571.

53. Wang Ching-wei, *China's Problems and Their Solution,* pp. 120–21.

54. Chiang Kai-shek, *Chiang Tsung-t'ung yen-lun hui-pien: Chuan-chu* [A collection of President Chiang's essays arranged in topical order: Special writings] (Taipei, 1956), 1:148–56.

55. *Tu-li p'ing-lu* [Independent Critics], no. 4, p. 46.

56. T'ang Liang-li, *Reconstruction in China* (Shanghai, 1935), p. 2.

57. Alexander Eckstein et al., eds. *Economic Trends in Communist China* (Chicago, 1968), pp. 65–69.

58. *Chung-hua min-kuo hsien-hsing fa-kuei ta-ch'üan* [Complete compilation of presently active laws and regulations of the Republic of China] (Shanghai, 1934), pp. 15–193.

59. Wang Ching-wei, *Wang Ching-wei hsien-sheng chiang-yen chi,* pp. 227–29; *Kuo-wen chou-pao* 12:7.

60. Ibid., 12:9.

61. *TSM,* 3:106–11; Ch'en K'o-hua, op. cit., 3:25–26; Liang Ching-tun, "Ho-Mei hsien-ting" [Ho–Umezu agreement], *Chuan-chi wen-hsüeh* [Biographical Literature] 11:5.

62. *TSM,* 3:117–20; *Kuo-wen chou-pao* 12:29.

63. Chou Fo-hai, *Wang-i chi* [A collection of past events] (Hong Kong, n.d.), pp. 71–72.

64. Kung Te-po, *Wang Chao-ming hsiang-ti mai-kuo mi-shih* [The secret history of Wang Ching-wei, his surrender to the enemy and sell-out of the country] (Taipei, 1963), p. 20; *Kuo-wen chou-pao* 12:50; Chin, op. cit., 2:175–76.

65. Chiang Kai-shek, *Chiang Tsung-t'ung yen lun hui-pien: Yen-chiang* [Speeches], 3:275.

66. Tung, op. cit., pp. 203–31. See also *The Chinese Year Book, 1937,* p. 1270, for members of the National Military Council.

67. Li Chih-chung, op. cit., pp. 343–51.

68. Kung Te-po, *Hui-i lu* [Memoirs] (Hong Kong, 1964), 2:65–66.

69. *Chieh-fang jih-pao* [Emancipation Daily], ed., *Tsung chiu-i-pa tao ch'i-ch'i* [From September 18 to July 7] (Peking, 1949), p. 34.

70. Li, op. cit., p. 351.

71. Tung, op. cit., p. 252; Feng Yü-hsiang, *Wo so jen-shih te Chiang Chieh-shih* [The Chiang Kai-shek I knew] (Hong Kong, 1949), p. 48.

72. Lyman P. Van Slyke, *Enemies and Friends: The United Front in Chinese Communist History* (Stanford 1967), pp. 76–91. Also see my review in *Journal of Canadian History* 3:2 (September 1968), pp. 131–32.

73. Soong Mei-ling's hint to Chiang in Sian of the dangerous developments in Nanking and of the importance of an immediate departure from Sian without arguing about terms with Chang Hsueh-liang, and T. V. Soong's confidential report on the movement of Nationalist troops under the orders of Ho Ying-ch'in, can be found in Chiang's diary, "Hsi-an pan-yüeh chi" [Records of a half-month in Sian], *Chiang Tsung-t'ung yen-lun hui-pien: Tsai-chu* [Miscellaneous writings], 6:37, and *Hsi-an shih-pien san-i* [Three reminiscences of the Sian Incident] (Hong Kong, 1962), which contains Chiang's diary, Soong Mei-ling's memoir, and a critic's comments on Chiang's policy toward Chang Hsueh-liang after the incident; pp. 20, 111–18, 170–71.

74. Professor Chang Fo-chuan of the University of British Columbia informed me that Hu Shih personally conveyed to him the information about T. V. Soong's conversation with Chang Hsueh-liang and about Soong's handling of Chang's investments abroad. Professor Chang was a colleague of Hu Shih's at Peking University in the 1930s.

75. *Hsi-an shih-pien san-i*, pp. 150–52; Tung, op. cit., p. 269.

76. For Wang Ching-wei's Japanese peace efforts and his subsequent collaboration with Japan, see my articles, "Chou Fo-hai: The Diplomacy of Survival," in *Diplomats in Crisis: United States-Chinese-Japanese Relations, 1919–1941,* ed. Richard D. Burns and Edward M. Bennett (Santa Barbara, 1974), and "Wang Ching-wei and Chinese Collaboration," *Peace and Change* 1:1 (Fall 1972):17–35.

77. For my interpretations of the rise of Mao Tse-tung and of the development of his ideology, see "Modern China: Ideology and Diplomacy" (cassette), *Flightapes* (Sunnyvale, Ca., 1972).

10.

In his essay John Boyle discusses two peace advocates who were operating at important levels in the Japanese military establishment and Foreign Ministry respectively during the escalation of the China war in 1937–1938. One, General Ishiwara Kanji, played a key role, as a colonel, in the plotting and carrying out of the Manchurian Incident; the other, Ishii Itarō, was Asian Bureau chief. From their separate vantage points they both came to appreciate the depth of Chinese nationalism and to see the folly of the "quick victory" thinking that deluded their colleagues and superiors in the military and civilian sectors of Japan's leadership. They were surprisingly articulate and outspoken; though their efforts were short-circuited, it is clear they were seeking a constructive way out of the spreading China war.

John Boyle took his M.A. at Harvard and his Ph.D. at Stanford. He is the author of *China and Japan at War, 1937–1945: The Politics of Collaboration* (1972) and has contributed articles and translations to *Monumenta Nipponica, Pacific Historical Review,* and *Japan Interpreter*. He has taught Asian history at California State University (Chico) since 1968 and is currently writing the section on occupied China for the forthcoming *Cambridge History of China*. A preliminary version of this essay was written for the conference China and Japan: Their Modern Interaction, sponsored by the Social Science Research Council at the University of Chicago in May 1974.

Peace Advocacy during the Sino-Japanese Incident

John Hunter Boyle

I.

The walled town of Wanping ("Obliging Peace") is situated about twelve miles southwest of Peking. In 1937 there were two bridges spanning the Yungting River just outside of town. One was a steel railway bridge only a few yards distant from a junction of two important lines which commanded the southern approaches to Peking. The other bridge, more picturesque than strategic, was already old when Marco Polo admired its graceful arches and stone lions seven centuries ago. It was in this vicinity that a Japanese garrison, permitted there under a strained interpretation of the Boxer Protocol of 1901, was conducting maneuvers on the night of July 7, 1937. From the darkness a volley of shots was heard by the Japanese soldiers at about 10:30 P.M. When the Japanese commander summoned his troops for a roll call, it was discovered that one of the soldiers was missing from the ranks. Accordingly, the commanding officer asked permission of the Chinese commander of a nearby fort to search for the missing soldier; when permission was refused, the Japanese shelled the Chinese installation. The studies by Yale historian James B. Crowley have shown that the incident at the Marco Polo Bridge was not a repetition of the Manchurian Incident of 1931—not, in other words, a staged incident used as a pretext to widen the Imperial Army's control over Chinese territory.[1] Nevertheless, the shots fired on July 7, 1937, set in motion a chain of events that veered out of control a month later and plunged China and Japan into an eight-year war.

It is a measure of the madness and confusion of war that we do not know who fired the first shots of that war. It is another measure of the madness of a war that cost nearly two million military dead that the missing soldier evidently disappeared from the ranks for no more than a few minutes. If the account of Morishima Morito, then counselor of the Japanese embassy in China, is correct, he merely went into the bushes to relieve himself.[2] At any rate, we still do not know the name of this historic individual who occupies a position of importance as the immediate cause of war roughly comparable to that of the Archduke Ferdinand in 1914.

The Marco Polo Bridge Incident did not precipitate an instant eruption of all-out war. For more than a month there was more negotiating than fighting and skirmishing was confined to a limited area in North China, the scene of numerous clashes between Japanese and Chinese forces in the previous decade. For reasons we will examine shortly, Japanese military strategists were most anxious to avoid an expansion of the North China Incident (as it was first called) into a full-scale war with China. Matsukata Saburō, a distinguished Japanese journalist, tells of having been dispatched by the War Ministry to North China shortly after the Marco Polo Bridge Incident to explain the Japanese version of the incident to Western newsmen and diplomats in China. A spokesman for the War Ministry assured Matsukata that his propaganda mission would take no longer than two weeks to complete, as the army was determined to settle the incident with great haste. Thirty-three years later, Matsukata recalled the outcome of his "brief" mission in an interview with this writer: "I was there for the next eight years."[3]

We do not know enough about the process by which "incidents" apparently capable of solution in a fortnight somehow mature into eight-year wars. The Sino-Japanese War (1937–1945) offers a valuable case study because of the wealth of documentary evidence available. In addition to the documentation made public in connection with the International Military Tribunal for the Far East after the war, there has been an immense amount of archival material published by the commercial Japanese press in the past decade or so.[4] The Japanese sources make Tokyo's wartime leaders and their strategic thinking an open book.

The North China Incident did, of course, expand into a "China Incident" in August 1937 as fighting broke out in Shanghai. But this did not end the determination of antiwar advocates in Japan (and in Nationalist China) to find a peaceful solution to Sino-Japanese differences. Before turning to two of these advocates, let us consider some of the general factors which help to explain why peace advocacy made sense in the Japan of 1937–1938.

Japan confronted a number of dilemmas and paradoxes in 1938. One of the principal goals of Japanese strategy on the mainland was to check the growth of Chinese nationalism and Communism—the two movements having coalesced in a shaky united front in the early months of 1937. And yet, by mid-1938, some Japanese were pondering the irony that the greater Japan's military commitment to the struggle against China, the more vigorous Chinese nationalism became. In the early months of the war, farseeing Japanese and Chinese predicted that the war would be protracted, one which neither the Chinese Nationalists under Chiang Kai-shek nor Imperial Japan would win. Both would be exhausted and broken by a long war and would in the end forfeit control of China to Communism.

By 1938, the Japanese were rapidly growing disillusioned and resentful of the unpopularity and inefficacy of the client regimes. There was much grumbling about the venality of Chinese collaborators, who, to many Japanese, lacked commitment to the goals of the "New Order in East Asia" proclaimed by the emperor in November 1938. With few exceptions, the Chinese collaborators were regarded by the Japanese as hungry, opportunistic job-seekers who could not be trusted for the long pull. Not surprisingly, there was an unmistakable air of shabbiness and transience about each of the several collaboration regimes established by Japan in the first years of the war.

In Japan, the National General Mobilization Law enacted in March 1938 signaled the collapse of parliamentary government and ushered in an era of government controls and extreme austerity. The demands of military procurement on the economy of a singularly have-not nation were severe and growing. Raw cotton and cotton cloth were removed from the domestic market, iron became as "scarce as gold," and chemists in the Ministry of Agriculture were "tanning rat skins in their search for a leather substitute." "It is hard now to buy an iron frying pan," wrote a *New York Times* correspondent; "a month from now it will be impossible."[5] The Home Ministry advised factory owners in late 1937 that "twelve hours should be the maximum" workday, but indicated that two hours of overtime were permissible "if unavoidable." Even then the regulation was criticized as inappropriate to wartime economy. Rest periods and dinner hours were canceled and the "14-hour working day was not at all uncommon."[6] The retail commodity price index nearly doubled in 1937 compared with 1936; in 1938 the increase was nearly triple the 1936 rise.[7] Small-business failures multiplied as government bureaucrats scrambled to weed out inefficient enterprises and thus gain the advantages of scale in production. For a few sensitive souls the prohibition of neon lights on the Ginza was a welcome product of the war—"an enlightened act of our unenlightened military government," wrote novelist Nagai Kafū in his diary. But for most it was a symbol of a grim austerity that promised to become much worse.[8]

Finally, and most important, by 1938 it was clear to many in Japan that the Imperial Army's involvement on battlefronts and garrison duty in a dozen Chinese provinces was creating a dangerous vulnerability in the vent of a war against the Soviet Union, which top army strategists judged not merely probable but certain within another three or four years. Strategists like General Ishiwara Kanji contemplated with horror the prospects of a two-front war and warned that Soviet power in the Far East was superior to Japan's—a calculation borne out by the Russian victories in numerous clashes throughout 1938–1939 but notably at Lake Khasan (Changkufeng) in the summer of 1938 and a year later at Nomonhan.

These were some of the reasons that impelled Ishiwara and others to urge a peaceful settlement of the conflict with China. The same premises, however, sometimes can be made to support different conclusions. General Ishiwara, for example, argued that Japan lacked the economic capacity to prepare for the inevitable war with the Soviet Union in the north and at the same time face a hostile China in the south; Japan must therefore befriend China. Others, however, accepted Ishiwara's premises about the danger of a two-front war but drew the opposite conclusion: since a hostile China was a menace to Japan, it had to be annihilated.

By 1938, the annihilation advocates were showing signs of succumbing to their own propaganda about the "light at the end of the tunnel." The troops had not returned home by New Year's Day as most had expected when they disembarked in China in the summer and autumn of 1937 but still there was widespread optimism born of confidence in the spiritual powers of the Japanese soldier and a corresponding contempt for the Chinese adversary. The Japanese "Chankoro" is the equivalent of the English-language "Chink" and was used with the same contemptuous overtones. In Hino Ashihei's widely read war reportage (translated into English as *Wheat and Soldiers*), "Chankoro" could be the objects of contempt whether they resisted the Japanese or welcomed them. Hino writes of his surprise at being greeted with smiles by the inhabitants of certain towns during the brief Hangchow campaign in late 1937:

> Such a thing could never be if any enemy occupied Japanese towns, and the men, women and even children would never forget that they were enemies and would be hostile to the very end. Japanese would sooner die than be friendly with an enemy. We would be friendly with Chinese individuals and indeed came to love them. But how could we help despising them as a nation when they would sell their smiles and flattery to any enemy for the price of their own skins when the destiny of their nation [was] in the balance. To us soldiers, they were pitiful, spineless people.[9]

Official pronouncements by Premier Konoe Fumimaro relegated Chiang Kai-shek to the status of a local warlord—and the Imperial Army had a wealth of experience in dealing with local warlords, almost all of it satisfying and reassuring from the point of view of the army. Consequently, when the annihilationists talked in 1938 about their *tai-Shi ichigeki ron*—that is, about defeating China with "one great blow"—there were not many to challenge their optimism. True, the "one great blow" was to have been the capture of the enemy's castle-town, Nanking, and something had gone wrong. Chinese resistance had not crumbled as predicted. But that was only a minor miscalculation. Surely, when Hsuchow fell, the Chinese would realize that they were beaten. After all, Hsuchow was a vital rail junction and throughout Chinese history had the reputation of being a pivotal stronghold. When Hsuchow fell, a dynasty could not long survive.

Hsuchow fell to the Japanese in May 1938 but somehow the Chinese ignored the lessons of their own history and continued their resistance. And so the drive on Hankow, the new capital, was launched. In October it and Canton, the last great coastal city held by the Nationalists, fell to the Imperial Army and the familiar lantern parades were held throughout Japan to celebrate the imminent defeat of China. We may surmise that those who gathered at the Imperial Palace in Tokyo to shout "Banzai" to the emperor across the moat felt a little less sanguine about the outcome of the China Incident each time they gathered there for victory celebrations. And yet, as General Imai Takeo writes in his postwar memoirs, "Our persistent use of the very phrase 'China Incident' reflected our self-delusion that we could solve things quickly." In short, Imai writes, Japan "refused to recognize that it was really in a war" until it was impossibly mired on the continent.[10]

II.

In China, the winter of 1937–1938 marked the high tide of the "united front." With the advantage of hindsight we now know that the Nationalist-Communist alliance was built on shaky ground, but for a few months, as Theodore White said, "China enjoyed the most complete unity of spirit and motive that it had ever known."[11] The spirit, needless to say, was the spirit of resistance to Japan. "Our armed forces have withstood the formidable enemy, and have used flesh and blood as armor and fortress. The second line steps up as soon as the first line fails. Their bodies may perish but the spirit never wavers," declared the Manifesto of the Extraordinary National Congress of the Kuomintang when it met in April 1938.[12] The resistance was not always so valiant as the manifesto suggested, but Colonel Joseph Stilwell's "estimate of the general situation" in March contained an impressive list of "factors favorable to the Chinese":

> General determination to resist to bitter end, educated and moneyed classes gradually taking part, more students in ranks, enormous man power, military training of reserves going on everywhere . . . more spirit visible in the ranks and among wounded, many new divisions nearly ready, loyal cooperation by the Reds, good example of execution of

Han Fu-chü [who surrendered much of Shantung province without a fight], no apparent depression due to loss of men and territory, guerrilla war in Shansi growing serious. . . .[13]

Here, then, we have the ingredients of a protracted war: Chinese will to resist to the death and Japanese failure to pay proper heed to that determination.

But there *were* gaps in the armor of China's resistance. In Nanking first, and then in Hankow and Chungking, was the Low-Key Club (*ti-t'iao chü-lo-pu*), as a group of Kuomintang civilian leaders styled themselves. The designation was meant to suggest that the prevailing approach to the war with Japan was "hysterical" and in need of toning down.[14] Meeting informally at the home of one of its guiding spirits, Chou Fo-hai, the members seem to have been bound together most closely by their common fear that the Chinese Communists were the one group that stood to gain by a protracted war between China and Japan. As the two nations fought themselves to exhaustion and as China descended into chaos, it would be the Communists who could best take advantage of the situation. A few years ago, this writer interviewed one of the leading spokesmen of the Low-Key Club, Kao Tsung-wu, then the Asian Bureau chief of the Foreign Ministry, and found that his anti-Communist sentiments had lost none of their vigor during the past three decades. Kao feels now as he did then, in fact, that neither Chinese nor Japanese regular troops touched off the Marco Polo Bridge Incident but that Communist troops "firing from a blind spot" were responsible.[15] As evidence of the gap in the armor of resistance, Kao and Chou Fo-hai (a trusted aide-de-camp to the Generalissimo and deputy director of propaganda of the Kuomintang) were already in the winter of 1937–1938 beginning the first cautious approaches to Japanese, approaches which would lead to the inauguration of a collaboration regime in 1940 headed by the distinguished Kuomintang statesman and patriot, Wang Ching-wei.

Corresponding to the Chinese Low-Key Club was a small group of Japanese diplomats, army officers, and civilians who were looking for a peaceful solution to the China Incident and were known by a variety of names, sometimes as the "anti-expansionists" (*fu-kakudai ha*) or the "peace and friendship faction" (*wahei shinzen ha*). Their beliefs—and the rejection of their beliefs by the army and the government—throw into sharper focus some of the reasons why the "incident" on the mainland lengthened into an eight-year war. Let us now examine the positions that two of these men were taking in 1938. One was a soldier, General Ishiwara Kanji (already mentioned), and the other was a Gaimushō official, Ishii Itarō.

III.

Ishiwara masterminded the Manchurian Incident and helped create Manchukuo. But he had changed in the years since 1932. For at least two major reasons, Ishiwara rejected in 1937 the kind of aggression against China which he fostered in 1931. The first was that, as we have seen, Ishiwara concluded that a war with the Soviet Union was a certainty and would come in 1941. Now, Ishiwara did not share with many of his army colleagues their overweening faith in the efficacy of *Yamato damashii*—Japanese spirit—as the key to military success. As a promising young officer (second in his class at the Military Academy), Ishiwara was sent to Europe for study and attaché duty. He developed a keen appreciation of European military history and strategy—his notebooks suggest that he was as familiar with the battle tactics of Wittgenstein and Scharnhorst as most Japanese officers were with Tōgō and Ōyama.[16] Perhaps as a result, Ishiwara thought less in terms of spiritual power and more in terms of airplanes, tanks, radios, rubber stockpiles, maritime transport capability, five-year plans, and total economic mobilization.[17] After assessing such factors in 1936, he became convinced that Japan could not generate enough war resources to prepare for the inevitable war against the Soviet Union and *at the same time* face a hostile China. Thus, he began to formulate the concept of the East Asia League (Tōa Remmei), a union of Japan, China, and Manchukuo, which would revitalize Oriental civilization and defend it against encroachment by Western imperialists and by Bolsheviks.

A second reason for Ishiwara's reappraisal of Japan's China policy was his awareness of the growing strength of Chinese nationalism. During the months after the Sian Incident when he served as the chief of the operations bureau of the general staff, Ishiwara challenged one of the major postulates of the expansionists, who held that the Chinese Communists were closely tied to Soviet Communism and therefore that the link formed at Sian between the CCP and KMT represented a Sino-Soviet threat to Japan. It was not so, said Ishiwara. The anti-Japanese united front in China had only an accidental relationship to any third power: it was, as Ishiwara wrote in early 1937, simply a "variation of the Kuomintang."[18] Whether the creation of a new China would result in a policy of hostility toward Japan was a matter which Japan, not the Soviet Union, would determine. The issue was whether Japan would "discard its past policy of imperialist aggression and thereby display the sincerity of the true Japan." Specifically, Ishiwara urged "liquidation of the notion" that North China constituted a "special zone." Japan must cease its encouragement of independence for the five provinces of North China and must "make it clearly understood that the area presently being administered by the Hopei-Chahar regime is naturally a part of the territory of the Chinese Republic and must therefore be placed under the central government of China."[19]

When the Marco Polo Bridge Incident shattered Ishiwara's plan for reconciliation with Kuomintang China, he concentrated on preventing an expansion of the war front and on encouraging Konoe to undertake peace negotiations. As Chinese resistance stiffened in the opening weeks of the war, the expansionists talked of a Blitzkrieg campaign (or, as it was called in Japanese, sokusen-sokketsu, rapid war, rapid settlement). "We need only dispatch more troops, take Peking, and the rest of the country will be on its knees," the China section chief of the general staff solemnly told Ishiwara.[20] Two years later, in an interview with Prince (Captain) Takeda, Ishiwara expressed his disagreements with such statements. "The Manchurian Incident had given them an idée fixe and so they concluded that the war could be ended in a hurry. I thought that this showed a shallow understanding of the national character of the Chinese," he said. Once hostilities began, it was inevitable that the war would be a protracted one, but the China section persisted in believing that, once Japan took North China, China would be "economically bankrupt." "They even cited figures," continued Ishiwara. But they were always "basing their ideas on the easy successes we had had in Manchuria."[21]

About ten days after the Marco Polo Bridge Incident and thus well before the conflict spread hopelessly out of control, Chiang Kai-shek summoned the nation's leaders, including the Communists, to an unprecedented conference at his summer headquarters in Lushan. In his address on July 17, Chiang repeatedly used the phrase "limit of endurance" to describe the way China felt about Japanese encroachment. For China to tolerate the loss of even one more inch of Chinese territory would be an "unpardonable offense against our race," he declared.[22] The speech was made public in Japan but "hardly anyone paid attention to its grave significance," lamented Gaimushō official Ishii Itarō. "It sounded like a 'bluff.' "[23] Three days after Chiang's address at Lushan, General Ishiwara was in the office of War Minister Sugiyama Gen (Hajime) pleading the case for caution. In order to avoid Japan's becoming "bogged down in China just exactly as Napoleon had been in Spain,"[24] Ishiwara advised that all Japanese troops in North China be pulled back to Manchukuo. There is little reason to believe that General Sugiyama, known by a variety of nicknames indicating his dull wit, had any appreciation for Ishiwara's well-chosen historical analogy. At any rate, the advice of Ishiwara was rejected and, accordingly, he took his arguments to Premier Konoe Fumimaro.

Ishiwara urged Konoe to undertake a direct, personal mission to negotiate peace with Chiang Kai-shek. Konoe, the son of a well-known friend of China (Konoe Atsumaro), was relatively free of the contempt for the Kuomintang that was so common among Japanese political figures. Ishiwara regarded him as the "one man" who could successfully negotiate with Chiang. Ishiwara explained the details of his proposals to Konoe's cabinet secretary, Kazami Akira; before the day was out Konoe was convinced of the merits of the plan and, though ill, ordered an aircraft readied for the flight to Nanking. The plan, however, aroused a storm of protest from expansionists in the army, and Konoe and his advisers were forced to reconsider. In the end, they correctly assessed the beleaguered position of Ishiwara on the general staff and decided against the peace mission. "For years, one of Konoe's advisers told him, Generals Terauchi, Sugiyama, and Umezu [regarded as expansionists] have been trying to establish their 'line' and Tōjō is their choice. To them, Ishiwara is a 'nuisance.' He is treated by them as a stepchild. He is like a candle in the wind ready to be snuffed out at any moment."[25]

In September 1937, the candle was effectively snuffed out. Ishiwara's views were so out of step with the prevailing opinion within the army general staff that a friend of Ishiwara's, visiting the general staff that month, reported that he was "shocked" to discover that "only General Kawabe Torashirō and one or two other subordinates agreed with Ishiwara's opinions. All the rest of the personnel were undermining the Chief's [Ishiwara's] plans."[26] The mainland commands, especially the Kwantung Army, where Ishiwara established his reputation a few years earlier, took the lead in calling for a "chastisement" (yōchō) of China, a phrase and an attitude heard increasingly from this time.

At the end of September 1937, Ishiwara was transferred from the "Center" in Tokyo to an assignment under General Tōjō in the Kwantung Army. The transfer was tantamount to exile. From that time his voice was muffled, heard by a group of comrades but largely ignored in the higher councils of army and government. In mid-1938, Ishiwara was back in Tokyo, evidently recuperating from an illness. In public addresses Ishiwara railed against the folly of the Hsuchow and Hankow campaigns. "Even if Hankow is captured, I regard it as highly unlikely that Chiang Kai-shek will fall. And even if Chiang falls, I hardly think that 400 million Chinese are going to capitulate," Ishiwara told his audience. The fault lay with politicians who had no knowledge of military strategy, no awareness of the strength of Chinese resistance, and no appreciation of Japan's unpreparedness to fight a full-scale war in China. "Politicians shouting 'Take Hankow' and 'Take Canton' are merely trying to cover up for their own incompetence. For politicians [such shouts] are like an injection of morphine or camphor. In the end, the people are riled up in this contrived fashion."[27]

Those who wished to "chastise" China encouraged and magnified the public clamor for victory and compensation and spoke darkly in the councils of government about the dangers of leaving the people discontented. As the public came to believe the official propaganda that Chiang was a "local warlord," they naturally came to expect a quick victory and harsh surrender terms. Such an atmosphere was easier to generate and exploit than it was to dispel. "But," said Ishiwara, "no matter what sacrifices we have made [in the war], it will not do for us to make greed a part of our basic philosophy. . . . It is base for us to argue that because we have lost 100,000 in the war we must grab some Chinese territory." The Allies inflicted a harsh treaty on Germany after World War I, Ishiwara observed, but it hardly behooved Japan to behave in the same predatory fashion. Ishiwara's speeches are sprinkled with invidious comparisons between the Western and Eastern nations. The nations of the West were powerful but lacked the spiritual resources of Japan. Yet Japan was ignoring its "moral" (*dōgiteki*) dictates, Ishiwara said, in seeking to preserve special privileges on Chinese soil and in failing to understand how the war was affecting "the sense of dignity of the Chinese people."[28]

In 1939, Ishiwara was transferred from his position on the Kwantung Army's staff and given garrison duty in Kyoto as commander of a provincial arsenal. Two years later, on the eve of the Pacific War, he was reduced to the ranks of the inactive reserves. His charges concerning the misguided war policy and inept national leadership continued throughout the war and nearly resulted in his imprisonment. As it was, he spent the war under *Kempeitai* surveillance. To understand Ishiwara's disgraceful retirement, one need only recall that his criticisms were voiced at a time when thousands of Japanese were dying in the cause of a war that was officially proclaimed as holy. One can imagine the fury of his army colleagues when they heard of his address before the Kyōwa-kai (Concordia Society of Manchukuo) in May 1938. He was saddened by the war, he said, but it gave him "great pleasure" to realize that "our 400 million Chinese brethren, since the Manchurian Incident and especially since this present incident, have come alive after being on the verge of death . . . China's peoples have opened their eyes but now it is the Japanese who are dozing." With biting sarcasm, Ishiwara spoke of meeting an eminent Chinese intellectual and suggesting to him that Chiang Kai-shek award "China's highest medal" to a certain Japanese general who had taken an important role in unintentionally awakening the Chinese to such vigor by taking the hard-line "chastise-ment" position.[29]

IV.

Few in high places shared Ishiwara's appreciation for the awakening nationalism of the Chinese. One who did was the Gaimushō's Ishii Itarō. As Asian Bureau chief, Ishii of course frequently set forth his views of the war but nowhere are they so cogently expressed as in a long memorandum which he prepared for the newly appointed foreign minister, Ugaki Kazushige. Ishii's "Ikensho" (statement of opinion), written in the spring of 1938, is an uncommon document for several reasons.[30] Unlike the wooden documentary style of most Foreign Office studies, Ishii's "Ikensho" is a lively, opinionated, almost passionate profession of the heart as much as the mind. It bristles with pungent metaphor: Japanese economic policy in China in recent years, for example, reminded Ishii of *tako hai* (an octopus eating his own legs) because the expansion of the yen bloc was drying up Chinese purchasing power and causing Japanese exports to China to plummet. But above all, the "Ikensho" is remarkable for its insight and candor. Like the reports on the Chinese Communist movement filed from Chungking and Yenan between 1943 and 1945 by American Foreign Service officers John P. Davies and John S. Service, Ishii's memorandum was a vigorous and forthright statement of a minority opinion that was ahead of its day.

Ishii's principal task in the "Ikensho" was to fortify the new foreign minister with reasons for breaking the *aite ni sezu* policy Konoe had established earlier in the year.[31] According to this policy, Japan would no longer seek a solution to the war through any negotiations with Chiang or the Kuomintang government. Instead it would seek a settlement with a new regime—perhaps with the puppet government in North China, the so-called Provisional Government (of Wang K'o-min); perhaps with the puppet regime in Nanking, the so-called Reformed Government (of Liang Hung-chih); perhaps with some other creation to be headed, as rumor had it, by retired warlord Wu P'ei-fu. Shifting his metaphors to the language of the sumo ring, Ishii explained that, so far as the Kuomintang was concerned, the *aite ni sezu* policy came as a sudden, unexpected betrayal of their expectations for peace; it was like *uchiyari*, a lightning-quick move in which one wrestler flips the other out of the ring. But what the Japanese government accomplished by this dramatic move which terminated German mediation efforts was simply to "constrict its possible alternatives to react to a changing situation. Now all we have," Ishii complained, "was the one policy of *oshi* (shoving)." Ishii compared the *aite ni sezu* policy to the magnificent but empty gestures which a flamboyant, clumsy sumo wrestler might make in some rustic third-rate ring (*inaka no miya sumo*).[32]

Ishii ticked off the alternatives which the new foreign minister could pursue. Placing any hope in such a "devaluated" figure as Wu P'ei-fu—as many in the army did—was folly, Ishii argued. The Chinese look on people like Wu as "old men who don't know when they are finished," said Ishii;[33] to resurrect such a political relic would be laughable. Wu's own arrogant assumption that his reemergence would solve the Sino-Japanese problem must be diagnosed, said Ishii, as a case of lingering intoxication with his past glories. Those who supported Wu did so on the grounds that warlords all over China but especially in Szechwan would join Wu in a great anti-Chiang alliance. Ishii conceded that many warlords had long years of association with Wu and were in fact displeased with the centralization that had taken place under the Kuomintang. It was an "error in timing," however, to expect that they would rise up against the Kuomintang at this juncture, insisted Ishii.[34] The warlords would move against the Kuomintang only if it were on its last legs, and at present it was far from that. It was in fact keeping a close watch on the warlords, especially those in Szechwan, and whatever else they were, the warlords were opportunistic. Their loyalties to Wu would never be sufficient to impel them to move against the superior Kuomintang armies. In addition, the warlords still remaining outside of the KMT were so divided by jealousies and conflicts that they could hardly be expected to join Wu in any united front worthy of the name.

After disposing of this and a great many other possible alternatives facing the new foreign minister, Ishii concluded that the only viable policy Japan could follow was to recognize that Chiang Kai-shek alone was leading the Chinese people, cancel the *aite ni sezu* policy, and negotiate a peace settlement with Chiang. It was useless to insist on the retirement of Chiang from the political scene in China as a precondition to reopening negotiations—a face-saving condition that was steadfastly demanded by Japan. Even assuming that the Chinese assented to this demand, Ishii declared, Japan's best interests would not be served. Whoever succeeded Chiang would be "unavoidably weak" and unable to control China. As a result, all China would fall into a state of economic and political bankruptcy. In the confusion and disorder, only the Communists would have "both ideology and organization" to take advantage of the situation. When this happened, Japan would be the "receiver" (*kanzainin*) of the bankrupt nation. It would take "any number of years and an enormous amount of energy" for Japan to suppress the disbanded armies, pacify the land, handle welfare problems and, above all, cope with the "immediate enemy," the Chinese Communists, who might well gain the backing of the Soviet Union.[35]

"It is undeniable," Ishii advised Ugaki, that Chiang Kai-shek was the one leading a "national revival" of China. To insist on his retirement from politics would be entirely self-defeating. The Chinese people would see it as a punishment administered by Japan and the hard-line elements would never allow Chiang, on whom the "reverence of the Chinese people was focused," to resign. Rather, they would drive the nation to even more die-hard resistance. Ishii's conclusion was: "What we must do is to rescue Chiang and try to work with him."[36] For too long, said Ishii, we have hated him as someone who "used Japan as an instrument for unifying the nation." The fact was that Chiang earnestly hoped for amicable relations with Japan, Ishii said, reminding Ugaki that the Chinese leader had on more than one occasion sent personal representatives to him for precisely that purpose. "We cannot regret too much that we have pushed Chiang to the point where he had to declare [in his address] that China had reached the limits of its endurance," wrote Ishii.[37]

Ishii pleaded with the new foreign minister to reject the comfortable prevailing notion that Japan's aims in China were selfless. The government and the army repeatedly said that Japan had no territorial ambitions in China, noted Ishii, but that was a lie. "We are going to subjugate China"— that is the mood of Japan today, he wrote. Thus, far from obeying the emperor's injunctions to bring about peace based on generous respect for Chinese national integrity, Japan was moving more and more in the direction of a "take-everything-you-can-get attitude" (*monotori shugi*), a "get-what-you-can-before-the-other-fellow-does attitude" (*sakidori shugi*), and a "get-the-lion's-share attitude" (*wakemae shugi*).[38] In the tightly clamped-down atmosphere of 1938, such candid national self-criticism by a responsible government official, even in the security of a confidential memorandum, was rare if not unique. It accused Japan of the same predacity as the Western imperialists and exposed as sham the official pretensions of Japan as a good neighbor of China. The emperor himself, Ishii reminded Ugaki, had declared before the Diet that Japan's only purpose in China was to secure a stable peace and achieve "fruitful co-prosperity."[39]

It would take courage, said Ishii, for Japan to discard its predatory attitudes and people would have to risk their political lives in order to back down from the *aite ni sezu* policy. But only if Japan's leadership could summon that courage could the nation avoid a hopelessly protracted war. There was, of course, the problem of "face" (*taimenjō*), which made it difficult for either side to advocate peace but Ishii prescribed a good Oriental solution to ease that difficulty—the use of third-party mediators, Germany and Italy. "They are our friends . . . and if they say we should do something, then what can we do?" But the steps toward peace must be done before the fall of Hankow, Ishii stressed. "I have a great fear that once Hankow is captured, we will have reached a point of no return."[40]

V.

Both Ishiwara and Ishii displayed uncommon insight into the vitality of Chinese nationalism and the need for Japan to get in step with that force rather than obstruct it. Both general and diplomat saw the fatal weakness in the prevailing myth that equated battlefield success with victory. And both saw their advice rejected and witnessed the fulfillment of their predictions as Japan became ever more mired on the continent.

While the two leaders deserve praise for their attempts to steer Japan away from protracted war, we should not ignore some questionable elements in their thinking. For example, Ishiwara's dissatisfaction with civilian leadership of the nation led him to argue that the army general staff dictate national policy. Second, we must remember that Ishiwara wanted peace with China not as an end but as a means—to enable Japan to wage the inevitable war with the Soviet Union. And, third, given Ishiwara's hatred of Communism, he would surely have found unacceptable any solution to the China Incident which did not provide for the total extirpation of Communism in China. One can only guess where Ishiwara's ideas would have led Japan, but a general staff dictatorship, a second Russo-Japanese war, and Japanese involvement in a renewed civil war in China do not add up to a felicitous fate for Japan.

Furthermore, neither Ishiwara nor Ishii, for all their respect for Chinese nationalism, advocated the one thing that would satisfy the demands of Chinese nationalists, namely, the relinquishment of Manchukuo. Nowhere in Ishii's "Ikensho" was such a proposal made; nowhere in Ishiwara's antigovernment speeches is anything of the sort suggested. On the contrary, Ishiwara argued that Manchuria was a land of Manchurians, Mongols, and Koreans colonized by China. Japan had moved into it in order to save it from falling into the hands of the West, and now it was simply "a joint Sino-Japanese colony."[41] It was the mark of moderation that he should concede that Manchukuo was in any sense Chinese. Not unless one looks to the tiny membership of the decimated and ineffectual Japanese Communist Party does one find a group of Japanese who favored withdrawal of the Imperial Army from Manchukuo. No matter how desperate the Japanese position in the eight-year war became, no matter how earnestly Japanese peace missions sought to find a negotiated solution to the war, relinquishment of Manchukuo was never seriously considered until July 1945—and even then it did not have the backing of the Japanese government. In any case, by that time Chungking was in no mood to negotiate a separate peace with Japan and within a month Soviet troops poured over the Manchurian border and ended Japanese options once and for all.

Fully to analyze the reasons why the views of moderates like Ishii and Ishiwara were rejected is beyond the scope of this essay but some tentative thoughts may be in order. First of all, the evidence is overwhelming that Japan drifted into the mainland quagmire exactly as Ishii and Ishiwara predicted, in a state of mindless optimism. This seems to be a common pitfall of powerful nations when they go to war. We have only to recall the expectation in the United States that American soldiers would be "home by Christmas" in the case of the Korean War and the talk of "light at the end of the tunnel" in the early stages of the Vietnam War to realize that the Japanese anticipation of an easy victory was not an exceptional miscalculation.

Once lured into conflict by the comfortable assumptions of an easy victory, the nation's leadership found it politically impossible to accept a negotiated peace that did not in some way compensate Japan for the terrible loss of life and expenditure of national treasure. Japanese leaders, both civilian and military, desperately needed to be able to go to the emperor and to the people with proof that the nation's sacrifices had not flowed from miscalculations at the top. China could have obliged the Japanese leaders by recognizing the "independence" of Manchukuo or acknowledging that Inner Mongolia and North China constituted special zones in which Japan possessed certain economic and military rights. Or, at very least, she might have agreed to the resignation of Chiang Kai-shek. Unfortunately for Japan, acceptance of those demands was out of the question for anyone who wished to preserve his political authority in China. When Chiang Kai-shek's longtime rival, Wang Ching-wei, finally accepted those demands as the basis for the establishment of a collaboration regime in 1940, he was immediately discredited and lived out the remaining four years of his life branded by most Chinese as a traitor.

A further reason why the peace advocacy of Ishiwara and Ishii failed in the China Incident was that the "rhetorical advantage" was always with their opponents, the expansionists. The phrase was used by Arthur Schlesinger, Jr., in attempting to account for the reasons why the Kennedy administration embarked on the disastrous Bay of Pigs operation.[42]

The "tangibles" and "intangibles" were of course different in 1961 from what they were in 1937–1938 but Schlesinger's point applies with considerable validity to the earlier period. The "advocates of adventure" like War Minister Sugiyama could point to an impressive string of Imperial Army victories and confidently assure the emperor the the "China Incident will be all over within a month." The anti-expansionists like Ishiwara and Ishii, however, were forced on the defensive with their cautionary advice against underestimating the reserve of strength that lay hidden in a China that most Japanese firmly believed to be beneath contempt because of its disunity, corruption, and backwardness.[43] For at least a century, China's weakness was accepted as fact by Japanese. For at least that long, but increasingly since the turn of the century, Japanese regarded Chinese vulnerability to foreign encroachment as the principal menace facing the Japanese Empire. That Ishiwara and Ishii failed to challenge such durable certainties with the scarcely tested and scarcely credible notion of Chinese resurgence is perhaps not surprising.

In the opening days of the war, T. V. Soong raised these issues in conversations with a Japanese friend of China, Saionji Kinkazu, then exploring the possibilities of a peaceful solution to the incident. The great obstacle to peace, as Soong saw it, was that both the Chinese and Japanese military had misconceptions concerning China. "The Japanese military," Soong said, "still hold to their preconceived ideas about the Chinese Army. They think that if you hit us once we will surrender and do what you want." The Chinese Army had "studied hard" since the Manchurian Incident. "It knows that it is stronger and it has the confidence that it won't be beaten this time. So, the Japanese Army underestimates the Chinese Army, and the Chinese Army overestimates itself. . . . Here is where the great danger lies," Soong concluded correctly.[44]

Another difficulty faced by the peace advocates, this one more peculiarly Japanese than the above, has to do with the premium in Japanese society placed on social harmony and conformity. Once a consensus materialized in favor of "chastisement," the advocacy of peace was easily and naturally seen as disruptive. This was especially true in the case of General Ishiwara, who pleaded his cause in public and who was not known for his capacity for compromise or circumspection, traits essential to the lubrication of social machinery in harmony-conscious Japan. Ishiwara was a man of great learning, a soldier of monumental self-discipline who lived by strict rules and freely displayed contempt for those who did not share his vision of impending national calamity. "You admired him but you felt uncomfortable with him" was the way one contemporary summarized the general's personality.[45] Given his uncharacteristic disdain for consensus, it was not hard for his enemies to regard him as an eccentric and to dismiss his views as alarmist.

One final insight into the reasons why peace advocacy failed is suggested by the attitudes of national superiority that were all too evident in the Japanese mentality in the 1930s. The fixation on chauvinistic slogans (like *kokui hatsuyō*, enhancing the national prestige) as statements of ultimate national goals could easily frustrate the goals of peace advocates like Ishiwara and Ishii. Shigemitsu Mamoru, decrying the wartime preoccupation with glory in his country, has perhaps come closest to summing up the reasons why the China Incident became an eight-year war:

Unhappy Japan! She not only misunderstood; she was impatient and intolerant of restraint. Always it was "glory" that mattered. In national policy, in the plan of campaign, it was "glory" that decided. This it was that molded the mentality of the people in the time of war. It was splendid, but endurance and wisdom would have been more valuable.[46]

Notes

1. James B. Crowley, "Japanese Army Factionalism in the Early 1930's," *Journal of Asian Studies* 21 (1962): 309–26; *Japan's Quest for Autonomy* (Princeton, 1966). In his controversial book *Japan's Imperial Conspiracy* (New York, 1971), David Bergamini argues that the emperor of Japan "had directed his General Staff to plan the war in early 1935" and insists that the plans which resulted "included even a description of the provocation which would be staged at the Marco Polo Bridge" (p. 6). Bergamini's thesis, however, must be regarded with extreme skepticism in view of the almost unanimous censure accorded his book by Asian specialists. See, for example, reviews by James B. Crowley, *New York Times Book Review* (24 October 1971), p. 3; Alvin D. Coox, *American Historical Review* 77 (1972): 1169–70; Shumpei Okamoto, *Journal of Asian Studies* 31 (1972), 414–16; and Richard Storry, *Pacific Affairs* 45 (1972): 272–76.

2. Morishima Morito, *Imbō, ansatsu, guntō: ichi gaikōkan no kaisō* [Conspiracies, assassinations, and swords: The recollections of a diplomat] (Tokyo, 1946), p. 131.

3. Author's interview with Matsukata, Tokyo, February 1970.

4. For an annotated listing of these sources, see the "Bibliographical Note" in my *China and Japan at War, 1937–1945: The Politics of Collaboration* (Stanford, 1972), pp. 395–400.

5. *New York Times,* 31 July 1938, cited in Alvin D. Coox, *Year of the Tiger* (Tokyo and Philadelphia, 1964), p. 133.

6. Tsuru Shigeto, *Essays on the Japanese Economy* (Tokyo, 1958), p. 215.

7. Itō Mitsuharu, "Munitions Unlimited—The Controlled Economy," *Japan Interpreter* 7 (1972): 360. The rate of increase was 5 percent in 1936, 9.4 percent in 1937, and 14.6 percent in 1938.

8. Edward Seidensticker, *Kafū the Scribbler: The Life and Times of Nagai Kafū, 1879–1959* (Stanford, 1965), p. 154.

9. From an unsigned review in *Oriental Affairs* (Shanghai), April 1940, p. 217. Hino Ashihei was the pen name of Tamai Katsunori.

10. Imai Takeo, *Shina jihen no kaisō* [Reminiscences of the China Incident] (Tokyo, 1964), p. 97.

11. Theodore White and Annalee Jacoby, *Thunder Out of China*, 2d ed. (New York, 1961), p. 53.

12. Milton J. T. Shieh, *The Kuomintang: Selected Historical Documents, 1894–1969* (Jamaica, N.Y., 1970), p. 183.

13. *Papers Relating to the Foreign Relations of the United States: Diplomatic Papers, 1938* (Washington, D.C., 1954), 3: 115–16.

14. The membership and beliefs of the Low-Key Club are discussed in Boyle, op. cit., Chapter 9, and in Gerald Bunker, *The Peace Conspiracy: Wang Ching-wei and the China War, 1937–1941* (Cambridge, Mass., 1972).

15. Author's interview with Kao, Washington, D.C., December 1969. See also Inukai Ken, *Yōsuko wa ima mo nagarete iru* [The Yangtze still flows] (Tokyo, 1961), p. 91. Inukai's book is a valuable firsthand account of the Japanese "peace movement."

16. The notebooks, essays, and speeches of Ishiwara have been collected in Tsunoda Jun, ed., *Ishiwara Kanji shiryō: sensō shiron* [Historical materials on Ishiwara Kanji: On theories of battle] (Tokyo, 1968).

17. See Horiba Kazuo, *Shina jihen sensō shidō shi* [Operational history of the China Incident] (Tokyo, 1962), 1: 65–78, for the economic surveys prepared by Ishiwara and his staff.

18. Tsunoda, ed., *Ishiwara Kanji shiryō: kokubō ronsaku* [On national defense] (Tokyo, 1967), p. 202.

19. Ibid., p. 198.

20. Usui Katsumi, "Nitchū sensō no seijiteki tenkai" [Political developments in the Sino-Japanese War], in Nihon Kokusai Seiji Gakkai, ed., *Taiheiyō sensō e no michi* [The road to the Pacific War] (Tokyo, 1962), 4: 117, citing unpublished documents in the Senshishitsu (Office of Military History), War History Archives, Tokyo.

21. Bōei-chō, Bōei kenshūsho, Senshishitsu [Office of Military History, Institute for Defense Studies, Defense Agency], *Daihon'ei rikugunbu* [War Department, Imperial General Headquarters] (Tokyo, 1967), 1: 459–60.

22. Chiang Kai-shek, *The Collected Wartime Messages of Generalissimo Chiang Kai-shek, 1937– 1945* (New York, 1945), 1: 24.

23. Ishii Itarō, "Ikensho" [Statement of opinion], in Gaimushō, ed., *Gaimushō no hyakunen* [One hundred years of the Ministry of Foreign Affairs], (Tokyo, 1969), 2: 323.

24. Inaba Masao, Kobayashi Tatsuo, and Shimada Toshihiko, comps., *Gendaishi shiryō* [Documents on contemporary history] (Tokyo, 1964), 10: 27.

25. Saionji Kinkazu, "Kizoku no taijō" [Departing the nobility], in *Shōwa no dōran* [The Shōwa Upheavals], ed. Imai Seiichi (Tokyo, 1969), p. 272.

26. Imamura Hitoshi, *Imamura taishō kaisōroku* [Memoirs of General Imamura] (Tokyo, 1960), 2: 284.

27. *Ishiwara Kanji shiryō: kokubō ronsaku*, pp. 249–51.

28. Ibid., p. 252.

29. Ibid.

30. For the text of this important document, see *Gaimushō no hyakunen*, 2: 315–37. Its full title is "Kongo no jihen taisaku ni tsuite kōan" [Plan for countermeasures for the present incident].

31. The *aite ni sezu* declaration was made on January 16, 1938. The phrase literally means "no dealing with [the Kuomintang]."

32. Ishii Itarō, op. cit., pp. 315–27.

33. Ibid., pp. 325–26. This is perhaps too bland a translation for Ishii's pungent "old men who douse themselves in cold water like youngsters and then take ill."

34. Ibid., p. 326.

35. Ibid., pp. 328–29.

36. Ibid., pp. 333–34.

37. Ibid., pp. 329–30.

38. Ibid., p. 332.

39. Ibid., p. 331. Ishii referred to a speech by the emperor on September 4, 1937.

40. Ibid. pp. 329–30.

41. *Ishiwara Kanji shiryō: kokubō ronsaku*, pp. 246–47. From a May 10, 1938, speech to Manchurian students studying in Tokyo.

42. Arthur Schlesinger, Jr., *A Thousand Days* (New York, 1965), p. 256.

43. Robert J. C. Butow, *Tojo and the Coming of the War* (Princeton, 1961), p. 254. General Sugiyama's optimism about an easy victory was evident again in the deliberations that preceded Pearl Harbor: he advised the emperor that the United States could be defeated within "five months." The emperor did not fail to note that Sugiyama's earlier prediction had been misguided. See Hattori Takushirō, *Dai Tōa sensō zenshi* [The great East Asia war], 4th ed. (Tokyo, 1966), p. 100.

44. Saionji, op. cit., p. 274.

45. Author's interview with Matsukata.

46. Shigemitsu Mamoru, *Japan and Her Destiny* (New York, 1958), p. 270.

11.

In the following essay, Yoji Akashi traces the tortuous course of the last peace effort between Japan and China prior to the end of the Pacific War. Of all the "meddlers" in the diplomacy of the era of Sino-Japanese conflict Miao Pin was perhaps the most unlikely as a peacemaker. Nevertheless, he obtained the ear of the Japanese premier himself and was ushered by the latter into the highest councils of the Japanese government.

Whether Miao's failure was due to his own inadequacies or to the ineptness and arrogance of Japanese officialdom is a point that may be argued from various angles, as indicated by Han-sheng Lin's commentary, and the reader is invited to form his own conclusions. Few can doubt that Japan and China could both have been spared much destruction and loss of life if the Miao "peace operation" had had a better fate.

Yoji Akashi is professor of history and government at the Faculty for Foreign Studies and Center for Japanese Studies, Nanzan University, Nagoya, Japan. During 1976–1977 he was visiting professor at the University of Malaya in Kuala Lumpur. He received his M.A. and Ph.D. in international relations from Georgetown University, Washington, D.C. His previous publications include *The Nanyang Chinese National Salvation Movement, 1937–1941* (1970) and "Bureaucracy and Military Administration in Southeast Asia" in *Japan in Southeast Asia, 1930–1945* (1974).

A Botched Peace Effort: The Miao Pin *Kōsaku,* 1944–1945

Yoji Akashi

I.

During the Sino-Japanese conflict of 1937–1945, Japan made a number of efforts at settlement. Of all the *wahei kōsaku* (peace operations), the Miao Pin *kōsaku* was the most bizarre. The principal figure was Miao Pin, once a Kuomintang (KMT) high official, who in 1923 while serving as civil affairs commissioner in Kiangsu was impeached for having accepted bribes. After the Sino-Japanese hostilities broke out in 1937, Miao went to Peking and joined the Japanese-sponsored North China Provisional Government. He was also associated with the Tōa Remmei (East Asia League), General Ishiwara Kanji's creation, the ideals of which, it is said, Chiang Kai-shek supported fully.[1] In Peking, Miao was supported by Japanese funds in organizing the Hsin-min-hui (New People's Society), in which he served as vice-chairman. Some of the puppet leaders deemed Miao a threat to their position and tried to assassinate him. In 1940 Miao fled to Nanking.

Introduced by Colonel Imai Takeo, a staff officer of the Sōgun (China Expeditionary Forces), Miao obtained a post in the Nanking government. Wang Ching-wei appointed Miao vice-chairman of the Legislative Yuan. Subsequently Miao became vice-director of the cultural committee of the Tōa Remmei established in Nanking at the request of Wang, who held Ishiwara in high esteem. In these capacities Miao came to know high Japanese embassy officials. Aware of Miao's connection with General Ho Ying-ch'in, KMT defense minister and Generalissimo Chiang's protégé, Nakamura Toyokazu of the embassy asked Miao to establish contact with high officials in Chungking. When this overture was uncovered by Nanking special police, to the embarrassment of the puppet government, Wang

267

dismissed Miao and relegated him to a sinecure as vice-chairman of the Examination Yuan.

Having little to do in Nanking, Miao went to Shanghai during 1942. In the great Chinese metropolis, where Japanese and Chinese intelligence agents were active, Miao made contact with KMT operatives and offered them his services;[2] his motives may have combined self-interest with sincerity. Miao seems to have concluded that Japan would eventually lose the war; perhaps he wanted to "make points" by offering his services to Chungking in the hope that he would be pardoned for his crime of collaboration. His conscience may have been troubling him, or he sincerely wanted to save both China and Japan from the Communists and the Western powers before both Asian countries exhausted themselves. Since Miao (like Chou Fo-hai,[3] number-two man in the Nanking government and a defector turned collaborator) had held high office in the puppet regime and was close to senior Japanese government and military officials, KMT agents may have accepted his services because of his intelligence value to the Chungking authorities.

Miao's involvement in the *wahei kōsaku* stemmed from a fortuitous event in the autumn of 1943—his intercession with Japanese associates to free a Chinese who had been arrested by Japanese gendarmes on the charge of belonging to Tai Li's Lan-yi-she, a gestapo-type KMT organization known as the Blue Shirts. This action led to occasional meetings in the French concession between Ch'en Ch'ang-feng, a senior officer of the Blue Shirts, Miao, and Tamura Shinsaku, a former *Asahi Shimbun* reporter and *Shina rōnin* (China drifter), now a free-lance writer. Tamura indicated that he could provide links to Ogata Taketora, state minister in the Koiso cabinet and his former superior on the *Asahi*, as well as to Prince Higashikuni, uncle of the emperor. Tamura must have been dropping names (without authorization) in an effort to impress Ch'en with Japan's serious and honest desire for peace. Ch'en assured Tamura, in turn, that he could "help open a channel of communication between Japan and China."[4]

Tamura apparently intended to bring his powerful friend Colonel Tsuji Masanobu of the Sōgun into the scheme after the groundwork had been laid. But when Tsuji was transferred to the Southeast Asian theater in July 1944,[5] Tamura went to Tokyo to see Ogata, who showed an active interest in the Ch'en–Miao–Tamura conversations. Recalling a meeting he had had with Miao in Shanghai the previous summer, Ogata thought that Miao's special relationship to Chungking had won him "singular recognition within the Nanking government."[6] Ogata brought the matter to the attention of Premier Koiso Kuniaki, who had met Miao once or twice in 1939. After securing Koiso's concurrence but not that of the foreign minister or the service ministers, Ogata on August 14 wrote to General

Matsui Takurō, chief of staff of the Sōgun, asking for air transportation for Miao to Japan to exchange views on peace with Ogata. When Matsui finally replied in September, it was to suggest that "awkwardness" be avoided by having Miao go to Japan of his own volition, not as an official guest.[7]

While the Japanese Supreme War Council was approving a policy that allocated the initiative in political operations vis-à-vis Chungking to the Nanking regime, and while the Sōgun was stalling Miao's flight, General Shibayama Kaneshirō, former military counselor to Wang Ching-wei and now vice-minister of war, pressed Ogata to drop the Miao affair. Foreign Minister Shigemitsu Mamoru also resented the Ogata–Koiso foray into diplomacy. The Japanese military and the foreign minister distrusted Miao and doubted the authenticity of his connection with KMT high officials.[8] Hence the Miao operation was dropped for the time being, although Ch'en and Tamura still met regularly at Miao's residence.[9]

Unwilling to abandon the Miao *rōsen* (route), Koiso asked retired Colonel Yamagata Hatsuo, a Military Academy classmate, to go to China to study the possibilities of ending the war.[10] Leaving on August 25, Yamagata spent forty-seven days in China, conferring with prominent Chinese individuals including Miao. Yamagata's report to Koiso in mid-October stressed that the Nanking government had lost popular support and that the Japanese had alienated the Chinese. Thus settlement of the hostilities was the only way to save the long-range situation.[11] Koiso was also impressed by the facts that General Ugaki Kazushige, his mentor, had recommended that the Nanking regime be dissolved, after his return from a trip to China; that General Hata Shunroku, former commander of the Sōgun, had expressed gloomy counsel about the Nanking government;[12] and that Wang Ching-wei was near death, leaving the puppet regime incapable of initiating *wahei kōsaku.* But when Koiso presented these views to the Supreme War Council on December 13, a rift became evident between the Japanese premier, the foreign minister, and the army. Eventually the council decided that the Japanese ambassador and the army and navy supreme commanders in China were jointly responsible for implementing political operations toward Chungking, while the Sōgun commander was to coordinate matters between Nanking and Tokyo.[13] Koiso then sought in vain to reshuffle the War Ministry and the Ministry of Greater East Asian Affairs, only exacerbating interpersonal relations in the process.[14]

Undaunted, Koiso resorted again to unconventional private diplomacy, sending Yamagata back to China as his personal representative "to obtain intelligence useful to *wahei kōsaku* and to meet Miao Pin in Shanghai to investigate the authenticity of the information" Ogata had received.[15] The military authorities in Japan and in China did everything possible to obstruct Yamagata's trip. Not until mid-January 1945 did he reach Shanghai, shuttling between there and Nanking for three weeks. The Sōgun's rebuff of Yamagata constitutes *gekokujō*, the defiance of higher authority by subordinates so characteristic of Japanese army politics.[16]

In the course of conversations between Yamagata and Miao, who impressed him by his sincerity and personality,[17] matters of tremendous moment were discussed in an atmosphere of fantasy characteristic of what George F. Kennan has called "dilettante" diplomacy. Oral "gentlemen's agreements" were reached concerning the Japanese evacuation of China and the future of Manchukuo, for example, that could only reflect the understanding of the highest authorities in Chungking and of the Supreme War Council in Japan. In the case of the Chinese, such an understanding can only have been tacit at best; in the Japanese case, it did not extend much beyond Koiso, Yamagata, and Ogata. Miao insisted that he had an "unofficial understanding from the Generalissimo to go to Japan" for further discussions with Japanese leaders on the basis of the draft proposals; Japan should demonstrate its sincerity by dissolving the Nanking regime, after which China would reciprocate.[18] In any case, Miao stressed, the present talks should be concluded by March 31, after which the powers supposedly vested in him by Chungking would expire. But again the Japanese military authorities delayed Yamagata's transportation, and he did not reach Tokyo until February 20—a loss of three precious weeks in all.[19]

After receiving Yamagata's favorable report and consulting with Ogata, Koiso decided to invite Miao to Tokyo, partly to "test the authenticity of his claim" that he had radio contact with Chungking and partly to use him, if his contacts proved genuine, to establish a direct communications channel with Chungking.[20] Only after deciding the matter on his own authority did Koiso contact the foreign minister and the service ministers—another serious mistake in a country where the premier was not a dictator and where consensus was typical of governmental decision making. Consequently, a negative response to Koiso's plan was only to be expected. Koiso felt obliged to call upon Prince Higashikuni to press War Minister Sugiyama to authorize Miao's trip. Sugiyama and Shibayama agreed with reluctance, after imposing a crucial precondition: Miao was to be invited for the collection of intelligence, not for the negotiation of peace.[21]

In Shanghai, Miao organized a seven-man party which was to fly to Japan.[22] Their departure was delayed for two weeks, while Japanese military police ordered the group reduced to three and then sent all of the members home. Some saw this interference as a conspiracy hatched by the Sōgun, the military in Tokyo, and the local embassy.[23] When the party was finally cleared to leave in mid-March and was on the point of boarding an army transport plane, Japanese military police refused passage to everybody except the disgruntled Miao. General Matsui, commanding the 13th Army in the Shanghai area, and no advocate of the Miao *kōsaku*, appears to have been directly responsible for the interception by the gendarmes.

In addition, General Okamura Yasuji, commander in chief of the Sōgun, did not intercede in the incident even though he had orders from the war minister to transport the full seven-man mission. Personal enmity between Okamura and Koiso may have had something to do with Okamura's behavior,[24] adding complexity to an already involved episode. The hawkish Okamura lacked political perspective on the larger issues of war and peace.[25] Thus he did not deign to reply to two peace feelers transmitted to him personally by Chiang Kai-shek (in Ch'en Yi's presence) and by General Ho, the former received in early February, the latter in early March. The KMT communications may have had no connection with the Miao operation, or they may have been designed to gather information from the Japanese. Still, Okamura admits in his diary that the Chinese side told him after the war that the two letters conveyed Chungking's true intention of arranging peace.[26] But Okamura never reported the conciliatory Chinese messages to his superiors in Tokyo at the time.

Although Koiso protested the army's repeated interferences to Shibayama, only Miao was ever allowed to travel to Japan, and even then by a nonmilitary transport plane. When he arrived in Tokyo on March 16, he came empty-handed—without even a radio transmitter and receiver, so essential for contact with Chungking.

Miao was whisked to the Shibusawa residence where, as an official guest, he remained during most of his two-week stay. The first person he met was Ogata. Miao reviewed his *wahei kōsaku*, emphasizing that he had been "informally instructed by Chairman Chiang to complete, within a certain period, the negotiations with the Japanese government" on the basis of the Miao–Yamagata draft plan for general peace.[27] Then Miao produced "a telegram from Chungking" as evidence of his credentials. The cable, marked with a secret code name, instructed Miao to "proceed with talks in accordance with the principles agreed upon with Yamagata in Shanghai and to make no concessions," while requesting him to keep Chungking informed of the progress of the negotiations.[28]

Before leaving Ogata's office, Miao expressed his views on the war, which predicted fairly accurately the military strategy the Allies were to follow in defeating Japan. Miao in essence emphasized the following points: (1) Okinawa was the next target of American operations; (2) the United States had *at the moment* no landing-operation plans for the Chinese mainland. Should a Japanese cease-fire be a preliminary step for concluding a general peace, China would not permit the landing of American troops on the mainland after Japan had withdrawn her troops peacefully, *for Chiang was not at all anxious for American landings and joint military operations;* and (3) the Soviet Union would invade Manchuria when the American assault on Japan reached a decisive moment.[29]

Miao's prognosis regarding the course of the war led Nakamura Shōgo, Ogata's secretary, to believe that Chiang Kai-shek was genuinely afraid of a change in the balance of power between Chungking and Yenan, should Japan be defeated. If Japan continued to fight to self-annihilation, China might become a battleground between Japanese and American troops. In that case the power balance would be tipped in favor of the Communists, because China's pivotal region would be reduced to ashes, and the American landings, especially if made in the north, would bring U.S. troops into close contact with the Communists for reasons of strategy. Such American military cooperation with the Chinese Reds would legitimize Soviet aid to the Chinese Red Army. Therefore, Nakamura theorized, Chiang wanted to achieve a Sino-Japanese rapprochement that would eliminate the possibility of American landing operations and ground warfare in China. This scheme would preserve the KMT's favorable balance of power vis-à-vis the Communists and check their power.[30]

On the second day after his arrival, Miao met Prince Higashikuni, an active participant in the Miao *kōsaku.* Higashikuni endeavored to gain a clear idea of Miao's motives and whether there was any basis for undertaking negotiations. The dialogue ran as follows:

Higashikuni: Will Chungking want to make peace with Japan?
Miao: Yes.
Higashikuni: Why does Chungking want to make peace with Japan?
Miao: Chungking has no desire to see Japan utterly destroyed, since China's self-preservation depends upon Japan's continued existence. Japan is China's breakwater. If peace is concluded now, we can also prevent the debouchment of the Soviet Union.
Higashikuni: In view of the fact that you were invited to Japan by Premier Koiso, why did you desire to see me before talking with anyone else?
Miao: Because no politician, military officer, or diplomat can be trusted, except the Emperor. His Majesty is the only one on whom we can rely. Since it is impossible for me to see the Emperor personally, I wish to present the question to Your Highness and to request you to convey my message, without adding comments, to His Imperial Majesty.

The prince replied that despite his kinship as uncle to the emperor, he could not, under Japan's constitutional system, bypass the cabinet on such a matter. Miao answered that Chungking was ready to negotiate if and when a Higashikuni cabinet was formed because the Chungking government trusted him. Before Miao took his leave, Higashikuni expressed his wish not only for Sino-Japanese peace but also for world peace and asked him to tell Chiang Kai-shek to assume the initiative. By the time the tête-à-tête was over, the prince had been favorably impressed by Miao as a man who sincerely spoke his mind, not as the manipulator and opportunist he was generally supposed to be.[31] He likewise had little doubt about Miao's legitimacy as Chiang's representative.

On the third day, Koiso finally received Miao—the only time Koiso saw him during the two-week visit despite the fact that Koiso had invited him as his guest. Exactly what was discussed during the Koiso–Miao conference, at which Ogata was also present, is not known except that Miao was "disappointed" in Koiso because the premier did not trust him completely and showed no decisiveness in removing the opposition from the military and the Foreign Office. When Miao reportedly pressed for resolute action by Koiso in effecting a breakthrough in the *wahei kōsaku*, the premier was apologetically evasive; he asked Miao to see Shibayama in order to persuade the opponents. This is a strange and irresponsible reply, for Koiso knew that the vice-minister of war was one of the principal figures who opposed the Miao *kōsaku*.[32]

After the meeting, Miao complained: "The prime minister is utterly powerless. How can Chungking negotiate if the prime minister whom I have trusted is so impotent and evasive?" The meeting convinced Miao that the premier of Japan had "no authority whatsoever" in decision making.[33] The observation was correct. Since Koiso had reason to be evasive, Miao gained the impression that the premier was irresolute. Koiso was not completely convinced of Miao's credentials, and he wanted to gain a better picture of Miao's motives as well as of Chungking's. Strange as it seems, the proponents of the Miao *kōsaku* made no attempt to provide a radio transmitter, a radio operator, or a cryptographer to establish Miao's legitimacy and credentials. Moreover, the premier, conscious of the difficulty of convincing the military to swallow peace conditions, could not commit himself to Miao until he received sanction from the Supreme War Council.

Koiso, advised by Ogata, decided to take the matter to the Supreme War Council, scheduled to meet on March 21, in order to secure its approval, and he asked Ogata to draft peace proposals. Ogata, Shibayama, and Miao subsequently discussed and approved Draft Plans to Be Implemented for Achieving General Peace with China, which the war direction section of the general staff had prepared the day after Miao's arrival at Tokyo. Except for a few amendments, the draft contained essentially the same principles which Miao had agreed upon with Yamagata; it deleted the provisions dealing with asylum for Nanking government leaders and with the Provisional Government's calling upon the United States and Britain for an immediate peace. Added to the new proposals was the following principle:

> Should [the KMT government] accept the main principles concerning the dissolution of the Nanking government, the cease-fire, and troop withdrawals, the Japanese government shall . . . send a special envoy bearing the Prime Minister's letter of credentials to Chungking. . . . While the government must not hesitate to make contact from suspicion of Chungking's sincerity, in view of the extreme importance of the matter it should not at the same time engage in negotiations before ascertaining Chiang Kai-shek's true intention.[34]

II.

On March 21, Koiso convened the fateful meeting of the Supreme War Council only after Higashikuni had made strong, private representations on behalf of Koiso to General Sugiyama and to General Umezu Yoshijirō, the army chief of staff.[35] The premier delivered the opening speech outlining the peace proposals which had been distributed to each member of the council. Then Ogata, who attended the meeting at Koiso's request, explained in detail the circumstances under which he had first met Miao years before and how the premier had invited him to Japan. Silence fell upon the meeting, and everyone sensed the coolness between the Koiso–Ogata group and its opponents; none of the members seemed to "pay attention to the mimeographed peace proposals." It is not surprising that the original injunction against the negotiation of peace with Miao had not been lifted. Breaking the silence, Umezu asked whether China would not become an American military base after Japan withdrew her forces unilaterally from the continent. Sugiyama then questioned whether Miao had qualifications and whether he was not a spy for Chungking. "In what capacity," the war minister asked, "did he come to Tokyo? Until this point is clarified, I have grave reservations about discussing matters of such extreme importance with you." Koiso was taken aback by Sugiyama's remark and by what he believed to be the war minister's sudden change of position with regard to inviting Miao. After all, Sugiyama had given his approval to Koiso for inviting Miao and had reaffirmed his consent when Higashikuni and Ogata explained the *kōsaku* to him.[36]

There was no time for Koiso to rebut Sugiyama, for Shigemitsu interposed. He wanted to "set the record straight," he said. He had never stated that he would "concur only if the war and navy ministers were favorably inclined"; he had never been "consulted" by Koiso and Ogata about the Miao *kōsaku*. "I have no knowledge whatsoever," the foreign minister declared, "about inviting Miao Pin to Japan. I wish to make this point clear in view of the grave war situation and as the foreign minister responsible for advising His Majesty [on foreign affairs]." Shigemitsu's implication that Koiso must have committed "a serious infringement" on the exclusive responsibility of the foreign minister to advise the emperor on foreign affairs caused Koiso's face to turn white. This was a grave charge which might engender a crisis leading to the dissolution of the cabinet. The premier, attacking the foreign minister's insinuation that he had violated the latter's prerogative, began to defend his position, saying that this was the "strangest thing" he had ever heard of. Not giving Koiso the opportunity to complete his sentence, Shigemitsu continued his own tirade, stating point by point what was wrong with the whole affair and where Koiso had deviated from the established position of the government with regard to political operations toward Chungking. He reminded the premier that the council had adopted the policy and had reported to His Majesty that political operations toward Chungking should be carried out in principle on the initiative of the Nanking government.

Then the foreign minister turned his verbal barrage against Miao Pin, denouncing him as untrustworthy and characterizing him as a political mercenary and a peace peddler who had betrayed the trust of the Nanking government and still possessed malice against that government. Shigemitsu charged that Tai Li, with whom Miao was said to have been maintaining contact, was a "most treacherous" man and a "born intriguer."[37] This denigration of Tai Li revealed Shigemitsu's ignorance about the powerful police and intelligence chief. Nor did the Japanese embassy, Foreign Office, or army intelligence know much about Tai Li,[38] who was termed "little more than Chiang Kai-shek's *alter ego*."[39] Shigemitsu's ignorance illustrates the poor quality of the Japanese intelligence-gathering apparatus and analysis, phenomena which had frequently contributed to the failure of *wahei kōsaku* efforts with Chungking.

Finally, Shigemitsu produced cablegrams, drafted by Shimizu Kunzō of the embassy and by General Imai of the Sōgun and dispatched by Ambassador Tani, to substantiate his charges against Miao's questionable credentials and character. There were, Tani reported, many peace mongers, all of whom were trying to induce Japan to make greater concessions and to arrange peace at her expense. Unless Japan did so, they insisted, Chungking would not come to the rescue of a "man [Japan] who lives with his mistress [Nanking] but is casting amorous glances at another woman [Chungking]." There was, Tani pointed out, no guarantee in return for Japan's concessions except a vague understanding that Chiang Kai-shek, viewing the matter in terms of the broader issues of Asia, might offer a helping hand to Japan. None of the peace peddlers, the ambassador said, was in a position to speak with authority; they were all trying to gather information from Japan for selfish and pecuniary motives. Characterizing

Miao as "typical of this kind" of peace monger, Tani warned Shigemitsu to exercise extreme caution and prudence in dealing with the turncoat Miao. To engage in negotiations with him in a desultory way would not only "expose Japan's weakness" but also "render benefit to Chungking and to the Anglo-American powers, bringing incalculable diplomatic consequences for Japan."[40]

No sooner had the foreign minister finished his declaration than the premier, visibly shaken by Shigemitsu's stinging rebuke, rose to his feet. Betraying emotion, Koiso said: "The purpose of inviting Miao Pin is to find Chungking's real motives, and it is my understanding that you raised no objection to bringing him [to Tokyo]."[41] Interrupting Koiso, Navy Minister Yonai asked whether Japan could get a guarantee from Chungking of China's neutrality after Japanese troop withdrawals and whether it was wise for the premier to have invited Miao without even verifying the legitimacy of his functions. Shigemitsu uttered the last word: "I am afraid that we are giving away information to the enemy. I cannot help but be terrified at the thought that his information should reach the United States through Chungking." Stung by these acid remarks, Koiso left the conference room indignantly and abruptly, saying that he had another appointment. The whole session had lasted only forty minutes, most of which was consumed by Shigemitsu's blustering speech.[42]

When this confrontation was over, all of Koiso's efforts during the last few months to bring Miao to Tokyo appeared to be near collapse. The meeting only served to widen the chasm between the two antagonist groups and strained personal relations between them. The Miao Pin affair created an unbridgeable disunity within the government at the highest level and at the most critical juncture of the war. The Koiso cabinet itself was on the verge of collapse.

For the rest of Miao's stay in Tokyo, Koiso seemed to avoid seeing him.[43] Miao was left with the vice-minister of war, with whom he made no progress regarding *wahei kōsaku*. Shibayama not only declined to discuss the matter but also spoke ill of Koiso. Such talk only served to strengthen Miao's disillusionment with the Japanese premier, whose prestige had declined rapidly in governmental and military circles.[44]

Meanwhile Ogata, not ready to give up what appeared to him to be the final chance to conclude peace before Russian entrance into the war,[45] made a last desperate effort to persuade Generals Sugiyama and Umezu through Prince Higashikuni. The prince again made private representations on Ogata's behalf and urged Lord Keeper of the Privy Seal Kido to mediate. Higashikuni was disturbed, he told Kido, by the fact that Miao, regardless of his disrepute, had not been accorded the respect due a government guest.[46] Ogata himself tried to change Yonai's mind. All came to naught. Yonai told Ogata that the position of the cabinet vis-à-vis Miao would force its resignation if the premier should pursue the present course.

The navy minister seemed to harbor no particular ill feelings toward Miao, though like all the others he had lingering doubts about his credentials and character. Ogata had no hard evidence to dispel Yonai's concern. Yonai, however, seemed to object particularly to one of Miao's peace proposals—the dissolution of the Nanking government—because his cabinet had recognized the Nanking regime in 1940 as the sole government of China.[47] In the end the navy minister advised Ogata not to get involved in the Miao Pin affair.[48]

The war minister and chief of the army general staff were more adamant than the navy minister; they were unimpressed and unmoved by persuasion, apparently on the advice of their subordinates.[49] In Sugiyama's case, his opposition seemed to be partly personal, deriving from a rivalry which had developed in the 1930s. Sugiyama detested Koiso's penchant for political intrigue and was unhappy that he, a field marshal on active duty and the second senior ranking general in the rank-conscious army hierarchy, had to serve under a reserve general. Sugiyama's dislike intensified when Koiso tried, in vain, to remove him from the war minister's post. Sugiyama made known to Shigemitsu his grudge against Koiso.[50]

Koiso was tenacious in clinging to the Miao *kōsaku.* Perhaps encouraged by General Hata's written report on China, the premier decided to report the whole affair to the emperor in order to solicit his support. According to Nakamura, the Hata report was generally in agreement with what Miao had said and with what Koiso had maintained, i.e., that the Nanking government was neither capable of nor had any desire for negotiating peace with the KMT government.[51]

On April 2, the day after tens of thousands of American fighting men hit the beaches of Okinawa (as Miao had predicted to Ogata soon after his arrival),[52] Koiso was received in audience by the emperor. The premier told him of his difficulties with the military leadership and with cabinet colleagues in obtaining a voice in the direction of the war and a consensus in the Miao *kōsaku.* Regarding the latter question, Hirohito inquired whether the premier intended to pursue the negotiations with Miao, and Koiso replied affirmatively. After the audience, the emperor said to Kido that what Koiso reported to him differed from what other members of the Supreme War Council had told him. Consequently, the emperor enjoined the premier "not to get deeply involved in the affair." In response to the emperor's request for Kido's advice whether he should tell Koiso to terminate the Miao *kōsaku,* Kido suggested that he hear the opinions of the foreign, army, and navy ministers before announcing his final decision to the premier.[53]

On the following day, the emperor heard the views of the three cabinet ministers; each expressed objections to the premier's peace venture. The emperor then summoned and told Koiso to "send Miao Pin back to China," because all three ministers were opposed to his peace maneuver.[54]

Koiso, who for some time had been thinking that he would either have to reorganize his cabinet or resign, decided to give up as premier. On April 5, he resigned and his cabinet fell.

The emperor's decision against the Miao *kōsaku* was less dramatic than those that brought the end of the February 26 young officers' rebellion (1936) or that terminated the war in August 1945. When opinion was divided in the councils of government, such as occurred in the case of the Miao Pin affair, the emperor—advised by his ministers and by the lord keeper of the privy seal—could bring to bear his august, mysterious influence. The emperor exercised this power against Koiso, whose cabinet could not reach a consensus on the Miao *kōsaku*.

In helping to make the imperial decision, Kido had the power to decide whom the emperor should and should not see and listen to, and when he should see his ministers. Thus Kido was able to regulate the flow of information reaching the emperor. Because Kido was Shigemitsu's close friend, it should not be surprising that Kido's attitude toward and opinion of the Miao Pin affair were influenced or even biased by Shigemitsu, who kept his palace comrade informed. According to Ishiwata Sōtarō, minister of the imperial household, it was on "Kido's advice to His Majesty" that the emperor told the premier that Miao should be sent back, thus contributing to the downfall of the Koiso cabinet and, with it, to the end of the unreal affair.[55]

III.

More than a quarter of a century later, proponents and opponents remain divided on whether Japan should have accepted Miao's mediation in the spring of 1945 to terminate the war with China and with her allies, through China's good offices. If she had done so, the argument goes, Japan could have been spared the holocaust of the two atomic bombs and could have prevented Russia from entering the war. I think not.

Despite apprehensions about Miao's questionable representation and character, the Koiso–Ogata group wanted to give the Miao *kōsaku* a try, even if it meant sacrificing the Nanking regime, which neither Koiso nor Ogata supported.

Ogata was a realist with a newspaperman's instinct. That instinct suggested the possibility of achieving peace through Miao Pin, but realism and instinct were not matched by an understanding of China's position in international politics. China would not accept a separate peace with Japan and a provisional settlement of the war including the dissolution of the

Nanking regime, as Miao proposed. Ogata's realism was, paradoxically, mere wishful thinking, perhaps induced by Miao's smooth talk.[56]

As for Koiso, he erred on at least two counts which antagonized the opponents, particularly Shigemitsu. First, he ventured into dilettante diplomacy, consulting in advance neither the foreign minister nor the army leadership, because (as Koiso said) Shigemitsu was not a man with whom one could have a heart-to-heart talk, while the military did not "enjoy the trust" of the KMT government.[57] Better communications could have minimized the bitterness between Koiso and Shigemitsu, if not saved the Miao *kōsaku*.

Second, Koiso like Ogata thought the Nanking government could be forsaken without moral compunction,[58] i.e., *bunchi gassaku* (federation of local regimes)—the army's standard formula of divide-and-rule practiced in the 1930s for the administration of China, according to which any regime was expendable. Shigemitsu saw in the Miao *kōsaku* the specter of *bunchi gassaku* and denounced it as an infeasible formula for the disposition of the China problem.

To political realists like Koiso and Ogata, foreign officials in Tokyo and Nanking were too concerned with upholding moral commitment, thus making the war a deeper quagmire and losing the opportunity for settlement. "Give up a worthless regime," they seemed to be saying, "for the substance of real advantage."

The army high commmand, both in Tokyo and Nanking, was unwilling to face the reality of surrendering to the KMT government; its concern with saving the army's hollow prestige and honor was too strong to admit defeat in China. Therefore the army consistently took a negative attitude and obstructed the *kōsaku* in every way.[59]

Shigemitsu's objection was threefold: his antipathy toward anyone who engaged in unauthorized *wahei kōsaku*,[60] moral commitment to the Nanking government, and the problem of the unverified character of Miao's representation. Partly deriving from his professional jealousy and cliquishness "characteristic of foreign office bureaucrats,"[61] Shigemitsu detested Koiso's *wahei* diplomacy of dilettantism and regarded it as an infringement upon his prerogatives. Furthermore, he had a particular distaste for the arrogance and sycophancy of Tamura, who had been known to the foreign minister when he was ambassador to Nanking until 1943. Shigemitsu characterized Tamura as a *Shina goro* (China hooligan). Tamura's participation strengthened the foreign minister's distrust of the Miao *kōsaku*.[62]

Shigemitsu's opposition was based on morality. It is perhaps on this score that he won the emperor's support, for Hirohito upheld moral principles too. In theory, the foreign minister's concern for moral justice was unassailable; Japan could not go back to her old policy of *bunchi gassaku*. "[Japan] could not," Shigemitsu wrote, "abandon her aim of appealing to

the Chinese people through the government [of Nanking]," to which his
own government and its allies had extended diplomatic recognition.[63] To
discard that regime by withdrawing recognition from it, in Shigemitsu's
and Hirohito's view, would be unjust. It was better, they believed, to uphold
justice even if defeat were certain than to betray an ally and win peace at
the sacrifice of a friend. Nevertheless, the honoring of moral principles is
one thing; refusing to propose an alternative and completely boycotting the
Miao kōsaku is another. The foreign minister offered no constructive
alternative to Miao's peace overture. As a result, several precious months
were wasted, partly because of Shigemitsu's position against forsaking the
Nanking government. For this negative attitude, Shigemitsu must bear
responsibility.

The foreign minister's position on wahei kōsaku toward the Nanking
and Chungking governments was totally divorced from reality. His insistence on convincing "Chiang Kai-shek of the futility of his anti-Japanese
resistance" and "appealing to the Chinese people through the Nanking
government" for peace was unrealistic. Chiang's resistance against Japan
constituted the moral strength of his leadership, and he had no reason in
1944 and 1945 to change that policy. By 1940, the Nanking regime had
already become a puppet government in the eyes of the Chinese people.
Since then, it steadily lost prestige and popular support until it existed only
in name. How could such a government appeal to the Chinese people,
whom it had alienated?

Like his colleagues in opposition to the scheme, Shigemitsu simply did
not believe that the Chungking government would delegate authority, not
even an informal and tacit understanding, to a dubious character such as
Miao, who had betrayed the KMT government and the Wang Ching-wei
regime. Miao was trusted, Shigemitsu maintained, by neither Chungking
nor Nanking. Friend and foe alike, who were acquainted with Miao,
described him as a "man not to be trusted," a "peace peddler," a "political
mercenary," an "opportunist," a "small fry," an "enigma," and the like.[64]
Shigemitsu and others, in supporting their position, cite the first postwar
trial that condemned Miao to death as a traitor to the KMT government;
therefore, they insist, the trial vindicates their contention that Miao was not
a bona fide representative of the Chungking government, although they
concede that Miao did have some sort of connection with Chungking's
higher authorities.[65]

An investigation of the summary trial and execution of Miao may
throw some light (and perhaps add confusion and mystery as well) into the
dark corners of this bizarre peace maneuver. Like other Nanking government high officials, Miao was arrested after Japan's surrender. But at Tai
Li's directive he was given preferential treatment; Miao was optimistic
about his fate and expected to be released soon.[66] Suddenly, however, Miao

was indicted on the charge of treason, not of an unauthorized *wahei kōsaku,* on April 3, 1946. Five days later he was sentenced to death.

The proponents of the Miao *kōsaku* argued some connection between Miao's sentence and the untimely death of Tai Li and Ch'en Ch'ang-feng, whom Miao had rescued from the Japanese military police, on March 23 in an airplane crash, officially confirmed on April 1. One may conjecture that Tai opposed Miao's trial; therefore, his death enabled Tai's rivals, including the Ch'en brothers, who controlled the central police, to prosecute Miao ostensibly for treason in order to seal his lips about *wahei kōsaku.* They must have feared political repercussions should Miao, if indicted for *wahei kōsaku,* publicly reveal the closely guarded secret of wartime *wahei kōsaku* in which Chiang himself was said to have been involved. Such public disclosure would irreparably damage the KMT's national interest at a time when the Nationalists with American aid were fighting the civil war against the Communists, and when public opinion in China and America was beginning to turn against the corrupt KMT government. For these political considerations, it is said that Chiang personally ordered Miao's death sentence, which was carried out on May 21.[67]

If this is true, why was Tsiang Chün-hui, the man who was supposed to accompany Miao to Tokyo at the Generalissimo's request, not executed? Was it because Tsiang could be trusted to keep his mouth shut, whereas Miao with his loose tongue might divulge the secret? Until the KMT government archives covering the wartime period are opened to scholarly scrutiny, the weight of evidence rests with the argument that the Miao *kōsaku* was a hoax.

The real cause for failure is as much a matter of Miao's dubious representation as of Japan's internal problems—Koiso's lack of political leadership, his inability to control the army high command and Foreign Office officials in Tokyo and Nanking, and personal and bureaucratic rivalry and jealousy. Koiso, prominent in the intrigues of army politics and in the Manchurian Incident, was not a man to inspire confidence; in his diary Shigemitsu revealed an abiding distrust of him. This mistrust prevailed generally among his cabinet colleagues. Lack of confidence in the premier's political leadership had a direct bearing on his inability to control the military high command and diplomats in Tokyo and Nanking. Still, Koiso alone should not be blamed for his difficulties. The system of the government and of the military was as responsible: no decision could be reached if any member of the cabinet disagreed. The premier might dismiss a dissenting cabinet minister to get a consensus, but he could not dismiss the military. Even if he succeeded in dismissing a war or navy minister, he could not appoint a new one, because the military would resort to the time-honored method of refusing to name a successor, thus forcing the resignation of the cabinet. In decision making, many captains were steering the ship of state. Japan's premier had no power to initiate peace. Chiang Kai-shek, Wang Ching-wei, and Miao Pin had learned a bitter lesson from Konoe and Koiso. It is indeed tragic that personal and bureaucratic rivalry and jealousy made the Miao *kōsaku* an unnecessarily bitter contest with no useful purpose.

Furthermore, most Japanese leaders failed to evaluate the situation in Chungking correctly. KMT China in 1944–1945 was different from that of 1938, when China was fighting alone. China now was in alliance with the Great Powers, who were winning the war in Europe and Asia. Chiang had no reason to abandon the United States on the eve of the latter's triumph. He had no reason to accept from Japan less than unconditional surrender. Probably he wished to preserve Japan as a deterrent against the Soviet threat, but even if he wanted to advocate peace, the Generalissimo was not free to do so. There were many variables, all weighing against China's national interest and Chiang's self-interest. Would the Chinese Communists let Chiang negotiate peace unilaterally? Would the rightists follow Chiang's orders? Would the rank and file in the army and the party respect him if he should conclude a separate peace? Would the United States make an alliance with the Communists to fight on against Japan? Would Li Tsung-jen or other military leaders emerge to lead the nation in war?

Chiang could possibly do one thing—mediate between the United States and Japan, if the latter would offer favorable terms to China, including complete and immediate withdrawal of Japanese troops from China and the reversion of Manchuria. But Japan's peace proposals were not liberal enough for Chiang to advocate peace negotiations seriously and openly.

In sum, the Miao *kōsaku,* like other futile *wahei kōsaku* attempted during the war, represented another chapter in the politics of illusion—illusion based upon wishful thinking and lack of understanding of Chungking's true position.

Notes

1. Yokoyama Shimpei, *Hiroku Ishiwara Kanji* [Untold history of Ishiwara Kanji] (Tokyo, 1971), p. 257.

2. Takamiya Tahei, *Ningen Ogata Taketora* [Ogata Taketora the man] (Tokyo, 1958), p. 194; Japan, Sanbō Honbu [Army General Staff], *Haisen no kiroku* [Record of defeat] (Tokyo, 1967), pp. 239–40; Imai Takeo, *Shina jihen no kaisō* [Reminiscences of the Sino-Japanese War] (Tokyo, 1964), p. 196; Kin Yūhaku, *Dōsei kyōshi no jittai: O chomei no higeki* [The reality of the shared fate: The tragedy of Wang Ching-wei], trans. Ikeda Atsumori (Tokyo, 1960), pp. 206–7; *Yomiuri Shimbun, Shōwashi no Tennō* [The emperor in Showa history] (Tokyo, 1967), 1: 199; Tamura Shinsaku, *Oroka naru sensō* [A stupid war] (Osaka, 1950), pp. 100–101; Howard L. Boorman, ed., *Biographical Dictionary of Republican China* (New York, 1970), 3: 36–37.

3. For information on Chou Fo-hai, see Shū Futsu-kai (Chou Fo-hai), *Shū Futsu-kai nikki* [Chou Fo-hai diary], trans. Yoshida Tōyū (Tokyo, 1953), 20 December 1940; Kin, op. cit., p. 252; Boorman, op. cit., 1: 408; correspondence with Han-sheng Lin, 16 April 1971.

4. Tamura, op. cit., pp. 118–34; Tsuji Masanobu, *Ajia no kyōkan* [Common feelings of Asia] (Tokyo, 1950), p. 234.

5. Tsuji, op. cit., p. 234.

6. Ogata Taketora Denki Kankōkai, *Ogata Taketora denki* [Biography of Ogata Taketora] (Tokyo, 1963), pp. 106–7, 129. Ogata recorded his first impression of Miao as follows: ". . . he is professional and secular. But he is never an idealist."

7. Nakamura Shōgo, *Nagata-chō ichi-banchi* [No. 1 Nagata-cho] (Tokyo, 1946); p. 125; Maruyama Shizuo, *Ushinawareta kiroku* [Lost record] (Tokyo, 1950), p. 212; Higashikuni Naruhiko, *Ichi kōzoku no sensō nikki* [War diary of an imperial prince] (Tokyo, 1957), p. 153; Ogata Taketora, *Ichi gunjin no shōgai* [Life of a military officer] (Tokyo, 1955), p. 125; Tamura, op. cit., pp. 140–41.

8. Tamura, op. cit., pp. 142–43; Takamiya, op. cit., p. 221; Hattori Takushirō, *Daitōa sensō zenshi* [Complete history of the greater East Asian war] (Tokyo, 1968), p. 662.

9. Tamura, op. cit., pp. 142–43.

10. Yamagata was an old China hand whose career on the continent went back to 1900. After he retired from the service, he continued to maintain interest in China, serving as adviser to dissident warlords in the southwest and working for a Chinese iron ore–mining company.

11. Yamagata Hatsuo, *Chūgoku* [China] (Tokyo, 1967), p. 167.

12. Ugaki Kazushige, *Ugaki Kazushige nikki* [Ugaki Kazushige diary] (Tokyo, 1971), 3: 1648–49; Watanabe Wataru, "Tai-Shi seisaku no kihon yōkō" [Principles for China Policy], 15 October 1944 (unpublished); Hata Shunroku, "Hata nisshi" [Hata diary], 30 September 1944 (unpublished).

13. Shigemitsu Mamoru *Japan and Her Destiny* (London, 1958), p. 328; *Ogata*, pp. 131–32.

14. Koiso tried in vain to persuade the army to reinstate him on active service—a necessary step to his becoming war minister in his own cabinet—and to allow him to join the decision-making Imperial Headquarters. The army turned down both of Koiso's requests. Sugiyama told Shigemitsu of his ill feelings; Shigemitsu, op. cit., p. 328.

15. Koiso Kuniaki, *Katsuzan kōsō* [Autobiography] (Tokyo, 1963), p. 813.

16. Ibid.; Takamiya, op. cit., p. 198; *Shōwashi no Tennō*, 1:198.

17. Yamagata, op. cit., p. 174.

18. Tamura, op. cit., pp. 160–64; Takamiya, op. cit., p. 199; Yamagata, op. cit., pp. 174–77; Sanbō Honbu, op. cit., pp. 239–40; Sammonji Shōhei, "Hōmurareta Myō Hin kōsaku" [Miao Pin operation buried], *Jinbutsu Orai*, February 1956, p. 109.

19. Why Miao specified March 31 is not clear. Aoyama Kazuo, who was in Chungking during the war years and was close to KMT intelligence circles, explained that it was related to a Chinese power struggle. Aoyama Kazuo, *Bōryaku jukurenkō* [Espionage expert] (Tokyo, 1957), pp. 237–38. Others like Sammonji said that the date had no special meaning, other than prodding the Japanese to expedite the peace talks, because the Chinese were aware of Japan's secret approach to the Soviet Union. Chungking saw in it a real danger of the rise of Soviet power in China. Correspondence with Sammonji Shōhei, 26 July 1969. Still another interpretation is that the deadline was set because the Russo-Japanese neutrality pact (April 1941) was to expire, with legal denunciation possible in April 1945. In view of Stalin's denunciation of Japan in November 1944, the Soviet Union (Chiang Kai-shek feared) was not going to renew the pact, thus freeing Russia to enter the Pacific War—a decision Stalin was about to promise to Roosevelt and Churchill at Yalta (February 11). *Shōwashi no Tennō*, 1:203.

20. *Asahi Shimbun* Hōtei Kishadan, *Tōkyō saiban* [Tokyo trial] (Tokyo, 1948), 5: 20; Kyokutō Kokusai Gunji Saiban, *Kyokutō kokusai gunji saiban sokkiroku* [Shorthand record of the International Military Tribunal for the Far East] (Tokyo, 1968), p. 366; Koiso, op. cit., p. 814; Tamura, op. cit., p. 169.

21. Shigemitsu used to call Miao a *gorotsuki* (hooligan) and a "peace peddler." Shibayama had no use for Miao. Interview with Yazaki Kanjū 22 November 1969. *Shōwashi no Tennō*, 1:200, 208. Koiso described the relationship between Shigemitsu and Shibayama, on the one hand, and Miao, on the other, as something of a "cat-and-dog relation." He declined, however, to elaborate on the cause of the personal enmity between them, saying that "I prefer not to discuss it in detail." The ill feelings of Shigemitsu and Shibayama no doubt stemmed from

what they believed to be the opportunistic character and questionable credentials of Miao, who maintained contacts with *Shina rōnin* like Tamura and "treacherous" men like Tai Li. Interview with Nakamura Shōgo, 2 August 1972. Deputy Premier Yonai Mitsumasa was skeptical of Miao's character; like Shigemitsu, he questioned the manner in which the premier had handled the whole affair; but was mild in his opposition, as he did not seem to want to offend Ogata, his close and lifelong friend. As early as December 1944, General Imai accompanied Ambassador Tani Masayuki to Tokyo on a mission to stop the Miao *kōsaku.* They told Koiso that the Sōgun and embassy staff unanimously opposed the *kōsaku* through Miao, whom neither the Japanese nor Chinese side trusted. Imai later tried to persuade Ogata to give up the Miao *kōsaku.* Imai, op. cit., pp. 198–99; *Shōwashi no Tennō,* 1:220; Higashikuni, op. cit., pp. 176–78. Tani was another person Koiso sought to replace, but Shigemitsu blocked the attempt.

22. For the reconstruction of the following story, I have relied on Takamiya, op. cit., pp. 210–16; Ishikawa Masatoshi, *Seiji naki seiji—Kimura Takeo hyōden* [Biography of Kimura Takeo] (Tokyo, 1963), pp. 182, 319–20; interview with Tsiang Chün-hui, 3 December 1968; correspondence with Tsiang Chün-hui, 11 January 1969.

23. For charges and denials of sabotaging the mission, see Takamiya, op. cit., p. 199; Koiso, op. cit., p. 815; Yamagata, op. cit., p. 178; Sammonji, op. cit., p. 109; Imai, op. cit., p. 200; interview with Imai Takeo, 5 September 1968.

24. Interview with Yazaki Kanjū, 12 November 1968; Yazaki Kanjū, *Manshū Shina jihen kembunki—kattate okitai kotodomo* [An account of my experiences in the Manchurian and China incidents—Things I want to tell] (Tokyo, 1963), p. 15.

25. Nashimoto Yūhei, *Chūgoku no naka no Nipponjin.* [Japanese in China] (Tokyo, 1958), 2: 117.

26. Okamura Yasuji, "Senjō taiken kiroku" [My experiences on the battlefield] (unpublished), pp. 30–35; Okamura Yasuji, *Okamura taishō shiryō* [General Okamura's diary] (Tokyo, 1970), 2: 217–18. General Ho was a graduate of the Japanese Military Academy as was General Ch'en Yi. His presence with Chiang is significant because Ch'en was a leading Japanophile who enjoyed Chiang's confidence and was Okamura's close friend.

27. Nakamura, op. cit., pp. 177–78.

28. Sammonji, op. cit., p. 109; the code name was *Yi-yen* (righteousness and benevolence).

29. Nakamura, op. cit., p. 177 (emphasis added). See Charles Romanus and Riley Sunderland, *Time Runs Out in CBI* (Washington, D.C., 1959), as cited in Barbara Tuchman, *Stilwell and the American Experience in China, 1911–45* (New York, 1971), p. 481. Chiang "disliked the idea of an immense intrusion of foreigners no less than the court of Peking had disliked it before him."

30. Nakamura, op. cit., pp. 181–82.

31. Higashikuni, op. cit., p. 176; *Ogata,* pp. 133–36; Kido Kōichi, *Kido Kōichi nikki* [Kido Koichi diary] (Tokyo, 1966), 2: 1182–83. Miao also met Ishiwara Kanji. Yokoyama, op. cit., p. 377.

32. Sammonji, op. cit., p. 110; Higashikuni, op. cit., p. 177; Nakamura, op. cit., p. 108; *Ogata,* p. 158.

33. *Ogata,* p. 158.

34. Sanbō Honbu, op. cit., pp. 239–40.

35. Higashikuni, op. cit., p. 178; *Ogata,* p. 138.

36. *Shōwashi no Tennō* 1:213–14; Tamura, op. cit., p. 172; *Ogata,* p. 137; Ōtani Keijirō, *Shōwa kempeishi* [History of the military police in Shōwa] (Tokyo, 1966), p. 481; interview with Tanaka Keiji, 20 July 1972. Ogata had a talk with Sugiyama prior to the conference of the Supreme War Council and told him, in reference to Miao's qualifications, of lessons he had learned from reading Chinese history: "Lately, I read *Chan-kuo-ts'e* [The stratagem of the warring kingdom]. In China, rarely does the ruler of a kingdom come out personally to negotiate peace, alliance, or coalition. At first, a commoner, privately approached by the ruler or by a minister, conducts preliminary negotiations. Only after the negotiations reach a point where the conclusion of an agreement is possible, do official talks begin. Such is the principle of negotiations practiced in China. In view of the fact Japan and Chungking are at war and we have declared we would not deal with Chungking, how do you expect Chungking to send an official envoy for negotiations from the beginning?" Why Sugiyama changed his mind is not known. Perhaps he had been under pressure from below. The Sōgun sent a staff officer to Tokyo on the heels of Miao's departure for Tokyo in order to present its view against the Miao *kōsaku.* Sugiyama was known as *Guzu Gen* (Gen the Laggard) and *Benjo no dōa* (toilet door). These epithets imply that Sugiyama had no firm conviction or principles of his own, and that he could be swayed either way, as susceptible to outside or inside pressures as a swinging door.

37. Shigemitsu, op. cit., p. 328.

38. Interview with Shimizu Kunzō, 12 December 1968. Shimizu, first secretary of the embassy, confessed that the embassy did not have enough information about Tai Li to assess his relationship with Chiang Kai-shek.

39. Statement of Linda Berenson at panel, "The Military in Modern Chinese Politics," meeting of Association for Asian Studies, 29 March 1972.

40. Ambassador Tani to Foreign Minister Shigemitsu, 15 March 1945; Tani to Shigemitsu, 17 March 1945, in Gaimushō, *Shūsen shiroku* [Historical record of ending the war] (Tokyo, 1966), pp. 221–23; Satō Kenryō, *Taiheiyō sensō kaikoroku* [Reminiscence of the Pacific War] (Tokyo, 1968), p. 323; Imai, op. cit., p. 199; interview with Shimizu Kunzō, 12 December 1968. In these cablegrams Shimizu, who drafted them, referred to Miao by his alias, Chou Lin, by which name the Chinese politician was reportedly better known among circles of disreputable peace peddlers. The use of the alias was meant sarcastically against Koiso and Ogata, who Tani and Shimizu thought were ignorant of the local situation. *Shōwashi no Tennō,* 1:221. Tamura characterized Shimizu as "good-for-nothing except as an interpreter." Shimizu had been in China since 1912 and had been serving as interpreter for the embassy since 1934. Here again is the personal enmity that hampered the Miao *kōsaku.* Tamura, op. cit., p. 157.

41. Koiso, op. cit., p. 812. Koiso writes in his memoirs that he had secured from his colleagues in the Supreme War Council an understanding that if any one of the constituent members were contacted regarding peace negotiations, he was free to act. I have found no evidence to corroborate Koiso's claim.

42. *Shōwashi no Tennō,* 1:219; Ōtani, op. cit., p. 481; Nomura Masao, "Tai Jūkei tandoku kōwa no yume" [A shattered dream for a separate peace with Chungking], *Jinbutsu Orai,* August 1965, p. 91.

43. Interview with Nakamura Shōgo, 20 July 1972.

44. Statement of Aiuchi Jūtarō in Murata Shōzō, *Hitō nikki* [Murata's Philippine diary] (Tokyo, 1969), p. 604. Aiuchi was the only Japanese who accompanied Miao to Tokyo.

45. The Japanese had no knowledge of the secret provisions of the Yalta Agreements signed in February, although they were aware of the possibility of Russian entry into the war at any time. Miao predicted this possibility to Ogata upon his arrival in Tokyo.

46. Kido, op. cit., 2:1182.

47. *Ogata*, p. 137.

48. Interview with Nakamura Shōgo, 20 July 1972.

49. Lieutenant Colonel Yamazaki Jūsaburō, desk chief of the China Section of the general staff, advised his superiors not to trust Miao. Interview with Yamazaki, 24 October 1968. Sanbō Honbu, Sensō Shidōhan, *Daihon'ei kimitsu sensō nikki* [Secret war diary of the Imperial General Headquarters], 20, 21 March 1945, in *Rekishi to Jinbutsu* [History and Personality], November 1971.

50. Takamiya, op. cit., p. 181; Shigemitsu, op. cit., p. 328.

51. Nakamura, op. cit., p. 187.

52. Japanese Imperial Headquarters had not expected U.S. landing operations on Okinawa. Hattori, op. cit., p. 802.

53. Kido, op. cit., 2:1185; *Tokyo saiban*, 5:21; Koiso, op. cit., p. 827.

54. Koiso, op. cit., p. 827.

55. Ishiwata Sōtarō, "Ishiwata Sōtarō jutsu Kyokutō gunji saiban" [Ishiwata Sōtarō's statement at the Far Eastern Military Tribunal]. *Naigai hōsei kenkyūkai shiryo*, no. 124, in *Shūsen shiroku*, p. 230. Even at the moment of Miao's departure, the army refused to provide air transport service. The new war minister, Anami Korechika, prevailed upon his subordinates and provided air transportation. Just before his departure on April 19, Miao met Yamagata, and they exchanged poems, regretting the failure of the negotiations and pledging a brotherly alliance. The poems are reproduced in Sammonji, op. cit., p. 110. The original is in Yamagata's possession. Miao remained two extra weeks in Tokyo at Prince Higashikuni's request, even after Koiso dissolved his cabinet.

56. Takamiya, op. cit., p. 196; *Ogata*, pp. 129, 139; in interview with Nakamura Shōgo, July 29, 1972.

57. Tanemura Sakō, *Daihon'ei kimitsu sensō nikki* [Secret war diary of the Imperial Headquarters] (Tokyo, 1952), p. 215. Interview with Nakamura Shōgo, 20 July 1972.

58. Koiso was one of the Yonai cabinet members who had remained skeptical of the cabinet decision which extended diplomatic recognition to the Nanking government.

59. Sugiyama was reported to have expressed his regret, shortly before committing *seppuku* (disembowelment) in 1945, for having adopted a negative view of the Miao *kōsaku;* Tamura, op. cit., p. 175.

60. At the Supreme War Council, Shigemitsu specifically criticized Baron Miyakawa, Prince Konoe's younger brother, and Ogawa Aijirō, a former researcher for the South Manchurian Railway. The foreign minister's criticism was by implication directed at Konoe, with whom Miyakawa and Ogawa worked closely. Konoe at this time was in communication with a certain Captain Ishimasa, who urged him to use the good offices of Hsu Ch'ung-chih, a KMT elder statesman, to bring the war to an end. "Chūgoku wahei to senkyoku dakai ni tsuite" [On the solution of the China problem and the war situation], 20 March 1945, in Yōmei Bunko, *Konoye Fumimaro kō kankei shiryō mokuroku"* [Historical documents relating to Prince Konoye Fumimaro] (unpublished).

61. Nakayama Masaru, *Chūgoku no sugao* [China as it is] (Tokyo, 1957), p. 115; interviews with Tsuchida Yutaka, 13 January 1969, and Sugihara Kōta, 27 December 1968. Foreign office bureaucrats were cliquish against noncareer men when the latter were appointed foreign

minister or ambassador, or when someone other than their own conducted diplomacy. See Hosoya Chihirō et al., eds., *Nichibei kankeishi kaisen ni itaru jūnen (1931–1941): Seifu shunō to gaikō kikan* [Ten-year history of U.S.-Japan relations to the outbreak of the war, 1931–1941: Government leaders and foreign policy organization] (Tokyo, 1971), vol. 1.

62. A former *Asahi* reporter and colleague of Tamura's conceded his disagreeable disposition. Interview with Kurai Ryōzō, 12 December 1968. Colonel Okada Yoshimasa, who after Tsuji's transfer to Burma urged Miao to continue his contacts with Chungking, said that Tamura's participation in the *kōsaku* proved to be a liability leading it to failure. Interview with Okada Yoshimasa, 21 October 1968.

63. Shigemitsu, op. cit., p. 328. Ogata, however, reported that Lin Pai-sheng, minister of information and Wang Ching-wei's close friend, had said in the spring of 1944 that the Nanking government problem could be resolved for the sake of improving Sino-Japanese relations. *Ogata,* p. 130.

64. Interviews with Tsiang Chün-hui, 3 December 1968; with Imai Takeo, 5 September 1968; with Sugihara Kōta, 27 December 1968; with Iguchi Hiroji, 26 December 1968; with Shimizu Kunzō, 12 December 1968; with Nakamura Toyokazu, 13 January 1969; Okamura, op. cit., p. 33; Ugaki Kazushige's statement in *Shōwashi no Tennō,* 1:203; Kodama Yoshio's statement in *Shūsen shiroku,* p. 236.

65. Interview with Imai, September 15, 1968; Shigemitsu, op. cit., p. 353; Maruyama, op. cit., p. 215.

66. Chin Hsiung-pai, *Wang Cheng-ch'uan shih-mo-chi* [Rise and fall of the Wang Ching-wei regime] (Hong Kong, 1956), pp. 152–53.

67. Ibid., p. 153; Maruyama, op. cit., p. 215; Takamiya, op. cit., p. 218; interviews with Hsia Wen-yun, 13 November 1968; with Tsiang Chün-hui, 3 December 1968.

Commentary on the Yoji Akashi Essay*

Han-sheng Lin

I fear that I do not share the belief of Professor Akashi that the Miao Pin *kōsaku* was a hoax. The case is so complicated that other interpretations are possible. As demonstrated in the preceding chapter, Premier Koiso Kuniaki regarded Miao's mission seriously, as a viable alternative; only after the voicing of strong objections by the Japanese foreign minister and by the military, coupled with the emperor's intervention, did Koiso abandon his peace plan and resign the premiership. Had Miao been successful in his initial attempt at negotiation, the Chungking government probably would have paid much more attention to his endeavors.

I tend to agree that Chiang Kai-shek believed he alone could save Japan and that Chiang wanted to help the Japanese negotiate with the Allies to end the war. Evidently the Generalissimo hoped to resolve the question of the Nanking puppet government with as little resistance as possible, to use Japanese forces to guard North China and Manchuria until he was ready to occupy the recovered territories, and thus to prepare for a military showdown with the Yenan regime. Of course Chiang could not and

---

*Han-sheng Lin's commentary was prepared strictly from the viewpoint of Chinese domestic politics. He has chosen not to deal with other aspects of the Akashi chapter, such as the "contradictions" in tone if not substance between the epilogue and the main text; the Japanese authorities' ignorance of the process of politics in Chungking—errors which Lin feels that Akashi perpetuates; and the assertion that Chiang Kai-shek fully supported Ishiwara's organization of Tōa Remmei, although Akashi produces no Chinese sources to substantiate such an assertion. Lin admits that, in his commentary, he has not given Akashi sufficient credit for his diligent researches and for his insight into Japanese politics; but Lin stresses that limitations of space caused him to focus his remarks on areas with which he is best acquainted.

would not deceive the Allies, and he undoubtedly would have encountered difficulty in convincing the Allies of the merit of negotiating with Japan at this point; but it would have been enormously beneficial both to Chiang and to Japan if he had succeeded. Miao Pin simply was not the proper instrument to accomplish the task; he was not important enough in Chinese politics to have communicated directly with the Generalissimo.

Miao was a political commissar under General Ho Ying-ch'in during the Eastern campaign and served as commissioner of civilian affairs in Kiangsu province under the Kuomintang, but had been disgraced. During the period of Japanese control, Miao was a collaborator in Peking, but was again disgraced while serving Wang Ching-wei's Nanking government. It was therefore difficult for the Chinese authorities to trust him; perhaps Shigemitsu Mamoru comprehended this better than the Japanese premier did. In addition, Miao's service under General Ho was twenty years past, and the two men evidently had not been in contact after Miao's dismissal in Kiangsu. As for Ho, he had his own difficulties in trying to initiate peace negotiations with the Japanese. Ho was known as a pro-Japanese leader before the Sino-Japanese conflict, and his actions were under constant scrutiny by the Communists and the advocates of war. Consequently, Ho had to exert himself to demonstrate his patriotism during the War of Resistance. Furthermore, at the time of the Sian Incident (1936), Ho was a strong advocate of bombing Sian regardless of Chiang Kai-shek's personal safety. Although he continued to serve the Generalissimo as minister of military affairs, Ho no longer enjoyed Chiang's complete confidence. In fact, Chiang gradually transferred his reliance for military counsel to Generals Ch'en Ch'eng and Hu Tsung-nan; his continued employment of Ho as nominal chief derived in part from Ho's connections with the Whampoa cadets.

Miao Pin mainly contacted the followers of General Cheng Chieh-min, a leader of the Blue Shirts. Both Cheng and General Tai Li were certainly aware of Chiang's strategy of helping the Japanese to end the war in order to strengthen his own political position, but they could not operate overtly because the Communists were suspicious of them and the Allies were unaware of their efforts. Cheng and Tai could easily have reached Chiang if they had had a favorable agreement in hand but, before any tentative accord was reached, they probably proceeded with the clandestine attempt at peace negotiations, on their own initiative. When Miao finally traveled to Japan, Tai had already contacted Chou Fo-hai of the Nanking government, the regime authorized by the Japanese Supreme War Council to negotiate with the Chungking government on Japan's behalf. At this point, Wang Ching-wei died, and Chou virtually took charge of the Nanking regime, which he operated in accordance with directives from Chungking. Chou was a leader of the Whampoa group (including the Blue

Shirts) and of the C.C. clique, as well as a political confidant of Chiang Kai-shek himself, before his departure from Chungking. After the organization of the Nanking regime, Chou maintained contact with Chungking through various channels, such as the Blue Shirts, the C.C. clique, and General Ku Chu-t'ung of the Third War Zone.

The Miao mission was therefore not the product of a conflict between the Nanking and Chungking factions, as it may have seemed, although the possibility that the Cheng group and Tai Li were competing for "points" cannot be completely ruled out. At any rate, if the Japanese conditions for peace had been acceptable to Chiang, either Tai or Cheng could have presented them directly to the Generalissimo. Hence the principal issue remains: Japan was not ready to abandon its interests in North China and Manchuria, and the Japanese military leaders had not yet accepted their defeat. Good evidence is seen in General Okamura Yasuji's attitude of disregarding Chiang's peace overtures. Additionally, Japan's internal conflicts were so deeply rooted that the Japanese authorities simply could not forge a united front for peace, even at this moment of national disaster. The behavior of the Japanese emperor also did not serve to unite the peace forces.

In conclusion, I should like to stress that even if Miao Pin had been successful in securing favorable terms, he would not have played a major role in the final phase of the peace negotiations. Miao was actually an "initial explorer" whose activities the Chungking government could repudiate easily; were he to fail in his mission, he would readily be made the victim. Indeed, after the war, Miao's wife overestimated his value to the Chungking government and foolishly published some documents intended to demonstrate his service to his country; their disclosure apparently caused his early execution. It was a pity that the Japanese government, until the very end, failed to realize that the crucial obstacle to peace was Japan's own inability to achieve a consensus; it could have consummated its peace negotiation through Chou Fo-hai instead of through such a dubious character as Miao Pin.

V. The Faces of Force

12.

Whereas most of the other essays deal with individual or institutional efforts to achieve balance between China and Japan, Coox's contribution examines the naked use of force in the eight-year Sino-Japanese conflict which began, more or less by accident, in the summer of 1937. After discussing the irreconcilable historiography of the war, most particularly its proximate causation, from the three-cornered standpoint of Chinese Nationalist, Communist, and Japanese interpretations, the author surveys the hostilities themselves, with emphasis upon the climactic years of 1937–1938. Japan, bogging down ever further, soon found that it could not win the war, while China would not lose it. In the process, Japan experienced serious difficulties on the home front and in the armed forces. Among the problems encountered by the Japanese Army were manpower shortages, qualitative deterioration, munitions and equipment insufficiencies, and baleful effects on strategic thinking. The results of escalation and attrition were intensified by the absence of concerted, realistic military or civil planning; Japan was learning, to its frustration, that it is far easier to commence than to terminate hostilities. Japan underestimated Chinese capabilities and will, and misunderstood the burgeoning sense of nationalism which animated both the Kuomintang and the Communists. In desperation, Japan sought to escape the hole it had dug and widened it, in the form of the Pacific War. The consequences were disastrous for the Japanese, who had learned little from the experience in China. Not only did Japan fail to impose its type of brutal balance upon the Asian mainland, but it contributed, albeit unintentionally, to the triumph of

Chinese Communism, one of Japan's avowed foes in the first place. Mao Tse-tung agreed that the Japanese militarists' invasion was largely responsible for the ultimate victory of the People's Republic of China.

Alvin D. Coox earned his Ph.D. from Harvard University, and resided for a dozen years in Japan after the war. He is the author of *Year of the Tiger* (1964), *Japan: The Final Agony* (1970), and *Tojo* (1975). He collaborated with Hayashi Saburō on the English edition of *Kōgun: The Japanese Army in the Pacific War* (1959) and coedited the two-volume anthology, *The Japanese Image* (1965–1966). The Greenwood Press is bringing out Coox's next book, *The Anatomy of a Small War: The Soviet-Japanese Struggle for Changkufeng/ Khasan, 1938.* Professor of history and director of the Center for Asian Studies at San Diego State University, Coox won the California State University Trustees' Outstanding Professor Award in 1973. He wishes to thank the San Diego State University Foundation for faculty grants-in-aid, which facilitated the acquisition of Japanese documentation for this essay.

Recourse to Arms: The Sino-Japanese Conflict, 1937–1945

Alvin D. Coox

I.

The descent of Japan and China into the worst war in their long histories provides a classic instance of escalation and attrition. Surprisingly, what Mao Tse-tung termed "not just any war [but] specifically a war of life and death" remains forgotten or unknown abroad, far overshadowed by more finite and hence more manageable campaigns of the Pacific War such as Iwo Jima, Okinawa, New Guinea, and Imphal. Four years after the fateful clash at the Marco Polo Bridge, an American national news magazine admitted that

> World War II's biggest front, its oldest battle, its hugest protagonist are unknowns. . . . To an unknowing world it is the army nobody knows. The world at large does not know it, because the small corps of foreign correspondents in China feel they must stick close to big cities to get big stories. Chinese politicians are ignorant of the war front because they consider their job to be in Chungking. The war front is days away from Chungking except by plane, and China has no planes to spare for junkets. Even foreign military observers almost never get to the front, and send home distilled views of that war.[1]

Nevertheless, this Sino-Japanese conflict lasted more than eight years, until Japan was overwhelmed, largely in other theaters of operation, in August 1945.

The Japanese military effort in China was of immense cost, major duration, fierce intensity and scope—what used to be called a war in simpler days. Yet the Japanese never declared war on China.[2] To this day they call the hostilities "Shina jihen," the China Incident. Further complicating any study of the Sino-Japanese hostilities is the polemical nature of its recording, for the struggle was essentially three-sided, involving Chinese

295

Nationalist and Chinese Communist forces against the Japanese invaders and against each other. It is not difficult to judge which of the Chinese principals defeated the other on the mainland by 1949 in the civil war, but each continues to insist that it won the war against Japan. According to PRC sources, the 8th Route Army, the New 4th Army, and guerrilla units fought 125,165 battles and engaged 64 percent of the Japanese troops in China and 95 percent of the puppet formations, thus constituting "the main force in the War of Resistance Against Japan."[3]

Chinese Nationalist sources retort that, in the autumn after the outbreak of the Sino-Japanese conflict, Mao Tse-tung admitted secretly to his political officers: "The Sino-Japanese War affords our party an excellent opportunity to grow. Our fixed policy is to devote 70 percent of our effort to our own expansion, 20 percent to coping with the Kuomintang, and 10 percent to fighting the Japanese."[4] On the basis of reports from the U.S. Observation Group in the Communist base area of Yenan, General Albert Wedemeyer "knew that Mao Tse-tung, Chou En-lai, and the other Chinese Communist leaders were not interested in fighting the Japanese because their main concern was to occupy the territory which the Nationalist Government forces evacuated in their retreat."[5] The senior Nationalist general Ho Ying-ch'in derides the astronomic claims of the Chinese Communists, whose forces he calls "untrained, undisciplined, poorly equipped," and without "an efficient organ of command." How could the Communists, Ho asks, have killed 1,704,117 enemy soldiers, since the guerrillas were outnumbered by about 3 to 1, were "always on the run," and were widely scattered? Significantly, Japanese forces surrendered to the armies of the Republic of China (ROC) in 1945, not to the Communists, although Chu Teh called himself "Commander-in-Chief of Anti-Japanese Forces in the Liberated Areas of China."[6] Even American journalists not unsympathetic to the Chinese Communists were obliged to admit that the latter

> could not challenge any important Japanese garrison post or Japanese control of the railway system defended by earthworks and heavy armament. Though they could blunt a Japanese spearhead or turn it aside, they could not stop it. . . . At peak periods of Japanese activity perhaps 40 percent of all the Japanese in China were battling Communists or garrisoning Communist-held land. But during the significant campaigns it was the weary soldiers of the Central Government who took the shock, gnawed at the enemy, and died.[7]

For their part, the Japanese elevated the fighting against China to the level of a holy war. General Matsui Iwane went to China, he said, to "chastise the lawless Chinese troops and to impress upon the Nationalist Government the necessity for reconsidering its attitude towards Japan." On trial after 1945 for war crimes committed in China, Matsui defined what he called the true nature of the hostilities as a fight between brothers within the "Asian family." . . . It has been my belief during all these years that we must regard this struggle as a method of making the Chinese undergo self-reflection. We do not do this because we hate them, but on the contrary because we love them too much. It is just the same as in a family when an elder brother has taken all that he can stand from his ill-behaved younger brother and has to chastise him in order to make him behave properly.[8]

Tōjō Hideki agreed that

> there was real fighting to be sure, but it was considered to be a family quarrel, in which the younger brother, China, was being made to reconsider its various illegal acts typified by such anti-Japanese phrases as *kō-Nichi* (oppose the Japs) and *hai-Nichi* (expel the Japs). The basic purpose was always the fostering of good neighborliness and friendship and for that reason the thing was never called a war nor was there a declaration of war.[9]

In Premier Konoe's words, Japan was striving "to help China recover from degeneration."[10]

A month after the Marco Polo Bridge clash the Japanese Foreign Ministry insisted that the cause of all the "untoward events" stemmed from Nanking's desire to inflame Chinese public opinion and to enhance its power base, in collusion with the Communists. The contempt for Japanese national strength had led to "an increasingly arrogant and insulting attitude" manifested in provocations, insults, and "acts of unpardonable atrocity." Although the Japanese deplored the situation and bore "no ill will toward the innocent Chinese masses," Japan's patience was exhausted. Nurturing no territorial designs, Japan wanted only to induce "truly harmonious collaboration" among Manchukuo, China, and itself.[11]

Professor Maruyama Masao warns that the moralizing by the Japanese military and civilian leaders was not "trumped up for the occasion":

> . . . the suppression of foreign peoples by Japanese military might was always "the promulgation of the Imperial Way" and was regarded as an act of benevolence towards the foreigners in question. The attitude was unconsciously caricatured in a speech by General Araki in 1933: "Needless to say, the Imperial Army's spirit lies in exalting the Imperial Way, spreading the National Virtue. Every single bullet must be charged with the Imperial Way and the end of every bayonet must have the National Virtue burnt into it. If there are any who oppose the Imperial Way or the National Virtue, we shall give them an injection with this bullet and this bayonet."

"Men who could think this way," concludes Maruyama, "would not be satisfied until they had imbued each individual slaughter with the mystique of the Imperial Way."[12] In the long run, the Japanese leadership was taken in by its own slogans.

In view of the self-righteousness of the three parties engaged in China, it is not surprising that even the origin of the hostilities of 1937 attracts no agreement.[13] In its original protest to the Great Powers, the Chinese

Nationalist government charged that the Japanese garrison at Peking "had no shadow of right" to be conducting field exercises in the area of the Marco Polo Bridge (Lukouchiao). Claiming to be looking for "a suppositious missing Japanese soldier," the Japanese forces intended "to use the inevitable refusal as the jumping-off point for further invasion" of China. The Japanese pretended to minimize crises which they continuously engineered; localization was a mere "subterfuge invariably attempted for baffling Chinese unity and confusing world opinion."[14] About ten days after the clash at the Marco Polo Bridge, Chiang Kai-shek told a group of ROC officials that the incident had been fomented by the Japanese as "a pretext for achieving their objects in North China, namely the enlarging of the concessions which they claimed [there] in virtue of the Tangku Truce terms [of 1933], the expansion of the limits of the independent East Hopei administration, and the expulsion of General Sung [Che-yüan] and of the Twenty-Ninth Army."[15]

Today the Chinese Nationalists and Communists can only accept the old interpretation that the Japanese were entirely responsible for the Marco Polo affray. Although General Ho calls the clash of July 7 a "sad but sacred" day, he insists that the affair was brought about "by the ambitions of the Japanese militarists. They hoped to take advantage of the Communist rebellion on the Chinese mainland to conquer all of China through open aggression."[16] Official Nationalist military histories assert that the Japanese garrison in the Peking-Tientsin region attacked the Marco Polo Bridge "on the pretext of a military exercise."[17] We are not privy to the innermost thoughts of the ROC military leaders but, immediately after World War II, General Ho is known to have asked Lieutenant General Nemoto Hiroshi about the truth of the Marco Polo episode; presumably not even the KMT side is acquainted with all of the facts.[18]

Although colored by ideology, the Chinese Communist account of the outbreak of hostilities in 1937 does not differ in basic outline from the Nationalist version. "Penetratingly analyzing the new situation," Mao Tse-tung "pointed out that the Japanese imperialist attempt to reduce China to a Japanese colony heightened the contradiction between China and Japan and made it the principal contradiction." Japanese imperialism, in the summer of 1937, "unleashed its all-out war of aggression against China. The nationwide War of Resistance thus broke out."[19]

The official Japanese version of 1937 attributed the underlying trouble to the Nanking government's anti-Japanese policy, which was said to be rooted more deeply than at the time of the Shanghai crisis of 1932. Hinting at the Japanese Army's real perception of events, General Sugiyama Gen (Hajime), the war minister, charged that the Chinese were overestimating their "national strength resulting from increased national unity, expansion of military preparations, especially in the air forces, and improvement of army organization and equipment." The first affray at Peking was blamed upon unexpected Chinese firing at Japanese units, who "reciprocated the Chinese challenge." Subsequent Chinese "provocations" necessitated Japanese "punitive operations."[20]

Although even the more dispassionate Japanese postwar histories still charge that Japanese troops (from a company numbering a mere 135 men) were shot at first by the Chinese in July 1937, they generally say little more than that the hostile fire emanated from the direction of a unit of Sung Che-yüan's 29th Army.[21] Nationalist forces are no longer identified as the indubitable culprits. As Colonel Hayashi Saburō puts it, "suspicions have not been dispelled that the whole thing was a ruse devised and executed on their own by a few willful men, rather than by the authorities of either Japan or China."[22] The senior staff officer of the Japanese garrison at the time, Major General Hashimoto Gun, remembers

> a strange event which happened while the Japanese and the Chinese forces were in a state of mutual suspense. [Gunfire] was repeated almost every evening. I heard rumors that it was probably done by Chinese students or by Communist elements. I think there existed a third party's intrigue to provoke a conflict between the Japanese and the Chinese forces.[23]

General Kawabe Masakazu agrees that there was no evidence the "unlawful firing" came either from the Japanese or the Chinese unit; "it almost seemed that a third party which did not belong to [either army] was firing from the intermediate area between. . . ."[24] From a survey of all available data, Professor Kimitada Miwa has concluded that, even if it cannot be proved that the Chinese Communists provoked the Marco Polo affair, "the party assiduously endeavored to produce a situation in which it seemed only natural and inevitable for a showdown to take place."[25] It does not seem unfair to conclude that the troubles in the Peking area derived from a combination of Chinese warlordism and banditry, competition between Kuomintang and CCP elements, provocations by Japanese hirelings and free-lance adventurers, and clumsy training exercises by the Japanese Army garrison.

None can argue against the existence of a superheated political and military climate in the Peking region in July 1937, but it is difficult to accuse the Japanese side—particularly the central authorities—of premeditated aggression at this particular time and place.[26] While Chiang Kai-shek was warning his compatriots of the danger that "the Peiping of today will become a second Mukden,"[27] Foreign Minister Anthony Eden told the British House of Commons, about two weeks after the Marco Polo Bridge affair, that according to all indications, the confrontation had not been provoked by either the Japanese or the Chinese government.[28] Once-secret Japanese Army (IJA) records reveal that the high command in Tokyo was truly taken by surprise when the fighting broke out at Peking. High-ranking officers on duty in the Japanese capital at the time mention repeatedly the confusion, disarray, and lack of unity of thinking on the part of the army general staff (AGS).[29] Naturally, contingency plans existed, but they had not been updated and the general staff expected no war with China. The Japanese garrison in North China had been instructed, since 1936, to be trained for hypothetical operations against the Soviet Union, not China. The Japanese troops which were conducting night maneuvers near the Marco Polo Bridge were proceeding under those guidelines.[30]

Of course there were hawks in the Japanese high command who savored the idea of "settling" the Chinese problem once and for all and who regarded the 1931 incident as a perfect precedent for swift and forceful action now. Some envisaged using the affray of July 1937 as the basis for establishing a buffer zone between Manchukuo and North China. But AGS doves such as Ishiwara Kanji felt that full-scale hostilities against China were unmanageable, irrelevant, or at least premature, that the Russians were pulling the Chinese strings, and that even the Kwantung Army in Manchuria was little better than a paper tiger confronting the huge ground and air forces of the USSR across the borders in Siberia.[31] Although an American military observer discerned evidence of deliberate planning in the Japanese "display of logistic efficiency" in North China in 1937,[32] it is incorrect to compare the unfurling of the "China Incident" with that of the "Manchurian Incident." Whereas in 1931 Mukden and other key points were overrun in about a day, "talk and skirmish" tactics characterized almost the entire month of July 1937, despite the fact that Tokyo's policy of localization lacked consistency, by postwar Japanese admission.[33]

When the first serious clashes erupted at Peking, the strength of the entire Japanese garrison force in North China amounted to only 5000 or 6000 men, built around a single infantry brigade. At Shanghai, in August, the Japanese Navy had no more than 4000 bluejackets ashore.[34] Available to the Chinese central authorities were ground forces that were not negligible quantitatively: 75,000 troops in the Peking district, and a total manpower pool which numbered 2,000,000 regulars and 500,000 ready reserves. During the initial phase, according to Chinese records, about 40 percent of the regular forces or 800,000 men were available for combat.[35]

Ostensibly to protect Japanese interests and to save the lives of 12,000 residents in North China, the high command in Tokyo decided to dispatch about 15 air force squadrons and three ground divisions to the continent as an "emergency measure," e.g., two divisions to Shanghai (August 13) and one to Tsingtao (next day).[36] Already, in July, other forces had been rushed to North China by the Kwantung Army and the Korea Army. Even in the AGS there was considerable opposition to these troop movements; the reinforcements, arriving on the heels of Japanese military mobilization, inevitably caused the Chinese to doubt the sincerity of Japanese local negotiators. According to Japanese sources, press officers in the Japanese War Ministry may have done their best to exacerbate matters publicly by releasing inflammatory communiqués without the knowledge of their superiors.[37] Hotheaded officers in Tokyo were also said to be using direct lines of communication privately to egg on other young staff officers in the North China garrison.[38] The Domei news agency did not help to cool the situation with its exaggerated reports of massive Chinese troop movements.[39]

On the Chinese side, too, hawk struggled with dove, "blind optimist" versus defeatist. The confused and the irresolute, according to Mao Tse-tung, were convinced that resistance would mean subjugation, while the exponents of a quick Chinese victory engaged in idle talk and lacked "courage to admit that the enemy is strong while we are weak." In addition, there were honest patriots who feared the danger of compromise and doubted the possibility of Chinese political progress; Mao insisted that the anti-Japanese war and Chinese national reconstruction were interconnected. In any case, capitulation to the Japanese "devils" was out of the question, lest every Chinese become "a slave without a country."[40] As for Chiang Kai-shek, the Generalissimo had long been pursuing the policy that "unless the critical moment for sacrifice has arrived, we do not speak lightly of sacrifice, in order to avoid the premature outbreak of war." Given the agreement which had led to the formation of a united front, however, and the apparent obduracy of the local military forces now in confrontation, the Nationalist authorities decided to order national mobilization, exploiting China's superior manpower and huge territory to wage a sustained war of attrition. "While wearing out the enemy on the one hand," the KMT strategists agreed, "we should improve our combat effectiveness on the other, awaiting the opportune time to shift to the offensive. . . ." In the initial stage, key locations should be held, terrain advantages should be exploited, the enemy's hope of a quick victory should be thwarted.[41]

At first the Japanese Army's strategic idea was to strike fast and to capture a number of vital points while the Japanese Navy covered landings, protected lines of sea communication, and provided naval air support. On the basis of the experience in Manchuria and at Shanghai in 1931–1932, the Japanese hawks judged that full-scale hostilities would be unnecessary. Local operations and threats of force were expected to awe the Chinese and cause the central government to lose heart and sue for a cessation of hostilities on terms favorable to the Japanese.[42]

Although the Chinese fought desperately and suffered immense losses, they could not check the invaders. Japanese troops soon overran North China, Shantung, and the great port city of Shanghai, where Chiang Kai-shek committed and lost some of his finest troops.[43] Nevertheless, contrary to the expectations not only of the Japanese but of the world at large, the Chinese did not yield. Many Japanese now believed that only the conquest of the Nationalist capital at Nanking would end Chinese resistance.

Japanese reinforcements poured in, Nanking fell quickly in December 1937, Chiang Kai-shek fled, and the inflamed Japanese soldiery went berserk in the city. The scale of commitment in the Shanghai-Nanking locale is suggested by the casualties: in just six weeks of fighting, the Japanese 9th Division, which fought its way into Nanking, counted 13,300 Chinese corpses, but suffered over 12,300 casualties of its own. According to the notes of the Japanese commander, in the fighting for Shanghai and Nanking the Japanese armies lost a total of 21,300 men killed and over 50,000 wounded.[44] The Chinese admitted suffering casualties exceeding 367,000 during the same period.[45]

Victory eluded the Japanese, although Tsingtao fell in January 1938, and Amoy, Kaifeng, and vital Hsuchow in May, thereby allowing the invaders to link their northern and central battle fronts. The opinion was now heard frequently among Japanese military authorities that a campaign against Hankow was inevitable. In the Chinese provisional capital the American ambassador consulted his attachés and concluded that the Japanese intended to use the capture of Hankow as a symbol of the termination of the military phase of operations in China.[46] Of the importance of the summer and autumn offensives of 1938 the Japanese were fully aware. Colonel Inada Masazumi, section chief of the AGS operations bureau, had been working on the presumably last major Japanese drive, to secure the Wuhan complex of Wuchang, Hanyang, and Hankow. It was to boost Japanese morale and to deal the Chinese a truly decisive blow, says Inada, that the operations were devised; even during the Hsuchow campaign, Hankow was on his mind. Inada's idea was to seize crucial objectives with a view to early consummation of a political settlement.[47] The fall of Hankow, it was expected, would cause even the misguided, insincere, and Red-tinged Nationalists to see reason. At long last, stability in the Far East would become a reality, under the rubric of *hakkō ichiu* (eight corners of the world under one roof). Chiang Kai-shek's stubbornness and the unexpected Chinese refusal to capitulate were galling to the Japanese, however. One widely read commentator declared later: "Chiang Kai-shek! You are a black ingrate. Your anti-Nipponism is enough to cause your benefactor, Dr. Sun Yat-sen, to weep in the nether world. . . . We advise you with all our heart, but we are in a hurry."[48]

The campaign for Hankow involved the largest Japanese military strength ever massed for a single action during the hostilities in China: two field armies totaling 9½ divisions, supported by great amounts of shipping, munitions, and equipment. Plans to take Canton in the south were held up until the success of the main Hankow offensive could be gauged.[49] Both Hankow and Canton fell by the end of October 1938; Walter Lippmann told Americans that "Japan has won the war."[50] But the end of hostilities was still not in sight. Although there was some despondency in Nationalist circles, Chiang Kai-shek established a new provisional capital at Chungking. According to Chiang's military estimate of the situation, the Japanese lost confidence, halted their offensives, and went over to a policy of "sustained operations."[51] It took the Japanese Army two years to push even halfway closer to Chungking; in June 1940 they reached Ichang, still about 300 miles away. Japanese ground forces had proceeded no farther west by the time the war ended in 1945. One particularly sensitive IJA colonel asks, rhetorically but sadly:

> Why, oh why, didn't we cut the China Incident short, after we had attained our initial objectives? It was senseless of us to get lured into the hinterland. Wasn't the creation of our "dream empire" in Manchukuo enough? All we ever ended up with was real estate, not popular support from those we "liberated."
>
> We really believed that Hankow would be the last clean-up operation, and then we might concentrate again on the building of Manchukuo. But it was Nanking all over again, quite the reverse of what the Japanese operations staff had thought. Chiang Kai-shek was supposed to give up but instead the Chinese fled to Chungking. We bogged down, deeper and ever deeper, in that endless morass of attrition.[52]

Important elements of the Japanese Navy were diverted from their primary high-seas mission to support the ground forces engaged in China. Possessing air supremacy, the Japanese sent flights of as many as 150 bombers to hit Chungking and other inland cities between May and August of each year. "Fatigue bombing" and "blockade bombing" were conducted mainly during the years 1939–1943, but air power could not interdict the enemy's logistical capability or break his will to resist. The Chinese used manpower and cross-country mobility to move supplies. After the Japanese Navy blockaded the Chinese coast and the army seized all major coastal ports and enclaves, except British Hong Kong, the Chinese resorted to overland supply from the interior, including the Burma Road and the routes from Russia.

II.

Why did the Japanese, with their vaunted technical, industrial, and mechanical advantages, fail in China? Ten months after hostilities broke out, Mao Tse-tung already discerned five major Japanese errors in the field: piecemeal reinforcement, absence of a main direction of attack, lack of strategic coordination, failure to grasp strategic opportunities, and failure to annihilate Chinese formations after their encirclement. Although, Mao admitted, the Japanese made some improvements, "much of the enemy's strategic and campaign command is incompetent," and many of the Japanese mistakes were of their own doing. The invaders suffered from "internal contradictions" among landlords, bourgeoisie, and warlords; they underestimated Chinese capabilities and were short of troop strength.[53]

The Japanese would certainly have agreed with Mao's fifth point. At the outset the AGS did not contemplate committing more than 11 divisions, or an absolute maximum of 15 if the reserves were drawn upon. Yet, by the end of 1937, the Japanese already had to dispatch 16 divisions and about 700,000 troops, approximately the number of men in the entire standing army to date. By the end of 1939, Japanese forces in China numbered 23 divisions, 28 brigades (the equivalent of another 14 divisions), and an air division. The number of troops in China rose to 850,000.[54] This level of commitment was maintained until around 1943, when transfers to other theaters began, under American military pressure in the western and southwestern Pacific regions. Still, at war's end in 1945, the Japanese Expeditionary Army in China was the largest of the Japanese armies stationed overseas: 1,050,000 officers and men (19 percent of the entire Japanese Army of 5,550,000); 26 infantry divisions (15 percent of 169); plus one of Japan's four tank divisions, and one of the 15 air divisions. In addition, 64,000 Japanese naval personnel were on duty in China.[55]

At the same time, however, the Chinese Army had been built up to 354 small divisions, 120 corps, 31 brigades, and over 112 regiments, numbering some 3,000,000 men in all. The core of the Chinese Communist forces alone was estimated by the Japanese at 500,000.[56] This, despite the immense casualties incurred on both sides. Chinese sources state that 60 percent of the Chinese regular army was lost in the fighting for Shanghai and Nanking in 1937, and that 28 percent of the total Chinese military strength as of 1940 was lost during that one year. Japanese divisions reported losses of only 1 in 20 and 1 in 40 in action against the Chinese. During the first 16 months of the fighting, the Japanese estimated that the Chinese suffered military casualties totaling 823,000. This figure is close to the Chinese admission of 1,102,000 casualties during the first 18 months. In all, the Chinese regular army, according to postwar ROC sources, suffered the following losses between 1937 and 1945, expressed in round numbers: killed in action—1,325,000; wounded—1,762,000; missing—130,000. The total number of Chinese military casualties therefore exceeded 3,217,000 officers and men. This figure reflects only regular losses, not those incurred by guerrillas or local defense units. In addition, the Chinese estimate their civilian dead and injured at 5,788,000. Overall Chinese casualties were caused as much by sickness and desertion as by hostile action. Dorn explains:

> Because of the lack of any medical care worth the name, most of the seriously wounded had died. All stragglers and prisoners had been shot or beheaded by the Japanese. Horrible as such action was, it was no different from what they themselves meted out to Japanese under reverse circumstances. As a matter of fact, the Chinese usually shot their own seriously wounded as an act of mercy, since "they would only die anyway."[57]

Beyond the demographic considerations there was the well-known and successful trading of space for time by the Chinese Nationalists and

Communists. Early in the conflict General Ishiwara said he dreaded a full-scale war against China, since Japan was in no position to commit itself fully and might become caught in a bottomless swamp, as had happened to Napoleon in Spain. Colonel Hayashi Saburō describes the Japanese experience in China:

> The Chinese took the best possible advantage of their vast and boundless terrain. They preserved their own fighting strength while wearing down the Japanese troops with frequent shifts of force and fluid tactics of advance or retreat, depending on the situation. Because of the Fabian tactics of the Chinese, most of the annihilation operations of the Japanese Army ended in failure; only narrow belts of territory could be captured. The prompt settlement of the China Incident by force, as originally envisaged by the Japanese Army, thus failed in the long run.[58]

In other words, the Japanese were thinking in terms of a Cannae, a Carthaginian victory of annihilation. The Chinese were resorting to the less spectacular but calculated strategy of attrition to dissipate, overextend, and exhaust Japanese power. After the loss of the Wuhan complex, Nationalist leaders espoused a strategy of so-called magnetic warfare designed to attract the invaders to a specific point where they might be outflanked and encircled.

A Japanese Army chief of staff has said that high-command attitudes toward China were characterized by optimism and disdain in general. A section chief at AGS headquarters in Tokyo, for example, reacted to the news of the dangerous clash at the Marco Polo Bridge by telephoning to say that "something interesting" had just occurred. Later a section chief visited the general's office and berated the staff for opposing the dispatch of troops to China. "You just do not know what the Chinese are like," complained the section chief. "That is why you are voicing such negative opinions, in anticipation of serious trouble. But I tell you, the incident will be settled if Japanese shipping loaded with troops merely heaves to, off the Chinese coast." This notion that China did not count was held widely by Japanese government circles, the military, and the general public.[59]

Yet the Chinese armies, for all of their huge losses, low morale, and constant defeats, were gaining steadily in both experience and capability. In 1938, having profited from the past year of warfare, the Chinese Nationalist Army "decided to assign corps as strategical units and divisions as tactical units with the intention of increasing the firepower and mobility of the front line units."[60] By 1941, wrote a foreign correspondent, the Chinese had made a "spectacular discovery": ". . . for a nation in which military leadership has classically been an affair of coin and cunning rather than martial skill . . . China could turn out first-class officer talent."[61] Behind the scenes, foreign material assistance and loans, mainly Russian at first, were reaching the Chinese. To the Japanese, the Chinese manpower pool appeared limitless, as well it might, for China drafted 14,054,000 men between 1937 and 1945, according to official Chinese sources. By the end of

1938, F. F. Liu suggests, the Japanese Army was actually overestimating the Chinese defenders.[62]

Part of the Japanese military's original confidence, and hence grandiose designs, stemmed from a low evaluation of the Chinese Army's abilities. One Japanese commander recalls that his single infantry regiment, 3500 men strong, engaged three Chinese so-called divisions under general officers, during the Hsuchow offensive, and "made mincemeat" of them. The statistics bear him out. Dorn speaks of the Chinese Army's "feudal" thinking and political influences. Other American professional soldiers judged that the Chinese had "never been able to coordinate their defense" and that "the efforts of the majority have consistently been nullified by the negligence, stupidity, failure to obey orders, or failure to fight on the part of a few." Wedemeyer found few Chinese senior officers who seemed "efficient or professionally well trained."[63] Apart from local successes by the Nationalists in April 1938 at Taierhchuang (ignored by Communist sources) and by the 8th Route Army at Pinghsing Pass in September 1937 and in southern Shansi next spring (for which the Nationalists take partial credit), the poorly trained and ill-equipped Chinese local armies could accomplish little in defense of the northern plains. Faulty coordination and lack of unity were costing the Chinese "almost irreparable damage in trained soldiers and material."[64]

While, as Mao admitted in 1938, the Japanese field forces were impressive in unit and small formation tactics, the invading armies were never able to trap and destroy the foreign-supplied Chinese main formations, despite constant sweeps and unceasing attrition. ROC sources note that by 1945 there had been 23 campaigns, 1117 major battles, and 38,931 engagements. From the Japanese side it was reported that in 1939 alone, the North China Area Army had fought 17,500 separate engagements; in 1940, over 20,000. Yet movement at night by the Japanese remained dangerous. Seizure of railroads and key points did not prove decisive. Instead of fighting for lines and points, the Chinese sought to control entire areas and cause the foe to become hopelessly bogged down. "China is like a blanket," foreign correspondent Gunther wrote; "the Japanese hold the seams, i.e., the canals, the railways, the rivers, the great cities." As Theodore White put it, "the Chinese could not win, but they would not quit."[65]

Japanese military planning was disjointed, short-range, and unrealistic. The conduct of hostilities was characterized by widening cleavages between the government and the high command, between the War Ministry and the AGS, between the authorities in Tokyo and those in the field. To start the fighting was easy; to terminate it, immensely difficult. As one IJA commander admits, the Japanese "are apt to begin a battle without visualizing the end of it, and we are not much concerned with what we are going to have to meet." By 1938 liaison conferences in Tokyo often reached an emotional stage. With staff officers speaking ill of each other, the civilian authorities could only look on impotently. The command was at loggerheads over the question of approval for further offensive operations on the continent, while the area armies were arguing for a linkup of their enclaves. The operations bureau staff, however, judged that there ought to be a sizable rotation of troops, to cope with problems of deteriorating discipline and morale, as had been seen at Nanking. Until fresh reinforcements could be provided by late summer 1938, the field armies should concentrate upon village pacification in zones already occupied and upon building up the new local regime. Thus, the local armies were still striving for a clear-cut military decision, which they thought was within their grasp, while the AGS was beginning to favor a negative policy of endurance.[66] A vicious circle ensued; the greater the area the Japanese managed to carve out, the more troop strength they needed. It was not unknown for local IJA commanders to launch a new, manpower-rich operation in China whenever the authorities in Japan spoke of de-escalating hostilities on the continent. The more the Japanese high command sought to limit the field forces, the more the China Expeditionary Army tried to deal "one last blow"—to knock out the elusive enemy regulars or guerrillas. Whereas Japanese military commitments to the China theater remained ad hoc in nature, cumulatively they came to equal a major proportion of total national strength, as we have seen.

In the absence of a sensible military policy, the Japanese ought to have developed successful modes of civil administration and of counterinsurgency activity. But the central authorities never devised a systematic and standardized approach; local commanders' "solutions" inevitably stressed force, fear, and intimidation. A Chinese general, Wu Te-chen, remarked that the trouble with the Japanese was that they "think they know China too much." According to a postwar analysis, "the most striking feature of Japanese counterguerrilla efforts regardless of the merits of individual military techniques or policies instituted in a few selective areas, was that the Japanese had neither an overall plan nor a system of operations."[67] Consequently the Japanese struggled, unsuccessfully in the main, to cope with three problems of military government: first, to win the hearts and minds of the natives; second, to pacify and safeguard liberated zones; third, to buttress a friendly (that is, pro-Japanese) government, the puppet regime established in Nanking in 1940. But had not Bismarck once said, "You can do anything with bayonets except sit on them?" The bankruptcy of Japanese policy in North China is suggested by the cruel slogan of "three-all" (sankō): "Burn all, loot all, kill all."[68]

III.

The Japanese commitment of overall military and economic strength to China led to serious problems in numerous fields. On the home front there were raw-material insufficiencies, consumer-goods shortages, budgetary-outlay restrictions, a gold-flow problem, and difficulties with civilian morale and with hoarding.[69] On the battlefront the armed forces suffered from many dangerous complications.

The Japanese field armies, although numerically reinforced, became weaker, overall, than they had been in the early stages of the hostilities. Severe casualties played a major part. According to Japanese sources, IJA units which fought at Shanghai suffered casualties equaling their table-of-organization strength. Thus the Wachi Regiment of the 11th Division had an initial strength of 3500 officers and men, but incurred losses amounting to 1100 killed and over 2000 wounded. To maintain the regiment's strength, eleven sets of replacements totaling 2500 to 3000 men had to be provided. In another Japanese division, the 3d, which fought at Shanghai, the Ishii Regiment lost 1200 killed and 3000 wounded, against an initial strength of 3500. At Shanghai alone, the Japanese attackers lost 9100 killed and 31,300 wounded.[70]

In the four and a half years until 1941 the Japanese already suffered 190,000 men killed in China, 520,000 wounded, and 430,000 sick.[71] Between 1937 and 1945 the Japanese Army lost 385,000 officers and men killed in combat in China; the navy, another 8000 dead. A further 54,000 Japanese soldiers died in China *after* the war. The total number of Japanese military dead in China amounted to 447,000 or 39 percent of the overall number of 1,130,000 IJA dead in World War II.[72] Other critical losses were incurred in terms of sick, injured, or wounded soldiers who had to be evacuated to the homeland. For example, in the zone of the Northern Area Army alone, 18,000 sick men were evacuated in 1938, 23,000 in 1939, and 15,000 in 1940, for a total of 56,000 evacuees in those three years. Another 23,000 were sent back from North China because of wounds or injuries.[73] Japanese records are always reticent about Imperial Army prisoners; Nationalist Chinese forces report the capture, by May 1945, of 22,293 Japanese troops.[74]

Illustrative of the Japanese high command's concern over the China campaign was the fact that from 1937 the Japanese Army, which since 1925 had possessed only 17 standing divisions, suddenly had to build its strength to 24 divisions, of which 16 were sent to China. From 1938 the overall number of army divisions increased by another ten, to 34 divisions. Total army manpower rose from 950,000 in 1937 to 1,130,000 in 1938.[75] Replacements and reserves were generally green, lacking not only training but also experience. Simultaneously and inevitably, a dilution in the quality of the IJA officer corps resulted from the "overnight" army increases. For instance, the Military Academy graduated only 388 lieutenants of all arms in 1936; 471 in 1937; only 426 in 1938; and 461 in 1939. Not until 1941 would the annual crop of academy graduates be trebled.[76] As early as 1936 Marquis Kido Kōichi learned from General Honjō Shigeru, then senior imperial aide-de-camp, that there were conspicuous defects in the army's state of preparedness, especially an insufficient number of officers. Honjō had asserted that all units lacked Military Academy officer graduates. The shortage of regular officers had to be made up from one-year volunteers as well as from master sergeants.[77] Major General Ugaki Matsushirō has described problems in the type and quality of IJA training:

> Company-grade officers were generally trained intensively and carefully, both in headquarters and in units, but field-grade officers (especially those above the rank of regimental commander) received comparatively brief training. Although training for battalion commanders was conducted prior to the China Incident, regimental commanders were not trained until thereafter. Despite the keenly appreciated necessity to train division commanders, such a program was never instituted. During the campaigns in China, in fact, a number of division commanders merely parroted the tactical views of their staff officers. All in all, during the China Incident, a relatively large incidence of weakness in Japanese Army officer training was revealed.[78]

Shortages of munitions affected the overall Japanese posture from the early period of hostilities in China. IJA officers recall that there was scarcely enough ammunition for the regular divisions, let alone the Moloch of Hankow. In 1937, according to War Ministry sources, the entire Japanese Army possessed ammunition stocks sufficient for 15 divisions engaged in combat for only about eight months. It would take another eight or nine months for Japanese production capability to catch up with and stay abreast of operational consumption by a full 15 divisions, if that; yet there were already 16 divisions in action in China by the end of 1937. The results are not surprising. A terrible munitions crisis was caused by the stubborn Chinese defense of Shanghai, where the Nationalists proved to be "not the Chinese of 1931." As early as mid-September 1937 the Japanese forces at Shanghai were rationed to several shells per artillery piece per day. IJA units in North China had to transfer ammunition to the central front, leaving the equivalent of only one battery's ammunition quota per division in the north.[79]

The Japanese Army was consuming all of its artillery ammunition stocks in China, even the corps reserves which had been earmarked for a possible war with the Soviet Union. In August 1938, when the Japanese

Korea Army became involved in a very serious clash with the Russians at Changkufeng, one IJA officer contacted Tokyo with a desperate plea for supplies of antitank ammunition. His request was rejected by the War Ministry. The reason given was that even the November 1938 ammunition production quota had been allocated for the Hankow campaign. Field Marshal Hata Shunroku, who commanded the Central China Expeditionary Army in 1938, remembers that the Hankow offensive obsessed him that year. "I recall suffering from grievous shortages of mountain artillery ammunition in particular," says Hata, "and I asked Tokyo for replenishment. They referred me to the Kwantung Army, which turned me down!"[80]

The AGS operations bureau chief asserts that the campaigns on the mainland were draining the high command of all reserve supplies of expendable material. "What a terrible danger this posed in the north, no matter how good our troops were!" writes a general in the War Ministry. To which it must be added that Japan was then in the throes of an almost irreconcilable internal struggle between the demands of mechanization and those of air power. The hostilities in China prevented a free choice.[81]

IJA shortages of equipment can be illustrated by one occurrence which few inside the army were in a position to know, and which of course the general public never heard anything about. During the critical Hsuchow operation of 1938, the fundamental material weakness of the army was demonstrated by the situation of the tank corps. To conquer Hsuchow, the Japanese forces in China had committed all available armor. Attrition was inevitable, as the result of mechanical or combat causes, but replacement tanks were lacking locally. Hurried messages were dispatched to headquarters in Tokyo but, there too, ordinary replacements were unavailable. Therefore the authorities in Japan collected whatever last tanks they could, even those from the service schools, ostensibly to participate in the annual review held in Tokyo on the occasion of the emperor's birthday on April 29. But when the parade was over, the tanks kept moving, from the Yoyogi parade grounds straight to Shinagawa train station. There the tanks and crews were loaded aboard waiting trains and shipped directly to the combat front in China! They arrived in time to participate in the attack on Hsuchow, which finally fell on May 19, three weeks after the parade for the emperor in Tokyo.[82]

The Japanese experience against China was in many ways atypical of any larger war which Japan might have to face. For example, because the Chinese lacked planes and tanks in quantity, the Japanese tended to think in terms of an unrealistic aerial and armored supremacy. Partly as a result, the Japanese Army did not devise substantial *Panzer* formations embodying heavy or medium tanks, and did not organize a long-range strategic air command. Essentially, the Japanese were still relying on infantry, cold steel, "human bullets," and the so-called Yamato spirit. Most of all, the Japanese came to despise the fighting qualities of the Chinese soldiery. By projection, this led the Japanese to look down upon and underestimate all other possible enemies, such as the Russians, the British, and the Americans. The Japanese had no true conception of their potential enemies. "A national trait of the Japanese is that they are not interested in intelligence," observed an IJA officer after the war. "There is a Chinese proverb: 'If you know your enemy and you know yourself, you will win a hundred battles.' . . . We always fought without sufficient information." Military requirements also outdistanced estimates consistently. The Japanese Army was chronically weak in logistical planning. One of General Yamashita's headquarters officers once said: "Japanese staff officers generally find logistics planning dull and thoroughly distasteful; so they skip it."[83]

There was another very important consideration in the minds of the planners in Tokyo: China was not Japan's prime foe. Especially since the Kwantung Army conquered Manchuria, the Soviet Union was Japan's main hypothetical enemy. In China, from 1937, the USSR sent Matériel, aircraft, and pilots to engage the Japanese as so-called volunteers. The preponderance of the Japanese Army, over 20 divisions, had always been reserved against the eventuality of a two-front war with the USSR. While exercising this restraint upon the Soviet Army, the Japanese simultaneously were waging the campaign against China, with the balance of the armed forces. Nevertheless, Chinese resistance could not be overcome as swiftly as hoped, and fierce Chinese counterattacks hurt the Japanese locally. Therefore the Japanese high command could no longer avoid committing a portion of troop strength reserved previously for anti-Soviet operations, from the start of the Hsuchow operation of March–May 1938. From this period can be dated the Japanese Army's abandonment of hope of localizing the hostilities in China. Until then, says an IJA staff officer, the annual Japanese operations plan could be drawn up by the AGS on the assumption that the Kwantung Army would be allocated the strength necessary for a counteroffensive capability against the USSR. As soon as the hypothetical enemy struck at Manchuria, the Japanese Army would commit forces from other areas to support the Kwantung Army's plans. Even during the Hsuchow operation, when the Japanese were still not overcommitted in China, it was conceived that divisions could be redeployed to Manchuria in the event of a national emergency versus the Soviet Union. But after the drafting of the Hankow plan, which required such massive troop and matériel strength, it became impossible for the Japanese high command to envisage the earlier war plans.[84]

Ishiwara has identified a number of the reasons for the Japanese Army's botching of the operational direction in China: (1) insufficient control by the central authorities, especially by the war ministry;[85] (2) meddling by the Kwantung Army;[86] (3) lack of broad-based training by the Army War College for a war of attrition, as opposed to emphasis on decisive battles; and lack of capability to develop unified geopolitical judgments;[87]

(4) failure to learn from history; e.g., from the Manchurian, Changkufeng, and Nomonhan incidents.[88]

In the Japanese homeland the authorities labored on mobilization matters necessary to raise and dispatch many new divisions to China, while a number of high IJA planners shuddered privately about the dangers of Soviet Russian intervention and of two-front war. A Japanese staff officer describes the problem:

> The hostilities in China were strangling us, swallowing our national industrial buildup efforts; the China front devoured our production. The AGS operations staff, who had always been focussing their attention on the Soviet Union, knew very well that we ought not to get too deeply involved in China, which hardly posed the threat that the Russians did. But some of the other general staff sections were aggressive toward China. Nor can one deny that there were, unfortunately, some field officers in China, as well as officers on the high command, who shortsightedly welcomed the China Incident.[89]

The last remark refers particularly to some cynics in the War Ministry who argued that a small-scale but drawn-out conflict in China would help Japan to build up its national strength against the Soviet Union.

Even the Japanese emperor is said to have expressed certain doubts about the military course of events. At a liaison conference in late February 1938, the monarch asked the war minister whether it was really feasible to contemplate *three* national efforts simultaneously; that is, protracted hostilities with China, preparations against Soviet Russia, and an expansion of the Japanese Navy. Sugiyama, the war minister, reportedly attempted to temporize, saying something to the effect that every effort would be made, after consultations with the cabinet. One participant came away with the feeling that this reply left the emperor extremely dissatisfied. After all, this was the same General Sugiyama who had assured the monarch, at the time the fighting in China broke out, that the affair would be settled within a month or so.[90]

As the Japanese were to find in the war against America, the endpoint of hostilities is far more difficult to establish than the starting point. The Japanese consul in Tsingtao conveyed the impression to an American official, early in 1938, that "the Japanese, while desiring peace, were puzzled as to how to achieve it."[91] After World War II, Admiral Nomura Kichisaburō told U.S. interrogators that the Japanese Army

> wished to end the China War quickly, but at the same time they wished to get something out of it. . . . They thought the job would be much easier than it was and they thought that they could accomplish things without much cost. However, I don't think they planned to go as far as they did. . . . I was told that they considered it could be finished within six months. . . . In order to save face, they were forced to continue.[92]

General Kawabe said after the war: "I thought then, and I think now, that if only we could have adopted a very long-range and broad view, firmly unifying the intention of cutting off the China Incident and facing things resolutely, then the situation would not have reached such a critical pass."[93]

Historian Hata Ikuhiko speaks of "the agony of Japan, which was facing this dead-end but could find no useful policy for settlement, and was all the while wandering around without being able to evolve a firm and unified scheme of war guidance."[94]

Many postwar Japanese critics castigate the shortsightedness of the military in allowing have-not Japan to become involved in an extraneous and imprudent war of attrition on the continent. Maruyama remarks that

> what made the absence of long-term planning and the lack of effective leadership so conspicuous was precisely [the] inability to regulate the means in terms of clearly perceived objectives. Thus the use of brute force to carry out policy became more and more commonplace, until finally there was no turning back; military power had become an end in itself.[95]

There is a certain fatal connection between the stray shots fired in the vicinity of the Marco Polo Bridge in July 1937 and the mushroom clouds that engulfed Hiroshima and Nagasaki in 1945. In the largest strategic sense, Japan's involvement in the China hostilities escalated into the catastrophic Pacific War.[96] It was therefore only fitting and proper that Chiang Kai-shek should have been deputized by the United Nations to accept the surrender of the 1,283,240 Japanese troops stationed in China, Taiwan, and North Vietnam, and that General Hsu Yung-chang should have participated in the formal ceremonies where the Japanese government and high command signed the instrument of capitulation aboard U.S.S. *Missouri* in Tokyo Bay.

The foredoomed effort by Japan to impose its kind of brutal balance on China united the Chinese populace psychologically in a Japanophobic patriotism unseen in recent history. One Japanese military historian calls Chinese nationalism, so underestimated by the Japanese Army, the greatest single cause of the failure by Japan to settle the hostilities.[97] While an early collapse of Japan did not occur, new hope was stirred in China by the entry into World War II of the United States and other antifascist powers. ROC and Communist tying-up of over one million Japanese troops was no negligible contribution to Allied victory in the Pacific. Nationalist forces joined in reconquest operations in Burma and fought to clear the Ledo Road from India to Kunming; by early summer of 1945 they had recovered Kweilin and Liuchow and were liberating Kwangsi. A campaign against Canton, to be followed by roll-up offensives northward to Manchuria, was being readied when the Japanese capitulated.[98]

Once the Japanese danger had been checked and then eliminated, the uneasy, insincere alliance between the Chinese Nationalists and Communists came apart. By 1945 the Communists were showing contempt for instead of fear of the Kuomintang government, on the eve of another four years of warfare to decide the political fate of the mainland. Japan's unintentional contribution to the outcome of the civil war was never better explained than by Mao Tse-tung. When a group from the Japan Socialist Party visited Peking in 1961, Chairman Mao politely declined their apologies for Japan's evil past. "It is Japan whom we must thank," he insisted, "for without the invasion of China by the Japanese militarists, we might still be living in the caves."[99]

Notes

1. *Time,* 16 June 1941. Theodore H. White agrees fully; see *Thunder Out of China* by him and Annalee Jacoby (New York, 1946), pp. 61–62.

2. Nationalist China finally declared war on Japan, 9 December 1941.

3. Among many such PRC sources, the most interesting is perhaps Lin Piao, "Long Live the Victory of People's War!" originally published in 1965 in *Renmin Ribao* in commemoration of the twentieth anniversary of victory in the Chinese People's War of Resistance Against Japan (Peking, 1967), p. 18. Mao gives the same statistics on pinning down Japanese and puppet forces as of 1943. There was some change in ratios, according to Mao, at the time of the Japanese offensives of 1944, when 56 percent of Imperial Japanese Army (IJA) troops (320,000 of 580,000 men, and 22½ of 40 divisions) were engaged by the Communists; the latter still were fighting 95 percent of the puppet armies. *Mao Tse-tung: An Anthology of His Writings,* ed. Anne Fremantle (New York, 1962), pp. 150–51.

4. Chiang Kai-shek (Chiang Chung-cheng), *A Summing-up at Seventy: Soviet Russia in China* (London, 1957), p. 85; "Chung Kuo Kung Chan Wen Ti Wen Chien" [Documents on the problem of the Chinese Communist Party], presented to People's Political Council, March 1941, published by Supreme National Defense Council, 1944, cited by Tien-fong Cheng, *A History of Sino-Russian Relations* (Washington, D.C., 1957), pp. 226, 368 n. 6; Ho Ying-ch'in, "Commemorating the July 7 Anniversary of the Outbreak of the War of Resistance Against Japan and Refuting . . . the False Propaganda of the Chinese Communists," *Free China Weekly,* 9 July 1972, p. 2. Mao's statement is found in many Republic of China (ROC) sources; see *PLA Unit History* (Taipei, n.d.), p. 7, which charges that the Chinese Communists "were fighting the Japanese on the surface." Also see Hsu Long-hsuen and Chang Ming-kai, comps., *History of the Sino-Japanese War (1937–1945),* trans. Wen Ha-hsiung (Taipei, 1972), pp. 537–38, which states that "whenever the Chinese Armed Forces fought against the Japanese, the Communists attacked the flanks of our forces. It was not possible to guard against such attacks."

5. Albert C. Wedemeyer, *Wedemeyer Reports!* (New York, 1958), p. 285. Also see Samuel B. Griffith, II, *The Chinese People's Liberation Army* (New York, 1967), pp. 75–77.

6. Ho, op. cit., p. 4. Ho Ying-ch'in was chief of the general staff and later commander in chief of Chinese ground forces. Also see Hsu and Chang, op. cit., pp. 547–49, 559, 561–71.

7. White and Jacoby, op. cit., p. 207. The authors add that during the campaigns of 1937–1938 and 1944, "more than 70 percent of Japanese effort was concentrated against the troops of Chiang Kai-shek and his warlord allies" (p. 210).

8. Maruyama Masao, "Japan's Wartime Leaders," trans. Ivan Morris, *Orient/West* 7:5 (May 1962): 40, citing International Military Tribunal for the Far East, *Transcript,* 7 November 1947; Alvin D. Coox, *Year of the Tiger* (Tokyo and Philadelphia, 1964), pp. 139–40.

9. Based on interrogation of Tōjō, cited by Robert J. C. Butow, *Tojo and the Coming of the War* (Princeton, 1961), p. 102 n. 37; Coox, op. cit., p. 140.

10. Cited by Coox, ibid., p. 140.

11. Statement by Japanese government, 15 August 1937, *International Conciliation,* (November 1937): 718, cited in *Documents on International Affairs, 1937,* ed. Stephen Heald (London, 1939), pp. 658–60. Also see Otto D. Tolischus, *Through Japanese Eyes* (New York, 1945), Chapter 13.

12. Maruyama, op. cit., pp. 39–40; Coox, op cit., pp. 140–41.

13. See John Boyle's essay this volume. John Gunther presents his journalistic account in the famous *Inside Asia* (New York and London, 1939), pp. 234–35. Han Suyin heard a picturesque version that "the manoeuvres developed towards realism, and live ammunition was used on both sides"; *A Mortal Flower* (New York, 1972), p. 409. Also see T. A. Bisson, *Japan in China* (New York, 1938), pp. 8–15; *League of Nations Official Journal,* Special Supplement no. 177, Subcommittee Rpt. of 5 October 1937, in Heald, op. cit., pp. 686–89.

14. Chinese memorandum to Powers signatory to Nine-Power Treaty, 16 July 1937, *New York Times,* 17 July, cited in Heald, op. cit., pp. 652–54.

15. Arnold J. Toynbee, *Survey of International Affairs, 1937,* (London, 1938) 1:187.

16. Ho, op. cit., p. 2.

17. War History Bureau, Ministry of National Defense, ROC, *Military Campaigns in China: 1924–1950,* trans. Lt. Col. W. W. Whitson, Patrick Yang, and Paul Lai (Taipei, 1966), p. 51; Hsu and Chang, op. cit., pp. 163, 175, 177, 179.

18. Author's correspondence with Imaoka Yutaka.

19. Lin Piao, op. cit., pp. 6–8.

20. Statement to the Imperial Diet, 27 July 1937, *Contemporary Japan* (September 1937), 360, cited in Heald, op. cit., pp. 654–58.

21. Japanese Research Division, Military History Section, Hqs. USAFFE/8th U.S. Army, *North China Area Operations Record, July 1937–May 1941* Japanese Monograph No. 178, (1955), p. 1.

22. Hayashi Saburō in collaboration with Alvin D. Coox, *Kōgun: The Japanese Army in the Pacific War* (Quantico, Va., 1959), p. 9; first published by Iwanami Shoten as *Taiheiyō sensō rikusen gaishi* [Outline history of the ground battles of the Pacific War] (Tokyo, 1951).

23. IMTFE, *Transcript,* 23 April 1947, p. 20,634, cited in Hayashi, op. cit., p. 196 n. 26. Also interview with Imaoka.

24. IMTFE, *Transcript,* 22 April 1947, pp. 20,535, 20,544, cited in Hayashi, op. cit., p. 196 n. 26.

25. Kimitada I. Miwa, "Brief Notes on the Chinese Communists' Role in the Spread of the Marco Polo Bridge Incident into a Full-scale War," *Monumenta Nipponica,* 18:1–4 (1963): 327–28. Also see Hata Ikuhiko, *Nit-chū sensō shi* [A History of the Sino-Japanese conflict] (Tokyo, 1961); Uno Shigeaki, "Chūgoku no dōkō" [The China movement], in Nihon Kokusai Seiji Gakkai, *Taiheiyō sensō e no michi* [The road to the Pacific War] (Tokyo, 1962), 3:332–41, hereafter cited as *TSM;* James B. Crowley, "A Reconsideration of the Marco Polo Bridge Incident," *Journal of Asian Studies,* 22:3 (May 1963): 277–91.

26. Crowley, op. cit., p. 291.

27. Toynbee, op. cit., vol. 1, p. 187.

28. Ibid., p. 183.

29. Bōei-chō, Bōei kenshūsho, Senshishitsu [Office of Military History, Institute for Defense Studies, Defense Agency], *Daihon'ei rikugunbu* [War Department, Imperial General Headquarters] (Tokyo, 1967), 1:430, 432–33.

30. Hayashi, op. cit., p. 9; Hata, op. cit., p. 248; Tsunoda Jun, ed., *Ishiwara Kanji shiryō* [Historical Materials on Ishiwara Kanji] (Tokyo, 1967), p. 447.

31. *Daihon'ei,* 1:430, 432, 445, 460; Inaba Masao, ed., *Okamura Yasuji taishō shiryō* [Okamura Yasuji materials] (Tokyo, 1970), pp. 394, 397; Inada Masazumi, "Nikka jihen to sanbō honbu no fun'iki" [The Japan-China incident and the atmosphere inside the AGS], in Nakamura Kikuo, *Shōwa rikugun hishi* [The untold history of the army in the Showa era] (Tokyo, 1968), pp. 213–30. I have treated the matter of Soviet Far Eastern forces in "Effects of Attrition on National War Effort: The Japanese Army Experience in China, 1937–1938," *Military Affairs,* 32:2 (Fall 1968): 60, 62 n. 16. Also see Akira Iriye, "The Failure of Military Expansionism," in *Dilemmas of Growth in Prewar Japan,* ed. James William Morley (Princeton, 1971), pp. 113–14. My interviews on this topic included Inada Masazumi, Kohtani Etsuo, Hata Ikuhiko, and Imaoka.

32. Frank Dorn, *The Sino-Japanese War, 1937–41: From Marco Polo Bridge to Pearl Harbor* (New York, 1974), pp. 4–5.

33. Hayashi, op. cit., pp. 9–10. Arnold Toynbee comprehended from the outset that the cases of Mukden (1931) and Peking (1937) were far from similar; op. cit., 1: 184.

34. *Daihon'ei,* 1:435.

35. The Japanese estimated Chinese regular forces at 1,700,000, ibid. Chinese military sources indicate the following ROC units at the commencement of hostilities; the numbers in parentheses refer to forces actually available: infantry divisions—182 (80); cavalry divisions—9 (9); separate brigades—46 (9); artillery brigades—4 (2); artillery regiments—20 (16); aircraft—600 (305 combat types); Hsu and Chang, op. cit., pp. 172–73. Only 10 of the 182 infantry divisions were equipped fully; most were understrength, some by as much as 50 percent; Harry H. Collier and Paul Chin-chih Lai, *Organizational Changes in the Chinese Army, 1895–1950* (Taipei, 1969), p. 188.

36. *Daihon'ei,* 1:436, 439, 444.

37. Ibid.,1:440.

38. Yabe Teiji, *Konoe Fumimaro* (Tokyo, 1952), 1:400–401.

39. *Daihon'ei,* 1:441.

40. Mao Tse-tung, *On Protracted War* (Peking, 1963), lectures delivered in Yenan, 26 May–3 June 1938. Lin Piao, op. cit., pp. 8–9, gives an excellent précis. Also see *Mao Tse-tung on Revolution and War*, ed. M. Rejai (Garden City, N.Y., 1970), pp. 240–41. The Chinese hawk vs. dove confrontation is discussed fairly in *Daihon'ei*, 1:440–41.

41. Hsu and Chang, op. cit., pp. 164–65.

42. Hata, op. cit., p. 246; *Daihon'ei*, 1:462; *Ishiwara Kanji shiryō*, p. 411, from question-and-answer sessions between Ishiwara and Prince Takeda, autumn 1939.

43. For new information on the German advisers' role and on Alexander von Falkenhausen's advice against defending Shanghai, see Billie K. Walsh, "Erich Stoelzner and the German Military Mission in China" (M.A. thesis, San Diego State University, 1971), pp. 144–48.

44. The Japanese 9th Division sustained losses of 3833 killed and 8527 wounded, between September 27 and approximately November 10. Data on Shanghai fighting from notes of Matsui Iwane.

45. According to Chinese Board of Military Operations data for July–December 1937, 124,130 were killed and 243,232 wounded, for a total of 367,362; Chinese Ministry of Information, *China Handbook, 1937–1945* (New York, 1947), p. 301.

46. Ambassador Nelson Trusler Johnson to Secretary of State Cordell Hull, 19 July 1938, in *Papers Relating to the Foreign Relations of the United States: Diplomatic Papers, 1938* (Washington, D.C., 1954), 3:230–33. Hereafter cited as *FRUS*.

47. Interview with Inada Masazumi. Also Hata Ikuhiko *et al., Nit-chū sensō* [The Sino-Japanese conflict], pt. 2 of *TSM* (Tokyo, 1963), 4:44–45, 368.

48. Taka'ishi Shingorō, chief of *Tōkyō Nichi-Nichi*, 4 February 1938, cited in Otto D. Tolischus, *Through Japanese Eyes,* (New York, 1945), pp. 123–24; and Mutō Tei'ichi, open letter to Chiang Kai-shek, 8 September 1941, ibid., p. 129.

49. Hata, op. cit., pp. 292–94.

50. *Time,* 7 November 1938. But *Time* also printed a statement by War Minister Itagaki Seishirō which was not only cautionary but also strongly anti-Chiang.

51. Hsu and Chang, op. cit., p. 253. Imaoka states that by the end of 1939, Japanese offensive operational plans were completed.

52. Imaoka interview.

53. Mao Tse-tung, op. cit., pp. 132–37.

54. Hata et al., *TSM,* 4 (pt. 2): 24, 41, 63; and Hata, op. cit., p. 249.

55. Hayashi, pp. 149–50, 182.

56. ROC data from *Military Campaigns in China*, p. 94; Japanese data from Hayashi, op. cit., p. 148. Even ROC wartime propaganda admitted that until the Hankow campaign, Japanese casualty rates were only one-third the Chinese; Chinese News Service, *China After Five Years of War* (New York, 1942), p. 51. For a contemporary roundup of estimated Chinese casualties, see *New York Times,* 9 July 1938 (Hankow dateline). The best surveys of the Communist forces are found in Chalmers A. Johnson, *Peasant Nationalism and Communist Power: The Emergence of Revolutionary China, 1937–1945* (Stanford, 1962), pp. 72–77; and Griffith, op. cit., pp. 72, 74, 336–38 n. 33; *PLA Unit History,* p. 8. Also see Hsu and Chang, op. cit., p. 547.

57. Dorn, op. cit., p. 65; Hsu and Chang, op. cit., p. vii; *China Handbook, 1937–1945,* p. 301; White and Jacoby, op. cit., pp. 133–40. Japanese estimates of Chinese casualties between July

1937 and June 1941 were 3,800,000, of which 2,015,000 were killed; Inaba Masao, Kobayashi Tatsuo, and Shimada Toshihiko, comps., *Gendaishi shiryō* [Documents on contemporary history] (Tokyo, 1966), 13:444.

58. Hayashi, op. cit., p. 12.

59. Kawabe Torashirō, *Ichigaya Dai kara Ichigaya Dai e: Saigo no sanbō jichō no kaisōroku* [From Ichigaya Heights to Ichigaya Heights: Memoirs of the last deputy chief of staff] (Tokyo, 1962), pp. 137–38; Tateno Nobuyuki, *Shōwa gunbatsu* [The Showa militarists], *Gekidō hen* [The terrible shock] (Tokyo, 1963), p. 251.

60. Collier and Lai, op. cit., p. 188.

61. *Time,* 16 June 1941.

62. Hsu and Chang, op. cit., p. 173; *China After Five Years,* p. 51; *China Handbook, 1937–1945,* p. 351; F. F. Liu, *A Military History of Modern China, 1924–1949* (Princeton, 1956), p. 201.

63. Dorn, op. cit., pp. 65, 370–71; White and Jacoby, op. cit., pp. 142–43; précis contained in Johnson to Hull, 19 July 1938, *FRUS, 1938,* 3:231; Wedemeyer, op. cit., p. 325. General Okamura told Wedemeyer after the war that "usually one Japanese division could defeat four or five Chinese" (ibid., p. 326).

64. Liu, op. cit., pp. 200–201; *China Handbook, 1937–1945,* pp. 350–57; Dorn, op. cit., pp. 61–64; Ho, op. cit., p. 3; Wedemeyer, op. cit., p. 284; Griffith, op. cit., pp. 62–64; Walsh, op. cit., pp. 169–81; Miyazaki Kiyotaka, *Shina hakengun kaku tatakaeri* [Thus fought the China Expeditionary Army] (Tokyo, 1966); Chen Wan-ming, "The Battle of Pinghsingkuan Pass," *China Reconstructs* (August 1971): 2–6.

65. Mao Tse-tung, op. cit., p. 137; Hsu and Chang, op. cit., pp. vii, 576; Gunther, op. cit., p. 242; White and Jacoby, op. cit, p. 77.

66. Hata et al., *TSM,* 4 (pt. 2): 42–43, 367–68; Imaoka interview; *Daihon'ei,* 1:454; Hallett Abend, "Japanese Divided on China Tactics," *New York Times,* 1 July 1938.

67. Gene Z. Hanrahan, *Japanese Operations Against Guerrilla Forces,* Operations Research Office, Johns Hopkins University, Technical Memorandum ORO-T-268 (Chevy Chase, Md., 1954) (Declassified), p. 15. Also see Michael Lindsay, "China (1937–45)," in *Challenge and Response in Internal Conflict,* vol. 1, *The Experience in Asia,* (Washington, D.C., 1968), Chapter 6; White and Jacoby, op. cit., p. 54; Johnson, op. cit., pp. vii, 55–58.

68. Kanki Haruo, ed., *Sankō* (Tokyo, 1957); White and Jacoby, op. cit., p. 205; Griffith, op. cit., p. 71; William W. Whitson with Chen-hsia Huang, *The Chinese High Command: A History of Communist Military Politics, 1927–71* (New York, 1973), pp. 75, 164–65.

69. Coox, op. cit., Chapter 9.

70. Data on Shanghai fighting until November 8, 1937, from Shimada Shigetarō diary. For a contemporary set of estimates, see *New York Times,* 10 July 1938.

71. Sanematsu Yuzuru, *Yonai Mitsumasa* (Tokyo, 1966), p. 52.

72. Imai Takeo, *Kindai no sensō* [Modern war], vol. 5, *Chūgoku to no tatakai* [The war with China] (Tokyo, 1966), p. 372. General Okamura estimated IJA losses to the Chinese guerrillas at less than 50,000; White thinks the true figure must lie between that and the huge Communist claim to have inflicted a half-million casualties on the Japanese; White and Jacoby, op. cit., p. 210. Interestingly, the Japanese Army suffered only 826 men killed during the entire Sino-Japanese War of 1894–1895.

73. *Gendaishi,* 9 (pt. 2): 466–68.

74. *China Handbook, 1937–1945,* p. 300. There is, of course, better reason to believe this figure than the inflated Chinese estimates of IJA dead and wounded.

75. Data supplied by Imaoka.

76. Interviews with Katakura Tadashi, Giga Tetsuji, and Imaoka. Also Kusano Gorō, "Ichigaya Dai yuraiki" [Records of the genesis of Ichigaya Heights], *Maru* 11 (February 1958): 224–32; "Meiji kengun yori gun kaitei made ni okeru rikugun heiryoku hensen gaikenhyō" [Condensed chart of the changes in army strength from the establishment of the army in the Meiji Period to dissolution], *Maru,* Special Supplement no. 106 (December 1956): 199; Shikan Gakkō [Military Academy] data supplied by Hata Ikuhiko.

77. Kido Kōichi, *Kido Kō'ichi nikki* [Kido Kōichi diary] (Tokyo, 1966), 1:459–60, entry for 2 February 1936.

78. Japanese Research Division, Military History Section, Hqs. USAFFE/8th U.S. Army (Rear), *Japanese Studies on Manchuria,* vol. 5, *Infantry Operations* (1956), 77–78. General Ugaki suggests that deficiencies dating back to the 1920s "were brought to light during the China Incident."

79. Satō Kenryō, *Tōjō Hideki to Taiheiyō sensō* [Tōjō Hideki and the Pacific War] (Tokyo, 1960), pp. 83–84; Hata, op. cit., p. 249; *Ishiwara Kanji shiryō,* p. 444.

80. Interviews with Hata Shunroku, Iwasaki Tamio.

81. Interviews with Hashimoto Gun, Miyashi Minoru.

82. Interview with Imaoka.

83. See Hayashi, op. cit., pp. 27, 45.

84. Interview with Imaoka.

85. *Ishiwara Kanji shiryō,* p. 437.

86. Ibid., pp. 435–36. Also see Kawabe, op. cit., p. 138.

87. *Ishiwara Kanji shiryō,* pp. 443–44.

88. Ibid., p. 445.

89. Interview with Imaoka. For discussion of the dual IJA strategic thinking, see Iriye, op. cit., pp. 113–14.

90. Harada Kumao, *Saionji kō to seikyoku* [Prince Saionji and the political situation] (Tokyo, 1950–1952), 6:248; Hata et al., *TSM,* 4 (pt. 2): 43, 368.

91. Consul Sobokin to Hull, Tsingtao, 13 January 1938, *FRUS, 1938,* 3:17–18.

92. Admiral Nomura Kichisaburō, "Observations on Japan at War," Tokyo, 8 November 1945; U.S. Strategic Bombing Survey (Pacific), Naval Analysis Division, *Interrogations of Japanese Officials,* 2:385, cited in Coox, op. cit., pp. 27–28.

93. Kawabe, op. cit., pp. 138, 152.

94. Hata et al., *TSM,* 4 (pt. 2):42.

95. Maruyama, op. cit., p. 41. Also see Yamamoto Katsunosuke, *Nihon o horoboshita mono: gunbu dokusaika to sono katei* [What brought about Japan's defeat: Military dictatorship and the

process leading toward its collapse] (Tokyo, 1949), p. 321. For fuller discussion of the topic of "Whither Japan?" see Coox, op. cit., ch. 2.

96. Colonel Horiba Kazuo, AGS war direction section chief in 1938–39, has stated that the outbreak of the Pacific War "signified the failure of the Sino-Japanese War"; cited by Iriye, op. cit., p. 117. Also see the remarks by Fujiwara Akira, "The Role of the Japanese Army," in *Pearl Harbor as History: Japanese-American Relations, 1931–1941,* ed. Dorothy Borg and Shumpei Okamoto with Dale K. A. Finlayson (New York, 1973), pp. 194–95.

97. Correspondence with Imaoka. Also see Lieutenant General Masataka Okumiya, JASDF (Ret.), "The Lessons of an Undeclared War," *U.S. Naval Institute Proceedings* 93 (December 1972): 27– 28.

98. Hayashi, op. cit., pp. 145–50; Hsu and Chang, op. cit., pp. 165–66, 576.

99. One version of this widely told story will be found in Ho, op. cit., p. 2. Lin Piao wrote, op. cit., p. 3, that "the Chinese people's [Communists'] victory in the War of Resistance paved the way for their seizure of state power throughout the country." For CCP vs. KMT attitude by 1944, see White and Jacoby, op. cit., p. 212.

13.

The next essay, by Martin Bagish and Hilary Conroy, is inserted here as a further "balancer" of perspective. Several of the essays in the preceding section, particularly those by Lin, Boyle, and Akashi, and to a certain extent that by Kahn, are concerned with "peace advocates" and their attempts to end the Japan-China war. These efforts are, and should be, treated with respect, and explored in depth.

Coox's essay, however, has reminded us that whatever may be said about peace overtures, Japan was engaged in all-out war in and against China from 1937 to 1945. Japan was the aggressor; indeed, the Tokyo war crimes tribunal, convened after the Pacific War, found the Japanese leaders guilty not only of war crimes and aggression but also of conspiracy to commit aggression. Questions of guilt and responsibility are discussed in this essay.

Martin Bagish is a Ph.D. candidate in East Asian history at the University of Pennsylvania. He spent two years as an exchange student at Kanazawa University, and has been working on a doctoral dissertation on the question of command responsibility for war crimes, with special emphasis on the cases of Japanese leaders tried in the war crimes trials at Tokyo and Manila.

Hilary Conroy is professor of Far Eastern history at the University of Pennsylvania, where he has taught since 1951. He is president of the Interchange for Pacific Scholarship and past president of the Conference on Peace Research in History. He has been a Fulbright Scholar at Tokyo University, a senior specialist at the East-West Center, Honolulu, and is the author of several books and articles on Japanese expansion since 1868, coauthor with Woodbridge Bingham and Frank W. Iklé of *History of Asia,* 2 vols., rev. ed. (1974), and coeditor with T. S. Miyakawa of *East Across the Pacific* (1972).

Japanese Aggression against China: The Question of Responsibility

Martin Bagish and Hilary Conroy

Although there were earlier manifestations of Japanese power plays against China, the long one, which culminated in the seizure of Manchuria and large sections of what used to be known as "China Proper," began with the Mukden Incident (September 18, 1931). From that moment until 1945, there was continuous and unrelenting Japanese pressure, military as well as diplomatic and political, against China which, stripped of rhetoric and excuses, sought to bring more and more Chinese territory and larger and larger numbers of Chinese people under Japanese control.

Such a large-scale, long-range endeavor suggests, on the surface, that there must have been a conspiracy at work or at least a plan operating or operated at high levels in the Japanese government, with shifting personnel perhaps, but with high-level backing at all times. This was indeed adjudged to have been the case by the International Military Tribunal for the Far East (IMTFE).

This "war crimes" tribunal, sitting in Tokyo from May 1946 to November 1948, convicted twenty-three out of twenty-eight accused Japanese leaders of an overall conspiracy to wage aggressive war, and twenty-two of these of directing that conspiracy into aggressive war against China.[1] In addition, one of the accused, General Matsui Iwane, commander in chief of Japanese forces in central China (1937–1938), while acquitted of being a part of the overall conspiracy, was convicted of "disregard of duty to secure observance of and prevent breaches of the 'Laws and Customs of War.'" This was with specific reference to the infamous "Rape of Nanking," and Matsui, along with six of the others, was sentenced to death by hanging as one of the worst of the war criminals.

Others sentenced to death and hanged were General Tōjō Hideki, army minister (1940–1941) and premier (1941–1944); Hirota Kōki, foreign minister (1933–1936) and premier (1936–1937); General Itagaki Seishirō, Kwantung Army chief of staff (1936–1937) and war minister (1938–1939); General Doihara Kenji, chief of Kwantung Army "special services" (1931–1933) and later army commander in Manchuria (1938–1940);[2] General Mutō Akira, "billeting officer" at Nanking (1937–1938), chief of the military affairs bureau of the army ministry (1939–1942), and field commander in Southeast Asia and the Philippines (1943–1945); Kimura Heitarō, Kwantung Army chief of staff and vice-minister of war (1941–1944).

Others, convicted of the overall conspiracy charge and given prison terms, included Marquis Kido Kōichi, secretary to the lord keeper of the privy seal in the early 1930s, minister of education (1937), of welfare (1938), home minister (1939), and lord keeper of the privy seal (1940–1945); Hiranuma Kiichirō, vice-president privy council (1926–1936), president (1936–1939), and premier (1939); General Koiso Kuniaki, Kwantung Army chief of staff (1932–1934), minister of overseas affairs (1939–1940), and premier (1944–1945); General Araki Sadao, war minister (1931–1934) and minister of education (1938–1939); General Minami Jirō, army minister (1931), Kwantung Army commander in chief (1934–1936), and governor-general of Korea (1936–1942); Tōgō Shigenori, ambassador to Germany (1937), to the USSR (1938), foreign minister (1941–1942, 1945); Ōshima Hiroshi, military attaché at Berlin (1936) and ambassador to Germany (1938–1939, 1941–1945); Shiratori Toshio, propagandist, diplomat, ambassador to Italy (1939); General Umezu Yoshijirō, Kwantung Army commander and ambassador to Manchukuo (1939–1944).

Two of the accused, Matsuoka Yōsuke, Japan's walk-out representative at the League of Nations (1933) and foreign minister (1940–1941), and Admiral Nagano Osami, navy minister (1936–1937) and navy chief of staff (1941–1944), died during the course of the trial. Ōkawa Shūmei, propagandist and participant in various "direct action" plots of the 1930s, also escaped a guilty verdict because he was found to be mentally unbalanced, though his writings helped the prosecution establish the existence of the general "conspiracy" for which the others were convicted.

Of the twenty-eight originally accused, only Matsui and Shigemitsu Mamoru, the career diplomat who was serving as foreign minister at the time of Japan's surrender in 1945, were judged not to have been a part of the general conspiracy. But Shigemitsu, ambassador at Nanking in 1931–1932 and 1941–1943, was convicted of plotting aggression against China.[3]

Having reached the judgment that a "conspiracy to wage wars of aggression for the purpose of domination of East Asia, the western and south western Pacific Ocean and the Indian Ocean, and certain islands in those oceans as charged in count 1 of the Indictment" had been established,[4] the tribunal further concluded as regards China:

> The war which Japan waged against China, and which the Japanese leaders falsely described as the "China Incident" or the "China Affair" began on the night of 18 September 1931 and ended with the surrender of Japan in Tokyo Bay on 2 September 1945. The first phase of this war consisted of the invasion, occupation and consolidation by Japan of that part of China known as Manchuria and of the province of Jehol. The second phase of this war began on 7 July 1937, when Japanese troops attacked the walled city of Wanping near Peiping following the "Marco Polo Bridge Incident," and consisted of successsive advances, each followed by brief periods of consolidation in preparation for further advances into Chinese territory.[5]

While these statements in the judgment, the twenty-three convictions on count 1 (overall conspiracy), and twenty-two convictions on count 27 (aggressive war against China) seem to prove beyond a shadow of a doubt that the tribunal believed there had been such a Japanese conspiracy against China, examination of the trial record and the separate opinions of the several justices indicates that the matter was not so clear as these make it seem.

Actually only two of the twenty-three (Ōshima and Shiratori) were convicted exclusively of conspiracy. Though they were sentenced to life imprisonment, Judge Radhabinod Pal, representing India on the tribunal, argued that there was no such crime as conspiracy in international law, and the president of the tribunal, Sir William Flood Webb, stated in a separate opinion that "because the emperor had not been indicted, however, none of his ministers should suffer the death penalty."[6]

Webb, as Richard Minear has pointed out in his careful analysis of the trial, was convinced of Emperor Hirohito's authority and guilt in whatever war crimes had been committed, and he did not accept Prosecutor Joseph B. Keenan's contention that the emperor had "been in the power of gangsters." However, Webb did not at the time openly contest the decision of the prosecution not to try the emperor or even to call him as a witness, which represented a political decision of the Allied Powers. It may be significant that Webb was recalled to Australia during the period (November 1947) when the decision was made not to call the emperor for testimony.[7]

Many years later, in 1971, Webb provided an introduction to David Bergamini's sensational book *Japan's Imperial Conspiracy,* which accuses Hirohito of masterminding a gigantic conspiracy to conquer China and wage aggressive war. In his introductory remarks Webb does not entirely endorse Bergamini's interpretation, but he states that "inasmuch as the accused were only subordinates who had obeyed orders and inasmuch as their leader had escaped trial, strongly extenuating circumstances had to be taken into account in awarding punishment."[8]

The juxtaposition of the Minear–Bergamini books on the question of

Japanese war crimes, particularly of conspiracy to wage aggressive war, is a fascinating one. Minear's, a serious scholarly work, emphasizes not only defects of the trial procedure but "fundamental misconceptions" that lay behind it, especially the "misconception" that there was a Japanese conspiracy to wage aggressive war from as early as the Manchurian Incident (1931) or even the Chang Tso-lin assassination (1928). Agreeing in general with the dissentient judgment of Justice Pal, Minear concludes that the trial was biased, political, unfair to the Japanese defendants, and a bad precedent.[9]

Bergamini, on the other hand, endorses the conspiracy theory and purports to "prove" that conspiracy was planned and executed at the highest government and military levels in Japan, with the emperor party to it and indeed the mastermind. He regards the trial as a sort of coverup for the emperor's complicity and any sympathy he may have for the victims of "victors' justice" (such as for General Matsui, whom he considers to have been a dupe) is more than offset by his exasperation that the worst culprits, the emperor and coconspirator relatives, such as Princes Asaka, Kanin, and Higashikuni, were not brought to trial.

Professional reviews of Bergamini's study have been critical of both his grand-conspiracy theory and his methodology. One calls his book "fiction" with an "imaginative plot."[10] Bergamini defended his thesis at a meeting of the Columbia University Seminar on Modern Japan on March 10, 1972, and his book, translated as *Tennō no inbō*, has enjoyed considerable popularity in Japan.[11]

The conspiracy controversy is of interest to our present analysis in two respects. If there were a grand "imperial conspiracy" for conquest at work in Japan, then (1) the Japanese peace efforts described in this collection must be dismissed as merely sham and subterfuge, and (2) the "Rape of Nanking" and other horrors committed by Japanese military forces in China cannot be considered merely accidental ravagings of undisciplined troops. Bergamini makes the specific accusation that Emperor Hirohito appointed his uncle, Prince Asaka Yasuhiko, to supersede "little General Matsui" in direct command of Japanese forces at Nanking and carry out the brutal rape of the city's populace that occurred, thus to teach the Chinese a lesson and break their spirit. Matsui, his argument goes, had originally issued proper orders to his troops but, being both inept and ill (with tubercular fever), he was kept in the dark about the atrocities by Asaka and his henchmen. He was, in effect, "kicked upstairs" to the overall central China command. Emperor Hirohito and Premier Konoe were "in" on this arrangement as on other phases of the "imperial conspiracy," according to Bergamini.[12]

The Nanking affair as well as the general Japanese command responsibility question deserve to be reviewed thoroughly in the light of post–Pacific War developments, but here we shall pursue the ramifications of only two of the questions involved, both of which turn out to be matters of degree: (1) the extent (enormity) of the "Rape"; (2) the extent of Japanese "imperial" complicity. The first question must be put in chronological context before it can be answered. While it is true that greater, indeed far greater, "crimes against humanity" have been carried out since 1937, Nanking certainly ranks as one of the worst crimes against a helpless population in recorded history prior to World War II. Bergamini, after reviewing various figures and accounts, puts the number of Chinese killed at 150,000, with at least 5000 women raped. Although his general theory may be fiction, the figures Bergamini gives on the Nanking casualties are not. The Tokyo trial put the figures at 200,000 killed and 20,000 women raped. Contemporary reports give vivid reality to the death and horror done.[13]

Japanese excuses for their behavior are not convincing. One was that Chinese soldiers threw away their uniforms and melted into the civilian population of Nanking, with great numbers of them "escaping" into an area of foreign institutions, legations, universities, and hospitals. Administrative responsibility for this area, which comprised 3.86 square kilometers, had been given over by the mayor of Nanking to a committee of foreigners on December 1 as the Japanese approached, and it had been disarmed and declared a "safety zone" by the committee. Records of the committee show that the Japanese repeatedly violated the safety zone with searches, seizures, killings, and rapes.[14] What they did outside was far more and worse.

Another excuse was that Chinese looters were everywhere and the Japanese were "restoring order."

Although he was never indicted or prosecuted, Prince Asaka was interrogated by a representative of General MacArthur's postwar headquarters (SCAP), Colonel Thomas H. Murrow, on May 1, 1946. Asaka admitted that he was in direct command of the Japanese forces in Nanking from December 1937 through February 1938, but said that he took orders from General Matsui, who entered Nanking with him on December 16 and who thereafter conducted the overall central China command from Shanghai. Asked when he was given command of the forces attacking Nanking, Asaka first said on November 10, but then corrected this to December 2.

> I got orders to take command of this Army on the 2nd of December in Tokyo and I reached there [China] on the 5th or 6th of December . . . I joined my army at Wusih.
> Question: Wusih is sixty or eighty miles east of Nanking. Who did you succeed?
> Answer: General Matsui. General Matsui was the commanding general of this army. . . . My predecessor was General Matsui and General Matsui was promoted to higher office, commanding the combined forces.[15]

Asaka was not asked, nor did he say, why he was given the direct Nanking command. Bergamini charges that Asaka's appointment was "overriding all other authority in a wave of imperial influence" and that after his arrival at the China front on December 8 and being informed that

300,000 Chinese troops were about to be surrounded and pinned against the Nanking city walls, "a set of orders went out under his personal seal, marked 'secret, to be destroyed.' They said simply, 'Kill all captives.' "[16] From this, Bergamini establishes a direct line of command from Hirohito through Asaka to two sadistic lieutenants of Asaka, Lieutenant General Nakajima Kesago and Colonel Mutō Akira, who carried out the "kill all captives" orders after Nanking was taken.[17]

At his interrogation Prince Asaka admitted that he had given orders to use Chinese prisoners "as laborers" to "unload materials in the Shanghai and Nanking areas." There were no systematic atrocities or orders for such. The only "unlawful acts such as rape" which he had heard about were reported to him through General Matsui's headquarters. There had been "quite a few" of these, but "all men under me who did such acts were court martialed," he said.[18]

It is obvious in retrospect that Prince Asaka's interrogation was far less severe than his position as commander of the Nanking troops should have justified. His evasive answers were not challenged and there was no followup to the single interrogation session. Undoubtedly decisions made in Washington in the fall of 1945, crystallized in a directive from the Joint Chiefs of Staff to General MacArthur dated October 6, "You will take no action against the Emperor as a war criminal," explains the dilatory handling of Asaka's case.[19] Clearly Asaka was as guilty as Matsui, perhaps more so, for the Nanking atrocities. Even if he did not know about them, as he claimed, his position was such that he had the direct command responsibility.

Whether this also implicates the emperor is a moot point. Hirohito's record on the Manchurian Incident has been restudied recently, and the evidence is that he not only admonished the military for its perpetration but, emphasizing his role as a "constitutional monarch," refused to use his imperial authority to authorize the advance of Japan's Korea-based forces into Manchuria.[20] On subsequent issues such as Japan's withdrawal from the League of Nations, the termination of treaties, the young officers' rebellion (February 26, 1936), the Marco Polo Bridge Incident, and the making of the Axis alliance, Charles Sheldon has restudied the evidence and found the emperor a consistent advocate of caution and moderation, unhappy with and negative toward military moves.[21]

Hirohito's critical role in backing the peace advocates in Japan's "decision to surrender" in August 1945 is well known.[22] His only inconsistent act, other than the appointment of Asaka, is the one wherein he enjoined Premier Koiso to "send Miao Pin back to China." But this was on the advice of three ministers and Lord Privy Seal Kido.[23]

Thus, while it is clear that the decision of the Occupation authorities not to try the emperor saved Asaka and perhaps other imperial relatives from trial before the International Tribunal and perhaps from the gallows, it does not necessarily follow that Hirohito authorized or approved the Nanking massacre. His moat-surrounded palace was far away from the scenes of carnage Japanese troops were engaging in and his imperial advisory structure could have effectively insulated him from the whole Nanking operation. Also, his record otherwise does not seem to support the idea that he was a master of imperial conspiracy and subterfuge in general. On the other hand, the reasons for the appointment of Prince Asaka to the Nanking area command remain obscure. According to Chinese figures, some 26 Japanese divisions, totaling 832,000 troops, were in China as of December 1937. The following year, 1938, the number increased to 976,000; it passed the 1,000,000 mark in 1939, and in 1944 rose to 1,856,000.[24] Even if these figures are exaggerated by as much as 50 percent, and they certainly are not, they are enough to indicate that Japan was engaged in conquest on a large scale and continuing basis.

While "young officer" plots and the *gekokujō* (lower echelon overbearing the higher) phenomenon may account for the Manchurian Incident and other bizarre happenings of the early 1930s, the senior officers known as the "Control Group" had regained control of the army and their civilian counterparts of the other elements of government by 1937. Since, as postwar studies have abundantly shown, decision making in Japan was by consensus of the military and civilian leaders, probably more rather than fewer of them were guilty of executing, if not planning, the escalation of the China war from 1937 on. Hence, the list of China war criminals tried by IMTFE should have been longer, not shorter. Certainly it should have included Prince Asaka; Emperor Hirohito, probably not. Professor Maruyama Masao has argued convincingly that there was no joint conspiracy. Political power was too unplanned and disorganized for that. It was rather, he says, an "underlying pathology" which drove Japan on in escalating the war.[25]

Notes

1. International Military Tribunal for the Far East (IMTFE), *Judgment* (mimeograph, 1948); Solis Horwitz, "The Tokyo Trial," *International Conciliation* (November 1950): 475–584, summary table p. 584; Richard H. Minear, *Victors' Justice: The Tokyo War Crimes Trial* (Princeton, 1971), pp. 193–99.

2. Regarding Doihara's rather mysterious China activities between these years, see B. Winston Kahn's essay in this volume.

3. For biographical data, see Miwa Kai and Philip P. Yampolsky, *Political Chronology of Japan, 1885–1957,* Columbia University, East Asian Institute, Study no. 5 (1957); Horwitz, op. cit., pp. 578–84. The chart on p. 584 puts Hiranuma's premiership in 1938; this should be 1939. On Shigemitsu, see Alvin D. Coox, "Shigemitsu Mamoru: The Diplomacy of Crisis," in *Diplomats in Crisis: United States-Chinese-Japanese Relations, 1919–1941,* ed. Richard Dean Burns and Edward M. Bennett (Santa Barbara, 1974), pp. 251–73; on Hirota, see "Hirota Kōki: The Diplomacy of Expansionism," Lee Farnsworth, op. cit., ibid., pp. 227–49.

4. Horwitz, op. cit., pp. 557–58; cf. IMTFE, *Judgment,* pp. 1138–42.

5. Horwitz, op. cit., p. 558; cf. IMTFE, *Judgment,* , p. 521.

6. Minear, op. cit., p. 117. See also R. Pal, *IMTFE Dissentient Judgment* (Calcutta, 1953), pp. 220–21, 251, 553–54.

7. Ibid., pp. 116–17.

8. David Bergamini, *Japan's Imperial Conspiracy* (New York, 1972), p. x.

9. Minear, op. cit., pp. 155–59.

10. Review by Shumpei Okamoto, *Journal of Asian Studies,* 31 (February 1972): 414–16; other important reviews are by James Crowley, *New York Times Book Review,* 24 October 1971; Alvin D. Coox, *American Historical Review* 77 (October 1972): 1169–70; Herschel Webb, *Pacific Historical Review* 42 (February 1973): 124–25.

11. See *Chūō Kōron* [Central Review], April 1973, p. 367.

12. Bergamini, op. cit., pp. 6–9, 22–24, 29–50.

13. Bergamini, op. cit., p. 46; IMTFE, *Proceedings,* p. 21572; H. J. Timperley, *Japanese Terror in China* (New York, 1938); Dr. Lewis C. Smythe et al., *War Damage in Nanking Area, December 1937–March 1938* (Nanking, 1938); Suzuki Akira, *Nankyōdai gyakusatsu no maboroshi* [The specter of the great Nanking massacre] (Tokyo, 1973); Shushi Hsü, ed., *Documents of the Nanking Safety Zone* (Shanghai, Hong Kong, and Singapore, 1939); Shushi Hsü, *Japan and Shanghai* (Shanghai, 1938); Lin Chao-pin, "My Personal Observations of the Japanese Attack on Nanking, 1937" (in Chinese), *Chuan Chi Wen Hsüeh* 23 (July 1974):15–21.

14. Timperley, op. cit., p. 17.

15. National Archives CIS File no. 44, pp. 3, 5, 7; see IMTFE, International Prosecution Section, *Exhibit,* file 919.

16. Bergamini, op. cit., pp. 23–24.

17. Ibid., pp. 35–40, 43–49.

18. CIS File no. 44, pp. 2–3.

19. National Archives, File 000.5 (War Criminals in the Far East), War X7298, 6 October 1945.

20. Hilary Conroy and Toru Takemoto, "An Ounce of Prevention: A New Look at the Manchurian Incident," *Peace and Change* 2:1 (Spring 1974):42–46.

21. Charles D. Sheldon, "Japanese Aggression and the Emperor, 1931–1941, from Contemporary Diaries," *Modern Asian Studies* 10 (February 1976): 1–40.

22. Robert J. C. Butow, *Japan's Decision to Surrender* (Stanford, 1954), pp. 206–9, 228–33.

23. See Yoji Akashi's essay in this volume.

24. Republic of China Board of Military Operations, *China Handbook, 1937–1945* (New York, 1947), p. 306. Also see figures in Alvin D. Coox's essay this volume.

25. Maruyama Masao, "Thought and Behaviour Patterns of Japan's Wartime Leaders," in *Thought and Behaviour in Modern Japanese Politics,* ed. Ivan Morris (London, 1963), pp. 86–90. For other discussions of Japan's decision-making structure see Yale Maxon, *Control of Japanese Foreign Policy* (Berkeley, 1957; Westport, Conn., 1973), esp. pp. 124–29; Chihiro Hosoya, "Twenty-Five Years after Pearl Harbor: A New Look at Japan's Decision for War," in *Imperial Japan and Asia,* comp. Grant K. Goodman (New York, 1967), pp. 52–63; Mushakōji Kinhide, "The Cultural Premises of Japanese Diplomacy," *Japan Interpreter* 7:3–4 (Summer–Autumn 1972):282–92.

VI. Chill and Thaw

14.

The intricate diplomacy by which John Foster Dulles and Japanese Premier Yoshida handled the problem of "Two Chinas" at the San Francisco Conference and in subsequent negotiations at Taipei is the subject of Yu San Wang's essay. This diplomacy of the early 1950s really solved no problems in the long-term relationship between Japan and China; indeed it probably complicated them, but it provided the first moves by Japan in China diplomacy after the Pacific War.

Yu San Wang was born in Kiangsu, China, and later moved to Formosa. He came to the United States as a college student, received his A.B. from West Virginia Concord College (1959), M.A. from the University of Massachusetts (1960), and Ph.D. in international relations from the University of Pennsylvania (1968). He has taught at Dakota Wesleyan University and at Fairmont State College, West Virginia, where he is now professor and director of the Division of Social Sciences.

Ending the State of War between Japan and China: Taipei (1952)

Yu San Wang

I.

United States foreign policy toward China immediately following World War II was based on the idea that the best hope for a united and strong China was for the Nationalist government to come to terms with the Chinese Communists. It was for this purpose that President Truman sent General George C. Marshall to China in late 1945. During the year he spent in China, Marshall became convinced that the positions of the parties were equally irresponsible, irrational, and irreconcilable.

In August 1949, the State Department published a "China White Paper" for the purpose of defending the United States stand on the issue of the Nationalist defeat on the mainland. But U.S. policy toward China changed as soon as the Korean War broke out. On June 26, 1950, President Truman ordered the 7th Fleet to prevent any attack on Taiwan. At the same time, he revealed that the Chinese Nationalists had been called upon to desist from attack against the mainland. The president said that the future status of Taiwan would have to await the restoration of security in the Pacific area, a Japanese peace treaty, or action by the United Nations.[1] Afterwards, the United States established a policy of nonrecognition of Communist China.

The appointment of John Foster Dulles as foreign policy adviser to the secretary of state on April 6, 1950, primarily served the purpose of restoring bipartisanship in government. Six weeks after President Truman assigned him the task of negotiating a peace treaty with Japan, Dulles announced at a press conference (May 22) that both Nationalist and Communist China would be invited to the Japanese peace conference. But with the entrance of

Communist China into the Korean conflict, the United States, in view of its nonrecognition of Peking, considered the Nationalist government on Taiwan the only legal government of China able to participate in the peace treaty with Japan.[2] Dulles pushed ahead toward the final drafts of the peace treaty and the security pacts, involving the United States and Japan, the United States and the Philippines, and the United States, Australia, and New Zealand. However, he was well aware that Britain's draft would open up the problem of including Communist China in the peace conference. To avoid further delay of the peace treaty, Washington finally gave up the idea of inviting the Nationalist government to the conference.

The British recognition of Communist China in January 1950 was based, to a major degree, on hopes of uninterrupted and advantageous trade with the latter. The Labour government had, as always, a low opinion of the stability of the Nationalist regime, and had ostentatiously avoided any commitment to it. Prime Minister Attlee, in a speech in the House of Commons, said that the Communist conquest in China would not be considered a disaster for British interests, and could not be prevented; it should therefore be accepted with good grace.[3]

This situation—the two major Western powers at variance in their attitudes toward mainland China—was politically advantageous to Peking. The Korean War brought them together again in a joint effort to resist Communist aggression in the Far East, but at the same time it further reduced the chances of American recognition of the Peking regime. In the early stage of the conflict the British strongly advocated United Nations intervention to halt local aggression and thus avoid an armed clash involving either the Soviet Union or Communist China.

The British attitude toward China's participation in a peace treaty with Japan was clear. Britain, as a member of the Far Eastern Commission, opposed Dulles's joint invitation. The British insisted that the Peking government alone should participate in the conference.[4]

Britain completed its own draft of the Japanese peace treaty in April 1951, and sent copies to the governments of the Commonwealth and to the United States. The British draft listed China as one of the "Allied and Associate Powers" and referred to "the People's Republic." During the debates in Commons in July 1951, the majority of the Labourites opposed any attempt to invite the Nationalist government to the peace conference and they opposed government's making any concession to the United States by leaving the question open to the Japanese after the peace treaty went into effect.[5]

In their support of Peking at the Japanese peace conference, the British were apparently convinced that Communist China was many times the size of Japan in territory and manpower, and vastly richer in natural resources. Although China had been weak in the past, she was rapidly finding herself as a nation and developing a certain cohesion. If she could be taken out of the Communist orbit, the whole balance-of-power picture would be changed radically.

Two explosive issues remained between London and Washington. The first concerned shipping and other economic controls over Japan. The British position was that Japanese shipbuilding capacity should be cut back to what it was in the 1930s, around 250,000 tons annually, instead of the 800,000 tons annual capacity Japan reached around 1940. The United States felt that Japan would have difficulties in rebuilding her trade with China and that the matter of shipbuilding should receive careful consideration. The other was the problem of which China was to receive Taiwan and the Pescadores, which were to be returned by Japan to China in accordance with the Cairo declaration (1943).

Nevertheless, a final compromise was reached before the first meeting of the San Francisco Conference. Many factors contributed. The first was that the British were disappointed by the fact that the Chinese Communists did not make any concessions to them with regard to trade and investments. In fact, the Communists were determined to force the British to abandon their assets.

Second, the Commonwealth countries were themselves divided over the recognition of Communist China. The majority, who still recognized the Nationalist government on Taiwan, had little doubt that the United States would continue to support Taipei, and they were loath to see the Nationalist position on Taiwan and the Pescadores compromised by Communist China's participation in the peace conference. British policy in the Far East depended heavily on the support of the Commonwealth because of London's weakness in the postwar period; therefore Britain had to reckon with the majority opinion on the China issue.

Third, the outbreak of the Korean War and the intervention of the Chinese Communists forced the British to reexamine the settlement with Japan. To expedite the peace treaty, London showed a greater willingness to cooperate with Washington in the Far East and prepared certain concessions to the latter, especially with regard to Chinese representation at the peace conference.

The United States, on the other hand, saw the move of the Communists in Korea as an intent "to increase the encirclement of Japan and thus to keep her out of the camp of the Western powers."[6] Washington therefore insisted that the Korean crisis provided more reasons for hastening the treaty with Japan. In so doing, the United States had to make concessions to Britain and other non-Communist countries for the purpose of gaining their cooperation at the peace conference.

When the conference opened at the Opera House in San Francisco on September 4, 1951, decisions on China had already been reached. In accordance with the provisions of the Japanese Peace Treaty concerning China, in Article 2 Japan renounced all rights, titles, and claims to most of its former territories outside of the home islands. These included Korea, Taiwan, the Pescadores, the Kuril Islands, South Sakhalin, the Spratly and Paracel Islands, although final disposition of Taiwan and the Pescadores was not made.

There was no quarrel between the United States and Britain over the legal right of China to sign the Japanese Peace Treaty at San Francisco, but the exclusion of both Taipei and Peking from the treaty was based on political differences. Chinese reaction began throughout Taiwan as soon as the text of the proposed treaty with Japan was published and it became known that Nationalist China would not be invited to the forthcoming San Francisco Conference. The Nationalist government made a public protest and insisted that, as the only legitimate government of China, it should participate in any multilateral peace settlement with Japan. The Nationalist argument rested on the following bases. First, the Nationalist government, not the Peking regime, had declared war on Japan and actually fought. Second, China, under the Nationalist government, joined the other Allied Powers to found the United Nations, and was still a member. Third, the Nationalist government was recognized by a majority of the countries which had declared war on Japan. Fourth, the Nationalist government had designated the Chinese Communists as puppets of the Soviet Union. Fifth, the Peking regime, condemned by the United Nations as an aggressor in Korea, would not be qualified to represent China. Sixth, it was the opinion of the Nationalists that active supporters of the Peking regime constituted only a relatively small minority of the total population and that most Chinese on the mainland disliked Communist rule.

The San Francisco treaty caused Japan enormous difficulties in deciding with which China it should negotiate a peace treaty. The Japanese government believed, however, that the best course of action was to operate within the framework provided more by world conditions than by developments within its own boundaries. Therefore, Japan took a wait-and-see attitude.

Japan was deeply worried about the Sino-Soviet Treaty of Friendship, Alliance and Mutual Assistance (1950), which was directed against her and against the United States as well. The Shanghai *Ta-kung pao,* in an open letter on August 21, 1951, warned Japan that a separate peace without Communist China and the Soviet Union would mean a declaration of war against both countries.

Further, the Japanese understood that Nationalist China was not invited to San Francisco because of British opposition. A British-Japanese conflict might develop if Japan decided to negotiate a peace treaty with Nationalist China. Tokyo, in fact, believed that the future economic policy of Japan in the Pacific area required Anglo-Japanese cooperation after the peace treaty went into effect. Japan, having experienced difficulty in establishing trade relations with Peking, was compelled to seek markets in Southeast Asia, the British area of economic interest for more than a century. Japan knew it would be unwise to provoke British anger, thereby jeopardizing future Japanese economic expansion.

And third, before the Sixth Session of the U.N. General Assembly was held in Paris on November 6, 1951, it was the general belief that the Communist bloc, due to their failure in San Francisco, would do everything they could to secure a United Nations seat for Peking. Prime Minister Yoshida intended to deny in the Diet that Japan had the right to choose the Chinese government with which she would sign a peace treaty. Yoshida insisted that the Japanese government should wait for the decision by the United Nations.

II.

General MacArthur had advocated peace with Japan as early as 1947, and he also wished to have Nationalist China included in a peace treaty. The temperaments and ideologies of the general and of Dulles were well suited, especially in their approaches to the Sino-Japanese problems. MacArthur, after his dismissal, continued to influence Republican senators "not only because of his wide experience in the Far East and Japan, but also because of his heroic stature in [their] eyes. . . ."[7] Partly as a result of the general's role, the Republicans in the Senate finally induced the Japanese government to conclude a peace treaty with Taipei.

Dulles and Foreign Secretary Morrison agreed in June 1951 that neither Peking nor Taipei should be invited to the San Francisco Conference, but the Japanese government should be left free to negotiate a separate peace treaty with either the Nationalists or the Communists, "in the exercise of the sovereign and independent status contemplated by the treaty." On his return from London, Dulles conferred with several senators, among them Bridges, Knowland, McCarran, and Hickenlooper of the Far Eastern Subcommittee, and assured them that after the San Francisco Conference the Japanese would immediately conclude a separate peace treaty with Nationalist China.[8] In late July 1951, Dulles wrote to Yoshida about the Anglo-American compromise and asked him not to hasten a peace treaty with Peking. Yoshida replied that the Japanese government had no intention of concluding a bilateral treaty with mainland China.[9]

In early August, Fitzmaurice and Tomlinson of Britain and Dulles and

Allison of the United States held a conference in Washington. Tomlinson asked Dulles how "we interpret the United States-United Kingdom understanding about China until the coming into force of the main treaty."[10] According to the American memorandum of the conversation, Dulles stated:

> I do not think that it is possible to give any categorical answer to this question. The principle involved is that there should be no Allied coercion upon Japan to adopt an arbitrary course in regard to China which might prejudice Japanese best interests for the future. Under those circumstances a good deal would depend upon the degree of freedom which might, in fact, be restored to Japan after the signature of the Treaty, but before the coming into force, particularly if the latter was considerably deferred.[11]

Speaking before a meeting of the Washington representatives of the National Organization on the Japanese Peace Treaty, on August 23, 1951, Dulles explained why China was not included at the San Francisco Conference:

> . . . I have no doubt that it will be charged that we cannot go ahead to make peace with Japan in the absence of China. Well, it is obviously very regrettable that China will not be represented at San Francisco. But to conclude that the other powers cannot make peace with Japan until there can also be peace with China may be in effect to say that there will never be peace with Japan and that the occupation of Japan must go on indefinitely.
>
> Now, the reality is that the Treaty of Peace which we have does take into view the point of view of China. We have been constantly in touch with the representatives of the Nationalist Government and we believe that their representatives have in this matter presented adequately and authentically the point of view of China and many of the provisions of this Treaty have been modified from our original draft in order to take into account the view of China. . . .[12]

During the question period, Dulles was asked if the United States would put pressure on Japan to sign a separate peace treaty with Nationalist China. He said that the United States would wait until after the San Francisco Conference, since he did not wish to jeopardize the Anglo-American compromise by making the United States position public prematurely.[13]

On September 9, the day after the conclusion of the San Francisco Conference, Morrison and Dulles, en route to Washington, discussed the Japan-China problem. According to Dulles's memorandum, Morrison hoped that nothing would be done to crystallize the Japanese position toward China until after the treaty came into force. Dulles, however, told Morrison:

> There was the reality which had not been disguised, namely that the present Government of Japan was strongly anti-Communist and did not want to favor or encourage the Communists either in Japan or on the Asian mainland. Against this the Japanese Government was on good relations with the Nationalists. We could not suppress indefinitely the natural desire of the Japanese Government which, we were assured, included at least such recognition of the Nationalist Government as would

assure their good will in various U.N. organizations where that government had a vote and a voice which the Japanese needed on their behalf as applicants for membership in U.N. agencies. Also, we were assured the Japanese would want quickly to put trade, diplomatic and consular relations with Formosa on a normal peace time basis. None of this, however, necessarily implied Japanese acceptance of the Chinese Nationalist Government as empowered to speak for, and to bind, all of China. I recalled that I had expressed this point of view in London.[14]

When a treaty between Nationalist China and Japan did not material-ize, fifty-six senators sent President Truman the following letter on September 12, 1951:

As members of the United States Senate, we are opposed to the recognition of Communist China by the Government of the United States, or its admission to the United Nations. Prior to the submission of the Japanese Treaty to the Senate, we desire to make it clear that we would consider the recognition of Communist China by Japan or the negotiating of a bilateral treaty with the Communist Chinese regime to be adverse to the best interests of the people of both Japan and the United States.[15]

During October and November, Dulles was in constant touch with members of the Senate Foreign Relations Committee about a bilateral treaty between Japan and Nationalist China. Senate leaders from both parties urged Dulles to make another trip to Japan to persuade the Japanese government to sign a limited peace treaty with the Nationalist government, but Dulles told them it would be unwise to go to Tokyo before Britain ratified the Japanese treaty.[16]

On December 6, ten days after the British approved the treaty, Dulles left Washington for Tokyo, in the company of Senators H. Alexander Smith and John J. Sparkman. Officially, Dulles denied that his trip had anything to do with the Tokyo-Taipei treaty; he insisted that it was designed to gather information for the use of the Senate in considering ratification.[17]

On December 11, Dulles, conferring with Sir Esler Dening, British ambassador to Japan, said that he and Senators Sparkman and Smith proposed to suggest to Yoshida that the Japanese government might find it in its best interests to make clear its intention not to make a bilateral peace treaty with Peking. In view of the vast number of problems between the United States and Japan, most of which would involve congressional action, and in view of the attitudes of Congress on the subject of China and the apparent stand of the Japanese government itself, it should instead negotiate a settlement with the Nationalists. Dulles added that there should also be a bilateral treaty between Japan and Nationalist China, with the understanding that it applied to territory now or hereafter under the actual control of Nationalist China.[18]

Two days later, Dulles outlined his proposal in a meeting with Yoshida. Yoshida told Dulles that Japan intended to sign a treaty with Nationalist China; Dulles immediately reported this to Dening and asked urgently for the views of Britain. On December 17, Dening advised Dulles that London had instructed him not to have further conversations with Dulles in Tokyo.[19]

On December 19, Dulles and Senators Sparkman and Smith paid a farewell visit to the prime minister. Yoshida told them that his government intended to deal with the China matter along the lines which he and Dulles had discussed and that he expected to clarify the Japanese government's position soon and would communicate with Dulles. The prime minister strongly hoped, however, that Britain would acquiesce in the proposed Japanese position, as it was embarrassing to be confronted by opposing American-British positions.[20]

The Dulles-Sparkman-Smith trip was the decisive factor in effecting a Tokyo–Taipei peace treaty. In his own record of the trip, Dulles indicated that he was pleased with his success. Upon his departure from Tokyo on December 20, Dulles denied that he had pressured the Japanese government to hasten recognition of Nationalist China.[21]

In early January 1952, during the official visit of Prime Minister Churchill and Foreign Secretary Anthony Eden to the United States, the American government proposed that the Nationalist regime be allowed limited participation in the signing of the Japanese-Nationalist peace treaty. On January 10, Secretary Acheson, Dulles, and others of the State Department met with Eden and Sir Oliver Franks. Dulles presented the position on behalf of the United States:

> The many responsibilities which the United States is discharging in Japan and the importance of cooperation between the Japanese and the United States governments create a situation where it is obviously in the interest of both governments that their foreign policies as regards China should be substantially the same. The Japanese Government, in fact, wants, for its own internal reasons, to pursue a policy similar to that of the United States. Prime Minister Yoshida will soon make clear Japan's attitude toward China which will indicate the general conformity with the United States policy to the extent of dealing with the Nationalist Government within the scope of its actual authority, now or hereafter, and not dealing with the Communist regime.[22]

Eden indicated that he recognized the forces which would tend to draw American and Japanese policies into alignment as regarded China, but he could not agree to the desirability of Japan's making any commitment before the multilateral treaty came into force. Although he insisted he would have to maintain his position in this respect,[23] Eden gave the impression that he would not press the British position strongly on Japan or feel aggrieved if the Japanese government did not follow the British line.

With Japan's decision to negotiate a separate peace treaty with Nationalist China, and with British cooperation to allow a limited peace treaty between Taipei and Tokyo, the difficulty of getting the United States Senate to ratify the Japanese treaty was removed.

III.

Immediately after the San Francisco Conference, Nationalist China had deemed it necessary to make an advance arrangement with Japan about the status of the Chinese mission in Japan prior to the coming into force of the Japanese peace treaty; the latter would terminate the jurisdiction of the Supreme Commander for the Allied Powers as soon as Japan regained her independence. As a result of conversations between Taipei and Tokyo, it was agreed that the Japanese government would continue to recognize the status of the Chinese mission after the treaty came into force and until the proposed Nationalist-Japanese peace treaty took effect.

In a letter to Dulles, dated December 24, 1951, Yoshida stated that Japan desired to have a full measure of political peace and commercial intercourse with Nationalist China. Justifying the Japanese intention, Yoshida said:

> At the present time it is, we hope, possible to develop that kind of relationship with Nationalist China, which has the seat, voice and vote of China in the United Nations, which exercises actual governmental authority over certain territory, and which maintains diplomatic relations with most of the members of the United Nations. . . .[24]

On January 8, 1952, Yoshida told his New Year's press conference:

> As long as China is a Communist country and disturbs the peace and order of foreign countries, Japan cannot hold intercourse with her. . . . We will hold intercourse with any country, Formosa or others, provided that the other party does not disturb the internal peace of this country.[25]

On January 23, 1952, Yoshida, in a major policy address before the new session of the Diet, made an announcement that he "would invite the Nationalist Government of China to accept the proposal for a treaty of amity with Japan as soon as legally possible."[26] It was the closest to an official declaration yet made that Japan would negotiate with the Chinese Nationalist government.

On January 25, the Nationalist government accepted the Japanese overtures. Before the opening of the peace talks, Nationalist China sent an official note to Japan which included the following important points:

1. Japan must recognize the Republic of China as one of the principal Allied powers and conclude a bilateral peace treaty with her.
2. The bilateral treaty should be concluded before the San Francisco Peace Treaty came into force.

3. The Government of the Republic of China would not accept a limited peace treaty.
4. The Government of the Republic of China was ready to conclude a bilateral treaty with Japan as early as possible.[27]

Japan was thinking of signing a limited peace treaty with Nationalist China and of concluding a similar one with Communist China later. Thus the Japanese government would not recognize the Nationalist government as representative of all of China, but would include Taiwan, the Pescadores, and other territories under the effective control of the Chinese Nationalists. On February 6, the Japanese government made these statements:

1. The Japanese Government will legally conclude a limited peace treaty with the Nationalist Government.
2. In Article 2 of the multilateral Treaty, "Japan renounces all rights, titles and claims to Taiwan and the Pescadores, but no final disposition of these areas was made in the Treaty at San Francisco." Therefore, Japan believes that the final disposition of these islands should be made by the United Nations. Due to the fact, however, that these territories have been actually under the control of Nationalist China which retains diplomatic relations with many of the Allied powers, Japan will possibly conclude a peace treaty with that government.
3. Under Article 26 of the multilateral Treaty, Japan has an obligation to sign a peace treaty with any country which had not signed the San Francisco Treaty but had adhered to the United Nations Declaration of January 1, 1942, and was at war with Japan, but the bilateral treaty between Japan and Nationalist China will not be necessarily the same as those of the present Treaty.
4. After Japan signs a limited peace treaty with Nationalist China, it would not prevent Japan from trading with Communist China.[28]

The Nationalist government responded immediately:

1. If Japan does not wish to conclude a formal peace treaty with the Republic of China, there is no need for the Japanese mission to come to Taipei.
2. The National Government of the Republic of China represents the whole of China.
3. The proposed Sino-Japanese peace treaty must be on the same terms as those of the San Francisco Treaty.[29]

What worried Yoshida was that the United States Senate had not yet approved the Japanese peace treaty. He therefore made a slight concession to the Nationalist government in order to promote more favorable conditions for ratification. As a result of consultations between Taipei and Tokyo, the Nationalist-Japanese peace conference was officially opened on February 20, 1952, in Taipei.

The Chinese foreign minister, George Yeh, at the opening session of the peace conference handed the Japanese delegation the Chinese draft of a full peace treaty for study. This draft contained seven chapters and twenty-two articles. It proved unacceptable to Japan. In the first place, the primary intention of Tokyo in negotiating a bilateral peace treaty with Taipei was "to recognize the latter's sovereignty only over the territory it actually controlled."[30] Further, the Japanese argued that the beginning of the Sino-Japanese War was December 9, 1941, when China formally declared war on Japan, Germany, and Italy. Finally, Japan wanted a simple treaty of no more than seven articles, dealing directly with Nationalist-Japanese problems.

On March 1, Kawada Isao, head of the Japanese peace mission, handed Yeh a copy of the Japanese draft with thirteen articles as the basis for discussion. The Nationalist Chinese immediately rejected it. First, although China did not declare war on Japan before December 9, 1941, the actual conflict between China and Japan started with the Manchurian Incident of September 18, 1931, which led to Japanese absorption of Manchuria and to the Marco Polo Bridge Incident of July 7, 1937, an event that marked the spread of war throughout China. Japan must be held responsible for both the undeclared war of 1931–1941 and the declared war of 1941–1945.

Second, Yoshida had indicated in his letter to Dulles that Japan, by Article 26 of the San Francisco Treaty, would conclude a treaty with Nationalist China. Thus a Nationalist-Japanese peace treaty, under this article, must be "on the same or substantially the same terms." Third, Nationalist China would not accept any Japanese reservation on the possibility of writing a peace treaty with the Communist regime on the mainland. All negotiations must be based on the Chinese draft.[31]

The talks were slow and produced nothing; neither Taipei nor Tokyo was ready to make concessions. Each side sought to bring American pressure to bear on the other. The negotiations might have broken down, had the United States not taken steps to mediate.

The United States, worried about the lack of progress, intended to do whatever it could to accomplish a Nationalist-Japanese treaty by the date on which the multilateral treaty took effect. During the negotiations, Karl Lott Rankin, United States minister to Nationalist China, was instructed by the State Department to mediate.

The difficulties came to the attention of certain members of the Foreign Relations Committee who sympathized with the Nationalist Chinese position. During the second week of March, Senator H. Alexander Smith visited both Tokyo and Taipei and worked effectively with high Japanese officials in Tokyo, while more discussions took place in Taipei and Washington.[32]

Prime Minister Yoshida called a cabinet meeting on March 8 to discuss the deadlocked situation. As a means of expediting matters, Wajima Eiji, director of the Asian Affairs Bureau of the Foreign Office, was sent to Taipei to advise the Japanese delegation.

Japan and Nationalist China agreed that there would be no explicit statement about the start of the war. However, Japan accepted the fact that it began with the Manchurian Incident. She also agreed to the Chinese-claimed reparations in the form of goods and services, according to the pattern of the San Francisco treaty.[33] Furthermore, Japan agreed to renounce all special rights and interests in China, and also would recognize all treaties, conventions and agreements concluded before December 9, 1941, to be null and void. The Nationalist government would take over all Japanese properties in Taiwan, while Japan, under Article 2 of the multilateral treaty, would renounce all rights, titles, and claims to Taiwan and the Pescadores. It was also agreed that the treaty should be applicable to all the territories which were at present, and which might hereafter be, under the control of the Nationalist Chinese. This would not affect Nationalist China's sovereign right over mainland China.[34]

On March 28, hope of an early conclusion of a treaty suddenly disappeared: Kawada received instructions from Tokyo that the newly reached agreements were totally unacceptable. Because of the firm Chinese position and of American pressure, Japan sent Wajima Eiji back to Taipei on April 5 to assist Kawada. He brought with him the following new Japanese instructions, which were presented to the Chinese delegation on April 6:

1. Japan would not accept the terms in the treaty insofar as they implied recognition of unlimited Chinese Nationalist sovereignty over all Chinese territories.
2. The Republic of China must terminate her claimed reparations against Japan in the form of goods and services.
3. Japan still believes that the actual beginning date of the war between China and Japan should be December 9, 1941.[35]

The Nationalist government made the following concessions on April 12:

1. The date of the beginning of the Sino-Japanese War would not be listed in the treaty.
2. The Chinese Government agrees that the peace treaty would only be applicable to the territories "which are now, and which may hereafter be under the control of the Republic of China," and the phrase "the sovereign right of the Republic of China," and the phrase "the sovereign right of the Republic of China over mainland China" would be taken out of the Treaty.[36]

On April 20, Prime Minister Yoshida sent a telegram to the Japanese delegation stating that the following provision must be renegotiated:

1. In the agreed Exchange of Notes, ". . . the present Treaty shall, in respect of the Republic of China, be applicable to all the territories which are now, and which may hereafter be, under the control of its Government," should be changed to ". . . the present Treaty shall, in respect of the Republic of China, be applicable to all the territories which are now, or which may hereafter be, under the control of its Government."
2. The following article should be omitted from the Treaty: All property, rights or interests in Japan of the collaborationist regime created in China, as a result of the so-called "Mukden Incident" of September 18, 1931, such as "Manchukuo" and the "Wang Ching-wei regime," shall be transferable to the Republic of China.[37]

This action brought negotiations to another deadlock and drew serious denunciation and protest from Taipei. The real intention of Yoshida's telegram was to delay the conclusion of the Nationalist-Japanese negotiations until the multilateral treaty went into effect on April 28. As soon as Japan regained independence, she would, as a sovereign state, negotiate a treaty with Nationalist China and would be free to sign a similar treaty with Communist China should she wish.

On April 25, Rankin visited Yeh and indicated that the United States was concerned about the deadlocked negotiations. He added that unless an early conclusion of the treaty was reached, the State Department would take necessary steps to mediate.

On the day of Rankin's statement, both Taipei and Tokyo made concessions to each other, and the following final agreements were reached on April 27:

1. The Japanese Government accepts the following Agreed Minutes: All property, rights or interests in Japan of the collaborationist regimes created in China, as a result of the so-called "Mukden Incident" of September 18, 1931, such as "Manchukuo" and the "Wang Ching-wei regime" shall be transferable to the Republic of China.
2. The Nationalist Government agrees to the Japanese Government's request that "or" should replace "and" in No. 1 of the Exchange of Notes to read as follows:
   The present Treaty shall, in respect of the Republic of China, be applicable to all the territories which are now, or which may hereafter be, under the control of its Government. [38]

After almost ten weeks of negotiations, Nationalist China and Japan finally signed a treaty of peace in Taipei on April 28, 1952, ending the state of war between them. [39]

This treaty was a product of considerable compromise between them. The real significance of the treaty, however, did not lie in its contents. It lay in the fact that Japan, given the choice at San Francisco to deal with either Taipei or with Peking, chose to negotiate a treaty with Taipei. This choice was made with the knowledge that the Communist world would hardly be pleased and it revealed the fact that Japan was committed to the side of the West under the deep influence of the United States. This conditioned Japanese foreign policy for twenty years in dealing with the problem.

Notes

1. *United States Policy in the Korean Crisis,* Department of State Publication No. 3922 (Washington, D.C., 1950), p. 27.

2. The John Foster Dulles Papers, I.L.I. News Conference, 1950: Papers (Princeton University), contain Addresses and Speeches, Correspondence, Documents, Conference Dossiers, Subject Folders and Press Releases, as well as other important materials. At the news conference, Dulles declared: "The United States recognizes and only recognizes the National-ist Government of China, so that naturally we would only deal with that Government in diplomatic talks regarding the Japanese Treaty. . . ."

3. *Commons Debates,* 31 November 1949, Vol. 469, Col. 162.

4. *The Times* (London), 17 November 1950.

5. *Commons Debates,* 17 July 1951, Vol. 471, Col. 217.

6. Dulles Papers, 8: Supplementary File of Papers and Other Materials in the Possession of John Foster Dulles, 1951.

7. Bernard C. Cohen, *The Political Process and Foreign Policy: The Making of the Japanese Peace Settlement* (Princeton, 1957), p. 241.

8. Dulles Papers, 9: Conference Dossiers and Subject Folders, 1951: Trip to London.

9. Ibid., 2: Correspondence, 1951. Yoshida to Dulles, 5 August 1951.

10. Ibid., 9: Conference Dossiers and Subject Folders, 1951: The Drafting of the Peace Treaty with Japan.

11. Ibid.

12. Ibid., I.B.I. Addresses and Speeches, 1951.

13. In a note to Dulles, 17 January 1952, Senator Tom Connally asked: "It is reported that when Senator Jenner made his original broadcast, he was informed by you that the Japanese

would sign a peace treaty with the Nationalist Chinese before we ratified the Japanese Treaty. Walter Trohan reported this in the *Times Herald*, 30 August 1951: Is this correct and why has it not been done?" Dulles confirmed the statement, 22 January 1952. See Dulles Papers, 2: Correspondence, 1952.

14. Ibid., I.G. Notes and Memoranda, 1951.

15. *Congressional Record*, 14 March 1952, p. 2363.

16. Dulles Papers, I.G. Notes and Memoranda, 1951.

17. For the text of the statement by Dulles upon his departure from Washington, see Department of State, *Press Release*, no. 1074, 6 December 1951.

18. Dulles Papers, 9: Conference Dossiers and Subject Folders, 1951: Trip to Tokyo, December, 1951.

19. Ibid.

20. Ibid.

21. Ibid., I.G. Notes and Memoranda, 1951.

22. Dulles Papers, 9: Conference Dossiers and Subject Folders, 1952: The British-American Conference on Japan's Foreign Relations with China, 10 January, 1952.

23. Ibid.

24. For the text of Yoshida's letter, see *Department of State Bulletin*, 28 January 1952.

25. *New York Times*, 9 January 1952.

26. Japanese Diet, House of Representatives, 13th Session, *Minutes of Proceedings*, no. 1 (21–25 January 1952), p. 23.

27. Nationalist Chinese Ministry of Foreign Affairs, *The Official Records of the Nationalist-Japanese Negotiations* (Taipei, 1953), p. 40.

28. *Asahi Evening News* (English edition), 7 February 1952, p. 1.

29. *Official Records of the Nationalist-Japanese Peace Negotiations*, p. 47.

30. *New York Times*, 22 February 1952. This was Yoshida's indication at the Japanese Diet, 21 February 1952.

31. *Official Records of the Nationalist-Japanese Peace Negotiations*, pp. 87–89.

32. *New York Times*, 7 March 1952.

33. *Nippon Times*, 18 March 1952, p. 1.

34. *Central Daily News*, 25 March 1952, p. 1.

35. *Nippon Times*, 7 April 1952; *Official Records of the Nationalist-Japanese Peace Negotiations*, p. 103.

36. *China Post*, 13 April 1952; *Nippon Times*, 13 April 1952.

37. *Nippon Times*, 21 April 1952.

38. *Official Records of the Nationalist-Japanese Peace Negotiations*, pp. 119–22.

39. For the full text of the peace treaty, see the Ministry of Foreign Affairs, Republic of China, *Treaties between the Republic of China and Foreign States, 1927–1957* (Taipei, 1957), pp. 248–57.

15.

In this essay Yung H. Park discusses the politics of the China question in Japan during the 1960s, with special attention to the policy of *seikei bunri* (separation of politics and economics) which evolved as the initial Japanese approach to relations with mainland China. He shows how the increasingly pro-Taiwan policies of Premier Satō spoiled whatever early promise this approach had, and discusses the tensions that developed in Japan as public opinion came to favor improved relations with Peking.

Park was born in Korea, did his undergraduate work at the University of Montana and took his M.A. and Ph.D. degrees in political science at the University of Illinois. He has been a professor of political science at Humboldt State University at Arcata, California, since 1966, and chairman of his department since 1970. He did field research in Japan, Korea, and Southeast Asia in 1969–1970, 1971, and 1972–1973. He is coauthor of *An Area Handbook for the Republic of Korea* (1969), and has published articles on Japanese administration, education, and policy making in Japanese and American scholarly journals. He is preparing a book on educational policy making in Japan.

The Roots of Détente

Yung H. Park

I.

It has sometimes been argued that but for the Nixon shocks, the Tokyo government would not have altered its long-standing policy toward China. This argument, however, does not take into account other external influences on Japan's China policy and the domestic political climate regarding the China issue. Although Washington's changing orientation toward China was decisive in Japan's China posture, the roots of a Sino-Japanese détente were already laid in the Japanese political system during the 1960s. Various political forces, supportive of Sino-Japanese rapprochement, were responsible for changes, though gradual, in Tokyo's orientation toward Peking. What was a decidedly minority opinion on the China issue during the 1950s gained acceptance as a majority opinion by the early 1970s, and a government intent upon staying in power could not ignore this changing domestic climate.

In the 1950s, Japan's China posture was dictated by her basic policy, popularly known as the separation of politics and economics (*seikei bunri*). Tokyo's rigid adherence to *seikei bunri* was largely in accord with the consensus of the major participants (e.g., the Liberal Democratic Party, organized business, and the bureaucracy) in Japan's foreign policy making and was generally endorsed by public opinion, as shown by contemporaneous polls.[1] Variations in Japan's China policy, determined by the government's perception and assessment of domestic power configurations and the international environment, depended largely upon who was premier. From their formal positions of responsibility, Japanese premiers have taken more and more actual control of foreign policy.

It is not surprising that when Ikeda Hayato became premier in 1960, he made it clear that his government would not deviate radically from the tradition of maintaining close ties with Taipei and Washington and of keeping politics out of economics in dealing with China. However, conditions affecting the Japanese political system of the early 1960s differed notably from those of the 1950s. As a consequence, the Ikeda government's China posture bore little resemblance to that of his immediate predecessor, Kishi Nobusuke, during whose administration Sino-Japanese trade was suspended abruptly.

After the turmoil over security treaty revision subsided, public attention focused again on China. Although the LDP retained its majority in the Diet in the 1960 general elections, there was a growing feeling of discontent with the absence of contacts and of trade with the mainland. The new premier quickly adopted a "low posture," paying due respect to the opposition parties and especially the Japanese Socialist Party (JSP), which had long advocated changes in Tokyo's China policy. Though he was one of the disciples (the other was Satō Eisaku) of Yoshida Shigeru's Washington-first diplomacy, Ikeda revealed his intention to attempt to break the impasse in Sino-Japanese relations. Thus, Liu Ning-i, chairman of the All-China Federation of Trade Unions, was granted an entry permit to attend an anti-atomic bomb convention in Japan, despite protests from Taipei.[2]

There was, in addition, a mood of optimism in Japan, attributable to the expectation that President Kennedy's eagerness to change America's traditional China policy would create an atmosphere favorable to improvement of Sino-Japanese relations. Indeed, Kennedy's choice of foreign policy aides was encouraging: Adlai Stevenson and Chester Bowles, who had both called for a new China policy.[3] China's changing domestic and external orientation also contributed to the new mood in Japan. Slowly recovering from the excesses of the Great Leap Forward, the Chinese Communist Party (CCP), under the leadership of Liu Shao-ch'i and Chou En-lai, launched a series of pragmatic policies to make China's economic development more predictable. This meant abandoning the earlier hard-line approach toward Japan—the suspension of trade in 1958 had damaged the Chinese economy—and emphasizing economics, rather than using trade only as a lure for political gains. China's deteriorating relationship with the Soviet Union was influential in the return to a moderate posture. Further, China hoped that the JSP would benefit from her hard-line position, but the party did poorly in the 1960 election.[4]

China's renewed interest in Japan was manifested in a variety of ways. On National Day 1960, several Japanese groups were invited to Peking, where they and their Chinese counterparts issued a public appeal for peaceful coexistence and improved relations between the two countries.[5] During his stay in Japan, Liu Ning-i carefully refrained from making derogatory remarks about the new Ikeda government and the LDP, while denouncing Washington's "imperialistic" policy toward the Japanese and Chinese peoples. Liu's visit, the first by a leading Chinese since 1958, was hailed widely as a sign of Peking's return to people's diplomacy.[6] Chou En-lai subsequently announced his "three principles of Sino-Japanese trade," according to which trade between the two countries in the new period could be guaranteed by an official agreement and by private agreements. Chou stressed that "the resumption of trade would be advantageous to both peoples."[7]

Domestic developments in Japan also played a significant role in the Ikeda government's China posture. Ikeda was under increasing pressure from the opposition parties, the pronormalization factions of the LDP, and business to act on his pledges. The opposition's favorite target was the alleged absence of autonomy in Japan's conduct of foreign affairs, an argument supported even by the antimainstream factions of the LDP. Nakasone Yasuhiro, a leading member of the Kōno Ichirō faction, charged that "the cause of uneasiness in the Far East lies in the antagonism" between Washington and Peking, and that Japan should mitigate this antagonism rather than take sides. Nakasone contended that in dealing with China, "Japan should look to the example of Britain."[8] Japanese industries and trading firms, adversely affected by the suspension of Sino-Japanese trade, were among the leading advocates of improved relations with China. Faced with growing competition in the European market, Japanese business was increasingly interested in gaining access to the China market, while those businessmen closely allied with Taiwan and Washington warned that Peking's interest in trade was dictated solely by political motives.

Ikeda responded to the growing clamor by actively supporting the so-called cumulative approach. Convinced that Sino-Japanese détente would be impossible without a thaw in the relationship between Peking and Washington, Ikeda set out to persuade Washington to change its traditional orientation toward China. During his visit with Kennedy in 1961, Ikeda reportedly conveyed the situation in Japan, arguing that Washington should seriously reexamine its China thinking and that it was "unnatural" to keep Communist China with her 600 million people out of the U.N. for long.[9] The Japanese envoy to the U.N. echoed Ikeda's argument in the General Assembly in the fall of 1961, while noting that Nationalist China should not be overlooked. The Kennedy administration politely ignored Ikeda's suggestion and the United States succeeded in 1961 in having Chinese representation designated an "important question" requiring a two-thirds majority for favorable action.

Japanese optimism soon gave way to the realization that Washington would not alter its traditional China policy.[10] Washington's negative response did not deter the Ikeda government from actively supporting nongovernmental cumulative contacts between Japan and China. When Matsumura Kenzō, doyen of the pro-Peking faction of the LDP, was invited to Peking in the fall of 1962, he was given Ikeda's "virtual blessings." The Chou–Matsumura conference, the first high-level talk since 1958, heralded the new era of cumulative people's diplomacy. The two agreed to exchange newspapermen and to promote trade between their nations. Despite rumblings from Taipei and the pro-Taipei faction led by Kishi Nobusuke and Kaya Okinori, the LDP responded favorably to the Chou–Matsumura communiqué. Secretary-General Maeo Shigesaburō, leader of the mainstream Ikeda faction, welcomed the agreement as contributing to the normalization of Sino-Japanese relations.[11]

Then a business delegation, led by Takasaki Tatsunosuke, an LDP advocate of improved relations, went to Peking to work out specific implementations of the spirit of the Chou–Matsumura agreement. The trade agreement signed by Takasaki and Liao Ch'eng-chih, a vice-chief of the Chinese staff office of foreign affairs, spelled out terms for trade between the two countries: (1) for 1963–1967, barter trade should be in the vicinity of $180 million annually; (2) Japan would export chemical fertilizer, agricultural chemicals, steel, and agricultural machinery, while China would export coal, iron ore, soy beans, corn, salt, tin, etc.; (3) Japanese plant export involving deferred payment would be subject to further negotiations; (4) the Liao–Takasaki memorandum and subsequent agreements should not be abrogated unilaterally.[12] Ikeda pledged his support as long as implementation of the L-T memorandum, as it was popularly known, did not require direct governmental involvement.[13]

Under those terms and the so-called friendly firms trade formula, initiated between China and certain Japanese companies, trade between the two countries expanded slowly, and by 1964 Japanese exports to and imports from the mainland exceeded those to and from Taiwan.[14] Encouraged by that steady growth and nudged by business, the Ikeda government decided in July 1963, despite the Foreign Ministry's serious reservations, to approve an export contract between the Kurashiki Rayon Company and China that involved the sale of a vinylon plant on a five-year deferred-payment basis. These developments were enthusiastically greeted by Japanese business and the pro-Peking elements of the LDP. The Japan Economic Research Council (Nihon Keizai Chōsa Kyōgikai), supported by the major business associations, stressed in its September 1963 report that Japan's trade with Communist nations, especially China, should be given greater encouragement. The report reflected the current thinking of zaikai, influenced by the growing trade between China and Western Europe and by the White House decision of September 18, 1963, to encourage trade with Communist nations. This enthusiasm was dramatically shown in 1964, when Nan Han-chen, chairman of the China Council for the

Promotion of International Trade, visited Japan on the occasion of the Chinese trade fair there. He conferred individually with leaders of such business associations as Keidanren (Federation of Economic Organizations) and Keizai Dōyūkai (Japan Committee for Economic Development), and with such LDP notables as Fujiyama Aiichirō, Kishi's foreign minister, Miki Takeo, Kōno Ichirō, and Satō Eisaku, It is significant that most of these LDP faction-chiefs had not previously espoused a pro-Peking cause within the LDP.

The tempo of Sino-Japanese trade did not slow down. Encouraged by Tokyo's approval of the Kurashiki transaction, other industrial giants including Tōyō Engineering, a leading fertilizer-maker, and Hitachi Shipbuilding signed export agreements involving deferred payments with China. Peking, while criticizing Tokyo's cooperation with Washington against China in the U.N.,[15] demonstrated on several occasions its enthusiasm for the growing economic ties with Tokyo. In 1963, Peking created the China-Japan Friendship Association, headed by none other than Liao, to promote people's diplomacy with Japan. In April 1964, Liao and Matsumura signed a series of agreements for exchange of trade missions and newspapermen. The two nations exchanged correspondents in September 1964, and in the following year, Peking dispatched its trade mission to Tokyo. Although the Ikeda government refused to send an official trade mission to China, it indicated clearly that the Japan mission would have its blessing.[16]

All these developments were given wide publicity in Japan and had significant impact on the growing popular desire for normalized relations with China. National consensus accepted Tokyo's support of the cumulative diplomacy most conducive to that end. Even such ardent pro-Peking members of the LDP as Matsumura, Utsunomiya Tokuma, and Furui Yoshimi, who played leading roles in the improvement of Sino-Japanese relations during the Ikeda era, supported Ikeda's basic China posture, while they denounced Kishi's.[17] However, the Ikeda government, like its conservative predecessors, did not have complete freedom in dealing with China. Ikeda found it imperative to reassure Washington and Taipei that his government was not about to recognize China, and remained concerned with maintaining amicable ties with these two allies. The Taiwan government, however, was disturbed by Tokyo's authorization of Export-Import Bank (a governmental corporation) loans for China trade, as well as by Tokyo's decision to repatriate Chou Hung-ching, a visiting Chinese technician seeking political asylum, to the mainland. Interpreting these occurrences as signs of Tokyo's drift away from Taiwan and aided by the rightists in the LDP, Taipei protested to Tokyo in the strongest terms. Taipei's fear was heightened by France's recognition of Peking in January 1964 and by Peking's conciliatory attitude on the Taiwan question.

To appease Taipei and the pro-Taipei Kishi–Kaya elements of his party, Ikeda prevailed upon his mentor Yoshida to pay an informal visit to Taipei as his personal envoy in February 1964. He reportedly assured Chiang Kai-shek that Tokyo would not abandon its traditional allies. Upon his return, Yoshida sent Chiang what was later known as the Yoshida letter, pledging on behalf of the Tokyo government that "government loans such as Export-Import Bank loans will not be available for further financing of plant exports to China" for the remainder of 1964.[18] On March 5, 1964, Ikeda issued a "unified governmental view" on China, which (1) reaffirmed the separation of politics and economics, (2) pledged to maintain the existing friendly ties with Taipei, and (3) indicated that Japan would consider normalizing relations with China only after the latter was admitted to the U.N.[19] Furthermore, rejecting Kaya's plea that the premier himself go to Taipei, Ikeda dispatched his foreign minister, Ōhira Masayoshi, in July 1964, to reaffirm Japanese-Taiwanese friendship and confirm Yoshida's pledge. In August Chang Chun, Chiang's personal adviser, visited Tokyo. Relations with Taipei, unduly restrained during the previous year, were restored to normal by late 1964.

These external constraints, and the pressure of the pro-Taipei elements of the party, were directly responsible for the Ikeda government's sudden failure to respond favorably to Peking's active gestures. Tokyo quietly ignored Chou's proposal for a governmental trade agreement. Further, Ikeda responded to Chou's May 1964 proposal for initiation of Peking-Tokyo ambassadorial talks—once welcomed as consonant with cumulative diplomacy—by indicating that Japan was not ready for them.[20]

Although Ikeda's freedom of action was circumscribed, it was during his administration that a sound foundation for people's diplomacy and trade between China and Japan was laid, although no progress was made in government-to-government contacts. The sector of business benefiting from the L-T memorandum, and those involved in "friendly firms trade," gradually emerged as powerful voices for better relations with China. Hitachi Shipbuilding and Tōyō Engineering, having seen their contracts with China called off as a result of the Yoshida letter controversy, concluded that meaningful trade ties with China would be possible only in an atmosphere of improved political relations. These firms and others joined the growing minority advocating the normalization of Sino-Japanese relations.[21] Both Ikeda and Ōhira stated that "once China is welcomed as a bona fide member of the U.N., Japan will naturally have to normalize relations with China."[22] Quite possibly, the premier felt that Peking's admission to the U.N. was simply a matter of time.

II.

Prior to becoming premier in 1964, Satō showed considerable interest in improving relations with China. When Nan visited Japan in 1964, Satō, then a member of the Ikeda cabinet, was one of the few LDP *jitsuryokusha* (faction-chiefs) rushing to meet him while his pro-Taipei colleagues stayed away. During his talks with Nan—unprecedented for an incumbent cabinet minister—Satō stated, in a show of extraordinary courage, that *seikei bunri* was no longer a viable policy and that Sino-Japanese relations would improve only when those elements were merged.[23] In his first major policy statement as premier, Satō pledged to pursue a forward-looking China policy. Peking took a wait-and-see attitude in the early days of Satō's government. But the cabinet early on denied an entry permit to a CCP delegation, led by Peng Chen (a leading CCP member and then mayor of Peking), planning to attend a JCP convention. Further, Satō's foreign minister Shiina Etsusaburō admitted publicly that Japan's endorsement of the "important question" formula was really designed to keep China out of the U.N.

China's response was swift. Charging that the Satō government was in fact pursuing an anti-China policy,[24] China suspended trade talks, and several leading Chinese including Liao cancelled visits to Japan. The LDP, rallying behind the premier, called off the proposed visit to China of LDP Dietman Kuno Chūji, rumored to be Satō's personal emissary. The party also withdrew its members from a delegation of the Dietmen's League for the Promotion of Sino-Japanese Trade scheduled to pay a goodwill visit to China in December 1964. Furthermore, Secretary-General Miki Takeo instructed LDP members to sever ties with the league and with similar organizations.[25] Meanwhile, Matsumura warned that Satō's rightist leanings jeopardized existing Sino-Japanese ties and argued that Sino-American détente, if mediated by the premier, would contribute to international peace. In another talk with Satō, Matsumura mentioned that the rejection of Peng Chen's visa application was bound to chill the future of the Sino-Japanese relationship.[26]

While assuring the party's pro-Peking group of his friendly policy toward Peking, Satō convinced the Chinese that he was indeed their enemy. In January 1965, he denied Export-Import Bank loans to Dainihon Bōseki and Hitachi Shipbuilding, and later he formally acknowledged the validity of the Yoshida letter.[27] The textile, fertilizer, and shipbuilding industries, already suffering from Ikeda's action against the use of governmental loans, reacted angrily, although he tried to convince them that their losses could be compensated by "a more lucrative trade with Taiwan."[28] A series of actions by Satō vis-à-vis Taiwan left no doubt in the minds of Chinese leaders that he was more eager to strengthen ties with Taiwan and the United States than to improve relations with Peking. When Ishii Mitsujirō and Kishi went to Taipei to attend a meeting of the Japanese-Taiwanese Cooperation Committee (Nikka Kyōryoku Iinkai) in December 1964, they carried Satō's personal letter to Chiang stating that his government hoped for closer ties with Taiwan. Peking was further annoyed by Satō's behavior during his first American visit in January 1965. Ignoring urgings by Matsumura and others to be more assertive on the China question, Satō merely reaffirmed in his joint communiqué with Johnson the long-standing friendship with Taiwan and stated that his government had no plans to go beyond the current level of unofficial contacts with China. The communiqué also contained their pledge to maintain close cooperation in their China policies.[29] What infuriated Peking was Satō's speech before the American-Japan Society of New York. Satō, deviating from his prepared and more moderate speech, emphasized that Japan was "more concerned than the U.S. with Communist China's aggressive tendencies."[30]

The growing rapprochement between Japan and South Korea, obviously prompted by Washington's policy of encouraging friendly ties between its two Asian allies, was also a matter of deep concern to China. The signing of the basic accord on normalization by Tokyo and Seoul was bitterly and consistently depicted by Peking as a step toward the creation of a North East Asia Treaty Organization (NEATO) under the aegis of the United States, whose primary objective was to carry out Washington's aggressive designs against the Chinese and Korean peoples.[31] The Satō government's unofficial endorsement of Washington's Vietnam policy was viewed as an obvious sign of Japan's collusion with Washington's "imperialistic" policy.[32] Satō committed the most unforgivable act in the eyes of Peking in 1967, the year the five-year period of the L-T memorandum expired: he visited Taipei—a step no incumbent premier had ever taken. Although he refused to concur with Chiang's views on China in toto, Satō agreed on the need for closer political, economical, and cultural ties between Japan and Taiwan.[33] Understandably, Peking soon labeled the Satō government "the worst and most anti-Peking regime" in the postwar history of Japan.[34]

During his second Washington visit in May 1967, Satō agreed with Johnson that precautionary measures must be taken by China's neighbors so that they would not be intimidated by her nuclear capability.[35] For Peking, the Johnson–Satō communiqué smacked of a NEATO. The state visit of Chiang Ching-kuo (Chiang Kai-shek's son and heir apparent) to Japan shortly after Satō's return from Washington did not help to dispel Peking's suspicions regarding NEATO.

China's animosity toward the Satō government reached a peak in the fall of 1969. Satō's actions, perceived as particularly hostile, came at the very time when the international environment surrounding China was changing rapidly in her favor. Following the enunciation of the Guam Doctrine, the Nixon administration indicated that it was interested in ending the cold-war relationship with Peking.[36] Moreover, Canada and Italy, two of Washington's close allies, were on the verge of recognizing Peking as the sole legitimate government of China. The Satō government again decided without many qualms to cosponsor the "important question" resolution in the U.N., while support for Peking was mounting.[37] As his brother proceeded to Taipei to attend a Japan-Taiwanese Cooperation Committee meeting, Satō went to Washington to confer with the new president. He stressed in his joint communiqué with Nixon that the security of Taiwan and South Korea was essential to that of Japan; the committee issued the most blatantly anti-Peking communiqué in its history, in which the Japanese participants endorsed Taipei's overplayed desire to return to the mainland.[38] The Japanese delegation, including both pro-Taipei LDP *jitsuryokusha* and leading businessmen, also promised on behalf of the Tokyo government to make a large governmental loan available to Taiwan.[39]

Although the rapid deterioration of Sino-Japanese relations was attributable in large measure to Satō's decided slant toward Taipei, China's erratic, xenophobic behavior during the Cultural Revolution did much to impair the relationship. Moderates like Ch'en Yi, Nan Han-chen, Liao Ch'eng-chih, and Kuo Mo-jo who had an important voice in China's Japan policy were temporarily replaced by "cultural revolutionists" whose radical activities seriously jeopardized people's diplomacy with Japan. Another consequence of China's behavior during this period was a "precipitous drop in Peking's prestige, and the creation of a decidedly unfavorable image in many quarters of the world, including areas which Peking had previously sought to cultivate." Japan was one of the affected areas: a leading poll taken in September 1967 rated China as the most disliked nation.[40] The expulsion of Japanese correspondents from China and the arrest of several "friendly firms" representatives stationed on the mainland did not help to alleviate the ill-feeling toward China. Of all the groups that had championed Peking as the only legal government of China the JCP was most adversely affected by China's radical turn. While Peking became vehement in its antirevisionistic and anti-Soviet campaigns, the JCP pressed for the formation of an anti-imperialistic international united front linking all Communist parties including Moscow. The JCP politely turned down China's suggestion that the party assume a more militant and revolutionary line. During his China visit, JCP Secretary-General Miyamoto Kenji reminded his Chinese hosts that "an armed rebellion was not appropriate in the realities of Japan" and the JCP was more interested in expanding its influence by way of the parliamentary approach.[41] Soon after Miyamoto's return, contacts between the two parties were suspended. But the JCP did not change its basic China position (i.e., recognition of Peking as the only government of China), although its enthusiasm toward China became more apparent than real, and it was far less inclined than the JSP to comply with Peking's terms for normalization in toto.

The Cultural Revolution also affected the JSP by sharpening interfactional rivalries and disputes on party policies toward China. While the rightist Eda, Kōno, and Katsumata factions were critical of the revolution and its radical ramifications, the leftist Sasaki faction and the extremist Peace Comrades Association (Heiwa Dōshikai) endorsed the revolution as a great "socialist movement" under Mao's leadership.[42] As a result, the JSP failed to wage a united campaign in support of China. Also hit by China's xenophobic interlude were various popular organizations affiliated with leftist parties and advocating the normalization of Sino-Japanese relations. For example, the JCP-controlled Japan-China Friendship Association split into a pro-JCP group and a splinter group called the Orthodox Headquarters of the Japan-China Friendship Association. Although they both supported recognition of China, their differing outlooks undercut their effectiveness in championing the cause of China.

III.

The Liberal-Democratic Party. Beginning in the early 1960s, intraparty dissatisfaction with the party's official endorsement of the government's China policy became increasingly organized. Critics grouped together because the party's official foreign policy organs, the Investigating Committee on Foreign Affairs (Gaikō Chōsakai) and the Foreign Affairs Division (Gaikō Bukai), largely dominated by factions supporting the incumbent premier, resisted discussion of problems related to China. In February 1960, the Society for the Study of the China Problem (Chūgoku Mondai Kenkyūkai), an informal grouping of ex-Progressive Party (Kaishintō) elements of the LDP, came into being. Members of factions other than the pro-Taipei Ishii faction formed the Society for the Study of Ways to Improve Japanese-Chinese Relations (Nitchū Kaizen Kenkyūkai). The two groups later merged into the Society for the Study of Japanese-Chinese Problems (Nitchū Mondai Kenkyūkai), which soon disbanded largely under pressure from the party leadership to keep the China debate within the official framework of the party.

In January 1965, concerned party members, largely from the Kōno, Matsumura, Ōno, Miki, and Fujiyama factions, created the Asian-African

Problems Study Group (Ajia Afurika Mondai Kenkyūkai), to press for greater diplomatic autonomy for Japan and the speedy normalization of Sino-Japanese relations. However, it was not yet prepared to write off Taiwan. The group's founding membership of nineteen quickly grew to seventy-seven, an indication of considerable intraparty dissatisfaction with the government's China stance. Diametrically opposed to this group was the Asian Problems Study Group (Ajia Mondai Kenkyūkai), led by Kaya Okinori and dominated by the Satō, Ishii, and Kishi–Fukuda factions. Doubtful that China was a peace-loving nation, the Asian Group insisted that Japan play an active role in keeping China out of the U.N. and maintain closer political and economic relations with "free world" nations.[43]

Although a minority, the Asian-African Group was nevertheless a powerful promoter of intraparty debate on China during Satō's regime. The 1966–1968 debate leading to substantial changes in the China stance of both the party and the government was attributable in large part to the group's pressure. Returning from Peking after signing the 1968 trade agreements with China, Furui, a leading spokesman for the Asian-African Group, personally urged Satō to put an end to what he called the "anachronous separation of politics and economics" and to assume a more positive posture in dealing economically and politically with China. Specifically, Furui advocated immediate rescission of the controversial Yoshida letter. Joining Furui and his supporters was Nakasone Yasuhiro, a rising faction-chief and minister of transportation—very susceptible to pressures from transportation and shipbuilding industries. Challenging the *raison d'être* of the Yoshida letter still endorsed by Satō and the Foreign Ministry, Nakasone publicly supported the authorization of Export-Import Bank loans for China trade. Nakasone was soon joined by Minister of International Trade and Industry Shiina Etsusaburō and Finance Minister Mizuta Mikio, both under growing pressure from the industries. Satō found it imperative to abrogate the controversial letter in 1968, although he refused to state explicitly that loans would be authorized for the China trade.[44]

The decision to initiate Vietnam peace talks in mid-1968 provided powerful momentum to the intraparty and governmental debate on China. One outcome of the partisan concern was the creation of another informal organ, the Discussion Group for New Policy (Shinseisaku Danwakai), a cross-factional body headed by Akagi Munenori, a leading Asian-African Group member. It was committed to studying ways for Japan to cope with post-Vietnam problems and was predicated on the assumption that a Vietnam settlement would lead to Sino-American détente.

Another upshot of the China debate was the adoption in May 1968 of a "unified LDP view" on the China issue by the Investigating Committee on Foreign Affairs. It urged that efforts be made to bring China more into the mainstream of international activities and to coexist with her in accordance with a policy of mutual respect and noninterference with each other's domestic affairs. As for the use of Export-Import Bank loans, the unified view merely stated, without naming China, that such loans be used to promote Japan's foreign trade.[45]

Nixon's initial China moves had a significant impact on the LDP critics of the government's China posture. Major figures in the Asian-African Group—Furui, Tagawa Seiichi, and Utsunomiya Tokuma—sensing a vital link between Nixon's desire to end the domestically unpopular Vietnam War and his China gestures, predicted that an effective dialogue would soon be established between the two powers and that China would find her seat in the U.N. sooner than the Satō government anticipated. Guided by their remarkable foresight, Furui and others were deeply concerned that Japan would fall behind Washington in opening diplomatic ties with Peking.[46]

Much to the embarrassment of the party leadership, LDP critics of the government's China policy went beyond intraparty activities in December 1970, when they and the opposition parties formed the Dietmen's League for the Normalization of Japanese-Chinese Relations (Nitchū Kokkō Kaifuku Sokushin Giin Remmei). The league proposed to "urge the government to take such measures as may be necessary to restore diplomatic relations" with Peking and to promote, through suprapartisan activities, a "national consensus" supporting speedy recognition of China.[47] United in its criticism of the Satō government's China stance, the league emerged as a powerful parliamentary challenger to the Taiwan-first policy. The government was also disturbed by the LDP members' close collaboration with the parliamentary opposition in attacks upon government policy and especially by the adverse effect such collaboration was bound to have on the public image of the ruling party.[48]

Also significant for the pro-Peking cause within the party was a widening disagreement among leading members and powerful faction-chiefs on the China issue.[49] Fujiyama, Kishi's foreign minister at the time of the 1960 political turbulence, made the most dramatic shift in views—from close association with Kishi's pro-Taipei policy to a highly critical opinion of the government's China stance. Still hesitant about committing himself to a decidedly pro-Peking stand, however, he refused Furui's suggestion that he visit China in 1966. By 1970, Fujiyama decided to join pro-Peking members of the LDP and openly challenged Satō's China policy. He accompanied Matsumura to Peking to confer with Chou En-lai and sign the controversial 1970 Sino-Japanese communiqué. By December 1970, Fujiyama emerged as the leading LDP Dietman working for normalized Sino-Japanese relations when he was elected chairman of the nonpartisan Dietmen's League. In July 1971, he was a prime mover in the abortive attempt to adopt a Diet resolution recognizing Peking as China's sole legitimate government. In the fall of 1971 Fujiyama headed a league mission to China, where it was agreed that Sino-Japanese relations should be established at the earliest possible date on the basis of China's "four principles of Sino-Japanese relations."[50] In October, when the opposition parties tried to discredit the Satō government's China policy through no-confidence motions in the Diet, Fujiyama led eleven other members of the LDP in boycotting the vote in a show of protest against the government.[51]

Miki Takeo, ex-Kaishintō LDP factional leader closely associated with Matsumura, as early as 1960 chided Premier Kishi for following a "backward-looking" policy toward China. After his departure from Satō's cabinet in 1968, Miki's attacks upon Satō's pro-Taipei position gained momentum. By January 1971, Miki asserted that "the Peking government is the legitimate government of China."[52] Nakasone was still another *jitsuryokusha* advocating radical changes in the government's China policy, and was one of the main influences in the government's decision to rescind the Yoshida letter in 1968. In November 1971, Nakasone went so far as to contend that Tokyo should initiate efforts to recognize Peking.

A fourth *jitsuryokusha* to challenge Satō openly was Ōhira Masayoshi, leader of the Kōchikai, a faction which had supported Satō's premiership. Alleging that the government's failure to deal effectively with both external and domestic problems contributed to "the lack of public confidence in politics," Ōhira, with an eye on the post-Satō premiership, severely criticized Satō's alleged reluctance to cope with the China question on the basis of a one-China formula. Ōhira stressed that Japan should not be a party to any scheme to keep Taiwan in the U.N.[53] Maeo Shigesaburō, a *jitsuryokusha* serving in the Satō cabinet, also came to question the wisdom of Satō's pro-Taiwan policy. Intraparty dissatisfaction also affected the junior members of the LDP parliamentary group. Organized in the Shōwakai (Showa Society), an informal cross-factional group led by such "mavericks" as Kōno Yōhei, Yamaguchi Toshio, and Shiotani Kazuo, they were increasingly dismayed by the continued domination of the party's official foreign policy organs by those close to Satō. After the Nixon announcement, the youthful dissidents became more vociferous in attacking what they felt was Satō's insensitivity to the rising domestic and international mood for closer ties with Peking.[54]

Still another testimony to growing intraparty defiance of the government was the fact that pro-Peking elements, especially those representing Japan in periodic negotiations for nongovernmental trade agreements with China, had progressively moved closer to Chinese positions on various aspects of the Sino-Japanese relationship. As early as 1968 the Japanese delegation including Furui and Tagawa accepted China's political terms of the trade agreement, among which were that Japan would not participate in plots to form two Chinas, and that Japan should not take a hostile attitude toward China. In 1969 when the 1968 agreement was up for renewal, the Chinese demanded that the Japanese delegation accede to political terms more in tune with China's long-standing positions. As a result, in addition to reaffirming the terms of the 1968 communiqué, the Japanese joined the Chinese in castigating the Tokyo-Taipei peace treaty as "hostile to the Chinese people" and in acknowledging Peking as the only legitimate government of China, and Taiwan as an inseparable part of China. Moreover, the Japanese expressed "an understanding" for the Chinese position that the Satō government was collaborating with "American imperialism" by maintaining the security treaty and that the treaty was an obstacle to improved relations between Tokyo and Peking.[55]

In 1970 the Japanese mission, headed by Furui, concurred with the Chinese that "the revival of militarism" in Japan constituted a serious threat to Asian peoples. Noting that the Satō government was pursuing an antagonistic policy toward China, the Japanese renewed their pledge to work for the speedy normalization of Sino-Japanese relations. The 1971 joint communiqué was far more critical of the Satō government's alleged collusion with "American imperialism" and asserted that Japan's treaty with Taiwan should be abrogated immediately.[56]

In addition to the factors discussed above, it is noteworthy that pro-Peking elements of the party as well as middle-of-the-roaders visited China in increasingly large numbers, especially after the end of the Cultural Revolution in 1969. Although they did not go as far as Furui, Tagawa, and Fujiyama in endorsing Peking's positions, they did make clear their dissatisfaction with the current Sino-Japanese relationship.

Thus, by the early 1970s the intraparty politics of the China question had placed pro-Taipei elements on the defensive. It is important to remember that the party operated within the general climate of opinion formed by the rest of the Japanese political system. Most influential in affecting the thinking of the ruling party was the business community.

The Business Community. Like the LDP, the business community, though united in its desire to expand trade with China, was seriously divided in its approach to the restoration of diplomatic relations with China in the 1960s. Those corporations trading heavily with the United States did not see eye to eye with those interested in expanding trade with China. Likewise, those industries with heavy investments in Taiwan were less willing to normalize diplomatic relations with China on the terms of her one-China position.[57]

In the early days of the Satō government, the business community generally supported its China stand. Business groups speaking through Keidanren, Keizai Dōyūkai, Nisshō (Japan Chamber of Commerce and Industry) and Nikkeiren (Japan Federation of Employers' Associations) endorsed the traditional policy of separating politics and economics. A minority view, largely confined to the firms actively involved in the China trade, insisted that the absence of normal relations with China seriously impeded the growth of the potentially lucrative China trade.

Peking was aware of the close ties between *zaikai* and the LDP government and of the powerful roles the former plays in the latter's decision making. Thus, as China reacted negatively to what she deemed the anti-China policy of the Satō government, she toughened her position in dealing with Japanese business. Talks for further L-T trade were suspended and China insisted that without normalized political relations trade would not be allowed to expand. It did not take long for the firms involved in L-T trade (i.e., those firms having close ties with the LDP government) to recognize the steady decline in the proportion of L-T trade to the total trade volume since 1964, the year Satō came to power.[58] They were well aware that the decline was directly attributable to Peking's policy of leaning to "friendly companies" at the expense of those involved in L-T trade.

During negotiations for the 1968 L-T memorandum trade agreement, China's policy of denying trade to firms not meeting her political demands assumed definite shape. The price expected from Japanese corporations for participating in the trade consisted of abiding by the principle of the inseparability of politics and trade and working for the restoration of Sino-Japanese relations. Japanese industries heavily dependent on L-T trade, e.g., chemical fertilizer industries, all expressed their willingness to accept Peking's political conditions. In 1968 China brought up the subject of the Yoshida letter by indicating that she was prepared to reconsider cancelled contracts involving the export of Japanese plants and ships if Tokyo would abrogate its policy on governmental loans. Japanese industries interested in plant exports, especially textile producers, responded favorably to this gesture. The machine-building industry, suffering from poor European sales, began to show an active interest in the China market, as evidenced by the vigorous bidding among leading machine-producers for shares of the market at the 1965 Japanese fairs in China. Shocked at the 40 percent drop in its overseas orders during 1967, the shipbuilding industry (one of Japan's largest export industries, doing well in China until 1965, when it was shut out) emphatically argued that the Yoshida letter should be abrogated.[59]

This sector of *zaikai* emerged as the leading critic of the Satō government's China posture. It was partly the pressure from this group, working through and with sympathetic elements of the LDP and the bureaucracy, that was responsible for Tokyo's nullification of the Yoshida letter in 1968.

In March 1970, the Chinese established new criteria for the development of trade contracts with Japanese firms in the form of Chou En-lai's Four Conditions for Sino-Japanese Trade. One of these strictures was that Japanese firms with heavy investments in Taiwan would be excluded from trade with China. New-Japan Steel, for example, was completely shut out of the China trade because of its close ties with Taiwan, South Korea, and the United States. Other firms were allowed to trade with China despite their failure to observe Chou's principles. While Mitsui and Mitsubishi (the so-called hawks of *zaikai,* trading heavily with Taiwan and South Korea and therefore less interested in China trade) criticized the strictures, other industrial giants were not prepared to do the same. One by one, they indicated they were ready to comply. Even Japan Air Lines, a governmental corporation, made it known in early 1971 that it would abide by them.

Following Canadian recognition of Peking in 1970 and especially the Nixon announcement of July 1971, *zaikai's* China stance was affected by an additional factor: potential competition with the United States in the China market. Toyota and Nissan nervously watched deepening trade ties between China and Canada, where U.S. automakers had large-scale investments. Specifically, the Japanese automakers were concerned that their American counterparts might beat Japan in laying claims upon the China market through their Canadian subsidiaries. This apprehension was heightened by the unexpectedly rapid sequence of events leading to Nixon's visit to China in February 1972, and was an overriding consideration in the Japanese automakers' hurried reorientation toward China, despite their extensive ties with Taiwanese and South Korean auto-producers.[60]

Nixon's China gestures affected *zaikai* in other ways. Japanese corporations with close business ties to the United States no longer felt constrained in their rush to China, as evidenced by the sudden increase in the number of Japanese firms assenting to the four principles of Chou En-lai. Nixon's Southeast Asia policy also prompted *zaikai* to redefine its traditional ties with Taiwan. Foreseeing serious business competition with China in Southeast Asia following general peace settlements in Indochina, Japanese business leaders increasingly recognized normal relations between Tokyo and Peking as essential to any attempt to coordinate their Southeast Asian economic activities with the Chinese.

In addition, a growing number of leading businessmen wielding much influence in the LDP government advocated accommodating Peking's political stipulations if Tokyo's failure to do so would exclude Japan from the China market. Thus the business community responded favorably to the league's pleas for funds. Many began to entertain the thought that the Satō government was a serious obstacle to improved relations with China—especially in view of Peking's unending attacks on Satō himself rather than his government,[61] and its new stringent proviso that trade would not be allowed to expand and that Sino-Japanese relations would remain "abnormal" until Satō was replaced. At the same time, China hinted that she would not be averse to Japan's continued economic ties with Taiwan after the abrogation of the Tokyo-Taipei treaty, so long as they did not involve massive Japanese investments there.

What disturbed Satō most was the rapid breakdown of the earlier cohesion among the leading *zaikai* supporters of his China policy. The first to break away was Keizai Dōyūkai, and then *zaikai's* elder statesman, Nagano Shigeo, chairman of New-Japan Steel and also of Nisshō. Nagano was a leading member of the Japan-Taiwan Cooperation Committee (Nikka Kyōryoku Iinkai) and the Japan-South Korea Cooperation Committee (Nikkan Kyōryoku Iinkai), both condemned by China. Publicly advocating China's entry into the U.N. and recognition of China as the only government of China, he indicated in September 1971 that New-Japan Steel was ready to abide by Chou's four principles.[62]

The much-publicized *zaikai* mission to Peking in November 1971 was a vivid demonstration of *zaikai*'s growing interest in China as well as of its impatience with the current Sino-Japanese relationship. Upon returning from China, Shōji Takeo, head of the mission, was emphatic, as the Chinese had hoped, about the need to normalize relations with China, echoing the new Chinese position that Japan's "investments in Taiwan would not be adversely affected" by the normalization of Sino-Japanese relations on the terms of China's one-China position.[63] Osaka-based Kansai businessmen, while in Peking in September, also promised to "exert pressure upon the Satō government" to normalize relations with China.[64]

Zaikai's consensus-building on the China question was finally achieved with the acceptance of Chou's principles by Mitsui and Mitsubishi, and with the *volte face* of Uemura Kōgorō, chairman of Keidanren, in May 1972. Besides the growing pro-China mood in the business sector, many leaders were losing confidence in Satō's leadership. Largely in response to China's incessant attacks upon the premier, they ruled out normalization during the tenure of his government, a task that they felt could only be fulfilled by a post-Satō government more congenial to Peking. This explains why business leaders looked forward to the premier's early retirement.[65]

The Bureaucracy. Within the Satō government, intrabureaucratic division over the China issues was apparent. While the Ministry of International Trade and Industry (MITI) and other bureaucratic sectors close to business were sympathetic to its desire to expand trade with China and to improve the political climate of the Sino-Japanese relationship, the Foreign Ministry, known to have been rather oblivious to the domestic political implication of Japan's foreign policy, continued to support Japan's traditional policy of cooperation with Washington and Taipei.[66] For instance, the MITI and Finance and Transportation ministries were displeased with Satō's decision, shortly after he assumed office, to endorse the Foreign Ministry's recommendation on the validity of the Yoshida letter. The letter was a focal point of contention between the two conflicting bureaucratic sectors from then on. The MITI pressed for the scrapping of the letter and the authorization of Export-Import Bank loans; the Foreign Ministry was opposed on the ground that these actions would gravely jeopardize Japan's relations with Washington and especially Taipei. When MITI minister Miki made it known in August 1965 that his "administration is not bound to the letter," the Foreign Ministry quickly announced that "the moralistic implications of the letter cannot be ignored."[67] The "unified" position later adopted by the government merely stated that "the government is not legally bound to the letter." However, in its elaboration the Foreign Ministry stated that, although the "private" Yoshida letter was not binding legally, its moral aspects would not be neglected, and that applications for bank loans would be acted upon by the premier himself "after most careful consideration."[68]

When the controversy over governmental loans flared again in 1968, the Transportation Ministry was in the forefront of the movement within the bureaucracy for the use of bank loans. The movement, joined by the MITI and Finance, resulted in the formal repudiation of the Yoshida letter and the softening of the government's position on loans. Nudged by business, and aware that Satō's continued hesitancy hampered closer trade ties with China, the MITI began seriously to question the wisdom of the government's pro-Taipei and pro-Washington orientation. As China tightened the political strictures in the trade agreements, the MITI became noticeably sympathetic to those corporations forced to uphold China's insistence on the inseparability of politics and economics, while the Foreign Ministry harshly criticized China's political use of trade. While aware of the economic importance of Taiwan to Japan, the MITI was more interested in the potential (albeit unknown) of the China market. It was critical of Japan's continued cooperation with the United States and Taiwan in the U.N. that China would interpret as hostile to her.

Signs of dissension began to manifest themselves even within the Foreign Ministry. The dominant group, represented mainly by the U.N. and American bureaus, endorsed the traditional orientation toward Taipei and regarded close cooperation with Washington as the cornerstone of any foreign policy; the minority group, led by the Asian Bureau and especially its China Division (Chūgoku-ka), was less sympathetic to Taipei and more interested in improved relations with Peking.[69] By 1970, conflicts between the two groups became serious. For example, on the ever-controversial issue of Chinese representation in the U.N., the intraministerial groups were diametrically opposed to each other. Whereas the dominant group, supported by Satō, advocated a two-China formula and supported cosponsorship of the important-question resolution to keep Taiwan in the U.N., the Asian Bureau was inclined toward a one-China formula.

The question involving China trade was also a point of conflict between the China Division, then headed by Hashimoto Hiroshi, and the majority view endorsed by the dominant group and the top leadership of the Foreign Ministry. While a June 1971 report denied the prospect of significant growth in trade with China, the China Division took a contrary position as early as May 1970. Taking note of a general upward trend in China trade during the 1960s, the division's report attributed the increase to the "complementary nature of the economic needs of the two nations" and to "their having close geographical and historical relations." As for the prospects, "Japan can expect China, with its huge population and wealth of natural resources, to be a substantial trading partner, and trade levels will probably continue to rise."[70]

Despite the China group's growing doubts, the Foreign Ministry continued to be dominated by the pro-Taipei and pro-Washington elements. However, the dominant group and the ministry were dealt serious blows by the so-called Nixon shocks—his China announcement and his economic moves. The leadership was severely castigated by Satō and his right-hand man, LDP Secretary-General Hori Shigeru, and by other LDP leaders for "the lack of foresight" on international matters vital to Japan. The most serious blow came in the fall of 1971, when the U.N. rejected the controversial Japan-cosponsored important-question resolution and adopted instead the Albanian resolution admitting Peking as the sole legal government of China.[71]

The Opposition Parties. Although the opposition parties were united in their desire to normalize relations with China during the Satō period, their approaches differed considerably. The Japanese Socialist Party (JSP), long known as the leading domestic ally of China, was most supportive of both her claims and her criticisms of Tokyo's basic foreign policy orientation. Specifically, as early as 1960 the JSP advocated in its controversial Asanuma declaration that the nullification of the Japan-Taiwan treaty was the essential precondition to restoration of Sino-Japanese relations. The JSP was most actively involved in "people's diplomacy" with China. During its numerous missions to China the JSP periodically reaffirmed its endorsement of Peking's one-China position. Within the Diet the JSP served as the leading critic of the government's China stand although, with its perennial minority strength, it was denied participation in governmental decision-making. Through its labor affiliate, Sōhyō (General Council of Japanese Labor Unions), with over 4 million members representing 38 percent of the nation's organized workers, the JSP often launched extra-parliamentary campaigns to arouse public opinion in support of normalized Sino-Japanese relations. The largest of these campaigns, the National Conference for the Restoration of Japanese-Chinese Diplomatic Relations (Nitchū Kokkō Kaifuku Kokumin Kaigi), was initiated in December 1970, and was cosponsored by the Sōhyō and pro-JSP groups, although other opposition parties did not participate.[72] In addition, shortly after the formation of the National Conference, another nationwide movement involving the JSP and pro-JSP mayors and local assemblymen was launched to arouse public support at the grass-roots level for speedy normalization of relations with China.

In the early years of the Satō government, other opposition parties were less eager to endorse Chinese terms on normalization. In this sense, these parties were a mitigating influence upon the pro-Peking position the JSP was advocating. Opposing the JSP's position, the moderate Democratic Socialist Party (DSP) pursued a basically two-China policy during most of the 1960s and its contacts with China were limited.[73] Although by the late 1960s its position was more closely aligned with that of China, the party, as late as February 1970, argued that while Peking was the legitimate government of China and therefore entitled to represent China in the U.N., "the question involving Taiwan is both an international and domestic question that should be solved peacefully in accordance with the free will of the people on Taiwan."[74]

The DSP's China views experienced rather drastic changes following Nixon's announcement. The shift was largely attributable to the currency of the China issue and to the sudden rush to her by other opposition parties, especially by the Kōmeitō (Clean Government Party), which had followed a moderate policy toward China. When Wan Kuo-chuan came to attend the funeral of Matsumura in August 1971, DSP chairman Kasuga expressed his desire to visit China and concurred with the Chinese view that "Taiwan is nothing more than a province of China."[75] In addition to affirming Kasuga's statement, the DSP Central Executive Committee in its October 1971 meeting formally adopted the position that "the Japan-Taiwan peace treaty should be abrogated in the course of restoring Sino-Japanese diplomatic ties."[76] Going a step further, the Kasuga-led DSP mission which visited China in spring 1972, concurred fully with the Chinese view that "the Japan-Taiwan treaty, which is illegal and invalid, should be nullified [as] the essential preliminary to the restoration of Sino-Japanese diplomatic relations."[77]

The Kōmeitō's positions were hardly distinguishable from the DSP's in the early 1960s. On the Taiwan question the party favored giving the Taipei government a de facto status to safeguard Japan's interests on the island. Beginning in the late 1960s, however, the party, largely moved by the growing popularity of the China issue, adopted an increasingly active role in promoting the pro-China cause. Peking was now depicted as the only legal government of China, and Taiwan as "China's domestic problem" and of no concern to Japan. In 1970 the Kōmeitō set up the National Council for the Normalization of Japanese-Chinese Diplomatic Relations (Nitchū Kokkō Seijōka Kokumin Kyogikai). Composed of some 200 scholars, journalists, and artists, the council's purpose was the "waging of a suprapartisan campaign to arouse public opinion" in support of normalization. By the end of 1971, regional councils were established in major cities, and no less than 2000 celebrities had pledged their support. In June 1971, prior to his trip to China, Kōmeitō chairman Takeiri Yoshikatsu publicly endorsed for the first time the scrapping of the treaty with Taipei. In Peking the Kōmeitō mission assured the Chinese that their party supported China's basic positions on Sino-Japanese relations and was determined to "stop the rising militarism in Japan."[78]

The Japanese Communist Party (JCP), which turned avowedly anti-

Peking at the beginning of the Cultural Revolution in 1966, remained the only opposition party less than eager to champion Peking's terms for normalizing Sino-Japanese relations. While still committed to a one-China formula and the abrogation of the Tokyo-Taipei peace treaty, the JCP warned against "a hasty normalization of Japanese-Chinese relations without solving fundamental issues existing between Japan and China," an obvious criticism of other parties zealously accepting Peking's terms.[79]

The Press. Japan's leading dailies, *Asahi, Mainichi,* and *Yomiuri,* important agents of political communication in Japan, generally betray an antigovernmental leaning on most foreign policy issues. The China issue was no exception. As early as the 1950s, the dailies deplored the abnormal state of relations with China and berated the government for failing to assume a forward-looking posture toward her, although they did not go so far as to insist that Japan accept China's terms for normalization.

By the beginning of Satō's premiership, the press emerged as a leading advocate of Peking's political terms for normalization and a critic of the government's China posture. *Asahi, Yomiuri, Nihon Keizai,* Japan's *Wall Street Journal,* and the Kyōdō Tsūshin, Japan's largest wire service, were much in tune with Peking's positions in their editorials.[80] The dailies had endorsed Chou En-lai's three political principles editorially and tacitly ever since 1964, when an agreement on exchange of reporters was first signed. These principles were reaffirmed secretly by the dailies in 1968 in return for the stationing of their newsmen in Peking.[81]

Although *Mainichi* was not a party to the 1968 "secret" agreement, its editorial stance on China did not differ significantly from that of the dailies that had accepted the Chou principles. This was due in large part to the currency of the China issue as well as the competitiveness of Japanese journalism. In fact, beginning in January 1970, all the leading dailies initiated unusually active China coverage, and news derogatory to China was conspicuous by its absence.

Public Opinion. During Satō's incumbency, public opinion changed dramatically in favor of Peking, and the minority view critical of the government's policy grew to be the dominant public sentiment by 1971. A *Mainichi* survey taken in November 1964 showed that 30 percent endorsed "a speedy restoration" of Sino-Japanese relations and another 30 percent supported greater economic and cultural interactions before diplomatic ties were established, the remainder representing other views and the uninformed.[82] A survey conducted by *Yomiuri* in April 1964 revealed that 63 percent supported China's entry into the U.N.[83] The *Asahi* polls taken between January 1970 and September 1971 were most revealing of the changing public mood. The poll, taken at the height of "ping pong diplomacy" in May 1971, showed that as many as 70 percent of LDP supporters favored the normalization of Sino-Japanese relations. Of those polled, 33 percent endorsed the Chinese position that Peking was the only legal government of China, while only 22 percent were opposed. The results of the 1971 survey represented a drastic contrast to the June 1970 poll, which showed that as many as 46 percent were opposed to Peking's one-China claim, while 19 percent supported it.[84] According to an August 1971 *Asahi* survey, conducted shortly after the Nixon announcement, 63 percent supported immediate initiation of negotiations for the restoration of Sino-Japanese relations. An equal percentage of the respondents endorsed Satō's visit to Peking with a view to restoring diplomatic ties with China. When questioned about Satō's leadership, 36 percent felt that under Satō's premiership Japan's China policy would not change, while 21 percent were opposed to this view, with 38 percent not responding.[85]

IV.

The changing domestic climate was reflected increasingly in the Satō government's China gestures. Beginning in 1970, the government began to vacillate between the traditional pro-Taipei orientation and a forward-looking posture toward China. In fact, Satō's departure from his traditional stand became progressively noticeable in proportion to the growing clamor for improved relations with China. In his 1970 annual policy speech before the Diet, Satō stressed that he "expected the Peking government to assume a cooperative and constructive" attitude toward other countries. He also stated that while "maintaining friendly relations with South Korea and Taiwan," his government planned to promote increased contacts and exchanges of personnel with China. These "cumulative efforts," he hoped, would lead to "an improvement of friendly relations" between the two countries. In the speech, the premier purposely called China "the Peking government" for the first time and made no reference to the separation of political and economic relations. Furthermore, he did not rule out the possibility of governmental contacts with China.[86] Foreign Minister Aichi Kiichi told Taipei's envoy to Tokyo that his government would adhere to the policy of maintaining and promoting friendship with Taiwan but that there was nothing wrong with Tokyo's desire to initiate governmental contact with Peking through their legations in a third nation.[87] In fact, there is reasonable evidence that the Satō government made several attempts to establish ambassador-level contacts with Peking in 1969 and 1970.[88]

Peking ignored Tokyo's interests and gestures. Instead, it denounced Satō's alleged collusion with Nixon to create two Chinas, Tokyo's continued support of Taipei's U.N. membership, and the alleged revival of militarism in Japan.[89] Peking also made it clear that Satō, in view of his commitment

to Taipei and his close identification with pro-Taipei members of the LDP
led by his own brother, would never be able to bring about the normalization of Sino-Japanese relations.

Apart from the considerable support for Taipei still existing in the
LDP and *zaikai,* the two major pillars of the conservative government,
Satō's own assessment of international politics dictated his reluctance to
make any concessions on Taiwan. As China recovered from the turbulence
of the Cultural Revolution, and as her dispute with Moscow continued to
intensify, Satō seriously entertained the possibility that Peking, despite its
anti-Satō verbiage, might consent to normalizing relations with Japan,
with the Taiwan issue unsettled. Satō assumed that Peking, in order to avoid
being hemmed in by its neighbors, might agree to normalization on less
desirable terms.[90] The Satō government believed that, in the words of
Kimura Toshio, "as far as Asian problems are concerned, Japanese-
American cooperation is the most essential requirement" and that "the
Chinese question will never be solved without mutual understanding and
cooperation between Japan and the U.S."[91] Tokyo, interpreting Nixon's
China gestures as mostly preliminary, assumed that it would be some time
before Washington and Peking could sit down for serious talks on outstanding issues. Tokyo steadfastly presumed that Japan would be invited to
participate as Washington's primary Asian partner in every important
phase of Sino-American negotiations. It was for this reason that the Nixon
announcement was all the more disappointing to the Satō government.

Afterward, the government's China stand, though still committed to
maintaining "close and amicable ties" with Taiwan, came to reflect the
changing mood of the major pillars of the conservative government. In
response to the critics' charge that Japan was being overtaken by Washington in approaching China, Satō stated that he too was willing to go to
China to discuss normalization with Chinese leaders. In an October 1971
speech, Satō accepted for the first time that Peking was the legitimate
representative of China and expressed the hope that the fate of Taiwan
would be settled "through negotiations between the parties concerned."[92]
However, Satō's decision of September 1971 to cosponsor with the United
States the two-China resolutions (to keep Taiwan and admit China in the
U.N.) was unpopular even among his traditional supporters.

While deciding to cosponsor the ill-fated resolutions, Satō concluded
that the rapidly changing domestic political climate dictated more positive
China moves on his part, though he remained cautious not to upset the pro-
Taipei members of the LDP and an important sector of *zaikai* still
committed to the support of Taipei. Even before the U.N. voted to replace
Taipei with Peking, Satō sent a message to Chou En-lai, in the name of LDP
Secretary-General Hori Shigeru, in which Satō accepted two of China's
preconditions for normalization (i.e., Peking is the only government of
China, and Taiwan is a province of China) and expressed his willingness to

meet the third condition (i.e., abrogation of the Japan-Taiwan treaty) "in the course of negotiations" between Tokyo and Peking. The letter also indicated that the secretary-general wished to visit Peking to open government-to-government communication.[93]

Satō was given a humiliating rebuff by Chou. The Chinese premier told Minobe Ryōkichi, JSP governor of Tokyo and the carrier of the letter, that Satō and the Hori letter could not be trusted.[94] China would not negotiate with Satō but his successor would be welcome in Peking as long as he accepted the three basic principles. This argument was repeated over and over by Chou to other Japanese visitors including members of the LDP and *zaikai* leaders. Satō's critics as well as a growing number of his traditional supporters came to conclude that Satō was a lame-duck premier. It was obvious that China's Japan strategy centered on a dual objective: to end the Satō government and to normalize relations with Japan under a premier acceptable to China. Indeed, China's adamant anti-Satō posture facilitated the fall of the Satō regime.[95]

Notes

1. Douglas H. Mendel, Jr., *The Japanese People and Foreign Policy* (Berkeley, 1961), pp. 215–44.

2. Arai Takeo, "Sengo Nitchū kankei-shi" [A history of postwar Sino-Japanese relations], *Sekai*, no. 324, November 1972, p. 148.

3. See Adlai Stevenson, "Putting First Things First: A Democratic View," *Foreign Affairs* 38: 2 (January 1960): 191–208; Chester Bowles, "The 'China Problem' Reconsidered," *Foreign Affairs* 38: 3 (April 1960): 477–78.

4. "Sengo Nitchū kankei no tenkai to kokkō seijōka" [Development of postwar relations and the normalization of diplomatic relations between Japan and China], *Chōsa geppō*, no. 205, January 1973, p. 5.

5. *Asahi Shimbun*, 5 October 1960.

6. Ibid., 30 July 1960.

7. Ibid., 30 August 1960.

8. Nakasone Yasuhiro, "Japan and the China Problem: A Liberal-Democratic View," *Japan Quarterly*, 8: 3 (July–September 1961): 265–71.

9. *Mainichi International Edition*, 1 July 1961.

10. When Dean Rusk, Kennedy's secretary of state, was asked if his administration might consider changing its attitude toward China in the near future, he emphatically replied: "None whatever, none whatever. And Peking has made it clear that they would not themselves even consider such a matter quite apart from our attitude unless we were to abandon Formosa, which we are not going to do; so that is not an active question at all." See *Department of State Bulletin*, 17 July 1961, p. 113.

11. *Asahi*, 20 September 1962 (morning and evening editions).

12. Ibid., 10 November 1962.

13. Arai, op. cit., p. 149.

14. Matsumoto Shigeharu, "Japan and China," in *Policies Toward China: Views from Six Continents*, ed. A.M. Halpern (New York, 1964), p. 138.

15. See the editorial in *Jen-min Jih-pao*, 4 January 1962. In the September 13, 1961, issue of the same paper, Peking called Ikeda "a reactionary" and compared him to Kishi. Later, Peking stated that "Premier Ikeda says he is trying to improve Sino-Japanese relations with a forward-looking attitude, but this is not true. He is solely concerned with winning more electoral votes. . . . The so-called forward-looking approach of his is really designed to antagonize China and to create two Chinas in deference to the U.S." See *Jen-min Jih-pao*, 23 December 1961.

16. Arai, op. cit., p. 149.

17. During his talk with Chou En-lai on July 10, 1961, Utsunomiya reportedly said that "Premier Ikeda is forward-looking, and China is well advised not to take any action that might have a dampening effect on his forward-looking approach." See Chūgoku Sōgo Kenkyūkai, [China Mutual Study Society], *Chūgoku no jittai to Nitchū shinkankei no arikata* [The realities of China and the current state of Sino-Japanese relations] (Tokyo, 1962), 12: 77. According to Tagawa Seiichi, an aide to Matsumura and later a leading LDP advocate of improved Sino-Japanese relations, one of the major reasons Matsumura supported Ikeda's bid for a third term as LDP president was the premier's positive China policy. See Tagawa Seiichi, *Matsumura Kenzō to Chūgoku* [Matsumura Kenzō and China] (Tokyo, 1972), p. 119.

18. "Sengo Nitchū kankei no tenkai to kokkō seijōka," op. cit., p. 6.

19. *Asahi*, 5 March 1964 (evening edition). For an elaboration of the unified governmental view, see Halpern, op. cit., pp. 160–64.

20. *Asahi*, 4 June 1964 (evening edition).

21. *Yomiuri Shimbun*, ed., *Nihon no jinmyaku: Zaikai* [Japan's terrain of personalities: Business community] (Tokyo, 1972), pp. 271–72. Matsubara of Hitachi was one of the leading advocates for the scrapping of the controversial letter.

22. *Asahi*, 31 January and 13 February 1964.

23. Samejima Keiji, "Nit-Chū fukkōeno michisuji" [The road to the restoration of Sino-Japanese diplomatic relations], *Chūō Kōron* [Central Review], December 1971, p. 91. See also Tagawa, op. cit., pp. 120–21.

24. See *Jen-min Jih-pao*, 21 November 1964.

25. *Asahi nenkan* [Asahi almanac] (Tokyo, 1965), p. 297; *Asahi*, 4 December 1964.

26. *Asahi*, 20 November and 2 December 1964.

27. Tagawa, op. cit., p. 121.

28. Samejima, op. cit., pp. 91, 92.

29. *Asahi*, 14 January 1965 (evening edition). See *Jen-min Jih-pao*, 20 January 1965, for Peking's reaction to Satō's Washington visit.

30. Ōta Takehide, "Jimintō" [Liberal-Democratic Party], *Chūō Kōron*, December 1971, p. 112.

31. *Jen-min Jih-pao*, 23 June and 13 November 1965.

32. Arai, op. cit., p. 150.

33. *Asahi*, 8 September 1967.

34. Arai, op. cit., p. 150.

35. Ibid.

36. For Nixon's elaboration of the Guam Doctrine (or the Nixon Doctrine) as it is applied to Asia, see Richard Nixon, *U.S. Foreign Policy for the 1970s: A New Strategy for Peace* (Washington, D.C., 1970), pp. 53–76. For a discussion of these indications, see the author's "Ties with Red China, Not Easy Task for Japan," *Korea Times,* 25 January 1970.

37. One Japanese observer noted that in 1969 Tokyo was more eager than Washington to endorse the important-question formula. See *Mainichi Shimbun,* ed., *Chūgoku mondai* [The China problem] (Tokyo, 1970), p. 46. Japan's U.N. envoy "seriously doubted that the admission of China into the U.N. at the present time will make any positive contribution to enhancing the prestige of the U.N." (ibid., p. 57). *Chūgoku mondai* is a record of proceedings of a round table discussion sponsored by the Mainichi Shimbun-sha in the spring of 1970. The participants included representatives of all political parties as well as a number of leading students of Sino-Japanese relations.

38. For the Nixon-Satō communiqué, see *Asahi,* 22 November 1969. In its December 10, 1964, meeting the committee urged the United States to take a tougher posture against China in view of her growing nuclear arsenal. The committee also advocated that all conflicts in Asia were solely attributable to China's aggressiveness and that all "free" nations should unite to contain her aggression, and urged that the Tokyo government refrain from taking any conciliatory step toward China and from getting involved in trade deals with the mainland. See *Asahi,* 11 December 1964. During the committee's tenth meeting in 1965, Adachi Tadashi, chief of the Japanese delegation, reportedly referred to China as an armed madman and a real destroyer of international peace. See Fukui Haruhiro, *Party in Power: The Japanese Liberal-Democrats and Policy-Making* (Berkeley, 1970), p. 246.

39. Samejima, op. cit., p. 92.

40. Robert A. Scalapino, "The Cultural Revolution and Chinese Foreign Policy," *Current Scene* (1 August 1968), p. 7.

41. "Sengo Nitchū kankei no tenkai to kokkō seijōka," op. cit., p. 6. See also *Akahata,* 4 November 1967.

42. For a good analysis of JSP politics, see Chae-jin Lee, "Factional Politics in the Japan Socialist Party: The Chinese Cultural Revolution Case," *Asian Survey* 10: 3 (March 1970): 230–43.

43. *Asahi,* 24 December 1964. For factional representation in the Asian-African and Asian groups, see Ogata Sadako, "Japanese Attitude toward China," *Asian Survey* 5: 8 (August 1965): 395.

44. *Asahi,* 15 March (evening edition) and 16 March 1968; 4 April 1968 (evening edition).

45. Ibid., 26 May 1968.

46. For a discussion of the moves by Nixon and their impact on Japan, see the author's "The Response of Japan and South Korea to the Changing Orientation of the Sino-American Relationship" (paper presented at the annual meeting of the Association for Asian Studies, Western Conference, San Diego, October 1971). For Furui's remarkable foresight, see *Chūgoku mondai,* pp. 54, 92–94.

47. Utsunomiya Tokuma, "Nitchū kōwa wa isoganeba naranai" [Peace between Japan and China must be speedily concluded], *Sekai,* no. 313, December 1971, p. 41. For an excellent analysis of the league, see Yamamura Tokuzō, "Giin dairengō no shiwaku" [The thinking of the Great Federation of Dietmen], *Chūō Kōron,* February 1971, pp. 98–105.

48. Yamamura, op. cit., p. 103.

49. LDP factions usually do not function as "policy groups," and factional lines on policy issues are not clear. See *Yomiuri Shimbun* Seijibu, *Seitō* [Political parties] (Tokyo, 1966), pp. 86–89.

50. These principles were: Peking is the only legitimate government of China representing the entire people of China; Taiwan is a province of the Peking government; the Japanese-Taiwanese peace treaty, which is illegal and invalid, should be abrogated; Taiwan should be expelled from all organs of the U.N. See *New York Times*, 4 October 1971.

51. Vote-boycotting, though not unprecedented, is seldom resorted to by LDP Dietmen as a form of protest against the government. Thus, the absence of 12 members, though a small segment of the LDP parliamentary group, must be considered a serious sign of intraparty opposition to the government's policy. Five of the 12 dissidents were affiliated with the Miki faction, while Miki himself voted against the no-confidence motions. For reasons given by the dissidents for the action, see *Sandē Mainichi*, 21 November 1971, pp. 16–21.

52. Apparently unaware of Miki's long record of opposition to the government's China policy, Sheldon W. Simon argues that Wang's visit was responsible for "the apparent conversion" of Miki into a pro-Peking champion. See Simon's "China and Japan: Approach-Avoidance Relations," *Current Scene* (7 January 1972), p. 3.

53. *Asahi*, 2 September 1971.

54. Ōta, op. cit., pp. 122–23. For a view representative of this junior group, see Kōno Yōhei, "Aeteyū 'Jimintō kaitō-ron' " [I dare to advocate "Dissolution of the LDP"], *Bungei Shunjū*, January 1972, pp. 144–51.

55. See *Asahi nenkan* (1970), pp. 293–94, for a summary of the joint communiqué.

56. For a summary of the 1970 communiqué, see *Asahi nenkan* (1971), pp. 301–2; for the 1971 communiqué, see *Asahi nenkan* (1972), p. 261.

57. For a discussion of *zaikai*'s role, see *Asahi*, 7 September 1972. Commenting on the role of *zaikai* in the politics of the LDP, Robert Scalapino notes that "the commercial and industrial groups have the greatest single influence on the Liberal-Democratic Party, especially in the field of foreign policy." I agree with this view. For Scalapino's discussion, see his "The Foreign Policy of Modern Japan," in *Foreign Policy in World Politics*, ed. Roy C. Macridis, 4th ed. (Englewood Cliffs, 1972), p. 348. For a good analysis of intra-*zaikai* divisions on the China issue, see Yamamura Kenichirō, "Saihensei ni yureru 'yūkō shōsha' " [Friendly firms in the midst of reorganization], *Asahi Jānaru* (7 April 1972), pp. 85–90.

58. See Japan, Ministry of Foreign Affairs, Asian Affairs Bureau, China Affairs Division, "The Present State of Japan-China Trade," *Current Scene* (1 May 1970), p. 6.

59. *Asahi*, 4 August 1965, and 21 February 1968.

60. Yamamura Kenichirō, op. cit., pp. 85–86.

61. For an analysis of China's attacks on Satō, see Osanai Takayuki, "Chūkyō wa kokkō o nozonde inai" [Communist China does not wish to normalize relations], *Jiyū* 13: 5 (May 1971): 37–38.

62. *Asahi*, 3 September 1971.

63. Shōji stated: "Premier Chou En-lai told us that he hoped we would try to convey the demand of the [Japanese] people for normalization of [Sino-Japanese] diplomatic relations to political leaders. We feel we ought to do this for the sake of Japan's future." *Asahi*, 23 November 1971.

64. Yamamura Kenichirō, op. cit., p. 90.

65. Ibid.

66. Hans H. Baerwald notes that in foreign policy matters disputes between the Foreign Ministry and the MITI are "not uncommon." See his article, "Japan," in Wayne Wilcox et al., *Asia and the International System* (Cambridge, Mass., 1972), pp. 32-60.

67. *Asahi,* 3 August 1965.

68. Ibid., 4 August 1965.

69. According to Tagawa Seiichi, high-ranking Foreign Ministry officials were either afraid or reluctant to approach Matsumura for current information on China after his return in 1970. The only exceptions were Japan's consul-general in Hong Kong and the China Division's chief Hashimoto. See Tagawa, op. cit., pp. 134-46.

70. "The Present State of Japan-China Trade," p. 7.

71. To argue that the decision was solely or even primarily influenced by the Foreign Ministry's optimistic assessment is to assign a dominant role to the ministry in the making of the important-question decision. There is reasonable evidence that Washington's intense campaign of persuasion, personally conducted by Secretary Rogers, played a critical role in Satō's decision. See *Asahi,* 22 (evening edition) and 23 September 1971. Furthermore, when the ministry submitted what Hori deemed unduly optimistic reports to the premier, it may have followed what it felt was a course of action desired by him. As one official said, "In studying the issue of Chinese representation at the U.N., we have been greatly perplexed because the attitude of Prime Minister Satō has not been clear. At one time he showed a positive stance; at another time his stance was drawn back." See *Japan Times Weekly,* 23 October 1971.

72. Yamamura Tokuzō, op. cit., p. 98.

73. For DSP views at this time, see Sone Eki, "Japan and the China Problem—A Democratic Socialist View," *Japan Quarterly* 8: 3 (July–September 1961): 286–97.

74. *Asahi nenkan* (1972), p. 267. For an elaboration of the party's views by its foreign affairs chairman, see Nagasue Eiichi, "Nihon gaikō to kakushin saihensei" [Japan's foreign relations and the reorganization of progressive forces], *Jiyū* 13: 3 (March 1971): 46–47.

75. *Asahi,* 30 August 1971 (evening edition).

76. *Asahi nenkan* (1972), p. 276.

77. For the text of the DSP-China communiqué, see *Asahi,* 14 April 1972.

78. Ibid., 4 July 1971.

79. *Asahi nenkan* (1973), p. 222.

80. For an analysis of press views on China, see Irie Michimasa, "Chūgoku mondai odoru masukomi" [Mass media dancing to the tune of the China problem], *Jiyū* 13: 5 (May 1971): 28–35.

81. *Los Angeles Times,* 14 April 1972. See also "Sengo Nitchū kankei no tenkai to kokkō seijōka," op. cit., p. 7.

82. *Mainichi,* 14 December 1964.

83. *Yomiuri Shimbun,* 19 April 1964.

84. *Asahi,* 3 June 1971.

85. Ibid., 21 September 1971.

86. Ibid., 2 February 1970 (evening edition).

87. *New York Times,* 30 June 1972.

88. *Asahi,* 22 September 1972 (evening edition).

89. *Jen-min jih-pao,* 1 November and 11 December 1970.

90. Kimura Toshio, deputy director of the cabinet secretariat under Satō, referred to his government's knowledge of contacts initiated between Moscow and Taipei that might lead to trade ties between the two. See *Chūgoku mondai,* p. 76.

91. Ibid, p. 62.

92. *New York Times,* 20 October 1971.

93. *Jiji nenkan* (Tokyo, 1973), p. 45. See also *New York Times, 21 November 1971.*

94. Fujiyama said Chinese leaders had told him that "Premier Satō always contradicts his previous Diet statements on China, and we cannot tell if he has really changed his [anti-China] positions." See *Asahi,* 21 September 1972.

95. Indications are that pro-Peking members of the LDP advocated Satō's speedy retirement and refused to support Satō in his efforts to establish contacts with China. For example, they refused to serve as intermediaries between the premier and Wang Kuo-ch'uan, who represented China at the funeral of Matsumura. See "Nitchū o dannenshita Satō taisei" [The Satō regime that gave up on Sino-Japanese normalization], *Sekai,* no. 312, November 1971, pp. 214–18.

16.

Yung Park's second essay probes the dynamics underlying new Premier Tanaka Kakuei's dramatic trip to Peking. Focusing on the domestic political climate in Japan, Park shows how the machinery and the will for rapprochement, set back by Satō's deference to Washington and Taipei, crystallized in the era of Tanaka, who was able to proceed with alacrity in response to signals received from Peking. From the Park essays, one sees how the roots took hold and how the various elements of the Japanese political structure contributed to the turnabout in China policy. Of course, an undercurrent of tension remains below the friendly verbal exchanges that accompanied the belated establishment of relations between Peking and Tokyo, but the important thing was that a Japanese prime minister had finally taken the trip to Canossa, and that a new start was at least possible in the long, long search for Sino-Japanese balance.

Park's essay is based upon a longer paper, "The Politics of the China Decision: Observations on Japanese Foreign Policy-Making," delivered before the annual meeting of Asian Studies on the Pacific Coast at San Diego in June 1974.

The Tanaka Government and the Mechanics of the China Decision

Yung H. Park

I.

As recently as 1970, Liberal-Democratic Party (LDP) Dietman Furui Yoshimi, long a leading advocate of a Japan-China détente, was severely reprimanded by many of his partisan colleagues for endorsing China's terms for the normalization of Sino-Japanese relations. Only two years later, in September 1972, the new premier of Japan, Tanaka Kakuei, made the historic trip to Peking which resulted in the establishment of diplomatic ties with China largely on terms long advocated by the Chinese.

The establishment of Sino-Japanese diplomatic ties would have been an impressive addition to what Satō Eisaku regarded as his major external accomplishment—Okinawa reversion—and would have made his "glorious exit" (*hanamichi*) possible. By spring 1972, China was the major foreign policy issue, and Satō's potential successors were judged by their ability to come to terms with it. All five front-runners—Fukuda, Tanaka, Ōhira Masayoshi, Miki, and Nakasone—capitalized on the China issue in their campaign strategies. Nakasone took the position that the post-Satō government would have to accept Chou's three conditions "in principle" before initiating normalization talks with China.[1] Fukuda accepted Peking as the legitimate government of China but refused to endorse the abrogation of the Tokyo-Taipei treaty. He merely advocated dealing with the Taiwan problem in the course of normalization negotiations, a position identical with Satō's.[2] Peking, deeply involved in the LDP presidential contest,[3] asserted that Fukuda was persona non grata and it would not deal with him. As a result, business leaders, though initially favorably inclined toward

Tōdai-educated, bureaucrat Fukuda, now leaned toward other front-runners agreeable to Peking.

Of the five contenders, Miki alone was invited to China during the party presidential campaign. He let it be known that, if he succeeded Satō, "he would be prepared promptly to meet all Peking's conditions, including a complete break with Taiwan, in order to establish relations with Peking."[4] Tanaka skillfully combined his presidential campaigns and the politics of the China question. To neutralize Peking, he successfully cultivated the impression among Chinese leaders that he was eager to normalize Sino-Japanese relations. In an April 21, 1972, meeting with Ōhira and Furui, held in utmost secrecy, Tanaka pledged to Furui, about to leave for China, that if chosen premier, he would appoint Ōhira, whose China views were well known to Chinese leaders, as his foreign minister, and work to establish relations with China. By committing himself to the formation of a "Tanaka–Ōhira axis," Tanaka hoped to impress Peking leaders and to garner China's support in the final party presidential contest.[5] In fact, Furui told his Chinese hosts that the Tanaka–Ōhira team was eager to bring about the normalization of Sino-Japanese relations. Tanaka also sent a personal message to Chou via the May 1972 Kōmeitō mission in which he reiterated his pledge to work for normalization. Chou's response was: "If, upon assuming the premiership, you are determined to wrestle with the normalization task, we will refrain from doing anything that might embarrass you."[6] With Peking thus neutralized, Tanaka proceeded to form a winning coalition of factions within the party.

The key to Tanaka's winning coalition was an agreement by Tanaka, Ōhira, Miki, and Nakasone stipulating that whoever was in the runoff against Fukuda would gain the support of the others. On June 29, Nakasone withdrew his candidacy in favor of Tanaka, delivering a large bloc of votes. The key to the anti-Fukuda coalition was the so-called *sampa* (tripartite) pact under which Tanaka, Ōhira, and Miki pledged "to initiate negotiations (with China) for the purpose of signing a Japan-China peace treaty."[7] Although the details of the agreement are not known, one may assume that Tanaka and Ōhira, who were consulting with each other as early as February, accepted Miki's most forward-looking China views as the cornerstone of the new mainstream-faction government's China posture.[8] In a functional sense, the tripartite pact, concluded at the peak of the party's presidential contest, virtually concluded Japan's decision making on the China question.

When Tanaka formed his government, with Ōhira as his foreign minister and Miki as his deputy premier, his major task was to achieve within his own party the necessary consensus on a new policy toward China.[9] This task was by no means easy. Although the dominant opinion within the party was in favor of normalizing relations with China even on the latter's terms, a significant minority, led by such right-wingers as Kishi, Ishii Mitsujirō, Kaya, and Fukuda, was adamantly opposed to writing Taipei off.

In his partisan consensus-building, however, the new premier was aided by a number of factors, both external and domestic. Peking's attitude toward Tanaka was vitally important. Chou wasted no time and extended an invitation for Tanaka and Ōhira to visit Peking without mentioning the three principles as a precondition. Chou also disclosed that China would waive any claim against Japan for war reparations, and that the U.S.-Japan security pact and the controversial 1969 Satō–Nixon communiqué would not hinder the normalization of Tokyo-Peking relations. Furthermore, he proposed to conclude with Japan a treaty of peace and friendship which would invalidate the Tokyo-Taipei treaty.[10] China's gestures were understandable, at least in part, in view of Tanaka's groundwork vis-à-vis China.

Washington's China posture was another external element working in favor of the new Tanaka government. The February 1972 Nixon–Chou communiqué declared that "there is but one China" and that "Taiwan is a part of China." Nixon also stated in the communiqué that Washington's ultimate objective was to "withdraw all its forces and military installations from Taiwan."[11] These statements dispelled whatever doubt the Japanese might still have had about Nixon's determination to achieve détente with Peking while leaving the Taiwan question to be solved by the Chinese themselves. Shortly after assuming his post, Ōhira announced that his government would proceed with the normalization of Sino-Japanese relations "at its own discretion" and keep Washington appropriately informed. Later, Ōhira assured Kissinger that improved Sino-Japanese relations would not impair the U.S.-Japan security framework. Washington gave no indication of displeasure with Tokyo's China gestures. Instead, Nixon shared Tokyo's view that Tanaka's China visit would contribute to the relaxation of tension in Asia and would not damage the transpacific alliance system even if Japan broke its diplomatic ties with Taiwan.

As for the domestic factors aiding Tanaka's consensus-building in the party, *zaikai* was a decisive one. *Zaikai,* whose consensus-building on China preceded the LDP's, played a powerful role in the party's decision making in a number of ways. The business community withdrew its support of Satō, which contributed to his "premature" retirement. Although they shunned active involvement in the party's presidential contest, *zaikai* leaders did not hesitate to express their preference for a premier better able to lead Japan in a growingly multipolar world and to cope with the China question. Some *zaikai* leaders even sided with specific positions advocated by presidential contenders. Addressing a Nisshō executive committee meeting, Miki, just back from Peking, stressed that "the only way to normalize relations with

Peking" was on the basis of Peking's three principles. Responding to Miki's speech, Nagano (chairman of the Nisshō) stated that "the Japanese-Taiwanese treaty is illegal and thus should be abrogated"[12]—the first time a major *zaikai* leader had made such a comment.

Most disturbing to pro-Taipei members of the LDP was the obvious tendency of *zaikai* leaders to shift support to the pro-Peking elements of the party. *Zaikai's* attempt to influence the LDP took an increasingly organizational form. A number of business-sponsored ad hoc groups were formed to serve as the "China lobby." Osaka-based (Kansai) businessmen, led by Saeki Isamu, chairman of the Osaka Chamber of Commerce and Industry, set up the Nitchū Mondai Kondankai (Society for the Study of Japan-China Problems) as a forum for Kansai businessmen and LDP supporters of normalization. Later, the society's membership was widened to include Tokyo-based *zaikai* leaders. Through the society and other groups and personal contacts with members of the LDP, *zaikai* was actively involved in the party's China debate and decision making. Business supported in other ways Tanaka's effort to seek the party's consensus. When the new government was formed, *zaikai* leaders, including chairmen of the four major business associations as well as heads of Japan's leading industrial giants, quickly rallied behind the new premier and formed the Ishinkai (Restoration Society).[13]

All the opposition parties recognized the new government's commitment to normalization, and, though motivated by varying partisan considerations,[14] followed the unprecedented policy of cooperating with the LDP government while urging the government publicly to accept China's three political principles. The press also welcomed the new government's basic China orientation, although some dailies (e.g., *Asahi*) urged that the government be more explicit in its intention on the Taiwan question.

Bolstered by public support—the new premier, noted for his dynamic personality, was immensely popular with the public—the government played an active and direct role in the party's decision making. Tanaka let it be known that he intended to move promptly on the China question. In July, shortly after he came to power, Tanaka created the LDP Council for the Normalization of Japan-China Relations (Nitchū Seijōka Kyōgikai), led by members of the LDP who supported an early normalization (e.g., council chairman Kosaka Zentarō of the Ōhira faction), for the purpose of intraparty consensus-building. Composed of more than 300 LDP Dietmen, the council was readily dominated by normalization supporters. Brushing aside the Foreign Ministry's suggestion that in view of China's demonstrated eagerness to conclude an early peace treaty with Japan, Japan had more to gain from a wait-and-see approach than from a hastily concluded normalization treaty, Tanaka personally instructed the ministry to proceed under the assumption that early normalization was inevitable. Tanaka also made it clear to the council that he correctly sensed an "overwhelming mood for normalization" in the country and was sympathetic to China's political principles, although, in deference to the pro-Taipei members of the LDP, he avoided making any more definite commitments to the principles.[15]

The pro-Taipei group, now a minority and in the camp of the antimainstream factions, did not give in easily. Although no longer opposed to normalization per se, Kishi, Kaya, Ishii, and others waged vigorous campaigns to dissuade the government from yielding to Peking on the crucial Taiwan question. The premier was personally urged by the Soshinkai and members of the Asian Parliamentary Union, two major pro-Taipei groups in the party, to go slow in his China approach and to exercise "utmost caution" in handling the Taiwan problem.[16] Understandably, the Fukuda faction emerged as a leader in the fight against the China bandwagon within the party. Composed of 65 lower-house members of the LDP and led by Fukuda, Tanaka's main rival for the party presidency, the Yōkakai warned against betraying "old friends" (i.e., Taipei) while supporting the establishment of relations with China.

Uninhibited by these moves, Foreign Minister Ōhira announced that "the Japan-Taiwan treaty will cease to have its validity when Japan-China relations are normalized." This position was later issued as part of the government's official "Basic Views on Normalization."[17] In an attempt to expedite the party's deliberation, Ōhira disclosed before the council (August 3, 1972) that his government had received an official Chinese invitation for the premier to visit China and was expected to respond shortly. Furthermore, even before the council's deliberation was over, the party's Executive Committee (Sōmukai), chaired by an Ōhira-faction leader, adopted a resolution (tōgi) in the name of the party welcoming the speedy normalization of Sino-Japanese relations and Tanaka's visit to China for this purpose.[18]

Acting under specific instructions from the premier, the council's progovernment leadership managed to reach a preliminary five-point decision in late August, to guide the government in reestablishing relations with China. While upholding the U.N. Charter and the 1955 Bandung principles of peaceful coexistence, the resolution called for: mutual respect for different political and social systems; noninterference in the domestic affairs of other nations; mutual nonuse of force or the threat of force; expansion of cultural and economic exchanges; and cooperation in the promotion of peace and prosperity in Asia. On the controversial Taiwan question, the resolution, not specifying conditions that would limit the government, noted the existence within the party of "the strong opinion that sufficient consideration should be given to maintaining Japan-Taiwan relations."[19] In an angry reaction to this part of the resolution, pro-Taipei council members charged that the council ignored "strong friendship for the Republic of China," and insisted that "utmost caution" be exercised in negotiating with Peking—no matter how long it might take—so that Japan's ties with the island would be maintained.[20]

A compromise reached later read: "In view of the close relationship between Japan and the Republic of China, negotiations should be conducted giving sufficient consideration to that relationship." On the very day the compromise version was adopted, Fukuda broke his long silence following his failure to capture the party presidency, and criticized the government's "hasty approach" toward China. Specifically, he advocated the so-called Three Principles on Normalization, which opposed the termination of Tokyo-Taipei relations, among other things.[21]

II.

The advent of a new premier in 1972 affected one important aspect of Japan's foreign policy, namely, relations with China. This seems to fit in with the postwar pattern of major changes in Japan's foreign policy occurring with the emergence of a new premier. The normalization of Japan-China relations was brought about not because Tanaka was a bolder kind of politician than his predecessors but because the domestic situation was ripe for a change of policy once the premiership changed hands. In view of China's unusual enthusiasm for a settlement with Japan after Tanaka came to power, Japan perhaps had more to gain from a slow approach than from a hasty one. Perhaps the Foreign Ministry's suggestion was valid. However, domestic political considerations (e.g., the China bandwagon and especially the consensus among the pillars of the conservative government) dictated that the new premier act promptly and decisively on the China issue. Thus, the premier was not the leader of the Japanese polity; he was the follower of the national consensus.

The decision to establish relations with China largely on her terms was made by Tanaka with the participation of Ōhira and Miki, two mainstream faction-chiefs whose backing was crucial to Tanaka's victory in his presidential fight with Fukuda. The premier and his close associates, the center of decision making, however, did not operate independently of the major elements of Japanese politics. The question is, Which of these elements had the most to do with the government's China decision? The government's decision was not significantly affected by the opposition parties, which could not develop a unified policy, or by the press, which had long advocated Tokyo's acceptance of China's political conditions prior to the initiation of normalization talks. The dominant influences on the government were undoubtedly the LDP and *zaikai*. The Satō government's vacillations between its pro-Taipei tradition and a forward-looking posture toward Peking reflected the gradual breakdown of consensus within the LDP and *zaikai*. Satō's willingness to go to China for normalization talks, the Hori letter, and his near acceptance of Chou's three principles were all dictated by the strong desire for normalization evidenced by the LDP and *zaikai*. Tanaka's decision came after the emergence of consensus within these two powerful elements. Only after the Tanaka government determined that the dominant view within the party favored the abrogation of the controversial Tokyo-Taipei treaty did it publicly proclaim that the treaty would be invalid when Sino-Japanese relations were normalized.

One leading student of Japanese foreign policy, Donald Hellmann, notes that in the politics of Japan's peace settlement with the Soviet Union the major business associations failed to influence LDP decision making "to any great extent." This was attributable, he argues, to several factors, including "the lack of continuing and clear procedures for consultation regarding major non-economic policy questions, the vague opinions voiced by the businessmen regarding this essentially political foreign policy issue," and "the self-contained nature of party policy-making exaggerated by the intensity of the factional struggles." He further suggests that "unless the form of ties with the Liberal-Democratic Party is substantially altered, business influence on major foreign policy decisions seems likely to continue to be limited despite its commanding position on domestic economic issues and essential financial backing given to the conservatives."[22] In the making of the Japanese-Soviet peace settlement, the business community was seriously divided over major issues. Although these differences were later narrowed "to the point where a unified stand was possible," this "contrived" unity carried far less weight than a "natural" consensus with the conservative decision makers. Hellmann himself points out that "the individual expressions of opinion which usually followed the conferences of the business leaders [on matters relative to peace talks] suggest a low level of political awareness and involvement."[23] If this was indeed the case, the "low level of political awareness and involvement" may well be another factor contributing to the inefficacy of the business leaders.

As a vital element of the so-called Japanese establishment or ruling triad, the business community, when backed by a consensus and motivated by a high level of interest, becomes a powerful factor in Japanese policy making in domestic and in foreign policy areas. Through their excellent means of overt and covert access to the LDP and its government,[24] business leaders have vigorously attempted to influence governmental policy making. Profitable international trade and economic prosperity have been the primary concern of Japan's foreign relations for a long time. The economic foundation of foreign policy has required (and dictated) *zaikai's* active participation (hence, influence) in Japanese foreign policy making. Business leaders were deeply involved with the China problem for largely economic reasons. The erosion of the dominant pro-Taipei settlement within the business community was reflected in the changing orientation of the Satō government's China posture, e.g., the rescinding of the Yoshida letter in 1968, and Satō's forward-looking China gestures after 1970. *Zaikai*'s feeling that Satō had served his usefulness contributed significantly to his failure to retire via *hanamichi*. *Zaikai*'s consensus-building, which preceded the LDP's, played a forceful role in directing the Tanaka government and in silencing those within the LDP who had misgivings about the action the government was about to take.

There is no indication that in the making of the China decision the bureaucracy played a major role. The Foreign Ministry, constitutionally designated as the major bureaucratic arm of foreign relations, was aware of its modest postwar status derived from its position of subordination to the ruling party and its government. It is true that the ministry's role during much of Satō's regime was substantial. Its essentially pro-Taipei and pro-Washington orientation was reflected in Satō's earlier China stance, but whatever influence the ministry had was derived largely from the current political climate of the LDP and *zaikai*. As the consensus within these two changed in the direction of seeking détente with China, however, the ministry was no longer accorded the prominence it previously enjoyed. As China became a high-level political issue requiring action by the premier, the Foreign Ministry was relegated to a supportive role, concerned primarily with the technical function of working out details. There is no evidence that the ministry's role went beyond that of translating Tanaka's views and wishes into concrete forms. In contrast to Satō, who relied heavily on the Foreign Ministry's policy suggestions, Tanaka and Ōhira regarded the ministry as an administrative agency in charge of the conduct of foreign relations and held firm control over the ministry, which they felt was noted for "duck paddling diplomacy."

The bureaucracy was far from united on the China issue. Even within the Foreign Ministry there were serious policy divisions, which in turn limited its influence in the China policy making. The economic aspect of Sino-Japanese relations forced the ministry to share many responsibilities with the economic ministries (e.g., Finance, MITI, and Transportation). In the politics of the China decision these agencies held policy outlooks distinctly different from those of the Foreign Ministry—another factor mitigating its influence. The economic ministries, viewing Japan-China relations primarily from an economic perspective, articulated to the premier the interests of that segment of business active in the China trade. During the Tanaka government the role of the economic ministries was confined largely to reinforcing the new pro-China consensus of the business community.

Japan's public opinion had changed rather dramatically, but there is no evidence that it played a significant role in the shaping of Tokyo's China policy. It is true that LDP Dietmen, like elected representatives in other democracies, are sensitive to the general tendencies of their constituencies on major domestic issues. Thus, no government, backed by a conservative Diet majority predominantly from rural districts, will initiate an economic policy adverse to the interests of the agricultural sector of the country. On foreign policy issues, however, a Dietman is given almost complete freedom, because "mandate uncertainty" is most common in these areas. Even when the electorate has expressed its mandate on a foreign policy issue, Dietmen can act with impunity against this clear mandate. China, though the major foreign policy issue in the 1970s, was hardly comparable in electoral importance to such bread-and-butter issues as rice-price, and LDP Dietmen thus did not feel compelled to support the normalization of Sino-Japanese relations because of public opinion. Viewed in this way, the China decision was made independently of the public mood. Thus, the relatively insignificant role of the opposition parties and the press in the shaping of the China decision makes sense.

Notes

1. *Asahi,* 9 June 1972.

2. Ibid., 22 June 1972.

3. *New York Times* (2 July 1972) reported that Peking "refrained from attacks on any of the leading candidates." Obviously the *Times* was unaware of Peking's intense covert activities to influence the outcome of the LDP presidential elections.

4. Ibid., 30 June 1972.

5. *Asahi,* 22 September 1972 (evening edition).

6. Ibid.

7. *Mainichi,* 9 September 1972.

8. *Asahi* reported that at the tripartite meeting of July 2, Miki was "most emphatic about having to solve the China problem." See *Asahi* , 9 September 1972.

9. Apart from its responsibility to the LDP, whose backing is needed under the present Japanese parliamentary system, the government's decision to include the LDP in the final stages of policy making was dictated by lessons from the politics of the 1956 Japanese-Soviet peace settlement. Overestimating the premier's authority in the conduct of foreign relations, Hatoyama proceeded to Moscow without a clear-cut mandate from his party, which was in fact badly divided over territorial issues. As a result, his negotiations with the Russians proved to be much more difficult. It was to avoid this unhappy experience that the Tanaka government took seriously consensus-building in the party. See *Asahi,* 7 September 1972.

10. *Japan Times* 18 July and 29 August 1972.

11. For the text of the communiqué, see *Peking Review,* 3 March 1972, pp. 4–5.

12. *Asahi,* 28 April 1972.

13. Ibid., 11 October 1972.

14. For a good analysis of these considerations, see *Asahi,* 22 September 1972.

15. *Asahi,* 22 September and 24 July (evening) 1972.

16. Ibid., 25 July 1972.

17. Ibid., 10 July and 4 August 1972. Public reactions to the views were uniformly favorable. For example, *Asahi* and other leading dailies welcomed them.

18. Ibid., 22 August 1972 (evening edition).

19. Ibid., 25 August 1972.

20. Ibid., 1 September 1972.

22. Donald C. Hellmann, *Japanese Foreign Policy and Domestic Politics* (Berkeley, 1969), pp. 151–52.

23. Ibid., p. 97.

24. For a discussion of these means of access in one domestic policy area, education policy, see the author's "The Central Council for Education, Organized Business, and the Politics of Education Policy-Making in Japan," *Comparative Education Review,* 19: 2 (June 1975): 296–311. For a general discussion of the relationship between the government and business, see Chitoshi Yanaga, *Big Business in Japanese Politics* (New Haven, 1969), pp. 66–94.

VII. Concluding Overview

17.

Surveying the recent past and then peering into the murky future, Tang Tsou, Tetsuo Najita, and Hideo Otake argue that it is improbable that East Asian politics will turn on Sino-Japanese rivalry. Sino-Japanese relations, they stress, form the common base of two triangular relationships, one governing the relations among China, Japan, and the United States; the other, among China, Japan, and the USSR. In either of these triangles, Japan occupies the most favorable position, and China the least advantageous. In view of Japan's favorable position and innate political wisdom, Japan should be able to resist political pressure by the superpowers and efforts to maneuver her into becoming the main antagonist of China. In both triangular relationships, Sino-Japanese relations are much less intense than the other two relations in terms of friendship or of enmity. Sino-Soviet conflict and rivalry are now the primary factor in East Asia. While Japan's policy of maintaining equal distance between the rivals has merit, it is not easy to implement. Since Japan's stance toward Taiwan is more favorable to the PRC than that of the United States, it is the latter which has become the target of Peking's maneuvers against Taiwan. The authors argue further that the two triangles with a common base form a quadrilateral relationship in the larger sense, although the role of the superpowers is still dominant. While Taiwan remains the stumbling block to long-range Sino-Japanese rapprochement, as the aviation issue demonstrated, the larger international system has taken precedence over the old regional approach. Hence, the history of the grim 1930s will not be repeated, and none of the unresolved issues, however thorny, is likely to lead to military conflict.

399

Lastly, the authors submit, Chinese leaders are not foolish enough to take actions or adopt policies which would cause the Japanese to go nuclear.

This article was originally prepared for the joint Japanese/American Conference, Japan, America and the Future World Order, held at the University of Chicago, October 4–6, 1973, and at Sophia University, Tokyo, April 25–29, 1974, and published under the joint editorship of Morton A. Kaplan and Kinhide Mushakoji by the Free Press/Macmillan and the sponsorship of the Center for Policy Study, University of Chicago, and the Institute of International Relations for Advanced Studies in Peace and Development in Asia, Sophia University.

Tang Tsou is the author of *America's Failure in China* (1963), for which he was awarded the Gordon J. Laing Prize in 1965. His other works include *Embroilment Over Quemoy* and *China in Crisis,* 2 vols. (1968). He is professor of political science at the University of Chicago.

Tetsuo Najita was born in Hawaii and received his Ph.D. at Harvard. His book *Hara Kei in the Politics of Compromise* (1967) was awarded the John K. Fairbank Prize in East Asian History for 1969. His articles on Japanese history have appeared in the *American Historical Review* (December 1968), the *Journal of Asian Studies* (November 1971, August 1972, August 1975) and in several compendia. A professor of history at the University of Chicago, Najita is also director of the Center for Far Eastern Studies there.

Hideo Otake is an assistant professor at Senshū University, Tokyo.

The authors wish to acknowledge research support given by the Center for Far Eastern Studies, University of Chicago, and Tang Tsou expresses his appreciation for a research grant from the Joint Committee on Contemporary China which enabled him to do his part in revising this article in the summer of 1975.

Sino-Japanese Relations in the 1970s

Tang Tsou, Tetsuo Najita, and Hideo Otake

I.

The years 1971–1975 will go down in history as a watershed in the development of East Asian politics, if not world politics as a whole. The China and Japan which have emerged in this new power structure stand in sharp contrast in their internal and external orientations. In domestic affairs, the common themes in the history of the two societies have not prevented China and Japan from becoming two important models of national transformation. In foreign affairs, the asymmetry of national powers and international positions is accompanied by sharp divergence in attitudes and approaches. A fledgling nuclear power with a backward and developing economy confronts the second most economically powerful nation in the non-Communist world whose defense power remains modest in spite of her rapidly increasing defense budget. The relative invulnerability of China with 800,000,000 people in a basically agricultural country of 3,600,000 square miles throws into sharp relief the extreme vulnerability of Japan with her dense concentration of population and industry. Yet prior to the energy crisis, the general view of the specialists was that the economic gap between China and Japan was likely to widen rather than narrow during the rest of the decade. But the energy crisis forcefully underscored the economic vulnerability of Japan. At the same time, the revised estimates of oil deposits in China have reopened the question of her economic potentials. But the answer must be sought by taking into account future agricultural development, importation of grains, and defense expenditures, as well as the probability of an increased rate of industrial growth following the stepped-up importation of modern machinery and plants for use in heavy and chemical industries.

The subjective orientations and objective positions of China and Japan in international affairs also contrast sharply. Since the establishment of the regime in October 1949, China has confronted a series of crises. Some of these crises have posed a real threat to her national security and others have prevented her from eliminating a rival regime and unifying the country. Yet brought up in adversity, accustomed to failures, inured to dangers, and experienced in achieving political gains with initially meager means in a protracted struggle, the Chinese revolutionary leaders have overcome some of these crises and have succeeded at the very least in maintaining the posture of a confident nation in accepting setbacks with equanimity, in making the best of unfavorable international situations, and in adjusting their operational policies to their present capabilities and current reality without forsaking China's national purpose. They take a long view of history in which the ebb and flow of immediate events are passing phenomena. They have formulated a series of positive and negative principles for major areas of foreign policy.[1]

Defeated in World War II, occupied by the United States, and subsequently obliged to enter the cold war on the American side, Japan had practically no alternative other than to support the American position. However, the Japanese government has seldom been an enthusiastic partner in this crusade. This was partly due to its careful cost-benefit calculations, but mainly due to two ideological elements: the strong pacifist-isolationist sentiment among the leaders and the population; skepticism about the American interpretation of aggressive intentions and military capacity of Asian, and particularly Chinese, Communism. Therefore, Japan has refused, as during the Vietnam War, to provide direct military aid to Asian governments in their wars against indigenous Communist movements. She also resisted the repeated demands of anti-Communist countries in Asia for international organizations such as the ASPAC or bilateral committees such as the Japan-Taiwan Cooperation Committee to take a more clear-cut position against Communism. Furthermore, Japan has kept her military defense capability to a minimum and has resisted the requests by the United States for further rearmament. In other words, Japan has developed her self-defense forces at a minimal level, calculated to maintain American military guarantees and friendship.

Relying on the alliance with the United States, Japan gave priority to industrial recovery and growth. Thus, Japan actively pursued an "economic diplomacy" in which foreign policies, including political matters, were evaluated in terms of economic advantage. Her leaders have sought to conduct this economic diplomacy within a stable international framework. Therefore, her foreign policy appeared purely pragmatic and often short-sighted, although this policy has actually been closely intertwined with a long-term vision of national economic well-being. As a practical matter, Japanese foreign policy has been one of constant adjustment to the forces of the international economy, as in the quest for raw materials and export markets, which gradually resulted in Japan's economic expansion in various areas of the world, especially in Asia and the United States. In sum, Japan's long-term foreign policy is best seen not in political terms, as is the case with China, the United States, or the Soviet Union, but primarily in the light of immediate and future economic needs. If Great Britain acquired her empire in a fit of absent-mindedness, it can be said that Japan became the world's second richest capitalist country and a world power in a period of "benign neglect" of *Realpolitik* and low posture in international affairs.

Despite the recent success in opening a dialogue with the United States and in establishing formal diplomatic relations with Japan, China still occupies the least favorable position in the maneuverings among the four major powers in the Far East. The Soviet military threat remains. In spite of the Shanghai communiqué, the Chou–Tanaka communiqué, and Foreign Minister Ōhira's statement to the press in Peking, no substantive progress has been made toward the solution of the problem of Taiwan. Indeed, the appointment of Leonard Unger as the ambassador to Taipei, the American agreement to establish two Chinese Nationalist consulates in Kansas City and Portland, the continued economic vitality of Taiwan, and President Ford's reaffirmation of American commitment to Taiwan after the collapse of the Thieu regime in South Vietnam have been developments contrary to Peking's expectations.

Japan's national fortune has followed a course totally unforeseeable thirty years ago. As Japan now enters a new era of equal partnership with the United States, the past neglect has left many foreign observers with a lingering impression of a Japan without political direction and in search of a role in international affairs which is still to be defined. Japan's strategic insecurity and her dependence on natural resources and markets outside her borders have made her vulnerable to drastic changes in international politics and economic policies whose effects are immediately felt, as the Yom Kippur War in the Middle East and the Arab oil embargo vividly showed. In comparison with China, the twofold problems confronting Japan are complex in a different way. One is to maintain a delicate balance between herself and both China and the Soviet Union, the Arab nations and the United States, and Communist and non-Communist nations in Asia, especially North and South Korea. To achieve an amicable balance, Japan must avoid unilateral provocation and maintain a rational and deliberate posture (sometimes leading to excessive delays) so as not to jeopardize the fruits of the past and the advantageous position of the present. The other is to compete with the large, basically self-sufficient powers, the United States, China, and the Soviet Union. Moreover, Japan's decision-making process is relatively cumbersome, since it involves intense competition among bureaucratic factional and partisan groups. Thus, Japan has to learn how to evolve long-range policies in a new era in which her political influence is bound to increase.

The question before us is, given the sharp contrasts in internal and external orientations and the asymmetry in national power and international position, how will Sino-Japanese relations evolve in the later 1970s? Will a fledgling nuclear power in pursuit of her national and revolutionary interests blackmail an affluent nation? Or, alternatively, will military power necessarily follow economic power? Will political domination inevitably come with economic penetration? Will a fully armed and nuclear Japan achieve hegemony in Asia and threaten the national security of China? In other words, will the present asymmetry in the types of national power be transformed into the hegemony of the one or the other in East Asia? Or will it lead to a shifting and complex equilibrium with the great capability in one sphere canceling out that in another realm and thus facilitating "peaceful coexistence" and further improvement in Sino-Japanese relations? Or will Japan become a neutral nation, forsaking the security treaty with the United States and the American nuclear umbrella? Or will the Sino-Japanese rapprochement soon lead to a tacit alliance or cohegemony over East and Southeast Asia in opposition to the Soviet Union and in competition with the United States?

II.

In attempting to answer these questions, we shall not follow that usual format of examining scenarios in which certain possibilities may become actualities, and then estimating the likelihood that these conditions will indeed come into existence. Instead, we shall examine only the possibility of intense Sino-Japanese struggle for leadership or hegemony in East Asia. In the context of this examination, our assessment of the other possibilities will become obvious. There are three reasons for this heuristic decision. First, Sino-Japanese rivalry for regional leadership is explicitly or implicitly considered by many scholars and influential men of affairs to be the crux of the problem. As noted by former Foreign Minister Shiina Etsusaburō, a pro-Taiwan leader of a minor faction in the LDP, "competition [with China] for Asia has already begun."[2]

Second, if this concept is accepted without qualifications, it may become a self-fulfilling prophecy in a relatively short period. An unqualified acceptance would lead the political actors to overlook other factors precluding or restraining such a rivalry and to adopt policies which would contribute to its rapid intensification. If, however, statesmen self-consciously resist and oppose what may be one of the many possibilities or even a highly probable development and if scholars assiduously analyze and direct their attention to the full complexity of the situation, they could, by their combined efforts, at least delay the actualization of that undesirable tendency and perhaps even prevent it altogether. Any complex situation contains conflicting tendencies and many possibilities. The highest form of statesmanship consists not of passive acceptance of the undesirable dominant tendency as historical inevitability but of creative development of new policies which will strengthen those tendencies leading to a desirable outcome and conducive to the realization of noble visions. In this respect, the task of scholars in the social sciences is not to describe a deterministic universe or to stress the inevitability of a particular outcome but to facilitate and encourage creative statesmanship. Both statesmen and scholars may fail in the end but they will fail with good conscience.

Finally, the methodological choice of focusing on one major possibility has the advantage of avoiding redundancy in the discussion of the various aspects of the complex situation and issues which would be unavoidable in a systematic examination of all the possibilities.[3]

Our method of exposition is to begin with the notion of Sino-Japanese rivalry and then to take into account other factors step by step so as to come to grips with the full complexity of the present situation. The notion of Sino-Japanese rivalry for leadership or hegemony in East Asia rests on a set of assumptions, leads to a set of policies, and contains a set of implications. It begins with the idea that East Asia forms a regional subsystem with China and Japan as the principal actors. One can follow Donald Hellmann and others who use the term "East Asia" to include China, Japan, Korea, Taiwan, and Southeast Asia. As such, this idea is purely descriptive and acceptable. Since China and Japan are neighbors "separated only by a strip of water," they naturally have profound concern for the political posture and military capability of each other. Since they are the two major powers whose territories lie exclusively in East Asia, they are sensitive to the foreign policy orientations and internal political developments in nations in that region, particularly in the buffer zone in Korea. A certain amount of conflict and competition is therefore quite natural.

But when the regional approach to Sino-Japanese relations is combined with the old-fashioned view of geopolitics and *Realpolitik,* the notion of Sino-Japanese struggle for leadership or hegemony in East Asia emerges. This notion assumes that because of geographic proximity, both China and Japan place political, military, and economic relations between themselves and with nations in East Asia above those with nations outside the region and that the importance of their ties with the latter lies primarily in the effects these have on developments inside the region.[4] Two other premises which start from different points, but ultimately reinforce the initial assumption, are sometimes added.

For Japan, it is assumed that the promotion of economic interests and relations entails, in the first instance, political influence and ultimately reliance on military power and that even in the latter part of the twentieth century, military power can effectively promote economic interests. For China, it is supposed that the export of revolution can always produce political control over a country which in turn can be used as an instrument to dominate that country's economy and to jeopardize Japan's economic interests. The corollary is that Japan will adopt a program of massive rearmament sufficient to protect her economic and political interests and to back up her conventional military power with nuclear weapons. China will push forward her revolutionary program in East Asia and use her political and military power to compensate for her economic weakness while seeking to develop her economy rapidly with the primary purpose of competing with Japan.

III.

While the possibility of Sino-Japanese rivalry for leadership or hegemony in East Asia cannot be ruled out entirely, particularly in the long run, there are several factors which militate against this possibility and which call into question the validity of some of its assumptions. First and most obviously, this analysis does not take sufficiently into account the presence of the United States and the Soviet Union in East Asia and the effects of their presence on Sino-Japanese relations. Despite the total elimination of her influence in Vietnam and Cambodia after the collapse of the Thieu and Lon Nol regimes, the United States remains a Pacific power—in Korea, in the Philippines, and on aircraft carriers on the high seas. Moreover, it is not likely that in the 1970s the U.S.-Japan security treaty will become inoperative or that the United States will abandon its bases in Japan and Okinawa. Despite the change in American administrations in 1977, the United States will probably maintain its commitment to Taiwan and consequently the defense treaty between Washington and Taipei, regardless of what happens to their diplomatic relations.

Conceivably, the United States could maneuver Japan into a rival position with China, making Sino-Japanese rivalry the main feature of East Asian politics. Indeed, American policies in the past have had such an implication. After Dulles became secretary of state, the United States strongly urged Japan to rearm on a large scale and to participate militarily in regional defense, and she demanded the establishment of diplomatic relations between Tokyo and Taipei as a precondition for a mutual security pact. More recently, during Nixon's first administration, Secretary of Defense Laird repeatedly urged Japan to step up her effort in rearmament and to play a greater role in East Asia.

Particularly intriguing is the inclusion in the Nixon–Satō communiqué of November 1969 of the statement that "the maintenance of peace and security in the Taiwan area is also a most important factor for the security of Japan." It seems that this so-called Taiwan clause was proposed by Japan as a concession to the United States in order to facilitate the return of Okinawa to Japanese control. Legally it served the purpose of linking Taiwan to Article 6 of the U.S.-Japan security treaty. It thus strengthened the legal foundation for American forces using Japanese bases to protect Taiwan in case of a Chinese Communist military attack. But in retrospect, this statement may have had more profound implications. We now know that within a few weeks of its inauguration, the Nixon administration formulated a new China policy. Kissinger told *Newsweek* in 1973 that "the Chinese knew what we wanted as early as June, 1969."[5] But, at the time, no one could confidently predict the Chinese response to America's initiative.

In this situation, the Taiwan statement had two implications. If a dialogue could not be established and détente could not be achieved, the Taiwan clause would involve Japan more deeply in the defense of Taiwan. More important, it suggested to Peking that the alternative to détente with the United States would eventually be a Taiwan under the joint guarantee and influence of Japan and United States. The latent political influence of Japan among Taiwanese based on past personal, political, educational, and cultural ties and on present economic interests would be openly, forcefully, and effectively asserted. The geographical propinquity of Taiwan to Japan, some Japanese leaders' fond memory of a Japanese-ruled Taiwan, and the existence of a fairly strong pro-Taiwan group in the LDP would make Japanese influence predominant, replacing the more remote, less intimate, and less passionate concern of the United States. Once established, Japanese political influence and military involvement in the defense of Taiwan would become intense, undermining Peking's aim of regaining Taiwan. Peking would therefore view Japan's involvement in the defense of that island as part of a rapid program of large-scale rearmament in Japan. Furthermore, with the Taiwan clause, Japan seemed ready to take the first step from self-defense to regional defense advocated by Dulles many years ago. The prospect before Peking would be rivalry throughout East Asia with a rearmed Japan, perhaps with nuclear weapons, at a time when China was threatened by the Soviet Union along her northern border and opposed by the United States elsewhere.

If this was indeed Peking's perception, it is not unreasonable to believe that the Taiwan clause in the Nixon–Satō communiqué gave Peking an additional incentive to make the subsequent decision to open a dialogue with the United States. If some sort of understanding with the United States could be reached over the issue of Taiwan and if détente with the United States could be achieved, the American effort to involve Japan more deeply in the defense of Taiwan would decrease or at least lose its justification in the eyes of the Japanese. Alternatively, Japan would be put in the unenviable position of antagonizing China on the sensitive issue of Taiwan and acting as a general rival of China while the United States was backing away from her uncompromising posture.

When the Chinese leaders studied the documents and books published in the United States, they must have come across both a signal and an implied threat. In the policy memorandum written by Richard Moorstein and Morton Abramowitz, which proved to be the general blueprint for the Nixon–Kissinger policy toward China, we find the following:

> Time may not be on China's side. Peking's leaders may feel the United States must eventually withdraw and leave Taiwan to its fate, but they also must have deep doubts about a resurgent Japan's growing interest in Taiwan. They have expressed fears that Taiwan would again enter a "Japanese sphere of influence" and about a resurgent Japan's growing interest in Taiwan. Concerned with reducing the likelihood of these eventualities, Peking might respond to partial solutions "in principle" that fell well short of actual reversion of Taiwan to the mainland at an early date or even any fixed date at all.[6]

It is not inconceivable that such a signal and an implied threat were conveyed to the Chinese through third parties or during Kissinger's secret trip to Peking in July 1971.

Confronted by the prospect created by the Nixon–Satō communiqué and subsequently elaborated in American published documents or communications, Peking launched a multifaceted policy. Premier Chou En-lai's trip to Pyongyang solidified the alliance with North Korea in the face of the common danger presented by the Nixon–Satō communiqué. The overthrow of Prince Sihanouk's government in March 1970 enabled Peking to play an active role in bringing about the Summit Conference of the Indochinese Peoples, thus sharply increasing her prestige and influence in Indochina. Within Japan, Peking gave verbal support even more unequivocally than before to the opposition parties and the dissident factions in the LDP. She launched an intensive propaganda campaign against the revival of Japanese militarism, which was said to be inevitably linked with the Satō government's intrusion into Taiwan, its commitment to South Korea, and its general ambition in East Asia. It is apparent to outside observers that in Peking's propaganda, potentiality was described as actuality. But the Chinese themselves were also clearly aware of this. As Premier Chou En-lai told James Reston in August 1971,

> When you oppose a danger, you should oppose it when it is only budding. Only then

can you arouse public attention. Otherwise, if you are to wait until it has already
developed into a power, it will be too strenuous.[7]

When stripped of its propagandistic elements, the series of articles and
speeches contained an analysis of Japan's future foreign policy which was
not basically different from the views of a few pro-Taiwan members of the
LDP or from some of the scholarly American analyses prior to the Shanghai
communiqué, which foresaw the inevitability of Japan's rearmament and
development of nuclear capability for the purpose of protecting Japan's
economic interests and supporting Japan's new role in East Asia.

One other aspect of Peking's policy was to continue to probe America's
intention in contacts through third parties, leading to Kissinger's secret
trip. In this process, Peking's penchant for secrecy served her well. Secrecy
prevented the opponents of Sino-American détente from voicing their
opposition and organizing themselves into a powerful political force. It also
became one of the main elements of the Nixon shocks. The shocks were all
the more severe for Japan because it was Washington which had kept Japan
from a rapprochement with China and because it was Japan's concession to
the United States in the Taiwan clause which triggered Peking's escalated
attack on the Satō government and opened up for Japan the prospect of
becoming Peking's principal non-Communist enemy.

After Kissinger's visit, Japan rather than the United States bore the
brunt of Peking's wrath, insofar as the issue of Taiwan and the question of
the two Chinas were concerned. Despite the principal role played by the
Nixon administration in working out the new two-Chinas formula in the
United Nations, announced by Secretary of State William Rogers in
August 1972, Premier Chou told Reston that "this statement issued by the
United States Secretary of State was a self-contradictory formula worked
out under the pressure of the talks between the Japanese Government and
the Chiang Kai-shek representative in Tokyo." He noted that Japan "has
started to harbor ambitions" over Taiwan.[8] Reston was surprised by the
"vehemence" of Chinese feeling and impressed by their real worry about
Japan.

Confronted with this severe verbal attack against "Japanese militarism," Japan's leaders denounced it as a misunderstanding of Japan's
position in international politics or as a mere propagandist campaign.
Japanese leaders also regarded this attack as unjustified because it was
China, not Japan, which had developed nuclear weapons and maintained
massive military forces. The Japanese leaders viewed the Taiwan clause not
as evidence of rising Japanese militarism but as a concession to American
pressure. They did not feel Japan had the capacity or intention to defend
Taiwan militarily in place of the United States. The memory of World War
II and lessons of the Vietnam War confirmed for them their view on the
undesirability of direct military involvement in defense of Taiwan.

Thus, after an initial shock and confusion, Japan's leaders accepted the new arrangements worked out by Nixon and Chou and sought to adjust Japan's political and economic policies to the emergent situation. They began to exploit new opportunites by establishing closer economic relations with non-Communist countries. Satō tried to contact Peking along this policy line, although perhaps not wholeheartedly, but was rebuffed. It appeared that in Peking's judgment Satō would soon resign and it would be more advantageous to wait for the next prime minister.

Prime Minister Tanaka's visit to China and Premier Chou En-lai's conciliatory policy succeeded in averting the potential if not the actual danger that Sino-Japanese confrontation over Taiwan and general rivalry in Asia would become the main axis of East Asian politics—a rivalry which would seriously jeopardize the internal development and foreign relations of both nations. They gave China and Japan a period to work out a relationship on a different basis. The summit meeting solemnized genuine compromise and mutual concession which produced no victory or defeat for either party. The establishment of a new relationship defused the issues of the revival of Japanese militarism and the U.S.-Japan security treaty.[9]

At present, a complex triangular relationship rather than Sino-Japanese rivalry is the principal fact insofar as the United States, China, and Japan are concerned. This pattern will most likely persist through the rest of the decade. By his brilliant diplomacy from November 1969 to September 1972, Premier Chou succeeded in averting the most threatening prospect of a confrontation with a rearmed Japan entrenched in Taiwan and backed by a United States committed equally to the defense of Taiwan and to limiting China's influence in East Asia. But in the new triangular relationship which now exists, China remains in an uncomfortable position. While her relations with both have been put on an entirely different basis from that existing before 1972, she is still confronted with two allies who are learning to work closely together and who enjoy intimate political, cultural, and economic relationships. The crucial issue of Taiwan, which we shall discuss in greater detail in a different context, has proved to be difficult to resolve. Peking is likely to pursue a policy of alternately improving her relationship with one of the two allies as a lever or inducement to move the other in the same direction. The contrast between Japan's willingness to reaffirm the principle of one China in signing the Sino-Japanese agreement on aviation in April 1974 and America's moves in bolstering the diplomatic and consular ties with Taiwan has been followed by a marked increase in the warmth of Sino-Japanese relations coupled with a visible cooling in the Chinese attitude toward the United States. This change in attitude may reflect a decision to place Sino-Japanese cooperation ahead of further rapprochement with the United States in Peking's scheme of priorities. President Ford's reaffirmation of American commitment to Taiwan on May 6, 1975, could only reinforce this decision.

In the long run, Japan occupies the most favorable position in this triangular relationship on condition that she take a position on Taiwan more favorable to Peking than that of the United States, as is the case today. Maintaining such a position would alleviate the fears of those Japanese leaders who say that the American nuclear umbrella as a protection against China might become unreliable in the distant future or that the United States would use it for bargaining in negotiations over serious economic issues which could not be settled in purely economic terms on their merits. It would be a less costly alternative to large-scale rearmament and nuclear development, which could not be undertaken without precipitating serious political conflicts in Japan and unpredictable repercussions elsewhere. Positively, it would give Japan room for maneuver in her relations with China during a period when Japan is redefining her role in Asia and in the world.

IV.

Sino-Japanese relations form one side of the triangular relationship among the United States, China, and Japan and among the Soviet Union, China, and Japan. In both triangular relationships, China's ultimate fears and hopes are presently riveted on her relations with the Soviet Union and the United States, the most significant factors shaping her foreign policies, while her relations with Japan are viewed in terms of their effects on her relations with the two superpowers. For Japan, there is scarcely any doubt that American-Japanese relations are accorded priority in her foreign policy while her relations with China and the Soviet Union are in a state of flux. To a large extent, Sino-American and Sino-Soviet relations will in the near future shape Sino-Japanese relations rather than the other way around, although China presumably hopes that in the long run greatly improved Sino-Japanese relations, amounting to a tacit alliance, will reinforce China's rapidly developing national power and bring about a progressive shift in the relative power balance between China and the two superpowers. The neglect of the Soviet Union's role in East Asia is another omission which vitiates the analysis and projection based on Sino-Japanese rivalry as the main feature in East Asia.

From China's point of view, the primary fact in East Asian politics and even world politics is the military threat from the Soviet Union and Soviet attempts to contain China. This perception persuaded Peking to change her policy toward Washington and was partly responsible for her concilia-tory policy toward Japan. Chairman Mao Tse-tung's New Year's instruc-tion in 1973 ("dig tunnels deep, store grains everywhere and never seek hegemony") was obviously issued with the Soviet military threat in mind.

Premier Chou En-lai in his political report to the Tenth Party Congress in August 1973 told the Chinese to be fully prepared "particularly against surprise attack on our country by Soviet revisionist social-imperialism."

Given the military capability of the Soviet Union in both conventional and nuclear weapons, readiness to use her military power in Hungary in 1956 and Czechoslovakia in 1968, and her theory of "limited sovereignty," the Chinese fear of the Soviet Union appears to be well grounded in reality. But even if a Soviet attack does not come, the disposition of Soviet forces along the Chinese border and the rumors and veiled threats of a Soviet attack serve many purposes. It has been our judgment since 1966 that one of the immediate and primary purposes of the Soviet troop dispositions and military threats has been to influence the struggle for power in China and thus her long-term political development and foreign policy orientations. The military dispositions along the Chinese border also reduce Peking's political influence and international prestige. The reentry of the Soviet Union under Khrushchev's successors into the Vietnam tangle was merely the beginning of the intensification of Soviet efforts to contain China. The North Vietnamese-Vietcong offensive in early 1972 was made possible by sophisticated Soviet weapons rather than by China's encouragement or perhaps even in spite of Peking's advice. The Soviet-Indian treaty of 1971 was a decisive stroke of Soviet diplomacy which turned the balance of power in South Asia sharply in favor of the Soviet Union and drastically against the Chinese. Brezhnev's proposal for an Asian collective security system is recognized by Peking as a move to check Chinese influence. The victory of the Vietcong and the North Vietnamese has been followed by rumors of intensified Sino-Soviet maneuvers for influence in South Vietnam. In the rest of the decade, Peking must continue to give priority to this military-political threat. She is also likely to view Sino-Japanese and Japanese-Soviet relations in terms of their impact on the Sino-Soviet conflict.

For the Soviet Union, it is to her advantage to enlist Japan as her junior partner in her conflict with China, to make Japan the primary target of Chinese hostility, and to dissipate Japan's political energy and resources in an artificially created conflict with China—a role for Japan analogous to that envisaged by Dulles in the context of Sino-American conflict in the 1950s. The Soviet invitation to Japan for joint development of oil and other resources in Siberia was a political move to use economic inducements to complicate Sino-Japanese economic and political relations. According to Muraoka Kunio, the supply from Tyumen would at most be only about 8 percent of Japanese oil imports in 1980.[10] But the strategic significance of a pipeline along the Chinese border or a new trans-Siberian railroad some distance to the north of the existing one was not lost on China.[11] Even if Japan's dependence on Soviet oil and gas is small, the USSR would use whatever leverage she gains in her dealing with Japan. The rapid development of economic relations between Japan and the Soviet Union would disrupt Japan's policy of maintaining "equal distance" between the Soviet Union and China.[12]

The political implications of this joint enterprise are not dissimilar to those of the Nixon–Satō communiqué of 1969. If China should react in the same fashion toward Japan as it did from November 1969 to early 1972, serious misunderstanding would develop between the two nations, one that another summit conference might not clear up. If this misunderstanding continued and deepened, the Soviet Union would succeed in her first step of promoting Sino-Japanese rivalry, turning Japan into a junior partner in the conflict. Moreover, a cooperative Japanese-Soviet economic relationship, when combined with Sino-Japanese misunderstanding, would hinder further development of Sino-American détente. The Soviet experts on the United States who showed their astounding shrewdness in engineering the profitable grain deals are certainly not unaware that many American experts and officials firmly believed that the United States should not move ahead of Japan in cultivating good relations with China. Thus, Japan is the key to the Soviet policy of isolating China in East Asia. If this diplomatic maneuver were successful, the Soviet Union would have solved her "China problem," and could turn her attention to other parts of the world. Confronted with the prospect of Soviet-Japanese-American "collusion" against China, Peking might find it necessary to make the best possible deal with the Soviet Union and the latter would again move to the middle position where it could exploit the Sino-American impasse over the Taiwan issue and China's traditional fear of Japan.[13]

The Japanese government is conscious of these political and military implications of the joint development of Siberia for China and the United States. Japanese leaders also fear "possible arbitrary actions by the Russians such as violating contracts, not paying agreed prices, and excluding the Japanese from sufficient inspecting facilities on joint projects."[14] Japan feels particularly vulnerable to these violations because she has few countermeasures to take. Thus Japan wants the United States to join some of the more important projects in part to mitigate Chinese protest and also to avoid the danger of being maneuvered by the Soviet Union in its conflict with China. Furthermore, since Japan does not wish to be overly dependent on the Soviet Union for raw materials, she is trying to diversify her suppliers of raw materials by embarking on joint ventures in South America, Canada, the Near East, Africa, Australia, Southeast Asia, and China. The Sino-Soviet conflict, however, has placed Japan in a strategically favorable position: she does not fear the excessive pressure of either China or the Soviet Union or both powers together in an anti-Japanese alliance. Thus, just as China seeks benefits from both Japan and the United

States to counterbalance Soviet moves, Japan pursues a policy of deriving advantages from both China and the Soviet Union, establishing closer relations to both without antagonizing either.

In any event, a protocol was signed on April 22, 1974, governing the conditions of a $1 billion loan from the Export-Import Bank of Japan to the Soviet Union to finance three projects involving the development of coal, gas, and forestry resources in Siberia. While a subsequent general agreement on the coal project was signed in accordance with the protocol, the gas project has not made much progress because it is predicated on American participation, which has not been forthcoming. The joint project to develop oil fields in Tyumen encountered even more serious obstacles. It subsequently became known that in April 1973 China contracted with Japan's International Oil Trading Company to deliver 1 million tons of high-grade, low-sulphur crude oil through December 31, 1973, at the low price of about $3.75 a barrel and without any other conditions.[15] In July, the Chinese government was reported to have promised to export to Japan 10 percent of the total oil produced in China. In 1974, 4 million tons were exported to Japan. In 1974, crude oil production in China was estimated at 65.3 million tons, an increase of 20 percent in one year. In October 1974 a tentative agreement was made for the export of a minimum of 8 million tons for 1975.[16] By one Japanese estimate, which is probably too high, China will produce 400 million tons of oil by 1980 and can be expected to export at least 40 million tons to Japan. According to a recent American estimate, China's total oil production by 1980 will be more than 200 million tons a year, of which approximately 50 million tons may be exported. With slight adjustments in consumption or output growth, the Chinese could raise the surplus to 65 million tons.[17] By comparison, the expected amount of crude oil imported by Japan from the Soviet Union will, at best, be 25 to 40 million tons a year in 1980. But a condition on the availability of oil from the Soviet Union could be a huge loan from Japan to finance the Siberian oil project, which would also have serious military and diplomatic implications. Japan has decided to hold off on the Siberian project partly and perhaps largely because of the prospect of buying China's oil without the diplomatic and financial risks inherent in the Siberian venture.

While she was fending off the Soviet maneuver to bind Japan with economic ties, Peking was planning a diplomatic countermeasure to frustrate the Soviet policy of establishing an Asian collective security system to contain China. From its first formal appearance in the Shanghai communiqué issued by the Chinese and American governments on February 27, 1975, the principle of opposition to efforts by any country or group of countries to establish "hegemony in the Asian-Pacific region" was unmistakably aimed by the Chinese at the Soviet Union.[18] Identical wording was included in point 7 of the joint statement signed by Chou En-lai and Tanaka Kakuei in Peking on September 29, 1972,[19] although the implicit meaning attributed to it by the Chinese was partially balanced by the preceding statement that the "the normalization of relations between China and Japan is not directed against third countries." In the negotiations on a treaty of peace and friendship envisaged in point 8 of the joint statement, Peking has insisted on a clause opposing "hegemony" by any power in Asia, arguing that the two nations must develop their relations on the basis of the joint statement rather than retreat from it. The Miki government refused to include such a clause. As of this writing, no progress has been made on the issue. Hence, Sino-Soviet relations have continued to influence the development of Sino-Japanese relations for better or for worse, as our analysis suggests.

We have suggested that the presence of the United States and the Soviet Union in East Asia has resulted in two triangular relationships and that Sino-Japanese relations, a subordinate side of these triangles, can be understood only in these contexts. The two triangular relationships, with Sino-Japanese relations as a common base, add up to a quadrilateral relationship in which the four sides are more important than the common base and have greater actual or potential influence in shaping the common base than the other way around. But the controlling relationship in this quadrille remains that between the two superpowers. Thus, militarily and in terms of its dominant political relationship, the world is still basically bipolar although other relationships are assuming greater importance. The impact of this global system on the regional system has been obvious, but the latter also has some effect on the former. The American endeavor to open a dialogue with China has been interpreted as an attempt to use China to redress the political balance which was in danger of shifting more and more in favor of the Soviet Union. It has also been interpreted as a move to make the Soviet Union more amenable to the U.S. overture to negotiate various issues. Whether or not these interpretations are correct, it is clear that America's new China policy was directed not at China alone. In order to preserve America's favorable position in this quadrilateral relation, any move toward a greater understanding with the Soviet Union must be accompanied and insured by some movement in improving Sino-American relations.

The global system also tends to dilute intraregional relationships. As Japan and China have become increasingly involved in global affairs, extraregional relationships will be more important than Sino-Japanese rivalry in East Asia. This is particularly the case with Japan, whose economic interests are primarily global rather than regional. What happens in the United States, the Middle East, and Western Europe more directly concerns Japan than does economic and political development in East Asia. In this regard, China's increasing interest in the Third World, with which she identifies, will not jeopardize the improvement of Sino-Japanese relations. For example, China's activities in Tanzania and Zambia have absorbed a proportionately large share of China's attention and foreign aid and have had no obvious adverse effects on Japan's position.

Given the Soviet military-political threat, China and the United States have a common interest in opposing the expansion of Soviet influence in every part of the world. But unless the United States could agree to a resolution of the Taiwan issue satisfactory to Peking, there is a limit to Sino-American rapprochement and cooperation. Hence, Peking's policies toward the United States have been ambivalent and have moved on several levels. On the one hand, she welcomes the maintenance of American military strength in Western Europe and explicitly acquiesces in the U.S.-Japan security treaty. On the other hand, she vehemently attacks both the superpowers while endeavoring to bolster the position and influence of the Third World of developing countries and the Second World of developed nations. She envisages a global configuration of power in which the Third and Second Worlds would use American-Soviet contradictions and stalemate to restrain effectively the two superpowers. This global vision implies that China will place greater value on Sino-Japanese than on Sino-American cooperation and trade—so long as the United States maintains her commitment to defend Taiwan. She hopes that Sino-Japanese cooperation will become the main feature in East Asian politics and one factor leading to a change in American policy toward Taiwan.

V.

We have outlined the existing and potential structure of relations in East Asia and the world at large which may affect the development of Sino-Japanese relations. We have concluded that intensive Sino-Japanese rivalry is not likely to be the main feature of East Asian regional politics. But there are several issues between China and Japan which must also be briefly examined. One is the generalized fear that the two contrasting political systems may not find it easy to coexist peacefully. This finds expression first in Japan's specific complaints and anxiety that China has in the past tried to interfere in Japan's internal politics and to influence Japan's foreign policy by supporting the opposition parties. Some Japanese leaders share a vague fear of a Communist revolution in Japan supported by foreign Communist regimes. The possibility that China would support a revolution led by the JCP seems remote to most observers, particularly in view of the strained relationship between the CCP and the JCP. But the growing strength of the JCP in the general elections and the unpredictability of either party's actions remind conservative Japanese leaders of the possibility of this so-called indirect invasion. For her part, China considered the peace treaty and the establishment of diplomatic relations between Japan and Taiwan a case of even more flagrant interference in the internal affairs of China.

As an understanding was being reached over the question of Taiwan at the Sino-Japanese summit meeting, the Chinese gave verbal assurances that they would not interfere in Japan's internal affairs. According to Prime Minister Tanaka, the following exchange took place: "We said [to the Chinese side]: 'We ask you not to interfere in our internal affairs. We ask you not to join hands with the JCP.' In response to this the Chinese side said: 'We will not interfere in the internal affairs of Japan. We will not export revolution, and even if we tried to, it cannot be exported.' "[20] But this affirmation of noninterference does not include the cessation of criticism of the JCP. Liao Ch'eng-chih told the *Yomiuri* Newspaper Reporters Mission that "our dear Mr. Miyamoto Kenji says that China's criticising the Japanese Communist Party is interference in internal affairs, but we will do this to the last. . . ."[21] After Tanaka's visit to China, the Chinese became circumspect even in their private remarks. According to Kimura Takeo, Premier Chou used such careful expression regarding Japan's domestic questions as, "I hope that you will listen to my statements as a mere reference, as they may become intervention in domestic affairs."[22]

In the future, China may well continue to cultivate Japanese opinion in all circles in order to influence Japan's foreign policy. Indeed, this is one of Peking's most effective measures to compensate for her lack of economic power and generally unfavorable position in quadrilateral relations. Shortly after the Chou-Tanaka meeting, *Jen-min Jih-pao* published a summary of past efforts of Japanese leaders to achieve normalization of Chinese-Japanese relations. It concluded with these words:

> The Chinese people will never forget the numerous Japanese friends who have paved the way for Sino-Japanese friendship and the restoration of diplomatic relations between China and Japan. . . . Of course difficulties of one kind or another will arise in future contacts after the restoration of diplomatic relations, but we are convinced that through the common efforts of the Chinese and Japanese peoples, all difficulties will surely be surmounted and new progress made.[23]

Thus, the issue of interference has been defused although it may well be revived if the question of Taiwan remains insoluble. The possibility of Chinese support for a Japanese revolutionary movement seems negligible in view of the relative internal stability of Japan, the strained relationship between the JCP and CCP, and the Chinese principle of "self-reliance" on the part of revolutionary forces.

The other issue which can cause complications in Sino-Japanese relations is competition in Southeast Asia and in the Third World as a whole for economic and political influence—a point frequently stressed by forecasters of intense Sino-Japanese rivalry in East Asia. Insofar as Southeast Asia is concerned, Indonesia, an important source of oil for

Japan, falls into a separate category. At the moment, Peking's political and economic influence there is almost nil. Without surface ships and transports, China poses no threat and can exert no military pressure. Insofar as China's military threat and pressure are concerned, the situation regarding the Philippines is not too different. This will remain so for many years to come. As for economic competition elsewhere in East Asia and the underdeveloped world, certain understandings seem to have been reached as a result of the summit meeting. As Nakasone said after his meeting with Chou En-lai, China would give economic aid to underdeveloped countries but would stress agriculture and light industries while Japanese aid would be centered on heavy industrial materials. The conclusion is that "Japan and China will not come into conflict."[24] But China also recognized that China and Japan follow two different methods of managing two different social systems. In addition, one rests on vastly superior economic power and technology; the other, on political skills and experience. Each has its own strengths and weaknesses. Chou told Kimura, "If Japan is to pursue profits too intensively, this will lead to 'exploitation' and cause repulsion among peoples in these areas (while laughing). . . . If this is to happen, this will be what China is waiting for."[25] Kimura reported that "Chou even went so far as to give me advice, saying . . . that it may be good for Japan also, if Japan carries out its economic policy, based on reciprocity and equality."[26] Many Japanese scholars came to similar conclusions some time ago.[27]

To Kimura, Chou described China's aid policy in the following terms: "China first makes what the other side needs, also China educates local persons; and when they master the professions they are engaging in, China leaves them in their countries for the benefit of their countries." Like many other domestic and foreign policies of China, this idealistic policy rests squarely on realistic economic and political calculations. Given her low level of economic and technological development, China cannot compete successfully with Japan or other economically advanced nations on purely economic and technical terms for markets, resources, and political influence in underdeveloped areas. By setting up a few demonstration aid projects in selected areas on unusually favorable terms, Peking established a standard of comparison which puts economic activities and aid by other nations in an unfavorable light. These examples would be welcomed by the developing countries as leverage for gaining better terms from developed countries, if not for their intrinsic economic importance. They will bolster Peking's political influence and claim to leadership in the Third World. They can be used to induce dissatisfaction with the economic activities and aid programs of the advanced nations.

If the people in a developing country should desire to assert their economic independence and to use their political power against the established economic interests of foreign powers in their country, the traditional methods of "gunboat diplomacy" or even large-scale military action no longer seem adequate in an age of rising nationalism and guerrilla warfare, if there is a strong and farsighted political leadership supported by a fully mobilized and organized population. The same conclusion applies to indigenous revolution with a popular base. The only alternative is for the advanced nations to pursue a policy of economic strangulation and of manipulation of the demands and preferences of specific political and social groups. Thus, the competition between China and Japan in East Asia and the Third World in general will not take on a military dimension but will be conducted in primarily economic and political terms, which may not be entirely unhealthy for them or for the underdeveloped nations concerned.

Korea, as a buffer zone between China and Japan, is another area of potential conflict. Their assessments of the importance of Korea and their policies are also affected by their overall diplomatic postures toward each other. This point is brought out clearly by events since the Nixon–Satō communiqué. From the Korean War to 1969, Peking looked at the Korean peninsula largely from the viewpoint of political and military confrontation with the United States. As a result of the Sino-Soviet conflict and the ambiguous position taken by North Korea in this dispute, Peking-Pyongyang relations were for a number of years less than intimate. The Nixon–Satō communiqué, which opened up the prospect of a Japanese-dominated Taiwan and South Korea, brought about a dramatic closing of ranks between Peking and Pyongyang against Japan as well as against the United States. The immediate endorsement by Peking, in the editorial in *Jen-min Jih-pao* (April 15, 1971), of the DPRK's policy of "independent unification of the Fatherland" suggested close coordination between the two nations.[28] In retrospect, one can see certain parallels between the aims, strategies, and tactics of Peking's policy toward Taiwan and those of Pyongyang's policy toward South Korea. Both called for "peaceful unification," contacts and negotiation between the parties of a divided nation, and withdrawal of American forces from the territories concerned. Ultimately, both wanted the United States to terminate the defense commitments. Both attacked Japanese imperialism and militarism. Peking demanded the abolition of the Tokyo-Taipei peace treaty; Pyongyang, the Japan-ROK treaty.

A more interesting but more speculative point emerges if one ponders these parallels in the light of the history of the Korean War. Most intriguing is the timing of the invasion of South Korea—it was launched before Peking could complete the elimination of the Chiang regime on Taiwan. This crucial decision, which in the opinion of many scholars was made by Stalin, led to the de facto separation of Taiwan from China, which has threatened to become a permanent situation. Even if one accepts the view of other scholars that Pyongyang advanced the date of invasion without Stalin's consent or even knowledge,[29] the Soviet Union must, from Peking's viewpoint, be held responsible for all the adverse consequences because of her commanding role in planning the Korean War, her control over supplies, and her failure to keep a close watch on the Korean armed forces.

In any event, the tremendous sacrifice and risk incurred by Peking in the Korean War helped save North Korea but jeopardized China's most important interest. North Korea became a drain on Peking's resources, but could not be considered a loyal friend of China in the Sino-Soviet dispute. The Chinese have constantly endeavored to learn from experience and seldom make the same mistake twice. Now, with full control of its own policies, Peking is not likely to place any move on the unification of Korea or some broadly defined and long-term Chinese interests in a unified Korea ahead of the unification of China, so long as this latter objective is within the realm of possibility.

Peking's endorsement of Pyongyang's policy of peaceful unification and the parallels in the two nations' policies toward unification indicate the sense of priority in Peking, although they are also rooted in other obvious military and political considerations. For Peking, they rule out the use of force in the Korean peninsula, indefinitely. Peking is certainly aware that peaceful unification between these two relatively equal parties is more difficult to achieve than between China and Taiwan, particularly in view of the strong American military presence and Japan's greater concern over South Korea. So long as China's peaceful unification has not been achieved, it is improbable that Peking would support North Korea in achieving unification and jeopardize the return of Taiwan. The only proviso to this guess is that neither the North nor the South Korean regime would collapse and no viable successor regime could be established to maintain the present stability in the Korean peninsula. This line of analysis, which we developed in the summer of 1973, has been confirmed by the events after the collapse of the Thieu regime. In the joint communiqué issued on April 26, 1975, at the end of Kim Il-sung's visit to Peking, the Chinese government "reaffirms its resolute support to the Korean people in their just struggle for the independent and *peaceful* unification of their father-land."[30] By implication, Peking again ruled out the use of force to unify Korea, at least for the time being.

In contrast to the relationship between China and North Korea, Japanese-South Korean relations since 1965 have been largely economic. At least, most Japanese leaders have defined them as such. The policy orientation identified in the general discussion of Japanese foreign policy governs Japanese policy in South Korea. That is, Japan depends on American guarantees for Korean security, which most Japanese leaders agree is essential to Japanese security. Despite repeated demands by the United States, Japan has been hesitant to commit herself to military cooperation with South Korean armies. However, Japan accepted the burden of helping to modernize South Korean military forces by supplying plants of heavy industries as aid, partly because Japan could thus in the long run increase her economic interest. At the same time, Japan established an unofficial trade agreement with North Korea in early 1972. Again, we encounter a basic trend of thought in Japanese leaders, namely, the best strategy toward Communist regimes is to increase trade with them, because Asian Communism derives much of its appeal and strength from nationalistic aspiration to be powerful and prosperous. Helping them in their nation-building through trade, it is believed, will decrease their belligerent posture toward Japan. At the present time, many Japanese leaders seem to feel that although a Communist South Korea might threaten Japan's security, Japan should not go beyond allowing American forces the use of their bases in Japan in accordance with the security treaty. Other Japanese leaders would support the following analysis by Muraoka Kunio, which would put an even narrower limit to Japan's action:

> At the moment any prospect of direct military participation by Japan in the peninsula is counter-productive; in Japan there will be no political consensus for it, and in Korea it will be unacceptable because of the past memory of Japanese rule. Moreover, a force hostile to South Korea is not necessarily hostile to Japan. Therefore, allowing the United States to use Japanese bases in such contingency (which the government would be inclined to do) would not meet the full support of the nation. Hence, any military cooperation with Korea would be deeply divisive in Japan, and would never become a possibility.[31]

Whether this relaxed attitude toward South Korea can survive the reexamination of foreign and military policies in Japan after the fall of South Vietnam remains to be seen.

VI.

With the possible exception of some Japanese-Soviet deals which would weaken China's defensive position, Taiwan is potentially the most disruptive issue in the ongoing Sino-Japanese rapprochement, one which could turn it into Sino-Japanese antagonism and rivalry in East Asia. Many observers recognize that China showed intense interest in effecting a rapprochement with Japan as soon as possible once the Tanaka cabinet was formed. Peking apparently expected that Japan's public position on Taiwan would go far beyond the Shanghai communiqué and thus lead eventually to changes in America's commitment to that island. Peking also hoped no doubt that as a consequence of this public position, Japan would follow a set of policies which would further weaken her various ties to Taiwan and facilitate the process of peaceful unification. For these reasons, China made significant concessions to Japan. She voluntarily renounced her demand for indemnities, although her bargaining position on this point

was weakened by Taipei's waiver of similar claims in the Tokyo-Taipei
treaty. She tacitly recognized the continuance of trade and economic
relations between Japan and Taiwan. She gave assurances of noninterference in Japan's internal politics. She showed understanding of Japan's
annoyance over Chinese analyses of Japanese militarism. She did not take
serious issue with Japan's right to self-defense or the U.S.-Japan security
treaty. Chairman Mao personally accepted Tanaka's explanation of his
phrase "cause trouble" in the latter's statement of apology for the damage
done to China in all the years of Japanese aggression and war.[32] The
Chinese negotiators resolved a terminological impasse by a decision to
express "politically" the termination of the state of war in the preamble and
to use the expression "the abnormal state of affairs" in paragraph one.[33]
The only major points on which China insisted were the clause regarding
the status of Taiwan in the joint communiqué and the sentence concerning
the termination of the Tokyo-Taipei peace treaty in Foreign Minister
Ōhira's statement during his press conference in Peking.

But the agreement on the Taiwan issue is so vague and general that
divergent interpretations are bound to arise. The only unambiguous result
was the establishment of diplomatic relations between Peking and Tokyo
and the termination of diplomatic relations and the peace treaty between
Tokyo and Taipei. Even paragraph three in the joint communiqué on the
issue of Taiwan[34] can be given an interpretation which minimizes its
significance. For example, Foreign Minister Ōhira stated: "Japan actually
has not said that Taiwan is a territory of the People's Republic of China. We
are only saying that it is a territory which ought to belong to China. There
is no difference at all from the past, and it is nothing more than shifting
diplomatic relations to Peking."[35] He affirmed that "we will not assist the
independence movement in Taiwan or have ambitions toward Taiwan."
This was a significant concession to Peking but there is nothing to prevent
various private groups from supporting the independence movement just as
they did in the past.

One of the questions which will assume crucial importance is the
applicability of Article 6 of the U.S.-Japan security treaty (the "Far Eastern
clause") to Taiwan and the status of the Taiwan clause of the Nixon–Satō
joint communiqué of November 1969. Immediately after his return from
Peking, Ōhira was asked: "Would it be all right to leave the 'Taiwan clause'
of the Nixon–Satō Joint Communiqué of 1969 as it is now?" Ōhira's answer
was: "It is quite all right. Relations between Japan and China were
normalized with the U.S.-Japan Security Treaty structure as it is. If it had
not been all right [for the Chinese side], the joint communiqué could not
have been drawn up." He was also reported to have said: "We attended the
negotiations with the standpoint of not impairing U.S.-Japan relations."[36]
On the same subject, Tanaka stated: "The U.S. stands on the premise that
China will not resort to armed force against Taiwan. . . . Such a situation

[as the invoking of the U.S.-Japan treaty] can be avoided; there is no possibility of such a situation arising."[37]

In November, the Tanaka government announced its "unified view" in the following terms:

> The Taiwan clause set forth the recognition of the top leaders of Japan and United States at the time in 1969. Since then, the situation surrounding Taiwan has changed, the possibility of armed conflicts arising has disappeared. In the light of this background, the recognition has also changed. Regarding the point whether it will not be interference in internal affairs, Taiwan is an inseparable part of the People's Republic of China and, basically, it is China's internal question. We hope that it will be settled peacefully between the parties directly concerned. Standing on this judgment, careful consideration will be given to the operation of the U.S.-Japan Security Treaty.[38]

In explaining this unified view, Ōhira expressed the government's belief that it was not desirable to argue a hypothetical situation. He asked for the opposition parties' understanding and assured them that "careful consideration will be given, keeping in mind friendly relations between Japan and China in the future." Regarding the Far Eastern clause, Yoshida Kenzō, director-general of the Asian Affairs Bureau of the Foreign Ministry, gave a similar answer to an interviewer.[39] Peking was far from satisfied with these interpretations. After an interview with Premier Chou En-lai, Kimura Takeo reported the following remark by Chou: "Concerning the fact that the Chinese side did not touch on the Security Treaty when Tanaka visited China, he stated that this is because Foreign Minister Ōhira stated that the Security Treaty will not apply to Taiwan."[40] Chou must have also assumed that Japan took a similar position on the Taiwan clause.

Hence, despite surface cordiality, the Sino-Japanese maneuvering on the question of Taiwan continues under different ground rules. As might be expected, Peking tries to weaken the various ties between Tokyo and Taipei, sometimes using economic inducements. Tokyo attempts to develop trade with Peking while keeping her economic advantages in Taiwan. In this respect, the delay in concluding an aviation agreement between Japan and China is illuminating. Liao Ch'eng-chih argued China's case in political terms: "It will be a problem if the line is extended as it is and planes were to fly from Haneda, Taipei, Shanghai to Peking. That would mean two Chinas, and we cannot accept that in any way."[41] Liao's interpretation of the Sino-Japanese understanding on the issue of Taiwan is as follows: "At the time of the restoration of the Sino-Japanese diplomatic relations last year, Foreign Minister Ōhira asked us to 'understand the questions of Japan's investments in Taiwan and its air route.' Toward this, the responsible persons of the Chinese side said that 'China cannot accept these questions legally, but it can understand that such questions actually exist.' "[42] In other words, for Peking, these questions are not excluded from future discussions and negotiations.

Accordingly, Peking at first demanded that the Tokyo-Taipei air route be cut, pointing to the precedent that China had been prevented from sending even a special flight to Japan prior to the restoration of Peking-Tokyo relations. After this demand was rejected firmly by Japan, Peking asked that changes be made on the flag and the name of the company painted on the Chinese Nationalist planes. Tokyo replied in effect that she was not in a position to impose a change. The two sides finally reached a compromise under which Foreign Minister Ōhira issued a statement declaring that "the Japanese government does not recognize the insignia on the Taiwan aircraft as a national flag nor does it recognize China Airline (Taiwan) as an airline representing a state."[43] Taiwan herself then took steps to cut the Tokyo-Taipei air route in the hope that the move would prevent the Diet from ratifying the agreement, or at least would strengthen the hand of the pro-Taiwan group (the Seirankai), and create serious difficulties for the Tanaka cabinet. This episode suggests that Peking would try to obtain the most favorable interpretation possible of the Sino-Japanese understanding on the question of one China so as to undercut Taiwan's international prestige and to isolate Taiwan. But it would accept a compromise which does not run counter to the phraseology of the joint communiqué and the Ōhira statement of September 1972. Peking achieved a diplomatic victory magnified by Taiwan's overestimation of the political power of the Seirankai, her willingness to be used by the Seirankai as an instrument in the struggle within the LDP, and her self-inflicted damage in terminating the Tokyo-Taipei air route.[44] The China-Japan air route has little short-term economic significance; both sides sought the agreement mainly for political reasons. To Peking, it meant a step, however small, toward the achievement of a one-China situation and toward the improvement of Sino-Japanese relations, one of the indispensable elements in the ultimate solution of the Taiwan issue. To Japan, it is a highly desirable move to induce the Soviet Union to compete for her favors, and to maintain her "equal-distance" diplomacy. It may also have been seen in the context of negotiations over China's export of oil to Japan. Hence, both sides reached a satisfactory compromise after negotiations lasting nineteen months, with China giving up her earlier demands and Japan assuming the risk of temporarily losing the lucrative Taipei-Tokyo air route.

Future negotiations and relations between China and Japan will continue to reflect the contrasts in the approaches and relative bargaining power of the two nations. Her newly acquired ability to export oil has given China bargaining leverage in the economic sphere. But she still needs imports from Japan more than Japan needs Chinese imports. To make up for her weak economic bargaining position, she must continue to appeal to Japanese opinion on the basis of the mutually agreed-upon principle of one China, the guilt feelings and goodwill of the Japanese, and a generalized Japanese anxiety over possible conflict with China. The internal divisions in Japan over China policy can also be exploited. Official and semiofficial contacts on all levels have become an important instrument of diplomacy. Thus, it came as no surprise that Peking sought to bring pressure on the Miki government over the issue of including in the peace treaty a clause opposing "hegemony" by any power in Asia by successfully persuading a JSP delegation to accept the Chinese position.[45] For her part, Japan relies on her present economic strength in dealing with Peking. As cultivating opinions takes a long time to produce results and even longer to translate these results into changes in public policies, Peking tries to proceed slowly and tentatively in order to obtain acceptable terms, or at least to wait until the results of her efforts are known. But since economic strength can produce immediate advantage, Japan desires quick agreements covering long periods of time. To date, the Chinese desire to compete with the Soviet Union and to prevent the rapid development of Soviet-Japanese economic relations has forced the Chinese not to delay an agreement with Japan for too long a period. This has weakened China's bargaining power.

In the long run, however, there is another factor at work. While the balance of economic strength is temporarily on the side of Japan, the balance of vital interests in Taiwan is on the side of China. The Chou–Tanaka summit meeting reflected this balance of vital interests. Although the relative importance of Taiwan to the economy of Japan has never been doubted by Japanese leaders, the strategic importance of Taiwan to the security of Japan is being reevaluated by some Japanese observers. At the same time, China's export of oil to Japan and import of heavy machinery in the next few years may make China a more important trade partner than Taiwan. The recovery of Taiwan will remain a primary Chinese objective while Taiwan's relative importance to Japan may further decline. Peking is apparently hoping that in the long run this balance of vital interests will enable her to achieve her objective.

What is the future of Taiwan? Our speculations on this subject are probably no better than oracle bone divination. But certain things can be said for the purpose of eliciting discussion. Peking's present policy of peaceful unification rests squarely on military realities in the Taiwan Straits, the continuing American commitment to defend Taiwan, and the general international environment. This situation will remain unchanged for some time to come. Peking wants to isolate Taipei diplomatically first. Peking may be hoping that with the development of great economic strength in the next few years, economic relations will appear more profitable with Peking than with Taipei. It is hoped that diplomatic and economic isolation, together with the concomitant decline in morale and economic strength, would make the political inducements offered by Peking to achieve unification more attractive than they are now.

But Peking, realistic about the prospect of peaceful unification, is apparently aware that the death of Chiang Kai-shek has increased rather than decreased the chances of the emergence of an independent Taiwan.

Many American observers asserted explicitly or said by implication that Peking had renounced the use of force over the issue of Taiwan or had reached an understanding with the American government to that effect. We have found no evidence that Peking has made such a commitment. Peking's policy at the present time, to achieve unification by peaceful means, does not rule out the resort to force, the threat of force, or such forcible measures as a naval blockade in the future.[46] The refusal to renounce the use of force is a necessary element in Peking's endeavor to persuade Taipei to negotiate a settlement. Moreover, the term "peaceful unification" has a special meaning when used by the Chinese Communists. It includes negotiation against the background of overwhelming military superiority on the Chinese Communist side. If the policy of peaceful unification cannot be successfully implemented, a shift to the use of force or the threat of force is possible. Such a shift is congruent with the Chinese Communist pattern of integrating "peaceful political struggle" and "armed struggle" and using alternately one of these as the principal form of struggle. The question is whether the military balance warrants such a shift.[47]

The long period in which a change in military balance will warrant a shift to the use of force to recover Taiwan will also witness many unforeseeable political developments and changes within China and Taiwan and in the world as a whole. If China succeeds in making a real breakthrough in her economic decline, the attraction of China for Taiwan will increase and the prospect of Taiwan's return will improve. Otherwise, a serious political constraint will be imposed on any attempt to regain Taiwan even if Peking acquires the necessary military capabilities. The sentiments of the Chinese mainlanders and Taiwanese on Taiwan will be another weighty political factor. The potential capability of the Nationalist government to make atomic weapons introduces an additional complication. No matter what sort of plan Peking has drawn up—peaceful unification or resort to force in the future—one of the most immediate and urgent tasks is to cultivate the favorable sentiment of the Taiwanese and Chinese mainlanders in the larger context of creating an overwhelming climate of world opinion that China is one and indivisible. This explains the tremendous efforts made by Peking in this direction and the political position taken by Peking in the negotiation over air routes. The general and vague principles embodied in the Chou–Tanaka joint communiqué and the Ōhira statement of September 1972 can be given concrete meaning only when they are applied to specific issues. Until China and Japan can reach substantial agreement on the many specific issues over Taiwan, a Sino-Japanese nonaggression pact would be out of the question. Conversely, Peking might be willing to offer political and economic inducements in the form of intimate cooperation throughout East Asia or some sort of informal alliance or cohegemony so attractive that Japan's economic stakes in

Taiwan would become insignificant by comparison. But Peking could not offer such inducements until her political and economic capabilities to act in the international sphere increase dramatically and the power of the Soviet Union and the United States suffer a corresponding decline. This is a possible development in the long run and should be watched carefully; but it will take time to materialize. If it should come to pass, the quadrilateral relations among the four powers in East Asia would undergo a drastic change and Sino-Japanese relations would become the dominant factor in East Asia. With this change, the global configuration of power will also take on a different shape, with China, Japan, and some countries in the Third World forming a center of power to balance the influence of the United States, the Soviet Union, and perhaps Western Europe.

VII.

The projection of Sino-Japanese rivalry in East Asia rests on various assumptions regarding the structure of power relationships in East Asia and on certain judgments and policy recommendations on specific issues over which China and Japan might come into conflict; it also has definite implications for Japan's defense program and political development. It assumes that China and Japan will come into serious conflict over a variety of issues throughout East Asia in which the interests of Japan and the United States might diverge and Japan might not receive U.S. military support. The logical inference is that Japan must acquire the necessary conventional military power to defend these interests. Since a program of rapid rearmament would likely give Japan superiority in conventional military capability, China would be tempted to resort to nuclear weapons or to nuclear blackmail in order to redress the balance and to uphold her interests. The inevitable result would be the acquisition of nuclear weapons by Japan.

In contrast, we have argued that, given the present structure of political relationships in East Asia, it is unlikely that Sino-Japanese rivalry would develop to such an extent that massive conventional and nuclear rearmament would become vital to Japan's defending her interests against China. We have also suggested that military power has serious limitations when it is used to protect economic interests or to deal with the unstable internal situation and possible revolutionary changes in East Asia. We have no intention of dealing with the technical problems of conventional and nuclear weapons. We shall only make several brief observations on the question of military power insofar as it bears on Sino-Japanese relations.

At present, China does not have the necessary conventional military power to pose any threat of an invasion of Japan. This situation will probably remain unchanged for the rest of the decade. In many discussions of the possibility of Japan's acquisition of nuclear weapons, the nuclear threat from China rather than from the Soviet Union has usually been cited as Japan's most likely incentive. This focus on China's nuclear threat probably stems from a feeling that the Soviet nuclear threat is of such a dimension that it looks like a "natural disaster" while the Chinese threat can be countered. It is also probably the outcome of a tendency to compare the United States with the Soviet Union and Japan with China, and the Japanese sense of equality with the Chinese in the structure of international power. In addition, it is a legacy of the Sino-American confrontation in which Japan associated herself closely with her American ally on all political issues and which intensified Sino-Japanese antagonism and obscured the chances of possible compromise. It is a response to Chinese propaganda attacks on Japanese militarism in the past which offended Japan's image of herself as a pacific nation. But this focus on the Chinese nuclear threat will probably be blurred as a result of long-term effects of the Sino-Japanese rapprochement in which the two nations seek to resolve the differences over various concrete issues through compromise or mutual concessions.

There is another point which deserves to be mentioned. China's decision to acquire and develop nuclear weapons was a response to the nuclear threat first from the United States and then from the Soviet Union. Any nuclear weapons systems sufficient to deter a nuclear attack from the Soviet Union and the United States would also be sufficient to cover Japan and other Asian nations. They do not represent any independent cost to China in economic terms. Obviously, China's acquisition of nuclear weapons has had visible political repercussions among her Asian neighbors. But these repercussions have been largely contained as a result of the general recognition of the serious threat under which China must formulate her military policies.

In contrast, a decision for Japan to go nuclear would be taken as a move directed primarily at China. If Muraoka Kunio is correct, "the level of force required to deter China would probably be substantially larger than that needed to deter the Soviet Union."[48] In view of past history, the political impact of such a decision on other Asian nations would be profound and not so easily contained. Moreover, China's future nuclear weapons program will be limited by her economic and industrial capabilities and her level of scientific and technological development, whereas Japan is not under similar constraints once Japanese scientists abandon their refusal to work on nuclear weapons. Even the nuclear superpowers would have to ask whether Japan would be content with being a second-rate nuclear power once she embarked on a program to develop nuclear weapons. If indeed Japan should go all the way, the international system would undergo another major change. We do not have the competence to discuss the question of "defensive" nuclear weapons, keeping the nuclear option open, technical feasibility, economic cost, and incipient vulnerability. But it takes only a layman's knowledge to assert that profound political changes would take place in Japan if and when she should decide to go nuclear.

The explosion of an atomic device in India in June 1974 brought to the surface the submerged trend toward proliferation of nuclear weapons. It has led to the postponement of Japan's plan to ratify the nonproliferation treaty. If India and other nations become nuclear powers, the pressure on Japan to acquire nuclear weapons will increase. But given Japan's internal political situation, her high level of economic and technological achievements, the absence of an implacable enemy, and the overwhelming public opposition to nuclear weapons, it is highly doubtful that Japan will go nuclear. It is more likely that in line with political advantage and opportunity costs, she will simply keep her nuclear option open, as she has tended to do thus far.

Maintaining this policy implies that Japan would continue to rely on America's nuclear umbrella for protection against the Soviet and Chinese nuclear threat, to depend on the United States Navy to protect the sea lanes, and to use Japan's overwhelming economic power to protect her own economic interests in underdeveloped countries. The reliability of America's nuclear protection has often been discussed. So has the desirability of establishing good relations with other nations in order to decrease the reliance on the United States and to reensure Japan's security. Insofar as Sino-Japanese relations are concerned, the only issue which could have led to a military confrontation was Taiwan. If a Sino-American military confrontation over Taiwan should occur and threaten to involve Japan as a result of the invocation of the Far Eastern clause of the U.S.-Japan treaty, the question of the reliability of the American nuclear umbrella would not arise. The problem would be whether Japan would be willing to allow the United States to use her bases for such purpose under the present formula of "giving careful consideration." As our previous analysis suggests, if a nuclear war threatens to develop over Taiwan, the United States, not Japan, must first answer the fateful question of how great a sacrifice she is willing to make to defend Taiwan.

For China, developing nuclear and conventional military capabilities is a matter of survival and a necessary means to achieve unification. But the tremendous cost in terms of financial and manpower resources is obvious to the Chinese leaders.[49] Vis-à-vis the United States, the level of force to be achieved would depend on the prospect of recovering Taiwan and on what would be required for that purpose. Nuclear force at this level will also present an objective threat to Japan. But the Chinese leaders are not likely to be foolish enough to use nuclear blackmail against Japan or escalate their conflicts with the Japanese government to such a level as to trigger a Japanese decision to acquire nuclear weapons.

VIII.

We have argued in this paper that it is improbable that East Asian politics will turn on Sino-Japanese rivalry. Instead, Sino-Japanese relations form the common base of two triangular relationships—one governing the relations among China, Japan, and the United States and the other governing the relations among China, Japan, and the Soviet Union. In both of these triangles, Japan occupies a more favorable position than China. It is true that as the power occupying the middle position, Japan is sometimes the object of pressure from the other two powers. There is also the danger that Japan will be maneuvered into becoming the main antagonist of China in either one or both of these triangular relationships. But given Japan's favorable position and her skill at negotiation, she will be able to absorb such pressures and perhaps even counter them. In both triangular relationships, Sino-Japanese relations are much less intense than Sino-Soviet, Sino-American, and American-Japanese either in terms of enmity or in terms of the long-term consequences of the interchanges. Sino-Soviet conflict and hostility is now the primary source of tension in East Asia. Japan's policy of maintaining equal distance between the rivals has a great deal of merit. But it is not easy to implement. Given the fact that since the Chou–Tanaka meeting, Japan has adopted a position less favorable to Taiwan than that of the United States, the latter is now viewed by Peking as the main obstacle in its maneuvers against Taiwan. These two triangles with a common base form a quadrilateral relationship. But the actions and policies of the two superpowers still dominate the relations among the four powers.

Within the above context, the Sino-Japanese rapprochement since the Chou–Tanaka meeting has yielded initial common understanding regarding the questions of interference in each other's internal politics, the defense power of Japan, the U.S.-Japan security pact and China's and Japan's respective roles in developing countries. China is now unlikely to place the unification of Korea ahead of the unification of her own country. Therefore, the problem of Korea will probably not cause serious Sino-Japanese conflict. The only bilateral issue which can cause serious trouble between China and Japan is Taiwan. Unless satisfactory solutions can be found for the many concrete problems that remain regarding Taiwan, Sino-Japanese rapprochement will not advance at a rapid pace in the foreseeable future, as, for example, toward the much-discussed goal of a Sino-Japanese nonaggression pact.

But none of the unresolved issues is likely to lead to military conflict. Because of China's unfavorable position in the quadrilateral relations, China's best hope lies in maintaining tolerable relations with Japan and the United States so as to fend off Soviet military pressure and counter Soviet efforts to contain China. The remaining years of the 1970s will witness neither an intense Sino-Japanese rivalry nor a sudden blooming of Sino-Japanese friendship. But the probability of a gradual increase in Sino-Japanese cooperation in East Asia is higher than that of intensification of Sino-Japanese conflict. Thus, the 1970s will be a decade of complex interactions among the four powers in which Japan will embark on her new, historic role as a pacific world power, maintaining an ambivalent and noncommittal stance toward both nuclear weapons and large-scale conventional forces; and China will continue to seek to demonstrate her ability to turn her much improved but still adverse circumstances into new opportunities for creative development.

In our view, then, Sino-Japanese relations in the 1970s will not be comparable to the 1930s. Power politics as they impinge on the East Asian region are more closely integrated with the larger international system. This basic fact calls into question the validity of the regional approach, which focuses almost exclusively on Sino-Japanese relations, a view that derives its inspiration from the analogy with Far Eastern diplomacy in the 1930s. We do not believe history will repeat itself.

Notes

1. These principles are opposition to hegemony of great powers; condemnation of spheres of interest; denial of any ambition to be a superpower; affirmation of her status as an economically backward country in the Third World; proclamation of support for "all oppressed people and nations" in their opposition to foreign aggression, interference, control, and subversion; the advocacy of the doctrine of self-reliance; the five principles of peaceful coexistence; the eight principles governing foreign aid; the renunciation of the first use of nuclear weapons coupled with the demand for their complete elimination; and support for a nuclear-free zone in Latin America. Flexible in their character and subtle in their implications, they are generally consistent with each other and serve the present interests of the nation without foreclosing future possibilities. They are used to stake out a claim for leadership of the Third World, establish a moral and political position for dealing with the other major powers on a basis of equality, and project an ideal future world order. The development of China's political influence in the Third World would compensate somewhat for her military and economic weakness relative to other Great Powers.

2. Donald C. Hellmann, *Japan and East Asia* (New York, 1972), p. 72, citing *New York Times,* 25 August 1965. Hellmann's book is built around this notion.

3. In our analysis, we shall not take into account certain extreme contingencies such as a possible but not highly probable all-out Sino-Soviet war, an unlikely total collapse of the Japanese economy, and the unthinkable consequences of a total change in China's political system. We cannot rule out entirely the possibility of the loss of power by the LDP to a coalition of "progressive" forces which would be preceded by many international and internal upheavals such as a worldwide uncontrollable inflation or depression, a precipitous decline in American influence, a corresponding rise in Soviet and Chinese power, irreconcilable conflict between Japan and the United States in the economic sphere, an irreversible process of economic deterioration in Japan, a sharp reduction in the standard of living of the majority of the people, the disintegration of the LDP following unbridgeable factional conflicts, and finally a resolution of the sharp differences in the orientations of the opposition forces.

China has already been confronted with the problem of the political successor to the late Mao Tse-tung. But the new leadership must still take into account the constraints imposed by the international power configuration. Given the ignorance of the outside world about China and the uncertainties confronting the Chinese themselves, it is our view that speculation on the policies of the successors to Chairman Mao is less meaningful than an assessment of the broad alternatives available to them and the impact of the policies of the other powers on the likelihood that one or the other of these options will be chosen.

4. For a perceptive analysis of the relative importance of geographical proximity and other factors such as technology and economic structure, see Charles Wolf, Jr., "International Transactions and Regionalism: Distinguishing 'Insiders' from 'Outsiders' " (Santa Monica, 1973), p. 4922/1.

5. *Newsweek,* 30 July 1973.

6. *Remaking China Policy* (Cambridge, Mass., 1971), pp. 4–5.

7. *New York Times, Report from Red China,* (New York, 1971), p. 95.

8. Ibid., pp. 82, 86, 95. A few weeks later, Chou told a group of Chinese visitors that if the United States withdrew from Taiwan and Japan stepped in, China would be ready to go to war with Japan.

9. According to Kimura Takeo, Premier Chou told him that "Japan forms a country, armaments for self-defense are necessary . . . this is a matter to be decided by the Japanese people and is not a matter in which another country should interfere." *Asahi,* 27 January 1973. See also *Nihon Keizai,* 26 January 1973; *Asahi,* 18 January 1973.

Liao Ch'eng-chih, the principal executor of China's policy toward Japan, said: "I cannot support the U.S.-Japan Security Treaty structure but its functions directed toward China have already lost substance, and we will not take particular issue with it at this late date. As a practical question, Japan will probably have to rely on America's nuclear umbrella for some time to come. . . ." *Yomiuri,* 12 March 1973.

After his trip to China, Tanaka found it possible to push forward the Fourth Defense Plan. Ambassador Ingersoll was reported to have said on February 5, 1973, that "the United States is not urging Japan to play a military role beyond the defense of its own country with conventional weapons." This statement was very different in spirit from the Nixon–Satō communiqué of November 1969.

10. *Japanese Security and the United States,* Adelphi Paper, no. 95, p. 13.

11. Liao Ch'eng-chih frankly told a Japanese audience that "if thought is given to the fact that an oil pipeline from Tyumen Oil Fields will mean the supplying of fuel to the Soviet Forces' aircraft and tanks to invade China, considerable measures to counter this must be taken, and Japan must keep clearly in mind that we will harbor 'bitter feeling' toward Japan too." *Yomiuri,* 12 March 1973.

12. This point was brilliantly argued by Mushakoji Kinhide in his article in *Asahi* Jyōnaru, 20 April 1973.

13. Senator Barry Goldwater declared on the Senate floor on June 3, 1975: "Communist China has done something that Europe has failed to do; namely, obtained the military respect if not fear on the part of the USSR. It is in our national interest in the foreseeable future that China remain a counterbalancing force." He expressed his concern that after Mao's death, a pro-Soviet faction could take power in China and that if the Sino-Soviet alliance should be revived, "this would represent the first—I repeat, the first—unbeatable alliance yet seen on this planet." *Congressional Record,* 3 June 1975, p. 2.

14. F. C. Langdon, *Japan's Foreign Policy* (Vancouver, 1973), p. 178.

15. *New York Times,* 12 May 1975.

16. Joint Economic Committee, *China: A Reassessment of the Economy*, 94th Cong., 1st sess., 10 July 1975, pp. 5, 240.

17. Ibid., pp. 5, 247.

18. *Peking Review*, 3 March 1972, p. 5.

19. The sentence reads: "Neither of the two countries should seek hegemony in the Asian-Pacific region and each country is opposed to efforts by any country or countries to establish such hegemony." *Peking Review*, 6 October 1972, p. 13.

20. *Asahi*, 1 October 1972.

21. *Yomiuri*, 12 March 1973.

22. *Asahi* 18 January 1973 (evening edition).

23. *Jen-min jih-pao*, 6 October 1972, p. 4, translated in *Peking Review*, 13 October 1972, p. 18.

24. *Yomiuri*, 19 January 1973.

25. *Asahi*, 18 January 1973.

26. *Tōyō Keizaei*, 17 February 1973.

27. For example, Professor Etō Shinkichi suggested (in *Jiyū*, May 1972) that "we should radically restudy and reform our economic and cultural cooperation policies." Muraoka Kunio wrote that "aid to Southeast Asia must be carried out so that the advancement of Japanese commercial interest is kept to the minimum" and expressed the hope that "economic cooperation would become an inherent component of Japan's security policy." *Japanese Security and the U.S.*, p. 32.

28. See the translation, "Korean People's Struggle for Unification of Fatherland Will Win," *Peking Review*, 23 April 1971, pp. 11–12.

29. This interpretation is effectively developed by Robert R. Simmons in his excellent book, *The Strained Alliance* (New York, 1975).

30. *Peking Review*, 2 May 1975, p. 9 (emphasis added). See also Vice-Premier Teng Hsiao-ping's speech, ibid., p. 12. For the analysis of Chinese policy by the American government, see *New York Times*, 29 April, 29 May, and 15 June 1975.

31. Muraoka Kunio, op. cit., p. 22.

32. Tanaka's report to the LDP General Assembly of members of both houses, *Asahi*, 1 October 1972.

33. Foreign Minister Ōhira's remark, as reported in *Tōkyō Shimbun*, 1 October 1972. He commented that "the other side was taking a more forward looking position than I had imagined."

34. This paragraph reads: "The Government of the People's Republic of China reaffirms that Taiwan is an inalienable part of the territory of the People's Republic of China. The Government of Japan fully understands and respects this stand of the Government of China and adheres to its stand of complying with Article 8 of the Potsdam Proclamation."

35. Ōhira Masayoshi, "Pekin, Washinton, Mosukuwa e no tabi" [Trip to Peking, Washington, and Moscow], *Bungei Shunjū*, December 1972, pp. 142–47.

36. *Asahi*, 1 October 1972.

37. Ibid.

38. Ibid., 8 November 1972.

39. *Toki no Ugoki,* 1 November 1972.

40. *Nihon Keizai,* 26 January 1973.

41. *Yomiuri,* 21 April 1974.

42. See also Shimizu Minoru, "LDP in Turmoil," *Japan Times,* 25 April 1974.

43. *Yomiuri,* 21 April 1974.

44. See also Shimizu Minoru, op. cit.

45. *Peking Review,* 14 May 1975, p. 6.

46. On the occasion of commemorating the twenty-seventh anniversary of the February 27 uprising in Taiwan against the Nationalist government, Fu Tso-yi, the ranking former Nationalist general on the mainland, issued a written statement warning his former Nationalist colleagues in Taiwan that "the Taiwan Straits are today no longer an obstacle to the liberation of Taiwan." This statement was given wide publicity by Peking and caught the attention of Western observers. For the statement, see *Peking Review,* 8 March 1974, p. 20.

47. For a report on the views of Chinese leaders which supports our analysis, see *Chün Pao* (N.Y.), 23 June 1975. *Chün Pao* is a pro-Peking biweekly.

48. Muraoka Kunio, op. cit., p. 24.

49. There are indications that there was a debate among top leaders from 1969 to 1971 over the extent to which defense industries should be rapidly pushed forward on a large scale at the expense of manufacturing machinery for agriculture and other industrial development.

Photographs

Photographs

Doihara Kenji,
commander of
the 5th Army

*From the collection of
B. Winston Kahn*

Foreign Minister
Fukuda Takeo

Japan Information Service

Foreign Minister
Ohira Masayoshi
emphasizes the
importance of
agriculture to
ECAFE development

Japan Information Service

V.K. Wellington Koo

*From the collection of
Pao-chin Chu*

Ishiwara Kanji

*From the collection of
John H. Boyle*

Ishii Itaro, ca. 1940

Courtesy the Ishii family

Tanaka Kakuei
meets Chou-En-lai

From China Reconstructs

From China Reconstructs

Tanaka Kakuei meets Chairman Mao

President
Richard Nixon
and Premier Sato
Eisaku at the
Western White
House

U.S.I.A. photograph

Prime Minister
Miki Takeo and
President
Gerald Ford,
Washington, D.C.,
August 1975

Japan Information Service

Index

Index